The Anatomy of Influence

The Anatomy of Influence

Decision Making in International Organization

by
Robert W. Cox

and
Harold K. Jacobson

and

Gerard and Victoria Curzon, Joseph S. Nye, Lawrence Scheinman,

James P. Sewell, and Susan Strange

New Haven and London, Yale University Press, 1973

Designed by John O. C. McCrillis
and set in Press Roman type by
The Peterson Research Group, Princeton, New Jersey.
Printed in the United States of America by
The Murray Printing Co., Forge Village, Massachusetts.

Published in Great Britain, Europe, and Africa by
Yale University Press, Ltd., London.
Distributed in Canada by McGill-Queen's University
Press, Montreal; in Latin America by Kaiman & Polon,
Inc., New York City; in Australasia and Southeast
Asia by John Wiley & Sons Australasia Pty. Ltd.,
Sydney; in India by UBS Publishers' Distributors Pvt.,
Ltd., Delhi; in Japan by John Weatherhill, Inc., Tokyo.

Contents

Preface

This is a book about influence in international organizations. It deals with eight specialized agencies in the United Nations family, attempting to understand the sources of influence and the ways influence is exercised by analyzing how decisions have been made in these agencies. Although it contains much information about the eight agencies, the book is not intended to be primarily a study of their growth and activities. A distinction should be made between an international organization considered as an institution with a continuous history and the political system that characterizes decision making in that organization at a particular phase of its existence. This study's focus is on the political systems of eight international organizations as they existed from 1945 through 1970. As the book appears, some of the systems studied here may be passing into history, though the organizations that gave rise to them persist. Since our aim is to generalize knowledge from comparative experience rather than to diagnose the problems confronting particular organizations, the fact that some of the cases are more historical than actual should not diminish the usefulness of inquiry into them.

The book is a collaborative work, prepared through a process of frequent interchange of perspectives and findings among the editors, the other authors of chapters dealing with particular organizations, and other scholars who have given liberally of their advice. Virtually every important aspect of the study was reconsidered at some time in the course of doing it. Points that seemed to have been settled were once more scrutinized. Even the aims of the study evolved. We and the other authors met on a number of occasions to discuss these issues. In the process, from being individual contributors to a volume of studies, we became a research team in which political scientists and economists worked toward understanding each other's concepts. Insofar as this book has achieved a common method and approach, credit must be given in the first place to the goodwill and tolerance of the other authors in submitting to the constraints of a joint enterprise.

The process of interaction of which this book is the result was made possible through the support of the Committee on International Organization of the Social Science Research Council. The SSRC provided funds to defray the cost of several meetings of the contributors and other related expenses. But its support went far beyond finance. Members of the SSRC Committee on International Organization—Lincoln P. Bloomfield, William Diebold, Jr., Ernst B. Haas, H. Field Haviland, Leland M. Goodrich, and Walter R. Sharp, and particularly its chairman, Inis L. Claude, Jr.—made important and often decisive intellectual contributions. Furthermore, prior research by Jacobson and Sewell on the organizations they treat in this volume was supported by the SSRC. We should also like to recognize the valued contribution of the committee's staff, Bryce Wood and Kay K. Ryland, in furthering our individual and group efforts. This book is in a very direct sense the result of the work of the Committee on International Organization of the SSRC.

Intellectual debts must also be acknowledged to Robert A. Dahl and Dankwart A. Rustow, whose thoughtful participation in group discussion with the research team helped toward a clearer definition of the concepts used in the study, and to Michel Crozier, whose ideas concerning the application of organization theory to international agencies helped us in devising the framework for comparative analysis.

Despite the conventions of academic preface writing, all of our counselors bear some share of responsibility for the outcome, because they stimulated us to move in certain directions, even though they did not control the final result.

A major problem of research about international organization is to gain access to and responses from "live" participating sources, mainly secretariat officials and delegates. The experience of the research team varied widely. We are all deeply grateful to the many delegates and international officials who willingly and candidly responded to our questions. Others, however, were clearly more suspicious of our attempts at independent inquiry.

This book is bound to disappoint some people who expect greater penetration into the political processes of international organizations. The authors can sympathize with such criticism and hope that other scholars will subsequently overcome the limitations of this study. Other critics may feel outraged by what may seem an indiscreet attempt to pull back the veil of formal procedures and to view as a political process what goes on in international organizations. With this reaction the authors have no sympathy. Willingness to submit to independent analysis is a sign of maturity and of self-confidence on the part of institutions and their representatives. Such maturity can legitimately be expected of the present generation of delegates and international officials and is fortunately widespread among them. The advance of political analysis not only satisfies scholarly curiosity, but also serves a broader public interest—enhancing the possibilities of public control over public institutions.

Rosannah Steinhoff edited the entire manuscript. All of the authors suffered momentarily under her questioning and gentle prodding, but we are convinced that because of her we have now said more clearly what we wanted to say and in much more readable fashion. Susan K. Lawrence and Catherine Ghébali have checked innumerable elusive facts, have done many computations, and have overseen the process of transforming a manuscript into a typescript with skill, diligence, and unfailing good humor.

Harold Jacobson wishes to acknowledge the support given him by the International Organization Program and the Center for Political Studies at the University of Michigan and by the European Center of the Carnegie

Endowment for International Peace in his work on the project. The International Institute for Labour Studies has provided Robert Cox with a base, giving a wide perspective on international organization, although the institute bears no responsibility for any views expressed in this book; he is grateful to have been able to adjust his contribution to the book so as to make it compatible with the requirements of his task at the institute. We both gratefully acknowledge the generosity of the Rockefeller Foundation in allowing us to use the facilities of the Villa Serbelloni for the final meeting of the contributors.

We hope that the methods of analysis we have used will prove applicable in the hands of other scholars to a wider range of international organization political systems than we have been able to encompass here and that our work may thus be a stimulus to the further development of empirical political theory concerning international organizations. We hope also that the properties and dynamics of different patterns of decision making that emerge in our findings—provisional though these may be in the onward march of theory—may be helpful to those concerned with building future international institutions and that knowledge of political processes may be used creatively toward international cooperation.

R.W.C.
H.K.J.

Abbreviations

ACABQ	Advisory Committee on Administrative and Budgetary Questions, United Nations
ACC	Administrative Committee on Co-ordination, United Nations
AFL–CIO	American Federation of Labor–Congress of Industrial Organizations
AMA	American Medical Association
BIS	Bank for International Settlements
BISD	Basic Instruments and Selected Documents, GATT
CAME	Conference of Allied Ministers of Education
CCIR	Comité Consultatif International des Radiocommunications (International Radio Consultative Committee), International Telecommunication Unión
CCITT	Comité Consultatif International Télégraphique et Téléphonique (International Telegraph and Telephone Consultative Committee), International Telecommunication Union
CECLA	Concilio para Económico Coordinación de América Latina (Latin American Economic Coordination Council)
CERN	(Centre) Organisation Européenne pour la Recherche Nucléaire (European Organization for Nuclear Research)
CGT	Confédération Générale du Travail (French Confederation of Labor)
CIAP	Comité Interamericano de la Alianca para el Progresso (Inter-American Committee on the Alliance for Progress)
CIO	Congress of Industrial Organizations
CMEA	Council for Mutual Economic Assistance (also known as COMECON)
CNNWS	Conference of Non-Nuclear Weapon States
COMECON	Council for Mutual Economic Assistance
CRU	Currency Reserve Unit
EBU	European Broadcasting Union
ECA	Economic Commission for Africa, United Nations
ECAFE	Economic Commission for Asia and the Far East, United Nations
ECE	Economic Commission for Europe, United Nations

ECLA	Economic Commission for Latin America, United Nations
ECOSOC	Economic and Social Council, United Nations
ECSC	European Coal and Steel Community
EEC	European Economic Community
EFTA	European Free Trade Association
ENEA	European Nuclear Energy Agency
EPTA	Expanded Program of Technical Assistance, United Nations
EPU	European Payments Union
ERP	European Recovery Program
EURATOM	European Atomic Energy Community
FAO	Food and Agricultural Organization
GAB	General Arrangements to Borrow
GATT	General Agreement on Tariffs and Trade
IAEA	International Atomic Energy Agency
IATA	International Air Transport Association
IBRD	International Bank for Reconstruction and Development
ICAO	International Civil Aviation Organization
ICFTU	International Confederation of Free Trade Unions
ICITO	Interim Commission for the International Trade Organization
IDA	International Development Association
IFCTU	International Federation of Christian Trade Unions
IFRB	International Frequency Registration Board, International Telecommunication Union
IGO	Intergovernmental organization
IICI	Institut International de Coopération Intellectuelle (International Institute of Intellectual Cooperation)
IIEP	International Institute for Educational Planning
ILO	International Labor Organization or International Labor Office
IMCO	Intergovernmental Maritime Consultative Organization
IMF	International Monetary Fund
INIS	International Nuclear Information Service, International Atomic Energy Agency

IOE	International Organization of Employers
IRAC	Inter-Agency Radio Advisory Committee, United States
ITO	International Trade Organization
ITU	International Telecommunication Union
LAFTA	Latin American Free Trade Association
LRIPC	Long Range International Payments Committee
NAC	National Advisory Council
NATO	North Atlantic Treaty Organization
NGO	Nongovernmental organization
NPT	Non-Proliferation Treaty
OAS	Organization of American States
OECD	Organization for Economic Cooperation and Development
OEEC	Organization for European Economic Cooperation
OTC	Organization for Trade Cooperation
PAHO	Pan American Health Organization
PASB	Pan American Sanitary Bureau
PASO	Pan American Sanitary Organization
PCPB	Preparatory Committee for Program and Budget, International Atomic Energy Agency
SAC	Scientific Advisory Council, International Atomic Energy Agency
SDRs	Special Drawing Rights
TAB	Technical Assistance Board, United Nations
UNCTAD	United Nations Conference on Trade and Development
UNDP	United Nations Development Program
UNESCO	United Nations Educational, Scientific and Cultural Organization
UNICEF	United Nations Children's Fund (United Nations International Children's Emergency Fund)
UNIDO	United Nations Industrial Development Organization
UNRRA	United Nations Relief and Rehabilitation Administration
WCL	World Confederation of Labor
WFTU	World Federation of Trade Unions

WHO World Health Organization

WMO World Meteorological Organization

1 The Framework for Inquiry

Robert W. Cox and Harold K. Jacobson

The growth of international organizations has been one of the significant changes in twentieth-century international relations and has been especially marked since World War II. During the nineteenth century and the first four decades of the twentieth, the number of international organizations grew steadily, until in the 1930s there were more than eighty. The pace of growth then quickened considerably, so that by the 1960s more than two hundred international organizations were in existence.[1]

This book is about decision making and influence in international organizations. The aim of the study is to identify influence, to weigh and assess it, and ultimately to explain how influence is acquired and exercised in international organizations. The method adopted to study influence is the analysis of how decisions are made.

Three terms must be clarified at the outset: *international organization, decision,* and *influence.* With regard to the first, this book does not attempt to deal with all of the more than two hundred existing organizations or even with a representative sample of them. The whole field of international organizations could be subdivided into a number of categories differentiated by membership, structure, and scope—and also by their saliency, their essentiality or utility, and the technicality of their subject matter. The organizations covered here represent a relatively narrow range within a rich and varied universe. They are:

> International Telecommunication Union (ITU)
> International Labor Organization (ILO)
> United Nations Educational, Scientific and Cultural Organization (UNESCO)
> World Health Organization (WHO)
> International Atomic Energy Agency (IAEA)
> International Monetary Fund (IMF)
> General Agreement on Tariffs and Trade (GATT)
> United Nations Conference on Trade and Development (UNCTAD)

Use of the comparative method requires that the things compared be similar enough to belong to the same species but differentiated by certain characteristics. These organizations have in common that they are functional rather than general in their coverage. Furthermore, all draw their membership on a worldwide basis—although none is fully universal—and may thus be

This chapter is very much the product of the collective enterprise which this book is. We gladly acknowledge the many intellectual contributions of our collaborators and others in this chapter.

distinguished from organizations with regional or other restricted forms of membership. Setting them apart from each other are significant differences in the composition of their memberships and in their institutional structures; marked differences in the breadth, essentiality, and technicality of their functions; and important differences in how salient the issues they deal with are for the central political authorities of member states.

ITU, ILO, UNESCO, WHO, and UNCTAD come considerably closer to being truly universal organizations than IAEA, IMF, and GATT. None of the organizations include Communist China (as of 1970, the cut-off date for this study); IMF and GATT do not include the Soviet Union and certain other Eastern European communist states. Several of the organizations have unique institutional features. ILO is characterized by its tripartite system of representation, according to which the member states are represented by delegates designated by employers and labor as well as by the government. UNESCO has a system of National Commissions; WHO, an elaborate regional structure; IMF, a system of weighted voting; and UNCTAD, a formally prescribed mechanism for conciliation. ILO, UNESCO, and UNCTAD have broad mandates in the fields of economic and social policy; the mandates of the other organizations are relatively restricted. States wanting to communicate with one another by means of telecommunications cannot ignore the activities of ITU; none of the other agencies' activities are quite so indispensable. The work of ITU, WHO, IAEA, IMF, and GATT requires a certain technical expertise, while that of ILO, UNESCO, and UNCTAD is less dependent on such skills. ITU, IAEA, IMF, and GATT deal with matters that can involve important aspects of state sovereignty and consequently are of great moment to the central political authorities of members. These differences in the organizations included in the study offer opportunities for significant comparisons.

Although the group considered here does not include regional organizations or other organizations with limited membership, such as the Organization for Economic Cooperation and Development (OECD), or an organization with a broad political mandate like the United Nations, it is hoped that the framework for analysis developed in this study may in time be applied to these other types of international organization. The limits within which the conclusions in this book are valid could then be more clearly established.

International organizations not only differ when considered as systems having a certain equilibrium at a given point in time (synchronically); they also change over time (diachronically). Changes may occur in the structure and processes of influence within a particular organization that can be explained in dynamic terms as well as in relation to other organizations. The international organizations studied here are thus considered as evolving systems during the period 1945 to 1970 (or such part of that period as they existed). Within this span, three base years—1950, 1958, and 1967—have been used as points at which to measure changes both in the structure of influence within organizations and in the characteristics of their environments.

The second term that requires preliminary clarification is decision. In one sense this term suggests finality, a settlement, the conclusion of a process, an outcome. From this point of view decisions have been looked at to discover their legal or formal authority and their content. Another aspect of a decision is as a new starting point in a continuing process, a point at which those options that remain open and those that have been foreclosed become clear. In this dynamic perspective failures to grasp opportunities, implicit decisions not to act, and failures to take decisions—in other words nondecisions—will be included within the concept of decisions. The legal or formal character and the content of the decision is less important than the balance of forces that it expresses and the inclination that it gives to the future direction of events. It is this latter aspect of a decision that is most relevant to an analysis of influence.

This study is concerned with decisions taken in international organizations. Such decisions are collective actions, differing in quality from the individual decisions taken by actors in the political processes of international organizations. A wide variety of forms of collective action are encompassed, including not only formal decisions by vote in assemblies, but also some decisions by bureaucratic authorities and definitions of policies by executive heads.

Since the structure and process of influence are the main objects of this inquiry, the practical consequences that flow from decisions need not be considered, not because the consequences of decisions made in international organizations are unimportant or unworthy of consideration but because they are beyond the scope of this study. If the purpose were to assess the value of international organizations, the impact their activities make upon national policies and thus ultimately upon the living conditions of peoples would have to be examined. This book is not, however, concerned with evaluating international organizations but with understanding better the process whereby their actions are determined. Thus it will not deal with the improvement of working conditions, with the expansion of trade, or with the effects of increasing international liquidity, but rather with how international labor standards are drawn up and enforced in the ILO, how trade regulations are made and applied through GATT, and how Special Drawing Rights are created and issued in the IMF. It will also be concerned with how such decisions come to be faced in these organizations and who has the most influence in determining their outcomes.

The third concept requiring clarification at this stage is influence. Influence is a crucial concept in the study of political phenomena, and volumes have been written about it. As used here, influence means the modification of one actor's behavior by that of another.[2] It is thus a relationship between actors—something that emerges in the political process, not something "given" or calculable at any time. Influence is to be distinguished from power. Power means capability; it is the aggregate of political resources that are available to an actor. These resources may be material or not. Power may be converted into influence, but it is not necessarily so converted either at all or to its full extent. Although those who possess the greatest power may also exercise the greatest influence, this is not logically necessary. One task of this study is to compare power with influence in international organizations.

Influence has specific scope: an actor influences another's behavior in some particular sphere of activity, or issue-area. Some actors may have resources enabling them to exercise influence in many domains, but at any one time they may be really concerned and willing to exercise it in only a few. An actor with relatively limited resources but greater intensity of concern may achieve greater influence in a particular area than another who has greater resources but less immediate concern. Intensity of interest may also explain why some actors are harder to influence than others who care less about the matter in question.

The elite are those who have the most influence. Who the members of the elite are is to be determined empirically. In international organizations they might be representatives of governments, representatives of private associations including commercial firms, members of international bureaucracies, or eminent individuals. Thinking of influence in terms of its scope suggests something about the nature of elites. No actors are likely to be influential to the same extent in all spheres, and thus the pattern of influence is likely to differ by issue-area.

Does this rule out the possibility of a single elite having general influence in an international organization? Not necessarily. It is conceivable that in organizations with limited functional scope a single elite will be influential in all significant decisions. This elite would then have general influence for that organization. Another possibility, however, might be a plurality of different elites. Each would be influential in a different category of decisions within an organization; but one category of decisions would have a certain preeminence, and the elite that influenced those decisions could then be considered as having general influence. This assumes a hierarchy among issue-areas or categories of decisions, in which some are dependent in the long run upon others.

Thus, the issue-area of who controls the machinery of government, that is, who is selected for the key posts of authority in the organization, might be regarded as supreme over other decision areas concerned with substantive matters. Those who control the governmental machinery may be able in the long run to influence or change the personnel who deal with such substantive questions, even though at a particular moment they may be blocked by a countercurrent of opinion. Conversely, there may be feedback from substantive issue-areas that affects selection to posts of authority. The relative intensity of interest in different substantive issues of policy may be a factor in this selection. If such a relationship of interdependence among issue-areas were to be established, those who most influenced decisions about the control of the machinery of government in the organization could be considered an elite of general influence.

Functions, Structure, and Evolution

Decision making in international organizations occurs within a context comprising the functions, the institutional framework and basic procedures, and the historical development of the agency. Because both the decision-making processes and the distribution of influence are initially shaped by these factors, considering them is an essential first stage in any analysis.

Given the nature of the international system, the creation of an international organization requires concrete action by states. Usually, although not always, such actions are consecrated in a treaty. In any case, understanding must be achieved about what is to be done and how.

International organizations have been set up to perform a variety of tasks: keeping the peace, promoting economic development, allocating the radio frequency spectrum, reducing obstacles to trade, ensuring that technology is used only for peaceful purposes, and facilitating the maintenance of stable exchange rates—to name only a few. While a certain level of agreement about what it is to do is necessary when an international organization is created, all parties need not share the same conception of the agreement. On the contrary, there are often sharp differences, and these differences can provide essential clues to future dynamic developments in international organizations.

Nor does an agreement about what an organization is to do necessarily represent all the ambitions nursed by the parties to the agreement concerning the ultimate functions of the organization. Many states may look upon international organizations principally as instruments for preserving their hegemony or improving their status. Moreover, personal motives, for example the wish to occupy top jobs, can operate along with considerations of state interests in creating new international agencies. Such motivations as these, whether expressed or unexpressed, are also important in shaping later developments in international organizations.

Whatever their specific tasks and fields of activity, international organizations can be divided into two broad categories according to the way in which they perform these tasks. Some organizations are established to provide a forum or framework for negotiations and decisions, others to provide specific services. This dichotomy establishes two ideal types: the *forum organization* and the *service organization*. Organizations in the first category provide a framework for member states to carry on many different activities ranging from the exchange of views to the negotiation of binding

legal instruments. States also often use such forums for the collective
legitimation of their policies or for propaganda. Organizations in the second
category conduct activities themselves; they provide common or individual
services or both. Inclusion in this second group depends upon who conducts
the services. If the services are carried out directly by individual states, even
though they may have been agreed to within the framework of an
international organization, that agency would not belong in the service
category. The organization itself must carry out the services. An agency that
collects, analyzes, and disseminates information would fit into this category
unless the information were intended mainly to facilitate discussions within
the framework of the organization, in which case it would be classified as a
forum organization.

In reality, of course, many international organizations fall into both
categories. ILO, for example, has an extensive technical assistance program,
but it also provides a framework for the negotiation of International Labor
Conventions. Similarly ITU, UNESCO, WHO, IAEA, and IMF execute
services in their own right and at the same time provide frameworks for
discussions and negotiations among their member states.

The distinction nevertheless has meaning, and the distribution of an
agency's endeavors between the two types of activity may significantly
affect patterns of decision making and influence. On the most elementary
level, the more an organization leans toward service, the larger its
international bureaucracy and the greater the bureaucracy's potential role in
certain types of decision making. This classification scheme also provides
helpful clues about how an organization can be studied—particularly what
bodies of theory developed in other contexts might be most germane.
Organizational theory can have great relevance for understanding decision
making in service organizations, and the more strongly an agency tends in
this direction, the more directly applicable this body of theory is.
Conversely, theories about negotiation, such as game theory, can be
extremely helpful in analyzing decision-making patterns in forum organizations.

This distinction between forum and service organizations relates to the
way in which agencies perform their functions, not to the importance these
functions have for member states and not to the authority possessed by the
agencies. Whatever their mode of activity, the importance and authority of
different organizations varies, and different states perceive them in different
terms. An agency that is regarded as crucial by one state may be considered
trivial by another, and there is similar variance in the responsiveness of states
to the decisions of international organizations. These differences too are
important.

They are immediately apparent when one examines the structure of
international organizations. The formal powers of the organization and its
organs, the extent of regionalism, the forms of representation, the voting

procedures, and the organization of the international bureaucracy, all tend to be prescribed at the time an international agency is formed. The initial understanding about how an international organization is to perform its functions inevitably represents compromises among conflicting points of view; all parties must be given some incentives to participate. If an organization is to have functions that might affect significant values, those in control of these values will generally demand structural and procedural devices to ensure for themselves the means of exerting special influence. How far they will press their demands and how successful they will be will depend upon the configuration of forces they face at the time. They might be dissuaded from pressing their claims too far by actual and potential counterclaims in the same functional area or in another. In general, the broader the mandate of the organization, the more likely will be such counterclaims. Conscience or conceptions of long-run self-interest can also serve as moderating forces. Whatever the outcome, these initial understandings provide the basic rules for subsequent decision making.

In some instances the parties to an agreement establishing an international organization will not only prescribe the structures and procedures for decision making but also attempt to specify doctrines according to which decisions should be taken. Thus the constitutional documents of IMF and GATT contain detailed codes of conduct, and the charters of several other international agencies tend in this direction. The more they lean toward such specification, the more the organizations' activities are likely to be set in a particular mold and the harder it will be to shift their direction.

Regardless of the rigidity of their charters, though, once international organizations are established, in many instances they evolve in ways that could not have been foreseen by their founders. To some extent this is because the interests and intentions of the member states change over time, sometimes because of developments within states or in relations among states. Moreover, states may modify their interests and intentions with respect to international organizations as a consequence of participation in them. As in other contexts interaction among actors can result in changed views. In addition, international bureaucracies created to serve international organizations may add new ambitions to those of the states: from the pursuit of specific technical goals the aim might be extended to the desire to make international relations more peaceful or to redistribute the wealth between rich and poor countries. Thus, once established, organizations take on a life of their own and develop their own inner dynamics.

Many of the major changes that take place in international organizations can be identified and measured in terms of the organizations' activities and accomplishments. An organization may change in its functions, either with respect to subject matter—by adding new areas of action or abandoning old ones—or with respect to modes of action—by switching, for example, from forum to service activities. Changes in functions can be traced in the programs of international organizations. There may be changes in the scale of operations, significant increases or, though not so likely, decreases in programs, for which budgets may provide an indicator. There may also be changes in the authority of an organization, either because members become more responsive to its decisions or because the organization begins to make enactments of a new kind that place more demands upon members. There is no necessary correlation between growth in scale and growth in authority; an organization's budget might grow at the same time that its importance for member states or its authority declined. Finally, there may be changes in the relative importance of an international organization within the issue-area or areas with which it is concerned. The extent to which the organization performs essential functions within the issue-area is relevant here. The existence or creation of another rival organization with overlapping jurisdiction would be an indication of significant change in this respect. Changes of the kinds suggested here may be explained by changes in membership of the organization, in the top personnel of the organization's bureaucracy, in the matters preoccupying member states, or in the new currents of ideas that may emerge.

Changes may be gradual, but one must watch for sudden discontinuities in an organization's history, significant changes in direction that could be termed turning points. Such turning points might occur in relation to any of the features mentioned in the previous paragraph—functions, scale, authority, or importance in the issue-area. They may also arise from dramatic and important changes in input—for example, in the intentions of major participants or in the membership of the organization. What constitutes a turning point is the abruptness, the unpredictability of a significant change, "an impulse which breaks through, untrammelled by the past."[3]

It has already been suggested that the environment of an organization—for example, the major preoccupations of governments, new currents of ideas, or such significant changes in the international system as the emergence of new nations—may affect its activities, or output. This relationship will be developed more fully below. Changes both in the environment and in the output of an organization may also be accompanied by an evolution in the rules for decision making within it. The complex relations between internal processes, on the one hand, and changes in the environment and in the organization's activities on the other, will have to be studied empirically. The importance of outlining the historical development of an international organization, particularly in terms of changing functions and structures, as a first phase in the study of decision making is to provide bench marks for the deeper study of these relationships.

Decision Making: A Taxonomical Analysis

Once the context provided by the functions, structure, and historical evolution of an agency is known, one can begin to consider patterns of decision making and the distribution of influence. For this purpose it is useful to classify decisions. The issue-area has proved a useful concept in studies of decision making in local and national politics,[4] and it is reasonable to assume that issue-areas are also significant in differentiating patterns of influence in international organizations.

Testing this notion in a comparative study, however, poses problems, for the concept of issue-areas has most often been applied in a relatively concrete and specific manner. For example, studies of local political systems have shown important differences between patterns of influence in decision making about educational and urban renewal issues. Attempts have been made to develop general typologies of issue-areas on the basis of the values at stake,[5] but these are difficult to apply empirically. A more manageable scheme for a comparative study of international organizations is to use a taxonomy of decisions based on the nature of the issues involved, a taxonomy that will also be comprehensive in the sense of covering all decisions of all the organizations studied.

This taxonomy divides decisions of international organizations into seven categories: representational, symbolic, boundary, programmatic, rule-creating, rule-supervisory, and operational.

Representational decisions affect membership in the organization and representation on internal bodies. They include decisions concerning the admission and exclusion of members, validation of credentials, determination of representation on executive organs and committees, and the manner in which the secretariat is composed, especially at the higher level.

Symbolic decisions are primarily tests of how opinions are aligned; no practical consequences in the form of actions flow directly from these decisions. The intention in symbolic issues is to test the acceptability of goals or ideologies intensely espoused by one group of actors or the legitimacy of long-accepted norms of dominant elites. In some cases these goals or ideologies may relate to broad issues of international politics, in others, to matters specific to the organization's field. In an organization with a mandate in the economic field, decolonization might be an example of a broad issue; improving the lot of developing countries would be an example of a goal specifically related to an organization. Some decisions that might fall within the definitions of other categories may be considered primarily symbolic; but as soon as the direct consequences of the decisions become appreciable, as for example in the controversies over the representation and participation of the communist states in ILO, these decisions fall into another category, in this instance, representational. The criteria for classification as symbolic are thus: the positive one of symbolic intention on the part of the decision makers; and the negative one of the absence of significant practical consequences flowing directly from the decision. The absence of direct consequences does not mean that symbolic decisions are unimportant. On the contrary, in the long run they may have profound consequences because of their effects on the milieu within which international relations are conducted.

This category of decisions can be singled out in order to test the hypothesis that symbolic issues tend to become acute during periods when the organization is adjusting to major changes in the environment that may entail shifts in the structure of influence and in the basic goals and policies of the organization. Such decisions may thus provide a particularly sensitive measure of changes in the internal distribution of influence.

Boundary decisions concern the organization's external relations with other international and regional structures on the matter of (1) their respective scopes, (2) cooperation among organizations, and (3) initiatives taken in one organization to provoke activity in another. All eight organizations considered in this project have some relation with the United Nations, and ITU, ILO, UNESCO, WHO, and IAEA receive substantial funds from the United Nations Development Program. A number of boundary issues arise in the context of these links. GATT and UNCTAD share overlapping jurisdictions, and to a lesser extent the same situation also exists among other organizations. When this occurs, boundary problems inevitably arise.

Programmatic decisions concern the strategic allocation of the organization's resources among different types of activity—the principal types are forum or service—and different fields of activity, which tend to be specific to each individual agency. Allocations usually result from negotiations among the actors concerning the main goals and division of emphasis among the programs of the organization. Budgets are often the framework within which programmatic decisions are taken.

Rule-creating decisions define rules or norms bearing upon matters within the substantive scope of the organization. The outcome of the decisions may in some cases be formal instruments such as conventions, agreements, or resolutions. Illustrations of decisions covered in this category include GATT's activity in the negotiation of agreements for tariff reductions, the establishment of Special Drawing Rights by the IMF, as well as the preparing of labor and health conventions by ILO and WHO. Rules may also be created in less formal ways; for example, speeches by the executive head or others that may never explicitly be the subject of votes may nonetheless articulate widely shared norms or goals with which the organization may come to be identified in the minds of many of its constituents. Such actions may in significant cases be considered as rule-creating decisions.

Some rule-creating decisions may resemble programmatic decisions because they seem to imply that certain priorities should be followed in making allocations; but decisions are considered to be programmatic only when they include a definition of priorities specifically for purposes of allocation, or, as is more usual, when they make an actual allocation in terms of budget or personnel.

Rule-supervisory decisions concern the application of approved rules by those subject to them. These decisions may involve various procedures ranging from highly structured to extremely subtle ones. The process of rule supervision passes through several stages, and organizations may develop distinct procedures for each of these stages.[6] The first stage is detection or gathering information about the observance or ignoring of rules. For example, are states complying with the frequency allocations agreed to within ITU? the standards set in International Labor Conventions? the safeguard provisions of IAEA? or the nondiscriminatory trading rules of GATT? Detection may be performed by states acting unilaterally or jointly, by the international bureaucracy, by a private panel, or by some combination of these.

Verifying whether or not the rules are observed is the second stage. This function may also be performed in various ways. Decisions could be entrusted to experts, to the international bureaucracy, or to representatives of member states, to list the most obvious alternatives. Proceedings could be public or private.

The final stage in rule supervision is applying sanctions or punishments for the violation of rules or awarding privileges for compliance with them. As in the other stages decisions about penalties and rewards can be made in several ways.

Operational decisions relate to the providing of services by the organization or the use of its resources in accordance with approved rules, policies, or programs. Examples are decisions about projects for specific technical assistance undertaken by UNESCO or other agencies or the granting of loans by IMF. They are essentially tactical allocations of resources made within broad strategic (programmatic) allocations. Frequently, such tactical, operational decisions are made largely between representatives of individual states and the international bureaucracy. In such decisions criteria referring to the pursuit of general goals may be diluted as a consequence of pressures for services and the need to retain clients' support.

Operational decisions may lead cumulatively to programmatic decisions. The inclusion of a program in an agency budget may be the culmination of a process in which the initiative came originally from an operational decision by the executive head or a segment of the international bureaucracy.

The extent to which operational decisions are effectively subordinated to programmatic decisions may indicate the degree of control that the executive head exercises over the bureaucracy. Weak control may lead to a dispersal of activities, which strengthens the relations between particular clients and segments of the bureaucracy but weakens the overall directing of resources. Strong control may give the executive head greater initiative to enlarge the tasks and enhance the autonomy of the organization.

In order to describe how decisions are usually arrived at for each of these categories of decision in a particular international organization, it will be useful to classify the actors involved, to consider the ways in which they may exercise influence, and to list the modes of decision making that may be employed.

The actors in international organizations may be classified according to the following categories:

1. representatives of national governments (who may be appointed by various ministries)
2. representatives of national and international private associations (including interest groups and commercial enterprises)
3. the executive heads of organizations
4. high officials and other members of the bureaucracy of each organization
5. individuals who serve in their own capacity formally or informally as advisers
6. representatives of other international organizations
7. employees of the mass media

Of course, not all of these classes of actors will be active in all organizations. For each category of decisions, however, the actors will fall into one or more of these classes, and it is important to know which of these categories of actors typically have the most influence on the outcome.

Influence can be exercised in many ways, but four of these seem particularly significant. In each decision some actor or group of actors must take the initiative and hence become the *initiator*. The real initiators are not always the formal initiators. For example, international officials sometimes prepare draft resolutions that are then submitted by members of national delegations. The identification of initiators consequently is a matter for critical inquiry, not a simple given fact. Some actors have the power, perhaps because of their strategic location in the line of communication or because of their control of extensive political resources, to block initiatives and hence to become *vetoers*. The term is not used exclusively in the formal sense of one having a legal power to veto, but in a practical, functional sense to denote one having the power to prevent a decision by whatever means he may require. There are some actors whose known or surmised views may have to be taken into account because of their control of resources or their formal authority, or for some other reason. They can be called *controllers*. Finally, others serve as go-betweens among the participants and as consensus builders. They are the *brokers*.

All of these different kinds of influence are important. Which is most important depends upon the total context of decision making, the way in which the particular political system under examination works, the patterns of interaction that are characteristic of it. Ideally it should be possible to distinguish and measure each kind of influence separately but according to the same scale. In practice this is not possible. But it is possible to clarify conceptually these four ways in which actors may be influential.

Initiatives and vetoes can be traced and ascribed to actors. The strength of the positive or negative influence that the initiative or veto implies depends upon an objective factor, the significance of the proposal; that is, how important it seems to the aggregate of actors in the decision-making process in terms of the consequences likely to follow from the decision. It depends also upon the subjective factor of how strongly the people who are for and against it feel about the matter. In order to compare strengths of influence it would be necessary to give some numerical expression to significance and intensity, an exercise that is not beyond the bounds of imagination.

Brokerage is a necessary and useful role, but is it influence? Do not brokers merely moderate and conciliate the influence of others? If we think of influence in the way proposed above, as the modification of one actor's behavior by the action of another, then brokers do exercise influence by bringing about modifications in the behavior of all actors involved in an issue. The more successful among them may add something to the resolution of a dispute that was not part of the intentions of either contestant but that helps both sides to come to agreement. A frequent way of resolving a dispute is to change the terms in which the problem is stated. Brokers themselves may stand to gain from the successful performance of their role, perhaps mainly through such long-term gains as an improved reputation and a consequent strengthening of the confidence they enjoy. A reputation for successful brokerage may give an actor a strategic position in the network of political communications; he may be increasingly consulted and kept informed by others. This constitutes for him a political resource, but a resource that depends upon the maintenance of his reputation. The influence of brokers may be constrained by their role. Theirs is a resource that is in danger of being expended once the attempt is made to convert it into positive or negative influence.

Initiating, vetoing, and brokerage imply activity in relation to a particular issue. The influence of the controller is different. It is conferred upon an actor by other actors' opinions of his potential for influence. It may also derive from the past history of an actor's behavior as an influential initiator, vetoer, or broker. Some actors may seek to become controllers and carefully cultivate their reputation for influence so as to be consulted upon important questions; others may, because of their power, have a controller's influence thrust upon them. A controller's influence is expressed in the difference between the way an actor actually behaves and the way he might behave if the controller were not part of the system or if his power and intentions were assessed differently. The government of one country might wish to initiate a certain proposal for action by an international organization but refrain from doing so because another country might oppose the proposal vigorously and successfully. More frequently, perhaps, initiatives will be shaped in such a way that they will meet the presumed views of controllers and therefore obtain their acquiescence or support. Thus, it is quite conceivable that some actors could have great influence in an international organization, though they actually initiated and vetoed very little.

Modes of interaction among actors may be divided into two broad categories, *analytical* and *bargaining*. When the first mode prevails, differences are settled by intellectual processes; facts are examined and rational techniques of analysis applied to them. Usually this mode is employed when the parties agree fundamentally about values and about the principles and criteria for decision. This is the mode of decision making used in a court of law or in a body of experts. When these conditions are not present, and especially when there are major conflicts of interests, rational techniques are much less likely to be determining, and bargaining is the normal mode of decision making. If agreement is to be reached, it will have to be on the basis of a compromise achieved more by barter than by rational argument.

In other areas of decision making it has been found that a formal procedure that appears to be analytical may in fact conceal a good deal of bargaining. We can expect that this phenomenon will also occur in international organizations, and thus it is important to look for evidences of bargaining in the preparation of decisions that are analytical in form.

This twofold classification is not the only possible one. Ernst Haas has suggested a classification into three decision-making modes conceived in terms of their integrative potential: the minimum common denominator, "splitting the difference," and "upgrading the common interest."[7] Haas was concerned primarily with outcomes and impacts of decisions.

The present study, however, is concerned primarily with processes rather than with outcomes or impacts. One purpose of the classification used in this book, for instance, is to relate modes of decision making to the relative influence of different categories of actors in each category of decisions. One would expect bureaucratic and expert influences to predominate when an analytical mode of decision making is used, and bargaining to be the mode when representatives of governments and interest groups predominate. To what extent are issues redefined so as to change the mode of decision making? Does a change in mode imply not only a change in the category of actors who affect the outcome but also perhaps a change in the nature of the decision—for example, from an operational decision to a programmatic decision? To find answers to questions such as these, the twofold distinction between analytical and bargaining modes suffices.

For each category of decisions, organizations tend to devise regular patterns of interaction. Thus, most decisions follow a routine. Occasionally, however, because of the newness or the importance of an issue, or for some other reason, routine patterns are discarded and others substituted. Crisis decisions would be a subset of this category. In this study we will be concerned with both routine and extraordinary interaction patterns.

Among the seven categories of decisions, some will be more important for particular agencies than for others. For example, rule-creating decisions are fairly important for all the agencies except perhaps UNCTAD, but rule-supervisory decisions are much more important for some than for others. IMF, IAEA, GATT, and ILO all have a major stake in international supervision and highly developed procedures for it. In other agencies it is less developed and seemingly less important. Symbolic decisions have been very important in ILO and UNCTAD but not very prominent in the work of the other organizations. Representational decisions also seem to be more salient in ILO than in the others. Programmatic decisions are a major focus of interest in UNESCO, WHO, and ILO; but they are of less concern in ITU, IMF, and GATT.

From the foregoing, it may be possible to sketch typical patterns of influence. Whatever the agency, we might expect to find that the same kind of actors were influential in the same category of decision. Government representatives would generally be most influential in representational, symbolic, and rule-creating decisions and less influential in boundary and operational decisions. Executive heads would be most influential in programmatic and boundary decisions compared to other types. International bureaucracies would be most influential in operational decisions and rule supervision when analytical techniques are used.

If such patterns of influences within each category of decision prove to be reasonably consistent, the general structure of influence within organizations—in particular the degree of domination by international bureaucracies or government representatives—would differ according to the relative saliency of the different categories of decisions for the organization.

All these suppositions are, of course, to be checked empirically in the studies of the individual agencies that follow this chapter. The patterns of interaction discovered in each of the international organizations and described according to the taxonomy of decisions will establish the structure of influence in each of them, disaggregating it by category of decision.

The next two sections of this chapter attempt to explain our mode of analyzing influence: first, through the actors in international organizations conceived as political systems, along with their sources of influence and their interactions within these systems viewed broadly as processes; and second, through the environments of these systems. The relation between these two levels of analysis can be expressed by saying that the extent to which the outcomes differ from what might have been predicted from an assessment of environmental forces—which exist independently of the existence of an international organization—is to be accounted for by process.

Actors and Their Sources of Influence

To consider international organizations as political systems raises certain conceptual difficulties. They are conglomerates, composed of bureaucracies and various conference structures. Nowadays the bureaucracies of international organizations tend to be recruited internationally; but, except for this feature, as political organs they are very much like national bureaucracies. The conference structures, however, have no direct analogue in national political systems. In form they resemble legislative bodies, and many of the procedures are the same. The participants in the conference structures of international organizations in most instances, however, are representatives of states who have more or less rigid instructions, and this feature makes these structures fundamentally different from national and local legislative bodies. Furthermore, only in exceptional instances do international organizations have actual authoritative control over substantial resources that might be needed to implement their decisions; generally such authoritative control is the prerogative of member states. Of the organizations treated in this project, only the International Monetary Fund has its own resources.

Because of the conglomerate nature of international organizations the term has been conceived to mean various things: (1) those appointed to act in the name of the organizations, usually the executive head and the international bureaucracy; (2) the direct participants in decisions, including the executive head, the international bureaucracy, and those who take part in the associated conference machinery (the assembly, the executive body or council, and other committees and commissions); and (3) a system of interaction including all of those who directly participate in decisions taken within the framework of the organization, and in addition all officials and individuals who in various ways actively determine the positions of the direct participants.

Although the third conception conforms less to common usage than the first two, it is the most realistic basis for defining international organizations as political systems. International organizations should be conceived of in a way that includes linkages with member states. Not to do so and to limit consideration of political processes to what happens in conferences eliminates some of the most important aspects of decision making. As already noted, representatives of states are as a rule instructed agents, and any conception that did not take this into account would be incomplete. Moreover, states are not monolithic. There may not be unanimity within a state about the policy that it should pursue in an international organization; and interdepartmental differences or differences between an important interest group and a department of government can have extremely serious consequences for decision making in that organization. As a final reason why a conception should include linkages with member states, the activity of international organizations frequently depends upon actions by member states, and a narrower conception would indicate greater autonomy for international organizations than they actually possess.

The definition of an international organization as a political system that includes national elements raises a problem concerning the identity of the states that are members of these organizations. For example, the "United States" that is a member of the IMF is a subsystem composed not only of officials of the Treasury and the Federal Reserve, but other financial agencies, and probably some Wall Street bankers and a few individuals—theorists or practitioners—who influence financial policy. The "United States" that is a member of the ILO is another subsystem that includes some officials of the departments of Labor, State, and Commerce, as well as George Meany, president of the AFL-CIO, and his foreign policy advisers; Edward Neilan, who is the employer delegate; and some officials of the U.S. Chamber of Commerce. These two subsystems may have only the most remote and tenuous relations with each other, at least under normal circumstances, through the national political system. Although such country subsystems are composed of individuals, it is often convenient to refer to the components of and actors in the subsystems, such as a government department, an interest group, or a segment of one of these, as limited collectivities. Doing this rather than singling out individuals implies that these limited collectivities achieve or enforce collective views. Country subsystems are subsystems both of the international organization to which they relate and of the national political system.

Other subsystems, such as those made up of officials of major international institutional groups—the Roman Catholic church, the International Chamber of Commerce, or even multinational corporations that play a role in particular international organizations—are similarly part of two overlapping political systems. In keeping with their formal functions, such subsystems may be generically referred to as *representative subsystems*. The most numerous and most important of these, of course, are country subsystems.

The direct participants in the decisions of an international organization may also be thought of as a subsystem that can be called the *participant subsystem*. This subsystem comprises those members of the representative subsystems who actually participate in the organization's decision-making processes, for example, as delegates at international conferences; it also includes other individuals, such as the executive head of the organization, who also take part directly in these processes. Again, although individuals are always involved, there may be occasions when it is accurate to refer to such limited collectivities as national delegations or segments of the international bureaucracy.

In terms of the broad concept used here, as a political system an international organization includes both its participant subsystem and its representative subsystems.

Conceiving of member states as country subsystems makes it easier to examine alliances between segments of these subsystems and of the participant subsystem, for example, an alliance that the international bureaucracy and certain functional departments of governments enter into on the basis of shared interests. Actors in the participant subsystem may be able to exploit cleavages within a country subsystem (or other representative subsystems) and to build up transnational alliances comprising segments from a number of representative subsystems as well as actors in the participant subsystem. The possibility that such alliances may develop is one of the most interesting aspects of the politics of international organizations. Some country subsystems will be more complex than others and some more open or penetrable by would-be alliance builders. Presumably there is some relationship between the degree of openness of a country generally and the openness of its country subsystem, but this and the whole subject need empirical examination.

The concept of a country subsystem must be related to the more commonly used juridical concept of a member state, and an analogous problem arises for other collectivities, such as interest groups, that participate in international organizations. The difference is essentially the distinction between those few individuals of the collectivity who shape and articulate policy in the international organization, in contrast to the collectivity as a whole, whose interest in the international organizations in question may be only marginal.

In terms of the concepts used here the states or other major relevant collectivities are considered to be parts of the environment of the international organization's political system. (The environment itself is treated in detail in the next section of this chapter.) Country subsystems are the linkages between environmental forces and the participant subsystems of the international organization. Representation is the process by which this linkage is effected.

Each state has power, or the capability of exercising influence, in international affairs broadly as well as in the specific field of the international organization in question. The country subsystem may mobilize these capabilities as resources for influence in the international organization. Such capabilities are always limited. Even the most powerful country cannot convert its power into influence operating simultaneously upon all the issues that might concern it. And many times competing claims will be urged within the national political system for the use of its power. For these and other reasons a country subsystem may not be able to command the full potential resources for influence that a state possesses. How far the state is prepared to convert its capabilities into influence within a particular international organization may often be determined by some authority higher than the country subsystem and outside it. That is, the high political authorities of the state may decide to limit their commitment or participation in an international organization or perhaps to press hard for certain goals through the international organization. How the high political authorities perceive the importance of an international organization for a state and the priority they are prepared to give to the exercise of influence in that body at the expense of other goals are environmental variables representing an important aspect of the conditions within which the country subsystem operates.

The country subsystem can take part in defining the national interests concerning the international organization and in placing demands upon the national political system for resources to influence decisions in the international organization. Simultaneously, within the international organization it articulates interests (which may be national, sectional, or both) on behalf of the national political system, and in so doing it may interpret their meaning. As a subsidiary task, the country subsystem also recruits new personnel into the political system of the international organization and socializes its individual members to the norms of the political system. The country subsystem is thus a channel transmitting support and demands from the national political system, representing part of the environment, to the international organization; and it is also a channel for demands that the international organization needs to make on the national political system.

A political system conceived in this way, while it corresponds to the realities of politics in international organizations and permits an appreciation of the rich relationships that develop, poses problems for comparative research because of its complexity. It is thus necessary to translate it into a more simplified set of working concepts that can be used in a comparative study.

As already noted, this study focuses upon two levels of explanation: one derives from interactions within the participant subsystem, the other from environmental variables. In regard to the participant subsystem, attention is especially focused on the sources of actors' influence, factors affecting their orientation and the structuring of relationships among actors through interaction within the system—in short, on the dynamics of process and on the effects of process upon the system itself. The country or other representative subsystems have a less central place in this inquiry, although their usefulness for explaining the resources and orientation of the actors in the decision-making subsystem should be underlined. Other studies might give a fuller place to this level of explanation.[8]

As conceived in this study, the actors are individuals who participate directly in the decisions of an international organization. The power of actors—that is, their capacity to exercise influence—is derived both from their position or office and from their personal characteristics. The representatives of some states or the occupants of some positions within international organizations will be important in certain decisions regardless of who they are. Even in these cases, though, the personal characteristics of individuals can enhance or diminish the power that would normally accrue to someone in their position. For example, Ambassador Goldberg had considerable power in the United Nations because he was the United States representative, but some of his power was also attributable to his personal qualities and skills as a negotiator and to his political connections.

Position includes as potentiality the resources of the collectivity represented by the individual and the priority given by the authorities of the collectivity to the use of these resources for influence in the organization. These resources can be of different orders: states may possess economic and military strength, which may be accorded deference in certain decisions; high international officials may command information and recognition, which allows them the initiative in proposing action or resolving conflict. Every position also carries with it its own history of previous attitudes and actions that predispose the behavior of the incumbent in certain directions; it includes also certain limitations in the form of binding instructions imposed by higher authorities in the collectivities represented.

Personal characteristics include skills necessary to carry out the duties and exploit the possibilities of a position: mobilizing the resources of the collectivity represented to achieve influence in the organization, shaping instructions for performing the duties of the position, and influencing the behavior of other actors.

An actor's power or his capacity to exercise influence is thus compounded of his position and his personal attributes. For the sake of clarity the relationship can be expressed in symbolic form:

$$P \pm A = C$$

Position or office (P) modified by (in this formula, plus or minus) personal attributes (A) equals the power or the capacity (C) of the individual actor. C is a function of P and also a function of A, but P and A vary independently. Although the form in which this symbolic statement is written assumes that A will add to or detract from P, in some circumstances the relationship may be multiplicative or more complex. This equation is not intended to create an illusion of precise mathematical treatment. Some of the concepts have not been, and probably cannot be, represented in a numerical form that would lend itself to mathematical application.

Among the personal attributes that might enhance an individual's power in an international organization are his personal charisma, ideological legitimacy, administrative competence, expert knowledge, long association with an organization, negotiating ability, and ability to persist in intransigence. The personal status he has acquired outside the organization through such things as wealth, election to an important office, scientific achievements, and possession of significant influence in an important collectivity will also affect his power. The advantages of these personal attributes vary with organizations. For example, negotiating ability might be especially valuable in organizations like GATT where consensus must be achieved, while the ability to persist in intransigence might be a telling factor in UNCTAD if the outcome was to be a declaratory resolution.

An actor's power attributable to his position may be represented symbolically here as:

$$X_c\,(G \pm S) = P$$

That is, the capability of the position of an actor (P) is a function of the priority (X_c) that the authorities of the collectivity attach to converting their capabilities in international affairs generally (G), as modified by their capabilities in the specific field of the organization in question (S) into influence in the organization. This anticipates somewhat the discussion of the components of the general and the specific capabilities of states to be presented in the next section, dealing with the environment, but it should be noted here that other kinds of power besides material power are included. Thus this symbolic statement can be used for other collectivities as well as states.

Substituting the components of the actor's position for P, the symbolic statement for an actor's power is:

$$X_c\,(G \pm S) \pm A = C$$

Like the authorities of the collectivities they represent, actors also exercise judgment about the conversion of their capabilities into influence. Here, we are referring to active influence in the sense discussed in the previous section. For both the individual actor and the authorities of the collectivity, the decision whether or not they should seek to use available resources to gain influence will depend upon several factors, including the intensity of their feelings about the issues at stake and their estimates of the probability and the costs of obtaining their goals. In estimating such probabilities actors make assumptions about the controller influence of others as well as about the likely extent of opposition and support. If they seek to exercise influence, the degree of their success will depend on how all the other influences within the organization are distributed on the issue at stake. For example, when faced with a united opposition, the representative of a powerful state might find it impossible to achieve an objective, whereas in other circumstances he would succeed easily.

Obviously, the influence that an individual actor actually exercises in the participant subsystem of an international organization may differ considerably from his capacity or power. Putting it in abbreviated fashion, the influence of an individual actor (I) is the result of his power (C) as modified by his decision to attempt to convert his power into influence (X_a) and by the distribution of all other influences within the organization on a particular issue (D). Symbolically, this can be expressed as:

$$X_a \cdot C \cdot D = I$$

The distribution of all other influences includes the pattern of alignments on a particular issue, as well as how other actors feel about it, the weight of their opinions, and their power. Thus it includes those who would support, oppose, or be indifferent. It also includes the deference accorded to the actor in question by other actors.

As the focal point of analysis shifts from the capacities of actors to their influence, attention must be given to their attitudes and perceptions and more broadly to process. Attitudes and perceptions are crucially important factors affecting actors' behavior; they have an effect, among other things, on whether or not the actors will seek to convert their capacities into influence. Process, the working out of strategies to obtain goals, the building of alliances, coalitions, and consensus, determines the configuration of forces within an organization.

The fundamental questions concerning attitudes and perceptions are how actors see the organization in question and how they understand its purposes and potentialities, particularly in terms of their own interests and objectives. The distribution and interplay between personal goals and public goals must be investigated in this connection. Personal goals involve such things as jobs, prestige, and tourism. There is every reason to suspect that personal goals play as great a part in international as in national or local politics. Public goals include those relating to both the substantive concerns of the organization and the interests of the collectivities that the actors represent. Concern for survival and growth of the organization as a whole or of subunits might be derived either from public or personal goals. Actors may have different points of view formed by their experience and professional training, as lawyers, economists, scientists, or engineers, for example, which mold their attitudes in certain directions. Actors may be grouped according to common perceptions of the organization and according to the intensity of their commitment to the organization and its goals.

A particularly significant case of regularities in perceptions and attitudes takes the form of organizational ideology. As defined here, an organizational ideology would contain—

1. an interpretation of the environment as it relates to action by the organization
2. specification of goals to be attained in the environment
3. a strategy of action for attaining these goals

Organizational ideologies might be narrow or broad. Functionalism is an ideology that is applicable to international organizations representing a variety of objectives. (The precise nature of these objectives is largely irrelevant, but they must be specific.) Functionalism stresses developing collaboration among states with regard to specific objectives as a means of gradually eroding the authority of nation-states in favor of world institutions. Marxist and populist ideologies compete with functionalism as other broad interpretations of the aims and strategies of international organizations. International organizations are seen in the Marxist view as expressing power relations between socialist and capitalist blocs; to the populist, they appear as a means of exerting pressure by the numerous poor upon the few rich. Along with these broad organizational ideologies are narrower and more task-oriented ideologies. Thus "education for development" is an ideology of UNESCO and to some extent of ILO, and nondiscrimination or the most favored nation are ideologies of GATT and IMF. It is of interest to ascertain whether such organizational ideologies exist, how they came into being, and how widely they are shared. Other important questions are whether they are especially linked with certain actors, whether they are publicized, and whether competing organizational ideologies exist.

Perceptions and attitudes are particularly important in identifying who pushes for what. No one assumes, however, that attitudes and perceptions impel actors in only one direction. On the contrary, actors may often be subject to conflicting pressures, and one of the reasons why special attention is given to organizational ideologies is to see the extent to which these pressures act counter to other motivational forces. A particularly interesting question is whether dual loyalties emerge with some actors, leading them not only to represent the views of their collectivity in the organization but also to exert influence on their collectivity in line with the consensus reached by the organization or in conformity with organizational ideology.

The formal structures and procedures of the organization are the institutional constraints within which the strategies of the actors are developed. But when attitudes are translated into strategies within these formal constraints, the actors create additional and often informal structures.

These structures created in the political process itself may be studied in various ways. In the first place, we look for persistent groupings of actors.[9] These may be formal groupings such as caucuses or informal networks involving an ingroup or establishment of actors who occupy key positions and who normally consult among each other about important decisions. Persistent groupings may enhance or decrease the possibility of an individual actor's exercising influence. An actor may find it easier to attain his objectives because of his membership in a coalition, or an opposing coalition may place obstructions in his path.

Such groupings determine, secondly, the configurations of influence within organizations, which may take forms approximating (1) unanimity; (2) one dominant coalition, possibly led by a dominant actor; (3) polarization between two rival coalitions; (4) a larger number of alliances, none of which dominates; or (5) crosscutting cleavages on different issues with no general pattern. The coalition policies of executive heads and members of international bureaucracies, as well as those of national representatives, are important factors determining these configurations.

Finally, there is the identification of elites made up of influential individual participants, elites that cut across groupings and configurations and thus show the stratification of influence in the organization. It is by knowing who is most influential that we can infer which resources are the most significant determinants of influence.

No single measure of the influence of actors in international organizations is entirely satisfactory, but several methods in combination should make it possible to take into account, if not correct, the inadequacies of each.

Analysis of voting has sometimes been thought of as one means of assessing relative influence.[10] However, in several of the organizations covered in this study votes are rarely taken, and in any case voting statistics are usually only useful to indicate the influence of states, not individual actors. Furthermore, analysis of voting cannot gauge influence exercised by those acting as brokers or controllers.

Other methods used in this study are similar to those employed in studies focusing on influence in other kinds of political systems. One of these methods is to note the formal structure of authority. Who holds the top offices in the hierarchy, including membership on executive bodies and the higher offices of the international bureaucracy? The limitations of this measurement are those that apply in any political system. Formal position in the hierarchy does not necessarily confer great influence. Some who are not influential will be included; and some who are influential may not appear.

Another device used in this study to measure influence has been to ask a panel of knowledgeable persons to list the individuals with the greatest general influence in each of the organizations. The weaknesses of the method lie in the variations in the competency of the judges and in the way they interpret "general influence." Its advantage lies in the possibility that the answers may identify influential individuals who do not occupy positions of formal authority. It must be borne in mind that this is a measure of reputation for influence.

A measure of behavioral influence has also been attempted for some organizations, based on the scores actors achieve for success in initiating and obstructing proposals. This method ignores broker and controller influence and as a consequence could yield rather different results from the measurement of influence by reputation. Another problem in applying this approach is distinguishing the relative importance of the proposals that are the subjects of initiatives and vetoes.

Finally, in some cases it has been possible to evaluate influence by closely studying the interactions involved in particular decisions. This method can yield greater insights into the processes of influence than other methods; but it is bound to be illustrative rather than comprehensive.

The other points of measurement of power and influence used in this book are to be viewed as rough approximations, offered because they may help illustrate a model of decision making that is too complex to allow for measurement of some of its more important variables and that directs special attention to process. The value of the study should rest on other grounds than the sophistication of its measurements.

The purpose of trying to measure influence goes beyond simply wishing to know which particular actors have the most influence at any particular time. Finding out more about the characteristics and sources of influence of each of the most influential actors is one step toward inferring more generally the relative importance of different sources of influence in different international organizations. What other sources· of influence compete most effectively with a position as representative of a powerful state? In which organizations do administrative competency or expert ability carry most weight? Which give preeminence to ideological legitimacy, that is, the definition and articulation of an ideological position, whether in the form of an organizational ideology or of one of the major ideologies of world politics?

Analyzing the backgrounds of the most influential actors and the roads they have followed to gain influence should give some clues to the relative importance of various personal attributes and should help to single out the positions or offices that are most likely to be springboards to influence. In some organizations these may be membership on the executive board; in others, posts in the secretariat. Some study of persons without influence may also be revealing, particularly if they might have been expected to be influential because of their positions.

Analysis of the political systems of international organizations on the above lines should show how the structures of influence within these systems arise and change. In part, this structure is determined by the capabilities and demands of the actors, that is, by input into the system from its environment. In part, it arises out of processes within the system itself. It would be particularly interesting to know how much is to be accounted for in terms of process alone; but this is very difficult to assess directly.

Environmental Impacts

The next step is to isolate that influence which is attributable to environment. International organizations are aspects of international relations or more broadly of world politics. To understand international organizations we must devise a framework that will make the decisions and actions taken through them intelligible in the context of events where they originate and which they may affect. International organizations are thought of in this study as systems that are not fully autonomous, but rather are subject to environmental forces that become major constraints upon and determinants of decisions.

These decisions, it is assumed, will reflect a pattern of expectations and demands that can be perceived in the world situation, for example, the desire of states for greater security from external violence or for freedom from

unilateral domination by one powerful country, or the desire for redistribution of the world's resources or for widespread acceptance of some
particular principles of political organization or ideology. The pattern of
expectations and demands—in particular, the relative strength of different
demands—and the extent of compatibility or of conflict among different
demands—is in turn assumed to be determined by certain objectively
ascertainable conditions in the world, including the relative military and
economic power of states, their level of economic development and social
mobilization, governmental effectiveness, and the basic principles of organization of different polities.

These objectively ascertainable conditions, which make up the environment of international organizations, can be thought of also as a system; they
can be described in terms of the stratification and characteristics of actors
and the patterns of interaction. The concept of the international system
corresponds very broadly to what is called in this study the environment of
international organizations. In the present context, however, the notion of
environment will include a number of factors that have not always been
considered by other authors to fall within the concept of an international
system, such as levels of economic development and distribution of different
types of polity.

This study does not limit the consideration of the equilibrium between an
international organization and its environment to a particular moment in
time. It is concerned with the historical development of international
organizations and with the changes in decision making and influence that are
associated with historical development. It is thus necessary to show how the
different key elements constituting the environment change and interact
through time. The environmental systems thus described will be concrete
historical systems that existed during the period encompassed by this study.
To avoid confusion, we shall not refer to the environment as a system, but
confine the term to the political systems of international organizations as
outlined in the preceding section of this chapter.

The separation between what goes into the international organization as a
political system and what goes into the environment is an analytical
distinction; it concerns the aspect of the entity considered rather than the
entity itself. States fall under both headings. Generally, characteristics of
states that are relevant to the functions and activities of an international
organization but do not involve active relationship with that organization are
elements of the environment. The machinery and personnel for participation
in an international organization are, on the other hand, considered part of
the organization's political or decision-making system and have been called
the country subsystem. Thus a state's gross national product, exports,
population, and type of polity are considered elements in the environment
of GATT or UNCTAD; its ministry of commerce, office of the president,
central bank, and other agencies, insofar as they are involved in briefing or

participating in delegations to GATT or UNCTAD, are part of the political systems of those organizations.

The environment can be considered to comprise a number of variables; some are common to all international organizations, and some are confined to particular organizations. Drawing this distinction between general and specific environments makes it possible to evaluate the relative importance of each in explaining decision-making processes and influence in international organizations. Classical functionalist theory would give greater importance to the specific than to the general environment. This is a proposition to be tested here.

We conceive the general environment in terms of states, their characteristics, and their broad policies. This is because states are the principal units in world politics, the dominant mode for organizing human and physical resources. They alone can become members of international organizations. This focus on states is, of course, a limitation. A case could well be made for including some transnational societal phenomena as important elements in the environment of international organizations, for example, religious movements, multinational corporations, or emerging forms of behavior and values. These are excluded from explicit consideration in this discussion of the general environment so that the concept may be expressed as simply and clearly as possible; but societal factors may arise in connection with the specific environments of certain organizations covered in the study.

Under the method proposed to describe the general environment the tasks are, first, to identify its key variables; then, to devise suitable indicators of change in these variables; and finally, to show the patterns made by changes in the variables, the time span of the study being divided for this purpose into significant historical periods. This scheme would make it possible to examine how changes in the general environment may help to explain changes in the structure of influence of international organizations. The general environment is dealt with in detail in the next chapter, and each chapter devoted to an international organization indicates something about that organization's specific environment. In this chapter the treatment of the environment is limited to pointing out the ideas underlying the concept.

Three major variables describe the general environment: the stratification of state power, the economic and political characteristics of states, and the patterns of alignment and conflict among states. These three variables are selected in the light of assumptions about the relations between certain preeminent characteristics of states and the behavior of states in international organizations. How correct these assumptions are will be established only when the evidence is in.

In the consideration of the first variable it is assumed that some relationship exists between the power of a state in international affairs generally and its power in international organizations. Since power is a primary factor in influence, there is likely to be a connection between a state's power in relation to other states and its influence in international organizations generally. The point of considering the stratification of power is to explore this relationship. We would expect the United States and the USSR, as powerful states, to have greater influence than Canada, Sweden, or India in any international organization, irrespective of its functional field; and we would expect Canada, Sweden, or India to have greater influence over decisions than Nicaragua, Gabon, or Cambodia. In order to test the validity of this assumption and its limits, it will be necessary to rank states according to their power.

The nature and components of power in international relations raise numerous difficult issues that have been debated at length. It would be presumptuous to attempt to resolve these issues within the compass of the present study and unnecessary to review in detail all the previous work on the subject. The ranking of power is constructed on the basis of concepts that are relevant to the purposes of this work, which explains and justifies the fact that it differs in some points from rankings devised by other authors.[11] The aggregate term *power* used here includes power in the form of such material resources as economic and military capabilities and also power in the form of such other resources as determination, reputation, or prestige.

The second major variable in the description of the general environment is the distribution of states according to their economic and political characteristics. Here it is assumed that the economic development of a state is important in determining the demands the state will place on an international organization, especially the type and priority of services demanded—for example, whether it would prefer an organization to be a clearinghouse for information or an agency for redistributing the world's wealth. Various questions merit exploration in this connection: Do the poorer countries tend to see international organizations as offering opportunities for pressure in favor of redistributing the world's wealth? If so, do they emphasize representational issues with the aim of gaining greater control over these organizations so as to use them more effectively for redistribution? Because of their concern with the initial accumulation of capital and technical skills, do countries in the early stages of modernization (as distinct from the poorest undeveloped countries, on the one hand, and those that have achieved sustained growth, on the other) place the heaviest demands upon international organizations for services to help fill these needs? Are there some states that are so concerned with internal problems of industrialization that they place fewer demands upon international organizations than either the poorer states in an earlier stage of modernization or the richer states? Are the richer states inclined to demand technically sophisticated services of international organizations? And are they more likely than poor states to stress rule-creating and especially rule-supervisory decisions, perhaps as means of protecting their own acquired positions?

It has also frequently been assumed that the internal polity of a state affects such aspects of its behavior in international organizations as its style of participation, its degree of commitment to the organizations, and its responsiveness to their decisions. International organizations have sometimes been seen as the creations of democratic states in their own image. Their assemblies have been compared figuratively with the elected assemblies of democratic polities—as parliaments of mankind. The ideals of international organization have been seen as the logical extension of the ideals of democracy—universal respect for the rights of the individual and the need to provide opportunities for his social fulfillment. But in practice can we find any discernible differences in the way democratic and nondemocratic states behave in and toward international organizations?

To examine the assumption giving rise to this question, it is necessary to classify states according to a typology of political regimes. This is no easy task. Classifying states according to levels of economic development is simple compared with the difficulties of conceiving and applying a typology of polities. Once again, we tread in an area where many issues have been raised and few resolved and where terminology as well as facts are much in dispute. Nevertheless, a classification has been possible here by building upon the work of others.[12]

Two dimensions of polities are particularly significant for the purposes of this study. In the first place, it is important to know whether the polity is democratic in the sense that there is a regularly accepted and reasonably orderly competition for political power. Second, when countries cannot be described as democratic in this sense, it is important to know whether the state is one that is in the hands of a revolutionary group seeking to mobilize the population with the aim of transforming society to fit its own ideology or whether it belongs in a third class, those where a more conservative group holds the reins and is preserving in broad outlines the existing structure of social power and wealth. These three types are called *competitive, mobilizing,* and *authoritarian.* It should be stressed that the criteria distinguishing them relate to internal politics, not to external alignments. The classification is designed to help uncover any meaningful relations between the internal character of the state's polity and its external behavior, particularly in international organizations.

Another set of questions arises in this connection. It has often been thought characteristic of revolutionary governments that they use foreign policy issues as a means of mobilizing domestic support. Will it, then, be found that the mobilizing regimes are most active in initiating and supporting symbolic decisions in international organizations? Will these regimes be more concerned than others that symbolic decisions and rule-creating or rule-supervisory decisions conform with their ideologies?

Conversely, it may be assumed that authoritarian regimes care less whether the positions they take in international organizations reflect the characteristics of the regime. They can tolerate a hiatus between the principles they formally support in an international forum and their practices at home precisely because their populations are not mobilized and articulate on the issues involved, and the regimes are not seeking to mobilize them. Ideological consistency will thus be less important for authoritarian regimes than for polities concerned with mobilization. Will it then be found that the delegates of authoritarian regimes in international organizations are relatively more free and less instructed than those of other types, that their actions depend more on their personal or idiosyncratic characteristics, and that they have greater opportunities to act as brokers?

In regard to competitive polities, it is often assumed that such polities are more penetrable, "open" societies and thus more likely to acquiesce in the authority of international organizations. There is more likelihood that groups within these societies will protest failures to observe international obligations. Will it then be found that competitive polities take rule-creating decisions more seriously than other polities do and agree only to decisions with which they feel they can comply? Will it also be found that for competitive polities changes of government and of policies at home are reflected in initiatives and support for rule-creating and programmatic decisions in international organizations?

Finally, a number of countries have changed their type of regime during the time span covered by this study. Have there been observable consequences in such international behavior by these countries, such as joining or leaving international organizations, changing their style of participation, or changing their demands?

Patterns of conflicts and alignments on major world political and ideological issues constitute the third variable used to describe the general environment. It is assumed that these patterns will have some effect on decision making in international organizations even when the subject matter of particular decisions may seem remote from the conflicts in which world political alignments originated. For example, many technical issues have acquired political overtones because of the East-West conflict. On the other hand, classical functionalist theory would have predicted that the more technical an issue is the more likely the chances are of avoiding the complications of politics. Thus the exact effect of these patterns on particular types of decisions at particular times and in particular organizations has to be considered.

Various writers on international relations have sought to describe the patterns of conflict and alignment among states in abstract terms. Usually, a dichotomy is created according to the writer's aesthetic and theoretical sensibilities between have and have-not, satisfied and dissatisfied, imperialist or self-extensive states and the status quo or self-preserving states. Morton Kaplan has gone beyond this with his conception of six political systems: the balance-of-power system, the loose bipolar system, the tight bipolar system, the universal system, the hierarchical system, and the unit veto system.13 He has developed patterns of interaction that pertain to each of these systems.

In the present study the patterns of alignment and conflict are described in more concrete terms, chiefly because it is difficult to fit abstract schemes to the empirical facts. Indeed, many other writers have not intended to provide descriptions of actual international political systems. For example, Kaplan viewed his systems primarily as heuristic models.14 Also, perhaps because the time span involved in this investigation is relatively brief, the more abstract schemes provide categories that are too gross and that therefore blur important distinctions. Even though states can be divided between the haves and the have-nots or between those interested in self-preservation and those seeking aggrandizement, the differences within each of the resulting groups are sometimes even greater than the differences between them. And although it is possible to describe the international political system in the late forties and early fifties as a loose bipolar system, this subordinates all other relationships to the Soviet-American, or communist-anticommunist clash. This clash was perhaps the most important conflict of that period; but it was not the only conflict, and even less was it the only relationship. Instead there were several overlapping patterns of relations. The first of these involved the clash between the communist states and that group loosely termed the West. The second centered on the struggle to end colonialism. The third was the related but different controversy between the rich and the poor states of the world, and the fourth was the issue of regional integration, particularly in Western Europe. Each of these patterns has had its principal actors. But for various reasons, including the nature of contemporary communications, all have tended to involve almost the entire world in one way or another, and consequently the patterns have been overlapping. The changing configuration of these patterns can be described in broad outline.

Since these patterns have not been congruent, it is impossible to create one wholly satisfactory scheme for classifying states according to their part in them. Still, some scheme is necessary to facilitate comparison, and the one that we intuitively regard as having the most general applicability is the following threefold division:

Western states: Australia, Austria, Belgium, Canada, Denmark, Federal Republic of Germany, Finland, France, Greece, Iceland, Ireland, Israel, Italy, Japan, Luxembourg, Netherlands, New Zealand, Norway, Portugal, South Africa, Spain, Sweden, Switzerland, Turkey, United Kingdom, United States

Socialist states: Albania, Bulgaria, Byelorussian S.S.R., Cuba (after 1960), Czechoslovakia, German Democratic Republic, Hungary, Mongolia, North Korea, North Vietnam, People's Republic of China, Poland, Rumania, Ukranian S.S.R., USSR, Yugoslavia

Other states: a residual category

In contrast to the classification of states according to type of polity, this classification refers to foreign policy alignments rather than to the internal political system of a state. Since foreign policy alignments grow stronger or weaker over time even if they do not shift, and since their strength and direction may differ on different issues, a classification by alignments is bound to be conceptually unsatisfactory. In practice, however, such a classification may prove to be more relevant to the divisions within international organizations than a classification based on the nature of polities would be, since the first is more directly related to the phenomena of behavior in international organizations. Its value may prove to lie less in conceptual clarity than in the extent to which it fits the facts.

The Western-Socialist-Others scheme of classification applies to both East-West and North-South cleavages. The Western group includes those countries that in the OEEC and NATO formed the core of the Western alliance from about 1949. It includes some other states that have been identified formally or informally with this alliance system, in particular, Australia, Israel, New Zealand, and Japan. In addition, the European neutrals (Austria, Finland, Sweden, and Switzerland) are included because it is assumed that these countries, though nonaligned in a military sense, are closely related to the Western group especially in economic matters. The Western group excludes some Asian countries that have been linked with the Western alliance system—such as Pakistan—since it is assumed that their primary identification in international organizations will be with the less-developed countries; for them the North-South cleavage will be more significant than the East-West.

The Socialist group includes the members of COMECON and related countries. In the case of the less-developed countries classified here, such as Cuba after 1960, it is assumed that the East-West cleavage has more importance for their foreign relations than the North-South. Yugoslavia is a debatable case but is included here on the grounds that it is more interesting to consider that country's behavior as a deviant from the Socialist group than as a member of either of the other two categories.

The classification Other states, though technically residual, in fact corresponds roughly to the less-developed countries, or in post-UNCTAD terms, to the Group of 77. South Africa, which by the purely residual test might have been classified there, has instead been placed in the Western category. In some instances it may be more meaningful to subdivide the group termed Others by regions: Asia, the Arab states of the Middle East, Africa, and Latin America.

Using the threefold alingment classification should help show the extent to which decisions of different kinds in international organizations reflect the major political cleavages affecting the world. This is, of course, only a first step toward explaining the degree of relevancy of these cleavages.

Changes in the three environmental variables can be traced through the time span of this study, which can then be divided into significant historical periods, each characterized by the specific way in which the key variables are related. This succession of historical phases provides points of reference that serve as guides in exploring the relation between changes in the general environment and the evolution of each international organization. Various questions arise in this connection.

One concerns the consequences that changing political alignments may have on the work and development of international organizations. The earliest phase of the period studied, corresponding to the cold war, was characterized by East-West bipolarity. In such a situation of political bipolarity, do international organizations have a tendency to become aligned with one of the blocs, in the active sense that the bloc uses the organization as an instrument of political warfare, or in the more passive sense that the organization's policies are most responsive to those of the dominant state in one bloc? In a situation of more diffuse international alignments, by contrast, do executive heads of international organizations and their bureaucracies tend to rely upon the support of nonaligned states, thereby perhaps achieving greater autonomy vis-à-vis the most powerful states? Firm conclusions concerning these questions cannot, of course, be drawn from the limited number of cases to be studied in this book; but careful examination of individual agencies may throw light upon the mechanisms underlying such relationships.

Other questions refer to aspects of functionalist theory, which places great stress upon the possibilities of depoliticizing international relations by concentrating on specific functional problems and letting experts or representatives of the relevant interests deal with them. Does it seem to be true that international organizations that conform with functionalist precepts are less likely to be affected by world political alignments or by the types of domestic political regimes characteristic of its members? In order to explore more deeply these functionalist theses, it is useful to distinguish between four concepts referring to the assigned functions of international organization and described by the terms *technical, functionally specific, essential,* and *salient.* Technical is taken to mean dependent upon a generally recognized body of specialized knowledge. Used in this sense the most technical subject matter would be that related to the physical and biological sciences. Functionally specific refers to the issue-area, for example, health, education, or labor, whereas technical refers to the knowledge required to deal with the issues. Essential suggests a problem that requires international cooperation for its solution, such as the delivery of mail between countries. Salient refers to the importance accorded to the subject matter of the organization's work by the political authorities of states. Insofar as functionalist theories are valid, it might be assumed that those international organizations that are most technical, functionally specific, and essential would be least affected by patterns of conflict and alignments and by the nature of political regimes. On the other hand, the more salient the subject matter, the more it would claim attention from the top political authorities in states, and thus the more likely it would be that world political alignments would affect the organization.

There are no completely satisfactory ways in which the concepts involved in these questions can be applied operationally. However, various indicators can be used as bench marks: membership, composition of executive organs, composition of the bureaucratic leadership, defined aims of the organization, scope of the organization's functions, programs emphasized, and budgetary allocations and contributions. In addition, turning points, in the sense used earlier, can also serve as indicators.

Most international organizations also operate in the context of an environment that is specific to the organization. For example, decision making in GATT is undoubtedly affected by the position of states in the world economy—their share in world trade and the proportion of their GNP derived from trade. The specific environment is conceived in quite broad terms to include such things as technological developments affecting communications in the case of ITU, and articulated bodies of opinion like labor movements in that of ILO. Two concepts developed with regard to the general environment can be applied to the specific environment: the stratification of power (or capabilities) and the pattern of alignments and conflicts. Indices can be constructed for specific fields in which organizations operate, and states can be ranked according to these. The relationships among states can also be broadly characterized.

The environment specific to an international organization may be either linked with or independent of the general environment. In most instances there is probably some relationship, but its strength will vary with different fields. The relation between decision making and the general specific environments can be examined empirically. One or the other could be more important, and the specific environment could act as an intervening variable. The indicators cited above can also be used for examining these issues.

Just as each organization has a specific environment, so it may be argued has each issue-area, or even—at the limit—each decision. The concept of specific environment can be applied with some flexibility. If the most relevant capabilities of states differ for different issues arising in an international organization, it may be preferable to use several indicators of specific capabilities, rather than a single composite indicator of organizationally specific capability. Similarly, certain cleavages in the specific environment of an organization may be more relevant to certain issues than to others.

Although figure 1.1 necessarily oversimplifies the relations, it summarizes the basic concepts utilized in this study.

Figure 1.1   Influence in International Organizations

Environment	Actors	Patterns of Influence in Decision-Types	The Structure of Influence

Participant Subsystem
(Shaped by Institutional Context)

Representative Subsystem 1

Representative Subsystem 2

Representative Subsystem 3

Representative Subsystem 4–*n*

General Environmental Variables

Specific Environmental Variables

Executive Head

Segment of the International Bureaucracy 1

Segment of the International Bureaucracy 2–*n*

Individual Advisers

Representational
Symbolic
Boundary
Programmatic
Rule-Creating
Rule-Supervisory
Operational

Persistent Groupings
Configurations of Actors
Levels of Conflict and Consensus
Elites

Feedback

The Structure of Influence

As a result of the analysis undertaken in this project, a description and an explanation of the structure of influence in each of the organizations being considered should emerge. The questions to be addressed are several. Is there a single elite with dominant influence, or is influence widely shared? In this context, how extensive is the influence exercised by the executive head of the organization and its bureaucracy? Is the structure of influence the same for all categories of decisions, or does it vary? What are the typical patterns of interaction? Do they show consensus or conflict? If there is conflict, how is it structured? Are alignments polarized or crosscutting? Do the alignments make the sides disparate in strength or evenly matched? How are all of these things to be explained? To what extent can they be explained by the environment within which the organizations operate? How important are the processes within the political system of each organization in explaining the generating and structuring of influence?

Answers to these questions should furnish grounds for some judgments about the likely outcomes of decision making in the international organizations being considered, particularly whether they will favor the status quo or redistribution. Furthermore, the span of time the project covers and the concern to explain how changes have taken place in the structure of influence should permit some reasoned speculations about the future. The data required on all of these issues should provide empirical grounds for generalizations. These in turn should yield a sharper definition of the variables involved in decision making in international organizations and a better understanding of the relationships among these variables, in other words, the rudiments of theory.

2 Power, Polities, and Politics: The Environment

Robert W. Cox and Harold K. Jacobson

This chapter presents the world political setting—the general environment—in which all international organizations operate. It does so in terms of the three key variables described in chapter 1: the stratification of power, the changing distribution of states according to their levels of economic development and types of political regime, and the world patterns of conflicts and alignments.

All features of this world setting have changed in some important respects since World War II. We want to investigage the commonly held assumption that changes in this setting bring about changes in behavior in international organizations. If we can pinpoint where changes have occurred in the environment, we may discover whether these changes relate to—or even explain—changes in the organizations to be studied. Thus, this chapter attempts to set forth indicators of change, insofar as possible in measurable forms.

For this purpose we need points of reference in time, so that we can measure changes over time. In the evolution of patterns of conflict and alignments, measurements are inappropriate; it is necessary rather to outline the salient configurations of international relations during the period of the study. From the standpoint of these configurations, dealt with in the last section of this chapter, the time span of the study seems to divide naturally into three periods: 1945-54, 1955-59, and 1960-70.

The other two variables, the stratification of power and the distribution of states according to economic and political characteristics, lend themselves more readily to measurement. Instead of attempting to average the measurements of these variables over periods of from five to nine years, it seemed that changes could be shown more precisely by focusing on three base years, one toward the beginning, one at the midpoint, and one at the end of the study's time span. As the earliest year 1950 was selected: it is halfway through the first postwar period in international relations, 1945-54; it is sufficiently remote from World War II not to have been affected by the immediate economic and political consequences of the war; it precedes the inflationary consequences of the Korean War; and it is a year for which basic economic data are available on a worldwide scale. The year 1967 was selected as the latest of the three base years because it was the most recent one for which data were available when the study was prepared. The halfway point between the other two base years is 1958, which falls within the second of the three selected periods of international relations.

In order not to overburden the text of this and subsequent chapters, the basic measurements of environmental variables that were constructed for this

Table 2.1

The Stratification of Power

Rank Order	1950 State	Rank Order	1958 State	Rank Order	1967 State
1	United States	1	United States	1	United States
2	USSR	2	USSR	2	USSR
3	United Kingdom	3	United Kingdom	3	France
4	France	4.5	People's Republic of China	5	People's Republic of China
5	People's Republic of China	4.5	France	5	Japan
7	Canada	6.5	Federal Republic of Germany	5	United Kingdom
7	Federal Republic of Germany	6.5	India	7	Federal Republic of Germany
7	India	8.5	Canada	8	Italy
9	Japan	8.5	Italy	9.5	Canada
12.5	Australia	10	Japan	9.5	India
12.5	Belgium	11.5	Brazil	11	Sweden
12.5	Brazil	11.5	Sweden	15	Australia
12.5	Italy	15	Argentina	15	Austria
12.5	Sweden	15	Australia	15	Netherlands
12.5	Switzerland	15	Belgium	15	Spain
16.5	Indonesia	15	Indonesia	15	Switzerland
16.5	Spain	15	Switzerland	15	Yugoslavia
20	Argentina	19.5	Mexico	15	Brazil
20	Mexico	19.5	Netherlands	21	Argentina
20	Netherlands	19.5	Spain	21	Belgium
20	South Africa	19.5	South Africa	21	Pakistan
20	Yugoslavia	26	Austria	21	Poland
27.5	Czechoslovakia	26	Czechoslovakia	21	South Africa
27.5	Denmark	26	Denmark	26.5	Czechoslovakia
27.5	New Zealand	26	German Democratic Republic	26.5	Denmark

27.5	Norway
27.5	Pakistan
27.5	Philippines
27.5	Poland
27.5	Turkey
27.5	United Arab Republic
27.5	Venezuela
34	Finland
34	German Democratic Republic
34	Israel
37	Austria
37	Cuba
37	Luxembourg
39	Nigeria

26	Israel
26	Norway
26	Poland
26	Yugoslavia
26	Venezuela
33.5	Cuba
33.5	New Zealand
33.5	Pakistan
33.5	Philippines
33.5	Turkey
33.5	United Arab Republic
37	Finland
38	Luxembourg
39	Nigeria

26.5	German Democratic Republic
26.5	Indonesia
26.5	Israel
26.5	Mexico
31.5	Cuba
31.5	Norway
31.5	Turkey
31.5	United Arab Republic
36	Finland
36	New Zealand
36	Nigeria
36	Philippines
36	Venezuela
39	Luxembourg

study, together with the methodological discussions relevant to these measurements, are placed in appendices. Appendix A gives the stratification of world power. Appendix B contains the stratification of state capabilities relevant to the specific environment for several of the international organizations treated in the chapters that follow. Appendix C shows the distribution of regimes by political and economic characteristics.

The Stratification of Power

As noted in chapter 1, in this study power means capabilities. This chapter is thus concerned in part with assessing the capabilities of states. In regard to the general environment, capabilities of states can be assessed in terms of material and other resources. In the composite index devised for the purposes of this study, considerable weight is given to gross national product (GNP), which may be thought of as a summation of a number of factors in material resources. Other material factors are also included in this index. GNP per capita is used as an indicator of ability to mobilize material resources. Population represents potential for development. The possession of nuclear weapons with their enormous destructive potential, or the ability to develop them, gives a state a particular military status. Finally, among nonmaterial resources, prestige differentiates the power of states in world affairs. The composite index contains components expressing all of these.

The rank orders for 1950, 1958, and 1967 that result from this composite index for the leading thirty-nine states in the general environment are shown in table 2.1. As can be seen, relationships among these thirty-nine states have been relatively stable, and changes have been gradual. This stability is evidenced by the following Kendall's tau beta coefficients of correlation:

1950-58	0.88
1958-67	0.81
1950-67	0.75

The most important changes are the rise in status of the People's Republic of China, of the Federal Republic of Germany, and of Japan, and the relative decline of the United Kingdom and Canada.

For states other than these thirty-nine, the scores on the composite index were small, and the differences among them were trivial. There were forty-three such additional independent countries in 1950, fifty-two in 1958, and ninety-two in 1967. The increase in their number was a consequence of the process of decolonization.

The Distribution of States by Their Economic
and Political Characteristics

GNP per capita is the most widely used measure of economic development. This study uses a fourfold classification of GNP per capita (in United States dollars adjusted to 1965 prices for purposes of comparability over time as well as space): the first category consists of countries with GNP per capita of less than $200; a second group comprises those with GNP per capita from $200 to $599, a third with $600 to $999, and a fourth with $1,000 and up. These divisions, though arbitrary, serve to categorize stages of development. The lowest category includes countries where poverty is deep and widespread and where it is hardly possible to speak meaningfully of development. The next lowest includes countries in the initial stages of modernization; the next higher comprises countries in an advanced stage of industrialization; and the highest, countries that have become developed mass-consumption societies. For some purposes it may be convenient to use a simple dichotomy, calling those in the two lowest categories "poor" countries, and those in the upper two "rich."

Political regimes of independent states, as noted in chapter 1, have been classified in a threefold division of competitive, mobilizing, and authoritarian polities. Nonindependent territories is a fourth category that can usefully be included to give the full picture of the international system at any given time, although it may not be relevant for some purposes, such as representation in international organizations.

Combining these two dimensions of economic and political characteristics gives a four-by-four matrix on which we can plot changes taking place between 1950, 1958, and 1967 in the distribution of the 154 political units in the international system (i.e. all states or geographically distinct territories with populations in 1967 of more than 200,000 in round figures). These distributions are shown in table 2.2. Examination of these matrices and of the data on which they are based suggests some significant changes in the environment of international organizations.

The major change has been the attainment of independence by former colonial territories, increasing the total number of independent states from 80 in 1950 to 131 in 1967, and reducing dependent territories from 74 in 1950 to 23 in 1967.

Next in importance have been increases in GNP per capita (in constant prices). By 1958, 24 percent of the independent countries that in 1950 were in the lowest category (less than $200 per head) had advanced to the next higher category ($200-$599); 27 percent of those that in 1950 had been second from the lowest advanced to the next higher ($600-$999); and 17 percent of those in the second highest category had passed into the highest ($1,000 and over). Similar rates of increase in levels of development occurred between 1958 and 1967; 27 percent of the independent countries advanced upward from the lowest category, 23 percent from the second lowest category, and 43 percent from the second highest into the highest category.

Table 2.3 shows that the increase in the number of independent countries, virtually all of them less-developed countries, has not resulted in an increase in the proportion of independent countries with the lowest GNP per capita. The effect that the trend toward independence has had upon the distribution

Table 2.2

Distribution of Political Units in the International System according to Economic Level and Polity

Year	Type of Polity	GNP per Capita $0-$199		GNP per Capita $200-$599		GNP per Capita $600-$999		GNP per Capita $1,000 and over	
		Number	Percentage	Number	Percentage	Number	Percentage	Number	Percentage
1950	Competitive	4	2.60	14	9.09	4	2.60	12	7.79
	Mobilizing	6	3.90	9	5.84	1	0.65	–	–
	Authoritarian	22	14.28	7	4.55	1	0.65	–	–
	Nonindependent	57	37.01	16	10.39	–	–	1	0.65
1958	Competitive	3	1.95	12	7.79	9	5.84	13	8.44
	Mobilizing	10	6.49	6	3.90	5	3.25	–	–
	Authoritarian	20	12.99	13	8.44	–	–	–	–
	Nonindependent	42	27.27	19	12.34	1	0.65	1	0.65
1967	Competitive	3	1.95	15	9.74	5	3.25	20	12.99
	Mobilizing	13	8.44	8	5.19	6	3.90	1	0.65
	Authoritarian	36	23.38	18	11.69	5	3.25	1	0.65
	Nonindependent	13	8.44	9	5.84	–	–	1	0.65

of levels of development has been offset by the effect of economic growth and the consequential movement toward higher levels of GNP per capita of a number of countries.

Table 2.3

Per Capita GNP of Independent Countries

Level (in Dollars)	1950		1958		1967	
	Number	Percentage	Number	Percentage	Number	Percentage
0-199	32	40.00	33	36.26	52	39.69
200-599	30	37.50	31	34.07	41	31.30
600-999	6	7.50	14	15.38	16	12.21
1,000 and over	12	15.00	13	14.29	22	16.79

Note: United States dollars adjusted to 1965 prices.

Since there are very few remaining colonies, it seems unlikely that the group with the lowest GNP per capita can increase much in future. As economic development proceeds, this will be a diminishing category. By contrast, the most substantial change has been the increase in the category with $600-$999, while the highest group has maintained its proportion of the total. In 1967, 29 percent of all independent countries were in these two highest groups, compared with 22 percent in 1950. These figures contrast with the widely accepted impression of a world environment composed of an increasing number of poor countries as a result of decolonization.

By contrast with the high rates of change in levels of development, changes in type of polity have been less numerous. Comparing the base years, changes occurred in type of polity in nineteen independent countries between 1950 and and 1967; some of these nineteen experienced more than one change.[1] There was no predominant pattern or trend in these changes. Six competitive polities became authoritarian; and six authoritarian regimes became competitive. Five authoritarian regimes were converted to mobilizing systems; and four mobilizing regimes were transformed into authoritarian polities (usually by military coup). Transitions between the mobilizing and competitive types were rare: the one competitive polity that became a mobilizing regime was Indonesia under Sukarno; and the one mobilizing system to become competitive was Argentina, which did so briefly following the fall of Perón.

The increase in the number of independent states through the emergence of new nations from former colonial status did more to alter the distribution of the three types of polity than did changes occurring in the political systems of the states that were independent in 1950.

Table 2.4 shows that the proportion of competitive polities in the international system has declined markedly, although their absolute numbers have increased. Mobilizing regimes increased sufficiently in number to enable them to do more than just hold their own as a proportion of the total. The authoritarian category showed the greatest growth, becoming the largest of the three groups. The number of polities in this category almost doubled.

Table 2.4

Types of Polity of Independent Countries

Type of Polity	1950		1958		1967	
	Number	Percentage	Number	Percentage	Number	Percentage
Competitive	34	42.50	37	40.66	43	32.82
Mobilizing	16	20.00	21	23.08	28	21.37
Authoritarian	30	37.50	33	36.26	60	45.80

Having considered separately changes in the two dimensions—level of development and type of polity—we can now infer certain relationships between the two from the matrices in table 2.2. It will be seen that political competitiveness is very rare in countries whose GNP per capita is less than $200 per annum. And while mobilizing regimes are more numerous than competitive political systems in this group, the overwhelming majority are authoritarian. Competitiveness is more frequent in the next higher group, with per capita GNP $200-$599, though the proportion of instances has been steadily decreasing since 1950. Mobilizing regimes are outnumbered by competitive regimes among countries in this category. Authoritarian regimes, the smallest group in 1950, have become the largest group in this economic category. While in 1950 and 1958 competitive regimes were in the majority at the next level of economic development ($600-$999 GNP per head), by 1967 the noncompetitive regimes formed the majority. This is explained by the movement upward of several European communist countries and by the military coups in Argentina and Greece. The group with the highest GNP per capita ($1,000 and over) is composed overwhelmingly of competitive political systems.

Differences in regional patterns of economic and political change are quite marked (see tables 2.5 and 2.6). By 1958 most of the Latin-American countries had moved up from the lowest level of development, clustering in the next higher group ($200-$599). Politically, authoritarian countries outnumbered the competitive throughout the period. The Arab countries of the Middle East also improved their economic levels; beginning the period mainly in the lowest group, they were spread evenly between that and the next higher group by 1967. (Kuwait is the exceptional case, since it is in the highest economic category.) Political systems were predominantly noncompetitive, with an increase in mobilizing regimes during the period. African countries remained predominantly in the lowest economic category, but by the close of the period a few had moved into the next higher class. African polities were overwhelmingly noncompetitive. Most were authoritarian. About 20 percent were of the mobilizing type in 1967. Asian countries remained mainly in the lowest group, with even fewer signs of development than appeared in Africa. Nor was there much significant change in Asian political systems. Meanwhile, most of those European countries clustered in the category with GNP per capita of $200-$599 during the immediate postwar period had moved into the highest and next highest levels by the late 1960s. This is the only one of the five regions under study in which competitive polities predominated.

Judging from the political and economic structure of the international system and the dynamics of relationships between economic and political factors suggested above, over the long run, perhaps the next twenty years, the relative decline in competitive polities may be reversed. Authoritarian regimes have been associated with low levels of economic development. In 1967, of the 131 independent countries 52 were in the lowest economic category, among them the majority of the authoritarian regimes. It seems likely that economic development during the next twenty years will reduce drastically the number of countries with less than $200 GNP per head. During this future period, crucial political choices will be taken by those countries passing through the second lowest level of development.

Patterns of Alignment and Conflict

Thus far we have been describing the characteristics of the states that are the primary units in the international system. The patterns of relationships among these states are an equally important part of the environment of international organizations. There have been four broad and persistent patterns of relations that might be termed the themes of the postwar era. The first of these involved the clash between the communist states and that group loosely termed the West. The second centered in the struggle to end colonialism. The third was the related but different controversy between the rich and the poor states of the world. These first three relationships define lines of conflict. The fourth, in contrast, was a trend toward regional integration. It made the most substantial progress in Western Europe; but it also received ideological expression in Latin America and in Africa, even though the institutions that further integration remained considerably less developed there than in Western Europe. In each of these patterns certain countries have had a principal place; but for a variety of reasons, including the nature of contemporary communications, each pattern has also involved in one way or another almost all of the states of the world. Consequently the relationships have been overlapping.

In a view of the environment of international organizations, the years since the end of World War II can be divided into three periods: 1945-54, 1955-59, and 1960-70. All of the patterns described above were present in each of the periods; however, since they were combined in different ways,

Table 2.5

Regional Patterns: Levels of Economic Development

Region	GNP per capita (in Dollars)	1950		1958		1967	
		Number	Percentage	Number	Percentage	Number	Percentage
Latin America	0-199	8	40.00	3	15.00	2	10.00
	200-599	11	55.00	15	75.00	14	70.00
	600-999	1	5.00	2	10.00	4	20.00
	1,000 and over	—		—		—	
	Total	20	100.00	20	100.00	20	100.00
Arab Middle East	0-199	7	77.78	5	55.56	4	44.44
	200-599	1	11.11	3	33.33	4	44.44
	600-999	—		—		—	
	1,000 and over	1	11.11	1	11.11	1	11.11
	Total	9	100.00	9	100.00	9	99.99
Africa	0-199	37	94.87	36	92.31	30	76.92
	200-599	2	5.13	3	7.69	8	20.51
	600-999	—		—		1	2.56
	1,000 and over	—		—		—	
	Total	39	100.00	39	100.00	39	99.99
Asia	0-199	19	85.36	18	81.82	16	72.73
	200-599	3	13.64	4	18.18	5	22.73
	600-999	—		—		1	4.55
	1,000 and over	—		—		—	
	Total	22	100.00	22	100.00	22	100.01

Europe (Eastern and Western)						
0-199	2	6.25	1	3.13	1	3.13
200-599	17	53.13	11	34.38	6	18.75
600-999	5	15.63	11	34.38	10	31.25
1,000 and over	8	25.00	9	28.13	15	31.25
Total	32	100.01	32	100.02	32	46.88
						100.01

Nonindependent countries that gained independence before 1967 are included for the three years. Of the 131 countries that meet these criteria, 122 were assigned to the following regions:

Latin America (20 countries): Argentina, Bolivia, Brazil, Chile, Colombia, Costa Rica, Cuba, Dominican Republic, Ecuador, El Salvador, Guatemala, Haiti, Honduras, Mexico, Nicaragua, Panama, Paraguay, Peru, Uruguay, Venezuela.

Arab Middle East (9 countries): Iraq, Jordan, Kuwait, Lebanon, Saudi Arabia, Southern Yemen, Syria, United Arab Republic, Yemen.

Africa (39 countries): Algeria, Botswana, Burundi, Cameroon, Central African Republic, Chad, Congo (Brazzaville), Congo (Kinshasa), Dahomey, Ethiopia, Gabon, Gambia, Ghana, Guinea, Ivory Coast, Kenya, Lesotho, Liberia, Libya, Madagascar, Malawi, Mali, Mauritania, Morocco, Niger, Nigeria, Rhodesia, Rwanda, Senegal, Sierra Leone, Somalia, South Africa, Sudan, Tanzania, Togo, Tunisia, Uganda, Upper Volta, Zambia.

Asia (22 countries): Afghanistan, Burma, Cambodia, Ceylon, India, Indonesia, Iran, Japan, Laos, Malaysia, Mongolia, Nepal, North Korea, North Vietnam, Pakistan, People's Republic of China, Philippines, Singapore, South Korea, South Vietnam, Taiwan, Thailand.

Eastern and Western Europe (32 countries): Albania, Austria, Belgium, Bulgaria, Byelorussian S.S.R., Cyprus, Czechoslovakia, Denmark, Federal Republic of Germany, Finland, France, German Democratic Republic, Greece, Hungary, Iceland, Ireland, Italy, Luxembourg, Malta, Netherlands, Norway, Poland, Portugal, Rumania, Spain, Sweden, Switzerland, Turkey, Ukrainian S.S.R., United Kingdom, USSR, Yugoslavia.

The following 9 independent countries were not included in any region: Australia, Barbados, Canada, Guyana, Israel, Jamaica, New Zealand, Trinidad and Tobago, United States.

Note: United States dollars adjusted to 1965 prices.

Table 2.6

Regional Patterns: Types of Polity

Region	Type of Polity	1950		1958		1967	
		Number	Percentage	Number	Percentage	Number	Percentage
Latin America	Competitive	6	30.00	9	45.00	9	45.00
	Mobilizing	2	10.00	1	5.00	1	5.00
	Authoritarian	12	60.00	10	50.00	10	50.00
	Total	20	100.00	20	100.00	20	100.00
Arab Middle East	Competitive	1	14.29	–	–	1	11.11
	Mobilizing	–	–	2	33.33	4	44.44
	Authoritarian	6	85.71	4	66.67	4	44.44
	Total	7	100.00	6	100.00	9	99.99
Africa	Competitive	–	–	–	–	1	2.56
	Mobilizing	–	–	2	22.22	8	20.51
	Authoritarian	3	100.00	7	77.78	30	76.92
	Total	3	100.00	9	100.00	39	99.99
Asia	Competitive	6	37.50	6	28.57	6	27.27
	Mobilizing	3	18.75	5	23.81	4	18.18
	Authoritarian	7	43.75	10	47.62	12	54.56
	Total	16	100.00	21	100.00	22	100.01
Europe (Eastern and Western)	Competitive	16	55.17	17	56.67	17	53.13
	Mobilizing	11	37.93	11	36.67	11	34.38
	Authoritarian	2	6.90	2	6.67	4	12.50
	Total	29	100.00	30	100.01	32	100.01

there is a basis for division into periods. Like most dividing points, those used here are somewhat arbitrary. Historical processes tend to be continuous, yet there are times when one or more aspects of the international political system become salient or lose saliency, indicating breaking points in developments.

1945-54

During the first period, 1945 through 1954, United States economic ascendancy was at its height. The United States GNP was more than three times as large as that of the USSR, the next state in rank order. The combined GNP of France, Italy, the United Kingdom, and West Germany amounted to only 42 percent of that of the United States.

With respect to patterns of relationships, the clash between the communist states and the West was the predominant feature of the period. As early as the Potsdam Conference in July 1945 tensions were evident between the Soviet Union on one side and the United States and the United Kingdom on the other. These tensions became more apparent at the London meeting of foreign ministers in September. Although the USSR and its Western allies continued to collaborate to some extent during 1946, relations in general deteriorated still further, and by 1947 the phrase *cold war* aptly described the situation. In March of that year the Truman Doctrine, which proclaimed that the United States would "support free peoples who are resisting attempted subjugation by armed minorities or by outside pressures,"[2] was enunciated. This doctrine was clearly aimed at communist pressure on noncommunist regimes. In 1947 the United States also inaugurated the Marshall Plan, more formally known as the European Recovery Program. Although the communist states were formally invited to participate in this program, it is questionable whether Congress would have appropriated the funds for it if they had accepted the invitation. In any case, the communist states chose not to participate, and Europe became increasingly divided economically as well as politically. The creation of separate institutions—the Organization of European Economic Cooperation in the West and the Council for Mutual Economic Assistance in the East—symbolized this division and reinforced the split.

As the gap widened, the Western states sought to redress the balance in conventional military forces. Unlike the Eastern European states, they had demobilized hastily after World War II. Matters of defense were arranged in coalition, first through the Brussels Pact, signed in 1948, and then through the North Atlantic Treaty, signed the following year. In 1949 the United States began a military assistance program for its allies.

Meanwhile, the civil war in China between the communist and nationalist forces continued, eventually culminating in the communists gaining control of the entire Chinese mainland in the fall of 1949. When the Korean War broke out the following June, cold war tensions reached a new height. In reaction, an increased drive to organize the noncommunist world resulted ultimately in a series of bilateral and multilateral alliances, including the South East Asia Treaty Organization and the Central Treaty Organization. The United States was the common partner in all of these alliances (though actually not a formal member of the Central Treaty Organization) and thus became the hub of the system. Tensions stayed at this peak for at least a year, until the Korean cease-fire began.

Some time in the winter of 1952-53 the cold war began to subside, and economic intercourse between the East and West began to increase. There was a change of government in both the Soviet Union and the United States in early 1953. In July an armistice agreement was signed in Panmunjom, Korea.

The other patterns of relationships described earlier existed during this period, but they were all secondary to the cold war. Asia was the focal point for the struggle to end colonialism. The decolonization of the Indian subcontinent was accomplished with relatively little friction between the United Kingdom and the nationalist movements. Indonesia and Indochina proved to be more contentious cases: in each, major violence occurred. Both conflicts, however, remained relatively restricted. The Soviet Union and the United States did not become significantly engaged in either. By the end of the period, the nationalist revolt had spread to North Africa, but only Libya had gained independence, and it had achieved its status more though the circumstances of World War II and divergence among the victorious allies than through a nationalist rebellion.

The rich state—poor state controversy was only beginning. The division existed, to be sure, and the gap between the economic levels of the two groups was becoming increasingly apparent. But the poor states had not yet mobilized themselves into an effective coalition. Moreover, even before great pressure for such action had been aroused, the richest state, the United States, inaugurated its technical assistance program addressed to the poor states' needs.

The movement toward European integration was in its infancy. The Organization for European Economic Cooperation was formed in 1948 as a consequence of the European Recovery Program. The Council of Europe was established the following year. In May 1950, France's Foreign Minister, Robert Schuman, proposed that France, Germany, and other countries merge their coal and steel industries, and two years later the European Coal and Steel Community came into being, uniting these sectors of the economies of Belgium, France, Italy, Luxembourg, the Netherlands, and West Germany.

1955-59

The second period chosen for examining the pattern of conflicts and alignments in world politics starts in 1955 and runs through 1959. At the beginning of the period the United States' economic ascendancy was beginning to diminish, and its position relative to other states continued to decline throughout the period.

The more significant changes, however, were in the patterns of relations. The cold war continued. Processes started earlier were brought to fruition, carrying on the chain of actions and reactions by various states: for example, West Germany was brought into NATO in 1955; in the same year the Soviet Union and the Eastern European states signed the Warsaw Pact. New initiatives, however, were in the direction of decreased tension and stabilization in Europe. An Austrian peace treaty was finally achieved in 1955. When in 1956 there was an internal reaction against Soviet influence in Poland and an uprising in Hungary, the West made no move to intervene.

Among the factors related to this trend toward stabilization, perhaps the most important was military technology. By the opening of the period, both the Soviet Union and the United States had developed thermonuclear weapons; each had the capacity to devastate the other, and each knew it—certainly this was so after the Summit Conference between Soviet and American leaders in 1955. The year 1955, therefore, seems an appropriate choice for the beginning of this period.

The so-called balance of terror established by this capacity had ramifications for the system of Western alliances. The fact that the United States had lost its strategic invulnerability made its promise and threat to defend Western Europe through its nuclear weapons seem less convincing and therefore weakened its position within the North Atlantic Treaty Organization. Furthermore, as a result of stabilization of the cold war the protection afforded by the nuclear giants seemed somewhat less essential to the smaller powers than it had in the past. The maxim that as the threat declines the cohesiveness of an alliance diminishes also applied.

In a sense the dimensions of the cold war changed during this period, for to an increasing extent the conflict was carried on away from Europe and through nonmilitary means. Much attention was focused on the Middle East, where a series of crises occurred; but the clash between the communist states and the West was not confined to that area, but permeated what came to be known as the Third World. One consequence was to strain the Western alliance system, for the interests of the United States and those of Western Europe in the Third World were much more divergent than their interests with respect to Western Europe itself. This conflict of interest was most evident during the Suez crisis of 1956, but it appeared on other occasions as well.

As the focus of the cold war shifted to the Third World, the struggle to end colonialism and the dispute between rich states and poor states inevitably gained prominence within the international political system. These concerns achieved additional prominence when a loose coalition of poor and anticolonial states began to form. Meanwhile a number of states from the

Southern Hemisphere began to act more or less as interest groups, aggregating and articulating demands. This movement followed two separate strands.

The first strand led to an attempt to mobilize the states of Africa and Asia. An initial step in that direction was the Asian-African Conference held in Bandung, Indonesia, in April 1955 (still another reason for selecting 1955 as the start of this period). In their speeches and in the final communiqué of the conference the delegrates clearly stated their positions and attitudes. They all talked about the necessity for greater progress toward economic development in their states and for increased financial assistance and commodity stabilization agreements, but they gave more emphasis to the struggle to end colonialism and found a greater degree of unanimity on this issue. The final communiqué vehemently declared "that colonialism in all its manifestations is an evil which should speedily be brought to an end."[3] This stress on anticolonialism was natural at that time because many of the Asian countries had only recently gained independence and most of Africa was still under colonial rule.

After Bandung, the loose coalition formed there continued to operate more or less as an interest group within the international arena. It gained new members as Morocco and Tunisia achieved their independence in 1956 and as Ghana and Guinea achieved theirs in 1957 and 1959 respectively; but while the process of decolonization was extended to Africa, it still moved at a relatively slow pace.

The second strand of the movement toward a coalition of states from the Southern Hemisphere involved Latin America. Here the emphasis was on economic development. Like the African and Asian group, the Latin-American states stressed the need for increased financial assistance and for commodity agreements. However, they virtually ignored the issue of colonialism, and rather than broadcasting their demands generally, they directed them specifically to the United States. In addition, they began to band together for joint efforts to achieve their ends.

Although the economic demands advanced by the two groupings of states were similar, there was little organized collaboration between them during this period. Among the reasons for this situation were the greater stress the African and Asian states placed on anticolonialism and the tendency of many of the leading states of that group to remain neutral in the cold war. Latin-American states, in contrast, were much more inclined to identify and align themselves with the West.

In 1954 the failure of the European Defence Community, an attempt to merge the military forces of the six states in the Coal and Steel Community, seemed to have ended the progress toward integration in Western Europe. Two years later, however, these six states accepted the treaties agreed to in Rome, establishing the European Economic Community, or Common Market, and the European Atomic Energy Community. The two treaties went into effect 1 January 1958. The first particularly would result in progress toward the comprehensive merger of the economies of the Six. Seven other European states—Austria, Denmark, Norway, Portugal, Sweden, Switzerland, and the United Kingdom—formed the European Free Trade Association. By the end of 1959, both groupings were firmly established.

In sum, then, the second period, from 1955 through 1959, was marked by a stabilization and a shift in focus of the clash between communist states and the West, an increase in the saliency of both the struggle against colonialism and the division between the rich and poor states of the world, and a continuation of the integration process among the Six of the EEC in Western Europe, together with a hardening of the division between the Six and the Seven of the EFTA.

1960-70

In the third period, from 1960 to 1970, all of the trends started in the second period continued, making the contours of the environment considerably different from what they had been during the first period. By 1965 United States dominance in the world economy was considerably less than it had been fifteen years earlier.

The trends in the patterns of relations established earlier also continued. It is true that cold war tensions mounted with the construction of the Berlin Wall in 1961 and with the Cuban missile crisis in 1962, but in 1963 the Partial Nuclear Test Ban Treaty was signed in Moscow, signaling a détente between the Soviet Union and the United States. The long-term movement toward relaxation of tensions that began with this treaty was limited principally by the war in Vietnam.

Partly as a consequence of this trend, the tendency toward the disintegration of the two alliance systems, already evident in the late 1950s, continued. The most significant defections from the tightly knit structures that grew up in the years immediately after World War II were that of France from the North Atlantic Treaty Organization and that of mainland China from the communist camp. In each case, perhaps the most divisive issue was the control of nuclear weapons. Neither the USSR nor the United States was willing actually to share control of these weapons with France or China or to transfer such weapons to them. France and China viewed the Partial Nuclear Test Ban Treaty as an attempt to limit the possibility of their gaining a nuclear weapons capacity. By 1967 France had withdrawn from the NATO integrated command, and as early as 1963 relations between mainland China and the USSR had deteriorated to the point of name calling. Another reason, of course, for the disintegration of the alliances, particularly in the West, was the declining relative strength of the principal partner. In addition, the Sino-Soviet split reflected an argument about relations between communist and noncommunist regimes. The Chinese clearly disagreed with the movement toward détente. In constrast to the Soviet-American situation,

Chinese-American relations showed little if any improvement.

In this third period the struggle to end colonialism gained major victories, but also ran into seemingly insurmountable obstacles. The period was characterized on the one hand by the onrush of states to independence, and on the other by the stubborn resistance to this movement in the southern third of Africa. The year 1960 was chosen as the starting point for the period because a record number of eighteen states achieved their independence in that year. During each year from 1960 through 1970 an average of three states gained their sovereignty, most of the new states being in Africa.

These new states swelled the loose coalition among the states in the Southern Hemisphere, particularly its African-Asian segment. As one immediate result, the demand to end colonialism began to be voiced in increasingly strident tones. But as fewer and fewer territories were left to be liberated and as the white minority regimes in the southern third of Africa showed that they were impervious to these demands, the cries became a ritual, and the African and Asian group turned more and more of their attention toward economic development. Consequently, the orientation of this group moved closer to that of the Latin-American states.

There was also movement on the other side. For a variety of reasons Latin-American states became more receptive to anticolonialism. In addition, in the changed context of the clash between the communist states and the West, the issue of alignment versus nonalignment became less divisive.

As a result of these developments, in the third period the two strands in the coalition of Southern Hemisphere states tended to merge. One bit of evidence for this view was Cuba's participation as a full member at the second conference of heads of state of nonaligned countries in Cairo in 1964. Argentina, Bolivia, Brazil, Chile, Jamaica, Mexico, Trinidad and Tobago, Uruguay, and Venezuela participated as observers. Collaboration between the Latin-American and Afro-Asian groups increased, adding strength to their efforts to aggregate and articulate their interests.

During the same period, attempts toward regional cooperation in Africa and Latin America continued, but marked achievement was lacking. In Western Europe, however, the integration process among the Six made headway. Despite quarrels and crises, the members of the European Economic Community continued and even accelerated steps to merge their economies. By the end of the period, for some purposes, particularly for the Kennedy Round trade negotiations, they had to be considered as one unit.

One might say, despite the risk in such broad comparisons, that in the third period the North-South struggle gained greatly in salience, the East-West struggle moderated, and the Third World countries refused to become aligned to its cleavages. Finally, new cleavages, which resulted when the countries of Europe and North America perceived the divergence of their interests on economic questions, became more prominent toward the latter part of this period.

The third period, then, was characterized by a dispersion of power, a rapid increase in the number of states, and more complicated and diversified patterns of relations. The elements of the new montage were all in existence in 1945; but after two decades some had faded, others seemed brighter, and all had been rearranged.

A Prospective View

One of the aims of this comparative study is to discern those relationships in political structures and behavior that would help in foreseeing likely future patterns of influence in international organizations. Our first step is to project the environmental conditions of decision making into the future. Speculations concerning the possible evolution of the environmental factors discussed above can best be directed first to the stratification of power; second, to the distribution of regimes by economic and political characteristics; and third, to the future structure of international relations (including patterns of conflict and alignment). A time span of the next fifteen to twenty years is the perspective adopted for these speculations.

While the bipolarity characteristic of the balancing alliance systems of the 1950s seems very unlikely to reappear, the predominant power of the United States and the Soviet Union is unlikely to be successfully challenged by any other power or power combination in the foreseeable future. The two superpowers will probably maintain a substantial lead over all other powers, although their strength (in GNP or military capability) in relation to others may continue to decline. Western Europe faces a political choice: whether to continue as a group of nation-states with nationally determined economic and foreign policies or to integrate politically and economically. The national economies of the major Western European countries are not large enough to provide the markets necessary to sustain investment in research and development sufficient to allow countries to enter the postindustrial society sustaining a rate of technological development comparable to that of the United States and the Soviet Union. Thus, without integration, either these economies will stagnate compared to the most dynamic economic systems, or if they continue to expand they will depend increasingly upon the technology and organization of United States corporations with multinational operations. Alternatively, if they elect economic integration, the present and prospective EEC countries would have a combined GNP greater than that of the Soviet Union, although still smaller than that of the United States. A third major power, Western Europe, is thus a possibility for the future. The political will of European leaders will determine whether or not this possibility is realized.

China, with its vast population and the apparent solidity of its modernizing regime, seems destined to become a fourth major power. Japan, in view of its recent rapid economic growth and the technological and organizational modernization of its economy, is likely to become a fifth major power during the next fifteen to twenty years; but its relatively small population may place limits on its upward movement in the scale of power. India might, over a much longer period, overtake Japan; but such an outcome seems unlikely in the next twenty years.

During the next twenty years economic development is likely to lead to a marked reduction in the number of countries in the lowest category of GNP per capita. (At present some 40 percent of all countries have a GNP of less than $200 per capita.) Movement upward from the lowest category marks the most potentially unstable phase of political development. For this reason we may expect internal upheavals in these states, in particular the seizure of power by ideologically oriented political elites or the overthrow of such elites, most probably by the military. The increase of domestic disorder in countries at an early stage of economic development will place greater demands upon the international system's ability to prevent the spread of such conflict and to devise ways of strengthening the political structure of states going through this difficult phase of early modernization.

This seems to have been the level of economic development at which the choice between the options of competitive and noncompetitive polities becomes decisive for the long run. In this choice the activity of international organizations may be influential. To the extent that international organizations foster and support autonomous institutions or countervailing elites, they may increase the chances that competitive political patterns will be selected. But it is equally conceivable that some activity by international organizations, merely by strengthening the state's administrative structures, will help maintain noncompetitive, authoritarian systems.

The near monopoly of competitive polities in the highest per capita GNP category ($1,000 and over) is almost certain to be broken, since a number of communist countries will move into this category. Higher levels of economic attainment may—as a result of organizational and technological pressures rather than of political choice—foster a decentralization of economic decision making in the more affluent communist economies. At the same time, tendencies toward increasing bureaucratization in capitalist countries may bring about some similarities in the structures of economic organization in the most advanced industrial states. Once this threshold in economic organization has been passed, ideological distinctions between the most powerful states will seem less and less important; but ideology may become the force by which those alienated from organizational power will be united in a transnational protest against the ruling technocracies or meritocracies.

If these are the possibilities regarding the units comprising the present international system, what estimates can we make about the way the system as a whole may be structured? And is it likely that new types of units will compose the future international system? The following propositions are suggested in this regard:

1. World order in a system dominated by five world powers, of which two will still be substantially more powerful than the other three, will rest on a consensual basis. If the expected abatement of ideological conflict between states takes place, consensus among the five is more likely to occur through a calculation and adjustment of interests without the complication of conflicts in ultimate values.

2. Disturbances to world order will increasingly arise from domestic conflict within both the least-developed and the most-developed countries, and these conflicts may have transnational revolutionary implications.

3. Regionalism—one possible pattern of development in the structure of world organization—implies a close association of political and economic power. In Western Europe regionalism may possibly produce a new world power. In Africa and Latin America, some subregional groupings may develop.

4. The multinational corporation presents an alternative structural pattern for the future, a functionally based economic, nonterritorial form of organization. This pattern may conflict both with regionalism and with the classical nation-state, since these attempt to plan and control economic growth on a territorial basis, while the functional principle introduces external influences into territorial units.

5. Some functional problems, particularly control of the biological and physical environment, are likely to require a response from the international system as a whole.

6. As a counterweight to the concentration of power in five major world powers and to the growth of regionalism, the desire for autonomy on the part of culturally or linguistically defined groups will persist and strengthen. Local resentments against control by remote and alien political authorities will tend to limit the range of matters on which such authorities take decisions and will lead toward a division of functions between local, regional, and international decision-making structures.

Thinking ahead, perhaps even beyond the next fifteen to twenty years, one possible structure of future world politics may be envisaged as no longer resting exclusively upon the nation-state, as in the past, but resting instead upon three different types of political systems: (1) large concentrations of territorially organized economic and political power, with world peace depending upon their consensus; (2) crosscutting lines of universal functional organization, some private—that is, not state-based, such as the corporations—and some public or state-based agencies for the performance of some tasks on behalf of the international system as a whole; and (3) a flowering of local autonomies, sovereign in certain primarily cultural issue-areas. Since each of these political systems is likely to be jealous and expansive, there would be continued adjustment of functional boundaries among them.

Alternatively, some of the forces identified above may combine to bring about a resurgence of the nation-state in a new nationalism. This tendency would be based upon a reaction by people in peripheral countries to perceived domination by the powerful central economies, by the major world powers in their spheres of influence, and by the multinational corporations. Strong national leadership, probably of an authoritatian or mobilizing type, would initially be more inward-looking than outward-looking in policy, more concerned with the rural and marginal populations and with establishing control over local economies than with integration into a world economy. To the extent that this tendency should predominate, the nature and problems of international organization would be affected. The demands of such regimes would be for services to support nation building and for aid in controlling and limiting transnational economic influences.

3 ITU: A Potpourri of Bureaucrats and Industrialists

Harold K. Jacobson

The International Telecommunication Union (ITU) could be regarded as a paradoxical organization. It is the oldest of the specialized agencies yet also one of the smallest. If Parkinson's Law—to which all international organizations are supposedly susceptible—has affected ITU, the pace has certainly been leisurely. Another apparent inconsistency is that although the International Telecommunication Union deals with matters that have immense commercial and political implications, it is one of the least-known members of the United Nations family.[1] To understand the processes of decision making in ITU, one must begin by exploring the facts that give rise to these seeming contradictions.

Functions, Structure, and Evolution

The International Telecommunication Union traces its origin to the Paris Conference of 1865 and to the convention signed at that time, which established the International Telegraph Union. By 1865, the political division of Europe into several separate states made international collaboration imperative if full advantage were to be gained from the development of electrical telegraphy. Messages sent by electrical telegraphy traveled at a velocity of about 300,000 kilometers per second. They could therefore crisscross Europe several times in less than a second, but only if political boundaries did not constitute insuperable obstacles. There thus would have to be at least a measure of agreement on the standardization of equipment, on operating procedures, and to a lesser extent on administrative procedures, including rates for services. Even though the technology of telecommunications has become vastly more sophisticated during the past century, this basic link between scientific developments and international collaboration has remained. The problems that ITU faces at present are infinitely more complicated than those considered in 1865, but in their broad outline the problems are unchanged.

Significantly, only one issue at the Paris Conference caused any contention: whether or not to establish a permanent commission. In the end, the French proposal to create such a commission was rejected, and it was not until the Vienna Conference three years later that the International Telegraph Union established a permanent bureau. While willing—or perhaps almost forced—to collaborate with one another, the member states of the union were extremely reluctant to take any action that might derogate from their sovereignty in this vital and sensitive field. This attitude has persisted to the present day, and it undoubtedly accounts for the restricted growth of the agency.

ITU has nevertheless grown over the years in the number of its members, in the size of its staff, and in the scope of its functions. In 1865, 20 states, all from Europe, signed the Paris Convention. In 1947 delegates from 72 countries and territories throughout the world joined in signing the International Telecommunication Convention drafted at Atlantic City, and in 1967 the ITU had 133 members. The Bureau of the International Telegraph Union when it was established in 1868 consisted of a director and a miniscule staff. By 1947 the bureau had grown to 56. In 1967 the staff of the ITU secretariat numbered 394, and in addition ITU was responsible for 208 technical assistance experts serving in the field.

The scope of the functions assigned to ITU has also increased over the years. At the Berlin Conference in 1885 the ITU began to draft regulations for the telephone. Further tasks were added when the International Radio Telegraph Union merged with the International Telegraph Union at the Madrid Conference in 1932. It was at this conference and as a consequence of the merger that the present name, the International Telecommunication Union, was chosen. More recently, in 1963, the ITU elaborated regulations for space communications. Thus ITU's scope has grown with technological developments and now covers virtually all forms of telecommunications. Despite this growth, though, the cautious attitude of member states first evidenced at the Paris Conference in 1865 has continued, and it is reflected in ITU's present mandate and structure.

In broad terms, ITU's mandate is "to maintain and extend international cooperation for the improvement and rational use of telecommunications of all kinds."[2] It is also charged with promoting "the development of technical facilities and their most efficient operation." More specifically ITU's functions are (letters refer to subparagraphs in article 4 of the International Telecommunication Convention):

(a) effecting the allocation of the radio frequency spectrum and registering radio frequency assignments

(b) coordinating efforts "to eliminate harmful interference between radio stations of different countries and to improve the use made of the radio frequency spectrum"

(c) fostering collaboration with respect to establishing the lowest possible rates

(d) fostering "the creation, development and improvement of telecommunication equipment and networks in new or developing countries"

(e) promoting "the adoption of measures for ensuring the safety of life through the cooperation of telecommunication services"

(f) undertaking studies, making regulations, adopting resolutions, formulating recommendations and opinions, and collecting and publishing information "concerning telecommunication matters for the benefit of all Members and Associate Members"[3]

With one exception, all of these functions are primarily directed toward providing a forum or framework for decisions and negotiations. Only (d), fostering "the creation, development and improvement of telecommunications equipment and networks in new or developing countries," involves providing services. It was not until after World War II that ITU began to engage in operational activities, and only in 1959 was this formally acknowledged by the insertion of subparagraph (d) in article 4 of the convention.

To perform these functions the members of ITU have created a complex institutional structure. As determined in 1965 by the Montreux Plenipotentiary Conference, ITU consists of: the Plenipotentiary Conference; the Administrative Council; Administrative Conferences; and the so-called permanent organs, which are the General Secretariat, the International Frequency Registration Board (IFRB), the International Radio Consultative Committee (CCIR), and the International Telegraph and Telephone Consultative Committee (CCITT).

The Plenipotentiary Conference is the supreme organ of the International Telecommunication Union. It consists of delegations of all members and associate members. It meets irregularly, roughly every five years, and determines the general policies of the union. In addition, it elects the secretary-general, the deputy secretary-general, and the member states of ITU that shall serve on the Administrative Council.

The Administrative Council consists of twenty-nine members. It meets annually and can be convened more frequently. It oversees the administration of the union and in certain instances acts on behalf of the Plenipotentiary Conference.

Administrative Conferences are held on either a worldwide or a regional basis. Their principal function is periodically to revise completely or partially the Administrative Regulations that comprise: the Telegraph Regulations, the Telephone Regulations, the Radio Regulations, and the Additional Radio Regulations. In addition, World Administrative Conferences dealing with radiocommunication elect the five members of the International Frequency Registration Board. Voting privileges in Administrative Conferences are limited to member states, although attendance is broader: among those permitted to attend are representatives of recognized private operating agencies.

The general functions of the international consultative committees are to study technical and operating questions and to issue recommendations concerning them. The CCIR and CCITT work through ad hoc working parties, study groups, world and regional plan committees, and plenary assemblies. Formal recommendations can be adopted only by plenary assemblies, which in addition elect the directors of the CCIR and CCITT. Recognized private operating agencies and scientific and industrial organizations, as well as the members and associate members of ITU, may participate in the work of the international consultative committees. Voting in plenary assemblies, however, is limited to ITU member states. However, if a state is absent, the recognized private operating agencies of that country may, acting as a whole, cast a single vote.

The secretariat of the International Telecommunication Union is almost a federation of four separate parts, each of which is headed by one or more elected officials. First, there is the General Secretariat, directed by the secretary-general and the deputy secretary-general, which in 1967 had a total staff of 220. The five-member International Frequency Registration Board heads the second largest component, with a total staff of 122 in 1967. Finally, there are the CCIR and CCITT. In 1967 these had staffs of 23 and 29 respectively. While the divided nature of the ITU secretariat is related to the historical development of the union, the persistence of this phenomenon cannot be separated from the resolve of the members to have so many elected officials. The elected heads of each component of the secretariat are chosen by and work with slightly different constituencies. They consequently follow somewhat different orientations.

The very complexity of the structure of the ITU and the multiplicity of elected officials are ways in which the members evidence their limited commitment to the organization. There are other indications as well. ITU is and always has been what might be termed a convention as opposed to a charter type of organization. In the latter, the members agree to a basic constitution, which usually includes fairly elaborate and stringent procedures for amendment. In contrast the entire convention is subject to revision each time that there is a Plenipotentiary Conference of the ITU, and only a simple majority vote is necessary. Changes in the convention have actually been gradual, but the potential remains for major alterations, including the cutting back of authority and the elimination of positions.

ITU's budget arrangements also reflect the limited commitment of members. Although budgets are voted annually by the Administrative Council, each Plenipotentiary Conference sets ceilings that apply until the next Plenipotentiary Conference. There are fourteen classes of contribution to each annual budget, ranging from one-half a unit to thirty units. Members are free to choose their own class of contribution. As one consequence of this system, although the United States regularly chooses the highest class of contribution, it contributes slightly less than 12 percent of ITU's budget. Underscoring the voluntary character of the financial obligations of membership, ITU provides no penalties for failure to pay annual contributions. Interestingly, private operating agencies, scientific or industrial organizations, and other international organizations share in defraying the expenses of ITU activities in which they participate.

Finally, article 51 of the convention provides evidence of a particular reluctance to allow ITU to develop its authority in matters that might involve national security. It allows members of the union to "retain their entire freedom with regard to military radio installations of their army, naval and air forces."

All of this is evidence that after more than a century people still have a reluctance to create an organ affecting telecommunications that would be beyond and possibly above governments—the same reluctance that made the delegates at the Paris Convention in 1865 unwilling to create a bureau for the International Telegraph Union. The reasons for this hesitancy are readily apparent. Communications are vital to the civil and military functions of government. To lose control of them is to surrender essential instruments of sovereignty. Yet the other feature obvious in 1865 is even more true today. To take full advantage of communications technology requires international collaboration. The mandate, structure, and authority of the International Telecommunication Union reflect these conflicting pressures on its members.

These features explain one seeming paradox mentioned in the beginning, the limited size of ITU despite its longevity. They also help to explain the second, the contrast between the immense commercial and political importance of the subject matter with which ITU deals and the relative obscurity that surrounds the agency. Beyond this fundamental fact, the very complexity of the ITU's structure and of the subject matter with which it deals helps to maintain the agency's obscurity.

Despite the reluctance of member states, the ITU has made important strides since the end of World War II toward becoming a more integrated and better articulated political system with broadening political functions. The Atlantic City Plenipotentiary Conference in 1947 was a major turning point in this regard. Three important innovations were introduced into the International Telecommunication Convention then: the International Frequency Registration Board was established; the Administrative Council was created; and the Berne bureau was transformed into an international secretariat. The result of these decisions was to make the ITU an international organization rather than an intermittent series of conferences. The Administrative Council in particular gave the ITU continuity that was previously lacking, and internationalizing the bureau made it potentially a more important political force. Even though in practice the IFRB did not perform all of the tasks that some had hoped it might, its creation substantially broadened the ITU's regulatory activities with respect to the radio frequency spectrum.

A second important turning point in ITU's postwar history occurred in 1951, when the Administrative Council authorized the union's participation in the United Nation's Expanded Program of Technical Assistance. This was the first step in adding service or operational functions to ITU's traditional forum functions. For the next decade, however, ITU's experts in the field were under the administrative control of the United Nations. Only as a consequence of decisions taken at the Geneva Plenipotentiary Conference in 1959 and in the Administrative Council the following year was the General Secretariat able to assume responsibility for field operations.

Recognition of these turning points is essential in explaining the development of the International Telecommunication Union. For example, the growth in the ITU's staff can only be accounted for in these terms.

A third turning point is perhaps equally significant, but in a different sense. In 1959 the World Administrative Radio Conference recommended that the Extraordinary Administrative Radio Conference be convened in 1963 to consider the problems of space communications. Had this decision not been taken, the ITU's activities would have lagged behind technical progress, a situation that would have left a tempting vacuum for organizational entrepreneurs outside the union. ITU thus far has done nothing with respect to space communications that could be considered substantially different from its traditional functions; the 1959 decision therefore did not enable the agency to engage in "task expansion." It did, however, enable it to keep up with changing technology.

Opportunities bypassed are less easy to identify. Selection of what would have been significant is a matter of judgment, and consensus in these matters is unlikely. Using the growth of institutional authority as the sole criterion, the two most important bypassed opportunities serve to document the points already made about the limited commitment of members to ITU. The first of these missed opportunities is the failure of the IFRB to go beyond its limited functions to become an instrument for management of the radio spectrum. The second is the failure of recent Plenipotentiary Conferences, particularly that held in Montreux in 1965, radically to alter the nature of the union, making it a charter rather than a convention type of organization, making its financial arrangements mandatory rather than voluntary, and molding the secretariat into a single body. Such decisions could have been the means of increasing the ITU's authority, thus making it possible for the organization to engage in task expansion. Should such decisions be taken in the future, they will surely mark a turning point in the union's history equal in significance to the 1947 Atlantic City Conference.

ITU's budget figures demonstrate in quantitative terms the significance of some of the turning points described above, particularly the addition of service activities to the union's mandate. In 1950 the total expenditures of the ITU were only $1,530,300. By 1958 these had grown to $2,302,100. During these years the union had only two sources of revenue: assessments on members and others participating in its activities and the sale of publications. In 1967 the ITU's expenditures totaled $11,103,000; of these funds $4,849,000, or 43 percent, came from the United Nations Development Program (UNDP). All but $300,000 of the remaining expenditures were financed by ITU's regular budget. The division between the regular budget and other sources of funds is also a rough measure of the relative share of the ITU's budget apportioned to forum and service activities, for no technical cooperation activities are financed from the regular budget.

Typically about 10 percent of ITU's regular budget income comes from the sale of publications; the contributions of private operating agencies and scientific or industrial organizations comprise another 3 percent. Assessments on members account for the remainder of the regular budget. When ITU member states are divided into three groups as in table 3.1, the shifting trends in the distribution of the union's assessed income can be seen. As the ITU's expenditures have increased, so has the relative proportion borne by Western states. This has occurred despite the fact that, with the increase in ITU's membership, Western states have come to constitute a declining portion of the total.

With this preliminary understanding of the nature of the ITU, we may now turn to an examination of decision making within the agency.

Table 3.1

Distribution of Assessed Income in ITU
(In Percentages)

	1950	1958	1967
Western	48	55	58
Socialist	11	10	10
Other	41	35	32

Decision Making: A Taxonomical Analysis

In considering the way in which different types of decisions are made within ITU, one must keep in mind the agency's complex structure and its multiplicity of organs. Each organ has its own structure and composition, and the body in which a decision is taken will affect the way in which it is made.

Representational Decisions

Until the redrafting of the International Telecommunication Convention at the Atlantic City Plenipotentiary Conference in 1947 any independent state could become a member of ITU merely by adhering to the convention and at least one of the sets of administrative regulations. Thus, decisions about the most basic representational issue, membership in the union, were not the subject of collective action, but were left solely to the applicant. This situation continues to apply to members of the United Nations, but since 1947 other states must have their application approved by two-thirds of ITU's members (by a mail or telegraphic ballot, or at a Plenipotentiary Conference). Since that time the union has had a number of controversies about membership.

The most contentious membership issues have involved Spain, Mongolia, the People's Republic of China, the German Democratic Republic, and the Republic of South Africa. In contrast, Italy has held continuous membership in the union, and Japan and the Federal Republic of Germany were readmitted without dissension in 1949 and 1952 respectively.

Although it had been the seat of the preceding Plenipotentiary Conference, Spain was barred from the Atlantic City Conference. Mongolia also failed to gain admission then. Both states eventually became members of the union, but only after they had been admitted to the United Nations. Communist China and the German Democratic Republic have occasioned controversies at various Plenipotentiary Conferences, but they have never gained admission. Nor have North Vietnam and North Korea.

In all of these instances, representatives of states have taken the initiative, and the controversies have all been settled by brute voting statistics. The votes have been determined more by broad alignments in world politics than by any specific factors peculiar to ITU. There is, however, considerable sentiment within the union favoring universality, and it is significant that, while the Republic of South Africa has been driven out of a number of other specialized agencies, it has been excluded only from certain ITU conferences and continues to participate in others. No attempt has been made to exclude Portugal from any of ITU's activities because of its failure to yield to anticolonialist demands.

There are many elections within ITU, and they evoke several different patterns of interaction. The union seems to have a large number of honorific posts that are usually filled without controversy by election in accordance with certain well-established patterns. For example, the chairman of a conference is customarily the chief delegate of the host country, and a provision to this effect has even been written into the International Telecommunication Convention.[4] Since 1960, private understandings appear to have been reached concerning the chairmanship of the Administrative Council and its committees, and as a consequence these elections have been uncontested. This was also the case in the council's early years. From 1955 through 1959, however, there were sharp divisions. One of the reasons for these was that France appears to have been more willing than the United States to give leadership positions to representatives of communist states.

Personal factors and individual interests or personal goals seem to play an extraordinary role in the choice of the elected officials of the ITU. The fact that on several occasions more than one national of a state has run for the same office illustrates this point. One reason for the importance of personal factors may be that the geographical composition of the Administrative Council and the International Frequency Registration Board is decided upon in advance of the elections, thus eliminating that element of competition. A corollary of this system is that if a region can reach agreement on its candidates, they are almost invariably accepted by the remainder of the membership. The bulk of the membership influences the choice only when the region cannot reach agreement. Another factor responsible for elevating the personal considerations may be the relatively limited formal power of the posts, which lessens the importance of programmatic difference among the candidates. Whatever the role of personal considerations, candidates seem to find it important to obtain the support of the United States; if they find it impossible to acquire support, they try at least not to elicit opposition.

To elect the secretary-general and the directors of the International Consultative Committees usually takes several ballots. Furthermore, positions shift to a significant extent before a winning coalition is finally mobilized. One suspects that a number of personal and national promises may be involved in the creation of such a coalition, and it is not unusual for a defeated candidate to receive an appointed post in the ITU some time after the election. The Montreux Conference even adopted a resolution suggesting that members of the IFRB who were not reelected be considered for appointment to the board's secretariat.[5]

Chairmen and vice-chairmen of the study groups of the international consultative committees are chosen by the plenary assemblies. Without exception the individuals chosen for these posts have attained prominence in their special fields and hold positions of responsibility in their own countries. More than 90 percent of them are Western nationals, reflecting the concentration of technical expertise in the West.

Structural change should also be considered a representational issue, since such change would alter the distribution of power within the union. Structural changes have been a major issue at two Plenipotentiary Conferences: Atlantic City in 1947 and Montreux in 1965. On the first occasion the five great powers (China, France, the USSR, the United Kingdom, and the United States) presented a plan that they had agreed on among themselves at a preliminary meeting in Moscow in 1946; and this plan was accepted in toto. On the second, both the secretary-general, Gerald Gross, and the United States fought hard to obtain reform, but beyond minor changes—relating, for example, to the size of the Administrative Council and the IFRB—the Montreux Conference merely agreed to appoint a study group to prepare a draft constitutional charter.[6] This group, whose report will be considered at the Plenipotentiary Conference scheduled to open in Geneva in September 1973, defined its task as being limited to distinguishing between those provisions of the present convention that should be included in a permanent constitution and those that should be included in less inflexible general regulations.

Symbolic Decisions

Because of the relative obscurity of ITU, there is not the same incentive for raising symbolic issues as there is in other organizations. Nevertheless they have been raised, particularly in Plenipotentiary Conferences and the Administrative Council.

In the immediate postwar years, what might be termed anti-European issues were the most prominent. They were the outgrowth of the feeling, particularly strong in the United States but also current in Latin-American circles, that ITU should become a global organization rather than primarily a European organization.

During the late 1940s and the 1950s, cold war topics were the dominant symbolic issues before the union. In the late 1960s, as decolonization proceeded, issues relating to this process entered the picture, particularly in connection with Portugal, Rhodesia, and South Africa. The mid-1960s also saw the adoption of a spate of resolutions suggesting that the union's work ought to be made more relevant to the concerns of developing countries.

As in the case of membership decisions, the protagonists in these actions have mainly been members of national delegations, and the pattern of decisions has followed that in other international organizations and in world politics generally. As the intensity of the cold war has diminshed and as the number of Southern Hemisphere states in ITU has grown, symbolic resolutions have increasingly evoked unanimous or near unanimous votes. The secretariat usually attempts to remain aloof from these controversies, although it did become involved in the South African imbroglio. Not unnaturally, both sides frequently seek to enlist the secretariat in their own cause. The secretariat's reluctance to become engaged is also understandable, given the nature of its work and the unlikelihood that it could use any symbolic decision for its own purposes.

Boundary Decisions

Boundary issues within ITU are particularly the province of the secretariat and the inner circle of national delegates who have a long and intimate connection with the union. They have handled the frequent and relatively routine issues arising from the overlap between ITU's activities and those of other specialized agencies, particularly the United Nations Educational, Scientific and Cultural Organization, the International Civil Aviation Organization (ICAO), the World Meteorological Organization (WMO), and the Intergovernmental Maritime Consultative Organization (IMCO), and there have been hardly any boundary conflicts. ITU's collaboration with ICAO, WMO, and IMCO has been particularly close and harmonious.

More serious boundary problems have arisen with the United Nations itself. The Transport and Communications Commission of the Economic and Social Council did not pose the threat that some within the ITU feared that it might. On the other hand, the regional economic commissions, particularly the Economic Commission for Africa and the General Assembly's Committee on the Peaceful Uses of Outer Space have taken actions that many in ITU regarded as challenging the union's primary jurisdiction in the field of telecommunications. In virtually every case the secretariat took the lead in asserting the union's claims, and the principal roles were played by the secretary-general and his personal assistants. The standard tactic used by the secretary-general has been to propose action by ITU that would duplicate that contemplated for another body. The union's regional program in Africa has been the result of playing out such a sequence. Each boundary conflict has also resulted in a slight increase in the union's public information program.

Actions relating to space communications taken by governments unilaterally or multilaterally outside of the framework of ITU have also been regarded by some within the union as a challenge to its jurisdiction. The International Telecommunications Satellite Consortium (INTELSAT) was founded by the United States and several other countries in August 1964. By 1967 INTELSAT had sixty member nations. INTELSAT has been governed by a committee in which each member's vote is proportional to its financial contribution, thus giving the United States a dominant voice. In April 1967 representatives of nine countries met in Moscow to discuss the formation of another international system; still other plans were debated by several Western European states and by some countries individually. There has been strong feeling among some in the ITU secretariat that the union ought to be involved in space communications in some way. Again, the secretary-general and his personal assistants have taken the lead in trying to bring the issue to the fore, and in 1968 they succeeded in having the Administrative Council authorize a second space conference to be convoked in 1971. Initially the United States and to a lesser extent the USSR were reluctant to have the ITU move in this direction, partially because of fear that it might reduce their freedom of action.

Programmatic Decisions

Perhaps the most general programmatic issue that ITU has had to face is the extent to which its activities should be oriented toward its less-developed members. One way in which this issue has been posed is the recurrent suggestion that ITU should have a technical cooperation program financed out of its own budget. In a sense, Hungary raised this issue at the Atlantic City Conference when it proposed that the new convention that was being drafted should provide for a telecommunication bank that would make long-term loans to enable member states to reconstruct and modernize their installations. That proposal was rejected with little debate, and subsequent proposals, phrased in more modest terms and more clearly oriented to the less-developed countries, have been given only slightly more consideration. The most recent debate and defeat occurred at the Montreux Conference in 1965. At the time there was strong support in the secretariat for the proposal.

One explanation for the negative attitude within ITU toward inaugurating its own technical cooperation program relates to the union's budgetary arrangements. Table 3.2 lists all of the states that had chosen contributions of ten or more units at the time of the Montreux Conference.

As table 3.2 shows, the distribution of financial burdens in ITU is very different from that in other specialized agencies. Middle powers bear a large share of the costs. Furthermore, the ITU contribution of many countries is a charge on the budget of the telecommunications administration, which is supposed to be self-supporting and perhaps even to show a profit. In programmatic matters involving costs these middle powers have a large voice, and it is generally a negative one. Significantly, after the Montreux Conference eight of the states listed in table 3.2 chose lower contribution classes.

Table 3.2

Leading Contributors to ITU's Budget in 1965

Country	Unit Class Elected
France	30
USSR	30
United Kingdom	30
United States	30
Brazil	25
Japan	25
United States overseas territories	25
Australia	20
Federal Republic of Germany	20
India	20
Canada	18
Argentina	15
China (Taiwan)	15
Pakistan	15
Netherlands	10
Sweden	10
Switzerland	10
Portugal	8
Portuguese overseas provinces	8
French overseas territories	5
Ukrainian S.S.R.	3
Byelorussian S.S.R.	1
United Kingdom overseas territories	1
Total for these members	374
Total for all members	557

This attitude has not, however, prevented ITU from dispensing technical assistance. Thanks to the forcefulness of the secretariat, ITU began to participate in the UN's Expanded Program of Technical Assistance in the early 1950s, and it later became an executing agency for the Special Fund. ITU now participates extensively in the United Nations Development Program (UNDP), and since 1966 the UNDP has contributed more than 40 percent of the funds that ITU has spent each year. UNDP's contribution has included funds given to the union to cover the administrative and operational costs of the technical cooperation activities. In keeping with the general attitude prevalent among the members of the union, the Montreux Plenipotentiary Conference reiterated that these expenses could not be borne by the union budget.[7]

It is striking how the nature of ITU has been altered as a consequence of its participation in UNDP. When the Expanded Program of Technical Assistance was first debated in United Nations circles, the ITU secretariat, and particularly an assistant secretary-general, Gerald Gross, took the initiative to gain the union's inclusion in the program. The Administrative Council and later the Plenipotentiary Conference authorized actions that the secretariat proposed, but the role of these bodies went no further than that. Of course, the secretariat could not have taken the initiative that it did unless national delegations had made supportive moves, particularly in the United Nations. United States representatives have always supported the secretariat in its desire to participate in the United Nations development activities, and the American delegate to the Administrative Council has always headed the council's technical cooperation committee. However, the United States has only favored ITU's engaging in technical cooperation activities within the framework of a centralized United Nations system. At Montreux, on the other hand, the United States was one of the most forceful opponents of the union's inaugurating a technical assistance program financed from its regular budget.

In 1959 the United States worked hard to have the union undertake activities concerning space communications, and especially to allocate portions of the frequency spectrum to facilitate the development and use of new technologies. More recently the secretary-general, Mohamed Mili, has played the same role of initiator. In both cases, however, an Administrative Conference could only be convened by a previous Plenipotentiary Conference or the Administrative Council, or by an action in which one-quarter of the members and associate members of the union individually addressed requests to the secretary-general. Thus, no matter who initiated the proposal for a conference, the next step involved mobilizing a coalition of member states. A conference is a way of posing certain issues, and it is there that a majority can formally settle them. So far as matters internal to ITU are concerned—for example, its structure or budget—that accurately describes the distribution of influence. If, however, the matter relates to regulation, influence would be distributed somewhat differently, as will be seen.

Another way in which the issue of ITU's orientation is posed is in the study groups of the international consultative committees. Their activities account for a high proportion of the union's work, and for a number of years some individuals within ITU have tried to shift the focus of these bodies more toward matters immediately relevant to the less-developed countries. However, an examination of the list of topics considered by the study groups reveals that most of them continue to be concerned primarily with issues of advanced technology. Although such concerns may indeed have some relevance for the less-developed countries (they are very likely to use any recommendations for standardization that result), they certainly are of greater interest to the more-developed members. The greatest contributions to the study groups come from the most technologically advanced members of ITU and from private operating agencies and scientific and industrial organizations within these countries. Because their inputs reflect their interests and problems, so do the outputs of the study groups. It is impossible for the secretariats of the international consultative committees to alter the situation. These staffs are simply not large enough to enable them to do more than carry out service functions. Often developing countries do not even send representatives to study groups.

Operational Decisions

The dependence of the ITU on UNDP funds for its service activities means that a large proportion of the operational decisions about which states should receive assistance and how much they should be given are out of the union's hands. All projects must originate with a request from the recipient government; in the end they must be approved by UNDP organs, particularly the resident representative and the Governing Council. About all ITU can do is to try to stimulate requests, but its efforts in this regard are hampered by the absence of a program financed by the union's own budget. Following the practice of most specialized agencies, technical assistance projects are used to try to stimulate requests for Special Fund projects. The secretary-general's travels, the periodic meetings of the union, and inspection trips provide occasions for discussions with members about things ITU might do, if only it were asked. Thus to the extent that anyone within ITU has influence in tactical decisions concerning its program, it is the secretariat, and particularly the secretary-general, the director, and members of the Technical Cooperation Department.

Rule-Creating Decisions

The International Telecommunication Union was established principally to perform regulatory functions, and such functions still make up a large proportion of its activities. Broadly, three concepts are involved: regulation, including the allocation of the frequency spectrum; standardization; and planning.

Drafting regulations has been part of the union's functions since its origin. These regulations deal with all aspects of telecommunications, from abbreviations used in radio telegraphy to watch hours for ship stations.

Other regulations allocate the radio frequency spectrum. Certain frequency bands are assigned for specific purposes: for example, maritime mobile, broadcasting, aeronautical, radio navigation, land mobile, amateur, and space. Some allocations are global. Others vary among three regions: region 1, consisting of Western Europe, Africa, the USSR, and Mongolia; region 2, the Americas; and region 3, the remainder of Asia and Oceania. Additional distinctions are made for the Tropical Zone, a band that varies slightly with the three regions, but that includes approximately the area between the parallels 30° North and 35° South. These allocations are agreed to in Administrative Conferences and are embodied in the Radio Regulations. Assigning specific frequencies to stations or users within the broad allocations is the responsibility of member states.

These regulations are so well established that, unless a new technological development like space communications raises new problems, little more than minor changes in existing rules are needed. In this perspective the Extraordinary Administrative Radio Conference, convened in 1963 to consider problems of telecommunications in space, was particularly interesting. Issues on that occasion were decided by majority vote. However, influence was distributed very unevenly.

The United States spent two years preparing for the conference. Besides work by the government to prepare the United States position, major studies were undertaken by the RAND Corporation, Lockheed, General Electric, and others. At one point General Electric had a staff of more than two hundred working on its study. Prior to the conference the United States position was submitted to all of ITU's members; the United States government also conducted a number of bilateral and multilateral negotiations that resulted in some modifications of the American position. In view of this extensive preparation it is not surprising that the position taken by the United States was extremely influential, and that the United States was not at all disappointed with the outcome of the conference.

ITU's work in standardization follows a similar pattern. As an example of what is involved, in the late 1960s a study group of the CCITT began to be concerned about direct dialing to establish intercontinental telephone circuits. Compatible equipment would be required, and to facilitate such a change the study group began to frame a recommendation. Great sums of money can hinge on these recommendations; to make even minor adjustments in the equipment of the Bell system of AT&T would cost millions of dollars; patent rights for new equipment are also involved. Formally, recommendations can be made only by the plenary assemblies of the international consultative committees and by majority vote there. In practice, however, the conclusions of study groups are usually accepted by the plenary assemblies.

As has already been noted, only a limited number of states participate actively in the study groups, and among these states the number that regularly submit comprehensive proposals is even more restricted. To give a concrete illustration, when Study Group VII (Standard Frequencies and

Time Signals) of the CCIR met in the summer of 1964, fifty-three papers were before it, and thirty of these had been submitted by the United States. No other participant submitted more than five papers. The list of states that offered papers is fairly typical: in addition to the United States it included the United Kingdom, West Germany, Czechoslovakia, Italy, Canada, Belgium, and Japan. Again, the United States was not dissatisfied with the outcome.

Planning is somewhat different. Since the early 1950s, ITU has periodically tried to project the requirements for telecommunications circuits. This is now done by compiling national statistics and reconciling them at national and global conferences. At most such a procedure could be called projective planning; no attempt is made to frame goals toward which all should strive, and the procedure does not commit anyone to anything. Hence, there is little stratification of influence.

With matters that do count in the framing of norms, however, influence is highly stratified. Influence goes to those states and private agencies that are technically prepared and that control the resources important in telecommunications, and extremely few meet these qualifications. Of course, these actors must be sensitive to the needs of others because they could always be voted down; but there is no substitute for technical knowledge and control of the physical resources involved.

Perhaps more remarkable is the fact that the process of creating norms has been so successful and has gone so smoothly. In recent years there have only been two conspicuous failures, when it has proved impossible to adopt recommendations: on the specifications for black-and-white television and for color television. Usually, however, the benefits of agreement are sufficiently widespread so that consensus can be obtained after a reasonable discussion. When questioned, participants in the process (who are, without exception, technically trained) will first respond that the agreements were reached on the basis of technical considerations. Subsequent questioning will reveal, however, their strong sympathy for each other's economic and political interests. Additional evidence of this sympathy is that recommendations will frequently have a built-in time lag for compliance, allowing for the gradual replacement of equipment. In negotiations such as the allocation of the frequency spectrum, which more nearly approach zero sum games where one player's gain can only be another's loss, political bargaining is more readily acknowledged.

Rule-Supervisory Decisions

Most of the norms created by ITU rely on self-enforcing mechanisms. If one wants to communicate, one must use compatible equipment; and it is not wise to broadcast on a frequency allocated to another use or assigned to another user. To a limited extent, however, the International Frequency

Registration Board is involved in norm enforcement activities. The board must be notified of new frequency assignments if they are to be used for international radio communication, if they might cause harmful interference with services of other states, or if international recognition is desired for them. The board then notifies all member states of this assignment, checking to see that it conforms with the International Telecommunication Convention and the Table of Frequency Allocations and that it is not likely to cause harmful interference with a frequency assignment already recorded in the master register that the board maintains. If the board's findings are favorable, the assignment will be recorded in the master register, the date being that of receipt.

Should the board find that the assignment is likely to cause harmful interference, it will return the notice to the authority that made the assignment; at the same time the board will communicate its findings and such suggestions for a solution as it may be able to offer. If a state insists on maintaining a frequency assignment despite an unfavorable finding by the board, it may nonetheless gain recognition for the assignment; the regulations provide that an assignment that has been in use for at least sixty days without complaint to the board that it has caused harmful interference shall be recorded in the master register.

If assignments are posted before being brought into use and then not brought into use within 120 days, the board may cancel the entry in the master register. The board may also cancel or alter entries if the use of an assigned frequency has been discontinued or if the use is not in accordance with the basic characteristics specified in the notification. However, any such action requires agreement by the notifying administration.

In 1967 the board received approximately forty thousand notices and gave favorable findings in some 70 percent of the cases. Prior to 1967, voting was frequently necessary to resolve these issues; since then however, the new five-member board has not had to resort to calling for a vote.

Once an assignment is entered in the master register, it has international recognition. In practical terms, such recognition gives the assignment a certain legitimacy. This is significant, for there is strong pressure against ignoring entries in the master register. However, if a party were determined to do so, ITU has no coercive powers to impose sanctions. States can report cases of harmful interference to the International Frequency Registration Board, but the most that the board can do is to study the problem and suggest possible solutions. The Radio Regulations leave it to the conflicting parties to solve the problem, merely admonishing them to act with goodwill.

It should be noted that the states themselves must monitor the uses actually made of the frequency spectrum. The members of ITU have never allowed the union to conduct monitoring; they are wary of any steps toward giving the organization substantial authority in this sensitive area.

Actors and Their Sources of Influence

All of the principal actors within the International Telecommunication Union have already been introduced: the elected officials and the appointed members of the secretariat; the members of national delegations, whether from telecommunications administrations or foreign offices; and representatives of private operating agencies, scientific or industrial organizations, and other international organizations. Representatives of national and international interest groups often concern themselves with matters under consideration by ITU. Examples of such groups are labor unions in the telecommunications field and associations of various kinds whose members use telecommunications, including amateur radio operators, small-boat owners, police, and radio astronomers. But such groups seldom have direct access to ITU bodies and must present their views through national delegations. For our purposes then, we may concentrate on the principal actors and, as a first step, categorize the resources available to them in decision making.

The Secretary-General

Six men have been secretary-general of the ITU since the end of World War II: Franz von Ernst (Switzerland), 1948-49; Léon Mulatier (France), 1950-53; Marco Aurelio Andrada (Argentina), 1954-58; Gerald C. Gross (United States), 1958-65; Manohar Balaji Sarwate (India), 1966; and Mohamed Mili (Tunisia), from 1966 to the present (1972).

It is difficult, on the basis of a sample of six, to make convincing generalizations about the qualities that contribute to the election of ITU's secretaries-general. In the first place, the mode of election has changed significantly. From 1947 until 1959, secretaries-general were elected by the Administrative Council. Since 1959 they have been elected by Plenipotentiary Conferences. The two bodies are obviously different voting constituencies. Second, two of ITU's secretaries-general succeeded to office on the death of the incumbent. The present secretary-general, Mohamed Mili, did this when Manohar Sarwate died in 1966, and Gerald Gross took office following the death of Marco Andrada in 1958. A year later, Gross won election in his own right.

Of the six men who have held the office, two were lawyers by training, while the other four had all received technical training in telecommunications. All of the latter had pursued careers in telecommunications in their own countries before becoming ITU officials. Andrada was one of the lawyers. The other, von Ernst, had become a journalist and politician and had been director of the Berne bureau since 1935. Both Mulatier and Gross were at one time vice-directors of the bureau, and these two also held the post of assistant secretary-general of ITU before they were elected secretary-general. Similarly, Sarwate and Mili both served as deputy secretary-general before becoming secretary-general. Andrada, Sarwate, and Mili all represented their countries on the Administrative Council and in a variety of other meetings sponsored by ITU before winning election to high office in the secretariat.

About all that can be deduced from this mélange is that technical training and experience seem to have become increasingly important qualifications for aspirants to the post of ITU secretary-general. Participation in ITU activities, including the Administrative Council, also seems to be helpful.

Examination of the characteristics and qualifications of defeated candidates produces no more in the way of useful generalizations, except that it is apparently difficult to attain the office of secretary-general by way of a directorship of one of the international consultative committees.

The powers of those who have been secretary-general of ITU have been determined in part by the nature of the office, which has been shaped by the union's historical development. The federal character of the ITU secretariat is a fundamental factor limiting the power of the secretary-general. The convention formulated in Atlantic City in 1947 provided for eighteen elected officials within ITU: the secretary-general, two assistant secretaries-general, a director for each of the three international consultative committees, a vice-director of the CCIR, and eleven members of the International Frequency Registration Board. The total number of elected officials was reduced to seventeen as a consequence of the 1956 merger of the International Telegraph Consultative Committee and the International Telephone Consultative Committee. It was lowered to fifteen in 1959 when the deputy secretary-general replaced the two assistant secretaries-general and the post of vice-director of the CCIR was eliminated. In 1965 the number was cut again, this time by six, when it was decided at the Montreux Conference that the International Frequency Registration Board should be reduced from eleven to five members. Even so, the ITU secretariat still has nine elected officials. Over the years these elected officials have often included defeated candidates for the post of secretary-general, who, of course, serve with the successful candidate, a situation that could well exacerbate the conflicts stemming from the lack of a clear-cut hierarchy on all issues and a consequent confusion in authority relationships.

This situation has naturally weakened the position of the secretary-general, and it has also led the incumbents to devote considerable effort toward becoming masters in their own house. Indeed, it was only in 1965 that a coordination committee, consisting of the secretary-general, the deputy secretary-general, and the directors of the CCIR and the CCITT and the chairman of the International Frequency Registration Board, was formally recognized. To strengthen the secretary-general's hand the article in the International Telecommunication Convention that recognizes this committee states that the committee can report to the Administrative Council only through him. The convention further empowers the secretary-general to act on urgent matters even in the face of a hostile majority on the committee. Less urgent matters on which the secretary-general does not have the support of two or more members of the committee must be referred to the Administrative Council for consideration, and the convention counsels the committee to reach decisions unanimously.

Members of ITU have also restricted the secretary-general by severely limiting the number of staff members who can be used for essentially political tasks. For example, it was not until 1968 that the union had its own legal officer, despite the fact that the union's traditional function was to provide a framework for preparing international regulations.

These circumstances aside, the role of the secretary-general in ITU's affairs seems to depend primarily on the incumbent's concept of the office and his personal attributes. All of the secretaries-general, with the exception of Gerald Gross and Mohamed Mili, appear to have had a very restricted concept of their office, confining themselves largely to routine administrative functions. A significant indication of this attitude is that the first press conference ever given by an ITU secretary-general was held by Secretary-General Mili on 21 November 1967.

Under these conditions, the ability of a secretary-general successfully to take initiatives depends largely on the network of personal relations that he can establish and maintain. The fact that Gerald Gross was a United States citizen was both an asset and a liability in this respect. Similarly his service as assistant secretary-general for more than ten years before his election both heightened and restricted his personal influence. Mohamed Mili's principal experience with the ITU before he became secretary-general was as a member of the Administrative Council. Insofar as it enabled him to establish contacts and to become involved—or to avoid involvement—in controversies, this may have been a better preparation for the secretary-generalship than work in the secretariat. Mili's nationality has enhanced his standing with the present majority in Plenipotentiary and Administrative conferences.

Other Elected Officials and the Staff

Even though they have won election in their own right, deputy secretaries-general of the ITU appear to have no independent power base. They are important officials; but they are clearly subordinate to the secretary-general, and their role depends to a considerable extent upon his wishes and on their personal relations with him.

The directors of the international consultative committees have considerable influence in their own sphere of activities, but it is difficult for them to extend their influence any further. Their relationship with their consultative committees can develop into a comradeship of functional specialists working on functional tasks. In their essentially coordinating roles the directors can exercise initiatives through subtle suggestions and by structuring communications patterns. Through these means they can be powerful forces in ITU working parties and study groups and in the plenary assemblies of their committees. The limited size of their staffs, however, restricts their ability to take initiatives. They are much more likely to be brokers and controllers within the consultative committees. Their resources are even more limited when it comes to decisions taken by Plenipotentiary and Administrative conferences and the Administrative Council. Here the close personal relations that can be built up in their own committees become relatively less important because other individuals also play significant roles.

Table 3.3 lists the individuals who have served as directors of the international consultative committees. The length of their tenure is impressive but easy to explain: prior to the 1965 revision of the International Telecommunication Convention their term of office had no limit. In 1965 it was decided that elections for directors of the international consultative committees should be held during every second plenary assembly, or about every six years. It is also significant that all of the directors of the international consultative committees have been nationals of Western states and of the leading powers in telecommunications. All have had technical training, and all have pursued technical careers prior to assuming their ITU posts.

Table 3.3
Directors of the International Consultative Committees

CCIF

    Georges Valensi (France), 1947-56

CCITT

    Léon Mulatier, assistant secretary-general serving as interim director (France), 1948-49

    Hugh Townshend, assistant secretary-general serving as interim director (United Kingdom), 1950-56

    Jean Rouvière (France), 1957-

CCIR

    Balt van der Pol (Netherlands), 1947-56

    Ernst Metzler (Switzerland), 1957-62

    L. W. Hayes (United Kingdom), vice-director, 1947-62, acting director, 1962-65

    Jack W. Herbstreit (United States), 1966-

The members of the International Frequency Registration Board (IFRB) do not have a power base analogous to that of the directors of the international consultative committees. Had the original conception of the board prevailed, they might well have been able to rely on a coalition of the victorious Allies in World War II for support. As it was, during most of the cold war the IFRB tended to look to the United States and the Western coalition when it needed to mobilize pressure to achieve the objectives agreed on by the majority of its members. More recently the board has looked to the developing countries for support. It may be significant that there has been no American national on the board since 1967.

Because his department has been responsible for more than 40 percent of ITU's annual expenditures since 1966, the head of the Technical Cooperation Department occupies a particularly sensitive and strategic position within the union. As in most organizations, the head of the Financial Division also has a strategic position because of his central role in the preparation of budgets. Other appointed officials within the ITU may have gained considerable influence over the years, but their influence owed more to their personal characteristics and relationships than to their official positions.

For most of those on the staff, the ITU is mainly a career service, composed predominantly of nationals of Western states. Of the 394 individuals who comprised the staff in 1967, 8 were elected officials, 363 had permanent contracts, and 23 had fixed-term contracts. Among these, 269 were working in the general service category or as members of the languages staff and thus were not subject to the principle of geographical distribution. Of the 125 who were so subject—and this number includes the 8 elected officials—95, or 76 percent, were nationals of Western states; 10, or 8 percent, were nationals of Socialist states; and 20, or 16 percent, were nationals of states classified earlier in this volume as Other. The states most heavily represented were Switzerland with 30 staff members, France with 18, the United Kingdom with 10, and West Germany and Spain with 6 each. No other state had more than 4 of its nationals on the staff.

Representatives of National Governments

Exactly how the government of a state will be represented in the International Telecommunication Union depends in many instances on the nature of the meetings and the type of activity involved.

Eighty of ITU's member states maintain permanent missions in Geneva, and presumably these can be used for day-to-day contact with officials of the union. It is significant to note, however, that only two of these missions, those of the United States and Japan, have staff members who could be considered full-time telecommunications attachés. The American mission has had such a post since 1963; the Japanese mission, since 1968. It may not be coincidental that the United States and Japan are leaders in telecommunications. Both also happen to be more distant from Geneva than most of the other leading states in this field.

There tends to be considerable continuity in the representation of states on the Administrative Council. Almost all who have this assignment are officials of their national telecommunications administrations. The United States, however, is always represented by an official of the Department of State, and several Latin-American states are also often represented by persons in their diplomatic services.

In all, some 337 individuals were accredited as members of national delegations to the Montreux Plenipotentiary Conference. Of these, 248, or

74 percent, were officials of national telecommunications administrations, and 61, or 18 percent, were members of their diplomatic services. The United States delegation of 22 members was the largest. Japan, with 15, had the next largest. The American and Japanese delegations each included three officials of private enterprises, a larger number than any other delegation.

Many of the same individuals would attend Administrative Conferences and plenary assemblies of the international consultative committees. However, others with special qualifications would be brought in if the subject matter of the meeting made it necessary.

Exactly how the position of a national delegation is determined varies with the state and the meeting. In most countries the national telecommunication administration assumes a dominant role, and the foreign office intervenes only when issues that it defines as political arise. These issues would usually fall in either the representational or the symbolic category. Since in many instances the chief delegate is the head of the relevant section of the national telecommunication administration, he can often establish his country's position by himself or in consultation with his delegation colleagues, if there are any. It is also generally true that the lower a state's level of economic and political development is the greater will be the freedom of its delegations to ITU meetings vis-à-vis their national capital. These two facts mean that in conferences attended by ITU's total membership, a large number of the participating states can establish their positions on many issues right at the meeting.

Perhaps the United States has the most complicated procedure for determining its position on issues before the ITU. The procedure is extraordinary not only in its complexity, but also because the Department of State has basic responsibility for the development of United States policy. Apart from the Department of State, several other government agencies participate in the formulation of American policy. All of these agencies are brought together in the Inter-Agency Radio Advisory Committee (IRAC). In addition, the Department of State has created national structures paralleling the international consultative committees, and IRAC and the Federal Communications Commission go to great lengths to ensure that the views of private industry receive an adequate hearing. As many as several hundred people may be at least intermittently involved for as long as two-and-one-half years in preparing the American position for a major conference. As a consequence of all this, United States delegations at ITU meetings certainly have among the most rigid and detailed instructions.

In any assessment of factors that lend weight to a national delegation's influence in ITU, certainly the state's standing in the environment would be the most important. Other assets—technical competence, for example—though also important, are almost by-products of this basic strength. When personal contact is useful, as it is particularly in plenary meetings, large delegations have an advantage.

The United Kingdom and France have important sources of strength in their ties with their former colonies. Many of the delegates who come to ITU meetings from newly independent states were trained in the British and French telecommunication systems, and they probably continue to use British and French equipment. Employees in their telecommunication systems may still receive training from the British and French. Thus there are sentimental and practical reasons that make these delegates especially receptive to appeals from Britain and France.

As in all international organizations, some people are able through charisma or other personal attributes to gain more influence in the ITU than would normally be accorded a delegate from their states. Perhaps the most successful recent delegate to ITU in this regard is Alpha Diallo of Guinea. Through his administrative and oratorical skills he has been able to organize the African group in Plenipotentiary and Administrative conferences, and as a consequence he has become a major force in the proceedings.

Representatives of National and International Private Associations

Private agencies operating in telecommunications can become members of the international consultative committees. They have full privileges except that they may vote in plenary assemblies only if the state that has recognized them is absent. However, since few important matters are decided in the international consultative committees by voting, this restriction is not very important. The participation of private operating agencies in the activities of the international consultative committees is widespread. Representatives of private operating agencies have even become chairmen of study groups, indicating the substantial role they can play.

Representatives of scientific or industrial organizations may also participate in activities of the international consultative committees, but only in an advisory capacity. For the individuals in these categories, perhaps the most important resources are the strength of their companies and organizations and their own personal qualifications.

Representatives of Other International Organizations

The final class of actors who play an important role in ITU proceedings consists of representatives of other international organizations. International organizations can be represented at all ITU meetings, and some of them send delegates to most such meetings. The organizations that have been most active in recent ITU sessions are:

United Nations
International Civil Aviation Organization (ICAO)
Intergovernmental Maritime Consultative Organization (IMCO)
World Meteorological Organization (WMO)

United Nations Educational, Scientific and Cultural Organization (UNESCO)

International Atomic Energy Agency (IAEA)

International Air Transport Association (IATA)

International Broadcasting and Television Organization (OIRT)

European Broadcasting Union (EBU)

International Scientific Radio Union (URSI)

The influence of representatives of these organizations depends very much on the issue, but in rule-creating decisions their influence is seldom very substantial. On the other hand, representatives of the UNDP are extremely influential in regard to decisions relating to ITU's technical cooperation, since the UNDP is the principal source of funds for these activities.

Attitudes

The discussion that follows pertains to the "ideological aura" of the International Telecommunication Union, in other words the views to which a substantial number of participants in any ITU proceeding would subscribe, although such views might not always prevail. These attitudes are a product of the nature of telecommunication, the long history of the union, and the fact that most of the participants in ITU meetings are actually involved in the manufacture or operation of telecommunication systems.

Perhaps the most essential article of faith in ITU is the proposition that international collaboration must and will follow technological progress. There is considerable pride within the ITU that over the years the time lag between new technological developments and new measures of international cooperation has lessened. A second principle in the ITU ideology, which in many ways stems from the first, is that the union should be a technical and universal organization rather than a political organization with restricted membership. As a corollary, it is held that the union should be most tolerant toward its members. Universal participation is recognized to be in everyone's interest, and in any case the union is virtually powerless to coerce its members. ITU's financial arrangements are one of the most striking examples of its tolerant attitude. The stress on the technicality of ITU's proceedings is one of the factors responsible for the playing down of symbolic issues.

In keeping with these major propositions, there is a firm doctrine within ITU that technical decisions can and should be taken on technical grounds and that it will be possible for experts to agree on technical issues. For several years the internal regulations of the International Frequency Registration Board stated:

Problems of a purely non-technical nature shall be decided by the Board on the basis of a two-thirds vote of the members present. In the consideration of problems having technical characteristics, the Board shall endeavour to reach its decisions by unanimous agreement. If, after reconsideration of such a problem over a period not exceeding 14 days, the Board fails to reach a unanimous decision, it shall immediately thereafter decide the problem on the basis of a two-thirds majority vote of the members present.[8]

In reality, of course, the distinction between technical and nontechnical issues is often far from obvious, but the important fact here is that IFRB's rules of procedure should have treated it as obvious. The period allowed for reconsideration is also interesting; it implies a belief that if experts disagree, an opportunity for further study should resolve their differences. The general doctrine involved here extends beyond IFRB and permeates ITU. For example, great effort is made in the international consultative committees to settle matters by consensus rather than by voting. To make a recommendation by majority vote signifies to the participants either that technical disagreements remain, although they could and should have been resolved, or that the decision was made for political or commercial reasons rather than on technical grounds.

All of these points have related to the nature of the ITU and to processes within it; another salient feature of the ITU ideology relates to the administration of telecommunication services. It is strongly believed in ITU circles that telecommunication services should and must be self-supporting in the long run, and the definition of the long run often seems very short indeed. This attitude has undoubtedly developed as a result of the personal experience and careers of many ITU delegates and officials. It affects ITU's activities by making commercial prospects one of the most important criteria for evaluating all future steps: there is strong presumption against doing something if its commercial value cannot be demonstrated in quite immediate terms. The doctrine also enters into the technical advice given by ITU.

The bias in favor of commercial interests impinges on ITU's relations with other international organizations as well. At various times the United Nations has offered to make its telecommunication network available to the specialized agencies, and on each occasion the ITU has objected. This warning was repeated in 1965 when the Montreux Plenipotentiary Conference reaffirmed

> that in normal circumstances, the United Nations point-to-point telecommunication network should not be used to carry the traffic of the specialized agencies in competition with existing commercial telecommunication networks.[9]

The doctrine also applies to ITU itself, for it is firmly established that the union should not be an operating agency.

Because it is widely shared, this organizational ideology is a unifying force within the ITU. However, it has prevented neither conflicts nor relatively persistent groupings of actors with respect to particular issue-areas.

When representational and symbolic issues have arisen in ITU, groupings among members have paralleled those differences in geography, language, and ideology that have been important in world politics generally. There has also been a relatively persistent grouping on the programmatic issue of whether or not the ITU should finance a technical cooperation program from its own budget. Several developing countries have favored such a course, with others among their ranks and all of the developed states in opposition. On some rule-creating decisions the possession of common equipment provides the basis for other persistent groupings.

The Organizational Elite

In an agency like ITU the significance of the concept of an organizational elite with general influence is questionable. As previously mentioned, some of the most important decisions taken within the ITU—particularly those relating to the creation of rules—are quite specific, and general influence is often of little consequence. The influence of an elite is most important for internal and administrative decisions. Because Plenipotentiary Conferences are held so infrequently and many of ITU's meetings are highly specialized, the individuals with general influence in the union are almost inevitably either elected officials or members of the Administrative Council.

As part of this study, a panel of notables[10] was asked to identify the twenty people who had the greatest general influence in ITU during 1950, 1958, and 1967. The list compiled from their answers named only five individuals who were not elected officials or members of the Administrative Council. Three of these were participants in Administrative Conferences,[11] and two were appointed members of the union's staff. Table 3.4 divides the twenty according to their position within the ITU for each of the three years. The shifts have obviously related to the structural changes in ITU over the years. They indicate an increased political control by representatives of states, which was among the effects these changes were intended to produce.

Table 3.5 shows the distribution of the twenty influential individuals for each of the years by the three broad groups of nationalities—Western, Socialist, and Other. The decline in the position of Western states, noted in other indices, is also evident here. One should note that 1950 was an unusual year, among other reasons because of the Soviet Union's boycott of the Administrative Council. Had it not been for this, the figures for the Socialist and Other states would probably have been slightly different for that year and therefore would have followed a more even progression in the following years. It might be noted parenthetically that the 1967 distribution was not drastically out of line with the distribution of budgetary contributions of the three groups.

Table 3.4

Twenty Most Influential Persons in ITU
(By Position)

Year	Elected Officials		IFRB		Appointed Staff		Administrative Council		Other	
	Number	*Percentage*	*Number*	*Percentage*	*Number*	*Percentage*	*Number*	*Percentage*	*Number*	*Percentage*
1950	6	30	5	25	—	—	9	45	—	—
1958	5	25	4	20	1	5	8	40	2	10
1967	3	15	3	15	2	10	11	55	1	5

Table 3.5

Twenty Most Influential Individuals in ITU
(By National Origin)

	Western		Socialist		Other	
	Number	*Percentage*	*Number*	*Percentage*	*Number*	*Percentage*
1950	16	80	—	—	4	20
1958	16	80	1	5	3	15
1967	13	65	2	10	5	25

It is also interesting to examine the specific nationalities of these influential individuals. In each year, four were French and three were British. There were four Americans among the twenty in 1950, but only three in 1958, and one in 1967. Each of the lists contained one national of Canada and one of Italy. A national of Australia was included in two of the lists. Two Swiss nationals were included in 1958 and one in 1967. Interestingly, none of the lists included a national of West Germany or of Japan. In each of the three years, at least one of the twenty influential people was a national of Argentina, and another a national of India. In 1958 the list included two Argentinians, and in 1967 two Moroccans.

Only one person was included in all three lists, René Petit, a Frenchman who has been a member of the IFRB since its formation. Eleven others were included in two lists: three of these were also nationals of France; three were nationals of the United States, two of Argentina, and one each of the United Kingdom, Canada, and India. There was a greater degree of continuity among those considered to be influential in the early postwar years in ITU than there has been recently. Seven of those included in the 1958 list had been on the 1950 list; only four of the names on the 1967 list were carried over from the earlier ones.

A good deal can be learned about the sources of influence in ITU by considering these lists and also by comparing the qualities of those named to the qualities of those who were not. Some familiarity with the ITU is obviously a requisite to the possession of influence. Everyone included on the lists has participated in the agency's activities for several years. Technical competence is also important. With the sole exception of Secretary-General Marco Andrada, all those listed were trained in some branch of telecommunications. All also had an intense personal commitment to their tasks. It is apparent, however, that holding an important position does not automatically place one among the organizational elite.

Environmental Impacts

Factors Specific to the Organization

The broad economic and political features described in chapter 2 have provided a general backdrop for decision making that is valid for the International Telecommunication Union during the past quarter-century. Several factors relating specifically to telecommunications have also been important. Before an analysis of the interaction between the environment and the ITU can be attempted, these need to be described.

First, we should reiterate that telecommunication by its very nature requires a measure of international collaboration. Second, the technology of telecommunications has progressed tremendously and with extreme rapidity in the years since World War II. Perfected television systems, transistors, automatic switching, and communications satellites are only a few of the

Table 3.6
Rank Order in the Environment Compared with Rank Order in Telecommunications

	1950		1958		1967	
	Rank Order in the Environment	Telecom-munications Rank Order	Rank Order in the Environment	Telecom-munications Rank Order	Rank Order in the Environment	Telecom-munications Rank Order
United States	1	1	1	1	1	1
Japan	9	6.5	10	4.5	5	2
USSR	2	8	2	3	2	3
Federal Republic of Germany	7	5	6.5	4.5	7	4
United Kingdom	3	2	3	2	5	5
France	4	4	4.5	6.5	3	6.5
Canada	7	3	8.5	6.5	9.5	6.5
Spain	16.5	24	19.5	21	15	8
German Democratic Republic	34	37	26	15.5	26.5	9
Australia	12.5	6.5	15	8	15	10
Poland	27.5	13	26	11	21	11
Czechoslovakia	27.5	10	26	9	26.5	12
Mexico	20	27	19.5	12.5	26.5	13
China	5	17.5	4.5	12.5	5	14
Austria	37	11	26	14	15	15
Yugoslavia	20	25.5	26	24	15	16
Brazil	12.5	37	11.5	27	15	17
Argentina	20	20	15	15.5	21	18
New Zealand	27.5	14.5	33.5	18.5	36	19
Finland	34	15	37	17	36	20
India	7	22	6.5	24	9.5	21
Italy	12.5	17.5	8.5	18.5	8	22
United Arab Republic	27.5	28	33.5	31	31.5	23
South Africa	20	25.5	19.5	28	21	24

Sweden	12.5	15	11.5	20	11	25
Netherlands	20	21	19.5	24	15	26
Switzerland	12.5	19	15	22	15	27
Norway	27.5	12	26	29	31.5	28
Philippines	27.5	33	33.5	36	36	29
Belgium	12.5	23	15	26	21	30
Denmark	27.5	9	26	10	26.5	31
Israel	34	31	26	30	26.5	32
Turkey	27.5	29	33.5	33	31.5	33
Venezuela	27.5	39	26	34	36	34
Cuba	37	36	33.5	32	31.5	35
Indonesia	16.5	30	15	35	26.5	36
Pakistan	27.5	34	33.5	37	21	37
Luxembourg	37	32	38	38	39	38
Nigeria	39	38	39	39	36	39

developments. The pace of technological progress has been phenomenal. The first transatlantic cable for telephone communications was laid in 1956. Prior to that time, telephone messages across the Atlantic were transmitted by radio. An active communications satellite, which could also conduct transatlantic telephone communications, was launched only six years later, and the "Early Bird" synchronous communications satellite began to provide regular service in 1965. This satellite increased by almost half the existing cable capacity for transatlantic telephone traffic.

Third, telecommunications facilities are distributed very unequally about the globe. To the extent that the control of resources constitutes power, this fact is important. The number of telephones in service and the number of radio receivers and television receivers produced have been chosen as indicators of the relative ranking of states with respect to telecommunications facilities. A composite ranking of the top thirty-nine states by these criteria is presented in table 3.6.

Clearly, a state's position with respect to telecommunications facilities is related to its overall capabilities, and the relationship was more pronounced in 1958 and 1967 than it was in 1950. Kendall's tau beta coefficients of correlation between rank order in the general environment and in telecommunications for the three years are: 1950, 0.46; 1958, 0.53; and 1967, 0.54. There are, however, some important differences between the rankings of certain states in the general environment and in the specific field of telecommunications. Japan is much more important in telecommunications than its position in the general environment would indicate. The positions of Spain, East Germany, Poland, Czechoslovakia, Mexico, Yugoslavia, New Zealand, and Finland show a similar discrepancy. Conversely, China, India, Indonesia, and Pakistan, populous states with low per capita GNP, rank lower in telecommunications facilities than in the general environment. This is also true of Italy, Sweden, Switzerland, and Belgium. The most dramatic shift in the field of telecommunications has been the growth of the position of Japan. Another significant change is the decline in the relative position of the United Kingdom. Both of these changes parallel those indicated for these states in the general environment, although Japan's ascent in telecommunications has been somewhat sharper than its growth in general.

The specific indicators underscore the leading position in telecommunications held by a somewhat limited number of economically developed states. Like all indicators of capability, these make the position of the United States seem especially strong. If anything, the indicators chosen here understate the position of the United States, since they do not show the tremendous lead that this country has in research and development in telecommunications, as evidenced by its dominant position in the field of space communications.

In view of the crucial role of the United States in the development, production, and operation of telecommunications equipment, it is important to understand the history of United States relations with international collaborative efforts in this field. The United States never joined the International Telegraph Union, partially because the union comprised mainly countries that had nationalized telegraph systems, but also because the vast continental boundaries of the United States made international collaboration much less important for it than for the European states. Observers from the United States government and from private companies did attend several of the conferences, including the Berlin Conference in 1903, and the United States became a member of the International Radiotelegraph Union, which ultimately resulted from that conference. When the two bodies merged in 1932, the United States became a member of the International Telecommunication Union. However, a residue of American hesitancy still remains. Although the United States signed and ratified the Radio Regulations beginning with their first formulation, it did not accept the Telegraph Regulations until 1949; and it still does not adhere to the Telephone Regulations.

A final aspect of the particular environment in which ITU must operate concerns the commercial features of telecommunications. Telecommunications can be a highly profitable business, particularly if one considers the revenues not only from the sales and rentals of equipment but also from the transmission of messages and programs and in some countries from advertisements. The telecommunications field includes a number of the world's largest corporate enterprises; for example, the American Telephone and Telegraph Company, General Electric, the Radio Corporation of America, the Marconi Company, Standard Telephone and Cables, Phillips, Siemens and Halske, Telefunken, and Sony. It is indicative of the commercial importance of telecommunications that, unlike the magazines published by other international organizations, the ITU's *Telecommunication Journal* is a glossy production, full of advertising.

The Stratification of Power

The stratification of power in the environment is reflected in the ITU in various ways. Membership in the Administrative Council does not necessarily guarantee influence; but since the council is the only organ of the ITU that is certain to meet annually, it is an important point of access. In 1967 all of the top ten states in the general environment except Communist China were members of the Administrative Council. Six of them (the United States, the USSR, the United Kingdom, France, Italy, and Canada) had held continuous membership since the council's establishment two decades earlier. Four other states not among the top ten in the general environment, but among the top twenty-five (Argentina, Brazil, Switzerland, and Yugoslavia) have also held continuous membership, as has Nationalist China.

Leading states—defined as the top ten countries in the general environment in 1967—have come to constitute a declining proportion of the Administrative Council's total membership, however, simply as a consequence of the council's expanded membership. Four elections for the

Administrative Council have been held, one at each of the Plenipotentiary Conferences since the end of World War II: Atlantic City in 1947, Buenos Aires in 1952, Geneva in 1959, and Montreux in 1965. In 1947 the size of the Administrative Council was set at eighteen. It was increased to twenty-five in 1959, and to twenty-nine in 1965. In the first election the leading states won six of the eighteen seats, or 33.3 percent. By winning seven seats in 1952 the leading states increased their proporation to 38.9 percent. Their total representation was increased to nine in the 1959 election, but since the council was also enlarged, their proportion declined to 36 percent. In 1965 their proportion declined even further to 31 percent even though their membership remained at nine because the council added still more members.

Another way in which the stratification of power in the environment is roughly reflected in ITU is in the nationality of the elected officials. Obviously this is at best an imperfect measure. One reason, as has been seen, is that factors other than national status are important in determining the outcome of elections; another is that the International Telecommunication Convention explicitly forbids elected officials and staff members to "seek or accept instructions from any government or from any other authority outside the Union."[12] Nevertheless, national status is one factor in elections; and because early socialization is important in shaping one's world outlook, the measure does have some meaning.

In 1950 nationals of the leading states occupied eleven out of the eighteen elective positions, or 61.1 percent. Eight years later eight of the sixteen elected officials (one post was not filled), or 50 percent were nationals of the leading powers. In 1967, nationals of the leading powers occupied five of the eight elected positions (again one post was not filled), or 62.5 percent.

The stratification of power in the environment is strongly reflected in ITU in other areas, but in these demonstration in quantitative terms is not so easy. For example, some of ITU's most important decisions involve the creation of rules. As is obvious from our earlier discussion, the leading states and private agencies within these states play a substantial role in this process. They are the principal initiators, and in some cases they also hold veto power. It would be pointless, for example, to create a rule about telephones if it were obvious that the United States would not follow it. The influence of the leading states and their private firms in these matters derives directly from their control of substantial resources in the field of ITU's activities.

Distribution of States by Economic and Political Characteristics

A second feature of the general environment is the distribution of states according to their economic and political characteristics. As will be recalled, the most significant change in the period covered by this study was the decline in the number of dependent states. Of the 154 political units classified in chapter 2, only 80 were independent in 1950. By 1958 this number had increased to 91. In 1967, 131 of the units were independent. The increase in ITU's membership has been an obvious consequence of this change. The increase in ITU's membership has also created stronger pressures within the union to do more about economic development, and more will be said about this later.

Tables 3.7 and 3.8 show the distribution of those ITU member states that have been classified in this study among the various economic levels and types of polity in 1950, 1958, and 1967.[13] The most striking change over the years in ITU's membership is the increase in the number of states classed

Table 3.7

ITU's Membership Classified according to Economic Level

Per capita GNP (in Dollars)	1950 Number	Percentage	1958 Number	Percentage	1967 Number	Percentage
0-199	23	35.39	29	33.71	46	37.10
200-599	25	38.46	31	36.05	41	33.06
600-999	5	7.69	13	15.12	16	12.90
1,000 and over	12	18.46	13	15.12	21	16.94
Total	65	100.00	86	100.00	124	100.00

Table 3.8

ITU's Membership Classified according to Polity

	1950 Number	Percentage	1958 Number	Percentage	1967 Number	Percentage
Competitive	30	46.15	37	43.02	42	33.87
Mobilizing	12	18.46	15	17.44	23	18.55
Authoritarian	21	32.31	33	38.38	59	47.58
Nonindependent	2	3.08	1	1.16	–	–
Total	65	100.00	86	100.00	124	100.00

as authoritarian and the decrease in the number classed as competitive. In 1950, authoritarian states constituted 32.31 percent of the total, and competitive states 46.15 percent. By 1967 these proportions were just about reversed: authoritarian states constituted 47.58 percent of the total; competitive states, 33.87 percent. This change, however, has had virtually no effect on ITU, because it is difficult to distinguish between the policies of competitive and authoritarian regimes. Had the proportion of mobilizing regimes changed more significantly than it did, the effect might have been greater, for even in as technical an agency as ITU, mobilizing regimes seem to pursue distinctive policies.

The second notable change is that between 1950 and 1967 the proportion of ITU's membership in the lower economic categories (i.e. with per capita GNP of less than $600) fell by about 4 percent, with a corresponding rise in the proportion of member states in the higher categories (with per capita GNP of $600 or more). This contradicts the popular assumption that the number of poor states in international organizations has increased dramatically. Of course the absolute number of states in all categories has increased; and in this instance absolute numbers seem to be more important than proportions, for pressures on ITU to do more toward promoting economic development have certainly increased.

Patterns of Alignments and Conflicts

Four broad patterns of relationships were identified in chapter 2 as being especially important in the environment of international organizations since the end of World War II. The first of these was the clash between the communist states and that group loosely termed the West. The second centered on the struggle to end colonialism. The third was the related but different controversy between the rich and the poor states of the world; and the fourth was the movement toward regional integration, especially in Western Europe. While all of these patterns of relationships have affected decision making in ITU, the first three have thus far had the most pronounced effects.

East-West Alignments. Since Communist China has never been a member, within the ITU, the USSR and the United States have been the focal points of the clash between the communist states and the West. The effects that developments in Soviet-American relations have had on the ITU and on patterns of decision making within it, however, have been subtle. The path from wartime collaboration to cold war and then to competitive coexistence can be seen; but the line—so clear in world politics—has been blurred and complicated by the structure of ITU and the nature of its subject matter.

For many of ITU's purposes its members can be regarded as black boxes: their ideological alignments and internal political systems make no difference. Technical and operating questions relating to international collaboration in telecommunications are hardly, if at all, affected by whether a regime is communist, socialist, or capitalist. The nature of the regime may have a greater effect on the administrative aspects of international collaboration, but here too its force can be minimized. Conflict between members, however, will affect ITU, particularly if telecommunications are used in their conflict. Another reason why ideologies play a less important role in ITU is that the technology of telecommunications makes for strong pressure toward universality within ITU: the members of the organization want and need to have most states as collaborators, and most states see the need to collaborate. Even adversaries desire to communicate with one another on a number of occasions. Furthermore, quite apart from their international operations, and regardless of any political conflicts, all countries must be concerned about what other countries do if they are to minimize the possibilities of harmful interference with their internal communications.

The USSR, Albania, Bulgaria, the Byelorussian S.S.R., Czechoslovakia, Hungary, Poland, the Ukranian S.S.R., and Yugoslavia all signed the Atlantic City International Telecommunication Convention in 1947, and all have been active members of the ITU throughout the period since the end of World War II, although for a short time Hungary was not listed as a member because it delayed in ratifying the convention. Mongolia became a member of ITU in 1964. Except for the People's Republic of China, the only important communist state that is not a member of the union is the German Democratic Republic. In view of that state's importance in the production of telecommunication equipment and its geographic position in the heart of Europe, its absence from the agency is of some consequence. In some ways the exclusion of Communist China and the German Democratic Republic is the most important effect that the clash between communist states and the West has had on the ITU.

Tables 3.9 and 3.10 summarize the elections to the Administrative Council and the IFRB in terms of the three groupings of states that have been used in other analyses in this study. In relation to their proportion of ITU's total membership, communist countries have always been overrepresented on both the Administrative Council and the IFRB; the extent of their overrepresentation on the council was greatest during the height of the cold war. Apparently the shift in the pattern of Soviet-American relations has had very little impact on these representational issues.

Soviet-American relations have in contrast affected the tone of ITU proceedings, particularly those of the Plenipotentiary Conferences and the Administrative Council. In 1946 the big five—Nationalist China, France, the USSR, the United Kingdom, and the United States—met in Moscow and agreed on the changes that they would like to see made in the International Telecommunication Union. This harmony continued to prevail with hardly any exceptions through the Atlantic City Plenipotentiary Conference the following year. However, the next conference, which was held at Buenos Aires in 1952, was marked by a number of sharp controversies between East and West. The atmosphere was considerably calmer in the 1959 Geneva Plenipotentiary Conference, and there was little difference in tone between that meeting and the conference held in 1965 in Montreux.

The tone of the meetings of the Administrative Council has varied according to the same pattern. As late as 1948 it was agreed that the Soviet representative should be chairman of the next annual session. That session, however, was marked by considerable vituperation; and the following year, in keeping with the general policy of the Soviet bloc, neither the representative of the USSR nor that of Poland participated in the council's

Table 3.9

Elections to the Administrative Council
(By National Origin)

	1947		1952		1959		1965	
	Number	Percentage	Number	Percentage	Number	Percentage	Number	Percentage
Western	8	44	8	44	10	40	10	35
Socialist	3	17	3	17	3	12	3	10
Other	7	39	7	39	12	48	16	55

Table 3.10

Elections to the International Frequency Registration Board (IFRB)
(By National Origin)

	1947		1959		1965	
	Number	Percentage	Number	Percentage	Number	Percentage
Western	4	36	4	36	2	40
Socialist	2	18	2	18	1	20
Other	5	46	5	46	2	40

session. The next few sessions of the council were characterized by sharp acrimony, but this gradually subsided. To a lesser extent the atmosphere of other ITU meetings has also been affected by Soviet-American relations.

In the many controversies within the ITU in which East and West took sides during the height of the cold war, the West triumphed almost without exception. However, it would be incorrect to say that the ITU was used instrumentally by the West in the context of this global confrontation. The greatest number of the controversies were initiated by the East: what happened was that its initiatives were rebuffed. Furthermore, few of the decisions taken during this period had direct and important consequences for the East; if it seemed that they might have such consequences, the East could always ignore the decisions, a course that they in fact pursued.

Soviet-American relations have had perhaps the most telling effect on the International Frequency Registration Board, which was created at the Atlantic City Conference in 1947. ITU, like its predecessor, the International Radiotelegraph Union, had carried out certain functions with respect to frequency allocation and registration since 1906. The pattern established then was that Administrative Conferences would settle how the segments of the frequency spectrum should be used, while the Berne bureau would take care of the task of registration.

According to the conception embodied in the 1947 Atlantic City convention, not only would the IFRB perform the bureau's traditional function of registration, but it would also enter, albeit gingerly, into the field of frequency management. Instead of serving merely as a passive depository, it would examine each notification submitted to it and could refuse to grant registrations. It could also cancel registrations if they were not being used. Furthermore, IFRB was mandated to furnish advice to members "with a view to the operation of the maximum practicable number of radio channels in those portions of the spectrum where harmful interference may occur." [14] The Americans, whose support was largely responsible for the creation of the IFRB, hoped that it would become something of a cross between the United States Federal Communications Commission and the International Court of Justice. Had the IFRB grown into the role envisaged by these planners, or even had it fulfilled all of the terms accepted at Atlantic City, the result would have been a significant expansion in the tasks of ITU.

However, the IFRB has played a much more modest role, and the cold war was at least one cause. At a very early stage it had become apparent that the Soviet Union was not in sympathy with the Atlantic City decisions, and it sought to block their implementation. Behind this action was the desire to restrict the ITU and the IFRB to the registration function as traditionally conceived, and to prevent the board from engaging in frequency management activities. Obviously the USSR wanted to protect its sovereignty in this sphere, and it was concerned about being outvoted in ITU and the IFRB. In 1949, after they had been defeated on a number of important votes, the USSR, Albania, Bulgaria, Czechoslovakia, Hungary, Poland, and Rumania withdrew from the Provisional Frequency Allocation Board. At the Buenos Aires Conference in 1952 the Soviet Union unsuccessfully sought to abolish the IFRB. At the 1959 Geneva Plenipotentiary Conference, the USSR made a similar proposal, which was also rejected. At this conference the United States countered by suggesting that the members of the IFRB should be elected for life, but this proposal was not adopted either.

It was not until 1958 that the USSR and other communist states within the Soviet orbit began to submit data on frequency use to the IFRB. Since neither East nor West could wantonly ignore the other side's use of the frequency spectrum, the practical consequences of their controversy over this matter were to make international institutions less important in relation to states in setting patterns of frequency use in the years after World War II.

A slightly ironic final note was added at the Montreux Conference in 1965. At this conference the United States was one of the leaders in a movement to abolish the IFRB. The Soviet Union, on the other hand, supported its retention.

Decolonization. Decolonization has been a second salient feature of the global political environment that has had an important impact on the International Telecommunication Union in the postwar period. On the most elementary level, decolonization has been responsible for the growth in the union's membership from 72 in 1947 to 133 in 1967.

The growth in ITU's membership was in turn the principal factor in the decisions to increase the size of the Administrative Council and also to alter its composition. As portrayed in table 3.9, from 1947 through 1959 the Administrative Council consisted of eight representatives from Western states, three from Socialist states, and seven from Other states. (The last category, it will be recalled, embraces all of Africa, Asia, and Latin America, except Japan and South Africa, which are included in the first category, and Mongolia, which is included in the second category.) From 1960 through 1965 the enlarged council consisted of ten representatives from Western states, three from Socialist states, and twelve from Other states. In the 1965 decisions, the representation of the first two categories was held constant, while that of the third was increased by four. Thus states classified as Other have had the most representatives on the council since 1959, and they have held a majority since 1965.

These changes in ITU's membership and in the composition of the Administrative Council have had important consequences in determining the type of symbolic issues raised in ITU and the manner in which they have been treated. Decolonization and development issues have largely replaced those stemming from the cold war.

Rich and Poor States. The inauguration of ITU's service activities and their subsequent increase are also related to decolonization, as well as to a third controversy—that between the rich states and the poor. These same two broad trends in world politics have also had a more subtle and potentially more profound impact on the International Telecommunication Union. Although the nature of a member's ideological orientation and political system is largely unrelated either to the role that the state might play in ITU or to the functions that the union might perform with respect to the member, a state's level of economic development is not as inconsequential. ITU was founded by states that were roughly similar in their economic development, and its tasks were defined to promote international collaboration among them. Such states continued to dominate ITU until well after World War II. It was only with decolonization and the entrance of large numbers of states from Asia and Africa that this situation changed. As it changed, and as the poor states became increasingly articulate in pressing their demands, the question of whether or not ITU ought to take a more positive role in promoting the development of its less-advanced members was raised. The relevance of the union's traditional functions as far as the majority of its members were concerned was also called into question.

Interestingly the change in the composition of ITU's membership also affected the controversy about the International Frequency Registration Board. The IFRB was not abolished at the Montreux Conference in 1965 largely because of the votes of the African, Asian, and Latin-American members of ITU. Developing states in general felt a pressing need for space on the frequency spectrum. They felt that the rich and established states, mainly because they *were* established, had more than their fair share of the spectrum. Rightly or wrongly the developing states saw the IFRB as a protector of their interests and as an instrument that they could use in their efforts to gain more space on the spectrum. They also saw the IFRB as a resource for technical advice that they badly needed. To a limited extent, then, decolonization has lent some support to the notion of institutional autonomy and authority for ITU.

Regionalism. The fourth broad trend in the world environment, the movement toward regional integration, has made very little difference in ITU. At most it has been partly responsible for the pressure to assist in the creation of regional telecommunication networks in Africa and Latin America.

The Structure of Influence and Patterns of Decision Making

By the choice of its members ITU has always been an organization with limited powers, and this situation seems unlikely to change in the immediate future. It is an extremely vital organization, to which almost all states feel that they must belong, and even those that do not belong usually comply with its decisions. They have little choice. At the same time, however, none of the members, particularly those who control the major telecommunications resources, are eager to give ITU strong independent powers. They need a framework for international collaborative efforts, but they have little intention of making the International Telecommunication Union very much beyond that.

These facts are very evident in the decision-making patterns within the agency. In general the elected officials and staff have little independent power. On symbolic and representational issues, which may make headlines but which have little impact on the important matters considered in ITU, influence is broadly shared. On the most important issues, however, influence is extremely stratified and is closely tied to national governments and the major private firms in the field.

Whether or not this will continue to be the case is difficult to predict. ITU's political organs have little control over the union's expanding service activities; but the secretariat would have difficulty in using this as a base for asserting its independence, for it does not have much control over these activities either. There is some basis for thinking that less-developed countries will become more and more assertive about the orientation of ITU's activities and about such matters as the use of the radio frequency spectrum. Their insistence on maintaining the IFRB, along with the large number of hortatory resolutions dealing with their needs that were proposed and adopted in the late 1960s may indicate the beginning of a trend. These states seem increasingly capable of attaining their ambitions; they have gained both formal access to power and a greater measure of influence within the union. What they lack is technical skill and control of important resources. The promise of the present situation is that the more-developed states will become increasingly responsive to the needs of their less-developed fellow members. Inevitably the authority of the organization would have to grow, for only a strong secretariat could counterbalance the weight of the leading states and private firms and thus increase the emphasis that is now given to the interests of developing countries. The danger is that the organization may develop an internal split, with one part stressing service activities and appealing to the needs of the less-developed countries, and the other stressing forum activities and appealing to the needs of the developed countries. Were this to happen, the two parts of the organization might pursue uncoordinated or even contradictory policies.

The nature of the participants in ITU curiously contributes to this danger. They are predominantly officials of national telecommunications administrations and representatives of private firms who tend to take a very narrow view of the union's functions and responsibilities. The organizational ideology reflects this attitude and, as ideologies do, reinforces the tendency. Given their vast resources, the United States, Japan, the USSR, West Germany, the United Kingdom, and France would probably have restricted aims for ITU in any event. But many middle powers, which in other organizations frequently follow courses favoring the growth of the organization and of its authority, do not do this in ITU because of the nature of their representatives and the way in which their policy is determined.

Whatever the future brings, it is clear that ITU will continue to be what it always has been, a vital forum for the coordination and adjustment of national policies. It already provides services, and it could become a telling force for the management of scarce resources if the member states wanted it to perform this role.

4   ILO: Limited Monarchy

Robert W. Cox

The International Labor Organization (ILO). is a relatively complex and relatively old international organization. No attempt can be made here to summarize its history, the evolution of its internal political processes, and the environmental forces that have shaped them. Fortunately, a substantial literature dealing with the organization already exists for those who wish to pursue these matters further.[1] In this chapter we shall focus on the years 1945-70, which saw the achievement of a certain equilibrium in the ILO's political system, a system we call limited monarchy. This term designates a political system in which influence is structured around one central figure—the executive head—who though he plays a leading role does so subject to very real constraints. This chapter attempts to delineate the characteristics of such a political system, considering the ILO as an exemplar.

Functions, Structure, and Evolution

Though we are concerned with the period 1945-70, some reference to the remoter past is necessary to explain certain basic features of the ILO. Proposals anticipating the ILO have been traced back to early nineteenth-century liberal humanitarians and paternalistic employers.[2] However, the ILO came into being in 1919 primarily because of certain concerns on the part of the victorious Allies in World War I: the fear that peace would be followed by widespread social conflict, the desire to protect Western Europe from the revolutionary situation emerging in the East, and the sense that some concerted action by the Allies was necessary to forestall these dangers. At the Paris Peace Conference the Allies agreed to set up a labor commission; and the British government came forward with proposals for an international labor organization. These proposals included the tripartite basis of representation, whereby trade unions and employers as well as governments would be directly represented, and envisaged the principal task of the new organization as the framing of international labor standards—both salient aspects of the organization which the conference established.

The political leaders' interest in the project was not sustained, however, and members of the labor commission found little response even in their own delegations.[3] This widespread indifference dissipated momentarily when the proposals reached the heads of government. Bela Kun had seized power in Hungary the day before. The ILO was Versailles' answer to Bolshevism.

The interest of the government leaders again waned as the ILO was brought into existence. However, the European trade union leaders—most prominent among them, Léon Jouhaux of the French Confédération Générale du Travail (CGT)—actively moved toward occupying a position of strength within the ILO. With employers' support, they succeeded in securing the appointment of Albert Thomas as first director. Thomas, a French socialist with a reformist and "national" orientation, had been a minister of munitions during the war, but at the time of his appointment he was in the political wilderness. His candidacy took the governments by surprise. Since they had not agreed among themselves concerning any candidate, and apparently had not given much thought to the requirements of the office, they acquiesced in Thomas's appointment.[4] He proceeded to use it as a base for initiative in international social policy, drawing strength from support of the International Federation of Trade Unions (Amsterdam International), which coordinated worker action in the ILO. This power of initiative on the part of the director and the political base he used represented important early modifications of the intentions of the founders.

Structure

In juridical form an intergovernmental organization, the tripartite system of representation and the tripartite organization of the internal procedures of representative organs make the ILO structurally unique. Each member state is represented in the International Labor Conference by four delegates: two are from the government, a third represents organized workers, and a fourth represents employers. The work of the conference itself is organized by groups, in which delegates representing government, employers, and workers meet separately to consider their points of view on the issues in the committees or plenary sessions of the conference. This activity has always been more important in the case of the Workers' and Employers' groups, which have tried to achieve a unified view on all major issues affecting their interests, than it has been for the Government Group.

The executive organ is the Governing Body, which is also tripartite in composition, in a ratio of two government members to one employer member and one worker member. A proportion of the government seats (formerly half but now ten out of twenty-four) are automatically allocated to the "states of chief industrial importance." The list of these is determined at infrequent intervals by a committee of statistical experts. The remaining government members are elected by the Government Group of the conference (without the participation of the "states of chief industrial importance"); and all the employer and worker members are elected by the Employers' and Workers' groups respectively. The composition of the other major committees and conferences of the ILO is determined by the Governing Body, which adheres to the tripartite principle, usually in the proportion of 1:1:1.

Turning Points and Changing Functions

The ILO's functions in the earliest years were largely limited to the negotiation of international labor standards in the form of conventions and recommendations. Director Thomas added the publication of his own analyses of the social situation and his proposals on social policy questions. Initiatives to move into new fields have often been linked with crises in the ILO's environment or with major events within the organization—in other words, with turning points in the ILO's history.

During the Great Depression of the 1930s, the first major crisis to affect the ILO, Thomas, followed by his successor Harold Butler, attempted to play a role in economic policy, but without much response or success. During the latter part of World War II, the ILO leaders tried again to secure a prominent place for the organization in influencing international economic and financial policy. The ILO's primary problem at this time was not expansion, however, but survival. The major decisions about postwar international organizations were being taken by the United States, British, and Soviet governments. The Soviet government was clearly hostile to the ILO, preferring that labor interests be expressed directly through the new United Nations machinery by the World Federation of Trade Unions (WFTU), in which Soviet trade unions participated along with those from Western countries. The Governing Body made overtures during 1943-44 in an attempt to attract the Soviet Union into the ILO, but was rebuffed. The American officials planning for new international arrangements in the economic and social fields were skeptical about the ILO's pretensions, and, in any case, United States policy counseled against opposition to firmly held Soviet views on what the United States government viewed as a secondary issue. British officials supported the ILO but were unwilling to press its claims against Soviet opposition and American indifference. Despite these unfavorable conditions, the ILO's leaders were nevertheless able to secure recognition of the organization as a specialized agency of the United Nations. Survival was thus assured, but the ILO's future role had yet to be defined.

In 1948 when David A. Morse, then acting secretary of labor in President Truman's administration, became director-general of the ILO, he initiated a program more oriented toward services. An initial bid to undertake the organization (including transport and settlement) of large-scale migration from Europe to the Americas was frustrated when the governments that were mainly concerned preferred to confide this task to an organization that would be more limited in membership and more subject to political control.

Failure to undertake a migration program was the ILO's first great "nondecision" of the postwar period. But Morse's other moves toward operational manpower activities, though more modest at the outset than the migration proposal, grew gradually into a large-scale and widely diversified technical cooperation program. Beginning with employment organization and technical training assistance to European countries in the postwar reconstruction period, manpower activities shifted to the less-developed countries in the 1950s. Other kinds of direct services to governments were added to manpower activities, which were conceptualized more broadly during the mid-1960s as human resources development. Technical assistance in other ILO fields, such as labor administration, social security, occupational safety, and health, was included in a larger and more comprehensive technical cooperation program.

In 1954 the Soviet government decided to enter the ILO accompanied by other socialist states, an action they were entitled to take as members of the United Nations; this action precipitated a crisis in the organization that remained acute for a decade. In ILO conferences the ideological polemics of the cold war took the form of a confrontation between the principles of tripartism and universality. Employers, many workers, and some governments supported the principle that respect by governments for the autonomy of trade unions and employers was a basic condition of participation in the ILO. Others urged the advantages of the widest possible membership, even at the cost of heterogeneity in ideologies and social systems.

After 1960, when a large number of African states entered the ILO, the focus of conference attention shifted from East-West polemics to the African attack on the policies of South Africa, Rhodesia, and Portugal. The African states pressed for more technical services and for decentralization of the ILO to give Africans more local control over such services.

The mid-1960s marks a final turning point in the period under study. Director-General Morse precipitated the negotiation of a new consensus within the organization on the program and a continuing dialogue about the structure of the ILO.[5] The debate about these issues reflected the growth of greater heterogeneity of ideologies and objectives among the membership. The proposals that Morse put forward as bases for the new consensus on programs gave even greater prominence to the service function.

Budget Trends

The gradual shift of emphasis from the setting of standards (the principal forum activity) to the provision of services is shown in the changing estimated distribution of ILO expenditures (expressed in percentages):

	1950	1958	1967
Forum	80	44	16
Service	20	56	84

These estimates result from the author's analysis of budget information. This information is not presented in official documents according to the same concepts for the three years, mainly as a result of the change from a heads-of-expenditure to a program budget, and so some problems of interpretation arise.

Despite their decreasing percentage of the total, the level of forum activities has been more or less stabilized since 1950. The increase in the total level of activity of the organization is accounted for by operational activities.

The effect of this trend on the ILO's sources of income is striking. The income budget can be divided between the regular budget, to which member states contribute, and revenue from extrabudgetàry sources, mainly from the United Nations Development Program (UNDP) and its predecessors. Percentages of income from these sources are shown in the following table:

	1950	*1958*	*1967*
Regular budget assessments	86	66	45
Extrabudgetary funds	14	34	55

Thus, by 1967 less than half of all activities were directly paid for by member states and controlled by their representatives through the budget, whereas in 1950 four-fifths of the activities had been supported in this fashion. Such a considerable shift in the financial basis of the organization could hardly be without significance to the structure of influence within it.

Decision Making: A Taxonomical Analysis

Representational Decisions

One source of representational issues lies in the desires of less-developed regions to have a greater voice in shaping the purposes and activities of the ILO. In the late 1940s the pressure came mainly from Asia; in the 1960s, from Africa. Demands from the developing countries included: regional machinery that would convey greater autonomy and be more responsive to local pressures; greater authority for the ILO conference in relation to the Governing Body; greater representation on the Governing Body; and representation in the International Labor Office.

The most intractable representational disputes, however, have concerned the place of the Soviet Union and other socialist states within the ILO. At first, the issue was whether the Soviet Union could legitimately fit into the tripartite structure, even though as a member of the United Nations it was formally eligible to join the ILO. Subsequently, the ground shifted to structural reform, and the Soviet group joined with some less-developed countries to press in favor of increasing the role of the International Labor Conference and diminishing that of the Governing Body. More and more, as opponents of the Soviet Union became reconciled to its presence in the ILO, the crucial issue became Soviet claims for increased representation in the existing structures.

The issue of Soviet membership was raised in 1954. As a step toward moderating the ensuing conflict, the Governing Body charged three indepen-dent persons to undertake an international inquiry into the status of trade unions and employer organizations. Voluminous monographs prepared under the supervision of the Office and many months of inquiry yielded the conclusion that so many shades and gradations of government intervention were possible in trade union and employer affairs[6] that a strict application of the principle of autonomy might exclude worker or employer delegates from a large proportion of members—by no means only those in the Soviet bloc. These findings persuaded the majority of governments to accept the interpretation of the ILO constitution that held that autonomy of trade union and employer organizations should be a goal rather than a prior condition of membership. No major issues of worker or employer repre-sentation were raised when single-party African states joined the ILO in the years that followed.

The initiative in raising the issue of Soviet representation was taken by trade union and employer delegates. The resolution of the issue was achieved through the mediation of a group of representatives of Western governments. The director-general and some other ILO officials played a broker's role; their influence could be considerable because the issues were posed in terms of constitutional interpretation and legal fact finding. Analytical techniques were used in a situation where the irreconcilable positions of the parties made a solution by bargaining unlikely. In addition, the director-general let it be known that he considered it a matter of high policy that the solution be consistent with the objective of universality of membership; and this position, to which most of the Western government representatives rallied, became the basis for settlement.

The handling of the Soviet issue can be compared with the situation after 1963, when African delegates moved successfully to condemn South Africa and force it out of the ILO. This issue was determined by weight of opinion in the conference. The outcome reflected particularly the much increased numbers of new nations in the organization's membership. Another factor was the disinclination of European or North American delegates to advance the principle of universality in the South African case in the face of African demands that were linked with the issue of racial discrimination.

The issues of representation on committees of the conference (and by extension on certain other tripartite ILO committees) has had a longer history. The Employers' and Workers' groups in the conference customarily have had the power of determining the representation from their groups on conference committees. The Employers' Group has consistently decided not to appoint Soviet employers' delegates.

Some Western government representatives again took a leading role in moderating this issue. They successfully worked out proposals to which all parties acquiesced in practice, though employers continued to oppose it in principle. Under the formula thus adopted by the conference, an appointed body of impartial persons—the Appeals Board—can grant seats on committees to delegates excluded by their group. Thus, in formal terms, an issue that could not be resolved by bargaining was to be dealt with by a body applying some objective criteria. In practice, there was no doubt that the Appeals Board would give satisfaction to the Soviet employers' delegates although perhaps not to the full extent of their demands.

Issues of representation on the Governing Body are decided exclusively among the representatives of governments and interest groups. Through a bargaining process prior to each election, interested delegates attempt to build up sufficient support to secure their election. The introduction of new members, particularly those from the Soviet group and the newly independent (mainly African) nations, brought new demands for representation and made this bargaining process more complex. Increasing the size of the Governing Body was insufficient to meet these demands painlessly. New demands could be satisfied fully only at the cost of disturbing such long-standing arrangements as the rotation of government memberships within the Scandinavian and Benelux countries. Beginning in 1963, no Western European government was elected to titular membership on the Governing Body, although four Western European countries had permanent seats as states of chief industrial importance. The communist-controlled World Federation of Trade Unions and the All-Africa Trade Union Federation have pressed for "proportional representation" among worker members on the Governing Body, but the International Confederation of Free Trade Unions (ICFTU) maintained its preference for majority vote on a slate of candidates, a procedure through which its monopoly of seats had hitherto been maintained. A Soviet worker was elected to the Governing Body for the first time in 1966, but the election of a Soviet member by the Employers' Group still constitutes one of the Soviet Union's unsatisfied demands.

The constituents keep a close eye upon the composition of the staff, particularly at the upper levels. For appointments to assistant director-general or deputy director-general, the director-general must consult with the officers of the Governing Body, that is, the chairman of the Governing Body and the vice-chairmen representing the Employers' and Workers' groups. The incumbents form an internal cabinet of advisers, with direct access to the director-general, and they are referred to collectively as the directorate. In 1947 the directorate consisted of four persons, all from Western Europe. The major additions to membership after 1954, from the Soviet bloc and Africa, brought pressures for enlarging the directorate. The Soviet Union very early demanded a post of assistant director-general to be filled by a Soviet national (since an American was director-general, and both a Briton and a Frenchman were members of the directorate). By 1960 Director-General Morse, judging that he could no longer deny this claim, proposed creating the new post. Both the Workers' and Employers' groups were against the proposal; and, though it was favored by the majority of governments, it did not pass. Lack of support from the United States government—influenced strongly on this issue by the president of the AFL-CIO, George Meany—was a special blow to an American director-general trying to play a moderating role on a cold war issue. Eight months later Morse resigned. The negotiations surrounding his return and reelection the next year (March 1962) doubtless involved assurances of United States government support, but the issue of a Soviet assistant director-general was not resolved. It remained as the King Charles's head of ILO politics. When, in 1970, Morse's successor appointed a Soviet assistant director-general as one of his first official acts, Meany's hostile reaction led Congress to suspend the payment of United States contributions to the ILO.

Symbolic Decisions

Symbolic issues have been contested with the same intensity as representational issues. During the early part of the cold war, socialist delegates proposed resolutions on peace, on condemning NATO, and on decolonization. In the 1960s symbolic issues relating to African questions became more prominent; for example, condemnation of apartheid and attacks upon the policies of white regimes of southern Africa. The election of the president and other officers of the conference also had symbolic significance, particularly when new groups of countries—the Soviet group and the Africans—were asserting their claims to status and influence in the organization.

The highest echelons of decision makers have dealt with the symbolic issues, in marked contrast to the way the so-called technical items have been handled. The election of the president of the 1966 session of the conference, according to one report, claimed the personal attention of President Lyndon Johnson, Secretary of State Dean Rusk, and Ambassador to the United Nations Arthur Goldberg, in addition to the high-ranking United States officials who were more obviously concerned.[7]

The priority given by the key decision makers to symbolic issues derives from their perceptions of what the ILO is all about. To the ILO official, the essence of ILO is the work it does, and this work can be thought of as responding to more or less objectively determined needs. Ideological cleavages and bargaining about representation seem to the ILO official hardly relevant to this work. The top-ranking trade union delegates, however, are active in a world in which political cleavages are refracted through the special prism of labor movements. Some, particularly those who have social-democratic backgrounds, have been fighting a battle similar to earlier union struggles to prevent communist infiltration of their organizations. Other groups of delegates have reacted in different ways to the ideological cleavage—either by taking sides or by adopting an actively neutralist position, which sometimes takes the form of raising other symbolic issues. Symbolic and representational issues are closely linked in the perceptions of many delegates as to what the ILO is about. Symbolic issues test the legitimacy of opposed views about the character and aims of the ILO. For the protagonists, the decisions on these issues provide the means of testing their relative strength within the organization, and perhaps also of measuring the extent to which they are prepared to identify their loyalties with the ILO. In their minds such issues may take precedence over questions concerning programs or labor standards.

It is probable that, for a time following the Moscow test-ban treaty of 1963, neither the Soviet Union nor the United States saw much utility in the ILO as an instrument of political warfare against the other. Regular consultation was informally institutionalized through meetings of the chief government delegates of the Soviet Union and the major Western powers. The purpose of these consultations was, so far as possible, to reach a consensus about avoiding symbolic issues, or at least avoiding political warfare. The director-general acted as a broker in bringing these key delegates together.

Boundary Decisions

From 1945 to 1949, the ILO's main boundary preoccupation was to secure from the United Nations practical as well as formal recognition of its competency in the labor field and a guarantee of nonintervention in its internal affairs. Beginning in the 1950s, the main boundary concern of the ILO (and that of other United Nations agencies as well) was to secure a satisfactory share of the funds coming from the Expanded Program of Technical Assistance and later the UN Special Fund (since combined as UNDP). Because these funds became the material base for shifting the emphasis toward programs in the field of manpower and human resources, the director-general had a considerable stake in cooperative relations with the United Nations.[8]

A third sort of boundary problems arose after 1964, as the Group of 77 less-developed countries, formed originally at the United Nations Conference on Trade and Development in that year, increased the pressure in the United Nations in favor of economic development. The creation of the United Nations Industrial Development Organization (UNIDO) implicitly challenged the ILO's competency in industrial training, which had become its major activity.

The bargaining strength of the ILO in a jurisdictional dispute with another international agency has depended upon the influence that ILO clients were able and prepared to use on its behalf compared to the influence that the rival agency could mobilize. In such a jurisdictional dispute, two potentially conflicting considerations arise. One is the desire to widen and diversify support by appealing to a broader range of clients. The other is to rely on intensity rather than breadth of support, which implies cultivating a restricted but at the same time faithful and influential following. In a jurisdictional dispute the United Nations, which has more regular contacts with the influential economic and foreign ministries of governments, might outdo the ILO on breadth of support. For the ILO, intensity of support—with a stress on tripartite uniqueness—is most likely to be effective. In practice, only the trade unions and labor ministries can provide such support. Neither are influential directly in the United Nations system (though some countries include trade union personalities in United Nations delegations); their support is more effective within domestic political systems. In a boundary dispute, the process of mobilizing support would be initiated by the director-general and the ILO officials dealing with external relations; the task then passes through the ILO country subsystems to the United Nations country subsystems, with the trade unions as the key links, and finally emerges among the government representatives in the UN General Assembly.

The ILO mobilized sufficient support within the UN General Assembly to avoid having its competency in the employment and training aspects of industrialization truncated in favor of UNIDO. An agreement was negotiated between the two organizations, and the ILO was able to continue its role in providing services for less-developed countries.

Correspondingly, the ILO gave less attention to the preoccupations of the industrially advanced Western countries. For these countries, the Organization for Economic Cooperation and Development (OECD) filled the gap, becoming a forum for exchanging information and evaluating such matters as active labor market policy and incomes policy. Thus in the issue-area of international labor affairs, parallel structures emerged alongside the ILO: UNIDO for the developing countries and OECD for the industrialized countries of the West. The relevancy and utility of the ILO for both groups of countries was thereby questioned; but during the 1960s Director-General Morse's diplomatic skill successfully obscured these challenges. The award of the Nobel Peace Prize to the ILO and the visit of Pope Paul VI to the ILO conference, both occurring in 1969, seemed to consecrate publicly the ILO's acknowledged place in the world.

Rule-Creating Decisions

The adoption of international labor standards in the form of conventions and recommendations was the original and, at least until the mid-1950s, the primary task of the ILO. As early as 1930, Harold Butler, the deputy director, wrote to his chief Albert Thomas: "I do not think that we can continue to rely on Conventions as the principal test of our activity and progress."[9] Butler's view has been echoed by many since then. During the 1950s the employers' delegates were most insistent on this point. Government representatives from industrialized countries were divided, some skeptical of new standards, others—often those who had a long personal association with the ILO—defending the tradition. Government representatives from less-developed countries often took the position that ILO standards were framed in the light of conditions in advanced countries and were inappropriate to their own. They demanded services, not standards. The worker delegates maintained the most united front in support of the ILO's traditional function. Yet those representing governments or interest groups who defended standard setting did not often come forward with suggestions for new standards. Increasingly, the initiative for new standards came from the ILO officials concerned with the organization's standards work.

Rule-Supervisory Decisions

The ILO has very comprehensive procedures for supervising the application of its standards. Governments are obliged to report the action they have taken to secure ratification of conventions and the extent to which their laws and practices conform with ILO standards. The procedures allow trade union and employer representatives to participate in the review of a country's conformity and also provide for evaluation by independent experts.[10]

ILO officials dealing with standards have been even more influential in all phases of the rule-supervisory process than in rule creation. Analytical techniques are prominent in this type of decision making. Reports from governments are analyzed by the Office. The Committee of Experts on the application of standards also plays a key role in initiating and conducting inquiries, but it does so in close association with the Office. Individual representatives of governments or interest groups can also initiate questions through the conference's committee on the application of standards. The membership of this committee has been probably the most stable of any conference committee. The ILO officials concerned have thus been able to work effectively as brokers and, in this capacity, to safeguard their basic principles of policy in the solutions that are reached. The procedures devised for considering alleged violations of trade union rights and extraordinary inquiries by independent commissions have the same general characteristics.

Operational Decisions

The project composition of the ILO's growing technical assistance program was determined largely by decisions reached between national government agencies in developing countries and those ILO officials who administer technical assistance and regional field offices. Projects for labor administration and for workers' education involved the ILO's traditional constituents—labor ministries and trade unions—in support of ILO's service functions; but these activities were small in proportion to resources allocated to manpower, productivity, and related services that appealed to other sectors of government more oriented toward the economy. Operational activities thus provided an opportunity for the ILO to broaden its constituent base. The network of field offices in the less-developed areas of the world was the instrument for strengthening these new connections.

Employers' and workers' representatives have had relatively little to do with the ILO's operational activities, either at the national level or in the ILO's tripartite organs. Indeed, the Governing Body, which is the formally authoritative organ on program matters, has had little to say in decisions concerning projects. Collective bargaining among delegates, like the bargaining that determines the allocations among the major programs included in the regular budget of the ILO, thus has had little impact on operational decisions.

External control over operational decisions has come from the United Nations system as well as from the recipient countries. The ILO's use of technical assistance funds has had to conform to priorities and purposes fixed through United Nations bodies, that is, by intergovernmental organs, and interpreted and executed by interorganization bureaucratic structures. The likelihood that projects will appeal to the UNDP has been a criterion for proposing them to government agencies. Paul Hoffman, the administrator of UNDP, and his officials thus have had the influence of controllers over ILO operational decisions.

Programmatic Decisions

The director-general has been the principal architect of adjustments in policy goals and programs. David Morse's annual reports to the International Labor Conference and his speeches in response to the debates on these reports provided occasions for testing consent, defining policy goals and program emphases, and setting these goals within the framework of a general ideology. The management reorganization carried out within the Office in 1965 gave Morse more effective means of mobilizing the resources available to the Office to support his program goals. A Research and Planning Department, reporting to the director-general, was set up; and a Program Committee, for which that department provided the secretariat, brought together the top officials under the chairmanship of the director-general. The director-general could use the Program Committee as a device to maintain an intrabureaucratic consensus on the program and also to effect marginal shifts of resources in support of his major program objectives. While the director-general has been initiator, the Governing Body has played the role of controller.

The interplay of influences and roles in programmatic decision making is illustrated by the decision to launch the World Employment Program. The genesis of this program lay with a few officials who thought the ILO might contribute most to the social aims of development by equipping itself to help governments work out employment-expanding policies and by arousing international pressures to make employment expansion a primary goal of development. Director-General Morse made public statements dramatizing the deterioration of the employment situation in less-developed countries and the dangers inherent in this situation. Both in Geneva and on his visits to member states he spoke with influential political leaders, stressing the availability of ILO help. These contacts, designed to gain the support of influential opinion, were frequently with top political leaders and elite audiences. The first major activity in the program, a mission by a group of experts to study employment policy in Colombia, was decided between Morse and President Lleras of Colombia. Morse was also able to convince his peers in the administrative committee on coordination that creating employment should be recognized as a goal of the Second United Nations Development Decade, and in this he had the significant support of Robert McNamara, president of the World Bank. Morse's role was thus to see the potentiality of the idea and then to build political support from the top.

In the development of this program idea, Morse kept the Governing Body and the ILO conference informed and secured from them the necessary budget allocations. He used the internal Program Committee as a means of gaining support within the Office for the program and also of shifting some resources from other programs. The idea was dramatized as the centerpiece and the proof of the ILO's forward-looking spirit at its fiftieth anniversary celebrations in 1969. Referring to many speeches in support of the idea, Morse proclaimed in his reply to the conference debate: "I interpret the work of this Conference as giving me a mandate."[11] He was speaking about a program intended to be the dominant feature of the ILO's work in the next decade.

Actors and Their Sources of Influence

Now that the typical patterns of interaction for various categories of decisions have been indicated, the next step is to explain the influence of the actors in these decisions. Actors are here considered as the individuals—delegates, international officials, experts, and others—who take a direct part in decision making. First, we will examine the resources available to each category of actors, along with whatever circumstances may incline them to convert these resources into influence. Second, we will point out the ways in which these individual influences become structured through the political system.

The Influence of Individual Actors

Employees of the mass media have not played a very significant part in influencing ILO decisions. All the other categories of actors that have been used in this study have been important.

National Government Representatives. Government representatives, as a category, have the greatest potential resources for influence: they have votes and they contribute the funds. The potentiality of these sources of influence has not, however, been fully realized. First, government members in the early period were disposed to share influence with the trade union and employer members. Second, the individual financial contributions of the majority of governments are so small that they hardly provide a basis for influence.

The small number of governments that contribute the bulk of the budget have had greater influence. This influence has affected the total size of the budget rather than its detailed content. The director-general has tried (not always successfully) to restrict the proposed budget to a level that could be accepted by the major contributors. Thus these contributors had an opportunity to make their influence felt at the initial point of informal consultation, when the director-general was estimating what budget figure he could safely propose; another opportunity arose during the consideration of the budget in the Governing Body's finance committee, when cuts were normally proposed and an attempt made to achieve consensus on the budget. At this second stage, however, the downward pressure of influence from the major contributors was likely to meet a counteracting upward pressure from the representatives of trade unions and developing countries. As a general rule, only financial imperatives that were expressed in firm instructions from the finance ministry, leaving no flexibility to the ILO delegate, would prove impervious to such negotiating pressures. Thus, finance could be a source of influence for the major contributors, but this influence was limited and counterbalanced by other pressures. When it took the form of an immovable environmental constraint (imposed by a political situation or by the general financial policy with which a government responded to a critical economic situation), it ceased to be a flexible instrument of influence for that particular major contributor. When during the 1950s Congress imposed a ceiling on the United States contribution to the ILO, this was an effective constraint upon ILO's expansion of the budget, but the ceiling also limited the influence of the United States on the composition of ILO programs until it was lifted in 1957.[12]

Personality has been a very important factor in the ILO. For many countries, the difference between active or passive representation can best be explained in terms of personalities. Although this has been especially true for the smaller countries, personalities have also been an important factor in the participation of some of the bigger ones. Sir Guildhaume Myrddin-Evans would be close to the top of any list of influential personalities in the ILO from the closing years of World War II until his retirement from government service in the United Kingdom in 1959. During the latter part of this period, he held appointments jointly in the British Ministry of Labour, the Foreign Office, and the Colonial Office; his main responsibility, however, was ILO affairs. Italy's chief delegate during most of the period covered by this study was Roberto Ago, an authority in international law. He also acquired a most influential position in ILO decision making. French government representatives have also included several very influential personalities. Paul Ramadier was a former prime minister; Alexandre Parodi, vice-president of the Conseil d'État. Henry Hauck, who was the alternate French government delegate from the beginning of this period until his death in 1967, held the formal position of labor attaché at the London Embassy, although he spent a large part of his time on questions concerning ILO and social affairs at the United Nations.

Government delegates, in addition to their participation in decisions by vote, have access to the director-general and can lay a variety of demands before him. Much of the director-general's time during the annual sessions of the conference has been taken up with such demands rather than with items of the agenda. (The weight of a demand is presumed to increase if it is presented by a minister in the government, and there may be thirty or more ministers attending the conference.) Further and even more auspicious occasions to press demands arise when the director-general visits member countries. Governments represented on the Governing Body have had much more frequent opportunities for access to the director-general.

What good has such access done them? It is difficult for the director-general to deny a request, but it is relatively easy for him to delay, often on the grounds of conflicting pressures. The director-general's information about the range of demands increases as more and more government delegates use their right of access to him. The inevitable diversity in the pattern of demands can enhance his own maneuverability when the values that can be distributed are limited—as is the case, for example, in a choice of conference agenda items or of committees to be convened, in the location of regional offices, or in appointment to high offices. On the other hand, when the values are not so limited—as when technical assistance allocations or appointments to lower posts on the Office staff are to be made—the director-general's influence over the decision becomes more constrained. In such cases, he will more often seek to make the decision impersonal or bureaucratic, that is, according to rules that incorporate some guarantees of equity acceptable to all governments. Thus access may give the director-general more influence over decisions than even the demanding government has. By stimulating a diversified pattern of demands when the values available for distribution are limited, the director-general could retain the effective deciding voice.

Interest Group Representatives. The ILO differs from other intergovernmental organizations in providing votes for interest group representatives of workers and employers from its member countries. In addition, international organizations of employers and trade unions have access to the ILO in a formal, nonvoting, consultative capacity. These organizations also attempt to inform, influence, and coordinate the nongovernmental delegates at ILO meetings. The Roman Catholic church has also been an influence in the ILO, although it has no formal relation to it. It thus should also be considered as an interest group from the standpoint of political analysis.

The influence of the individual national trade union or employer representative varies to some extent according to the importance of the organization he represents, his status in his own organization (elected officeholders have an edge over appointed officials in most organizations), his personal political skills in the international arena, his access to others who wield influence in his group and in other groups, and the length of his association with the ILO.

The principal international interest groups concerned with the ILO are the World Federation of Trade Unions (WFTU); the International Confederation of Free Trade Unions (ICFTU); the Christian international trade union organization, which was formerly the International Federation of Christian Trade Unions (IFCTU) and has now been reconstructed as the World Labor Confederation (WLC); and the International Organization of Employers (IOE).

The WFTU was formed as a result of contacts made during World War II among the British Trade Union Congress (TUC), the Soviet All Union Central Committee of Trade Unions, and the American CIO; and as the war ended, it emerged as the dominant force in international labor. At that time, both the Soviet trade unions and the CIO were beyond the orbit of ILO contacts. Some significant groups held aloof from the WFTU, including the American Federation of Labor, the established international trade secretaries, and the Christian international. Whereas the prewar Amsterdam (socialist) international had been a force for cohesion among labor movements within the ILO, the WFTU fostered cohesion outside the ILO and appeared as a rival to it, raising WFTU interests directly with the United Nations.

After the WFTU split over the Marshall Plan in 1949, its membership became confined to the communist countries and communist-controlled organizations in other countries. WFTU affiliates found no hearing among the majority of worker delegates in the ILO, and WFTU's access to the United Nations became more restricted. The WFTU remained outside the ILO, aloof and hostile.

The ICFTU, set up in 1949 in combination with the AFL by those who seceded from the WFTU, succeeded the prewar Amsterdam international as organizer of the ILO Worker's Group. With headquarters in Brussels, the ICFTU set up an office in Geneva to provide a secretariat for the group.

The case of the Christian trade union international, now the WLC, should be examined first of all in the context of relations between the Roman Catholic church and the ILO. Following the reentry into the ILO of the Soviet bloc countries in 1954, the support of the Catholic church became especially valuable to Director-General Morse in maintaining his stand for universal membership. Such support was important not only because of the influence the church exercised in the world as a whole, but especially because Catholics are numerous among both the leaders and the rank and file of American trade unions. Papal endorsement could help take some of the sting out of the charge that the organization was "soft on communism." Pope Pius XII gave a special audience to members of the ILO Governing Body at Castel Gandolfo on 19 November 1954. This audience took place during the session in which consideration was being given to an amendment to the constitution that would have made. it possible to exclude Soviet workers' and employers' delegates—and thus in practice the whole Soviet bloc. The pope's statement included these remarks: "It [the labor movement] must seek its objective on the plane where your Organization has placed it, that is to say, on the plane of universality."[13] The use of the term *universality* was either significant or fortuitous in that political context. Either way it was helpful to Morse's policy. Pope John XXIII in the encyclical *Mater et Magistra* (1961) later expressed "heartfelt appreciation" of the ILO; Pope Paul VI addressed the ILO's fiftieth-anniversary conference session in Geneva in June 1969.

If relations between the Catholic church and the Office were close and friendly, those between the Christian trade union international and the ICFTU have on the contrary been at times tinged with suspicion. Christian trade unionists were excluded from the Governing Body from 1949 to 1959, the period of ICFTU's exclusive dominance; but in 1960 an understanding was reached to include one Christian representative on the list.

From about 1962, the WFTU began to give up its attitude of distant hostility and to seek more effective influence in the ILO. WFTU-ILO relations reached a turning point in 1966. A Polish delegate was elected president of the conference over the opposition of the AFL-CIO and other ICFTU affiliates; and a Soviet trade unionist was elected by the Workers' Group to the Governing Body for the first time.[14] In October 1967 the Executive Committee of the WFTU adopted a new policy of making its presence more actively felt in the ILO. The report embodying the directives for this policy stressed the changed balance of forces in the United Nations and in other international organizations that had accompanied the admission of new states.

> To underestimate this political phenomenon would be tantamount to cutting ourselves off politically from these new forces which exist in Africa, in Asia and also in Latin America. It is not the imperialist States who place the greatest expectations in the United Nations and its specialized agencies. After 22 years of existence of the United Nations, one realizes that the imperialist powers are beginning to regard these international assemblies as troublesome and embarrassing since they are continuously exposed to accusations there.[15]

In the ILO, the report noted optimistically, "discrimination against the WFTU and its affiliated organizations" had been reduced, and there was a more "positive policy on the part of the ILO Workers' Group."

The role and effectiveness of the IOE in the ILO have also evolved considerably. From the beginning of the period under study the IOE functioned as a secretariat for the employers at the conference and Governing Body sessions. During the early years it was primarily a European body, with headquarters in Brussels; its contacts with the Office were minimal. The East-West conflict following 1954 gave the IOE a political role rallying "free' employer delegates. It began to strengthen its contacts in Latin America, Asia, and Africa. The headquarters were moved to Geneva in April 1964 and closer contact was established with the Office.

The Executive Head. The formal authority of the director-general is bestowed upon him by his election. The conservation and enhancement of his effective influence depend upon his behavior in office. David Morse used his power of initiative primarily to build and maintain a broad-based consensus, especially after the reentry in 1954 of the Soviet bloc, when East-West accommodation within the organization became his central preoccupation. The policies he defined at that time had some appeal to all major segments of opinion. The stress on universality was supported by the Soviet bloc and most Western governments, with the notable exception of the United States. For those opposed to the Soviet presence, principally Western employers and trade unionists, Morse's renewed accent on measures to promote freedom for trade unions and to abolish forced labor had appeal, since they were perceived as an ideological attack on communist methods. The less-developed countries (and also most employers) supported the expansion of technical assistance. The measure of Morse's success was that in 1957, though the organization was still widely divided on the issue of universality, the Governing Body decided unanimously to reappoint him for a five-year term.

After 1957 personal support for Morse dissipated somewhat in respect to the AFL-CIO and its president, George Meany. The publication of an ILO report on trade union rights in the USSR, which seemed to emphasize the social welfare activities and the prestige of the Soviet trade unions more than their submission to political control, sorely disappointed Meany's advisers. Morse's readiness to add a top-level post to the ILO staff, one intended to be filled by a Russian, further fed this suspicious attitude.

The AFL-CIO is the principal influence on the United States government's policy in ILO matters. Even though the United States government maintained its support for Morse personally, it would be likely to respond to pressures from the AFL-CIO on particular issues, and Morse could count on very few countervailing influences within the United States to support him on the Soviet issue. Although he enjoyed much personal goodwill, his political position gave him little effective influence in the United States government on the issue that was his principal preoccupation as director-general. When Morse announced his resignation in November 1961, the United States government responded with assurances of fuller support. So did many other governments. Although the breach with the AFL-CIO was not fully healed, Morse returned, and in March 1962 he was reappointed for another five-year term (1963-68). This time there were three blank ballots alongside the thirty-seven favorable votes.

From this point onward the range of interests expressed in the ILO became more diversified as the less-developed countries became more articulate in their demands. The director-general's chief preoccupation shifted from the East-West issues, on which the events of 1962 showed he had temporarily reached the limit of accommodation, and turned toward giving more satisfaction to the new member states, especially those in Africa. His actions were directed toward (1) bringing the African countries into the consensus and gaining their confidence by satisfying them on symbolic issues concerning South Africa and Rhodesia; (2) redefining the ILO's program goals to give first place to development of human resources and institution building as twin instruments of modernization; and (3) reasserting his leadership of the bureaucracy following the disturbing events of the interregnum and reshaping it so that it might carry out effectively the newly defined organizational goals.

Once again Morse took initiatives that were closely related to his efforts to build consensus. The new program goals would appeal to the less-developed countries, but would not exacerbate East-West tensions. Changes in the bureaucracy designed to give more central direction in support of the major goals were accompanied by a policy of fuller representation of African and other less-developed countries in the Office and by a promise to decentralize the administration of field operations by shifting it to regional centers. By the end of 1965 the three conditions mentioned above were substantially achieved.

The resources of the director-general derived primarily from his central position in the network of political communications within the ILO. He was the principal point of contact between opposing interests, a position that enabled him to play a broker's role in resolving issues. He had, or could readily acquire, information about the views and demands of the participants in the system, and thus he could take initiatives with a reasonable idea of the probable reactions. This potential for influence was reinforced by his power over appointments, the allocation of services, and the execution of programs, though these were all open to bargaining.

The primary qualification for making effective use of these resources is good judgment concerning the state of the ILO's political system and environment. In general, the more diversified the pattern of demands and conflicts, the greater are a director-general's chances of selecting goals that will command wide support or acquiescence and of avoiding those that involve intense conflict. This proposition seems to be borne out by the contrast between Morse's difficulties in 1962 on an issue on which East and West were polarized and his relative success in 1965 when the less-developed countries, particularly the African states, had become more articulate.

The weakness of the executive head's position is shown in any major crisis with a country subsystem if he lacks leverage within that subsystem. In such a case, he will reach an impasse. Worse, if the country subsystem is influential in the ILO, as is true of the United States, the subsystem may block the executive head's initiatives or undermine his authority.

Another potential source of weakness lies in the international bureaucracy itself. If the executive head is its effective leader, the principal political officers, who are carefully selected to correspond with the major aggregations of constituent interests, will keep him fully informed about trends in demands and opinions so that he can adjust his policies as necessary. They will also help influence the various groups and caucuses to support the organizational goals. But these conditions are difficult to achieve and maintain. The executive head may have to assert his leadership over the bureaucracy recurrently, especially if his reassessment of the state of the system demands any major shifting of goals. Morse took on the challenge of bureaucratic adaptation twice: once between 1950 and 1954, when a staff essentially oriented to setting norms was converted into a more operational agency; and again, as mentioned, between 1963 and 1965.

Segments of the Bureaucracy. The International Labor Office emerged from World War II as a small staff with a high sense of commitment to building a new world order. The staff members were united by their efforts to survive the debacle of the League of Nations, by the tradition of strong executive leadership, and by their conviction that they had a right to express collectively an independent international viewpoint on the postwar issues of social policy. This staff was schooled in a coherent organizational ideology, which can be called the ILO's traditional ideology because it gave preeminence to the organization's original role as a promoter of international regulations.

The fundamental doctrine of this ideology appears to be a reconstruction of eighteenth-century natural law theory, a vision of a future world order based upon principles of law that have been found to be common to all peoples and cultures. The Marxist view that law is a superstructure expressing power relations in each particular phase of a society's historical development and thus will inevitably be superseded in a transformed society is implicity rejected. Law is regarded rather as a kind of immanent force progressively realized through history. The very notion of ideology is alien to this concept, according to the principal deputy director-general, Wilfred Jenks, the concept's most prominent spokesman, who in 1970 succeeded David A. Morse as director-general of the ILO:

> Ideology belongs to time and place. We are not captive to time or place. We belong to everywhere and all time. The ILO has no ideology but it has ideals, and its ideals, which transcend ideologies, are fundamental, universal and eternal.[16]

The ILO, in this view, has a significant but limited role as custodian of that branch of the universal law that regulates labor conditions. However, it has a much more significant and much less limited role—indeed it has a historical mission—as the international organization that is most fully conscious of this particular vision of future world law. These broader implications are underscored by the ILO's emphasis during the past two decades on human rights rather than on those aspects of law more specific to labor.

This fundamental doctrine is by its nature esoteric. It is attractive especially to those who are directly concerned with the normative work of international organizations, but it does not have wide appeal among the personnel of national governments. The strategy that translates this ideology into action, however, has attracted broader support. This is the strategy of functionalism, as applied to the circumstances of the ILO. The ILO's efforts at the international level to promote social justice through international labor standards are envisaged in this strategy as joining and supporting the efforts of social reformers and particularly of trade unions at the national level. To be effective instruments of pressure within countries, trade unions would have to be strong and independent of state control or domination. The unions and the ILO thus had a common interest in freedom for trade unions. Together they would be a force transforming the world into a system of pluralistic welfare societies closely integrated internationally. In such a world, social conflicts would be resolved under law. The rights of individuals and freedom of association would be given international sanction. And the success of efforts to establish such a world could be expected to be a powerful factor for peace.

The new generation of career officials recruited by the ILO in the late 1940s was nurtured in these ideas. Members of this generation rose during the next twenty years to occupy many of the senior positions within the Office. By and large they remained committed to the traditional ideology and to its functionalist strategy. During the 1950s, the expansion of the service activities of the ILO introduced a new element into the staff: specialists in manpower organization and other aspects of labor policy, recruited in their years of maturity rather than as young persons starting a career. The job of these new recruits was to administer the growing technical assistance activities. Later still, during the late 1950s and early 1960s, the traditional ideology was challenged by ideas articulated by a small group of officials, mainly economists, whose preoccupation was how best to help the underdeveloped countries. This latter group thought in terms of fuller emphasis on policies for development of poor countries in a concept of social equity.

By the late 1960s, four segments of the International Labor Office staff could be distinguished according to their basic ideas and approaches, although these segments did not correspond exactly to the formal organizational subdivisions. These informal groupings can be identified as the standards, technical, field, and developmental segments. While the technical and field segments tended to be essentially pragmatic in their outlook and did not share any common professional orientation, both the standards and the developmental segments had coherent, and in some measure competing, ideologies. These two also had distinct professional identities: the standards segment identified with the legal profession; the developmental, with economics. It is important for the analysis of influence to distinguish these segments, but one should not lose sight of the persistence of a strong ethic of loyalty to the ILO and discipline in its service. These segments should be thought of as divergent tendencies, not as rival factions.

Eminent Personalities. When we considered government representation, we noted that in some cases personalities who are eminent in their own right act as government delegates, even though some of them have little functional relationship with the national agencies in the labor policy field. One reason why such persons were attracted into the ILO orbit lies in the interest that the novelty of the ILO aroused in international law circles after World War I. Some of the ILO's supporters came from the field of international law rather than from labor affairs. The proliferation of international organizations in the post-World War II period has perhaps diluted this special interest in the ILO and led to the building up of national bureaucratic structures concerned with representation in international organizations. Because of these factors the likelihood that independent personalities of general eminence will act as government representatives may diminish in the future.

Eminent persons in particular fields also take part in ILO decision making as experts called in to advise on policy issues or programs. The principal initiative in their appointment has come from the segment of the Office concerned with the subject matter the experts will examine. In some cases the director-general himself has initiated the appointment of an expert, but usually this occurs only when the matter in question has a politically important bearing on his specific policy aims. Such appointments have to be approved by the Governing Body, and they thus must be acceptable to it.

Workers' and Employers' groups have been increasingly insistent that persons from employers' and workers' circles be included on expert bodies, though not nominally as representatives of the organizations they come from. These groups seek to avoid allowing expert meetings to have a purely "technocratic" character. The composition of the expert committee is the key to acceptability of the conclusions. Perhaps because they see experts as rivals in the conferring of legitimacy, the tripartite organs manifest some lack of enthusiasm for expert meetings.

Representatives of Other International Organizations. Representatives of
other international organizations have played only a very limited role, often
one dictated primarily by protocol, in the ILO conference and Governing
Body. Their real influence has been felt in the various interagency
coordinating bodies. Among the most significant of these representatives has
been Paul Hoffman, administrator of the UNDP, which has been the source
of funds for almost half of the ILO's activities.

The Structure of Influence

The foregoing section suggests something about the sources of influence
among categories of individual participants in the ILO political system. How
these individual influences become clustered into configurations and how
influence has been stratified are the next questions to consider.

Persistent Groupings: Functionalism versus Regionalism. Persistent groupings can be thought of as formal or informal. Formal groupings are the
Employers' and Workers' groups—these are provided for in the ILO's
procedures. Less official, but equally formal, are a variety of caucuses.
Informal groupings are those that result from actual behavior: for example,
the disposition to vote alike. Such behavior will be influenced by formal
groupings as well as by other factors.

The Workers' and Employers' groups—in the conference, Governing Body,
and other ILO meetings—have served as institutional mechanisms for interest
aggregation. Since group meetings are private, the effectiveness of the groups
in aligning attitudes and votes can be judged only by the subsequent
behavior of their spokesmen and members. These internal processes within
the groups are among the more significant but least-known factors affecting
ILO decision making.

The practice of regional caucusing appeared later in the ILO than in the
United Nations. No regional caucuses, with the exception of the Latin-
American and Nordic groups, were of any significance before 1954. During
the 1960s, however, group caucusing became a more important ingredient in
decision making. The caucuses varied considerably in structure and range of
interests. All of them represented the extension of other international
political systems into the ILO. In some cases, the formal structure of the
caucus existed outside the ILO and independently of it. The Latin-American
group, the Geneva Group, and the Group of 77 were examples. The
Latin-American group is an all-purpose caucus dealing with all organizations
based in Geneva. The Geneva Group, comprising permanent representatives
of major noncommunist contributors, was initiated in 1964 to achieve
consensus on budget policy within that significant group. This group is a
more formal and specifically oriented version of an earlier Western caucus
that provided a means of consultation on political and electoral questions.
The Group of 77 emerged at the 1964 UNCTAD and has served to aggregate

the views of less-developed countries on matters arising in other international organizations as well as in UNCTAD.

Some caucuses have had substantial continuity, beginning with the formulation of positions through regular intergovernmental consultations in the region and following through with meetings of delegates in the course of ILO conferences. The speeches given by Soviet bloc delegates to the ILO showed evidence of rather detailed advance preparations concerning the issues to be stressed at Geneva. The African states have agreed on their ILO objectives through ministerial meetings of the Organization of African Unity and have then continued their actions through group meetings in Geneva; these consultations have covered such political issues as those concerning South Africa and Rhodesia, as well as such topics as field machinery and technical assistance. The Nordic states prepared their positions on ILO technical issues through the Nordic Council's machinery. Similarly, the Arab League has tried to bring about regular intergovernmental consultations on labor questions in the hopes of achieving advance preparation of positions on technical as well as political ILO questions; and the Organization of American States provided a framework for periodic meetings of the region's ministers of labor.

Voting behavior in the conference gives some indications about trends in the relative strength of regional loyalties compared with the solidarity of Employers' and Workers' groups. While there may often have been marked differences of opinion within the Employers' and Workers' groups, both have been able to maintain a remarkably strong cohesion among their members in the voting. If anything, this cohesion appeared stronger in 1967 than it was in 1950, despite the growth during the intervening period of competing poles of attraction, particularly in claims of regional loyalties. The Workers' Group has been slightly more cohesive than the Employers' Group on most issues. In 1950, some Asian employers separated from the group majority on representational issues, perhaps in reaction to the predominance of European leadership in the Employers' Group. Beginning in 1954, however, the reentry of the Soviet bloc reestablished unity among the noncommunist employers, though this unity was not as marked on issues other than those relating to socialist countries' representation. Unity among workers, by contrast, was strained by the issue of Soviet reentry; some trade union delegates from all regions supported the communist position against that taken by the ICFTU-inspired majority. The cohesion of the employers probably owes a great deal to the IOE, which gained considerable support among employers' delegates during the period when "free" employers were reacting strongly to the Soviet entry and continued to broaden its regional support in developing areas after the Soviet issue had become less salient to most employers.

The socialist voting bloc has been the most unified of all. The only other case of marked regional cohesion is among Arab states of the Middle East. Otherwise, regional cohesion has not been high, and the traditional ILO

Worker's and Employers' groups have prevailed over regionalist tendencies.

An Informal Network of Influentials. Because of the diversity of its representative elements, the ILO is a relatively complex international organization. Its procedures and patterns of negotiation and bargaining reflect this complexity. Knowing the ropes gives a delegate considerable negotiating advantages, but learning the ropes requires a long apprenticeship during which some delegates may gradually acquire dual roles and dual loyalties—they become committed to the ILO, even though they do not support ILO policy in all respects. Their criticisms of ILO policies are loyal criticisms, made with the intent to modify the directions of the ILO so as to enhance its appeal to the delegate's own constituency. Such delegates can become as much the apologists of the ILO vis-à-vis their own organizations as advocates of their constituents' policies in the ILO.

An informal network of influentials has consequently developed, consisting of those who have long experience on the Governing Body together with the director-general and the few ILO officials who deal constantly with them. These people are consulted in any important decisions. The threads of negotiation run through their hands. This applies not only to decisions formally taken by the Governing Body, but also to some decisions formally taken by the director-general (for which he wishes to gain broader support) and to decisions taken through the much larger conference, since Governing Body members act as the steering network in the conference. This informal network has not been a closed group, but entry into it has required a certain acculturation to its norms of behavior.

The possibility of recruitment into this network of influentials is enhanced by continuity of representation. Continuity has been highest in Western European delegations to the conference; and among these it has been highest of all for employers. Continuity has been lowest for African, Asian, and Latin-American delegations, but it has also been low for the United States, Canada, and Australia. [17] These facts undoubtedly biased the composition of the informal network in favor of Western Europe. The influentials have, however, consciously tried to broaden their contacts by recruiting among new additions to the ILO's membership, particularly those from the Soviet bloc and African states.

Dual roles and an informal network of influentials have been forces for integration within the ILO decision-making system. One weakness may be inherent in this integration: a delegate can become so exclusively an "ILO man" that he loses influence on substantive questions within his own constituency. This can happen when representation in the ILO becomes a full-time specialized function. The price of integration may then be ineffectiveness.

The processes of influence can best be understood through an examination of the main protagonists' roles. Which ones initiate? Who blocks initiatives? Who are the controllers? How are these respective roles played? Valid quantitative answers to these questions are virtually impossible. In ILO practice few decisions occur as a result of one actor's making a proposal that is first debated, then accepted or rejected by the other decision makers. The origin of most initiatives is very complex and rarely apparent from the public record. A tradition of building consensus has been carefully cultivated, and the process consists of many initial informal stages in the gathering of support for a new proposal. The informal network of influentials manages the process of forming a consensus; and generally overexposure as an initiator breeds failure.

This informal network of influentials may be called the establishment of the ILO's political system.

The Organizational Elite. Conceptually, the establishment should be distinguished from the organizational elite. The former is a network of personalities who together play the roles of brokers and controllers. What is important is the continuity and confidence of their mutual relationships. The organizational elite denotes all individuals (considered separately) who have great influence in the affairs of the organization.

An attempt was made to identify the organizational elite by asking a number of knowledgeable persons to name the individuals who had the greatest influence in the ILO with special reference to the years 1950, 1958, and 1967 (see table 4.1). This is an exercise obviously open to much bias, and the detailed results should not be taken too literally. The main value of this exercise lies in the inferences that can be drawn as to the characteristics or resources that make for influence.

Among the resources that account for the influence of this organizational elite, long association with the organization seems to have been a consistently and increasingly important factor. Another important source of influence is occupancy of a position that gives access to the director-general. These two ways of acquiring influence underscore the monarchic character of the ILO's structure of influence. The monarchic structure of influence is further accentuated by the fact that the director-general may be influenced directly by important personalities who have no immediate connection with the ILO; heads of governments or the pope, for example. Still another resource is ideological legitimacy; that is, the expression of an ideology that appeals to a significant number of participants, whether it relates only to the organization or is found in the general environment. Ideological legitimacy has been an even more pronounced source of influence since the 1954 Soviet reentry into the ILO raised some basic issues of organizational purpose and structure. Other sources of influence appear to have declined in importance during the period covered by this study. The influence of personal charisma is less evident, as is influence deriving from high personal status acquired outside the organization.

Table 4.1

Distribution of Influential Persons in ILO
(By Position and National Origin)

	1950		1958		1967	
Formal Position	*Number*	*Percentage*	*Number*	*Percentage*	*Number*	*Percentage*
International officials [a]	8	40	7	35	6	30
Government representatives	4	20	7	35	5	25
Employers' and workers' representatives	8	40	6	30	9	45
Origin by Group of Countries						
Western	17	85	14	70	16	80
Socialist	–	–	1	5	1	5
Other	3	15	5	25	3	15
Origin by Principal Countries						
United States	3	15	3	15	5	25
United Kingdom	4	20	3	15	3	15
France	6	30	2	10	3	15
Other	7	35	12	60	9	45

[a] Including two officials from organizations other than ILO in 1950, and two in 1967.

The Environment and Its Impact

To assess the impact of the environment on influence in the ILO it will be necessary to make some comparative measurements of influence in the organization and of the three environmental variables in this study—power stratification, politicoeconomic characteristics, and patterns of conflict and alignment. These measurements will show which environmental forces appear to have the greatest effect and may suggest explanations of the origins of these effects.

Power, Labor Policy Capabilities, and Influence

Stratification in the specific environment of the ILO is expressed through a composite index of states' capabilities in labor policy, compiled so as to yield a rank order for the years 1950, 1958, and 1967 (see appendix B). Capabilities are taken to mean resources relevant to labor policy (variables expressing potential) and effectiveness in using these resources (performance variables). This composite index includes measures of the importance of industry in a country, the work force that can be unionized, the strength in numbers and effectiveness of trade union and employer associations, the objective success of the state in dealing with issues of labor policy, and the international prestige of the country in this field.

To rank the influence of states in the ILO is more difficult. Indeed the use of a concept of state influence can be questioned with reference to an organization where only a minority of the most influential individuals are government representatives and where national delegations do not—or at least are not presumed to—act as units. Despite these reservations, a ranking of the twenty states reputed to be most influential has been made by consulting knowledgeable persons. Because of the greater conceptual difficulties in defining state influence, the results are probably even less satisfactory than the identification of the twenty most influential individuals by similar methods. Here too the purpose of the exercise is not to award prizes for influence but to learn something about its characteristics. By comparing the rank orders of power in the general environment, the capabilities of states in labor policy, and reputed state influence in the ILO, we arrive at the Kendall's tau beta formula rank correlations expressed in the following table:

	1950	*1958*	*1967*
World power and labor policy capability	0.35	0.46	0.54
World power and influence in the ILO	0.46	0.58	0.41
Labor policy capability and influence in the ILO	0.53	0.34	0.56

Considering the small number of countries ranked (fifteen to twenty for influence; thirty-nine for the general and specific environments) and the already mentioned problems in ranking influence, one should not pay too much attention to small variations in the coefficients of correlation. However, the table does suggest certain tendencies.

In the first place, there was a significant correlation, though a fairly weak one, between world power and labor policy capability in the early years. The link between the two is the level of industrial development, which is reflected in the power index through GNP and in the labor capabilities index through industrial production. But the weakness of the correlation suggests that labor policy capability is not merely an intervening variable transmitting the impact of state power but is independently significant. This implication strengthens the functionalist hypothesis, separating areas of international functional cooperation from the political issues of international relations.

Second, there was a significant correlation between labor policy capability and influence in the ILO for 1950 and 1967, although this was weaker for 1958. And finally, world power appears to have been somewhat less significant than labor policy capability in explaining influence in the ILO for 1950 and 1967, but more significant for 1958. Since 1958 marked the peak of the impact of the cold war within the ILO, it should not be surprising that influence within the organization was patterned on world political cleavages and thus reflected world power. Thus it might be inferred that, in the absence of acute issues of a general political character, factors in the ILO's specific environment tend to predominate.

Politicoeconomic Characteristics and Influence

The matrix of states, classified by type of polity and level of economic development, that was constructed to express changes in the general environment (see appendix C) can be applied to indicators of representation and influence in the ILO. Available indicators include membership of the ILO and membership of the Governing Body, which can be compared with the total number of independent states.

Four categories of countries are singled out within the matrix of table 2.2 because of their particular interest: (1) rich, competitive states, the last two cells in the first row; (2) authoritarian states, the third row; (3) mobilizing states, the second row; and (4) poor states, the first two columns. In figure 4.1 the comparisons of the three indicators are presented for each category in the forms of bar graphs representing percentages. The order in which the indicators are presented can be thought of as successive "selections" of potential influence. Membership in the ILO, though it approaches universality, is already a selection from among all independent states in the international system. Those individuals who are titular members of the Governing Body are a selection from the possible universe of participants in the decision-making system. Thus the bar graphs illustrate the skewing of influence through two successive selections.

Figure 4.1   Politicoeconomic Characteristics of States and Influence

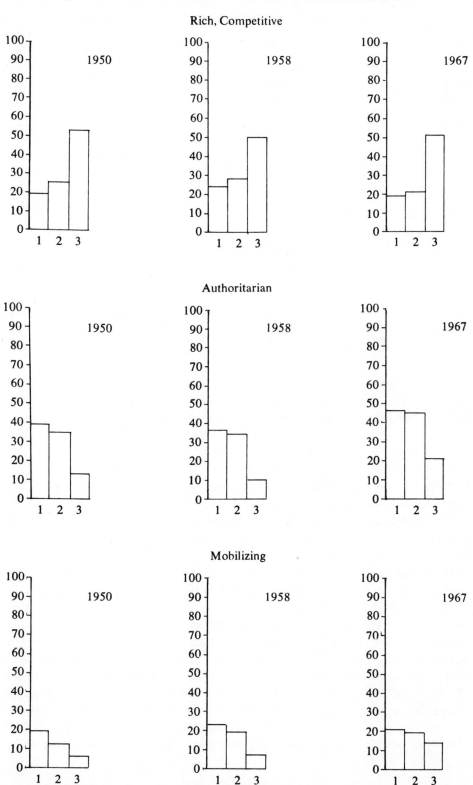

Figure 4.1 (Cont.)

Poor

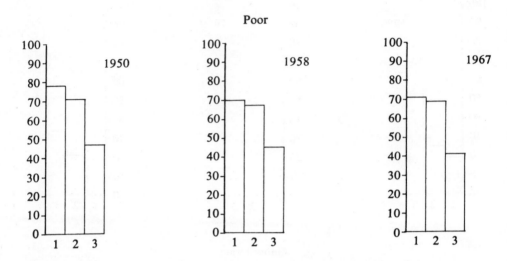

NOTE: Numbers under the bars refer to the following indicators of potential influence: 1, independent states; 2, ILO member states; 3, Governing Body titular members (by national origin). Bars represent the percentage in the category of countries mentioned.

The results of this skewing are striking: rich competitive polities have the greatest influence; authoritarian polities are weakly represented; mobilizing polities, though a small proportion of the total, have improved their position of influence since 1950 and now have representation corresponding to their proportion of the membership; and poor countries are much less influential than their total numbers would suggest. Of course, the individuals who are Governing Body members do not necessarily reflect the interests of the states from which they come. Nevertheless, the aggregate suggests a cultural milieu shaped according to values emanating from relatively rich competitive polities, and this milieu may condition both thinking and behavior as they relate to decision making.

Important as these factors shaping the culture of the organization are, one should not assume too readily that a state's type of regime will determine its action in the ILO. There is nevertheless some evidence that a connection exists. Type of polity shows up as an important factor in some representational decisions, especially those linked with freedom of association. The rich-poor dichotomy, as might be expected, shows up more strongly in some programmatic issues. Changes in type of regime may also affect the behavior of states in relation to the ILO. Under the Perez Jimenez dictatorship Venezuela withdrew from the ILO because of criticism concerning violations of trade union rights; it returned after it established a more competitive polity. Indonesia withdrew when the Sukarno regime reached its mobilizing phase and returned when military intervention overthrew that regime. In a number of other cases, changes in regime were followed by changes in delegations' styles of participation and in their personnel. This was particularly true of Egypt, Iraq, and Cuba after revolutions had installed mobilizing regimes, and of Ghana when military intervention overthrew Nkrumah and thus ended a mobilizing regime. Changes of style or even of personnel are less noticeable when regimes have moved between competitive and authoritarian types.

Political Alignments and Influence

The same indicators that were used to assess influence in relation to the politicoeconomic characteristics of states can be applied to the major world political alignments: West, East, and South, which correspond roughly to the Western, Socialist, and Other classification of states set up in chapter 1. This is done in figure 4.2.

The skewing shows an initial preponderance of Western states, which recedes toward the close of the period. Socialist countries improved their position, so that by 1967 they had a place roughly equal to their numerical status among independent states. The less-developed countries in the Other category lagged far behind in influence in relation to their numbers. This skewing may more closely reflect relative world power than a mere count of countries would do. Thus the informal processes of the ILO may be thought of as correcting in some measure the distortions of real power implicit in the formal equality of states.

The ILO was less Western in 1967 than in 1950, and the existence in 1967 of a significant organized and articulate minority of Socialist countries was another major difference. The influence of less-developed countries seems, however, to have remained relatively low in proportion to their numbers. This does not mean that the growth of the less-developed countries' component in ILO membership has been of no consequence: it has brought about a marked change in the preoccupations and activities of the organization without greatly changing the stratification of influence. Western states have supported changes in the ILO's work and even in some aspects of the organization's structure to meet the needs and expectations of less-developed countries. Western states remained the controllers, while some of the initiative passed to the less-developed countries.

Changing Patterns of Conflict and Alignment

As long as unity among the great powers lasted (1944-47), the ILO was at a disadvantage because the Soviet Union was not included among its members and was actively hostile to the organization. The organization's achievement during those years was survival. But as the world power configuration moved into its cold war bipolar phase (1947-54), the ILO's fortunes improved. The significance of the Soviet Union's absence from

Figure 4.2   World Political Alignments and Influence

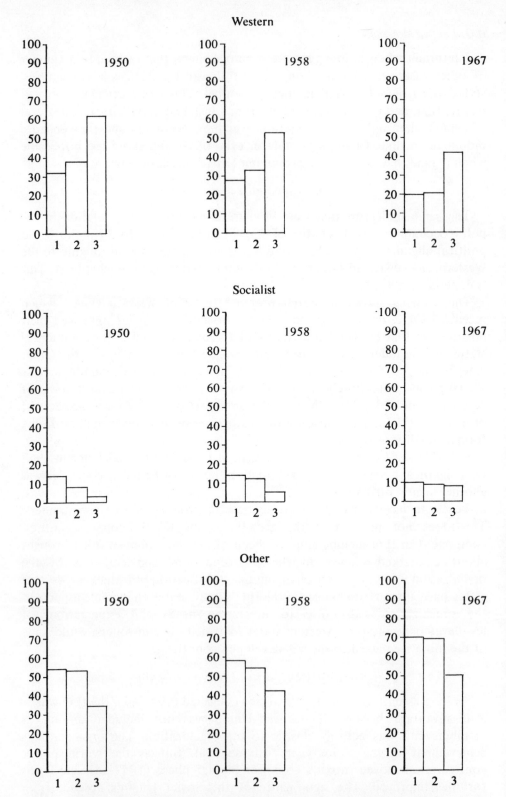

NOTE: Numbers under the bars refer to the following indicators of potential influence: 1, independent states; 2, ILO member states; 3, Governing Body titular members (by national origin). Bars represent the percentage in the category of countries mentioned.

membership changed. When the UN Economic and Social Council became a theater of political warfare between East and West, the Western powers preferred to shift to the ILO the responsibility for dealing with politically charged questions, such as those relating to trade union rights and forced labor. This phase of cold war bipolarity created favorable conditions for two of the ILO's major postwar programs: a normative human rights program and an operational manpower program. In the context of the cold war, stress on human rights was an instrument of political warfare that the Western powers could use to attack Stalinist labor camps and the Soviet concept of trade unionism. The manpower program was a complement first to the European Recovery Program and then to President Truman's Point Four.

One consequence of Soviet accession to membership in 1954 was to make cold war issues prominent within the ILO at a time when the cold war was abating in the world political environment. At the beginning of the 1960s, bipolarity was complicated by the emergence of the Third World as a more articulate force. The continuing prominence given to cold war issues in ILO debates conflicted with the growing demands of less-developed countries that priority be given to their problems. This discordance between the new pattern of demands from the membership and the ideological terms in which the main issues were framed in ILO debates brought about what may be called a lingering crisis of legitimacy. None of the main world groupings—West, East, or South—felt entirely secure in their allegiance to the organization. But none had clearly articulated goals for the ILO, and so this uncertain feeling manifested itself in a succession of representational and symbolic issues.

The ILO was never, during this period, merely a passive instrument of Western countries. The executive head was able to use the state of the power configuration in order to expand the ILO's work in the two major directions of human rights and manpower. Though politically based in the cold war cleavage, he pursued these programs for their own sake, not as political weapons; and these programs survived the cold war, in which they had their origin. Unlike heads of some other international organizations, the director-general of the ILO never tried to make his political base among the nonaligned; he always kept close contact with Western countries while reshaping programs so as more nearly to satisfy the demands of less-developed countries. An attempt to shift his main base of support to the latter might have brought about a crisis of confidence at a time when the ILO's continued allegiance to the Western concept of pluralism and to its own traditional tripartite structure appeared to some to be challenged by the new elements within the organization.

Patterns of Influence: Past, Present, and Future

Analysis of the environmental impact on the ILO shows conclusions rather different from those resulting from analysis of the ILO political system and its processes. Changes in the environment explain the evolution of the ILO's program and of the organization's relationship to world political alignments. On the other hand, the political system explains more fully the remarkably stable structure of influence on decisions. World politics set the framework for action, but the ILO has not been a passive creature of world politics. The ILO developed a political system capable at best of taking advantage of the opportunities presented by the condition of world politics and at worst of assuring its own survival.

Yet tendencies can be discerned and conditions may arise that could lead to change in the structure of the system. A first structural element with potential for change is the bureaucracy. There is evidence in the ILO to support the common assumption that all types of large-scale human organizations are growing more bureaucratic. The bureaucracy figures prominently as initiator of decisions concerning all the manifest functions of the ILO. The director-general and segments of the bureaucracy are also the principal brokers, while the constituent representatives in the informal network of influentials enter the picture mainly as controllers. The dramatic growth of service functions has been the principal impetus for the growth in size and capability of the ILO bureaucracy. This trend is underlined by the fact that the largest part of all ILO funds during the 1960s came directly from UNDP sources, not through the ILO regular budget. This increase in the functions of the bureaucracy and its greater role as initiator and broker should not, however, lead one to infer that there has been concentration of bureaucratic power. The crosscutting character of alliances in support of diverse ILO goals means that there has been no single organized monopoly of influence. The bureaucracy itself contains a plurality of interests that are to some extent rival and in any case distinct, and the constituents' control (mainly through the governing body) has the effect of perpetuating this pluralism within it.

A second structural aspect that contains the possibility of change is entailed in the relative roles of bureaucratic and representative bodies. Here there have been signs pointing toward a separation of interests: the bureaucracy concerning itself increasingly with programmatic and operational decisions (principally the growth of services); the tripartite bodies, with representational and symbolic issues. The normative work of the ILO, though diminished in importance relative to service activities in terms of resources expended, retained political importance as a bond between the bureaucracy and the representative bodies. But the main binding element was the existence of an informal network of influentials—the system's establishment. The acculturation of new members, representative of new constituent groups, into this network is one condition for continuity of this political system.

A third structural element is the role of the director-general. His is an indispensable but limited power within the system. It is indispensable because the system could not function without his initiating and brokerage activity, and it is limited by the state of the world environment, by any views intensely held by members of the establishment, and by the intrabureaucracy competition over which he presides as mediator and arbitrator.

Another condition for continuity is the ongoing negotiation of a broad consensus on the future aims and programs of the ILO. ILO programs must be backed by a broadly based coalition of forces. The director-general is the only element in the system capable of defining its purpose in terms of the consensus; but the structure of representation imposes severe limits on his ability to modify the bounds of possible consensus.

Bad judgment on the part of a director-general could result in changing a system that, in the last analysis, depends so much upon good judgment in this office. For example, any hint of pretensions to absolute monarchy could erode the broad support acquired for a form of limited monarchy during the 1948-70 period. Or if a director-general were to pursue sectarian goals and cease to function primarily as consensus builder, the political system of which he is the centerpiece could begin to disintegrate, seeking a new equilibrium.

So long as the establishment is adequately representative of powerful forces in the ILO's environment, a failure of leadership of this kind would probably be checked. The greatest risk to the system would be a simultaneous aberration in executive leadership and decline in representativeness of the establishment. The establishment under such conditions might continue effectively to monopolize influence in important decisions within the participant subsystem, while at the same time becoming increasingly deferential to the director-general's initiatives and less able or willing to inform him about the constraints limiting his action. The participant subsystem would then become more and more remote from the representative subsystems and from the real forces in the environment, and the director-general would become more likely to misjudge his situation and consequently to come into conflict with external forces.

Such an evolution would open yet a fourth structural possibility for change, namely, a major crisis between the participant subsystem and some powerful force in its environment. Since June 1970 such a crisis has arisen between the ILO and the United States. It began with the appointment of a Russian as assistant director-general by the newly elected Director-General Jenks, to which the United States Congress responded by suspending payment of the United States contribution to the ILO budget. The perspective necessary for analysis of this crisis is lacking because the chain of reactions it set in motion is as yet incomplete. Conceivably, the crisis could mark the end of the political system analyzed above. This system had attained substantial autonomy from its environment, or more specifically from states. Environmental forces were by and large content to let the participant subsystem take decisions without intervening. But there now appear to have been limits to this toleration. Once a crisis has brought so powerful an environmental force as the United States Congress into a posture of active intervention in ILO affairs, the status quo ante may prove difficult to retrieve.

5 UNESCO: Pluralism Rampant

Functions, Structure, and Evolution

The United Nations Educational, Scientific and Cultural Organization, now more commonly called UNESCO, was established in Paris on 4 November 1946. During its formative period Julian Huxley maintained that this organization, which he was leading, "must foster and promote all aspects of education, science, and culture, in the widest sense of those words." UNESCO's constitution outlines three organs, a General Conference, an Executive Board, and a secretariat. The General Conference comprises delegations from member states. There were 125 in December 1968. Initially the Executive Board consisted of 18 individuals elected by the General Conference; by 1968 the board numbered 34 representatives elected for staggered four-year terms from among the General Conference delegates appointed by member governments. The president of the General Conference sits in an advisory capacity on the Executive Board. In 1968 the UNESCO secretariat had reached a total of approximately 3,600 individuals—2,200 professional staff members and 1,400 office and technical staff members.[1]

Assigned Functions of the Organization

UNESCO, like other international organizations, was established largely to afford a permanent framework for negotiations among the governments of participating nation-states. Governments might exchange concessions to realize mutual gains—for instance, each might agree to allow freer entry from the other's country of individuals and objects bearing educational, scientific, and cultural values. These governments might set general standards or create rules dedicated to the regulation or guidance of certain behavior. Governments sometimes have utilized the UNESCO framework also as a sounding board for propaganda or for symbolic decisions. Although governments are UNESCO's primary actors, from the outset the organization was implicitly contemplated as an international actor at least partly distinguishable from member governments.

The negotiated exchange of mutual concessions for mutual gains and multilateral standard setting within UNESCO—even though in practice no less than in constitutional theory these are frequently stimulated by

I am indebted to the Social Science Research Council, to the Yale Office for Advanced Political Studies, and to Claës Nilsson, Robert Shapiro, Mietta Manca, and Paul Andrews for support and research assistance on UNESCO. I am also grateful to individual Unescans for their forbearance and their frequent cooperation.

secretariat officials personifying the organization—may tentatively be classed as forum assignments rather than service activities. Most international organizations are first resolution-making mechanisms, and UNESCO is no exception. Conventions and recommendations are envisaged by article IV, paragraph 4 of the constitution; periodic reports from nation-state members about action upon these as well as "on laws, regulations and statistics relating to educational, scientific and cultural life and institutions" are foreseen by article VIII.

Policy processes such as promoting programmatic and institutional extension today comprise an important portion of UNESCO's activities. An operational premise is evident even in constitutional terms. In article I, the organization is directed to collaborate "in the work of advancing the mutual knowledge and understanding of peoples . . . through all means of mass communication . . ." and "with Members, at their request, in the development of educational activities." It is also directed to suggest "educational methods best suited to prepare the children of the world for the responsibilities of freedom" and to assure "the conservation and protection of the world's inheritance of books, works of art and monuments of history and science." As a further task it is to initiate "methods of international co-operation calculated to give the people of all countries access to the printed and published materials produced by any of them."

Formal Framework for Decisions

By UNESCO's constitution, its General Conference is authorized to "determine the policies and the main lines of work of the Organization" and "take decisions on programmes submitted to it by the Executive Board." The conference may summon governments to represent themselves at international conferences on education, the sciences and humanities, and the dissemination of knowledge. It or the Executive Board may bring together nongovernmental organizations (NGOs) for the same purposes.

Executive Board assignments include preparation of the provisional General Conference agenda and examination of the director-general's proposed program and estimated budget. The UNESCO constitution exhorts its board to "be reponsible for the execution of the programme adopted by the Conference" by taking "all necessary measures to ensure the effective and rational execution of the programme by the Director-General."

UNESCO's secretariat is headed by the director-general, designated "chief administrative officer of the Organization" by the constitution. Either the director-general or his designated deputy participates without vote in all conference, board, and other UNESCO meetings. He formulates and submits proposals to the conference and board, including the draft program and budget already noted. By the rules of procedure he is authorized "at any time, with the approval of the presiding officer," to offer "either oral or written statements concerning any question under consideration" (rule 50).

The constitution instructs him to "prepare and communicate . . . periodical reports on the activities of the Organization" to members as well as to the Executive Board. Subject to admonitions about staff members' integrity, efficiency, competence, and geographic distribution, the director-general is charged with selecting personnel for the secretariat.

Besides the three representative organs just introduced—the General Conference, the Executive Board, and the secretariat—UNESCO's constitution suggests several other channels for representing claims. In addition to their status as observers at meetings, NGOs are authorized to "undertake specific tasks" for UNESCO and to participate on advisory committees created by the General Conference. The Executive Board is urged to consult "qualified persons concerned with questions within its competence." Each member state is responsible for "associating its principal bodies interested in educational, scientific and cultural matters with the work of the Organization, preferably by the formation of a National Commission broadly representative of the Government and such bodies." The constitution instructs members to arrange for national commissions or national cooperating bodies to "act in an advisory capacity to their respective delegations to the General Conference and to their Governments in matters relating to the Organization and . . . function as agencies of liaison in all matters of interest to it."

Beyond constitutional provisions, although they are now firmly established, the presence of permanent national delegations at UNESCO headquarters strongly suggests a development in representation that warrants separate acknowledgment. Permanent representatives facilitate continuing multilateral diplomatic contacts, cognizance of special meetings at UNESCO House, and access to the secretariat throughout the policy cycle. In 1967, ninety-four governments reported permanent UNESCO delegates. Substantiation for these claims, however, varied considerably.

Major Turning Points and Nondecisions

Constitution making is a primary, fundamental decision-making exercise into which constitution makers carry their predispositions and from which some semblance of these emerges, both in the written words and in the heightened expectations or disappointments of participants. UNESCO constitution making was no exception. The process and the document it produced thus serve as one perspective from which the turning points both before and after formal institutional inception can be discerned.

The Conference of Allied Ministers of Education (CAME), organized during the war by the British government, developed into UNESCO's constitutional matrix. Between 1942 and 1945 the British minister of education, originally R. A. Butler, presided over a series of meetings in London that were attended by representatives from continental European states. The United States, Soviet, and Chinese governments, among others, were invited to send observers and did so, although the USSR did not become a UNESCO charter member. Extra-European participation in discussions on certain postwar problems was thus initiated well before the formalities of constitutional adoption in London. During the CAME meetings and the establishment of UNESCO, that is, from October 1942 to November 1945, the aims of participating governments across a broad substantive sector of international policy were articulated in these London arenas and indicated by actions elsewhere.

To oversimplify somewhat, the French contrived to realize UNESCO's C for culture; the British and Americans demanded a separate E for education; the same two belatedly agreed that an S should be added for science; and the Americans pressed for and achieved a substantial (though titularly unrecognized) commitment to communcations.

The French saw a Paris-based postwar organization as the logical successor to, or even as a strengthened continuation of, the Institut International de Coopération Intellectuelle (IICI). IICI was authorized by the League of Nations to serve as secretariat for the league's International Committee on Intellectual Cooperation. It was financed by the French government and located in the Palais Royal. The institute was, as UNESCO is, valued as an instrument for extending French culture to an elite in all corners of the globe.

During the days of the League the United Kingdom and its dominions never voted together, as Lord Balfour once observed, except when opposing intellectual cooperation. But during the period of CAME, the British government was drawn toward educational reconstruction—and especially reeducation upon the European continent—as one means of forestalling war and as a response to the demands of an interested, organized, and articulate minority of the British electorate. Several representatives from continental states' ministries of education actively concurred in this emphasis upon education, or denazification, as it was revealingly called by the francophonic Belgian CAME representative. American participation in CAME was accompanied by the introduction of more ambitious goals like "mass education"; in these the British willingly and others necessarily acquiesced.

A CAME science commission emerged about nine months after the educators' conference had begun. The science commission developed into an odd and intriguing concourse of interests. One segment was particularly interested in realizing the prospect that Anglo-American scientific industry would replace German firms in continental markets. Another was driven by the desire, fanned by Britain's experiences since World War I, to rationalize the haphazard international diffusion of scientific discoveries, further the international movement of scientists, and provide institutional assistance toward achieving both goals. Science, at least as an element of culture and a focus for education, always had a place in CAME planning for a permanent postwar organization. At the London conference, a few months after Hiroshima, participants agreed to add an S to "UNECO."

From mass education to mass communication was a short step for some Americans. The U.S. Department of State, represented by William Benton and Archibald MacLeish, among others, sponsored a London conference resolution[2] urging the Preparatory Commission, in view of the "paramount importance of the media of mass communication," to "give special attention to establishing relations with mass media, including the press, the radio, and the cinema. Communications thereafter enjoyed an important organizational and programmatic status.

London preparatory conferees modified and polished the verbal statement of national aims that had already been partially aggregated in two constitutional drafts, a United States–CAME product and an eleventh-hour French one. Most foreign policy aims became UNESCO aims on a both/and rather than an either/or basis.[3]

Program possibilities overlooked by the constitution makers were seemingly envisaged in short order by Preparatory Commission participants, led by Sir Alfred Zimmern; by UNESCO's first director-general, Julian Huxley; and by NGO spokesmen. The First General Conference, in 1946, is said to have received 147 project proposals.[4]

Although constitution making and the establishment of UNESCO suggest a fully formed infant institution, several subsequent turning points, potential and actual, deserve special acknowledgment here. They are noted in summary fashion.

Among nondecisions, budgetary opportunities must be counted as among the foremost. The implications of financing are likely to be apparent throughout any discussion of international issues in which UNESCO has an assigned place.[5] In interviews during 1969 with the UNESCO representatives of twenty-one member states, thirteen counted inadequate financial resources as a major UNESCO disability. One, representing a state in the Southern Hemisphere, said, "Frankly, bilateral aid is better," because in such an instance the touchstone is completion of the project, whereas thrift, or even niggardliness, is the criterion for UNESCO.[6] Such policies, of course, raise the question of who precisely is responsible for budgetary nondecisions.

Standard setting and application, a procedural possibility pioneered by ILO, counseled for UNESCO by ILO's emissary C. Wilfred Jenks, and underwritten in rudimentary fashion by the UNESCO constitution's provisions for adopting norms and receiving reports from member states, has not been very fully developed to date.

A proposal by Americans for a UNESCO radio network[7] was received with enthusiasm by few others. Even Julian Huxley, usually excited by challenging schemes, greeted this one with coolness. No doubt UNESCO's history would be quite different if this had been a decision instead of a nondecision.

Significant nondecisions about membership were those on Communist China, North Korea, North Vietnam, and East Germany. On the other hand, the Soviet Union in 1954 reversed its decision not to join UNESCO, and at about the same time Czechoslovakia, Poland, and Hungary resumed active membership. Bulgaria, Rumania, and Albania joined shortly thereafter. When the change of government occurred in Cuba, the Castro government ended Cuban membership in IBRD but remained active in UNESCO.

The growth in membership of newly independent states generally, and of African states particularly, may be counted a UNESCO turning point. The seventeen African memberships recorded in 1960 as the Congo crisis unfolded and the seven more in 1962 dramatized the need and mobilized demand for UNESCO's services beyond their existing magnitude and scope.

Few UNESCO decisions are more important than choosing the director-general. Julian Huxley (elected in 1946), Jaime Torres Bodet (elected in 1948), Luther Evans (elected in 1953), Vittorino Veronese (elected in 1958), and René Maheu (elected in 1962, reelected in 1968), have each affected UNESCO by what they were and what they did. The men and their styles will be briefly considered later in this chapter. (They will be more fully examined in a subsequent work by the author.)

The creation and availability of financing outside the organization affected UNESCO's budget and program, especially by directing the focus of many activities toward work in the field. Critical turning points in external financing include the UN Expanded Program of Technical Assistance (first funded in 1950), the UN Special Fund (established in 1959), projects in education underwritten by auspices of the International Bank for Reconstruction and Development (i.e. IBRD and IDA) and authorized by a Bank decision in 1961, and a UNICEF decision to finance education in 1962. A discussion of extra-UNESCO financing is offered in the following section.

Evolution of Financing

Some major points and trends in UNESCO's financial evolution in terms of income are listed below. The classification of states noted in chapter 1 as Socialist, Western, and Other is used in this discussion.

Members' assessment percentages changed markedly between 1950 and 1958. With the participation of the Socialist states—in particular the Soviet Union—the Western states' total percentage dropped from 76 percent in 1950 to 65 percent in 1958. In the latter year, the Socialist states' percentage was 19 percent.

Among Western states during the 1950-58 period, the United States' assessment fell from 38 to 31 percent; the United Kingdom's assessment, from 13 to 7 percent; and the French contribution, from 7 to 5 percent—slightly more than West Germany's assessment percentage in the same year.

Other states—a list that grew between 1950 and 1958 and increased even more between 1958 and 1967—were assessed a *declining* percentage of the total over these years: 21 percent in 1950, 16 percent in 1958, and 13 percent in 1967. Some of this decline is accounted for by the changing China

(Taipeh) percentage. From 7 percent in 1950 it was dropped to 5 percent in 1958 and to 2.5 percent in 1967.

UNESCO expenditures also evolved in the 1950-67 period. External financial is reflected in expenditure budgets. During 1967-68 almost half the total UNESCO budget was funded from external sources. UNESCO's first regular expenditure budget (for 1947) was $6 million. For 1950 it was $8 million, and for 1958 it was $11 million. The greatest increments between 1947 and the present did not take place until after 1960. In 1967 the regular budget reached $31 million.

With the exception of international norms, relations, and programs, each major component in UNESCO's regular expenditure budget (education, natural sciences, culture and social sciences, and communications) has risen markedly since 1960. Most striking among these increases are the higher allocations for education: $1.2 million in 1950, $1.7 million in 1958, and $7.2 million in 1967.

External funds show a strong emphasis on "development." For 1967, a total of $12 million in external funds was allocated to development of human resources, including education and training. For the same year, $11 million from external sources went to scientific research and the application of science to development. Together these items constitute almost 40 percent of the total UNESCO budget.

Three general observations might be offered with regard to these selected data. First, the decline in the percentage of funds obtained through individual and composite Western assessment and the proliferation of external sources (including some intergovernmental accounts not subject to assessment according to state shares) diminish *relatively* the foundation for any government's "piper's claim" to policy prerogatives that might earlier have been advanced. Second, the decrease in the percentage of UNESCO's funding (both regular and external) that is underwritten by members other than those from Western or Socialist countries makes it increasingly likely that in General Conference plenary meetings majority votes can be mustered among members who are paying a small fraction of the cost of programs resolved upon. Third, some of these trends and figures on the output side make it evident that "development" has become a sacred cause in UNESCO, even if, for idiosyncratic reasons, this is less true in UNESCO than in certain other agencies.

Decision Making: A Taxonomical Analysis

The term *decision* conveys a sense of decisive action authorized if not actually taken during one salient moment of truth, a connotation that ill befits UNESCO—and for that matter any other political system we know about. This qualification does not, however, mean that it is fruitless to try to understand UNESCO through attempting to classify its undertakings. In this chapter categories conform to the terminology prescribed for the essays on individual organizations comprising this comparative study. Representational decisions, boundary decisions, and symbolic decisions can be regarded as actions undertaken with the purpose or effect of constituting, reconstituting, maintaining, or adapting the organization—the organization in this sense meaning something greater than its international officials and headquarters facilities. Rule-creating decisions, rule-supervisory decisions, programmatic decisions, and operational decisions are more intimately related to substantive outputs.[8]

As in other chapters, and in anticipation of a discussion of UNESCO actors, this taxonomic outline alludes to several decision-making roles: initiator, broker, controller, and vetoer. As we shall see, different types of decisions imply differing constellations of these roles, not to mention differing conjunctures of those who act through them. In view of the scope of this essay the material on actual UNESCO decisions obviously must be regarded as illustrative rather than exhaustive.

Representational Decisions

Most decisions regarding states' representation in UNESCO occur in home capitals; a few, which might be classed as symbolic, occur at UNESCO itself. The South African government, for instance, made its own decision to withdraw in 1956. Spain is a borderline instance. In 1950, the United Nations Economic and Social Council (ECOSOC) recommended Spain for membership in the specialized agencies; after a bitter fight in and beyond UNESCO, ECOSOC's recommendation was followed at the Seventh General Conference. The 1950 decision on Chinese credentials was taken in the Fifth General Conference, where the United States government successfully mobilized sufficient support to turn back the delegation from the People's Republic of China.

Representation on the UNESCO Executive Board, as well as chairmanship of the board and of its commissions, is determined by secret balloting. The General Conference votes for Executive Board candidates; the Executive Board then chooses its own leaders in a similar manner. Here, more than in the admission of Spain and the accreditation of China, the process of caucusing and informal communication is evident. Unlike the home-to-headquarters procedure on many questions answerable with an affirmative, a negative, or an abstaining vote, there may be no explicit government instructions, particularly for the list of Executive Board candidates. Caucuses certify their nominees informally; conference delegates write upon their ballots, in most cases, the names of those so certified to represent their "region."

The number of Executive Board seats has gradually increased from the eighteen established at the beginning in 1946 to the thirty-four that was the number in 1968. These seats provided direct representation for 64 percent of the total state membership in 1946, but only for about 20 percent in 1964.

What began as a remarkably propitious situation for would-be Executive Board members thus became progressively difficult for candidates. In 1968 only half the UNESCO member states had ever had a delegate elected to an Executive Board seat.

The composition of the Executive Board reflects increasing negotiation within and between caucusing groups. Even a more general picture, that of table 5.1, suggests change over time. New members with new claims demand accommodation; the response has been to enlarge the Executive Board and, less visibly, to rotate or split terms or to reduce another group's status. The slate proposed by the disciplined Africans late in 1966 demonstrated this last outcome with devastating effect by shutting out five Asian candidates—each unwilling to step down as a candidate.

Table 5.1

Composition of UNESCO's Executive Board
(By National Origin)

	1950		1958		1967	
	Number	*Percentage*	*Number*	*Percentage*	*Number*	*Percentage*
Western	11	61.11	9	45.00	10	33.33
Socialist	1	5.56	2	10.00	3	10.00
Other	6	33.33	9	45.00	17	56.67

When a high post in UNESCO's secretariat is created or an existing one is vacated, an informal process of consultation begins. Governments receive and screen volunteers or nominate candidates of their own choosing. Discussion takes place in the director-general's private circle, in the department concerned, and between permanent representatives and the director-general, the topic being the history of geographic distribution and its current status throughout the secretariat's upper reaches. The Executive Board then meets, with vitae of the candidates before it. Members extol the virtues of their respective candidates and try to sow seeds of doubt in the director-general's mind about candidates they oppose. Taking into consideration these claims and the qualifications of the candidates, the director-general decides.

UNESCO's directors-general are elected, ordinarily in somewhat ritualistic fashion, by the General Conference. The Executive Board, which nominates a candidate—or if that one should fail to be elected, a second candidate—provides a major arena for negotiations. First the board meets privately, perhaps at a chateau or villa, to discuss nominations, which are tendered as a rule through member governments. These talks may continue for some time before agreement is reached. During this stage some potential candidatures are ended, either by the negotiators or by the prospective candidate himself. Once agreement on a nominee is reached, a draft contract specifying the conditions and perquisites of his appointment is discussed by the General

Conference "at a private meeting," as the UNESCO rules of procedure assert. The conference vote proceeds by secret ballot.

Initiators of representational proposals are most likely to be the governments of member states or, when membership and credentials are sought, of would-be members. Candidatures for UNESCO membership subsets, preeminently the Executive Board, may be advanced by individual hopefuls themselves, though such persons must also be sanctioned by their governments through formalities outlined in the rules of procedure. Less formally, and somewhat less inevitably, the same is true of initiatives leading toward positions in the secretariat's upper reaches.

The role of vetoer in UNESCO is a minor one, without much possibility for drama. A permanent member of the United Nations Security Council can prevent a state from obtaining United Nations membership, thereby barring what might be called the ascriptive route to UNESCO membership. However, the government of a state thus barred can apply directly to UNESCO for membership. In such cases a potential vetoer would have to exercise influence over others' choices rather than casting a single negative vote. On accreditation questions, such as who shall represent China, a single actor who wishes to exercise a veto has even less leverage. A single government can of course veto its own national for a UNESCO post, especially one on the Executive Board. And an individual can also refuse an offer to participate in an international organization by vetoing himself. But these must be considered fairly marginal expressions of the role of vetoer. Even the government of a state high in the hierarchy of international power has on occasion proved unable to turn back a bid to place a man whom most other governments favored in the office of director-general.

The controller is a role that suggests weighty latent influence and anticipative reactions by others. As with other representational roles, the controller is usually played by a government or by that government's delegate. When a participant is intensely committed to mastery, this controller can sometimes prevail in matters of membership, credentials, and the selection of higher UNESCO civil servants. It is easier to block a proposed change of the status quo than to effect one. Perhaps that is the essence of controlling.

On representational questions the role of broker in UNESCO is likely to become fairly lively. Whether in international organizations or in the real estate business, brokers generally prefer a wide range of possible outcomes over no outcome at all, though like everyone else they will prefer some kinds of outcomes to others. In UNESCO the broker is not clearly identified with any chief contestant or even, initially, with any prominent solution. He may, for instance, stand back uncommitted while the agents of the great powers utilize normal diplomatic channels and assert themselves on behalf of their candidates for director-general. Deadlock activates the broker. More than other roles on representational matters, the broker's part is played by actors performing as individuals, not simply as governments' representatives. Some individuals fail at brokerage under the most promising conditions, while others succeed—in the sense of getting an outcome favorable to themselves and others—in quite inauspicious circumstances.

Boundary Decisions

UNESCO maintains a list of projects which its officers wish to undertake with the assistance of UNDP preinvestment contracting. UNDP men have their own priorities, and these are likely to differ from UNESCO's. Either party may initiate negotiations. Member governments or ministerial segments of governments sometimes serve as brokers, for they have something to gain by mutual accommodation of the two international organizations. Either UNDP or UNESCO can exercise a veto on outcomes, although in practice negotiation seems to produce not vetoes but new formulas.

UNESCO and FAO are currently in dispute over whose jurisdiction agricultural education falls within. At stake are institutional pride and UNDP financial support. In some governments the ministry of agriculture (which identifies with FAO) is responsible for agricultural education; in others the ministry of education has this responsibility. Certain governmental representatives recently interviewed at UNESCO complained of overlaps with other organizations, particularly in the issue-areas of demography and planning for the Second Development Decade.

With all the interfaces of education, science, culture, and communications, perhaps it is striking that so few UNESCO boundaries become occasions for disputes. At the quasi-universal and regional levels, UNESCO sponsors many joint activities. Just as IBRD or UNDP pays most of the bill in joint projects with UNESCO, UNESCO is likely to underwrite most of the expenses of its joint undertakings with the Organization of African Unity and the Arab League.

Boundary questions, unlike representational questions and the symbolic issues to be considered next, tend to be a special concern of the director-general and other secretariat officials rather than of member governments. Pillar governments may complain about wasteful redundancies, but they are rarely disposed to serve as brokers and either unable or unwilling to act as vetoers. Criticism of moves to expand organizational tasks or of inadequate coordination of agencies does, however, serve as a ready rhetorical adjunct to controllership.

Symbolic Decisions

UNESCO offers an unending series of issues whose theme is the collective legitimation of the world's doers of good or the delegitimation of its doers of evil.[9] For the governments of many new states membership in UNESCO, as in other international organizations, is a palpable sign that their status is recognized in the eyes of the world and of their own peoples. Sovereignty is thus epitomized and personified in a rite of independent national maturity and individual political manhood. For this reason deprivation of membership can easily be seen as a form of political castration. Ritual gestures toward denial of participation function to symbolize the wish that it is impossible or dangerous to accommodate.

For instance, Portugal's government had not shown much interest in UNESCO programs or in participation before 1965 when that government decided to assert its dormant claim to UNESCO status as an attribute of its United Nations membership. During the Fourteenth General Conference, late in 1966, Portugal's membership and even its delegation's right to be seated were hotly though unsuccessfully contested by parliamentary tactics as well as by walkouts by Africans and others. Following this interlude, business resumed pretty much as before.

As a symbolic issue the matter of Chinese representation for many years carried a short fuse that was frequently lit. Assessments on the United Nations scale proved onerous for the vestigial Chinese regime on Taiwan, and a UNESCO majority for some years accorded a reduced rate to Taipeh. Passed by UNESCO resolution, this assessment remained subject to repeal by the same method. Hence it invited references to the "bankrupt Chiang regime" and spasmodic campaigns for reversal.

Other issues may be classed as symbolic, even though when they are actually voted on (as few UNESCO questions are) they have impressive majorities, nearing unanimity, in their favor. Disarmament; peace and security; freedom from colonization or imperialism; and racial justice—these are issues which, if not "vetoed" or "controlled" before they reach the agenda, are resolved and thereby dissipated until the next UNESCO muster. To look for UNESCO brokers in symbolic matters would be to miss the point entirely.

Symbolic issues momentarily create polarities in which UNESCO participants are lined up against each other or banded together against some outside evil. The internal divisions, for instance on successive questions initiated nominally on behalf of the Chinese, serve as a test of relative strength to indicate the balance of forces at the time. Only a bold social scientist would try to name a UNESCO issue to date that mattered more to successive governments of the United States than keeping out the Chinese Communists. In other instances these morality playlets serve to reinforce both the principle in the minds of the protagonists (as well as their constituents) and, in a curious fashion, the tenuous community that convenes under the aegis of UNESCO.

Rule-Creating and Rule-Supervisory Decisions

Setting and applying standards occupies UNESCO far less than it does ILO. The best-known multilateral treaty adopted by UNESCO is the Convention against Discrimination in Education, a statement of human rights approved on 14 December 1960, by a vote of 60 to 0 to 2. By 10 January 1969, following the International Year for Human Rights, forty-eight states had ratified it. Other conventions include the International Convention for the Protection of Cultural Property in the Event of Armed Conflict, the Universal Copyright Convention, and a convention on performers' rights in which ILO spokesmen also figured.

New norms may be initiated by the secretariat, though ordinarily they are formally proposed by member governments. Some prospective standards emanate from nongovernmental organizations. Certain representatives of the World Confederation of Organizations of the Teaching Profession, for example, have proved especially active on behalf of general rules for the welfare of teachers. After a proposal's initiation, the duty of drafting its formal version is usually assigned to interested individuals representing governments. Linguistic representation is assured by the composition of the drafting committee. The draft is reviewed in the Executive Board, endorsed there, and passed to the next General Conference, where it is likely to be adopted without much difficulty.

Conventions (not to mention recommendations and resolutions) are more aptly described as ideals than rules. In UNESCO, contrary to the situation in some other organizations more heavily engrossed in standard setting and application, governments are most unlikely to be called to account when they fail to do what they had agreed to do. The effective veto comes not in setting standards, but in applying them through concerted action and in implementing them at home. No genuine regimen for review or surveillance in connection with standards has been authorized for UNESCO. Periodic reporting by governments is itself rudimentary when compared to that by ILO or Council of Europe members. While the job of directing UNESCO's Office of International Standards and Legal Affairs has belatedly been raised to carry with it the title of assistant director-general, no sustained effort has yet been mounted by secretariat or members to provide the organization with the necessary organs, procedures, and mandates to enable it to move fruitfully toward accomplishing its goals. A few governments seem to feel that the newly asserted human rights resolutions are too threatening to be allowed teeth, and that UNESCO, with its openness to intellectuals as well as to media and to foreign political systems hostile to current governmental officeholders, is much too dangerous to be encouraged in any endeavor more sweeping than practical programs and operations.

Programmatic and Operational Decisions

UNESCO's province has always seemed virtually limitless to most UNESCO civil servants; and indeed there might seem little that would not arguably fall within the purview of education, science, culture, and communications. Perhaps it is natural that developments or challenges in these substantive areas have frequently set off UNESCO claims, often successful ones, that the organization should assume responsibility for various international innovations. Thus, despite some lingering fears of overpoliticization through UNESCO's sanctioning of mass communications, certain UNESCO officials continue to eye communications satellites longingly.

In the issue-area of cultural affairs, UNESCO rose to the defense of Egyptian and Sudanese temples threatened by Aswan waters. UNESCO helped renovate cultural objects damaged in the northern Italian floods of 1966 and aspires to save sinking Venice.

Spurred by the interest shown in a 1963 conference in Geneva on science and technology for development, the UNESCO secretariat quickly made known its own competence for directing such efforts. Since about 1960 UNESCO has sought to remain in the forefront of international oceanographic efforts. And in 1968 the organization sponsored a meeting of experts to study pollution and other environmental problems, thereby staking a claim to yet another issue-area that is arousing wide public attention. [10]

These are, of course, only a few of the program lines promoted since Charles Ascher counted 147 proposals for projects back in 1946. In magnitude of conception such proposals start with the scheme to develop the Amazon in the 1940s; include such major projects of the 1950s as primary education for Latin America, research devoted to arid lands for the benefit of the Middle East and other parts of Africa and Asia, and mutual cultural appreciation between East and West; and range to the current Participation Program, which assists members in promoting individual projects at home. [11]

Programmatic and operational decisions in UNESCO are made by a process that involves both members of the secretariat and representatives of member states, although neither the resolutions of the General Conference nor those of the Executive Board adequately reveal the choices made or the procedure by which they are reached. Within UNESCO, the secretariat is fundamentally important in programming. When a new program line, such as hydrological or environmental research, is begun, authorization is of course sought in the General Conference, stimulating brokerage (if there is significant disagreement) and other parliamentary roles. Governments especially interested in certain programs frequently act as initiators and sometimes advance the secretariat's proposals. In UNESCO a striking number of General Conference resolutions state that the "director-general is authorized" to continue programs or to undertake them anew. Although increasing extrabudgetary funds are not the only reason why René Maheu is a strong director-general, they probably contribute to his strength by expanding and complicating some programmatic sectors and by attenuating the financial lines between national governments and UNESCO programs. One has the feeling that although controllers—or comptrollers—operate throughout the UNESCO cycle, no programmatic vetoer exists, except perhaps the director-general. Large contributors to UNESCO appear to have greater influence on the total magnitude of UNESCO's activities than on the way funds are allocated among types and fields of activity.[12]

Both foreign member governments and UNESCO officials apparently exercise some influence on operational action in the field. About 1,600 experts were working under UNESCO auspices at the end of 1967. In our 1969 interviews with twenty-one representatives of UNESCO members, seven reported that furnishing experts of their own nationality constituted one major way by which their "government works with UNESCO." None offered any statement, however, that his nation's experts deflected the host government in any respect.

UNESCO maintained twenty-one chiefs of mission in 1967. A representative from one member in the Southern Hemisphere observed that the UNESCO chief of mission in his capital works with the national commission and telephones advice directly to the national delegation in Paris.

Actors and Their Sources of Influence

Classification

National Government Representatives. There was a time when UNESCO people liked to think that they were representatives of the arts, sciences, and professions associated with UNESCO's programs rather than representatives of their respective nation-states. The Executive Board long perpetuated the myth that its members did not act for their governments, but followed their individual judgments on behalf of the General Conference, UNESCO's plenary. Few if any governments had resisted the exercise of selection and instruction procedures until 1954, when actual practice was constitutionally formalized. The professional vitae of nominees for its Executive Board, which UNESCO prints and circulates before each selection of new board members, still carry individual names followed by state names in parentheses. Today as in the past, governments are likely to nominate individuals for election to the Executive Board who can and do claim noteworthiness in their own right—even if these governments, in violation of the recognized rules of the game and sometimes to the detriment of their future chances to be represented on the board, occasionally replace the elected individual with a foreign-office technician.

General Conference delegations are customarily made up to display a range of professional and other attributes. But here similarities among them cease. In many delegations the substantive experts, who may be drawn from private life or the relevant ministry, play important parts. Rarely is this the case with the great powers' delegations, whose token luminaries seem overshadowed by the keepers of political orthodoxy. An exception is the usual French delegation, whose members constitute a magnificent cast of dignitaries, each seemingly exercising his own judgment in his sphere of competence, each evidently acting only in the interests defined by the government of France.

The delegations of the great powers tend to be larger and more fully instructed than those of other states. While a political department head from the foreign affairs office or from a substantive ministry of such a state may make an appearance, he is somewhat less likely to remain to direct his delegation than if he came from a smaller power's capital. When the head of a delegation is responsible back home for his government's positions in UNESCO, the delegations' instructions may of course be augmented or modified in Paris. During a recent General Conference one political disciplinarian reportedly pressed forward with a bit of orthodoxy from his capital only to be brought up short by the head of his delegation, who rejoined: "Excuse me,____, but I *am* [the capital city] on this."

General Conference delegates are frequently drawn from a member state's UNESCO national commission. Constitutionally the national commissions, which may include individuals and representatives of domestic groups interested in some aspect of education, science, cultural matters, or communications, are regarded as intermediaries between governments, peoples, and the organization. The invitation to each member state to "make such arrangements as suit its particular conditions" has led to wide variation in the size, composition, autonomy in relation to the home government, and vitality of the national commissions. Virtually all governments report the existence of a commission. Thus far, however, only a few of these commissions seem to take any part in formulating initiatives concerning programs and personnel. More often commissions have simply provided resonance in their group constituencies for their governments' declarations.

The status of national commission members in a General Conference delegation is one indication of that commission's potency at home. The Brazilian, French, Indian, Japanese, Scandinavian, and Swiss national commissions appear to be among the strongest; each biennially supplies its delegation to the General Conference with a goodly number of active representatives. In most other cases the commissions merely serve as a pool that the governments can draw on for prominent figures who will add luster to their General Conference delegations.

Final decisions on conference delegation personnel are likely to rest with the foreign ministry or its equivalent. Sometimes the executive intervenes. One major state's delegation-designate for the Fourteenth General Conference was radically modified by that state's chief executive at almost the last minute. The places of several notable commission members were taken by personal friends of the executive, including one person from the executive's home region who was better known for his fortune and his generous contributions to the ruling political party than for his interest in or knowledge of UNESCO matters.

Representatives of National and International Interest Groups. Although nongovernmental organizations (NGOs) are far from having the formal status within UNESCO that organized trade unionists and employers enjoy within ILO, UNESCO-accredited NGOs are noteworthy for their close symbiotic relationship with the organization, their variety, and their number. No other specialized agency maintains so many formal NGO ties.[13]

UNESCO's directives to nongovernmental organizations invite "consultation and co-operation . . . for the purpose of enabling UNESCO to secure documentation, advice and technical co-operation" and for "enabling organizations which represent important sections of public opinion to express the views of their members." NGOs participate in formulating and executing certain elements of the organization's program. A biennial conference of international nongovernmental organizations at UNESCO headquarters facilitates collective consultation on the draft program and budget; an NGO standing committee operates between these conferences. NGOs send representatives to some UNESCO meetings, and certain NGOs are authorized to submit written statements for the director-general to communicate to member states. Many NGOs have Paris offices, and some are housed by UNESCO. NGOs may be granted UNESCO subventions "to ensure the continuity of the beneficiary organizations whenever their activities are of special significance to its objectives and the execution of its programme." Between 1958 and 1963, $3,717,000 was allocated to NGOs by the Executive Board.[14] UNESCO extends contracts to "any specially qualified nongovernmental organization" for carrying out specific UNESCO program items. During the 1958-63 period, such contracts totaled $1,881,340.

The Executive Head and His Immediate Entourage. Paris was chosen as the site for UNESCO headquarters. But at a predominantly Anglo-Saxon luncheon meeting during the London establishment conference it was concluded that directors-general would speak English. Julian Huxley, who had succeeded Alfred Zimmern as secretary-general of the UNESCO Preparatory Commission, was named the first director-general. When Huxley accepted the post, he announced that he would be unable to continue in it for a full term: this, commented an observer close to the action, was the price the United States asked in return for its acquiescence in his selection rather than that of a nominee of American origin.

It has been said that Huxley had merely to walk across a room at a cocktail party to enlist a couple of enthusiastic recruits to the UNESCO secretariat. Those whom Huxley gathered about him were in general men who spoke English and shared at least one of his almost limitless intellectual passions.

Jaime Torres Bodet, the Mexican minister of education when tapped as UNESCO director-general in 1948, spoke French well and proudly, a fact more profoundly appreciated by the French than by the Anglo-Saxons at the time of his election. As director-general, Torres Bodet instituted a formal French-style *cabinet* and brought more cultural diversity into the UNESCO secretariat, including its upper echelons, than he found when he took office. He "Latinized" UNESCO's inner circles, as an English-speaking official overstated it some years later. Torres Bodet's tenure ended in 1952 with his resignation, and John W. Taylor of the United States served as acting director-general for several months.

UNESCO's next elected director-general was Luther Evans, an American, who emerged as the compromise victor after an extended deadlock. Without emulating Huxley's style of collegial relations, Evans opened the way to communication and consultation with lower secretariat echelons in a manner and to an extent that top executive leaders in the organization had never approached. The American later tried, and failed, to trim his way through a tempestuous crisis over personnel. Several citizens of the United States were ultimately dismissed from the secretariat for their refusal to respond to a congressional loyalty probe. This severely damaged the morale of the secretariat and left Evans extremely vulnerable. Although it scarcely offset Evans's blameworthiness for these dismissals in the eyes of many in UNESCO, Evans did an excellent job of assuring a smooth transition in 1954 toward Soviet participation in the organization. He was no budgetary expansionist, but he nonetheless animated early efforts to reorient UNESCO toward practical programs in Asia and elsewhere.[15]

Vittorino Veronese was chosen director-general in 1958. UNESCO's relations with the Roman Catholic church were never cordial during Huxley's tenure, but Torres Bodet's and Evans's efforts had brought about increasing cooperation, and with Veronese's election, relations entered a new era of cordiality. Italian criticism of French hegemony in UNESCO's cultural programs, too, was blunted by the fact of Veronese's director-generalship, if not as a consequence of his action. Each director-general has infused a sense of commitment toward UNESCO into a new part of the UNESCO "environment." But although Veronese was a remarkable orchestrator of small groups like the Executive Board, he found his new executive post a difficult, indeed an overwhelming, assignment. After several periods of enforced absence from active duty, a necessity induced partly by the taxing details and responsibilities of his new office, Veronese yielded to René Maheu of France.

Huxley and Torres Bodet were famous men who had been associated with UNESCO during its formative stage. Evans and Veronese had served their governments upon the Executive Board. Maheu had joined the UNESCO secretariat in September 1946 and moved rapidly upward. He was elected to a full six-year term in 1962. In 1968, Maheu became the first UNESCO director-general to be reelected.

Secretariat. Probably the most striking changes in the UNESCO secretariat over the years are those that reflect the shift toward operational activities and reorientation toward field work. At the outset there was little organizational concession to field operations. Director-General Torres Bodet in 1950 reported the creation of a small section attached temporarily to the office of the director-general to prepare for the forthcoming implementation of "the technical assistance scheme for economic development."[16]

But note the shift of UNESCO personnel toward the field. A UNESCO comparison of the number and proportion · of established posts at head-quarters and in the field for 1950 and 1968, shown in table 5.2, dramatizes the point. The 1968 figures suggest a remarkably field-oriented organization. It must be recognized that "away from headquarters" covers a multitude of roles. By some UNESCO staff members, New York is referred to as "Siberia."

Table 5.2

Distribution of UNESCO Posts in Paris and Afield

	1950		1968	
	Number	*Percentage*	*Number*	*Percentage*
Posts at headquarters	780	95	600	27
Posts away from headquarters	44	5	1,600	73
Total	824	100	2,200	100

Sources: Unesco, *Report of the Director-General on the Activities of the Organization from October 1949 to March 1950* (Paris: Unesco, 1950); idem, *What Is Unesco?* (Paris: Unesco, 1968), p.13.

Resources

Ability to Mobilize Votes. As suggested earlier, surprisingly few UNESCO decisions come to a vote. In analyzing the votes that do take place, one could all too easily misjudge influence and assign it to a delegation that "leads" only because it has moved out in front of a column that is already forming, as the Soviet Union has done time and again on decolonization issues. Voting leadership depends mightily upon what question is at issue because it is the particular question that structures participants' intensities of preference. Communist Chinese participation once was a question on which the United States pulled out all the stops. However, the United States representatives do not care about many other questions sufficiently to devote scarce resources toward achieving a preferred disposition of them.

In a sense, when the director-general must mobilize votes, he has already lost something. René Maheu was able to marshal huge majorities on behalf of budget and program expansion in the early 1960s, but these proved to be Phyrrhic victories: they soon evoked from restrictionists a backlash directed at him personally. He has since shown himself willing to restrain gratuitous majorities. If his own candidacy for reelection was the one question that impelled Director-General Maheu to rally all his forces, he is a powerful vote mobilizer indeed, for he won the Executive Board's recommendation and reelection by a unanimous vote in the Fifteenth General Conference.

Control over the Budget. Budget control is an important resource for influence, but it has proved a gross instrument. To convey to the secretariat early in the budget cycle what one's government will insist upon as its maximum financial contribution is fairly effective for that particular purpose, especially if it is concerted policy among most of the states that are financial pillars of the organization. But to prejudge programs by setting an arbitrary ceiling on one's contribution is likely, now as always at UNESCO, to cost something in the indignation it arouses in some quarters, including the office of the director-general. Moreover, even by imposing an early ceiling, governments are not able to choose what items will go in or stay out. That is a function of, among other things, permanent representation at UNESCO headquarters, special positions in the decision-making line, administrative competency, expert knowledge, and long association (both nationally and individually) with the organization.

Permanent Representation. Most member states now maintain permanent representation at UNESCO. Even among the great powers, however, there is great variation in the extent of staffing and the diligence with which programs in the making are scrutinized and shaped. The French and the Soviets are both exceptionally well-manned and seem to maintain close surveillance across the breezeway that separates, or joins, the permanent delegation building and UNESCO House proper. Americans are less numerous, and the permanent delegate for the United States has been known to comment upon the difficulty of keeping posted on evolving matters without a larger staff. The British are very lightly staffed. As of 1967, the permanent British delegate was based in London and commuted to Paris for meetings. His subordinate and a small secretarial staff were left to operate the permanent delegation office.

Strategic Posts. Among special positions in the decision-making process, strategic secretariat posts are no doubt the most important. The budgetary, personnel, and administrative segments of the secretariat seem to be Anglo-Saxon strongholds. Partly because of national or cultural pride, partly because these posts confer particular advantages in connection with programs, certain states or groups of states strive to maintain their men in posts that they almost feel are theirs by prescriptive right. The Latin Americans, for instance, are usually well represented in the education sectors; the Soviets have long been closely identified with science.

Other things being equal, the member state with a bureaucracy capable of sorting through the voluminous UNESCO documentation, drawing appropriate conclusions that will advance the state's defined interests, and setting in motion timely action will obviously be in a better position to affect outcomes than the state that simply lets documents pile up. Expert knowledge, properly engaged, is likely to yield successful sponsorship, acclaim, and preeminence within new programs. But the qualification is important.

Organizational Attitudes

Substantive Themes. Security was the fount of early UNESCO doctrines; development replaced security. According to its constitution, the organization's keystone purpose was "to contribute to peace and security." UNESCO's preamble set forth a rather literary thesis on war and framed a prescription for eradicating it. Only a hint of the future concern with development is discernible. Perhaps "peace building," with its functionalist overtones, is the best effort at doctrinal synthesis thus far. Phrases from the preamble and both popular and official preconceptions behind them served formulators of organizational doctrine for many years. "Free flow of ideas," "raising the standards of education, science, and culture," "democratic culture," "education for freedom," "peace through understanding," "freedom of information," "tensions" studies, and so on were readily calibrated for totalitarian aggressor targets on the Right and then on the Left. Even "fundamental education" and the early, abortive literacy initiatives of Zimmern, Huxley, and Torres Bodet were largely founded on the premise that literate people were peace-loving people.

These "bourgeois notions" did not go unchallenged. The Yugoslav observer carried his critique into UNESCO, labeling Huxley's synoptic effort "a kind of philosophic esperanto."[17] But it was membership for the Soviet Union and for Third World states, more than debate on UNESCO's purposes, that modified the orientation of this organization.

Today development is the touchstone of doctrinal ventures. Only "implications of disarmament" studies (which have a development angle, of course) and "peace research" are founded upon UNESCO's keystone purpose. To "education for development" had been added "educational planning." Slogans abound on behalf of the contribution that science and technology, communications (via space satellite and otherwise), and recently even book publishing might make toward the development of lower-income nations.

Procedural Themes. The vast and continuing gap between what some in UNESCO would like to accomplish and what their organization is financially and otherwise able to undertake helps to explain two recurrent procedural themes. The first might be called *NGOism.* Because from the outset UNESCO took on more than its members would sanction actually handling, NGOs—not far distant—were promptly called in to help. Necessity was crowned by arguments on the virtues of voluntarism, participative programming, and nongovernmentalism. This theme persists despite sporadic restrictionist onslaughts meant to cut back NGO subsidies.

The second theme is quite different from NGOism and perhaps contrapuntal to it. Program *concentration* might be considered a strategic effort to offset the centrifugal tendencies of UNESCO's promotional activity. Today the argument for concentration—that UNESCO cannot really accomplish anything unless it focuses its limited resources upon a single significant problem, or at most only a few—is most frequently heard among UNESCO restrictionists, particularly representatives from the United States, the United Kingdom, and the white Commonwealth countries.

UNESCO decisions during the middle 1950s to consolidate resources and efforts in a limited number of major projects illustrate one sort of concentration effort. Other thrusts toward concentration occurred when the General Conference established these program priorities: for education, in 1960, at the instigation of a British government just released from the burden of several African colonies and with the consent of General Conference representatives concerned about the sequence of events in the Congo; for science and technology, in 1964, with the encouragement of a director-general well aware of the organizational implications of the preceding Geneva Conference on Science and Technology for Development.

A final procedural theme should be included in this necessarily incomplete catalog. UNESCO, like other specialized agencies, has received substantial "preinvestment" contracting from the Special Fund. At present, it may be recalled, UNDP funds to UNESCO total approximately the same as regularly budgeted UNESCO resources. In order to minimize UNDP's impact upon his organizational mission, to prevent UNDP from preempting his choices, and to restrain UNESCO bureaucrats from free enterprising with UNDP officials for an individual department's special benefit, Director-General Maheu has advanced two doctrinal guidelines. First, he warns against "technocrats"— those who would, by his criteria, both immorally and mistakenly reduce all means to a narrow conception of development. Second, he has originated a new *institutional* orientation for the word integration, which he uses to underline the special authority and responsibility of his office in interorganizational relations. Like the unit rule that some governors invoke to hold their state delegations together at conventions to nominate presidential candidates in the United States, the concept has a principled sound. Like the unit rule, Maheu's idea has advantages for the corporate entity and its negotiating position. And like the unit rule, it helps the man on the top to control those beneath him no less than to act as their spokesman.

Actor Groupings

UNESCO, like other specialized agencies, precipitates caucuses of regional and special-interest groups. These were apparently begun with the purpose of electing individuals to the Executive Board and to other positions. More recently they have been used for concerting policy on programs and budget.

Task expansionists include most national representatives; virtually all NGOs in communion with UNESCO; the director-general and people in his bureaucracy involved in substantive programs; bodies of experts; and such international organs as UNDP, IBRD-IDA, the UN Children's Fund (all of which underwrite UNESCO projects), and the UN General Assembly (which infrequently resolves a new task for UNESCO or more fully sanctions an older one). The International Institute for Educational Planning (IIEP) also may be counted among expansionists.

This listing demands qualification. Expansionist national representatives and caucuses, NGOs, secretariat programmers, experts, and the international organizations cited do not wish expansion in all activities, only in the ones identified with their own respective preferences. Most would undoubtedly be restrictionists on other questions.

Restrictionists include some national representatives and their caucuses (eleven affluent representatives meet periodically to apply a brake against budgetary and program acceleration, as one put it; the socialist representatives caucus separately); the budgetary and administrative segments of the secretariat; and such other international organs as FAO and occasionally ECOSOC.

It should be noted that almost everyone is expansionist with regard to something. We have reviewed the UNESCO undertakings that are prized by the Western pillar governments. Russians, on the other hand, want more UNESCO science for the glory of the Soviet system.

The Environment

General Environment

One of the unwritten rules of UNESCO's electoral politics (although earlier inscribed for CAME's Inter-Allied Bureau) is that the great powers will be among the states named on secret ballots for the Executive Board. The United States, the United Kingdom, and France have served on the Executive Board from its beginning. China (Taipeh) was chosen in each election until the one immediately following the credentials battle of 1950; it has not been elected since. The Soviet Union was elected as soon as it joined UNESCO.

With the exception of a brief period, India has been represented on the Executive Board since 1946. Egypt, or the United Arab Republic, Brazil, Italy, Japan, and West Germany are other mainstays.

Great powers, once they are UNESCO members, have with relatively minor exceptions been rather well represented in the secretariat, even if seldom to the satisfaction of any single government or of its criteria of equity—the assessment scale or another brief.

UNESCO charter members, particularly the great powers, were influential in defining the organization's initial aims, largely because they participated in the London deliberations at which these were formulated. *Re*formulated aims, the scope of UNESCO's functions, and shifting emphases in its programs are due proximately to such factors as reassessments by individual secretariat officials and more distantly to external financing—through the calculations that this type of funding engenders. But reorientation is most fundamentally explained by the increasing visibility (or to put it operationally, the increasing UNESCO membership) of states with low per capita gross national products.

It might be recalled that the 1960 UNESCO General Conference voted a priority to education in UNESCO programming. That was the year of the great increase in African membership. It was also a time when the "education for development" codicil to a contemporary sacred calling was being diligently presented to external financing allocators by UNESCO secretariat officials, UNESCO-related experts, and nongovernmental organizations.

The hypothesis that the probability of an international organization's becoming aligned with the policies of one state varies directly with that state's dominance in the environment may perhaps best be considered for UNESCO by introducing a vignette that clearly seems to point in this direction, then qualifying the conclusiveness of this case as far as the hypothesis is concerned. For this example we look to a year emphasized in the joint study.

The United States, the Cold War, and UNESCO: A 1950 Vignette. An early American initiative to assign UNESCO the legitimizing role in an enterprise to establish a worldwide radio network had died a quiet death after 1946. About 1950, however, similar proposals appeared. These in turn were dropped before the end of the Korean War, at a time when vocal segments of the American public were turning against UNESCO because of what were frequently termed its communist tendencies. The following comments by observers from several vantage points sketch the temporary resurgence and the subsequent ebb of American interest in UNESCO as an instrument of United States foreign policy during the middle months of 1950.[18]

President Harry S. Truman conveyed a friendly and low-keyed message to the Eighth United States National Commission meeting in Washington during April 1950. Truman pledged the organization all the support at his command; he referred to the "vital importance" of UNESCO's work and stated that he wanted a Congress elected "that believes in international cooperation wholeheartedly." He predicted that UNESCO "could be successful in time," but cautioned: "We expect things to happen too fast. The United States is noted for its go-getters. . . . In organizations such as yours and the United Nations, if over a generation or two generations we come close to accomplishing our purpose, we have made great progress."

Senator William Benton, however, brought a different message to the same conclave. Benton warned his audience that "unless UNESCO boldly faces up to the political issues of war and peace" it would be "doomed to the ineffectuality of Arab scribes of the middle ages." He called the organization's publicity insignificant, and he proposed that the United States finance "certain extraordinary UNESCO projects."

At the Fifth General Conference during the spring of 1950, the cold war gripped UNESCO proceedings. The *Times Educational Supplement* (London) editorialized on 16 June about the "inquietude" that attended discussion of Communist Chinese representation, German reeducation, and similar sensitive questions: "It was seen to be a serious, and some thought undesirable, departure to execute the policy of one nation or group of nations which might not be the policy of the United Nations as a whole."

The Korean War gave rise to such American newspaper headlines as "U.S. Looks to UNESCO to Tell Korea Truth"; "UNESCO May Assume New Duties in Korea after [Executive] Board Meeting"; and "UNESCO's Aid Sought along Propaganda Front." The *Continental Daily Mail* observed on 29 July 1950 that UNESCO was becoming a veritable "psychological warfare organization for the Western Powers." On 14 August the *News Chronicle* (London) warned: "American insistence that UNESCO enter the cold war by spreading pro-Western, anti-Communist propaganda is producing a crisis which may almost wreck the Organisation." In a thoughtful article entitled "UNESCO and Peace," published in the *Fortnightly* for August 1950, Owen Hickey criticized the UNESCO secretariat's authorization to utilize public and private funds from outside the organization's budget. "So long as UNESCO shapes its policy independently of that of any bloc of nations it is a matter for congratulation if it finds Governments which are ready to put up money for its execution. But the temptation to be influenced by the preferences of a willing patron is strong and subtle."

From another quarter came different views. United States Secretary of State Dean Acheson told a press conference late in August that the program authorized by UNESCO's Executive Board would have a "powerful influence" upon teachers, writers, and others throughout the world, especially in areas "where the nature of the brutal assault on Korea has been obscured or distorted by communist propaganda." From its sounding of opinion the Paris edition of the *New York Herald Tribune* concluded: "Most observers do not believe that any accomplishment by UNESCO in Korea will be denounced as 'propaganda' by the Western powers or the other democratic countries supporting UN troops."

Byron Dexter, editor of *Foreign Affairs*, contended in a letter to the *New York Times* that the question of the day was whether the world's nations would be organized on a democratic or a communist model; if this was not the affair of UNESCO, the United Nations should be given "the necessary funds and apparatus (such as National Commissions) to do the work that UNESCO is not doing."

An Associated Press dispatch, basing its conclusion upon the UNESCO survey entitled *World Communications,* found that for a Campaign of Truth, "the means are not only at hand, but they have been charted. UNESCO has listed the newspapers, privately owned radio sets and seating capacity of motion picture theaters in the world. All could be used."

The *Boston Herald*, on 1 September 1950, judged Director-General Torres Bodet a willing collaborator. If UNESCO could go on to

> stimulate its member nations in a broader presentation of the actual Korean facts, [U.S.] ex parte propaganda gropings become less necessary. . . . It is far better for Hindus and Moslems to receive amplified, well-proportioned Korean war facts via the Indian and Pakistan radios, respectively, under UNESCO auspices, than from a U.S. Information Service or a U.S. controlled radio broadcast.

On the other hand, Ferdinand Kuhn, writing in the *Washington Post* about two months later, saw the organization "riddled with the 'neutralism' that afflicts many intellectuals today, especially in Europe. UNESCO had to be bludgeoned into taking action on the Korean War . . . and its secretariat in Paris persistently shrinks from fighting the present world-wide battle for the minds of men."

On the face of it, this vignette seems to indicate that UNESCO's decisions follow the orientation of a dominant state in the international system—the United States. But several qualifications must be entered along with any generalization from this single instance.

First, there is the limitation of time. Once one has traced the rise and decline of American influence on certain UNESCO decisions during 1950, one should raise the question of what happened both before and after. Was the United States equally successful at other times? And if not, can this be accounted for by showing that before and after 1950 the United States was relatively less dominant in the "environment"?

Second, there is the limitation of scope. Spotlighting the salient issues played up in headlines should not lead to the neglect of other issue-areas. Was the United States equally successful in these others? And if not, how can dominance in the environment be reconciled with any discrepancy between success in one issue-area and another?

Third, there is the question of the missing superpower. What effect did the fact that the Soviet Union was not a member during 1950 have upon the inclination and success of the United States in using UNESCO as it did? The Soviet absence from UNESCO would seem to have been acted upon in much the same fashion that the contemporary Soviet absence from the Security Council was utilized—as an opportunity to monopolize the cloak of United

Nations legitimacy to cover actions that were essentially those of the United States government. But is this dominance to be accounted for by stratification, by membership lag, or by some other notion?

Power or influence can provide a telling explanation of decisions only in relation to participants' *choice of instrumentality* and to the *intensity* with which these participants pursue their objectives through chosen instrumentalities. Some may regard a specialized agency like UNESCO as an irrelevant instrumentality in foreign policy, or at least they may consider it inferior to bilateralism or regionalism in the same policy areas. Or it may be that cultural aims, for instance, are given low priority among the various objectives of a participant's foreign policy, whatever the chosen instrumentality may be.

The case of UNESCO raises the question of how to account for an apparent shortfall of United States influence in comparison to expectations. This problem is eased if we adopt the view that, first, UNESCO is only one of many foreign policy instrumentalities that the governments of nation-states (including the United States) choose; and, second, UNESCO policy areas are identified with only a few of the objectives that these governments pursue intensely.

Without question, UNESCO's behavior is strongly affected by the governments, and perhaps by the types of states, that act in close operational proximity to the organization. But the most important impacts of this kind come through new participants—the socialist states in 1954, the African states about 1960, the Chinese People's Republic in 1971—and the access to the organization that this membership gives their governments. At this point of membership governments cease to be merely potent elements of the environment and become part of UNESCO itself.

How much does the degree of bipolarity help one to understand UNESCO's decision making? First let us outline two hypothetical patterns as alternatives, pattern A and pattern B. In both of these patterns the two superpowers with their respective allies are held in taut opposition within, as well as outside, the international organization in question. In pattern A, organizational decisions are reached only on the most innocuous matters.[19] Important action takes place elsewhere—through instrumentalities untrammeled by polarization. In pattern B, on the other hand, one of the two polar superpowers is able to exercise its will despite the opposition—no doubt the bitter opposition—of the other. Thus a range of highly controversial decisions bears the organizational imprimatur even though these decisions are made, or commanded, in the capital of the dominating superpower. The unsuccessful superpower perforce minimizes its losses, practices the tactics of exposing puppeteer and puppets, waits or works for better times, and in the meantime seeks to achieve most of its foreign policy objectives through other instrumentalities.

UNESCO diverges from both these patterns of tight bipolarity in an important respect. The changing international system was for many years imperfectly reflected in UNESCO's membership, above all because the Soviet Union was not a member. Whatever the character of UNESCO decisions, then, they could have approximated pattern A or pattern B, strictly applied, only after 1954. Given the qualification of Soviet nonmembership, however, UNESCO approached pattern B in the early 1950s. While UNESCO has been the forum for plenty of diatribe since then, it is as much a mistake to conclude that all subsequent decision making has been reduced to trivial outcomes by a deadlock of the superpowers (pattern A) as it is to maintain that one superpower has continued to dominate the other in UNESCO's choices (pattern B).

Decision making in UNESCO has evolved with loosening bipolarity and with the addition of new members. UNESCO began as an initiatve of European governments. Other great powers and the British dominions were subsequently invited to participate in discussions of postwar arrangements. Near the end of the war it was understood that Latin-American states would be invited. Many of these did attend the London establishment conference; five joined UNESCO in 1946, and others did so within several years. India became a UNESCO member the year before its independence. Egypt, Lebanon, Saudi Arabia, and Turkey were the other non-European UNESCO members in 1946. The United Nations "alliance" for educational, scientific, and cultural matters was of course launched without the states that were present enemies. Furthermore, its initial circle of members barely touched Asia and Africa.

Czechoslovakia and Poland joined UNESCO in 1946; Hungary, the next year. All three soon began to boycott UNESCO General Conferences, to fall behind in paying assessments, and to criticize UNESCO policies. In December 1952 the Polish government announced that it was withdrawing from UNESCO participation; Czechoslovakia and Hungary soon did the same.

The defeated states, whose wartime governments had been deposed and whose peoples were to a limited extent being "reeducated" under nominal UNESCO sponsorship, were admitted to UNESCO during this period. Italy's induction in 1948, Japan's in 1950, and above all West Germany's in the same year, must be regarded as important stages in drawing lines between a particular alliance within UNESCO and another particular alliance outside. Not surprisingly, the judgment on Chinese credentials at the General Conference of 1950 and the admission of South Korea in 1950, South Vietnam in 1951, and Spain in 1953 all sparked adverse comment from Eastern Europe and points farther east.

However, this period of tightening alliances also brought into UNESCO the following: Austria in 1948; Switzerland and Burma in 1949; and Indonesia, Sweden, and Yugoslavia in 1950. Switzerland and Sweden, active UNESCO participants once their governments had decided to enter, were important about 1953 in tempering some of the blasts from UNESCO about the cold war. India, a charter member, joined in this effort. Moreover, Iran, Iraq, and Pakistan, all to become members of Western collective self-defense arrangements in 1954 or 1955, helped to further, though they did not originate, the subsequent loosening bipolarity within UNESCO. Aside from its specific composition, UNESCO's increase in membership from 1947 to 1954, which amounted to forty-five new member states and brought the total to seventy-three, may also have helped lead to less tautness in relation to the two poles.

The Soviet Union's entrance into UNESCO in 1954, a year that also brought membership and a vote to the Byelorussian S.S.R. and the Ukrainian S.S.R., was succeeded by the membership applications of Bulgaria and Rumania in 1956 and Albania in 1958. With Soviet membership, the Finnish government apparently felt that Finland's neutral status would not be impaired by joining, and Finland became a member in 1956.

The loosening of bipolarity in international relations was strikingly illustrated and furthered by the entry of African members that enlarged most units within the United Nations complex about 1960. This influx of new members voicing new demands, in conjunction with other developments, sharply modified some UNESCO practices.

Increasing membership, dilution or attenuation of the superpowers' duopoly on political orthodoxy, and an ever more extended agenda of diverse program items have contributed to increasingly diffuse patterns of alignments and conflicts in UNESCO. Loosening bipolarity is more noticeable in some policy areas than in others. The UNESCO secretariat, led by the executive head and his advisers, has rather skillfully built up portions of its program on the basis of support from varying segments of the membership. However, in UNESCO, if not elsewhere, support is based at least as much on those who want a program element intensely as those who are not aligned and who remain indifferent. "Coalition building" probably conveys the wrong image for UNESCO; most decisions are not taken by vote, even when they are acclaimed by plenaries.

As diffusion progresses, the international bureaucracy has no doubt gained in autonomy. One reason is that its expertise becomes more and more important with the increase in complexity; another is its growing range of choices. Directors-general are left with further leverage in formulating programs when governments are unwilling, because they do not feel intensely about them, to devote scarce resources to surveillance of emerging policies.

Loosening bipolarity—or more intensive participation in UNESCO by socialist governments—has led to an interesting shift in style, at least in some public phases of decision making. During the mobilization of UNESCO facilities for the Korean Campaign of Truth and other programs predominantly set in motion by the United States, UNESCO was extolled for its service as a "political" organization, or chided for its reluctance to act as such. Since the Soviet Union joined, the conception of UNESCO that United States representatives and to a certain extent representatives of other North Atlantic governments prefer has been the idea of a distinctly nonpolitical organization. Politics in this usage, as before, connotes controversiality through the embarrassment of a sovereign state or its government. Now the Soviet representative is the one likely to assert that unless UNESCO as a political institution comes to grips with the "real" problems of war and peace, it will never amount to anything.

Specific Environment

Tables 5.3 and 5.4 align this study's "stratification" of states in the general environment with other rankings of states by certain capacities and achievements in education, science, and communications. All specific rankings except books published on pure and applied science are made on a per capita basis.

There are some rather striking divergences between the generally powerful and those with high specific ratings. Among the governments influential in UNESCO's literacy and other educational programs we would certainly find some from states that are far down in the specific rankings here. Brazil, India, Nigeria, and the UAR carry enormous weight on educational matters, partly because they are educationally needy. Neediness is not, of course, sufficient to endow one with influence. Most of these member states have exceptionally competent persons representing them in educational policy making, and all actively pursue the fruits of UNESCO's educational promotion. India and the UAR have allowed UNESCO to penetrate their national systems in order to gain assistance in the long-range planning of their educational programs. The experience will place their governments in even stronger positions to exercise influence within this substantive policy area, if they so choose. Three of these four influential participants, true enough, do exceed the threshold of "power" necessary to qualify them for the general environment list.

Some differences among rankings by specific indicators, moreover, raise interesting questions. For instance, the high number of science books published by the USSR, Poland, Czechoslovakia, and East Germany relative to other specific indications for these states may be related to socialist (and especially Soviet) interest and influence in UNESCO science programs. One might wonder whether the discrepancy between United States radio and television ownership rankings, on the one hand, and newspaper circulation rankings, on the other, runs parallel to any differences in the importance this government accords to various UNESCO communications programs. The same question might be asked of Canada and, conversely, of New Zealand. It would be fascinating to inquire whether annual cinema attendance per capita—perhaps the most idiosyncratic of these rankings—carries any

Table 5.3

Stratification in Specific Environment: Education

Stratification in General Environment (1967)		Students in Higher Education per 100,000 Population	
1	United States	1	United States
2	USSR	2	Philippines
3	France	3	Netherlands
5	People's Republic of China	4	Australia
5	Japan	5	New Zealand
5	United Kingdom	6	Argentina
7	Federal Republic of Germany	7	Japan
8	Italy	8	Israel
9.5	Canada	9	France
9.5	India	10	Canada
11	Sweden	11	Denmark
15	Australia	12	Austria
15	Austria	13	USSR
15	Netherlands	14	Belgium
15	Spain	15	Finland
15	Switzerland	16	Federal Republic of Germany
15	Yugoslavia	17	Yugoslavia
15	Brazil	18	United Kingdom
21	Argentina	19	Sweden
21	Belgium	20	United Arab Republic
21	Pakistan	21.5	Czechoslovakia
21	Poland	21.5	Switzerland
21	South Africa	23	German Democratic Republic
26.5	Czechoslovakia	24	Italy
26.5	Denmark	25	Venezuela
26.5	German Democratic Republic	26	Poland
26.5	Indonesia	28	Cuba
26.5	Israel	28	Mexico
26.5	Mexico	28	Norway
31.5	Cuba	28	Spain
31.5	Norway	31	Turkey
31.5	Turkey	32	India
31.5	United Arab Republic	33	South Africa
36	Finland	34	Pakistan
36	New Zealand	35	Brazil
36	Nigeria	36	People's Republic of China
36	Philippines	37	Indonesia
36	Venezuela	38	Luxembourg
39	Luxembourg	39	Nigeria

Table 5.3 (Continued)

Primary and Secondary Students as Percentage of Population		Percentage Literate Age 15 and over	
1	United States	6	Australia
3	Canada	6	Austria
3	New Zealand	6	Denmark
3	United Kingdom	6	German Democratic Republic
5	Australia	6	Finland
6	France	6	Netherlands
7.5	Japan	6	New Zealand
7.5	Federal Republic of Germany	6	Norway
9.5	Belgium	6	Sweden
9.5	Denmark	6	Switzerland
11.5	Czechoslovakia	6	United Kingdom
11.5	Sweden	6	Federal Republic of Germany
13.5	Finland	13.5	Japan
13.5	Norway	13.5	United States
15.5	Israel	15.5	Canada
15.5	Poland	15.5	Czechoslovakia
17	Netherlands	17	Belgium
18	Yugoslavia	18	Luxembourg
19	Cuba	19	France
20	Spain	20.5	Poland
21	Austria	20.5	USSR
23	Argentina	22	Israel
23	Switzerland	23	Italy
23	USSR	24	Spain
25	German Democratic Republic	25	Argentina
26	Luxembourg	26	Cuba
27	Venezuela	27	Yugoslavia
28	Italy	28	Philippines
29	Philippines	29	Venezuela
30	Mexico	30	Mexico
31	People's Republic of China	31	Brazil
32	South Africa	32	People's Republic of China
33.5	Brazil	33	South Africa
33.5	Turkey	34	Turkey
35	United Arab Republic	35	United Arab Republic
36	Indonesia	36	India
37	India	37	Indonesia
38	Nigeria	38	Pakistan
39	Pakistan	39	Nigeria

Sources: For students in higher education per 100,000 population, Bruce M. Russett, et al., *World Handbook of Political and Social Indicators* (New Haven: Yale University Press, 1965), p. 214; for primary and secondary students as percentage of population, ibid., p. 218; for percentage literate age fifteen and over, ibid., p. 222. Calculations on "specific environment" by Paul Andrews.

Table 5.4

Stratification in Specific Environment: Science and Communications

Number of Science Books Published 1962, 1963, or 1964		Total Circulation of Newspapers per 1,000 Population		Radios per 1,000 Population	
1	USSR	1	United Kingdom	1	United States
2	United Kingdom	2	Sweden	2	Canada
3	United States	3	Japan	3	Sweden
4	Japan	4	Luxembourg	4	Luxembourg
5	Poland	5	New Zealand	5	Denmark
6	Federal Republic of Germany	6	Norway	6	German Democratic Republic
		7	Australia		
7	Czechoslovakia	8	Switzerland	7	Belgium
8	France	9	Finland	8	Finland
9	Spain	10	Denmark	9	USSR
10	Mexico	11	United States	10	France
11	German Democratic Republic	12	Federal Republic of Germany	11	Federal Republic of Germany
12	Netherlands	13	Belgium	12.5	Austria
13	Sweden	14.5	Netherlands	12.5	United Kingdom
14	Italy	14.5	Czechoslovakia	14	Norway
15	India	16	Austria	15	Argentina
16	Yugoslavia	17	France	16	Switzerland
17	Denmark	18	USSR	17	Czechoslovakia
18	Turkey	19	Canada	18	Netherlands
19	Switzerland	20	Poland	19	Israel
20	Belgium	21	Spain	20	New Zealand
21	Austria	22	Argentina	21	Australia
22	Finland	23	Israel	22.5	Italy
23	Norway	24	German Democratic Republic	22.5	Japan
24	Brazil			24	Venezuela
25	Australia	25	Mexico	25	Poland
27	United Arab Republic	26	Italy	26	Mexico
28	New Zealand	27	Yugoslavia	27	Cuba
29	Argentina	28	Venezuela	28	South Africa
30	Venezuela	29	Cuba	29	Yugoslavia
31	South Africa	30	South Africa	30	Spain
32	Philippines	31	Brazil	31	Brazil
33	Indonesia	32	Turkey	32	United Arab Republic
34	Cuba	33	People's Republic of China	33	Turkey
35	Pakistan	34	Philippines	34	Philippines
36	Nigeria	35	United Arab Republic	35	People's Republic of China
37	Luxembourg	36	India	36	Nigeria
		37	Indonesia	37	India
		38	Nigeria	38	Indonesia
		39	Pakistan	39	Pakistan

Table 5.4 (Continued)

Television Sets per 1,000 Population		Annual Cinema Attendance per Capita	
1	United States	1	Australia
2	Canada	2	Israel
3	Sweden	3	USSR
4	United Kingdom	4.5	New Zealand
5	Denmark	4.5	Italy
6.5	Japan	6	United States
6.5	Federal Republic of Germany	7.5	Austria
8	German Democratic Republic	7.5	Luxembourg
		10	Czechoslovakia
		10	Norway
9	Australia	10	Spain
10	Netherlands	12.5	German Democratic Republic
11	Belgium		
12	Finland	12.5	Mexico
13	Czechoslovakia	14.5	Venezuela
14	France	14.5	Switzerland
15	New Zealand	17.5	Argentina
16	Norway	17.5	Cuba
17	Italy	17.5	Denmark
18	Switzerland	17.5	Sweden
19	Austria	23.5	Belgium
20	Luxembourg	23.5	Finland
21	Cuba	23.5	France
22	Venzuela	23.5	Poland
23	Argentina	23.5	People's Republic of China
24	USSR		
25	Poland	23.5	United Kingdom
26	Spain	23.5	Federal Republic of Germany
27	Mexico		
28	Brazil	23.5	Yugoslavia
29	Yugoslavia	28	Canada
30	United Arab	30	Brazil
31	Philippines	30	India
32	Israel	30	Japan
33.5	Indonesia	33	Indonesia
33.5	Nigeria	33	Netherlands
35	People's Republic of China	33	United Arab Republic
36	Turkey	35	Turkey

Source: For number of books of pure or applied science, *United Nations Statistical Yearbook* (New York: United Nations, 1965), p. 717; for newspaper circulation, Unesco, *Statistical Yearbook,* 1965 (Paris: Unesco, 1966), p. 526; for radios per 1,000 population, ibid., p. 584; for television sets per 1,000 population, ibid., p. 600 (no data provided for India, Pakistan, South Africa); for annual cinema attendance, ibid., p. 563 (no data provided for India, Pakistan, South Africa). Calculations by Paul Andrews. *Note:* All these data are for 1964 or for closest preceding year for which data were available.

analogous manifestations in UNESCO's cinematic program sectors. And how, we may ask but cannot answer, does the Philippines manage to send such a high proportion of its primary, secondary, and literate students to college or university?

The specific indicators of prowess are evidently not the most helpful guides to influence. But they do provoke questions about influence that are pertinent to any examination of the international relationships we abbreviate by the use of such acronyms as UNESCO.

Patterns of Influence

In the early days of UNESCO Julian Huxley prophesied that unless it developed "a general outlook and line of approach" the new institution that he headed would run the "danger of undertaking piecemeal and even self-contradictory actions." UNESCO rapidly became a plural system in which, as an astute veteran of UNESCO affairs once noted, "Everyone has his own hobbyhorse." Whether many simultaneously active hobbyhorses advance any agreed cause or merely create vertical motion and noise we must leave for another time and a different context.

Today the group with the best claim to composing a single UNESCO elite with general influence would be René Maheu and those close to him. They are the chief arbiters of UNESCO's immediate temper and direction. From them spring most major innovations. This interpretation, however, must be rather severely qualified. The director-general does not affect choices in some policy areas where many representational and symbolic decisions are made. Even in programmatic matters, where his influence is greatest, the director-general is in part restrained by the commitments and nondecisions of the past. This will be as true tomorrow as it is today. Furthermore, although he endorses program and budgetary proposals in all fields, in some he can know little about what happens, much less exercise his influence upon the disposition of cases.

No nation-state represented in UNESCO can claim influence to match the director-general's, even with these qualifications. Individual governments intensely value one sector or another of UNESCO's range of tasks. Partly because other governments are indifferent, a government that does concern itself may be a government influential in its chosen sector. On the other hand, such governments frequently do not find it feasible to deploy sufficient resources to give real meaning to their influence.

UNESCO will be affected programmatically and otherwise, though to an extent not yet foreseeable, by the UNDP-authorized Jackson Report (*A Study of the Capacity of the United Nations Development System*, 1969) and its call for more voluntary funds for UNDP action. The same report carries indications, however, that UNESCO and other specialized agencies including FAO might be relied upon relatively less in future operational programs. UNDP is thus likely to loom even larger than in the past as a factor in UNESCO decisions, although the actual disposition of Jackson Report recommendations is yet unclear. In view of past criticism directed at proliferating agencies with overlapping substantive jurisdictions, it will be interesting to observe how spokesmen for existing specialized agencies react to this report's sanctioning of new private association executors for projects contracted by UNDP.

Intensity of interest and thus of participation is the best guide to influence by governments. But relative influence is tested only where intensely pursued governmental objectives conflict. At these points the United States is likely to prevail over the Soviet Union. Exceptions include those symbolic questions that elicit exhortations to decolonize or abandon imperialism.

To end on a note suggesting headlines would be misleading. Most UNESCO decisions do not arouse general interest. Most do not entice the two superpowers into disagreements; on many issues one finds them about equally skeptical and detached. Nevertheless, although these same decisions fail to gain attention or real support in the great industrial states or among their governments, they are often of vast importance to other UNESCO members. The future of the United Nations Educational, Scientific and Cultural Organization depends chiefly upon the ability of the governments of the Southern Hemisphere to develop effective means of extending their influence beyond the plenary chambers of the General Conference.[20]

6 WHO: Medicine, Regionalism, and Managed Politics

Harold K. Jacobson

Functions, Structure, and Evolution

According to its constitution the objective of the World Health Organization (WHO) is "the attainment by all peoples of the highest possible level of health." Health is defined in the preamble as "a state of complete physical, mental and social well-being and not merely the absence of disease or infirmity." Few international organizations have been created with such far-reaching goals. They represent some of mankind's most fundamental aspirations, and for that reason they universally command at least token respect. The drafting of WHO's constitution in 1946 signified a desire to go beyond formal deference to these goals, however, and actively to promote their achievement through a global organization.

Like many of the steps taken in the immediate aftermath of World War II toward establishing new international organizations, those that culminated in the creation of WHO built on a tradition of earlier collaborative efforts.[1] Thus when at the San Francisco Conference in 1945 Brazil and China jointly proposed that a conference be convened to create an international health organization, there was already a record of some international collaboration, and an institutional framework was already in existence. The joint declaration submitted by the two delegations was unanimously approved and referred to the General Assembly for implementation. Action followed promptly. A technical preparatory committee held its first meeting on 18 March 1946; the International Health Conference opened in June, and the constitution of the World Health Organization was signed on 22 July 1946.

That the initiative in the creation of the World Health Organization would have been taken by Brazil and China, two developing countries, was significant and foretold a shift in the nature of the international collaborative efforts in the field of health. Prior to 1945 initiatives had largely come from the developed states, and the primary thrust of international efforts had been to protect the developed states in the Northern Hemisphere from the diseases of the poorer states in the Southern Hemisphere.

This concern of the developed states is expressed to a degree in WHO's constitution; but, as has already been indicated, the organization's purpose is much broader. Its broad objective—"the attainment by all peoples of the highest possible levels of health"—was accepted in 1946 with little controversy.

To fulfill this broad objective, twenty-two functions were assigned to the organization in chapter II of its constitution. Some of the most important of these are noted in the following excerpts:

(*a*) to act as the directing and co-ordinating authority on international health work;

(*c*) to assist Governments, upon request, in strengthening health services;

(*d*) to furnish appropriate technical assistance and, in emergencies, necessary aid upon the request or acceptance of Governments;

(*f*) to establish and maintain such administrative and technical services as may be required, including epidemiological and statistical services;

(*g*) to stimulate and advance work to eradicate epidemic, endemic, and other diseases;

(*j*) to promote co-operation among scientific and professional groups which contribute to the advance of health;

(*k*) to propose conventions, agreements and regulations, and make recommendations with respect to international health matters and to perform such duties as may be assigned thereby to the Organization and are consistent with its objective;

(*n*) to promote and conduct research in the field of health;

(*o*) to promote improved standards of teaching and training in the health, medical and related professions;

(*s*) to establish and revise as necessary international nomenclatures of diseases, of causes of death and of public health practices;

(*u*) to develop, establish and promote international standards with respect to food, biological, pharmaceutical and similar products;

(*v*) generally to take all necessary action to attain the objective of the Organization.

As can be seen, the organization was to have both forum and service functions and was charged with providing services to states individually (*c* and *d*) as well as generally (*f, g,* and *n*). Unlike many other specialized agencies, therefore, WHO from its very creation had the task of providing assistance directly to states. The poorer states would inevitably be the principal recipients.

To a certain extent this emphasis on assistance to poorer states was attributable to the states that took the initiative in calling for the creation of WHO. Since this emphasis also fit rather nicely into the historical development of medical science, it was to a certain extent in accord with the selfish interests of the richer states. As more and more has been learned about diseases, the emphasis in medical treatment has shifted from quarantine, to cure, to prevention. Consequently, a frontal attack on the health problems of the poorer countries provided more effective protection for the richer countries than had the limited measures attempted a century earlier. Furthermore, the rapidity with which diseases could be transmitted had increased dramatically with improvements in transportation, particularly with the development of air travel. The richer countries, however, were not wholly self-interested: WHO's mandate covered numerous health problems besides the communicable diseases of the poorer countries. Just how much support the richer countries would be willing to provide, however, beyond that dictated by their broadly defined self-interests, remained to be seen.

Although it was relatively easy to achieve consensus at the International Health Conference in 1946 concerning WHO's objective and functions, obtaining agreement about the organization's structure proved to be more difficult.

By far the most controversial structural issue concerned the status of regional organizations. Although there was general agreement that existing regional organizations (i.e. the Pan American Sanitary Organization) should be brought into relationship with WHO and that WHO's structure should provide for substantial regional decentralization, there remained considerable room for controversy about the degree of autonomy that regional bodies might have. The decisions finally embodied in WHO's constitution specified that regional organizations should be "integral" parts of the organization and decreed that the Pan American Sanitary Organization (the formal title that had been given to the Pan American Sanitary Bureau and the associated conferences of governmental representatives) should in due course be integrated. These decisions constituted a framework within which negotiations could be started between WHO and the Pan American Sanitary Organization. In contrast, the International Health Conference provided that WHO immediately assume not only the activities previously performed by the Office International d'Hygiène Publique and the Health Organization of the League but also the functions conducted by the United Nations Relief and Rehabilitation Administration in this field.

Certain other features of WHO's constitution are also worthy of note, even though (or perhaps because) their adoption was relatively uncontroversial. The World Health Assembly is empowered to adopt regulations concerning sanitary and quarantine requirements, nomenclature, and standards for diagnostic procedures, as well as standards for biological, pharmaceutical, and other such products moving in international commerce. These regulations are binding on all members of the organization unless they notify the director-general of rejection or reservation within a specified time. Because it was felt that participation in an international organization working in the health field should be universal, the membership requirements were minimal: United Nations members and other specified states need only accept the constitution; others must also have their application approved by a simple majority vote in the World Health Assembly. The stress on universality also explains the lack of any provision in the constitution for withdrawal from the organization. In keeping with this emphasis, WHO's constitution makes no distinctions among its members; none are given a favored position with respect to seats on WHO's Executive Board or ratification or amendment of the constitution. The constitution came into force when it was ratified by twenty-six members of the United Nations, and adoption of amendments requires only a two-thirds vote in the World Health Assembly and acceptance by two-thirds of WHO's members.

Some of these special provisions were sources of concern, particularly to the United States. The fact that WHO's constitution could be amended without the United States' concurrence, and that there was no provision for withdrawal, caused the Senate to recommend ratification with the understanding that the United States reserved "the right to withdraw from the Organization on a 90-day notice,"[2] and the president accepted this recommendation. Other alarms were voiced in the United States. It was obvious that the United States would be the largest contributor to WHO, and it was also apparent that the organization's emphasis on providing services would mean that its budget could attain substantial levels. Because of these facts, there was some sentiment for establishing a ceiling on the American financial obligation.[3] Although this move was rebuffed, absolute ceilings on the American contribution were written into annual United States appropriations for WHO through 1955, when the ceiling was changed to a fraction—one-third—of WHO's total regular budget. The fixed-sum ceiling never exceeded $3 million. The American Medical Association, whose representative was an integral part of the United States delegation to the International Health Conference, wanted to ensure also that WHO would limit its activities to problems of public health and preventive medicine and would not concern itself with "the care of the sick and the social organization related to the practice of medicine."[4] The AMA left no doubt about its opposition to any action by WHO that might promote socialized medicine. These several concerns partly explain why, even though the WHO constitution was signed on 22 July 1946, the United States did not complete its ratification until 21 June 1948.

Lingering doubts about the status of the Pan American Sanitary Organization were another reason for the United States delay. The states of Latin America were also concerned about the problem. Mexico was the first of the Latin-American states to ratify the constitution, but it did so only on 7 April 1948. On 2 June 1948 Brazil became the second Latin-American state to take this action. China ratified the constitution on the day it was signed, as did the United Kingdom. Mexican ratification on 7 April 1948 meant that the necessary twenty-six United Nations members had ratified WHO's constitution so that it could enter into force.

The basic structural features of WHO have already been outlined in the preceding discussion. The central organs of WHO are: the World Health Assembly, the Executive Board, and the secretariat. The assembly is composed of delegates representing all members of WHO. It meets annually and makes decisions on "important questions" by a two-thirds majority and on others by a simple majority. Originally, the Executive Board consisted of eighteen persons, designated by as many member states. In 1960 the number of board members was increased to twenty-four, and in 1967 the World

Health Assembly adopted another constitutional amendment increasing the number to thirty, although at the end of 1971 this amendment had not yet received sufficient ratifications for it to enter into force. The member states entitled to designate persons to serve on the board are elected by the assembly for three-year terms. WHO doctrine has it that persons serving on the board act in their individual capacities, not as representatives of their states, and that the board exercises "on behalf of the whole Health Assembly the powers designated to it by that body."[5] The distribution of formal powers between the World Health Assembly and the Executive Board is skewed somewhat in favor of the former. Most final decisions have to be made by the assembly, and the assembly alone can approve the budget. In many ways the Executive Board's mandate is to act as a steering committee for the assembly. The secretariat is headed by a director-general, who is appointed by the assembly on the nomination of the Executive Board. The conditions of his office are set by the assembly.

As envisaged in its constitution, WHO also has a highly developed regional structure. There are six regions: the Eastern Mediterranean Region, the Western Pacific Region, the Southeast Asia Region, the European Region, the African Region, and the American Region. Each regional organization consists of a regional committee and a regional office, headed by the regional director. In the American region, the Pan American Sanitary Bureau, in addition to performing its original functions, serves as the WHO regional office. The Directing Council of the Pan American Sanitary Organization—in 1958 the name was changed to Pan American Health Organization (PAHO)—serves as WHO's regional committee. By agreement with the Council or the Organization of American States (OAS), PAHO is also a specialized agency and the health arm of that body. Because of its historical development and special status, PAHO alone of WHO's regional organizations has its own regular budget, raised by assessments on member states, in addition to the funds that are assigned to it from WHO's budget. Although not a member of PAHO, Canada attends its meetings as an official observer.

The World Health Organization's evolution was marked by steady growth in the first years and has since experienced rapid growth. By 1950 WHO had 74 members. Eight years later this total had increased to 85, and in 1967 there were 126 members (two of these, the Byelorussian S.S.R. and the Ukrainian S.S.R., were inactive). The growth of WHO's staff and expenditures has followed a parallel pattern. In 1950 the WHO staff numbered 706; in 1958, 2,961; and in 1967, 4,367.[6] Similarly, WHO's total expenditures have risen from $9,219,913 in 1950 to $45,218,000 in 1958, and to $100,227,000 in 1967.[7]

As is frequently the case, these aggregate budgetary figures require some explanation. The funds expended by the World Health Organization come from a variety of sources. In the budgets of the late 1960s these sources were consolidated under four major headings: WHO's regular budget; technical assistance; Voluntary Fund for Health Promotion; and United Nations Children's Fund (UNICEF). The first category consisted mainly of funds raised by assessments on member states. The principal components of the second category were funds made available to the Pan American Health Organization and funds allocated to WHO from the United Nations Development Program. The third category consisted of funds voluntarily contributed to WHO and earmarked for special purposes, such as malaria eradication and the development of community water supply systems. UNICEF funds were those allocated by the UNICEF Executive Board for individual projects assisted jointly by UNICEF and WHO. Table 6.1 shows the proportional division among the various sources of funds administered directly or indirectly by WHO in 1967. As can be seen, in 1967 more than half of the funds administered by WHO came from the regular budget. This was not always the case. In the 1950s the regular budget usually accounted for about one-third of WHO's obligations. The proportion began to change in 1962.

Table 6.1

Sources of WHO Funds

Source of Funds	Percentage
Regular budget	51.04
Technical assistance	
UNDP	11.09
PAHO	
Regular budget	8.93
Voluntary funds	6.33
Funds in trust	2.30
Voluntary fund for health promotion	3.29
Amounts allocated by the UNICEF executive board	17.01
Total	99.99

Source: WHO, *Official Records,* no. 163, p. xxix.

The significance of the various sources of funds is that states make different contributions to each of them. For example, in 1967 the United States contributed 31.2 percent of WHO's regular budget, 66 percent of PAHO's regular budget, 37.3 percent of the UNDP funds, and 39.8 percent of UNICEF's funds.[8] More than 90 percent of the voluntarily contributed earmarked funds of WHO and PAHO have come from the United States.

As table 6.2 shows, the scale of assessments to support WHO's regular budget has maintained a relatively constant distribution among the three major groups of states. In terms of actual contributions, however, this table is somewhat misleading, for in 1950 none of the Socialist states participated in WHO and consequently none paid their assessments, nor did all of them participate in 1958 or 1967. The most interesting observation drawn from table 6.2 is that, even though the category labeled Other has come to constitute an increasing proportion of WHO's membership, its contribution to the regular budget has declined.

Table 6.2

Distribution of Assessed Income in WHO
(In Percentages)

	1950	1958	1967
Western	70.16	65.81	66.79
Socialist	10.33	18.45.	19.32
Other	19.51	15.74	13.89

Computations concerning the proportion of budgetary funds devoted to functions are difficult to make and require a number of arbitrary judgments. Even allowing for their rough quality, however, such figures clearly show WHO's emphasis on service activities. For instance, 91 percent of the funds at WHO's disposal in 1967 (including those from UNICEF) were expended on "operating" activities, that is, services to states either collectively (for example, epidemiological services and research) or individually in the form of technical assistance projects and fellowships. This percentage has remained relatively constant, except for a few early years when the organization was just getting under way and administrative expenses were a slightly larger proportion of the total. Similarly, the proportion of WHO's funds (again including those from UNICEF) expended at headquarters in Geneva vis-à-vis the proportion spent at the regional offices or in the field has also remained stable. In 1967 these proportions were 16 percent and 84 percent, respectively. Again, in the early years of WHO, headquarters absorbed a larger share of the budget. The high proportion of the budget spent away from headquarters demonstrates the emphasis that WHO puts on field activities, or services to individual states.

This discussion of budgetary data indicates that the growth of the organization has largely followed the path determined for it at its inception. The delegates at the International Health Conference wanted to create an organization whose principal purpose would be to provide services to member states, and that is the type of organization WHO has become.

Nevertheless, there have been significant turning points in WHO's history. Most of these marked advances, but some represented lost opportunities. The first significant date was 1947. An outbreak of cholera occurred in Egypt that year and underscored the crucial importance of completing the creation of WHO. Under the circumstances the Interim Commission of WHO provided emergency assistance. The second turning point was the completion of the agreement with the Pan American Sanitary Organization in 1949. This agreement committed the American states to pursue their collaborative activities in the health field within the framework of WHO.

Three important dates relate to WHO programs. In 1955 the World Health Assembly decided to undertake a malaria eradication program, and for the first time the organization mounted a large-scale campaign against a major disease. In 1966 the assembly confirmed

> that the role of WHO is to give Members technical advice, upon request, in the development of activities in family planning, as part of an organized health service, without impairing its normal preventive and curative functions.[9]

This reversed the position that the assembly had taken in 1952, when it refused to authorize a population program.

The final significant date is 1960. In that year thirteen newly independent states, mainly on the African continent, became members of WHO. Since then, with the progress of decolonization, there has been a steady stream of new members. This development has increased the ranks of the poor countries in the organization. It was also about 1960 that WHO's budget began to increase substantially. The two developments were not unrelated.

Decision Making: A Taxonomical Analysis

The decisional output of the World Health Organization has already been implicitly sketched in gross terms in our description of the functions, structure, and evolution of the organization. This broad outline will now be completed in more detail, before we proceed to analysis and explanation.

Representational Decisions

The basic emphasis on universality that prevailed when WHO's constitution was drafted has generally guided the agency's practice with respect to representational decisions. Among the United Nations' specialized agencies WHO's membership has been exceeded only by that of the International Telecommunication Union, the Universal Postal Union, and the World Meteorological Organization.

The Federal Republic of Germany, Italy, Japan, and Spain were all admitted to WHO in 1951 without controversy. In the late 1960s the most prominent nonmembers of WHO were the People's Republic of China, the German Democratic Republic, North Korea, and North Vietnam. Of these four, only the case of the People's Republic of China was debated regularly, and then only during the discussion of reports of the Credentials Committee. On these occasions several delegates would state their belief that the People's Republic of China should be represented in WHO, but they never went beyond that. And in the end, when the Credentials Committee reported having recommended the acceptance of, among others, the credentials of the delegates of the Republic of China (Taiwan), the committee's reports were always accepted, and without record votes.

Also in the late 1960s, the Republic of South Africa, though still officially a member, had ceased participating in the agency's activities. South Africa's de facto withdrawal was a direct response to the adoption of an amendment by the World Health Assembly in 1965 that empowered the assembly to suspend or expel a member if it "ignores the humanitarian principles and the objectives laid down in the Constitution, by deliberately practicing a policy of racial discrimination."[10] Even though it appears unlikely that the amendment will ever gain sufficient ratifications to become effective, its passage in the assembly achieved the objective sought by the sponsors of the move: the exclusion of South Africa, at least in the short run.

Earlier in WHO's history, other member states had refused to participate in its activities. In February 1949 the ministries of health of the USSR, Byelorussia, and the Ukraine informed the director-general that they were dissatisfied with the work of WHO and no longer considered themselves members of the organization. Prior to this, Soviet delegates had criticized WHO for devoting what they considered insufficient attention to the task of restoring the health services of the countries that had suffered German occupation. In 1947 Byelorussia, Poland, the Ukraine, and Yugoslavia received roughly one-third of the funds under the control of the Interim Commission of WHO. Subsequent decisions, though, made it clear that this proportion would rapidly decline. In the twelve months following the Soviet action in February 1949, Albania, Bulgaria, Czechoslovakia, Hungary, Poland, and Rumania also notified the director-general of their withdrawal. On each occasion, the World Health Assembly adopted a resolution urging the state to reconsider its position, and in 1954 the assembly made a further plea to these socialist countries to renew their participation.

When in the mid-1950s these socialist states indicated that they were interested in resuming active membership in WHO, one of the main issues that had to be settled was the status of their assessed contribution during the period of inactive membership. Technically, since there is no provision in WHO's constitution for withdrawal, these states were in arrears. Consequently they were not only subject to suspension of their voting privileges but ineligible to benefit from WHO's services. The assembly decided that these states need only make a token payment of 5 percent of the amount they were assessed each year that they were inactive; the total payment could be made in installments over a ten-year period. The general sentiment within WHO was that resumption of active membership should be made as easy as possible for the socialist countries. The United States had proposed the specific figure of 5 percent. Most of the socialist countries again began to participate actively in WHO in 1957, though Czechoslovakia waited until 1958, and Hungary until 1963. Byelorussia and the Ukraine have never resumed active membership.

Membership in WHO automatically entitles states to participate in the organization's regional activities; and states have been assigned to the region of their choice. Though this policy has created certain anomalies, serious difficulties have arisen in only two instances. In 1951 the Arab states announced that they would no longer sit in meetings of the Eastern

Mediterranean Committee if delegates from Israel were present. As a consequence, no meetings of that regional committee were held that year or in the two subsequent years. From 1954 through 1957 all of the states in the region met without Israel. Starting in 1958 the committee met in two subcommittees, one consisting of the Arab states and certain others, and one consisting of some of these same states and Israel.

In 1966, acting on a recommendation of the African Regional Committee, the assembly suspended the right of Portugal to participate in the meetings and activities of that committee. According to the resolution, this suspension would remain in effect until Portugal "furnished proof of its willingness to conform to the injunctions of the United Nations" concerning its territories in Africa. [12]

A second category of representational decisions consists of elections for offices. The most important of these concern the Executive Board, the director-general, and the regional directors. In addition, WHO has the usual elections for presiding officers of plenary and committee sessions and for rapporteurs. The organization's mode of conducting most of these elections could best be described as a system of carefully managed politics, designed to minimize open controversy and, some might argue, to maintain control within a core group.

Chronologically, the procedure starts at each assembly with the election of the Committee on Nominations. This committee consists of the same number of members as the Executive Board, and it is elected on the opening day of the assembly session. The outgoing president of the assembly nominates a list of candidates equal to the number to be elected, reflecting the same distribution among WHO's regions as that prevailing on the Executive Board (France, the USSR, the United Kingdom, and the United States are always included). Although additional nominations can be made from the floor of the assembly, this seldom occurs. The president's list has almost always been accepted.

The Committee on Nominations, once elected, proposes candidates for the offices of president and vice-president of the World Health Assembly, and those of chairmen of each of the assembly's main committees. Candidates for membership on the General Committee are proposed in the same way. By tradition the Committee on Nominations proposes only one candidate for each office, and almost without exception the committee's nominees are elected.

The General Committee consists of the president, the vice-presidents, the chairmen of the main committees, and a specified number of additional members. Through 1960 these additional members were sufficient to make the total fifteen; after 1960 the total was twenty. In addition to its functions relating to the management of the assembly's business, the committee plays a central role in the election of the Executive Board. As will be recalled, the assembly elects states, which then become eligible to designate individuals to serve on the board. The General Committee considers which states are willing to stand for election, and then it prepares a list for submission to the assembly. The list always contains 50 percent more names than the number of vacancies: nine names were presented when six were to be elected, and twelve when eight were to be elected. However, the committee "recommends" a group drawn from the original list and comprising precisely the same number of names as there are vacancies. By custom, the states that are not recommended withdraw. The assembly can vote only for states on the list submitted by the General Committee. Among other consequences, this system means that the distribution of the members of the Executive Board among WHO's regions is decided by the General Committee. The committee has gradually adjusted this distribution as WHO's membership has increased, so that the Executive Board roughly reflects the total membership. Parenthetically, it should be noted that the tradition has developed that no state—not even France, the USSR, the United Kingdom, or the United States—will stand for reelection to the board immediately on the expiration of a term in office. The four leading states always allow a year to lapse after the expiration of a term on the Executive Board before offering their candidature again. This custom has been ignored only once, by the United Kingdom in the early 1950s.

Table 6.3 shows the composition of the Executive Board during 1950, 1958, and 1967, divided into the Western, Socialist, and Other states categories. In terms of the board's activities, the 1950 figure for Socialist

Table 6.3

Composition of WHO's Executive Board
(By National Origin)

	1950		1958		1967	
	Number	Percentage	Number	Percentage	Number	Percentage
Western	8	44.44	7	38.88	5	20.83
Socialist	2	11.11	1	5.56	3	12.50
Other	8	44.44	10	55.56	16	66.67

representation is misleading, since of the two Socialist states entitled to designate members of the board, Poland and Yugoslavia, only the latter did so. The present purpose, however, is to show the outcome of WHO's electoral processes, and table 6.3 does that accurately. The most notable trend is, of course, the increased representation of states in the Other category. Given the nature of the system, this was not something these states have had to fight openly to achieve; rather it was the consequence of decisions taken within the General Committee.

The mode of choosing WHO's director-general follows a similar pattern. The assembly "appoints" the director-general on the nomination of the Executive Board; that is, the board presents a name that the assembly then

accepts. Two directors-general have been chosen in this manner, Dr. Brock
Chisholm, who was elected in 1948, and Dr. Marcolino G. Candau, who was
elected in 1953 and reappointed in 1958, 1963, and 1968. The meetings of
the Executive Board and the World Health Assembly to consider the
appointment of the director-general are private. However, candidates other
than the actual nominee could have been seriously considered only in 1948
and 1953.

Regional directors, the only elected officials of the WHO secretariat other
than the director-general, are appointed by the Executive Board "in
agreement with the regional committee."[13] In practice this means that the
board accepts the nomination of the regional committee. The director-
general always attends meetings of regional committees when nominations
of regional directors are being considered. Some of the nominations in
regional committees have been hotly contested. Except for the African
region during the period before the onrush of independence on that
continent, regional directors have always been nationals of states within the
region. Some of them have even been nationals of the state in which the
regional office is located.

The representational decisions described here have been routine decisions
that recur at regular intervals. In addition, WHO has occasionally taken
extraordinary—albeit negative—decisions of a representational character. In
1968 fourteen states (Argentina, Australia, Brazil, Canada, France, Italy,
Mexico, New Zealand, Nigeria, Panama, the Philippines, the United Kingdom, the United States, and West Germany) proposed a series of constitutional amendments whose principal provisions included biennial rather than
annual assembly sessions, biennial programming and budgeting, and a change
in the status of members of the Executive Board from that of individuals to
that of governmental representatives. In the debate many delegates alleged
that these amendments were designed to increase the influence in WHO of
the principal contributors to the budget. The proposed amendments gained
so little support that they were not even put to the vote. Indeed, some of the
states that at first asked to be included among the cosponsors subsequently
changed their view and asked to retract their names; and in the end the
original sponsors asked to have their proposals withdrawn. Similar attempts
earlier in WHO's history to shift the assembly to biennial sessions and to
change the nature of representation on the Executive Board have also failed.
Given this record, the possibility of major structural change in the World
Health Organization through constitutional amendment seems remote.

Symbolic Decisions

Symbolic decisions are rare in WHO. When they are taken, considerable
effort is usually expended by secretariat personnel and a number of
governmental representatives to minimize the salience accorded the issue and
the controversy associated with it. The assembly has adopted resolutions on

the radiation resulting from the testing of nuclear weapons, the epidemiological situation in Vietnam, and the health of Palestinian refugees in Israeli-occupied territories. The general subjects involved in these resolutions were among the most controversial in world politics since the end of World War II. The three topics (the only ones of this nature ever considered by the assembly) were originally introduced in WHO respectively by delegates of the United Arab Republic, the USSR, and Iraq. While these delegates sought the adoption of hortatory statements supporting their point of view, the resolutions that were ultimately adopted were drafted in technical terms, and in each instance they asked for studies by the secretariat. In all, the resolutions on these topics that have been successfully proposed in the World Health Assembly constitute less than 1 percent of the total adopted by that body.

Programmatic Decisions

WHO's main function is providing services to member governments; its forum functions are very minor. This basic programmatic decision was made by the assembled delegates in the International Health Conference when WHO was established, and it has not been reconsidered.

Another basic programmatic decision was taken in 1949 when the World Health Assembly, acting on a recommendation of the Executive Board, enunciated the policy that WHO should not normally provide medical supplies to recipients; its efforts should be concentrated on providing advisory assistance.[14] (Subsequently this statement was clarified to make clear that it was not intended to exclude supplies and equipment used for training and demonstration.) The communist countries immediately objected to this decision, and it may have been a factor in their subsequent withdrawal from the organization. On the other hand, the United States was insistent that WHO should not ordinarily provide medical supplies. The fear that the agency might take such action, and particularly that it might provide supplies for the Soviet Union, was one of the reasons for the delay in the United States ratification of WHO's constitution and was partly responsible for congressional insistence on setting an absolute ceiling on the United States contribution to the budget.[15]

The question of the provision of medical supplies was not reopened until the late 1960s. At that time the initiative came from delegates from African countries. In 1967 and 1968, when WHO's budgets were several times larger than those of two decades earlier, the World Health Assembly merely decided that the question of furnishing medical supplies might be considered, but no positive action was taken.[16]

These two basic programmatic decisions have provided a framework within which all others have been taken. The other decisions concern four broad issues that are separable but interrelated:

1. the level of WHO's activities

2. the division between services given to states collectively and individually.

3. the division of the services given to states individually among WHO's
six geographic regions

4. the emphasis to be given to various substantive areas

For any particular year all of these issues are more or less settled in WHO's
budget for that year.

As has been pointed out, WHO's budget comprises funds coming from a
variety of sources. The principal components are: the regular budget,
voluntary contributions, funds under the control of the Pan American
Health Organization, funds allocated to WHO by the United Nations
Development Program, and funds allocated by the UNICEF Executive Board
to projects jointly administered by WHO and UNICEF. WHO's program
therefore is shaped by the decisions about each of these sources of funds.
Decisions involving UNDP and UNICEF are made within political systems
that are different from that of WHO, although the systems partially overlap.
An important and distinctive aspect of the relationship between UNICEF
and WHO is that the former cannot spend money for health purposes
without the latter's technical approval. Finally, the WHO system itself is
decentralized, and regional offices play a substantial role in the formulation
of the budget.[17]   The director-general is in a strategic position because he is
able to serve as the connecting link among the various locales where
decisions relating to WHO's budget are made. The budget document he
prepares is called the Integrated International Health Program and includes
activities financed from all of the various sources. However they may be
financed, all WHO programs are administered in the same manner.

WHO's regular budget has almost always been the largest single component in the Integrated International Health Program. Thus, decisions
about it vitally affect the overall level of WHO's activities. Since the
director-general takes the lead in formulating the budget, suggesting targets
for each segment of the organization, it is on his initiative that new figures
and thus a new level of activity are proposed. The budget that he compiles is
submitted to the Executive Board, which can comment on it but not alter it,
and then to the World Health Assembly. Approval of the budget requires a
two-thirds majority vote of members present and voting in the assembly. In
most years WHO's regular budget has increased by about 10 percent, but in
each of four years, 1958 and 1961 through 1963, the budget was more than
20 percent greater than that of the preceding year. And in 1964, 1965, and
1966 the increase was close to 15 percent. Often, particularly in the late
1960s, the budget has been adopted despite opposition from the states that
are the major contributors—the United States, the United Kingdom, France,
West Germany, Canada, Japan, and Italy. Nevertheless, starting in 1967 the
assembly has been willing to accept the notion advanced by these states that

each year it should adopt an order of magnitude, expressed as a percentage of the present budget, to guide the director-general in formulating his proposals concerning the increase in the following year's budget. During debates on budgetary increases some of the major contributors opposing the increases have also made veiled threats that they might reconsider their position toward WHO.

WHO has somewhat contradictory doctrines concerning the other three broad programmatic issues that it must deal with. First, there is the notion that the World Health Assembly should establish global priorities and long-term work programs, and the assembly has periodically taken such action. A second doctrine is that the regional decentralization that was enshrined in the constitution should be an important consideration in the formulation of the budget. In keeping with this doctrine, regional budgets are approved by regional committees before they are submitted to the director-general for inclusion in the program and in budget proposals that he submits to the assembly. A final WHO doctrine affecting programmatic issues is that the organization should conduct projects only when governments request them; it should not force projects on any government.

Table 6.4 shows how the funds available to WHO in 1967 were allocated, exclusive of those that UNICEF provided for support to joint UNICEF-WHO projects. The emphasis on services to individual governments is easily visible; some 70 percent of the funds went for this purpose. The favored position of states in the PAHO region, largely a consequence of the fact that PAHO has its own budget, is also apparent.

Given the fact that the bulk of WHO's funds are devoted to services rendered to individual states or to small groups of states in the form of projects and that over 70 percent of these projects are of more than one year's duration, changes in programmatic emphases are made incrementally. Substantial changes are infrequent. Such changes do occur, however. In 1958 the African region received about 10 percent of all the funds devoted to services to individual governments, and earlier its share was even less. The funds allocated to Africa rose sharply in the period immediately following 1958. In this same period, when a large number of African states gained their independence, the most substantial increases ever made in WHO's budget were recorded, and the relative shares allocated in the American and European regions declined.

Among the various fields of activity, work concerning malaria has always been stressed, receiving from the outset about 10 percent of the funds devoted to services. The funds devoted to this problem increased even more, both relatively and absolutely after the Malaria Eradication Special Account was established in 1955 with a special contribution from the United States. The research program really began in 1958, again after a special voluntary contribution from the United States. In 1966 and 1969 the United States again made voluntary contributions, resulting respectively in larger alloca-

Table 6.4

Summary of WHO Program, 1967

	Amount Allocated	Percentage of Total
1. Policy-making organs	$ 798,845	0.95
2. Central administration	3,257,811	3.88
3. Operational activities	59,266,202	70.50
a. Services and assistance to governments		
African Region	$11,621,380	19.61%
American Region	20,536,013	34.65
Southeast Asian Region	7,409,199	12.50
European Region	3,740,041	6.31
Eastern Mediterranean Region	7,815,311	13.19
Western Pacific Region	5,077,808	8.57
Interregional activities	3,066,444	5.17
Total	59,266,202	100.00
b. Worldwide services	11,025,419	13.12
c. Assistance to research	7,233,028	8.60
d. Coordination, evaluation, and collaboration with other organizations	1,102,905	1.31
4. Other provisions	1,381,600	1.64
Total	$84,065,810	100.00

Source: WHO Doc. EB41/27.

tions to programs relating to smallpox and family planning. The relatively greater attention devoted to environmental sanitation and particularly to water supplies in the late 1960s has been made possible through an influx of UNDP funds. Although the director-general alone hardly had the power to bring about any of these developments, he was in a position to stimulate them; and it would have been difficult for these projects to make any headway if he had opposed them. When less substantial changes in programmatic emphases have been involved, his role has been even more important; for in framing budget proposals he is always a controller and can also be an initiator and a vetoer. If he wants to insert a new program—for example, an attack on a particular disease—he can do this. He can also veto initiatives of staff members. Once an initiative is launched, a careful effort must be mounted to form a consensus. Many such efforts involve a meeting of a committee of experts, and such meetings culminate in an assembly resolution. The director-general's role in this process of consensus building is crucial.

Operational Decisions

Thus far, the analysis of decision making concerning the Integrated Health Program has been at the macro level. It is also possible to view the program as an aggregation of individual projects. If one includes among such projects WHO's worldwide services and assistance to research as well as its field activities, they comprise more than 90 percent of the total program. On a micro level countless decisions have to be made about such questions as which countries get certain projects and which technical services are supported at each level. Questions in the latter, detailed category involve about 20 percent of the budget and are mainly the concern of headquarters. They tend to be settled among the director-general and his immediate subordinates.

The situation with respect to projects for countries singly or intercountry projects, which together account for about 70 percent of the budget, is more complicated. Countries submit requests to WHO. Of course they are likely to ask only for things that WHO provides, and the views of the WHO country representative may have a substantial effect on their request. These requests from countries are forwarded to regional offices, and the regional director bases the regional budget on them, within the framework of the guidelines established by the director-general. This regional budget is then considered and approved by the regional committee before it is forwarded to the director-general, who in turn incorporates it in the general budget.

Some choices must be made in these processes; for, on paper at least, there are always more projects than WHO's funds can support. Choices appear to be made at three crucial points: when the country's request or program is finally formulated, when the regional director composes his budget, and when the director-general composes his. Using the final budget as a base point for generalizations about the entire process, certain rules seem usually to have been observed with respect to allocations to countries within regions. First, the larger the country's population, the larger its allocation is. (In a graph showing the two sets of figures, however, the allocation curve would be much flatter.) Second, the fewer physicians a country has, the larger its allocation. Decisions that cannot be explained by the first rule can generally be accounted for by the second. When neither explanation applies, it is almost always because unusual political circumstances prevailed in the country concerned. To state these rules is not to minimize the importance of individual choices, but merely to indicate that certain broad constraints apparently affect these choices and that the ability of WHO to discriminate among countries other than on the basis of gross, open criteria is limited.

Rule-Creating and Supervisory Decisions

Three types of rule-creating decisions are taken within WHO. The most formal are regulations. These are adopted by the World Health Assembly and are binding on all member states in all respects, unless a member specifically rejects them or lodges reservations within a specified period. The assembly has adopted only two regulations: the International Sanitary Regulations (superseded on 1 January 1971 by the International Health Regulations) and the Regulations on the Nomenclature and Classification of Diseases and Causes of Death. Both of these have been revised periodically, and in each case the assembly has acted on the recommendations of a group of experts.

A second type of rule-creating decision takes the form of reports by expert committees and scientific groups. These are adopted exclusively on the authority of the committee itself. The director-general and the Executive Board might review a report before it was published, but they could not alter it. Many of these reports suggest ways in which particular health problems should be handled; sometimes they discuss treatments for specific diseases, sometimes more general topics. WHO's technical assistance personnel look to the reports of expert committees for guidance, as do persons in the field of health throughout the world, whatever their capacity.

Finally, the assembly occasionally adopts hortatory resolutions: for example, a resolution urging member states to enforce the application of ethical and scientific criteria for pharmaceutical advertising. Whatever the origin of the first resolution on a topic, specific principles are usually formulated by the secretariat or an expert group and approved by the assembly.

No decisions are taken in WHO that could be classified as rule-supervisory decisions. Compliance with WHO rules is a matter left strictly to the member states. There have been some proposals that WHO should provide assistance to member states in rule supervision, but no concrete steps have been taken in this direction. Some observers consider WHO's lack of enforcement power the organization's most serious weakness.

Boundary Decisions

Boundary decisions have arisen frequently in WHO. Health is a pervasive subject in any case, and the definition embodied in WHO's constitution, on which the organization's mandate is based, is the broadest possible. In addition, WHO's extensive field activities constantly bring it into close contact with other organizations.

Like other agencies in the United Nations system, WHO has negotiated formal agreements with agencies whose activities bring them into frequent contact with WHO. Such agreements delimit spheres of competence and define WHO's relationships with the Pan American Health Organization (the agreement formed the basis for PAHO's becoming a part of WHO), the United Nations, the International Labor Organization, the Food and Agriculture Organization, the United Nations Educational, Scientific and Cultural Organization, and the International Atomic Energy Agency. Each of these agreements was negotiated by WHO's secretariat and ultimately approved by the assembly. For some of them, selected members of the Executive Board were drawn into the negotiating process as advisers to the secretariat. In the cases of the United Nations Children's Fund and the United Nations Development Program, resolutions adopted by the assembly and the appropriate organs in the other organizations provide a framework for relationships and serve the same functions as the more formal agreements.

More important for the way things actually work out than these broad statements, though, are a vast number of specific decisions taken in the context of particular projects. The secretariat has challenged the plans and efforts of other organizations, and particularly of the IAEA, to undertake activities in fields that it considered to be within WHO's sphere of competence. A frequent mode of solving such controversies has been the appointment of joint committees, often composed of staff members of the two organizations. Within these bodies WHO representatives have vigorously sought to preserve what they felt to be the integrity of their organization. Examples are the ILO/WHO Committee on Occupational Health, the Joint FAO/WHO Expert Committee on Nutrition, and the IAEA/WHO Expert Committee on Medical Radiation Physics. Since 1964 WHO and IAEA have also maintained permanent liaison officers at each other's headquarters. Controversies about spheres of competence occurred less frequently after 1965, perhaps because lines of demarcation had by then been firmly drawn. The change may also have been related to the fact that the budgets of all of the United Nations agencies were vastly increased by that time and were substantial in absolute terms; many of the agencies had all of the technical assistance work they could handle.

Somewhat special boundary problems arise in the cases of UNICEF and the UNDP. These two organizations provide more than one-quarter of the funds available to the Integrated International Health Program. From the outset UNICEF and WHO agreed that they would engage in joint projects, with UNICEF furnishing the supplies and WHO the technical assistance. Broad policy questions are resolved by the Joint Committee on Health Policy, which consists of an equal number of representatives of the two organizations. More detailed questions are settled when UNICEF's area representatives and WHO's country representatives must agree on recommendations concerning the support of projects.

A central issue between WHO and UNDP is the extent to which UNDP's resident representatives will have jurisdiction over WHO projects that are financed by non-UNDP funds. WHO has staunchly asserted its independence in this matter, and WHO's country representatives have acted accordingly. A related but broader issue concerns the determination of what proportion of development funds channeled through the United Nations system should go through the UNDP and what proportion through individual agencies such as WHO. The director-general of WHO has argued for substantial increases in WHO's budget so that the organization would not become, in his view, excessively dependent on UNDP funds to support the program; and he has been supported by several government delegates as well as by the secretariat. The fact that WHO's regular budget has come to account for an increasing share of the Integrated International Health Program demonstrates his success.

Actors and Their Sources of Influence

Explanations for patterns of decision making and influence may be sought first by considering those who participate directly in WHO's activities or, in more technical terms, on the level of the participant subsystem. The principal actors in WHO are: governmental representatives, WHO officials and staff members, experts serving in an individual capacity, and officials of certain other international organizations, namely UNICEF and the UNDP. Employees of the mass media have never participated directly in WHO; and although nongovernmental organizations such as the International Hospital Federation, the International Society of Cardiology, and the World Federation for Mental Health have an official relationship with WHO and regularly send observers to its meetings, the part that they play in the organization's activities is generally minor. The discussion here will focus on the principal actors and analyze their characteristics, sources of influence, attitudes, and alignments.

Representatives of National Governments

Governments appoint representatives to the World Health Assembly and to regional committees. In addition, those governments that have been chosen by the assembly for this purpose designate individuals to serve on the Executive Board. Individuals serving in the first two capacities clearly fall within the definition of governmental representatives. Members of the Executive Board, however, have a more ambiguous status.

Almost without exception members of the Executive Board are governmental officials, but according to WHO's constitution they exercise their powers "on behalf of the whole Health Assembly." [18] The practical consequences of this vary with time, individuals, states, and issues. Some members clearly act as instructed representatives. On the other hand, there have been occasions when members of the board from the United States have taken one position when they acted in that capacity and another when they later served as official delegates to the assembly. Board members from developed Western countries seem to have the greatest latitude in arriving at their own policy positions. If nothing else, their independent status on the board is probably a factor of strength for them when they participate in country subsystems arguing for particular courses favored by health specialists. That this status makes some difference was evidenced by the fact that several Western countries sought, albeit unsuccessfully, to alter it by constitutional amendment. Although members of the Executive Board will be considered in this section as governmental representatives, their special status must constantly be kept in mind.

Governmental representatives in the World Health Organization are predominantly technical specialists. This can be seen in table 6.5. In this table individuals from member states and associate member states attending three WHO meetings in an official capacity—the January 1967 session of the Executive Board; the Twentieth World Health Assembly, which met in May 1967; and the Fifteenth Session of the Regional Committee for Africa, which met in September 1965—have been divided into three categories: medical doctors, other persons employed by functional ministries such as ministries of health or social welfare, and other persons employed by foreign ministries. Those in the last category, who have been listed as diplomats, constitute one-quarter or less of the governmental representatives at any of the meetings; medical doctors constitute at least 65 percent. If the number of medical doctors and the number of those on staffs of functional ministries are lumped together, they constitute three-quarters or more of the total number of representatives. Almost without exception, heads of delegations are either medical doctors or members of functional ministries, usually the minister or the deputy minister.

Medical doctors, the dominant category among governmental representatives to WHO, have common professional bonds. Medicine has certain common global standards; furthermore, given the nature of medical training, a large number of the representatives have had at least a portion of their professional preparation in similar if not the same institutions. Meetings of the World Health Assembly and regional committees are structured to emphasize a professional atmosphere. Time is allocated at each meeting for discussion of a specific technical subject.

Governmental representatives also tend to have lengthy and multiple associations with WHO. Individuals who have only one association with WHO are rare. Some people are delegates both to their regional committee

Table 6.5

Distribution of Governmental Representatives in WHO Meetings

	Medical Doctors		Functional Ministry Staff		Diplomats		Total	
	Number	Percentage	Number	Percentage	Number	Percentage	Number	Percentage
Executive Board (January 1967)	31	70.46	2	4.54	11	25.00	44	100
World Health Assembly (May 1967)	312	65.41	69	14.46	96	20.13	477	100
Regional Committee for Africa (September 1965)	46	80.70	9	15.79	2	3.51	57	100

and to the assembly, and some may serve on the Executive Board as well. In addition, if a delegate's country receives assistance from WHO, he may have been the one responsible for going over the plan for the coming year with the WHO country representative and approving it. There are also ways in which governmental representatives, as individuals, may have contacts with WHO. Some serve on the organization's numerous expert committees. Some may have been members of the secretariat at an earlier period in their careers; and those from poorer countries may have had a WHO fellowship or worked as a counterpart in a WHO project. One would expect that in WHO, as in most such cases, association with an organization would generally bring attachment to it.

The existing evidence on how governmental policies about WHO are determined suggests that ministries of health or social welfare and foreign ministries are jointly involved, in varying combinations of strength. In general, ministries of health are very protective of their position as the dominant voice in what they consider to be technical issues. Since these ministries almost without exception provide the officials who head the delegations, they are in a strategic position to enforce their views. Indeed, since the head of the delegation might well be the minister of health, he might even determine policy on the spot. Foreign ministries, however, generally insist on having their way on matters like the membership of Communist China and the Republic of South Africa. In the case of most Western countries foreign ministries are also responsible for seeing that policies relating to basic budgetary matters are carried out.

The characteristics of governmental representatives in WHO—the fact that they are predominantly professionals in the health field, their lengthy and multiple association with the organization, and their formal ties to functional ministries in their own countries—are important in shaping decision making in the agency. They explain the slight attention given to symbolic issues and the low-keyed manner in which such issues are treated. They also have an important bearing on the way in which representational issues are settled. The type of "managed politics" that prevails could only occur among a group sharing the same basic assumptions, accepting a commitment to common goals, and working in a spirit of trust. The professional character of governmental representatives in WHO also provides a built-in dynamism making for constantly increasing budgets: given their professional beliefs and commitments to the preservation of human life, few of the delegates could feel that the organization was doing enough and that its activities should not increase.

Among governmental representatives, influence depends both on their positions and on their individual characteristics. The representatives of certain states, particularly the United States, the Soviet Union, France, and the United Kingdom, have been influential regardless of which individuals occupied these positions. All participants in the organization's political processes are aware that these states and a few others provide the major budgetary support. These countries are also known to have high standards of health care. Furthermore, they tend to have the largest delegations at World Health Assemblies. A delegate with a large supporting staff can do many more things, such as establishing contacts with other delegations, than his less-equipped colleagues. In addition the United States and the USSR have had biomedical attachés permanently stationed in Geneva. The knowledge these attachés have gained through continuous contacts with the organization is a valuable resource for American and Soviet delegates.

Even though almost anyone serving as a delegate of a leading state would be influential, the people appointed to these positions almost invariably could command influence in their own right because of their substantial professional accomplishments.

The influence of delegates from other states depends largely on their personal qualities. Among the several sources of power, the most important in WHO are long association with the organization, professional accomplishments, and, especially for delegates from poorer countries, the ability to organize others and mobilize voting support.

The Executive Head

The World Health Organization has had two directors-general: a Canadian, Dr. Brock Chisholm, who served from 1948 through 1953, and a Brazilian, Dr. Marcolino Gomes Candau, who was first elected in 1953 and then reelected three times for five-year terms in 1958, 1963, and 1968. The two men have several things in common. Both received part of their education in the United States; both attained high positions in their national governments. Furthermore, both had served in WHO prior to their election as director-general. Dr. Chisholm was rapporteur for the Preparatory Committee for the International Health Conference. He was also Canada's delegate to that conference and the executive-secretary of the Interim Commission of WHO. Dr. Candau became the director of WHO's Division of Public Health Services in 1950, and the following year he was chosen to be assistant director-general in charge of the Department of Advisory Services. In 1952 he became the assistant director of the Pan American Sanitary Bureau, the regional office of WHO for the Americas. Both men had also demonstrated—beyond their professional talents—an energetic drive and important political skills.

In any organization the executive head is an important official, but the director-general is in an especially significant and influential position in WHO; and both Dr. Chisholm and Dr. Candau played a large part in making this so. Each contributed significantly to defining the powers and role of the director-general. WHO's regional structures were created during Dr. Chisholm's term of office. Throughout that process he firmly and successfully insisted that the organization should not become completely fragmented and that procedures to ensure cohesion should accompany those favoring decentralization. Thanks to his efforts WHO has uniform personnel and financial policies. Staff members can serve in various regions, and in fact WHO has a plan for rotating staff, especially in the administrative and financial services. Only one regional organization, PAHO, has an independent budget. As WHO has developed, backstopping and coordinating the organization's field activities have become the principal functions of the regional offices, which have not been allowed to gain independent policy-making powers.

WHO's greatest growth occurred when Dr. Candau was the director-general. Like his predecessor Candau fought to preserve the cohesion of the organization, though this time the challenge was expansion rather than regionalization. Through 1959 WHO's headquarters secretariat was organized into three broad departments: advisory services, central technical services, and administration and finance. At Dr. Candau's initiative the headquarters secretariat was reorganized starting in 1960. No longer was there a clear division between field and central services; rather, elements of the two were grouped together in functionally oriented divisions. This system has prevailed since then, ensuring the director-general's control over the secretariat.

Control over the secretariat is one of the important assets attached to the position of director-general. The regional directors are the only other elected secretariat officials. The director-general has ultimate authority over all other appointments, including appointments to the posts of deputy director-general, assistant directors-general, and directors of health services in the regional offices, who are immediately below the directors in the regional hierarchies. Especially with regard to these positions, his responsibility is direct as well as ultimate. The term of office of the regional directors, the deputy director-general, and the assistant directors-general cannot exceed five years.

Unlike many international secretariats, WHO's secretariat does not consist chiefly of personnel with permanent contracts. At an early stage in the organization's development, it was decided that to give most professional personnel permanent contracts might make it more difficult to keep the scientific proficiency of the organization at a high level. As staff members they would be deeply involved in administrative work to the detriment of their professional skills; therefore, they should not remain too long. This policy prevails in de jure though not completely in de facto terms. Over the years, roughly 20 percent of the professional personnel at headquarters and regional offices have had permanent contracts; for those working on projects the proportion was 5 percent. On the other hand, in 1969, of the total professional staff 29 percent had served more than five years and 23 percent more than ten years. An incidental effect of this personnel system is to strengthen the director-general's authority over the secretariat.

The director-general also makes all appointments to WHO's expert advisory panels and committees. These committees play a crucial role in WHO's substantive activities; but it is interesting to note that many of their members have multiple roles in the organization and serve on other occasions as governmental representatives. In fact, in 1950 the Executive Board adopted a resolution requesting that the director-general appoint board members to expert committees only in extraordinary circumstances.[19] This is not to impugn the choices that have been made by the directors-general, for the supply of highly qualified personnel is limited, but merely to draw attention to the interlacing of various roles in the organization.

Another source of strength in the office of the director-general is its central role in the budgetary process. The director-general initiates the process of formulating WHO's budget and establishes guidelines at this stage. Later he compiles the proposals of the headquarters staff and the regional offices. At both stages he has opportunities to make important judgments about allocations among functions and regions. The formal position of the director-general makes him an initiator, controller, and vetoer as far as programmatic decisions are concerned.

Finally, the distribution of powers between the World Health Assembly and the Executive Board as well as the composition of the latter strengthens the director-general's position in WHO. As will be recalled, the Executive Board can comment on the director-general's budget, but it cannot alter it, and in fact the board seldom recommends significant changes in the director-general's proposed budget. The assembly has ultimate budgetary power. The assembly has always been somewhat too unwieldy to exercise tight budgetary control; and since 1960 the states from Africa, Asia, and Latin America, the principal recipients of WHO assistance, have constituted by themselves the two-thirds majority required to adopt the budget. The manner in which the Executive Board is chosen assures that its members will go no further than friendly criticism of the director-general and that they will share his goals. Indeed, two members of the board always represent the board at the assembly, and when the board has recommended the director-general's budget they become strong advocates of it there.

Both of the directors-general have also had personal traits that have been important sources of strength. Some have already been mentioned. Beyond these, both men had the respect of the United States public health community, a vital asset since the United States has provided the largest budgetary support. Because he is a national of a developing country, Dr. Candau has been in an excellent position to work with the developing countries who hold the majority in the assembly. Both men have been committed to the organization and to its growth. Dr. Candau has presided over WHO with a fierce determination to protect the autonomy and the integrity of the organization and to advance its goals. Though it would be impossible to prove in any rigorous manner, his leadership certainly appears to have given vital impetus to the organization's growth.

Other WHO Officials and Staff Members

Although no other members of WHO's staff have rivaled the director-general, some have had important influence. At headquarters two individuals have stood out: Dr. Pierre Dorolle of France, who has served as deputy director-general, and Milton P. Siegel, an American, who was an assistant director-general. Siegel held his position from the time the WHO secretariat was created until his retirement in 1971, and Dr. Dorelle's tenure has lasted since 1950, when he joined the secretariat. By virtue of their long associations with the organization and their personal qualities each gained substantial influence. Dr. Dorolle has regarded himself as the director-general's alter ego. A quiet man, he has never challenged the director-general; but there can be no doubt that he has been important in the organization's inner councils. Siegel was in charge of the administrative and financial aspects of WHO from the outset. He introduced American administrative practices into the organization and deserves much of the credit for WHO's reputation for being a well-run agency. A masterful tactician, he was an exceedingly useful aide to the director-general in encounters with the Executive Board and the assembly.

Whoever the occupant is, the post of regional director is important. All communications from the field must pass through the appropriate regional office; they cannot be sent directly to WHO headquarters in Geneva. Thus the regional director occupies a crucial point in the organization's communications network. Acting on behalf of the director-general, regional directors have authority over all appointments of field personnel in their region. (Actual selection is made by a selection committee composed of the senior personnel in the regional office.) The regional director also compiles the budget for the region on the basis of the various countries' requests, and this budget is then reviewed by the regional committee. The regional director is in a strategic position in the budgetary process, but various constraints limit the freedom of all participants. The regional director owes his election to the regional committee and is thus unlikely to take action that would alienate its members. Each of the members of the regional committee has his own country's program to be concerned about; none of them is therefore likely to launch criticisms that might provoke retaliatory action from his fellow members. These constraints serve as pressures toward some variant of a fair-share system. They explain why, within regions, allocations to countries generally vary directly with population and inversely with the number of physicians. Nonetheless, regional directors clearly are controllers with respect to operational decisions.

Country representatives of WHO are also important in their own areas. They have general administrative authority over the WHO personnel in the country, and they usually have an office in the ministry of health, in close physical proximity to the minister. They interact frequently with local officials and play a vital part in shaping the country's request or program for the coming year. In this way country representatives can become initiators with respect to operational decisions and, in a cumulative sense, with respect to programmatic decisions.

Individuals

Once a person is chosen to serve on an expert advisory panel for WHO, he can be an important force in the organization's work. In 1967 there were forty-three such subject-oriented panels, with a total membership of 2,507 experts. Members of expert advisory panels contribute technical information by correspondence or in the form of reports on developments within their own fields. Expert committees and less formal scientific groups are convened to consider specific topics. They are appointed by the director-general from among the members of expert advisory panels. There were eighteen meetings of expert committees and fourteen scientific group meetings during 1967. Until 1960, the Executive Board's authorization was required before the report of an expert committee could be published; in 1960, to avoid delay, the director-general was given this power. He had always had authority over the publication of less formal documents. The report of an expert committee may not be altered without that committee's consent.[20] As has already been pointed out, these reports are WHO's most frequently utilized method of rule creation. They serve as guides for WHO's personnel and health workers generally. Occasionally, expert committees can even take initiatives in a programmatic sense. For example, WHO's expanded program in environmental health followed chronologically and substantively the conclusions and recommendations of an expert committee. Expert committees deal with technical issues and are composed of highly qualified individuals. Within expert committees, besides the usual qualities that make an individual effective in small groups, the most important attribute is technical competence. Decisions in these bodies, almost without exception, are made in an analytical manner. "Purely scientific questions" cannot be submitted to a vote; if agreement cannot be reached, divergent opinions are reported.

Representatives of Other International Organizations

Representatives of two other international bodies, UNICEF and the UNDP, play an important role in operational decisions in WHO. In a cumulative sense they may also be influential in programmatic decisions. Since their concurrence is necessary to gain financial support for certain projects, UNICEF area representatives and UNDP resident representatives are controllers and possibly vetoers. Conceivably, they could become initiators by suggesting projects, but this would have to be done subtly through local officials or WHO personnel.

Organizational Ideology

That there is an organizational ideology in WHO and that it is important in the organization's political processes should already be apparent. The goal specified by this ideology is clearly stated in the constitution: "the attainment by all peoples of the highest possible level of health." WHO's approach to this maximalist position toward health care is primarily preventive rather than curative. Beyond this, the specific subgoals in WHO's ideology tend to parallel those prevalent in the public health doctrines proclaimed and practiced in the United States, the United Kingdom, and the Soviet Union. The emphasis on campaigns against specific diseases, such as malaria, was drawn from the historical experience of the United States Public Health Service. Although the impact of the British and Soviet experiences has not been as notable, it has nevertheless been substantial. However, issues relating to the organization of health care services —particularly socialized medicine—have hardly been broached in WHO; this is in large measure a consequence of the United States' early insistence that such issues should not be considered in the organization.

A commitment to the broad goal enshrined in WHO's constitution almost inevitably carries with it a commitment to steadily increasing budgets for the organization. Considering the magnitude of the world's health needs, those firmly dedicated to its purposes never feel that WHO is doing enough. There is thus in the organizational ideology held by many WHO participants an almost insatiable demand for additional resources.

Furthermore, many of the participants in WHO seem to regard health as an absolute value; they feel uneasy about weighing the effects of resources devoted to health measures against the effects of utilizing those same resources for some other purpose. When pressed on this issue, such people will make the quite valid point that the benefits gained from better health are very hard to compare with those gained from a new productive facility or increased vocational training, for example, since the consequences of these latter efforts can be measured more easily in economic terms. Fundamentally the training and life-long commitment to health work of these individuals make it difficult for them to agree that in aggregate terms a country might reap advantages from giving priority to projects that would result in more direct economic benefits than those likely to result from health projects. These feelings are responsible for the widespread agreement in WHO that the organization should not become overly dependent on UNDP funds. They also have had something to do with the strained relations that have sometimes existed between WHO's country representatives and UNDP's resident representatives. In summary, many participants in WHO either have no theory concerning the relation between the growth of health care services and a broader social development or simply assume that such services should have an absolute priority.

Other aspects of WHO's organizational ideology are also related to the declared maximalist goal. That the organization should be universal and technical and that "political" intrusions should be kept to a minimum are logical corollaries. Consequently, politics of the type that dominate the General Assembly of the United Nations are seldom apparent in WHO.

However, politics can be taken to mean the settlement of basic questions about who gets what, and such issues are central in WHO. According to the ideology of WHO, these questions are settled in an almost totally analytic manner; and no one can deny that analytical techniques are utilized. In the end, however, a number of these basic questions are solved through processes that involve considerable bargaining among the participants, even though such negotiations may be low keyed and implicit. How else, for example, could the level of WHO's total budget or the allocations among regions be settled? In this sense, then, WHO is an eminently political organization, despite organizational ideology to the contrary.

Persistent Groupings of Actors

Because of the widespread adherence to the organizational ideology—which may exist only because the ideology sidesteps a number of crucial issues—any persistent groupings in WHO are muted. Certain rather long-lasting coalitions have formed, but these tend to be created to deal with specific and limited issues. Representatives of the major contributing states from both East and West frequently coalesce to fight budgetary increases or to limit them. Cooperation between East and West on these issues is implicit and tentative, while within the Western sector it is formalized within the Geneva Group. These restrictive efforts are always countered by an overwhelming coalition of delegates from recipient countries. On symbolic issues the divisions parallel those in world politics. Occasional representational issues may provoke divisions between delegates from richer and poorer states. Other divisions may develop along geographical lines and, within the African region, between delegates from French and English-speaking countries. However, there is no general alignment within WHO's subsystem of participants that would prevail for all issues. On the contrary, one sees an overriding unity, forged by the organizational ideology.

This ideology further affects those who participate in WHO by uniting them in a loose alliance against other members of their country subsystems who, though involved in the formulation of policy for WHO, have little actual contact with the organization. This is probably the most important persistent grouping in WHO. The members of WHO's participant subsystem tend to be committed to the organization and to argue in support of its goals against other members of their country subsystems who are less committed to the organization, perhaps because of their broader responsibilities. In the country subsystems of the developed countries that are major contributors to WHO, the principal argument concerns the level of budgetary support for the organization. In the poorer countries the controversy concerns the size of the health program, because they cannot accept any external assistance without incurring—at the least—opportunity costs. Projects require facilities and counterpart personnel, and they are seldom started unless it is assumed that the recipient country will carry them on after a certain period. In a sense, the members of WHO's participant subsystem can be viewed as a global pressure group for health programs.

Organizational Elite

Despite the overriding unity among the actors in the participant subsystem, it should already be apparent that in the World Health Organization, as in all large organizations, some actors are more influential than others. Thus it is possible to speak of an organizational elite in WHO, in the sense that some actors have broad influence within the organization. Certain actors become members of this elite because of their position, others because of their personal characteristics.

In 1967, in my judgment, based on seventy-five interviews conducted in Geneva as well as in the field and on lengthy study of the documents, the organizational elite consisted of thirty individuals. None of the individuals was new to the organization in 1967; and many of them had had a long association with WHO.

Several other aspects of the list are interesting. Of the thirty men included, only one was not a medical doctor; eleven (or 36.67 percent) were secretariat officials, and nineteen (or 63.33 percent) were representatives of governments. Given the power assets of their formal positions, the director-general, the regional directors (who have substantial power in their own regions), and the representatives of the United States, USSR, France, and the United Kingdom would have been included in the organizational elite, almost without regard to the personal qualities of the incumbents. The others owe their inclusion primarily to their personal attributes. Half, or fifteen of the thirty individuals, are nationals of countries classified as Other; two (6.67 percent) are from Socialist countries, and thirteen (43.33 percent) are from Western countries.

Given the importance of the position of individuals in determining which have greatest influence in WHO, and the long association of several members of the elite with the organization, a statistical analysis of those who in other years had influence comparable to that of the thirty top-ranked men in 1967 could not yield substantially different conclusions from those cited above. The nature of WHO's organizational elite has been relatively constant. The strength of the organizational elite within WHO, and more broadly of the organization itself, is intimately related to this stability.

Environmental Impacts

The environment of the World Health Organization, as of all international organizations, consists principally of states, their characteristics, and their broad policies. The nature of the World Health Organization's activities, the predominantly professional character of the participants in its decision-making processes, their commitment to its organizational ideology, and the quality, strength, and strategic role of the organizational leadership and elite all serve to minimize the impact of the general environment on the agency.

WHO's principal activity consists of providing services to states, and these services are rendered mainly in the form of technical assistance. Moreover, because this assistance is technical, it requires some expertise to comprehend. These facts significantly affect the way in which states as collective entities feel themselves related to the organization. Net recipients of WHO assistance—about 90 percent of the members in 1967—are likely to be concerned about the aid that they themselves receive and will make collective judgments about their own requests for assistance. But, if for no other reason than that they would not welcome other states interfering with their plans, they are unlikely to be much concerned about global aspects of WHO's activities, except as these will affect them directly. Thus their collective judgments will most often be limited to such general issues as the broad level of support for WHO's activities and the division of allocations among regions. Net donors are likely to limit their concern and their collective judgments to the same questions. Only those donor states that have extensive resources and see their role in world politics as reaching into all corners are likely to be concerned either about the division of allocations among various substantive fields of activity or about the meshing of WHO's activities with other efforts they are pursuing outside the organization. In short, the occasions when all member states in WHO are concerned, in the sense of taking collective judgments, will arise in connection with an extremely limited number of programmatic decisions.

Representational and symbolic decisions, because they are common to many international organizations and impinge on broader issues of world politics, are more likely to stimulate states to formulate collective judgments. But these collective judgments must then be implemented by governmental representatives who usually are medical personnel and have been socialized into WHO's organizational ideology. This means that their personal interest in such issues is likely to be marginal; and in any case they have been taught to believe that such issues should not disrupt the important substantive work of the organization. Further, because of the procedures in WHO, such issues are handled in a way that maximizes the power of the organizational elite, the bulk of whom have a strong commitment to the organization and to helping maintain its uninterrupted and tranquil progress. This elite, for example, plays a vital role in screening candidates for the Executive Board, and because of this system an individual has almost no chance of being put on the board before he has been socialized into the organization. Thus, even on issues on which all states are likely to take positions, the effects of their taking these positions tend to be muted.

Since the sources of most rule-creating decisions in WHO are expert reports, the states as such are almost totally excluded from the process, although they have the right to suggest topics. Operational decisions, which are numerous and important in WHO, are settled between individual states and country representatives, but within a broad framework. Differences among outcomes in these decisions tend to be more the result of idiosyncratic factors than of any generalizable phenomenon.

Boundary decisions involve states very much in the same manner as programmatic decisions do. First, the concern of states generally is limited. Second, all members are likely to take stands on any boundary issues that might affect the overall level of resources transferred from rich to poor states, with the poorer states almost uniformly favoring courses that will expand the total. Preserving WHO's autonomy is seen as such a course. Finally, only a very small number of states, namely the principal donors, will take a deep interest in such questions.

The Organizationally Specific Environment

Another reason why the general environment's impact on the World Health Organization is minimal is that the agency exists within the context of a specific environment that in some ways serves as an intervening variable. One element of this specific environment is the culture of medicine and health care. We have already introduced this element into the analysis, particularly in our treatment of the organizational ideology.

Another element of the specific environment is that states' capacity for influence in the field of health does not coincide perfectly with their capacity for broader influence. Of course absolute capacity, in the sense of control over physical and human resources, is important in this field; but in a setting dominated by professionals as this organization is, a country's reputation for professional performance and its actual professional performance are important additional elements of capacity. To show this in a rough sense, a rank order of the thirty-nine leading states in the general environment in the late 1960s has been prepared according to an index made up from statistics showing: the absolute number of physicians in each state, the number of inhabitants per physician, the infant mortality, and the life expectancy of females at birth. (The figures used in the construction of the index are included in appendix B.) The absolute number of physicians of a country and the number of inhabitants per physician are indicators of that country's ability to provide medical personnel for international health work, training, and research—and of course for health care within the country. The level of infant mortality and the life expectancy of females at birth are indicators of a country's reputation or prestige in this field. The stratification of states in the general environment compared to that in the specific area of health care is shown in table 6.6. The most obvious and significant difference between the two rank orders is that several small states that have a highly developed economy (Australia, the Netherlands, Czechoslovakia, Denmark, and Nor-

Table 6.6

Rank Order of WHO Member States in the General and Specific Environment

General Environment, 1967		Specific Environment, 1966	
1	United States	1	United States
2	USSR	2	Australia
3	France	3	France
5	People's Republic of China	4	Federal Republic of Germany
5	Japan	5	United Kingdom
5	United Kingdom	6.5	Netherlands
7	Federal Republic of Germany	6.5	USSR
8	Italy	8	Czechoslovakia
9.5	Canada	9	Denmark
9.5	India	10	Japan
11	Sweden	11	Norway
15	Australia	13	Canada
15	Austria	13	Sweden
15	Netherlands	13	Switzerland
15	Spain	15	Italy
15	Switzerland	16	German Democratic Republic
15	Yugoslavia	17	Israel
15	Brazil	18	Austria
21	Argentina	19	Poland
21	Belgium	20	Belgium
21	Pakistan	21	Spain
21	Poland	22	New Zealand
21	South Africa	23	Argentina
26.5	Czechoslovakia	24	Finland
26.5	Denmark	25	Yugoslavia
26.5	German Democratic Republic	26	Mexico
26.5	Indonesia	27	India
26.5	Israel	28	Philippines
26.5	Mexico	29	Luxembourg
31.5	Cuba	30	Venezuela
31.5	Norway	31	Brazil
31.5	Turkey	32	United Arab Republic
31.5	United Arab Republic	33	Pakistan
36	Finland	34	Turkey
36	New Zealand	35.5	Cuba
36	Nigeria	35.5	South Africa
36	Philippines	37	Indonesia
36	Venezuela	38	Nigeria
39	Luxembourg	39	People's Republic of China

way, for example) have higher standing in the specific field of health than they do in relation to the general environment. On the other hand, such large, poor states as India, Indonesia, and Communist China have a much lower ranking in the specific field than in the general environment. Kendall's tau beta coefficient of correlation for the two rank orders is .40, indicating that although there is some association between the two, there are also substantial differences.

Even allowing for these minimizing and intervening factors, however, one cannot deny that the environment does have an impact on the World Health Organization. The extent of this impact can be considered in detail under the three broad rubrics used to describe the general environment: the stratification of power, the distribution of states according to their economic and political characteristics, and the pattern of alignments and conflicts.

The Stratification of Power

What effect does the stratification of power, either in the general environment or in the specific environment, have on decision making and the pattern of influence in the World Health Organization? In 1967, twenty-one of the thirty individuals included among the organizational elite, or 70 percent, were nationals of the thirty-nine states listed in table 6.6. However, only twelve, or 40 percent, were nationals of the ten top states in the general environment. Whether these are regarded as high or low figures is a relative matter; but it is clear that nationals of the most powerful states in the environment do not dominate the organizational elite. On the other hand, the only states that are continually reelected to the Executive Board after absences of only a year and that almost always have one of their nationals serving as deputy or assistant director-general are the United States, the USSR, France, and the United Kingdom, four of the six top states in the environment. And eight of the thirty individuals included among the organizational elite in 1967, or 26.67 percent, were nationals of these four states (United States, three; France, three; USSR, one; and the United Kingdom, one). These four states also supply a large share of WHO's professional personnel. On 30 November 1966, there were 1,818 professionals serving WHO (including those in PAHO); of these, 568, or 31.24 percent, were nationals of these four states, divided as follows: United Kingdom, 213; United States, 209; France, 111; and the USSR, 35. The large number of British and American personel on WHO's staff may help explain why the public health doctrines of these two states are so pervasive in the organization.

The results of this stratification of power are also explainable by recalling that the leading states in the environment played only a limited role in determining either the level or the nature of WHO's activities. Indeed, in the late 1960s many WHO budgets were adopted despite the dissenting votes of these states. Yet their opposition was not completely without effect, for WHO's rate of budgetary growth did begin to taper off at that time.

The significance of the top states in the general environment can also be seen by looking at their budgetary contributions to WHO. In 1967, 5 members of WHO contributed 62.91 percent of the regular budget: the United States, 31.18 percent; the USSR, 13.29 percent; France, 5.42 percent; Germany, 6.60 percent; and the United Kingdom, 6.42 percent. These 5 countries also provided the bulk of WHO's other funds. In the budgetary politics of the 1960s, the wishes of these states could be overridden because the director-general had the initiative in proposing a figure and because the ultimate acceptance of the figure rested with those states that could comprise a two-thirds majority in the assembly. In a body of 126 members, 5 is not a "blocking third." However, there was a limit. If these 5 states were pushed to the point where they reconsidered their commitment to the organization, WHO's very existence might be jeopardized. No doubt this explains why the director-general was willing to go before the so-called Geneva Group (the representatives in Geneva of the major Western countributors to agencies of the United Nations family) to explain and justify his budget before it was presented to the assembly. He could go against the wishes of these states, but he could not alienate them. The figure settled on for budgetary growth was thus less than he and the net recipients considered desirable, but more than that favored by the major donors.

It is perhaps significant that since the establishment of the post of an assistant director-general responsible for administrative, budgetary, and financial matters, a national of the United States, the leading contributor to WHO, has held this office. The personal confidence that American governmental officials have had in him partly explains why American government officials generally feel that whether or not the United States agrees to WHO's expenditures, they need not worry too much about how its funds have been managed.

Of the leading states, the United States is the only one that has consistently sought to take the initiative in programmatic matters. It has proposed for the organization new major courses of action, for example medical research and the eradication of malaria and smallpox. With each such proposal, it has also made a substantial voluntary contribution to start the program, and on each occasion its initiative has been accepted by the organization. In the long run, the financing of these activities has been absorbed into the regular budget. Thus, through this process the United States has affected the organization's priorities.

When the United States has chosen to be a vetoer, as it has done in the representational issues concerning Communist China and East Germany, it has succeeded. How extensively it could play such a negative role is difficult to predict. In the first quarter-century of WHO's existence, there have been no other issues on which the United States has taken so clear a stand.

The Soviet Union, France, and the United Kingdom are all important in the World Health Organization, but more as controllers than as initiators or vetoers. They seldom propose new activities. Only the Soviet Union has sought to block activities, and it ceased this attempt after WHO's very first years. The approval of these three countries is sought, however, in most matters.

The United Kingdom is somewhat more important in WHO than its position in the general or the specific environment would indicate. One explanation lies in its budgetary contribution to the organization, which is the fourth largest. In addition, in WHO the United Kingdom frequently operates in close partnership with the United States, and the British gain strength from this alliance. Finally, the United Kingdom has consistently had more nationals occupying professional staff positions in WHO than any other country.

The two most notable "underachievers" in WHO are West Germany and Japan. Judging by their position in either the general or the specific environment, both would seem to have far greater capacity for influence than the amount they actually exercise in the organizaton.

Ranking the influence of other states in the World Health Organization is difficult because much seems to depend on the character of their representatives. It is worthy of note, however, that twenty-two members of the organizational elite in 1967, 76.67 percent, were not nationals of the four leading states.

Distribution of States according to Their Economic and Political Characteristics

As the distribution of states in the general environment has changed, so has the composition of the World Health Organization's membership. This can be seen clearly in tables 6.7 and 6.8. The statistics used for these tables include those states that were classified in the matrices in chapter 2 dealing with the general environment and that were actively participating members of WHO.[21] Thus, the totals are somewhat less than the actual membership of WHO during each of the years, but this does not distort the general proportions among the actual participants in the organization. Over the years the most notable change in the nature of WHO's membership concerns the political regimes of the member states rather than their per capita GNP. The proportion of states with competitive regimes has declined significantly, while the relative number of states with mobilizing and authoritarian regimes has increased.

This change, however, appears to have had very little effect on decision making within the World Health Organization. Symbolic issues and disputes about representational matters were raised with somewhat greater frequency in the middle and later part of the 1960s than in the previous ten years, but even so they hardly became a salient feature of the organization's activities. The professionalism so prevalent in WHO and the heavy emphasis on service activities have insulated the organization from the effects of changes in the political composition of its membership.

Table 6.7

WHO's Membership Classified according to Economic Level

Per capita GNP (In Dollars)	1950 Number	1950 Percentage	1958 Number	1958 Percentage	1967 Number	1967 Percentage
0-199	27	42.86	28	34.15	45	37.50
200-599	20	31.75	30	36.59	40	33.33
600-999	4	6.35	11	13.41	14	11.67
1,000 and over	12	19.05	13	15.85	21	17.50
Total	63	100.00	82	100.00	120	100.00

Table 6.8

WHO's Membership Classified according to Type of Polity

	1950 Number	1950 Percentage	1958 Number	1958 Percentage	1967 Number	1967 Percentage
Competitive	32	50.79	36	43.90	42	35.00
Mobilizing	3	4.76	13	15.85	21	17.50
Authoritarian	26	41.27	33	40.24	57	47.50
Nonindependent	2	3.17	0	0	0	0
Total	63	99.99	82	99.99	120	100.00

Given the significant increase in WHO's budgets in the early 1960s, one might expect the number of members in the lowest income categories to increase. No such relative increase has occurred, however. There has, though, been a substantial increase in the absolute number of member states in the category with the lowest per capita GNP: this figure has risen from twenty-seven to forty-five, or by two-thirds. Furthermore, those states that entered WHO in the 1960s, even though they fell into the same low-income categories as many that had been charter members of WHO or had entered during the 1950s, were nevertheless substantially poorer than the earlier entrants. One explanation of the increases in WHO's budgets can therefore be found in the absolute needs of its members, rather than in the political process within the organization.

The political process has also played a role. To see this we must look at the low-income countries in terms of geographical groups. In 1950 there were eight Latin-American states in the category with the lowest per capita GNP, constituting 29.64 percent of the group. In 1967 there were only two, constituting 4.44 percent. Latin-American states were less vocal than those from Africa and Asia in pressing their claims for assistance within the general framework of WHO. First, PAHO has its own budget, and any increased funds for this organization will definitely be spent in the Americas. Second, many of the Latin-American states have been closely aligned, particularly in the 1950s, with the principal contributor to WHO, the United States; and they have therefore been sensitive to its feelings about budgetary increases.

The Pattern of Alignments and Conflicts

The impact that the pattern of alignments and conflicts in the general environment has had on the World Health Organization has also been minimal. During the height of the cold war, the socialist states withdrew from participation in WHO. But they were entreated to return and were welcomed when they did. Moreover, before they left they had not been discriminated against in representational decisions or in any other category of decisions. Admittedly, though, their hopes that the organization might become for them a major supplier of medical matériel were dashed. Since the return of the socialist states to active participation, tensions between communists and anticommunists have occasionally arisen in WHO, but their total effect on the organization can only be described as trival.

WHO has been more sensitive to conflicts arising from a division between states in the Northern and Southern hemispheres involving decolonization and development. Representational and symbolic issues related to the struggle for a final end to colonialism gained some salience in the organization in the 1960s. Since the bulk of WHO's activities really involve the rendering of services to developing countries, with the developed countries paying the costs, almost all controversies about programmatic issues can be related to the broader North-South controversy about development. Yet these have generally been broached in a highly pro- fessional, rather than an emotional manner.

The fact that in the controversy between the Northern and Southern hemispheres, it is easy to lump the East and West together may very well contribute to the downplaying of East-West tensions in the organization. Another important explanation for the downplaying of East-West tensions is the socialization of the individuals in the participant subsystem. This socialization has also minimized the force of North-South conflicts. The trend toward regional integration in the world has had virtually no effect on WHO.

This detailed review has confirmed the initial proposition that the impact of the environment has been minimal. The environment sets certain brqad parameters, but otherwise whatever goes on within WHO is determined by the participant subsystem.

The Structure of Influence and Patterns of Decision Making

The dominance of the participant subsystem over the environment means that in decision making within the World Health Organization the executive head and the bureaucracy of the organization have considerable influence. WHO is therefore heavily dependent on the quality of its internal leadership. The first two directors-general have been skillful in building their political strength within the organization, maintaining a strong personal position within the organizational elite, keeping this inner group united, and using the organizational ideology to give cohesion to the agency as a whole. WHO's growth in the first quarter-century of its existence is in large measure attributable to Dr. Chisholm and Dr. Candau.

Neither Chisholm nor Candau suffered challenges by other members of the organizational elite. This can partially be explained by simple fortune, but another explanation lies in their considerable political acumen, which allowed them to avoid grounds for challenges. As long as WHO's organizational elite is cohesive, as it always has been, it can substantially control the organization. Indeed, to some extent it can even defy the environment. Thus the director-general's relationship with the organizational elite is crucial.

Aside from the quality of its leadership, the future of the World Health Organization in gross terms depends upon the attitude of a few crucially important states: namely, the United States, the USSR, France, and the United Kingdom. In a real sense, these states remain in a position to control the budgetary growth of the organization. To alienate them would have most serious consequences for the organization. Part of the director-general's job, therefore, must be to maintain good relations with them. As has been the case throughout the development of international collaboration toward improvements in health, these states have a genuine self-interest in work in this field, even though the benefits they receive may be indirect. The rich states of the Northern Hemisphere can easily be contaminated by the health problems of the Southern Hemisphere. As the rich states of the North see the situation, however, there are limits to their self-interest in improving health conditions in the South. The director-general's task is to see that these limits are not breached, but he must also try constantly to widen them. The director-general is aided in this task by two circumstances. The first is the commitment of members of the participant subsystem, including the representatives of the leading four states, to the organization. Because of this commitment, many government representatives to WHO almost can be viewed as the director-general's agents or lobbyists within country sub-systems. A second circumstance is that the attitude of several smaller Northern Hemisphere states, such as Denmark, the Netherlands, Norway, and Sweden, can almost always be counted on to be more favorable to the growth of the World Health Organization than that of the leading four states. This may be because the standards of health care in these smaller states are exceptionally high. Their more limited budgetary contribution may also be a factor. Whatever the reason, their position makes it difficult for the leading four states to take too negative a stand. Consequently, in many tactical situations delegates from these states are the director-general's most important allies.

Besides the director-general, the leading four states, and those Northern Hemisphere states committed to high health standards throughout the world, most of the other participants in the World Health Organization are the net recipients of WHO assistance. These states provide a ready majority in the World Health Assembly for proposals favoring the growth of the organization. The director-general's problem is not to muster this majority, but rather to prevent it from going too far. Were the director-general to become completely enamored with the majority, he might be led to take actions going beyond the tolerance of the leading powers. At a certain point the cohesiveness of the majority would also begin to crack. Particularistic ties with leading states would lead some to defect from the majority, and other states would drop out of the struggle for increased resources for WHO because the overall costs would be greater than the priority they were willing to assign to the goal.

The broad parameters of activities carried on by the World Health Organization have been and will probably continue to be determined by the interplay between the director-general and the three groups of states named above. This pattern could change if one of the four leading states were to take a different attitude toward WHO or if the "underachievers"—the Federal Republic of Germany and Japan—were to become more active and adopt a different orientation from that of the leading states. However, there have been no forewarnings of such developments. The entrance of the People's Republic of China could also change matters.

The structure of influence and the pattern of decision making in the World Health Organization is more diffuse for more detailed issues. These issues are largely settled within the participant subsystem. The position of the director-general is crucial here too, but influence is dispersed more widely among the organizational elite. In the first quarter-century of the organization's existence, this elite has demonstrated considerable capacity for both stability and self-renewal. The formal and informal rules of WHO favor these trends, and there is no reason why they should not continue. If, for some reason, the organizational elite ever faltered in either respect, it could seriously damage the organization and weaken the position of the participant subsystem.

In short, there appears to be no reason why WHO's political system in the future should not basically be a projection of what it has been in the past. It is a strong and stable system. The only caveat concerns the existence of certain crucial factors—the quality of the director-general, the attitude of the leading states, and the quality of the organizational elite—a change in any of them would have serious consequences for WHO. If there is no change, however, WHO will continue to be, as it has been in the past, an organization dominated by the ideology of medicine, by a strong commitment to regionally decentralized service activities, and by carefully managed politics.

7   IAEA: Atomic Condominium?

Lawrence Scheinman

The statute of the International Atomic Energy Agency (IAEA) came into force in July 1957. The agency is thus among the newer members of the United Nations family. It is unlike the other organizations treated in this volume in that it ranks as an autonomous agency within the United Nations system rather than as a specialized agency. The privileged status of the IAEA is indicated by the fact that it reports directly to the General Assembly and that it can, under certain designated circumstances, directly seize the Security Council.[1]

Three background features of IAEA are particularly relevant to an understanding of its evolution and development. First, while its most immediate source is the Atoms-for-Peace program of the United States, enunciated by President Eisenhower before the General Assembly in December 1953, its more remote source is to be found in the failure of the Baruch Plan of 1946 to win the necessary support. This plan would have allowed for international ownership and control of nuclear production and development as well as for the creation of a central nuclear authority. Instead, national development and control and nuclear proliferation became the norm. The Atoms-for-Peace program, as it evolved into the institutional form of the IAEA, can be regarded in some measure as an alternative to the Baruch Plan and, consequently, as an element in the continuing but still unsuccessful attempt to achieve nuclear disarmament.

Second, because it is linked only very indirectly to disarmament and arms control problems and is more directly focused on the peaceful development of nuclear energy, the IAEA is usually regarded as a technical agency. However, the above-mentioned characteristic along with the general acknowledgment that the infrastructure and technology of both the peaceful and the military atom are closely related and at points even indistinguishable and the fact that the technical and political aspects of the atom in many instances cannot be dissociated from one another, make it seem more appropriate to look upon the agency as an ongoing example of the political handling of technology.

Third, the IAEA is the product of calculated American policy. It is the first (though not the only) major institutionalized expression of an American policy to internationalize the benefits of nuclear energy and to take the lead in the peaceful nuclear field as well as in military nuclear capability. Thus the United States might hope to maintain the image of technological

The author wishes to thank the Carnegie Endowment for International Peace, and particularly its former president, Joseph E. Johnson, for their generous support of this study.

leadership and to capitalize on the commercial potentiality of the atom without simultaneously running the risk that such a policy would lead to military nuclear proliferation. With the American nuclear monopoly broken, the erosion of secrecy already under way, and the promise that the peaceful atom would become more reality than myth and that the dispersion of nuclear technology and facilities would be the tide of the future, the United States sought to channel this development and manage its implications through an institutional forum. The agency properly may be viewed, therefore, at least at its inception, as an expression of political policy by the United States, in which others joined. Whatever the balance of influence or the particular orientation of the IAEA at any given time, the characteristics sketched above are of a general and continuing relevance to the evolution, development, and behavior of the IAEA.

Structure, Functions, and Evolution

Formal Framework of Decisions

In formal terms the two principal deliberative organs of the IAEA are the Board of Governors and the General Conference. The statute of the IAEA vests authority to carry out its functions in the board; and the board's program and budget, subject to approval by the General Conference, constitute the framework of agency action. The IAEA's Board of Governors in fact predominates over the General Conference and the secretariat to a greater degree than is true of similar organs in most other international organizations. This is not to say that these other organs of the IAEA are powerless or without influence, but only that the formal prescription of the statute is largely reflected in actual practice.

One of the most striking features of the board, and one which has important implications for decision making in IAEA, is its composition. The board consists of twenty-five (originally twenty-three) members, of whom thirteen are designated by the outgoing board and twelve elected by the General Conference. The provisions for selecting the thirteen members designated by the board are complex. The statute divides the world into eight regions. Once the five most advanced nuclear states have been designated (regardless of region), the most advanced states in each of the regions not represented by the original five are named to the board. Thus, for each of the eight statutory regions the most advanced nuclear state is assured a seat on the board as long as it can maintain its regional lead. The two states that are major producers of source materials are also designated from among four named in the statute. One state is designated as a supplier of technical assistance. In practice this seat rotates among the four Nordic countries. The twelve members elected to the board by the General Conference are chosen with regard to the regional criterion except that two regions—Latin America, and Africa and the Middle East—must each be represented by four members on the full board.

Voting on the board is by simple majority except on matters relating to finance and the budget, amendments to the statute, and appointment of the director-general, where a two-thirds majority is required. The pattern during the past several years has been in the direction of decision by consensus rather than by formal vote. This reflects the dynamics of the agency's decision making, which typically relies on committees of the board and even more on informal extraconstitutional consultation.

The role of the General Conference is limited to control over the purse strings and authority to take decisions on matters referred to it by the board or "to propose matters for consideration by the Board and request from the Board reports on any matters relating to the functions of the Agency."[2] This authority has been frequently invoked, and the limited influence that the conference does have on agency policy and orientations stems from resolutions passed under this provision. Although the conference has the power to return the budget to the board with recommendations for change, it has never used this authority. The true value of the conference lies not in its limited formal powers, but in its role as a forum in which those not represented on the board can express their views and exchange information and in which member states can finalize bilateral or multilateral agreements in the nuclear field.

Assigned Functions of the Agency

The principal objectives of the agency, set out in article II of its statute, are "to accelerate and enlarge the contribution of atomic energy to peace, health and prosperity throughout the world" and "to ensure, as far as it is able, that assistance provided by it or at its request or under its supervision or control is not used in such a way as to further any military purpose." One of the difficulties the agency has increasingly faced is the maintenance of balance between development and control. Many of the nonnuclear underdeveloped states regard atomic energy as a potential means of rapidly and radically improving their standards of living and general prosperity (a view largely engendered by the United States with its Atoms-for-Peace program); the emphasis in the agency, therefore, is on development, and many resolutions of the General Conference reiterate this concern. For some of the nuclear powers themselves, the emphasis is more in the direction of control. This is particularly true of the United States and, in recent years, the Soviet Union, although if one analyzes the agency especially in terms of initiatives and support, it is clear that the United States feels much more keenly the promotional responsibilities of the agency.

The agency does serve as a forum for decisions and negotiations, but the bulk of its efforts are service activities. Its character as a decisional framework is demonstrated by its responsibilities in the regulatory fields: to establish safeguards systems as well as regulations, codes, and standards relating to the safe handling of radioactive materials; health and safety standards; civil liability codes; transportation regulations for international commerce; and standards for the management and disposition of radioactive waste. Regulations are not binding on the member states, but they do have a binding effect on agency operations and on agency assisted projects. They also serve as guides to national legislation or as the basis for international conventions.

If the forum concept is broadened to include not simply a framework for negotiation but also a medium for the exchange of views, then the IAEA can be seen as serving yet another forum function—that of providing a constructive and cordial meeting ground of scientists and political leaders of East and West.[3]

In the service field the agency has a statutory mandate to encourage and assist research on nuclear energy; to provide nuclear materials, equipment, facilities, and services; to foster the exchange of information; and to further the training and exchange of scientists and technicians. The agency is also charged with establishing or acquiring facilities, plant, or equipment useful toward carrying out its assigned functions and administering the safeguards system once it is adopted.

To these ends the IAEA developed programs to suit both general and more individual interests. A framework program was recommended by the Preparatory Commission in 1957 and adopted by the board and the General Conference. While there has been a modest expansion of programs, there have been no major or radical shifts. Emphasis has changed within the framework in response to technological advances or to pressures from groups of states, but the program has generally been fairly stable and evolutionary. Individual services are in great measure provided through a technical assistance program, which comprises assistance missions to assess nuclear possibilities and the establishment of regional study groups or training programs, but which mostly entails the supplying of experts, materials, equipment, training, and fellowships.[4] Technical assistance is financed almost entirely through a voluntary contribution fund and such UNDP funds as are made available to the IAEA. Common services include conferences, symposia, and seminars on a variety of subjects. Finally, the agency has its own laboratories in which a good deal of research is carried on under a unique research contract program. These programs are not of great monetary significance when compared with parallel national efforts, but they have symbolic value to the agency and provide a lever for exerting a coordinating role in nuclear research.

Evolution of the Budget

In keeping with the modest expansion of its programs, the budget of the IAEA is one of the slowest growing in the United Nations family. The average rate of growth between 1958 and 1968 was less than 8 percent. The greatest increase in the agency's budget came in 1968, when the growth over 1967 was 10.7 percent.

The IAEA budget has two components. One is the regular budget, which under the statute covers only administrative expenses and is funded by assessments on member states and from miscellaneous income. The other is the operational budget, which covers agency facilities (including a laboratory at headquarters, one in Monaco, and the International Center for Theoretical Physics in Trieste) and the agency's technical assistance program. Income for the operational budget derives from voluntary contributions of member states, special (in kind) contributions, and agency participation in UNDP. The latter adds significantly to the technical assistance side of the operational budget but represents only about 10 percent of the agency's total regular and operational expenditures. Despite the term *operational* applied to one part of the budget, a number of operational activities, particularly the agency's facilities, are increasingly funded from the regular budget.

The largest single contributor to the agency is the United States; its assessed contribution for 1967 was 31.87 percent or $2.7 million of a total assessment of $9.4 million. The Western states as a group contributed 67.73 percent of the 1967 regular budget; the Socialist states contributed 19.54 percent, and the sixty-three member states from countries classed as Other states contributed the remaining 12.73 percent.

The four nuclear weapon states in the agency (United States, Soviet Union, United Kingdom, and France) together contribute approximately 57 percent of the regular budget, a factor that is reflected in the relative weight of these states in the agency. The third largest contributor is West Germany, a nonnuclear weapon state. As we shall see, West Germany's level of contribution does not correlate with her level of influence in the agency. These comparisons are graphically represented in tables 7.1 and 7.2.

Voluntary contributions systematically fall 30 to 35 percent short of the $2 million target annually set by the General Conference. In 1967 approximately two-thirds of the member states contributed a total of $1.2 million. The United States traditionally has provided a large share of the voluntary budget. Until 1964 it had supplied a flat $500,000 and matched dollar for dollar all contributions over $1 million—up to a ceiling of $1.5 million, which never was attained. Since 1965, however, the United States contribution as a percentage of the total amount pledged by all member states, including the United States, has dropped progressively from 50 percent (1965) to 35 percent (1968), as Washington has made an effort to bring its voluntary payments into line with its assessed payments. The second largest contributor to the voluntary fund is West Germany, which, as a potential exporter of peaceful nuclear technology and nuclear reactors, has shown considerable though belated interest in the IAEA. This interest must be read partly in the light of the Non-Proliferation Treaty (NPT), whose implementation has a strong bearing on the constraints on West German nuclear development. Other states have paid far less than their proportionate share: France, for example, contributes only token amounts to the agency, and between 1960 and 1967 the Soviet bloc made no payments to the voluntary fund, except for $13,000 by Czechoslovakia in 1960 and $3,000 by Poland in 1961. Since 1967, however, the Socialist states have been contributing to the voluntary fund.

Table 7.1

Contributions of Groups to Regular Budget in IAEA
(In Percentages)

	1958	1959	1967
Western	67.47	68.31	67.73
Socialist	18.59	18.05	19.54
Other	13.94	13.64	12.73

Note: Figures are given for 1958 and 1959 because, although 1958 was the first year of agency operation, 1959 was the first year when finally adjusted assessments were applied.

Table 7.2

Contributions of Selected States to the Regular Budget in IAEA
(In Percentages)

	1958	1959	1967
United States	33.33	32.51	31.87
United Kingdom	7.21	7.22	6.49
USSR	12.89	12.46	13.43
France	5.26	5.9	5.5
Federal Republic of Germany	3.93	4.95	6.7

Note: Figures are given for 1958 and 1959 because, although 1958 was the first year of agency operation, 1959 was the first year when finally adjusted assessments were applied.

Technical assistance constitutes one of the greatest demands on the agency, but the organization has been unable to augment substantially its resources for this purpose; even UNDP funds have added only $550,000 to $900,000 a year for country programs. Whereas in 1959 the agency was able to meet about 90 percent of all requests for technical assistance, in 1968 the proportion it was able to meet amounted to only about 30 percent. During that time requests increased from $700,000 to $3 million, but resources remained roughly constant. The problem of funding technical assistance has been partly offset, however, by the board's approval of transferring a number of costly items from the operational to the regular budget: for example, laboratory costs and that part of the research contract program that was originally funded from voluntary contributions.

Thus, there have been no major quantitative jumps in the budget and only minor qualitative adjustments to meet an unsatisfactory financial situation. However, as a consequence of the NPT the near future may signal not only a quantitative jump in the budget but a shift in program emphasis of significant proportions as well.

Secretariat

The staff of the IAEA is headed by a director-general appointed for a four-year period by the Board of Governors subject to the approval of the General Conference. Two men have held this post: Sterling Cole, an American congressman, was the first director-general, serving from 1957 to 1961; the second is Sigvard Eklund, a Swedish scientist, who in 1969 was appointed to his third successive term. The five agency departments are headed by deputy directors-general although the head of the Safeguards Division is designated as inspector-general. While no single post is the specific preserve of any one country, the United States has held the post of deputy director-general for administration (and directorship of the budget within that division) since Cole's term of office came to an end. The Soviet Union has laid claim to the Department of Technical Operations. The Department of Research and Isotopes can be characterized as a West European post. The Department of Technical Assistance, created in 1965, is under the tutelage of an Indian national and likely will remain in the hands of a national from a less-developed country. Again by limited tradition, the position of inspector-general is filled by a national from a nonnuclear weapon state.

The agency staff has grown in the same proportion as the budget and program—very modestly. There were 161 professional staff members in the IAEA in 1958, and 228 in 1961; in 1968 the professional staff had increased only to 314.

Major Events and Turning Points

The original idea of the Atoms-for-Peace program, out of which the IAEA grew, was that the agency would serve as a bank for the deposit of fissile materials, which presumably would be drawn increasingly from the military arsenals of those powers possessing nuclear weapons. The banking concept eventually gave way to a brokerage concept, which was codified in the statute. A major role of the IAEA was to supply source and fissionable materials and to help ensure the continued availability of fuel supplies for national nuclear programs. These provisions were based on what turned out to be two erroneous expectations: that competitive and economic nuclear power was imminent and that source and special fissile materials would be in short supply. The expectation with regard to the economics of nuclear power arose from the 1955 Geneva Conference on the Peaceful Uses of Nuclear Energy. As things turned out, competitive nuclear power was still a distant promise, demand for source and fissile materials was correspondingly much lower than expected, and the euphoric bubble of the mid- and late-1950s burst. Thus, by the time the agency got under way, late in 1957, one of its principal tasks had already been undercut. The agency's response was to cast about for other, more modest and preparatory tasks.

A second turning point in the prehistory of the agency is a consequence of the policy of the United States. The Atoms-for-Peace program signaled a change in American attitudes toward peaceful nuclear assistance. In 1954 the McMahon Act was revised to allow for such assistance, and between 1955 and 1958 the United States entered into some forty bilateral agreements for the transfer of nuclear knowledge and information and for the sale of research reactors. In each instance arrangements were made whereby the United States would undertake to safeguard and inspect the nuclear facility of the recipient state. Thus, the second of the IAEA's main tasks was undercut. In short, economic and technological conditions, on the one hand, and the policy pursued by the leading nuclear power, on the other, limited the importance as well as the scope of activity of the agency before it had even got under way.

Since its inception there have been a number of turning points for the IAEA that center around its safeguarding role. A most significant event was the cessation of systematic Soviet opposition to the agency's safeguards system. Evidence of this shift appeared in early 1962, when the Soviet tone in board and conference meetings began to moderate; and the change became patent in 1963 at the time of the signing of the Moscow Partial Test Ban Treaty. This shift of Soviet policy not only facilitated intra-agency policy making, but it also lent increased legitimacy to the agency's safeguards system. In February 1964 a major step forward in safeguards was the extension of the existing system to reactors of more than one hundred megawatts, that is, to power reactors as well as to research reactors. In 1965 the entire safeguards system was reviewed and revised by the Board of Governors, and the new document was accepted without dissent on the board. The importance of this event is that the 1965 revised system constitutes the first program of international inspection supported by both East and West. Since 1965 this system has been steadily expanded to cover nuclear facilities other than reactors, and by 1968 the entire fuel cycle (with the exception of enrichment plants) was covered by the agency's safeguards system.

Two other events of immeasurable importance to the IAEA have flowed from the above developments: the systematic transfer of the United States' bilateral safeguard agreements to the IAEA under newly negotiated trilateral agreements and the designation of the agency as the appropriate safeguards body under the Non-Proliferation Treaty. The significance of this designation cannot be underestimated. Under the statute of the IAEA, safeguards are applied only under specified circumstances: when the materials and equipment were supplied to the recipient state by or through the agency;

when it is asked to apply safeguards by parties to any bilateral and multilateral arrangement; or when a state unilaterally submits its nuclear facilities voluntarily to the agency's system. The NPT, on the other hand, requires all nonnuclear weapon states that ratify the treaty to place their nuclear facilities under IAEA safeguards.[5] Once implemented, this provision will radically expand the scope of the agency's control activities and catapult it from its present modest position in the United Nations family to a place among the most important international agencies. The probability of increased importance has already affected the IAEA by sharply augmenting the pressure for an enlarged and more broadly representative Board of Governors. At the time of this writing, agreement has been tentatively reached to expand the board to thirty-three members.

Decision Making: A Taxonomical Analysis

While issue-areas, or more accurately the particular issue in question, can often determine the role played by different actors, some limited generalizations regarding the distribution of roles in the IAEA are possible. An important preliminary point is that activity in any form is related to interest, and the IAEA as a rule has been of only marginal interest to a large segment of its membership. This has meant that the active clientele of the agency has been rather small and that a number of these participants have played multiple roles more often than might otherwise have been anticipated.

The role of initiator is the monopoly of no single group or set of participants. The secretariat has been responsible for numerous initiatives, especially in the earlier years of the agency's life. The most wide-ranging initiatives have come from the Western states, particularly the United States, while the socialist countries have played a very limited role in initiating, and the few less-developed states that are active have focused nearly all of their attention on resolutions concerning assistance and development (i.e. redistribution). However, one must distinguish between two types of initiatives emanating from the Western states: The United States' initiatives incline toward expanding the role of the agency or toward finding things for the IAEA to do, as was the case during the period when most of the purposes for which the agency was created could not be fulfilled because of specific environmental circumstances. A second type of initiative, taken largely by the United Kingdom and South Africa, has been aimed not at expanding the role of the IAEA but at maximizing its capacity to perform efficiently and effectively within the framework of the limited role defined for it.

This suggests other roles commonly filled by these and the other Commonwealth countries—as potential vetoers of undesirable initiatives (usually defined in terms of cost) and also as controllers whose views, because of their control over needed resources and their reputed influence in the agency, the initiators must take into account. France and the Soviet Union have been active as controllers, their objective often being not so much to veto initiatives as to see that matters are kept in line and that the agency does not drift too far from its statutory purposes. When the prospect of a budget increase arises, Australia and Canada often join forces with the Soviet Union in an effort to curtail anything more than modest growth. The director-general, the deputy director-general for administration, and the director of the budget division (the latter two are Americans) centrally positioned in the secretariat's hierarchy can block proposals from within the staff and, in effect, serve as potential vetoers on programmatic initiatives arising in other secretariat divisions.

The role of go-between or broker is performed partly by the director-general and partly by such countries as Canada, India, or the Scandinavian states.

Representational Decisions

Membership in the IAEA is open to any state upon recommendation of the Board of Governors and approval of the General Conference. The issue of Chinese representation has been raised annually in the General Conference by members of the Soviet bloc but has been handled routinely in the form of a credential resolution deferring to the action of the General Assembly. More recently the socialist states have been advocating the admission of East Germany, but this has never been the subject of a serious debate, and no resolutions to this effect have been tabled. Efforts to circumvent the exclusion of countries such as China or East Germany, through draft resolutions providing that without exception all interested scientific organizations and scientists should be able to participate in scientific activities organized by the agency, have met with consistent failure.

Another type of representational issue that has permeated the agency's life, though without severely affecting it, relates to the status of intergovernmental and nongovernmental organizations. The issue about intergovernmental organizations has centered on EURATOM and the Soviet's refusal to accept the regularization of relations between EURATOM and the IAEA, primarily on the gound that as the EURATOM statute did not specifically prohibit the use of atomic energy for military purposes, the community did not qualify as an exclusively peaceful organization. Nevertheless, each year the board invites EURATOM to participate as an observer at the General Conference. The EURATOM case has not come up since 1967, when observer status was also accorded to COMECON. The nongovernmental organization issue stems from the refusal of the Western powers to grant consultative status to the World Federation of Trade Unions (WFTU). This led to an understanding that was tantamount to a moratorium on the granting of consultative status to nongovernmental organizations, and no such status has been granted since 1961.

Beyond these vestigial cold war issues lies a second range of representational issues, which relate to membership on the various organs of the agency. An African-sponsored resolution in the 1960 General Conference, noting that Africa and the Middle East were inadequately represented on the board, led to the board's recommending an amendment to the statute, which would add two more members from this geographic region. Similar efforts at the time of the conference on the statute met with failure.

Designation of membership on the board has raised a number of problems. One arose from an intraregional dispute between Argentina and Brazil as to which one was the "most advanced" in nuclear power in Latin America and consequently entitled to automatic designation on the board. A gentlemen's agreement whereby Argentina and Brazil would be alternately designated as their region's most advanced state resolved the issue. Whichever of the two was not so designated was always elected to the board by the General Conference.

A second issue related to South Africa, which is automatically designated as the most advanced in nuclear capability of all states in the region of Africa and the Middle East. Despite various attempts by other African nations to deny South Africa its traditional seat on the board on the ground that its racial policies rendered it incapable of representing the African states, South Africa has consistently retained its board membership. That it has been able to do so is primarily the result of a combination of two factors: one, the effort led by the United States and supported by a large segment of the membership to keep broader political issues out of the agency; and two, the feeling of the major powers, pressing for nuclear détente and agreeing that nonproliferation is an imperative, that they cannot afford to leave South Africa, a major uranium producer, outside the club.

Another issue, also relating to the designated seats on the board, was raised by the Congo in 1965. The statute names four states—Belgium, Portugal, Czechoslovakia, and Poland—and provides that two of these shall be designated annually as producers of source materials. The Congo proposed an amendment to the statute on the grounds that the circumstances under which this provision was drafted no longer obtained and that Belgium, for example, was holding a seat by virtue of the Congo's uranium deposits. The board declined to recommend any action, largely for the reason that, whatever the merits of the Congolese argument, the provision in question also served to maintain a balance between East and West, and any tampering with the statute would undo the delicate balance necessary to the agency's survival. Consequently, the board agreed to hold the issue in abeyance until a general review of the statute took place.

The interesting common feature in this and the preceding issue is the orientation of the de facto permanent board members, whether East or West, developed or underdeveloped, toward preserving the status quo. The United States, India, Argentina, and the Soviet Union have all taken a dim view of efforts to meddle with the representational provisions of the statute. Such efforts have been increasing, however, largely because of the greater political role the board will be called upon to play in connection with the Non-Proliferation Treaty. In this regard, 1968 proved to be a watershed year for the agency; the General Conference adopted a resolution calling on the board to review article VI and to study ways by which its membership could be made to reflect the progress achieved by many agency members since the statute came into force in 1957.[6] The permanent board members, unable to quell the demand for change, have nevertheless so far been able to channel the review along lines that preserve most of the underlying concepts of the present article VI even while expanding the size of the board.

The regional principle also applies to the board seats filled by election in the General Conference. Candidates are determined beforehand in regional caucuses, and the candidate agreed on normally receives a unanimous or nearly unanimous vote in plenary session. The practical effect of leaving representation to each individual region is to deny some technically advanced countries any opportunity to represent their region on the board. A glaring example of this problem is Israel, which has never represented its region or been elected to any office at any level because of the opposition of the Arab states. Cuba is another example: it was elected to the board in 1958 when relations with the United States had not yet deteriorated, but it has not been elected since then.

The issue of representation has also arisen at the level of the secretariat. The statute calls for recruitment on as wide a geographical basis as possible and for a minimum number of permanent contracts.[7] Both the less-developed countries and the Soviet bloc exercise surveillance over these provisions, and by and large the director-general has kept permanent staff to a minimum and fulfilled the mandate for wide geographic recruitment. As the figures in table 7.3 show, however, there are a number of marked imbalances in the secretariat.

The figure for Socialist states under C results from the policy of East European governments not to accept permanent appointments. Personnel policy is a highly sensitive and controversial issue, and except for the posts in the highest echelon, appointments are largely in the hands of the director-general. Many appointments to staff posts, particularly those of directors and classified as P5, are the subject of bargaining between the director-general and the member states, and the director-general uses this leverage to strengthen his role within the secretariat.

The only major representational issue in the secretariat came in 1961, when the retirement of Sterling Cole as director-general raised the question of his replacement. The Western states nominated Sigvard Eklund, but the less-developed countries put forth the Indonesian diplomat Sudjarwo as their candidate. Their argument, most clearly articulated by India, was that the developing countries were inadequately represented in the top echelons of the agency and that only the appointment of a national of one of those countries to the post of director-general could rectify the situation. Eklund's candidacy was sharply contested by the Soviet Union and the other two socialist states on the board, largely out of political considerations, for this was a time of trial between the Soviet Union and Dag Hammarskjöld. In the event, Eklund was elected by a vote of thirteen to three. His support came from the Western states and Latin America, with the socialist states casting the three opposing votes and with India, Iraq, and Ceylon abstaining. The Soviet Union had toyed with the idea of a troika for the agency but walked out of the General Conference after that body ratified the board's choice by a vote of forty-six to fifteen with five abstentions. The Soviet Union quietly returned to the following board meetings, and the issue has not been raised again.

Table 7.3

Distribution of Top Posts in IAEA

	Western	Socialist	Other
A. Distribution of the 267 posts classed as professional or higher, subject to geographical distribution (out of 314 posts at this level)	180	48	39
B. Distribution of the 24 highest posts in the agency	14	6	4
C. Distribution of permanent posts in the secretariat	49	1	8

Source: IAEA, *The Staff of the Agency*, INFCIRC/22/REV/8, 12 August 1968.

This did not resolve the problem of representation of the less-developed countries, however. In 1963, partly under continuing pressure from the developing nations, partly in response to enlightened Western concern about regional imbalance, and partly in the interest of greater efficiency, Eklund reorganized the secretariat so as to concentrate all technical assistance in a single department. As deputy director-general of the new department he named a highly qualified Indian national, Upendra Goswami. Because technical assistance is the agency function most relevant to the developing countries, the problem of representation at least at this level has subsided somewhat; and attention has increasingly shifted to the problem of the composition of the board.

In sum, most representational issues were initiated either by the developing nations or by the socialist states. The Western states on some issues and the permanent members of the board on others have been cast in the role of potential vetoers or brokers. The secretariat, on the other hand, has been only marginally involved.

Symbolic Decisions

Three features of the IAEA—the limited attention it commands, its meager publicity at least until 1968, and the private meetings of its board—combined to render the agency of little interest to states as a forum in which to conduct political vendettas. In the 1950s the socialist states tried to link IAEA activities to broad questions˙such as arms limitation and declarations not to use nuclear weapons; but these efforts did not reach the point of draft resolutions aimed at testing the acceptability of the goals to the membership at large. In the private confines of the board and in the public conference the Soviet bloc has consistently objected to technical assistance for Taiwan, South Vietnam, and South Korea and has used these occasions to attack the policy of the United States on Vietnam; but these interjections have been brief and mostly for the record only.

The closest the agency has come to reaching a symbolic decision of this genre was in 1967. In the midst of the Arab-Israeli war in June of that year the board met to pass on the technical assistance program of the agency. A piece of equipment donated to the agency by France had been awarded, purely on technical grounds, to Israel. The Arab states, supported by the Soviet bloc, attempted to reverse the secretariat's recommendation on the ground that Israel was an aggressor state and would use the equipment to further military plans involving nuclear force. Acquiescence of the board would have been tantamount to condemning Israel; and when the Arab-Soviet group sought to force the issue, the Western states, backed by a number of neutrals, voted to support the secretariat's original recommendation. The point that had been reaffirmed was that the agency's concern was limited to technical and scientific considerations [8] and that extraneous political controversy should not intrude in agency affairs.

This does not mean that symbolic issues have not arisen in the IAEA. Most symbolic issues have related to matters specific to the agency and have been addressed to such questions as the objectives of the organization, the appropriateness of agency action at given times, and more recently the scope of agency responsibilities in the nuclear field.

The less-developed countries, as a rule only modestly active, have been the principal initiators of actions designed to reaffirm the responsibility of the agency to the developing countries in matters of training, education, technical assistance, and general development. India, Pakistan, Mexico, and the United Arab Republic have been particularly active in sponsoring resolutions or provisos emphasizing the "extensive responsibilities of the agency in technical assistance" or calling for "special attention to the needs of underdeveloped countries." Of sixty-seven substantive resolutions passed by the conference between 1957 and 1967, for example, twenty-seven in one way or another related to the agency's developmental responsibilities. The director-general has frequently indicated in his public addresses that he shares these convictions.

Resolutions expressing satisfaction and support for agency policies or programs emanate largely from the Western states. In some instances these have related to action undertaken by the board in response to demands from developing countries (for help in the development of nuclear power, for example), but in others, like safeguards, they have been directed toward endorsing principles and procedures formulated on the board and of potentially wide application. Safeguards initiatives have been the special province of the United States, whose own ideas and practices are largely reflected in the agency's regulations.

While the IAEA has been a low salience organization for most of its life, the coming of the Non-Proliferation Treaty has altered this situation. Not only does the NPT specifically designate the IAEA as the agency responsible for overseeing the safeguards provisions of that treaty; it also raises the question of the role of the agency in implementing other treaty provisions, particularly its role in the development and management of peaceful nuclear explosions. Under article V of the NPT the benefits of peaceful explosions (which cannot be carried out by nonnuclear weapon states parties to the treaty) are to be attainable through "an appropriate international body with adequate representation of nonnuclear weapon states." The issue has been whether or not the IAEA is that "appropriate international body." A number of countries participating in the Conference of Non-Nuclear Weapon States (CNNWS) in September 1968, among them Mexico, Ghana, and Italy, contended for a variety of reasons that it is not—at least as it is presently structured.[9] Responding to this challenge from outside the framework of the IAEA (a challenge threatening an organization that was originally created to accommodate situations involving proliferation of nuclear weapons, and in which the United States holds preponderant influence), the United States introduced a resolution in the 1968 General Conference affirming the agency's particular competence in matters relevant to the peaceful use of nuclear explosions and calling upon the director-general to initiate studies preparatory to the performance of such a role.[10] Associated with this is the problem of the composition of the board: the equity of its structure has been contested with increasing frequency as the Non-Proliferation Treaty comes closer to implementation. The implications of the treaty for the IAEA thus are incalculable. Through the treaty the agency has its first real opportunity to come into its own and to rise from relative obscurity to the center of the international stage.

Boundary Decisions

Because the IAEA deals in a resource that can apply to many specific fields, such as health, agriculture, or industry, for each of which there exist specialized agencies, it is almost condemned to a continual adjustment of its jurisdictional boundaries. At the time the statute was drafted, the ILO, FAO, and WHO questioned whether the draft statute did not give IAEA a poaching license on their territory. With the support of a number of national delegations they managed to get IAEA's statute modified to require that in establishing or adopting standards for health, labor conditions, and the like the IAEA would be obliged to consult or collaborate with United Nations organs and the specialized agencies concerned.

Since its establishment the IAEA has come into jurisdictional conflict with the FAO and WHO. Resolution of these and any differences between the IAEA and other agencies is left largely to the director-general, subject to ultimate approval by the board. Differences with the FAO were resolved in 1964 by the creation of a Joint Division staffed and financed partly (but not equally) by each agency but housed in the IAEA and headed by an FAO official who formerly was in the secretariat of the IAEA. Although the Joint Divisions's program must be approved by the directors-general and governing bodies of both organizations, differences remain at a relatively low key, and the board of the IAEA is disinclined to interfere. Relations with WHO are still conducted through liaison officers, for the two agencies have been unable to reach a joint division type of accommodation; and relations between them are less harmonious.

The IAEA has had fewer jurisdictional confrontations with the other intergovernmental organizations such as ENEA or CERN, although ENEA for a time was highly competitive with IAEA, often seeking to preempt the agency on popular or attractive projects. The more prominent exception to the general infrequency of jurisdictional confrontation is EURATOM, which has its own safeguards provisions and which consequently cuts into the universality of the IAEA's system. This is a point that the director-general has not failed to make on a number of occasions. Because of the United States' support of EURATOM and the general influence of the EURATOM states in the IAEA, the board has never been called upon to take a position on this problem.

In view of the limited nature and relative unimportance of IAEA during much of its lifetime, there have been few points of contention between the agency and the United Nations. More recently, however, the United Nations seems to have become aware of the existence and potential importance of the IAEA, a development whose implications became manifest in the Conference of Non-Nuclear Weapon States in 1968. The conference, originally intended to deal with questions related to the security of states not possessing nuclear weapons, was gradually extended to cover programs for peaceful uses of nuclear energy as well. This agenda item was the source of a number of resolutions implicitly challenging the jurisdiction and mandate of the IAEA. The United States resolution on peaceful explosions, discussed under symbolic decisions, and subsequent action by the United

States and the Soviet Union at the Twenty-third General Assembly to quell an attempt to create a special committee on nuclear development (sponsored by Italy) were the main efforts made to preserve the IAEA's position as the primordial agency responsible for nuclear development. This is one of the rare instances in which the initiative on a boundary question came from member states rather than (but not to the exclusion of) the secretariat.

Programmatic Decisions

Because its original main purposes of brokerage and control were unattainable as a result of changes in the specific environment of the agency, the initial problem of the IAEA was largely to find work to justify its existence. Through a combination of entrepreneurship and ingenuity exercised by several persons in the top echelon of the secretariat and the strong commitment of the United States to support the agency, a program emerged on an ad hoc basis. It was geared partly to promoting certain secondary uses of atomic energy and partly to preparing countries for the eventual utilization of nuclear energy in general.

Since the problem in these earlier years was rather to find something useful for the agency to do than to select one course among a superabundance of alternatives, the assessment of priorities in programmatic choices was not a significant issue. There was, nevertheless, resistance to the direction of the chosen program. The developing countries admonished the board in one of the first resolutions of the General Conference that priority should be given to activities of relevance to the underdeveloped areas of the world.[11] In 1961, in response to increased pressure from the developing countries to pay greater attention to the practical applications of nuclear energy accessible to them, the agency shifted emphasis in its research contract program, stressing the application of radioisotopes in agriculture, medicine, and hydrology at the expense of work on safeguards methods and waste disposal.

Although on a few occasions the developing countries have mobilized themselves on behalf of common interests—most notably in the case of the International Center for Theoretical Physics in Trieste and in the creation of a regional radioisotope center for the Arab states in Cairo—generally speaking, these countries have not exerted great influence over the agency program. The explanation lies in their low level of interest, their lack of cohesion, and the absence of consistent, articulate leadership. They initiated and supported a large number of resolutions relating to the importance of agency assistance to developing countries in its first few years; but they became more cynical and less interested as time went on and the atom looked less like a panacea for their problems of economic development. The principal concern of the developing countries is for technical assistance, but the structure of the agency's budget precludes their use of many avenues of pressure, for all technical assistance activities must be funded by voluntary contributions. Furthermore, most of the developing countries receive technical assistance in the nuclear field on a bilateral basis and thus have a somewhat reduced incentive for exerting pressure on the agency in this regard.

Two points that have a general bearing on the programmatic development of the IAEA are: first, there is a symbiotic relationship between a conservative board and a conservative secretariat; second, to the extent that there are expansionist tendencies, they emanate either from segments of the bureaucracy (as distinguished from the director-general of the agency) or, with somewhat less consistency, from the United States. A considerable amount of control over the program is exerted within the secretariat through a Preparatory Committee for Program and Budget (PCPB), chaired by the deputy director-general for administration. This adds to the restraints exerted on programmatic decisions by external factors and creates a cadre of internal potential vetoers. The Soviet bloc opposes budgetary increases in principle; the Commonwealth countries, while basically opposed to anything more than a modest increase, usually make specific recommendations with respect to the program. Only the Latin-American states have been inclined to support the liberal orientation of the United States, which stands behind the estimates of the director-general and occasionally even recommends increases in programmatic sectors.

Differences over the budget are in reality differences over the program. For example, one of the principal charges on the agency's funds is the laboratory that was started despite Soviet opposition and with no support from the Commonwealth countries. The laboratory was able to get under way only because of an outright contribution from the United States. Soviet and developing country opponents have argued that much of the work done in the laboratory should more appropriately be allocated to developing countries and that the laboratory incessantly expands its scope of activity, moving away from the abstract concept of coordinator and toward an actual scientific center for research, which is allegedly beyond its mandate. A number of Western countries even beyond the Commonwealth subscribe to these criticisms, but the board generally manages to reach an accommodation that leans in favor of the laboratory. Part of the reason may lie in the fact that several of those Western states that take a narrow view of the laboratory indicate only that they would abstain, rather than vote no, if the budget were put to a vote. As a yes vote by only two-thirds of those voting is enough to carry the budget, the support of a dozen states generally suffices.

The issue of priorities has become more pronounced in the last several years as a result of the agency's allocating a rapidly increasing proportion of the budget to safeguards and introducing one of the few new programs (besides safeguards and radioisotopic uses) since its inception—the International Nuclear Information Service (INIS). The two together accounted for 80 percent of the increase of the 1969 budget over that for 1968. Both stem from American initiatives and have the unqualified support of the Soviet Union. The less-developed countries on the board have become increasingly concerned over these developments.

While it is still too early to discern any particular pattern of alignment on the allocation of agency resources, there is some evidence that as the superpowers draw closer together in their mutual search for détente, several of the advanced nonnuclear weapon states may come to identify themselves more closely with the views of the developing countries, at least insofar as safeguards are concerned. The picture that emerges from a review of the relationships in the programmatic sector shows a large number of cross-cutting cleavages, with the issue of priorities only recently becoming serious.

Operational Decisions

Operational decisions in the sense of tactical allocations of resources made within the framework of programmatic choices are largely in the hands of the secretariat, although this is in no way an immutable rule. The statutory relationship between the secretariat and the board, whereby the latter is vested with authority to carry out the functions of the agency, underlies the close watch the board has maintained over the execution of IAEA programs. Until 1964 the director-general was required to report to the board bimonthly on all major developments in the agency's work. Since then he has received some latitude: now he need only submit two such reports a year. [12] In practice if not in theory, however, the director-general and the secretariat have somewhat greater leeway of action than the formal provisions might suggest.

The agency's technical assistance program is primarily negotiated between the supplicants and the deputy director-general for technical assistance. The allocation of technical assistance in the form of experts, fellowships, training, or equipment is subject to unwritten rules aimed at ensuring equitable political and geographical distribution, rules over which the director-general exercises vigilance. The result is that while scientific criteria are employed in evaluating projects, they are compromised by these other considerations of distribution and balance.

The problem of balance and distribution also has intervened in the agency's research contract program, which is not classed as technical assistance. Research contracts are supposed to be awarded in the interest of resolving scientific and technological problems related to the agency's scientific work; logically they were nearly always negotiated directly with laboratories and institutes in the more advanced countries. In 1960, for example, more than 70 percent of the funds allocated for research contracts went to advanced states. Under combined pressure from the developing states and the secretariat, seconded by the Soviet Union and without serious Western opposition (because a refusal to contract with developing countries would be impolitic), the board in 1961 authorized the director-general to give preference to developing countries whenever the research could be reasonably expected to equal that which could be carried out in an advanced state. The general pattern now is that two-thirds of the funds spent on research contracts each year go to institutes in developing countries. [13] Yet of the ten countries that receive the lion's share of research funds, six are advanced states (Austria, Japan, Belgium, France, Czechoslovakia, and Italy) and a seventh (Israel) is not ordinarily considered to fit the concept of a developing country. [14] The distribution of symposia and conferences over issue-areas is also susceptible to the intrusion of geographic and political factors.

One of the more dramatic confrontations with respect to the tactical allocation of resources arose from a resolution passed in the Tenth General Conference (1966) calling for a review of the agency's activities. It originated in the discontent of some of the developing countries over their representation in the secretariat and on the board. The initial draft resolution declared that the agency's response to developing countries' needs was inadequate, and it called for a special review committee, including representatives of the developing countries. This draft resolution was channeled, through a series of modifications emanating from developing and developed countries, toward a constructive review of ways and means of increasing assistance to developing countries. One of the differences between the Afro-Asian states and the Anglo-Saxons, in particular, had been whether or not the IAEA's technical assistance program should have as its chief object the transfer of knowledge and skills, or whether the provision of equipment was also an important aspect. The compromise resolution on the results of the review, [15] cosponsored by Australia, India, and the United Arab Republic among others, allowed that equipment could be made available independently of expert services and asked that the director-general give particular attention to such requests without requiring any formal relationship between services and equipment. Only on the issues of equipment versus experts and the magnitude of the technical assistance program have the developing countries shown any cohesion.

Finally, individual members of the board have intervened in the operational sector for the purpose of changing the rules of the game rather than for protesting any particular resource allocation. A striking example is an initiative taken by the United States in 1963 to limit the allocation of all Type-I fellowships to nationals of those states that were receiving assistance under EPTA. Type-I fellowships are those funded out of voluntary cash contributions. This rule would have eliminated nationals from the Soviet bloc states from consideration for such fellowships, for at that time none of those states were participating in EPTA. Nor was any state in the Soviet bloc contributing to the voluntary program; yet a large number of the fellowships awarded by the secretariat in the previous years had gone to East Europeans. The secretariat's awards had been in great measure based on the criterion of quality; however, a number of officials felt some obligation to assist East Europeans to get contacts outside the Soviet bloc and training opportunities outside the Soviet Union. Although not all of the Western states were enthusiastic about the United States initiative, they ended by supporting it in the face of East European claims of discrimination in violation of the statute. Ultimately most of the East European states began participating in EPTA and thus qualified for Type-I fellowships again. To avoid another bout with the United States on this issue the secretariat has since established for itself a ground rule that unless a country is not in the Eastern bloc or is a developing state, no more than five fellowships can be awarded to its nationals.

These cases demonstrate several important facts: the balance between the secretariat and the member states with regard to operational decisions; the limits of the secretariat's autonomy; the influence that a large donor state can wield even in some of the secondary aspects of the organization's work; and the role of the often "silent majority" of less-developed countries in the IAEA.

Rule-Creating Decisions

There are two major interlocking dimensions of agency activity relating to the establishment of the conditions under which international nuclear transactions are to take place: (1) regulations, standards, and codes regarding health, safety, and the handling of radioactive substances; and (2) safeguards against diversion of nuclear materials from peaceful to military purposes. In both cases it must be an agency project or agency assistance must be involved before regulations are binding on member states, unless, of course, there is a voluntary submission. Safeguards raise highly sensitive political questions and carry implications for national sovereignty not found in the other regulatory fields, since they entail provisions for accountability and for international inspectors to be on national territory and in national facilities for the purpose of verifying national accounts and reports.

Whether safeguards or other regulatory issues are in question, the structure of influence in the agency is basically the same. The core group in this area, as in most agency activities, includes the United States, the Soviet Union, the United Kingdom, and Canada. France, because of its equivocal view on safeguards, stands somewhat apart on that issue. When safeguards were a major issue between the West on the one hand and the Soviet bloc and some of the developing countries like India, Indonesia, and the United Arab Republic on the other, France's reserved position enabled it occasionally to play a brokerage role; but as the Soviet position shifted in favor of safeguards and the French unenthusiastically endorsed the system, France lost some of its weight.

The United States has been the predominant influence in safeguards. At first this influence was exercised through the exertion of considerable pressure and the mobilization of votes both in the board and in the General Conference on behalf of safeguards principles and regulations. Soviet opposition forced the West to act as a cohesive unit, and this strengthened even further the American dominance over the agency's safeguards development. With the Soviet Union now supporting safeguards, not only must the United States share influence over the development and orientation of the system (though still maintaining a leading position), but it also has lost some of its ability to maintain a solid Western front on all issues involving safeguards.

Paradoxically the importance and implications of safeguards make them an area in which a fairly wide range of states wish to make their weight felt; but precisely because of the importance of safeguards to them the major powers have tried to maintain close control and to shape the safeguards system to their satisfaction, either through political bargaining, or more often (now that the principle of safeguards is established) through superior expertise. The emerging tension in this field is therefore between the nuclear powers and the 'threshold" or near-nuclear states, and it is this pattern that seems to be replacing the older confrontation between East and West.

In other regulatory fields the stakes are somewhat lower, and the opportunities for an interested and active lesser power to make its weight felt are increased. But partly because these fields are less interesting to many states and partly because they are highly technical and thus require sophisticated knowledge and experience, the same core group, joined by Japan, South Africa, Australia, and India, is left to dominate the scene. Influence in the sectors of rule creating other than safeguards is also partly determined by interest. Thus, in transport regulations the commercial states play an important role both at the political level and in the expert committees; in problems of waste disposal into the sea, maritime states and those states whose geological formations preclude or limit burial of radioactive waste beneath the ground are central actors. Again, however, simply because of the expertise necessary in nearly all nuclear matters, the leading nuclear powers are almost condemned to play a significant role.

The secretariat is also an important actor in rule creation. All work in the regulatory sector is carried out initially through panels of experts drawn from the member states, who either discuss the secretariat's drafts or are themselves responsible for producing a draft document. In the area of safeguards these experts are governmental officials and are closely instructed, thus narrowing the range of opportunities available to the secretariat to exercise influence. In other less sensitive fields, however, the secretariat can play a more active and influential role both as an initiator and as a mediator, and it has done so. Because all draft rules and regulations eventually must come before the board for approval, part of the secretariat's strategy (employed also in the programmatic sector) is to call on experts from states whose governors are thought likely to offer resistance.

Rule creation also involves establishing the rules of the game on matters internal to the agency. If the rules relate to the budget, then a different pattern from that noted above usually prevails. For example, when the United Kingdom and the United States tried to amend the statute so that all agency activities would be financed from a single assessed budget, they ran into a coalition of forces built around the Soviet Union, Canada, Australia, South Africa, and France. When the United States forced the issue in the board, eleven states including those named above either voted against the recommendation or abstained, and the United States decided not to press its case further.

Rule-Supervisory Decisions

The detection and verification of the observance or nonobservance of rules established by the agency are, where they are applicable, carried out by the secretariat. The agency has no direct legislative powers; but, as we have seen, the safeguards, health, and safety measures adopted by the agency do apply to agency projects and to cases where the agency has given substantial assistance. In the matter of safeguards, the measures also apply if a state voluntarily submits itself to the rules or enters into an agreement with the agency and a supplier state for the IAEA to safeguard and inspect the nuclear materials in question. The manner in which detection and verification in safeguards are carried out (through auditing procedures and direct inspection) is subject to agreements negotiated between the agency and the state in question, within the framework of the safeguards system adopted by the agency and with ultimate approval by the Board of Governors. Among the principal questions raised by the Non-Proliferation Treaty are just how verification should be accomplished and what kind of division of responsibility can be made between the national state and the IAEA.

The application of sanctions has not yet arisen in the agency. If it did, however, the board is vested with the authority to call upon the state in question to take corrective action, to curtail or suspend any further assistance to that state, to call for the return of all materials supplied by the agency, and to recommend that the General Conference suspend the member state in question. Decisions regarding penalties beyond these lie with the Security Council of the United Nations, to which the board is required to report once it has determined that the safeguards rules have been violated.[16]

Actors and Their Sources of Influence

With considerations of structure, function, evolution, and a taxonomical analysis of decision-making patterns behind us, we now can turn to the questions of who actually participates in the decisions of the IAEA and what are the bases of their influence. To what extent is influence a function of role, and to what extent does it depend on more random factors like idiosyncratic qualities and attributes? There are a number of participants in the IAEA's decision-making process, and they are grouped and presented here in descending order of importance.

National Government Representatives. National representatives to the IAEA tend to be divided between diplomatic and functional types with the balance in favor of the functional. At the 1968 General Conference, for example, forty-four delegations were headed by functional representatives and twenty-seven by diplomatic. Of these twenty-seven, however, fourteen were ambassadors from their nations to Austria, the host country, and in a number of these cases the alternate on the delegation was a functional representative. This suggests that at least some delegation heads were playing a ceremonial role. The same pattern prevails in the Board of Governors. Many of the major powers are represented by functional types, although it is sometimes a matter of scientist turned international envoy. The level of representation for the advanced nuclear states tends to be middle to high; for some of the less-advanced states, middle to low. As a generalization, the level of representation to the agency is a function of the degree of interest a state takes in the work of the IAEA.

For a number of states, such as the Soviet Union, there is a division of labor between the governor and the resident representative, with the latter speaking on behalf of the state at the annual General Conference on matters of political concern. Thus, at least to a degree, the functional representative does not take the lead in representational or symbolic issues. The functional representative does not, however, necessarily escape political dialogue. Interestingly, despite the increased politicization of the agency as a result of the Non-Proliferation Treaty and the Conference of Non-Nuclear Weapon States, there has not been any noticeable shift from functional to diplomatic representation. Dramatization of political questions relating to the big nuclear issues still tends to occur in better publicized forums like the General Assembly.

Approximately half of the member states have permanent representatives to the IAEA, but this is a highly magnified reflection of reality. Only a dozen or so states, largely the permanent board members, have a full-time resident representative; and only two states, the United States and the Soviet Union, have complete missions. Sweden and France, for example, have "half a man" each in Vienna. The role of the permanent representative varies considerably, and it is difficult to generalize categorically about his latitude of independent action, beyond saying that on secondary issues the permanent representative appears to have a fairly free hand and that this freedom does not seem to vary significantly between different types of states. One thing is certain, however: presence in Vienna is an important factor, especially since the agency's style of operation has shifted from frequent and lengthy board meetings to a pattern of continuous informal consultation among member states and between member states and the secretariat.[17] One essential function performed by the resident representatives is to keep momentum up and problems down.

Government representatives as a group are the most important participants in the decision-making process of the agency. At least to some degree they are relevant to all types of decisions and predominant in most. There are, of course, differences among governmental representatives, and one of the distinguishing criteria for influence is representation on the Board of Governors. This is true not merely because the statute vests authority in the board to carry out the functions of the agency but also because the board is de facto the seat of power in the IAEA. The possibility that someone not on the board could exert influence in the agency is not of course ruled out; but this tends to be a sporadic rather than a continuous influence, and it is often, though not always, exercised through a surrogate on the board. If there are limitations to this medium for exerting influence, its occasional effectiveness is not to be overlooked. Mere presence on the board, however, although it is by and large a necessary condition for the exercise of influence, is not sufficient in itself. Presence must be accompanied by an active interest in the agency.

The Director-General. Because executive authority is vested in the Board of Governors, with the director-general designated as chief administrative officer, his position vis-à-vis his governing body is considerably weaker than that of his counterparts in many other international organizations. This statutory limitation is compounded by the tendency of the board to insist on its prerogatives and occasionally to wield a heavy hand in relation to the director-general. One example of this is the reluctance, until recently, of the board to permit the director-general to authorize the transfer of even small amounts of fissile materials without first securing the board's approval. Similarly, the board's Technical Assistance Committee and Administrative and Budget Committee, particularly the last, exercise surveillance over the programmatic and assistance sectors of agency activity.

The first director-general, Sterling Cole, was reluctantly accepted by the Soviet Union "in the spirit of conciliation." Cole, who had an activist conception of his office, was at a disadvantage because of the cold war environment as well as his nationality. He was inclined to take initiatives rather than to devote his energies to building consensus; and he was particularly active with respect to safeguards, which he regarded as one of the most important purposes for which the agency was created. This led not only to confrontations with the Soviet Union and some of the developing countries on the matter of priorities, but also to some differences with the United States, which in the first few years of the agency's life was still pursuing a bilateral course on safeguards, while Cole was arguing vigorously for an international system.

The current director-general, Sigvard Eklund, takes a more passive view of his role. He is inclined toward conservatism and caution and is not disposed to grasp initiatives. This was manifest in his treatment of the question of the IAEA's relation to the Non-Proliferation Treaty. Rather than seize the opportunity of asserting the agency's role in the implementation of the treaty, Eklund committed himself to saying only that if the agency were called upon to assume responsibilities under the treaty, it would be prepared to do so. Thus, suggestions within the secretariat that the agency should independently initiate studies of its role and capabilities were soft-pedaled. For some time, on the other hand, Eklund has been, like his predecessor, openly critical of competitive safeguards systems, both bilateral and regional. His caution with respect to the NPT reflects a sharp perception of what the traffic will bear, as well as good political acumen, but it also fits the pattern of conservatism and restraint that has marked his administration.

Eklund conceives his job to consist principally of consensus brokerage, although even here his preference sometimes runs to letting the major powers work things out between themselves. His deference to the board has its rewards, however, for a sense of trust in Eklund has developed in the course of time. When one considers that the Soviet Union walked out of the General Conference following Eklund's election in 1961, his cordial relations with the Soviet Union are no mean achievement. In the long run, however, his personal conservatism and passive view of his role reduce the possibilities for Eklund to develop an independent power base, and they reinforce the statutory limitations placed on his office.

Segments of the Bureaucracy. While several departments in the secretariat had the potential for creating an independent power base, none of them have actually achieved this. In some respects the Department of Technical Assistance was an empire unto itself, but because it had to rely on voluntary contributions and its clientele had no effective means of pressing the donor states into augmenting those contributions, its own powers were limited. The two deputy directors-general in charge of the bulk of the agency's functional activities concerned with nontechnical assistance were powerful in their own realms and tended to negotiate a modus vivendi between themselves with respect to allocating research contract funds or establishing suggested priorities for panels, symposia, or conferences; they also were expansionist in orientation, but their power could be neutralized, either within the secretariat by the intervention of the director-general or by appeals of one or the other to sympathetic board members. One of these two, the Soviet deputy director-general, generally was regarded as "the Russian representative in the secretariat." This points up one of the characteristics of the secretariat: the tendency for members to align themselves with particular countries. One explanation for this is the rapid turnover of staff, owing to the director-general's interpretation of the statute to mean that the number of permanent posts, not merely the proportion of total posts, be kept to a minimum. This interpretation, by maximizing the number and frequency of appointments to be made, gives him some political leverage.

Another characteristic of the secretariat is the tendency toward a certain clubbishness among some groups, for example, the Commonwealth countries. These countries hold a disproportionate share of permanent or long-term appointments and a good number of the administrative posts—not to speak of the scientific ones. Besides having cultural links, they are also, as a rule, professional international civil servants who came from the United Nations or other specialized agencies when IAEA was started. While it is difficult to isolate the precise nature of their influence, beyond the fact that by knowing the ropes they can facilitate or impede initiatives, it is clear that such influence exists and that these individuals form a separate communications network within the secretariat.

Eminent Persons and Expert Advisers. The IAEA makes extensive use of panels of experts both in the preparation of programs and in their periodic evaluation. Except in the safeguards field, where participants are designated by and are representatives of national governments, most of the panels are appointed by the director-general. Theoretically, persons are appointed on the basis of technical expertise only; but in practice political and geographic considerations intervene. The expectation of the director-general that the imprimatur of these panels will facilitate the secretariat's task of securing the board's approval often proves to be correct, but it is also true that an unfavorable report from the panel can be damaging to the secretariat's case. Thus, panels constitute one of the more important resources of the secretariat and do exert an influence over agency decisions. How effectively the secretariat uses expert panels in its cause depends on the skills of the participants from the secretariat. Some outside experts who have served on these panels have remarked on the adeptness of the secretariat in fashioning the limited technical advice of experts into endorsed recommendations for wider action.

The agency also has a Scientific Advisory Council (SAC), composed in the past of such prestigious scientists as Isidore Rabi, Sir John Cockcroft, and Homi Bhabha, among others. SAC reviews the overall scientific program of the agency and passes scientific judgment on panels, conferences, and symposia. Despite its prestigious composition, however, SAC is less influential in agency decisions than the panels of experts convened for particular purposes. It rarely takes a strong position, and on one of the few occasions that it did—when it unanimously rejected the idea of a center for the study of theoretical physics—it was overridden. In general it can be said that SAC is influential if and when the director-general and the board choose to make it so; and this has not been their common practice, especially in recent years.

Representatives of Other International Organizations. As we noted earlier, the agency has run into a number of boundary problems, especially with the FAO and WHO. Representatives of both of these organizations have intervened in agency programs relating to their fields of concern, and there have been instances when this intervention had a bearing on what the IAEA did. In many instances external interventions connect with and reinforce intra-agency restraints on programs, and thus it is hard to fully evaluate the impact of these interventions. With the establishment of a joint FAO-IAEA division, FAO is now institutionally tied to the agency's decision-making process, but the IAEA is ordinarily the dominant partner in this arrangement.

Representatives of National and International Private Associations and Employees of the Mass Media. For most of its life the IAEA has operated without much publicity, and as a consequence employees of the mass media have had virtually no role in agency decision making.

Sources of Influence

Sources of influence in the IAEA fall into three groups: those that time has proved to be relatively important, those that are relatively unimportant, and those that have a latent and periodic importance. The factors that appear to have least relevance to influence in the agency are administrative competence, ideological legitimacy, and flexibility or inflexibility in bargaining positions. Exceptions can, of course, be found; but because we are speaking here in relative rather than absolute terms, they do not invalidate the rule.

There is no fundamental doctrine regarding the agency that assumes an ideological form, and hence there is no ground upon which one can acquire influence by articulating a widely shared set of beliefs. Conversely, the fact that some representatives may speak for a member state whose own legitimacy is contested by a large portion of the agency's membership has not had any significant bearing on the influence of that representative. The striking case in point is South Africa. On the other hand, it is clear that the director-general owes his credibility in part to his being able to represent the diverse priorities and concerns voiced in the agency and to strike an acceptable balance between the goals of development and control. Flexibility and intransigence in negotiating have rarely been significant as resources. Among the few exceptions are the single-mindedness of the developing countries in pursuing the idea of the International Center for Theoretical Physics in Trieste and of the United Arab Republic in pressing for a radioisotope study center in Cairo, although in this negotiation Cairo's willingness to meet any conditions in return for agency sanction was as marked as the perverse insistence on pursuing the policy. As for administrative competence, its absence creates a target for criticism, but its presence only modestly reinforces the position of an actor, whose influence must be based on other resources.

Several sources of influence that normally might be expected to predominate are best considered as latent or periodic sources in the IAEA.

These include control over budgetary contributions, control over other material factors relevant to the work of the agency, and ability to mobilize votes. Control over budgetary contributions is a limited and latent resource. It is limited in that certain heavy contributors, particularly the Federal Republic of Germany and the Republic of China, do not exert influence commensurate with the financial support they furnish. This is in the process of changing for the Federal Republic of Germany, and for both countries it is explainable by political considerations. Control of budgetary contributions is latent in the sense that major contributors do not bring their financial weight to bear in order to assert or impede policies or programs; rather, the known tolerance of donor countries is taken into account both by the secretariat in drawing up the budget for the board, and by the General Conference in approving the budget. Major donors can thus be said to play a controller's role through their financial power and to exercise their influence vicariously. Latent power can, of course, be converted into direct power, but generally the controller role prevails over that of initiator or vetoer.

Control over other than financial resources has two dimensions. On the one hand is a country's status. Technologically sophisticated nations participate as a routine matter in scientific and other panels, conferences, and symposia. Representatives or nationals of these advanced nations derive influence from the nuclear standing of their state and from the fact that the implementation of decisions may require reliance on the material resources controlled by those nations. On the other hand, there has generally been very little demand for nuclear materials, for reasons explored earlier. The agency has not become a major channel for the exchange of nuclear fuels or material, and technological advance has had only limited relevance, unless one considers the status or prestige noted above. If the latent promise for developing the peaceful applications of nuclear explosions under the Non-Proliferation Treaty were fulfilled largely through the auspices of the IAEA, this situation would change and would presumably allow the technologically advanced states—and specifically the nuclear weapon states—to exert influence on national programs and policies through their almost exclusive control over the explosive devices in question. Similarly, if the agency were to become a main channel for general nuclear development, the advanced states would gain leverage and influence through their control over needed resources.

The relative importance of sources of influence has varied in response to the changing style of decision making in the agency. This is particularly true of the ability to mobilize votes—an important asset in the cold war days, it has become a latent resource ever since the board moved away from formal voting to decision making by consensus. At the level of the General Conference, mobilization of votes on behalf of resolutions has occasionally been important, but the limitations on the role of the conference minimize the importance of vote mobilizing in that forum.

Given the informal, consultative, consensus-building style of decision making that characterizes the agency, certain resources suggested in our discussion on actors become of evident importance: permanent presence in Vienna, continuous active interest in agency work, access to influential decision makers, long association with the agency, and personal qualities. Permanent representation of an active, interested state virtually ensures consultation and participation. With few exceptions, however, full-time permanent representation is maintained only by permanent board members. In some instances (e.g. Japan, Argentina, Canada, India, and South Africa) the permanent representative is also on the Board of Governors. Neither France's nor the United States' governor is resident: the United States governor "commutes"; the French governor keeps in continuous touch through close relations with colleagues and key figures in the secretariat. In other cases (e.g. Brazil) the resident representative, though an alternate to the governor, serves in that capacity most of the time. Thus, what is determined through consultation at the level of permanent representatives has little chance of failing to be ratified by the board; and, because of the overlapping composition of the two groups, there is little risk that permanent representatives would go beyond the limits that the board would accept. An added consideration is the high degree of continuity of representation, especially for the United States, the Soviet Union, France, and the United Kingdom.

How effectively a representative can wield influence is partly a question of what he represents—the interest and status of his country or its budgetary contributions, subject to the qualifications earlier stated—and partly a matter of the person himself. The relevance of idiosyncratic factors increases as one moves away from the major powers. The influence of countries like Canada, Japan, and South Africa has varied with different representatives, and any weakening at the level of representation can significantly affect the influence of the country. Long association with the IAEA and expert knowledge reinforce the influence of particular representatives and members of the secretariat. Expertise is an especially important source of influence on scientific policy but is not tied to this sphere of agency activity. Melding of the art of advocacy with expertise and intimate knowledge of the organization's evolution strengthened the hand of the already influential British governor, for example. The United States and the Soviet Union appear to be the only two countries for whom the role factor takes precedence over idiosyncratic factors in accounting for influence, and even then it does not exclude other sources.

Having access to or holding a special functional position in the decision making of IAEA is also an important factor in accounting for influence. Permanent representation, membership on the Board of Governors, and long association with the agency all facilitate this access. At the level of the secretariat, some of the positions to which access is most desirable are those of director-general, deputy director-general for administration, and director of the budget. It is significant that since 1961, when the United States relinquished the post of director-general, the latter two posts have been held by American nationals. The importance of the deputy director-general's post is that any political question filters through that office; the budget post is important because any expenditure on programs comes under the scrutiny and jurisdiction of the director of the budget. Thus, the two together command a view of most agency activities. The fact that the person who is now deputy director-general for the second time alternates as assistant general manager for international affairs in the U.S. Atomic Energy Commission suggests the close relation between access and potential influence.

Organizational Ideology

Ideologically, the IAEA is a low-key organization. There is a certain folklore about the agency, shared by many representative and bureaucratic elites, that science and scientific organization can successfully serve as a common meeting ground for East and West and thus perhaps facilitate international understanding. This general belief reinforces the idea that scientific and technical questions ought to be decided on merit rather than on irrelevant political grounds; it also helps to minimize political confrontation on issues extraneous to the organization. Periodic intrusion on this orientation does not detract from its general application insofar as the scientific dimensions of agency work are concerned.

Folklore is not in and of itself ideology, however. If there is recognition of the value of the IAEA as a meeting ground and source of East-West contact, there is no self-image that the agency is in fact accomplishing great things. Nor is there any evident missionary zeal to change the world in terms of peace or prosperity through the benign atom. The executive leadership's preference for a cautious, pragmatic approach dispels any such image and in fact brings the agency closer in line with the political realities with which it must live. But this very caution and conservatism has precluded a coherent doctrine or ideology offering clear goals and a strategy for organizational action from emerging.

Few agency programs have taken ideological form. At first they were meant merely to ensure survival; later, as operations became routinized, they were also marked by the attitude of "atomic science for its own sake." In the absence of overall ideological direction, projects were justified more on their intrinsic merit than on their contribution to peace, health, and prosperity—although these statutory objectives might be satisfied in the context of given programs and the programs justified to the members in these terms. This pattern always has entailed a risk of subgoal dominance in IAEA. The policy of short-term appointments involves a similar risk. As individuals come into the agency to contribute their specific skills and find no general doctrine to guide their action, they begin to assume an attitude of "science for the sake of the project." This is not necessarily a self-serving interest in the narrow sense of that concept, but neither are many of the projects clearly developed in terms of explicitly defined organizational goals.

There is in the IAEA a latent division between development-oriented and control-oriented objectives. This split is more evident among representative elites than among secretariat officials. The two objectives have always been an underlying source of tension, particularly at the turn of the 1960s, when the statutory principles on safeguards were being made operational, and sharp differences arose in consequence between the West and the Indian–Indonesian–United Arab Republic front, joined by the Soviet bloc. It cannot be said, however, that safeguards were the source of sustained ideological opposition in the agency. With the general growth of safeguarding duties and the conclusion of the Non-Proliferation Treaty, which grants major safeguarding responsibilities to the IAEA, the division over the relative value and importance of development and control is becoming more pronounced. Increased responsibilities in safeguarding have led to upgrading that part of the secretariat concerned with safeguards and inspection, and both among the representatives and in the secretariat one may expect more articulate, more coherent, and perhaps more sharply defined ideological positions regarding the purposes and priorities of the IAEA in the future.

Organizational Elite

Who constitute the elite of the IAEA? With the assistance of a panel of knowledgeable individuals an effort was made to designate the twenty most influential persons in the agency for 1958 and 1967. It is interesting that in neither year could twenty individuals be discovered whose names elicited unqualified agreement regarding their relative influence. The figures in table 7.4 represent the consensus of at least half the panelists involved.

Table 7.4

Distribution of Elites in IAEA

	1958		1967	
Regional	*Number*	*Percentage*	*Number*	*Percentage*
Western	9	64.28	8	61.54
Socialist	3	21.43	2	15.38
Other	2	14.29	3	23.08
Functional				
Representative	11	78.57	8	61.54
Secretariat	3	21.43	5	38.46

In the regional distribution Western predominance remained constant. The only significant change was that the number of American nationals who were ranked among the organizational elite increased from two in 1958 to four in 1967. One of the four, however, was considered influential only in safeguards. A second of the four Americans was serving a second tour in the secretariat as deputy director-general for administration; and, as already noted, when he was not serving in Vienna, this official held a high position in the U.S. Atomic Energy Commission. Neither West German nor Japanese nationals figure among the twenty most influential persons in either period. France and Great Britain are represented on both occasions, and Canada only in 1958. Of the five Third World figures named in the two years, three were Indian.

The figures on functional distribution suggest an increase in the importance of the secretariat, but this interpretation is questionable. The agency's minor importance to most of its members and their consequently mild interest in it during most of the 1960s suggests that, rather than an absolute increase in its influence, the secretariat gained in stature through default by representative elites. By this reasoning a renewal of interest in the IAEA, such as the Non-Proliferation Treaty appears to have inspired, would reveal that the secretariat's greater importance was a short-term change rather than a reflection of a permanent trend. One also must take personnel policy into account in assessing these figures: the policy of keeping a minimal permanent staff and using short-term appointments, considered in conjunction with the highly governmental nature of atomic energy, reinforces the view that governmental representatives will play a pre-dominant role, whether on the board, in the secretariat, or in the missions. Finally, some consideration must be given to the highly personal nature of influence in the IAEA: in such circumstances changes of representative elites may, as with Canada, lead to a temporary loss of influence by a country, but it is not likely to mean much more than that.

Persistent Groupings

The same cluster of actors has dominated agency activity since its outset, but the pattern of alignments among them has varied over time and with different issue-areas. Bloc confrontation was common in the cold war period of the IAEA's history, but it was not an immutable principle. Bloc cohesion was never strong on such issues as the budget or the laboratories; there the Soviet Union and the Commonwealth countries frequently made common cause. The pattern of alignment on safeguards has been transformed with the growth of nuclear détente. Whereas in earlier days this issue polarized large segments of the membership around Western and Eastern positions, safeguards have more recently become the focal point for an emerging Soviet-American coalition.

Safeguards have given rise to such strange partnerships in the IAEA as India and South Africa and have been the source of some strain in the Western camp. Recent developments indicate that three groups of states may form on the question of safeguards, replacing the earlier bipolar pattern: (1) the Soviet-American position of positive and vigorous support for increasingly internationalized safeguards supported by other members of the Soviet bloc and such states as the Netherlands, Canada, and the Scandinavian countries; (2) Western and other states, such as West Germany, Japan, Italy, India, and South Africa, which constitute the threshold states in the agency and who find greater common cause in protecting their mutual interests than in supporting traditional allies (France never has been an enthusiast for safeguards, and recently even the United Kingdom, in keeping with its effort to join the European Economic Community, has shown reluctance to support Soviet-American conceptions); (3) a third group comprising the states of the Third World, which at best are indifferent to safeguards because credible nuclear status is so remote.

In the field of technical assistance a pattern aligning developed against undeveloped states takes form, although the latter group is so disparate and disinterested that it rarely becomes cohesive.

Caucuses as they are known in other organizations do exist in Vienna, but they are much less continuous, operating principally on representational issues. The Asian states are sharply divided among themselves: Japan leans toward the West, India pursues an independent course, and the balance of Asia has few vested interests and no leadership. African states also lack leadership and are noted more for their absence than for anything else. Arab cohesion is greatest on questions relating to Israel, and the only country capable of giving the Arab peoples effective leadership, the United Arab Republic, lacks the confidence of other regional states because of its self-serving conduct in the agency. Among the regional groups outside the Soviet bloc and the West, the Latin Americans give the greatest evidence of cohesion; their solidarity tends to benefit the United States.

The Geneva Group of contributors to international organizations functions in Vienna but on a more modest scale than elsewhere, for a number of reasons: the structure of the agency's budget, the preference for informal consultation, the fact that there is not fully overlapping membership between the Geneva Group and the permanent board members, and the desire not to provide dissident members of the Geneva Group with a platform for airing their views.

The secretariat is not systematically linked to any one group, although segments of it have close relations with particular representatives (often based on national identity); and the top echelon is, as we have seen, unwilling to move against the wishes of the superpowers. Despite increasingly fluid relations in the IAEA, the secretariat has not endeavored to build diversified coalitions of support from different groups on behalf of secretariat inspired objectives. This fact in turn derives from the agency's unadventurous and generally nonideological character.

Environmental Impacts

The fact that the IAEA is in many respects an alternative to the Baruch

Plan and is through its control responsibilities at least obliquely related to arms control makes it increasingly clear that certain features of the agency's specific environment are in fact parts of the general environment. The single most important development in the agency's specific environment was the emergence of nuclear détente between the United States and the Soviet Union, which facilitated not only the legitimation and growth of the agency's safeguards system but also the Non-Proliferation Treaty in which the IAEA plays an integral part. This development is most decidedly also a major component of the general environmental change in the past ten years. In the following pages we will consider three apsects of the IAEA's environment: the stratification of power, the distribution of states by economic and political characteristics, and the effects that certain patterns of interaction—among them the East-West struggle and the movement toward decolonization—have on the membership, aims, leadership, and style of the agency.

Stratification of Power

The stratification of power in the general environment has not changed in any significant way since the inception of the agency in 1957. This fact is faithfully reflected in the composition of the Board of Governors. Table 7.5 permits comparison among power in the general environment, capabilities in the specific environment, [18] and influence in the IAEA. The figures on the general environment are those given in chapter 2 of this volume and are tabulated for 1965. The ranking of states in the specific environment and of the order of influence in the IAEA, on the other hand, are based on the period from 1965 to 1968.

There is a rather marked similarity between the three lists, particularly at the upper levels. Seven states appear among the top ten on all three lists. Several countries that appear on the lists for the general and specific environments do not appear on the list of those influential in the agency: the People's Republic of China, which is not a member of IAEA, and Denmark, Austria, Switzerland, and Spain. Denmark takes turns with the other Nordic countries in occupying a designated seat on the board; and Austria, Switzerland, and Spain alternate with other European states on the board in elected seats. The Netherlands, which serves only periodically on the board, derives its relatively high ranking from its former governor and spokesman on nuclear matters, Ambassador Eschauzier, whose long and intimate association with the rather small elite in the nuclear world in general assures him access and a hearing for issues on which the Netherlands has an interest.

A number of states—Pakistan, the United Arab Republic, Mexico, and the Congo—that figure on the list of states influential in the IAEA do not rank among the top twenty in the general environment; and except for Pakistan they also have low status in the specific environment. Their presence on the one list is to be explained largely by the active interest of their

Table 7.5

Rank Order of States in the General Environment, in the Specific Environment, and in IAEA

General Environment		Specific Environment		IAEA	
1	United States	1	United States	1	United States
2	USSR	2	USSR	2	USSR
3	France	3	United Kingdom	3	United Kingdom
5	People's Republic of China	4	France	4	France
5	Japan	5	People's Republic of China	5	Canada
5	United Kingdom	6	Canada	7.5	India
7	Federal Republic of Germany	7.5	Federal Republic of Germany	7.5	Australia
8	Italy	7.5	Japan	7.5	South Africa
9.5	Canada	9.5	India	7.5	Japan
9.5	India	9.5	Italy	11.5	Argentina
11	Sweden	13	Australia	11.5	Brazil
15	Australia	13	Israel	11.5	Federal Republic of Germany
15	Austria	13	South Africa	11.5	Netherlands
15	Netherlands	13	Spain	15	Belgium
15	Spain	13	Sweden	15	Pakistan
15	Switzerland	18	Argentina	15	Czechoslovakia
15	Yugoslavia	18	Belgium	19	United Arab Republic
15	Brazil	18	Brazil	19	Mexico
21	Argentina	18	Norway	19	Congo
21	Belgium	18	Pakistan	19	Poland
21	Pakistan	21.5	Denmark	19	Italy
21	Poland	21.5	Netherlands		
21	South Africa				

representatives, although this cannot be said to be a constant characteristic of all of these countries. It would be closer to reality to curtail the list of influential states to the top dozen or so, with the caveat that when certain other states are represented on the board (such as Belgium or the United Arab Republic or Mexico), they exert influence largely because of the personality of their governors.

If one contrasts the ranking by influence in the IAEA and the ranking in the specific environment, the only blatant anomaly is Israel, which, because of pressure mounted by the Arab bloc, has been excluded from any official role in the work of the IAEA. Unlike the other notable distortions between these two lists—West Germany and Italy—that concerning Israel is not likely to be improved by the anticipated expansion of the Board of Governors, unless Israel is subsequently treated as a European state.

In sum, there is a reasonably high correlation between power in the general environment, capability in the specific environment, and influence in the agency. Kendall's tau beta coefficients of correlation are:

General Environment with IAEA Specific Environment	.77
IAEA Specific Environment with Influence in IAEA	.71
General Environment with Influence in IAEA	.68

The statute theoretically allows for adjustments in response to changing capabilities in the specific environment inasmuch as it provides that seats on the board shall be designated on the basis of technological advance; but where the general environment is concerned, the basic geopolitical situation that gave rise to the organization has not altered significantly enough since that time to warrant any striking change in either its principles or its operation.

Distribution of States

The progressive increase in the number of independent states in the world is reflected to a degree in the increased membership of the agency. The most dramatic changes are in the mobilizing and authoritarian groups and those with a low per capita GNP. Whereas in 1958 thirty-four of the sixty-six member states had polities other than competitive, in 1967 sixty of the ninety-seven members fell into noncompetitive categories, an increase from 52 percent to 62 percent of the total membership. Similarly, in economic grouping by per capita GNP, the number of states in the two lowest groups rose from forty out of sixty-six members in 1958 to sixty-one out of ninety-seven in 1967, or an increase from 60 percent to 63 percent of the total membership. The greatest increase was in the group with $200 to $599 per capita GNP, which grew from twenty-two to thirty-six between 1958 and 1967. This growth accounts for nearly one-half of the total increase of membership during this period.

How much qualitative impact did these increases in membership have on the IAEA? The composition of the executive and deliberative organs of the agency was affected very little, as we already have seen. The Board of Governors has remained constant at twenty-five since 1962, when the agency's membership stood at seventy-seven. Insofar as the secretariat is concerned, although agency membership rose from seventy in 1960 to ninety-seven in 1967, the number of states represented in the secretariat rose by only nine, from forty to forty-nine. More striking is the fact that only eight of the fifty-eight persons holding permanent appointments came from the Afro-Asian or Latin-American states; and only four of the forty-two holding fixed appointments for five years or longer came from those regions.[19]

The change in the distribution of states did have some effect on the allocation of resources and the emphasis given to various parts of the program. The general contours of the program have not changed; but within the framework that has prevailed during much of the life of the IAEA, emphasis has been shifted to accommodate the demands of the developing countries. This shift was particularly evident in research contracts and, as we have seen, in the distribution of the subject matter of conferences and symposia.

In budgetary allocations the change has been even more modest. The increased number of less-developed countries in the agency has heightened the demand for technical assistance. Since it has not been possible to extract larger voluntary contributions from member states, and the agency's share of UNDP funds has stabilized at about 2.2 percent, the board has sought to meet the increased demand by giving a more and more flexible interpretation to the concept of "administrative expenses," so as to facilitate the transfer of certain costs normally charged against the operational (voluntary) budget to the regular (assessed) budget. Conservatism toward increasing the regular budget minimizes the effect of this tactic, and only a small additional amount of money is released for technical assistance.

Demands of the economically developed states are predicated on an existing technological base, and stress is placed on the agency's role as a medium for the exchange and dissemination of information, a forum for establishing international standards for health and safety and as a point at which research on problems of general relevance can be coordinated. To the highly developed states, then, the agency is useful largely as a means of setting up the ground rules for nuclear commerce. Demands for the development and application of a comprehensive safeguards system, a regulatory function, are not (with a few exceptions) as widely heard among the more advanced states. Although most of these sympathize with the objective served by a safeguards system, the existing discrimination between nuclear weapons states and all other states in the application of that system is considered unacceptable in the long run.

In a technological field like nuclear power, demands will in large measure be related to the claimant's capacity to absorb the applicable technology.

Except for India, Pakistan, Thailand, the United Arab Republic, and perhaps Tunisia, the states with the lowest per capita GNP are the least advanced in nuclear science and the least able to absorb nuclear technology. These five exceptions, although their capabilities in this respect are by no means equal, are evidence that nuclear sophistication does not neatly correlate with level of economic development. These countries are not only more advanced than other countries in the same economic category, but also more advanced than many countries in the next highest economic category; and their demands on the IAEA differ from those of the states with which they cluster economically, tending rather to have more in common with demands of states like Poland, Czechoslovakia, Argentina, or Israel. Nevertheless, it is generally true that as one moves to the higher categories ranked by per capita GNP, an increasing number of states are in a position to absorb and apply nuclear technology. One generalization worth noting regarding demands on the agency is that the atomic energy authorities that are weak in their national systems or have lost support because of the domestic pressure to grant priority to other sectors are the most vocal and persistent in calling upon the IAEA. For some of these countries IAEA support can stimulate renewed interest at home or tide a creditable institution over a difficult period by means of research contracts or occasional assistance in procuring equipment. The Philippines is a case in point.

Increased membership has also brought about a larger proportion of authoritarian and mobilizing regimes in IAEA. The greatest increase has been among authoritarian regimes, which accounted for two-thirds of the new members between 1958 and 1967. It is not easy to ascertain what effect this influx or the change in the distribution of regimes will have on the agency. There are no apparent differences in the style of the General Conference, where most of these new states participate (if they bother to attend), and except for issues created by the Non-Proliferation Treaty, the meetings of the board have, if anything, tended toward increased harmony and consensus.

One interesting feature can be noted, however: mobilizing regimes tend to be the most active in the least substantive areas. The Soviet bloc countries are vocal on representational issues and on resolutions that are more fashionable than useful; Cuba occasionally takes unconventional positions on issues about which there is a relatively high degree of consensus; the United Arab Republic and Tunisia have endeavored to embroil the agency in the Middle Eastern conflict by urging that the board take steps that would implicitly condemn Israel as an aggressor. The very limited experience of the IAEA suggests that as states move from other types of regimes to mobilizing regimes, their activism increases accordingly; and that shifts, like Ghana's, from mobilizing to authoritarian regimes may lead to increased restraint. On the other hand, shifts from competitive to authoritarian regimes do not seem to affect the nature of a state's participation and activity in the IAEA:

Argentina, Brazil, and Greece illustrate this point. The representatives of some of the authoritarian regimes have played very constructive roles in the agency; this has been particularly true of the representatives of Argentina and South Africa, both of whom have helped to keep the agency on an even keel.

Patterns of Alignment

Two of the four patterns set forth in chapter 2 are of considerable importance to the IAEA: East-West conflict and regional integration (in the nuclear field). The other two patterns, decolonization and the controversy between rich and poor nations, have been, at least until recently, less important to the IAEA.

East-West Relations. Of the various environmental trends of the postwar era the most significant for the IAEA has been the evolution of East-West relations. This has been particularly true with respect to the defined aims of the organization, the scope of its functions, its program emphases, and the decision-making process. Responsiveness is most dramatically demonstrated in safeguards and control; indeed, the entire history of agency safeguards is permeated by the original confrontation and the eventual convergence of Soviet and American polities. Until 1962 Soviet bloc members on the Board of Governors systematically opposed the development and implementation of an international safeguards system. Subsequently, and particularly after the signing of the Moscow Test Ban Treaty of 1963, the Soviet Union lent increasing support to the concept of a safeguards system and to a central agency role therein. What had developed between 1958 and 1963 was a more marked détente between the two superpowers, especially about nuclear matters. Treaties on the Antarctic and Outer Space, the Test Ban Treaty and the Non-Proliferation Treaty are bench marks in the development of increasingly convergent Soviet-American views on nuclear problems. The IAEA profited considerably from this détente: Soviet support for the safeguards system added to the legitimacy of that dimension of agency activity and facilitated a steady expansion of the IAEA's safeguarding responsibilities. It also helped to undermine the resistance of some of the less-developed countries to the safeguards concept. Thus, in terms of organization aims, control has been reinforced. The assignment of safe-guarding responsibilities to IAEA under the Non-Proliferation Treaty goes beyond affirming organizational aims and constitutes an expansion of the scope of agency functions, in that safeguarding under the NPT is intended precisely to police an arms limitation agreement rather than to serve as an ancillary to developmental assistance.

A second area that demonstrates the link between the evolution of the agency and the evolution of Soviet-American relations is the changing pattern of decision making on the Board of Governors: the shift from a pattern of mobilization to one of consensus. Until the Soviet Union changed its position on the issue of safeguards and adopted a supporting rather than an antagonistic attitude, the board's proceedings were highly formal, and decisions often resulted from the mobilization of support for particular policies by the United States. In recent years the situation has grown more fluid: board meetings have been fewer and shorter; most of the agency's essential business is conducted informally through consultations among the secretariat and the various resident representatives of member states (particularly the Soviet and American missions); and decisions are reached by consensus rather than by formal vote. If the Soviet Union and the United States are agreeable to a particular program or orientation, then it is likely that this will become agency policy; if they are in disagreement, then the issue is unlikely to be raised.

A third effect of Soviet-American nuclear détente is reflected in the partial but positive collaboration of the superpowers in the programmatic area. Safeguards regulation and research on safeguard techniques, as well as the acceptance of budgetary allocations for safeguards, are the best examples, and information programs are another: both the United States (the initiator) and the Soviet Union are strongly backing the new INIS program, which will more immediately benefit the nations with advanced nuclear capabilities, especially the United States and the Soviet Union. In view of the conservative orientation of the board toward the size of the regular budget, under which both safeguarding and INIS are funded, it is evident that increased costs in these sectors may lead to modification of the overall program and the emergence of new emphases.

The vestiges of cold war issues nevertheless persist in the agency in areas not directly related to nuclear détente. This certainly is so with issues that are fundamentally symbolic or representational. In technical assistance also, as we have seen, cold war issues have continued to intrude; but once again the overarching interest of the superpowers in nuclear détente has muted their effect. In general, then, extraneous political tugs-of-war are not critical to the conduct of agency activities, and the positive impact of détente outweighs the negative effects of these skirmishes. A forceful demonstration of this point was made at the 1968 meetings of the General Conference. Although the meeting took place only a month after the Soviet invasion of Czechoslovakia, and in a city teeming with Czech refugees, debate and discussion were marked by the absence of any reference to the Czech crisis. The sum and substance of the link between IAEA and the evolution of East-West relations is the dissipation of ideological blocs, at least insofar as the most important aspects of agency work are concerned; a more diffuse pattern of alignments within the agency; a less formal decision-making pattern; and some evidence of a movement toward a Soviet-American duopoly in the IAEA.

Regional Integration. The movement toward integration in Western Europe has been a matter of increasing significance to the IAEA, particularly since the nuclear field is among those where integration has been attempted. The fact that EURATOM has been less than successful in fulfilling its original goals is of little comfort to IAEA, for it is precisely in the area of greatest import—safeguards and control—that EURATOM has been a competitor with the international agency. No EURATOM state has submitted any of its facilities to the IAEA safeguards system;[20] and the Non-Proliferation Treaty is so worded with respect to safeguards as to permit EURATOM to survive, and at the very least to serve as an intervening institution between IAEA and the five nonnuclear weapon states in EURATOM. The situation is further complicated by the fact that the United States supports both the regional organization of EURATOM (in pursuit of its goal of fostering European integration) and the international agency (in pursuit of its goal of nonproliferation and controlled nuclear development). Moreover, the United States itself contributed to undermining IAEA's claim to be the most appropriate organization to handle safeguarding when it transferred safeguarding responsibilities under its bilateral agreements with member states of EURATOM to that organization rather than to IAEA.

For two reasons EURATOM's impact on IAEA has been less marked in other fields of activity. First, in many areas, such as technical assistance, training, and applied research, the two organizations are not competitive. In matters like norms for health and safety they are even complementary. Second, EURATOM is much less cohesive in fields other than safeguards. The new INIS program, for example, has received varying support from the EURATOM states. In sum, the principal effect that regional integration has had on the IAEA has been to limit the scope of one of its most important functions—safeguarding.

Decolonization. Decolonization has affected the IAEA in the same way that it has affected most other organizations—it has helped to increase membership. This increase, however, has been less dramatic for the IAEA; of the forty states that achieved independence between 1958 and 1967, only seventeen had become members of the IAEA by 1968.

Despite an increase in total membership from sixty-six to ninety-eight between 1957 and 1968, the governing body, as we have seen, has increased by only two. Thus, during most of the life of the agency the Board of Governors has maintained the same basic composition: of the twenty-five seats on the board, the Afro-Asian and Latin-American states hold eleven, the socialist states three, and the Western states (including South Africa) eleven. Pressures to change derive not from increased membership as much as from the upgraded importance of the agency resulting from the NPT. As we noted earlier, South Africa's right to its seat on the board, granted because of its role as an important producer of source materials, has been contested

only sporadically and never very strongly. Despite the increased number of
Afro-Asian states in the IAEA, the South African and Portuguese questions
that have so penetrated certain other organizations in the United Nations
family are not profoundly significant in this agency. In discussing symbolic
decisions we suggested that one reason this issue has been muted is the low
salience and low publicity of the IAEA, which allow it to escape certain
political issues. Another reason is the absence of a large number of African
states from the agency; IAEA is not (at least not yet) an African oriented
organization.

Rich and Poor States. Rich versus poor is a question that until now has
not really been consequential for the IAEA. This is not to say that no
demands for capital and assistance have been forthcoming from the
less-developed states; but claims and demands on the agency have been
rather low in their intensity. Among the reasons for this, two were discussed
earlier. First, many of the less-developed countries are not capable of
absorbing nuclear technology in any meaningful way because they lack
either the industrial infrastructure or the technical personnel necessary to a
sustained nuclear program, or both. Second, the major promise of nuclear
energy lies more in power reactors and desalination than in the application
of radioisotopes to medicine, agriculture, or hydrology, important as these
uses may be. Until now, however, nuclear power has not been a competitive
form of energy except for some of the industrially more advanced states.

A third reason for the low intensity of demands is to be found in the lack
of leadership among the less-developed countries, and in their general
inability to articulate their demands effectively. The one state that could
have taken leadership, India, has done so only sporadically. India's nuclear
development so far outstrips that of any of the other less-developed
countries as to identify this country more closely with the advanced
nonnuclear Western states in this field. India's needs are different from those
of Ghana, Chile, or Ceylon, and its special security concerns make it a very
ambiguous state on such issues as nonproliferation and safeguards.

The United Arab Republic has attempted to assert leadership on several
occasions but has never succeeded in doing so, largely because of a problem
that is a fairly common affliction among many of the developing
countries—regional prestige. India and Pakistan, Brazil and Argentina,
Tunisia and Morocco, Turkey and Greece are all examples of paired
competitors for regional prestige and symbolic leadership in the nuclear
field. The result of these competitive situations is to dissipate the
opportunities for creating a united front. In more recent times such
countries as Mexico and Pakistan have assumed a "revisionist" role within
the agency, but these events have been too recent to have any evident effect.

Finally, there is a generally low level of interest in the agency among the
less-developed states—to many of them IAEA is a low saliency agency. This

is best demonstrated by the turnout at the annual General Conference, which for most countries is the only opportunity for direct contact with the agency, its secretariat, and the leading members. The 1968 conference, for example, was attended by representatives from only seventy-six of the ninety-eight member states. With the exception of Albania, all of the twenty-two absentees were from either Afro-Asian (fifteen) or Latin-American (six) states. This pattern has been a characteristic of conferences in past years. A further point of interest is that of these twenty-two absent members, all but two (Algeria and Cyprus) belong to the group with the lowest per capita GNP. These, of course, are the states least able to absorb nuclear technology or to articulate their demands effectively.

Despite this catalog of deficiencies, the developing countries have not been totally quiescent in the agency. Since the outset the General Conference periodically has passed resolutions drawing attention to the importance of serving the needs of the less-developed states and of employing the agency's resources to improve the standards of living in those parts of the world. That the board and the secretariat have been responsive to these demands is demonstrated by their shifting the orientation of research contracts, symposia, and conferences to make them more immediately relevant to the developing countries, their effort to do something about upgrading the technical assistance program and, within that program, the placing of greater emphasis on equipment rather than experts.

One further point is in order regarding the division between rich and poor states. In the nuclear field, when speaking of haves and have-nots, it is sometimes more appropriate to use military nuclear capability as a criterion of "have." Only four of the member states of the IAEA have nuclear weapons. While this distinction has always carried a certain weight in the agency, it has become increasingly important because of the Non-Proliferation Treaty. The NPT sanctifies the division of the world into nuclear weapon states and nonnuclear weapon states. The effects on such issues as nuclear fuel supply and the exploitation of various nuclear technologies—particularly peaceful explosions, used for such purposes as mining, land movement, and tapping underground minerals—are not yet clear, but many of the more advanced nonnuclear weapon states have taken an increasingly pessimistic view of the eventual effect of this division of the world into two classes of states. This concern became evident at the Conference of Non-Nuclear Weapon States held in Geneva in September 1968, where a greater unity began to develop among the have-nots than has normally been true in the agency. Despite wide divergencies between these states economically and industrially and their widely varying interests, one issue at this conference garnered considerable support—the demand for a review of the composition of the IAEA's Board of Governors. This review is currently under way and will very likely result in an expansion of the board. In this instance Italy and West Germany are even more committed than some of the

Afro-Asian states to the need for a change in the structure of the board. The entire effect of the Non-Proliferation Treaty on the IAEA is far from clear, but certainly it has sharpened a division already existing in the agency between the haves and the have-nots.

The pattern of alignments in the general environment has thus had some impact on the life of the IAEA. The earlier years were characterized by a cold war division, with the United States supporting the agency's activity by mobilizing votes. The second, more recent, period indicates a dissipation of bloc confrontation, a shift toward more cooperative action, and in some matters like safeguards the emergence of a Soviet-American duopoly. The earlier cleavage has not been replaced by any neat substitute; rather, patterns of alignment within the agency are more diffuse, shifting, and complex. The greater diffusion of alignment has reduced the tendency of the agency to identify itself with one or another of the power blocs—as it had done on many secondary issues, but especially on the problem of safeguarding, the only critical issue the agency faced in its first ten years. But the diffusion has not done anything to strengthen the secretariat's leadership, which until now at least has leaned toward conservatism and neutrality. Nevertheless, as the Non-Proliferation Treaty demonstrates, the opportunities for coalition-building have increased as disparate states have discovered a common interest in particular issues or become aware that their identity with their traditional allies no longer corresponds to reality. That treaty also demonstrates something else: the relative unimportance of the IAEA to most of its member states prior to the tabling of the NPT by the superpowers in 1968. Until then, issues like the composition of the board or the scope of the agency's responsibility were bandied about; but no group made any serious effort to upset the existing balance and impose a new one. With the NPT, however, the importance of the agency for many of its members has grown substantially.

The Structure of Influence

The IAEA emerges from the preceding analysis as an organization that is simultaneously sensitive to, yet autonomous from, its environment. Organizational growth, expansion, and significance has been heavily dependent upon the phenomenon of nuclear détente, which is an element of both the specific and the general environment of the agency. The attainment of higher plateaus of international relevance is thus in large measure a function of particular trends in the agency's environment and of the degree of consensus and mutually shared concern on nuclear matters among the leading nuclear weapon states and of their determination to use the agency as an instrument for the pursuit of those ends. This kind of generalization pertains not only to the decisions on rule creation and rule application (safeguards and control), but also to some of the more significant programmatic decisions (scientific information policy, for example).

We also have observed, however, that the IAEA has been able to operate in a relatively depoliticized atmosphere and that it has been more autonomous from other environmental forces that do not have an effect upon or directly relate to the level of nuclear détente. Thus it can be said that within the consensual framework of agency activity the participant subsystem (largely, but not exclusively, the representative elites) emerges as an important factor in explaining the decision-making process and the structure of influence in the IAEA. Consensus, in other words, intervenes as a limiting factor between the environment and the internal dynamics of the organization.

Influence in the agency is stratified, and the stratification does tend to correlate to a high degree with environmental status. However, another variable—interest—tends to intervene between environmental status and influence, once again limiting the explanatory power of the environment. A central characteristic of the first decade of agency life was that influence was largely a function of interest, and the latter more than environmental status-ranking explains the limited effectiveness of the vast majority of less-developed countries and even some of the more-advanced states in the IAEA. This is demonstrated by the case of South Africa on the one hand (greater influence than its status in the general environment would suggest) and of West Germany on the other.

The IAEA is today in a transitional state. Historically it has passed through several stages. Until 1961-62 the United States dominated in the agency in the context of cold war confrontation. The emergence of nuclear détente transformed the style of the agency and helped to isolate it from the prevailing world tensions. Most of the members were pleased with this turn of events, and its consequence was a more flexible and fluid situation in terms of internal agency dynamics—a situation that did not, however, upgrade the role of the secretariat. Commencing in the late 1960s an increasing uneasiness began to arise that nuclear détente implied not only the emergence of a Soviet-American condominium but also the increased disregard of the views of others. The source of this concern lay less in the specifics of agency activity than in the negotiation of the Non-Proliferation Treaty. The underdeveloped nations expressed concern that IAEA would be transformed into little more than an international policing authority for the NPT at the cost of its developmental responsibilities, while the near-nuclear or threshold states began to envisage inequities and discrimination in the development and exploitation of nuclear technology affecting their ability to compete on equal terms with the nuclear weapon states in the anticipated markets for nuclear power production.

One result of these events is the increased saliency of the IAEA to its constituents. A first measure of this impact is the decision to amend the statutory provisions on representation on the Board of Governors, partly by revising some of the prevailing criteria, partly by expanding the size of the board. These decisions remain subject to ratification by two-thirds of the membership. For our purposes it will suffice to suggest that at least in the short term the IAEA will become the arena of a dialectical relationship between an expanded scope of consensus (on the nature and extent of safeguards) and increased politicization. Whether this means that in future we will be able to explain the decision-making process or the structure of influence more through the participant subsystem than through the environment is problematical; that the IAEA as a consequence will acquire increased autonomy from its environment is unlikely.

8   IMF: Monetary Managers

Susan Strange

The International Monetary Fund (IMF) was the expression of American concern, even in the midst of World War II, that the postwar international economy should have an orderly and efficient monetary system and should suffer neither the violent shocks nor the uncertainties of the interwar period. This same concern had been felt earlier by Britain, the United States' predecessor as top currency state.[1] But Britain had been unable either at the Genoa Conference of 1922 or later to get European agreement on an effective international monetary organization. The result was that no permanent arrangements existed in the League of Nations system for intergovernmental financial diplomacy.

The Bretton Woods Agreement of July 1944 to set up the IMF was predominantly the product of Anglo-American discussions, and other countries were more or less invited to take it or leave it. Most decided to join, partly because access was otherwise denied to the Fund's twin organization, the World Bank. But in the years since, no one has doubted the necessity of the Fund, although it has been much criticized. The United States itself judged the organization unsuitable to deal with the most pressing postwar problem—that of financing the recovery of Western Europe. Later, the Fund was acknowledged to be inadequate to deal with all the stresses and strains of the 1960s and had to be extensively supplemented with additional machinery of international financial collaboration.[2]

Structure, Functions, and Evolution

Formal Framework of Decisions

The two bodies in the Fund formally responsible for taking decisions are the Executive Board and the Board of Governors. The Board of Governors, the deliberative assembly of the organization, meets once a year. Representation is based on the principle of one state, one governor (usually the minister of finance or economics, or in some cases the governor of the central bank), but not of one state, one vote. The governors wield unequal votes, based on a system of quotas. Together with the qualified majority voting arrangements, this has assured to the United States a predominant position and, on key matters, a veto. Certain basic decisions (such as expulsion of members and admission of new ones, revision of quotas, gold price changes and the election of executive directors) are reserved to the Board of Governors.[3] Any general revision of quotas in the Fund must be approved by the governing board by a four-fifths majority of the total voting power. Any change in the Articles of Agreement has to be approved by three-fifths of the members having four-fifths of the votes. And any "uniform proportionate change in par values," which means any change in the world price of gold—or, translated even more crudely, devaluation of the dollar in terms of gold—has to be approved by every member having more than 10 percent of the total voting power.[4] The governors may take decisions by correspondence (and often do so) or at their general annual meetings. These are held twice out of every three years in Washington and once in some other country.

All other decisions are taken by the Fund's Executive Board. This body is, in effect, in permanent session in Washington. Since the Fund is a service organization operating a large-scale "kitty," it produces a comparatively large number of decisions to be sifted and selected. Here, too, the Articles of Agreement provided that decisions should be taken by the weighted voting system based on members' assigned quotas in the Fund, though in recent years votes are hardly ever counted, and decisions are usually consensual. The Executive Board consists of appointed directors and elected directors both paid by the Fund. The appointed directors are nominated by and act for the five members with the largest quotas. The elected directors are nominated by and act for groups of member countries. Their votes cannot be split and must be cast as a unit.

The concept of quotas is central to the operation of the Fund and deserves a brief explanatory digression. Besides affecting its voting power, each country's quota also determines its subscription to the Fund, in gold and its national currency, as well as its borrowing rights from the Fund. For this reason agreement on the distribution of quotas is easier to reach than it would be if these quotas related solely to voting rights. Initially, the size of the members' quotas was worked out according to a complex statistical recipe combining factors for national income, monetary reserves, and foreign trade. In reality, United States officials had decided that to avoid congressional opposition, they could raise their own Fund subscription most painlessly by assigning to the Fund the surplus of over $2.8 billion that had accrued to the U.S. Treasury (as guardian of Fort Knox) when the dollar had been devalued against gold in 1934. They had then, in effect, calculated a formula that gave the United States a quota of about this size, and—in relation to the other countries—a dominant voice in the conduct of the organization. As a French delegate at Bretton Woods put it, "In the end, quotas were established more or less arbitrarily by the United States in a series of deals."[5]

Since the original distribution, quotas have undergone general increases three times: in 1958, 1966, and 1970. The formula has been revised, and special upward adjustments have also been made, in particular cases, for Germany, Italy, and many other countries. The effect has been to lower the comparative position of Britain and still more that of Nationalist China.[6]

Assigned Functions of the Fund

The function of the organization as it was originally conceived by its American author, Harry Dexter White, was to provide a stabilization fund on which members could draw and by means of which they could avoid sudden and too frequent destabilizing changes in their exchange rates. The kitty principle, by offering members access to a source of credit that would supplement their own monetary reserves, would provide the leverage for some international regulation of monetary policies. Reflecting the concerns and interests—both ideological and material—of the United States (and to a lesser extent of Britain and the developed European countries), the Fund was directed by its Articles of Agreement to the pursuit of three monetary objectives: liberalization, stabilization, and nondiscrimination. Its work would be helped and complemented by that of the World Bank and the proposed International Trade Organization.

Both Harry White and Maynard Keynes attached great importance to the regulatory functions of the Fund. And both perhaps overestimated its capability in this respect—White because his thinking derived from an earlier plan he had devised for imposing a little monetary order on unruly Latin Americans and Keynes because his plan for an International Clearing Union had deliberately asserted the equal responsibility of surplus and of deficit countries to make the necessary but uncomfortable adjustments to reestablish equilibrium.

Moreover, the assigned functions of the Fund were not formulated with sufficient precision—and could not be since no two cases were exactly alike—to avoid the subsequent need for highly political decisions as to who needed to do what to preserve a just and stable international monetary order while assuring a steady rate of economic growth. By the Fund's second decade of activity, the Europeans' persistent surpluses had given them the diplomatic power to contest United States views on these questions. The Fund's functions became the object of a continuing process of negotiation between the United States and the other developed countries including two former enemy states, Germany and Japan, and one nonmember, Switzerland. At the same time, the growing number of new, developing states that had joined the Fund exerted another powerful drive to redefine the functions of the Fund and make it serve the financial needs of the poor for system expansion no less than those of the rich for system preservation.

Evolution of the Budget

In most international organizations the limits of their capacity for task expansion are roughly set by their financial resources as revealed in the annual budget. Whether the budget grows or not is also apt to reflect the perception, by at least the leading members, of how closely their interests are affected by the organization.

The Fund is different. The organization's budget has not been in any substantial sense a constricting factor. Indeed, for its first ten years its finances showed a substantial and steadily growing deficit, approaching some $14 million by 1955. It is worth noting that this caused no real anxiety and was expected to continue for some time to come. Then, in the twelve months following the Suez affair and the British and French drawings, the Fund earned almost $8.4 million in charges on members' drawings. It added this to $5 million yielded by special interest-bearing bonds that the United States had exchanged for some of the Fund's idle stocks of gold.[7] This income was the consequence of the organization's activity and not—as it would have been with most other international agencies—a precondition for it. A much better indicator of the organization's importance has been the use made of its resources. Since the method of financing the Fund requires no annual levy but calls instead for an initial capital contribution, which can be increased only when it is decided to increase quotas, it is unlike most international organizations in that its financial capability is more like that of a business enterprise than of a club. The Fund, like any business, is based on the expectation that it will continue to make a profit by its operations and to command the confidence of the shareholders. A principal concern therefore is to operate the multicurrency kitty with conservative prudence. At first, resources at its disposal depended partly on the total amount of members' quotas and partly on how well-spread the drawings were between different currencies. More recently, the Fund's capability has also depended on the additional credits made through activation of the General Arrangements to Borrow (GAB), and in future it will additionally depend on the amount of Special Drawing Rights (SDRs) activated with the consent of the leading developed countries, notably the United States and members of the European Economic Community (EEC).

The deficit was accumulated while, as Fred Hirsch says, it was "largely passive and inactive" and under "strong American influence, almost domination."[8] In the period from 1947 to 1955, gross drawings from the Fund totaled only $1.2 billion, less than the total for the next single year, 1956-57. But in the next nine years annual gross drawings averaged $1.1 billion, and by mid-1966 the total gross drawings added since 1955 amounted to over $11.5 billion.

By then, the Fund had accumulated a general reserve of $180 million and, in good banking tradition, had put another $180 million away in a special reserve. By 1970 the total of the two reserve accounts had risen to about $600 million—a hoard on which other international organizations inevitably cast covetous eyes. The Fund has now become the only really rich international organization—a fact of which one is reminded by the thick gold-colored carpet used throughout its headquarters and by the Bretton Woods Recreation Center near Washington, a luxurious country club owned by the Fund.[9]

One result of the peculiarity of the Fund's financing is that this organization is not under the same pressure as it would be if its operations depended on annual budgetary contributions to maintain some rough equality in the distribution of benefits, at least among states of similar economic strength or importance in the organization. The disparity among various countries as beneficiaries of the Fund is striking. According to Hirsch, by mid-1966 Britain had taken over $4.75 billion in gross drawings from the Fund—over one-third of the total for all members. The next largest drawing was by the largest contributor, the United States, with gross drawings of $1.18 billion; next in size of drawings were India, with $1 billion; France, with $519 million; and Brazil, with $503 million. The disparity among drawings even applies within the group of developing countries. Of their total drawings up to 1967, 78 percent had been drawn by 10 percent of these countries.

Secretariat

Keynes's original hope had been that the Fund would be primarily a supranational service organization and that as much as possible of the day-to-day running would be left to a technical secretariat. As the British delegation put it at the Atlantic City Conference in 1944, "We want to aim at a governing structure doing a technical job and developing a sense of corporate responsibility to all the members, and not the need to guard the interests of particular countries."[10] In the later pursuit of this functionalist illusion Britain tried in vain to assert—against the opposing view held by the United States—that the job of executive director was a part-time one and that a good deal could safely be left to the Fund staff. In the first year the British director attended only 35 out of 160 meetings of the board. But though his rebellious example was followed by the Belgian, Mexican, Canadian, and Italian directors, the cause was hopeless. The United States view soon prevailed; and member governments, through their appointed or elected directors or their alternates, were attending meetings regularly and thus becoming directly involved in all substantial decisions of the Fund.

At first, therefore, the secretariat was very much overshadowed by the Executive Board, to whom it was subordinate, and operated mainly as the board's adviser. But article XIV of the Fund's agreement directed that five years after the Fund had begun operations, it should start consultations with member countries on exchange controls and restrictions still affecting nonconvertible currencies.[11] Since the secretariat had to staff and conduct the consultations, this increased activity inevitably brought about greater pressure of business. It began to adopt, at least for all routine and minor matters, the *lapse-of-time procedure.* In effect, this meant that the board backed up staff decisions automatically, unless an executive director having an objection or query was reasonably prompt in raising it.

In the mid-1960s, the Fund's consultative function was once again greatly developed, largely as a result of the increase in membership and, ironically, of Britain's own extreme indebtedness to the Fund. The rise in staff influence is partly evident in the pattern of staff expansion. From a total of 355 posts in mid-1947, half of which can be assumed to be clerical and menial, the number increased little at first, reaching about 500 after fifteen years. Then, from about 1963 or 1964 to the end of 1968, staff numbers doubled, reaching about 1,000. Similarly, there were nine departments of the secretariat in 1950, eleven in 1961, and fifteen in 1968. Table 8.1 shows how the fifteen departments were arranged.

Table 8.1

Arrangement of Departments in the IMF

Departments	Senior Staff
Functional Departments	
Exchange and Trade Relations	4
Legal	3
Research	4
Treasurer's (Members' drawings, etc.)	4
Statistics	1
	16
Area Departments	
European	5
Asian	4
Middle Eastern	3
African	5
Western Hemisphere	4
	21
Regional Offices	
Paris	1
Geneva	1
	2
Training and Technical Assistance Departments	
Central Banking Service	3
Fiscal Affairs	4
IMF Institute	2
	9
Housekeeping Departments	
Administration	2
Secretary's Department	2
	4
Managing Director	1
Deputy Managing Director	1
	2
Total senior staff	54

The Fund differs somewhat from others in the United Nations family in that it is not under such great pressure to observe the principle of equitable geographic distribution in selecting its staff. Although the formal obligation is there, the need of a mainly operational organization to maintain at least a minimum standard of professional competence has led to a predominance in its senior ranks of Americans, Europeans, and white Commonwealth nationals. This tendency has been increased by the habit of poor countries of recalling staff members from the Fund after a few years to take key posts at home in the finance ministry or the central bank. The Fund thus functions at times as a nursery for monetary managers, producing a worldwide "old boy network" of officials susceptible to its influence.[12]

The French have always alleged, and many other people have assumed it to be true, that the whole IMF, including the staff, is dominated by the Americans and other Anglophones. Brian Tew quotes Raymond Aron and the French press to show their view when Pierre-Paul Schweitzer, a Frenchman, became managing director in 1963. And Tew's breakdown of senior staff by nationality in 1968, shown in table 8.2, broadly supports these allegations.[13]

Table 8.2

Distribution of IMF Senior Staff by Nationality

United States	23[a]
United Kingdom	6
Canada	2
Australia	1
Total Anglophone	32
France	4
Netherlands	4
Federal Republic of Germany	1
Total EEC	9
Other European	3
Asian	7
Latin American	2
African	1
Total	54

[a]Five of these became naturalized United States citizens after joining the IMF staff.

Moreover, no Frenchman was appointed head of a department in the IMF until the French executive director had put in a complaint in 1953. And although Germany has had a major net creditor position in the Fund through most of the 1960s, the first senior staff post to go to a German was that of treasurer in 1969. At the time of writing, there were still no Japanese in senior staff positions.

Opinions differ concerning the caliber of the Fund's staff. No single writer has been quite as rude as the Jackson Report was about some of the United Nations staff, but some critics have alleged that staff members have been slow to react to changes and developments in the international economy.[14] My own judgment is that the operational character of the Fund makes it less subject than some international organizations to the sort of paper passing, empire building, and other demonstrations of Parkinson's Law that one finds in many bureaucracies. As civil servants with a concrete job to do, the staff shows a high standard of responsibility, integrity, and impartiality. Because they are drawn, as a rule, from central banks and national civil services, however, they are more used to carrying out political directives than they are to initiating policy measures in response to changes in the world outside.

Major Events and Turning Points

The Fund opened for business in March 1947. In that summer, hopes for an early end to the period of postwar transition were dashed: first, when Britain's attempt to introduce sterling convertibility under Hugh Dalton met with such disastrous results; and, second, when Secretary Marshall, in June 1947, declared the United States' readiness to assist a European Recovery Program. Before the summer was out, the United States had, in effect, realized the gravity of Europe's problems of economic recovery and taken a clear decision to deal with the special needs of Western European countries, not through the Fund or the United Nations, but through the new Organization for European Economic Cooperation (OEEC), which allowed it to negotiate the terms of American aid bilaterally with each beneficiary. This United States decision also involved the establishment a bit later, of new intra-European payments arrangements, allowing and encouraging discriminatory convertibility between European currencies. Thus, no sooner had it begun, than the Fund was put firmly on ice. It did not fully thaw out for the next decade.

At the end of its first decade, in 1957-58, two developments brought the Fund into greater activity and importance. One was the combined effect on sterling and the franc of the Suez fiasco and the Algerian war, as a result of which both Britain and France applied to the Fund for substantial drawings. The other was the long-delayed plunge by the European countries, including Britain, into currency convertibility with its attendant dangers of monetary imbalance.[15]

Four years later, in 1962, the Fund may be said to have reached not so much a turning point as a parting of the ways. On the one hand, this was the year when the General Arrangements to Borrow were negotiated among the Group of Ten (i.e. the United States, Britain, Canada, Japan, Sweden, and the five EEC countries, plus Switzerland—which is not, of course, a member of the IMF). The agreements[16] were a compromise between the French desire to take the whole arrangement outside the Fund and the determination of the managing director, Per Jacobsson, to associate the Fund with it. Essentially a multilateral swap arrangement, the GAB committed the United States to lend $2 billion, and Germany and Britain $1 billion each, out of a total of $6 billion. The Fund's managing director kept the final right to activate the GAB, but the real decision lay with the Group of Ten, meeting with him but without other Fund members. The GAB agreement followed the sterling crisis of 1961, which coincided with a mounting deficit in the United States balance of payments. The two events brought home the facts that the Fund did not have the resources to support both sterling and the dollar at the same time and that additional credit had to be negotiated outside it. At about this same time, while the world's rich countries were going outside the Fund for their mutual support, a large number of the poor countries came into it. Between the end of 1961 and 1963, twenty-nine developing countries had joined the Fund, increasing its membership from 73 to 102.

The year 1965 is notable in Fund history as the year of Secretary of the Treasury Fowler's speech to the Virginia Bar Association. Like Secretary Marshall's speech, this too presaged a significant departure in American foreign economic policy. After seven years in which the liquidity problem had given rise to endless arguments and countless plans among economists, the U.S. Treasury had at last come round to the view that a supplementary reserve asset, "paper gold," would be an aid rather than a threat to the dollar. If one of the earlier proposals for a Currency Reserve Unit (CRU) had not come from the French, appearing to American eyes as a deliberate scheme to supplant the dollar, perhaps the recognition might have come a little sooner.

The final outcome was an agreement in principle at the Rio meeting in September 1967 that Fund members should accept a new gold-guaranteed international currency as a unit of account among central banks, the allocation of Special Drawing Rights being in line with IMF quotas and subject to rules about their use and repayment. Since the French had failed to get support from other EEC members in opposing the SDR scheme, the way was open to agree on a detailed plan in Stockholm in March 1968, with the understanding that the Articles of Agreement should be amended to strengthen the power of the EEC, not only in controlling future activations of SDRs, but also in other major decisions of the Fund.

The other important turning point for the Fund was the decision in 1967 to embark on a scheme for compensatory finance when fluctuations occurred in export earnings, a scheme that had the effect of a discriminatory use of Fund resources in favor of poor primary-producing members. Another step down the same road was the decision to provide some finance for commodity buffer stocks. This decision was an initiative that the French took under pressure from France's African associates and because they wished to improve their relations with Latin-American and other developing countries.

Decision Making: A Taxonomical Analysis

The difference between decision making in the Fund and in most other international organizations derives from the peculiarity of the Fund's main assigned function—to run a multicurrency pool of funds on which members could draw in case of need and to use this kitty as a carrot that would induce the donkeys to accept a harness in the shape of rules of good monetary behavior. The important decisions, therefore, concerned three key questions: how big the amount of available funds should be; what sort of rules should be applied and how stringently; and which applicants for drawings should have priority.

The first two questions produced general policy decisions that could be recognized as such—though the process of deciding the rules of good behavior necessitated some flexibility before the best way was found, under differing conditions, to achieve the broad objectives set at Bretton Woods. In practice, the process of interpretation was often more creative than administrative, and the Fund's regulatory and supervisory activities have shown a constant search for flexibility in the application of the rules. [17]

The last issue—who should have first claims on the funds—seldom showed up in Fund records as requiring a significant policy-making decision. Yet by a series of small, local, operational decisions, which appeared to those involved to be of a routine, precedent-following kind, a policy was slowly hammered out, which applied the Fund's resources in a highly political manner. Without its ever being stated in so many words, the Fund's operational decisions made its resources available neither to those in the greatest need nor to those with the best record of good behavior in keeping to the rules, but paradoxically to those members whose financial difficulties were most likely to jeopardize the stability of the international monetary system.

This is one important reason why it is particularly difficult to classify neatly the major decisions taken in the history of the Fund. Not only is there the problem just mentioned of operational decisions that were also, cumulatively, both programmatic and regulatory (i.e. rule-creating and rule-supervising); another difficulty is that decisions concerning the size of the kitty, which I have considered in this analysis as programmatic, also directly affected Fund operations. Furthermore they also indirectly increased the Fund's power both to create new rules and, by its powers of supervision, to see them carried out.

As a subsidiary result of these taxonomical difficulties, the Fund provides less ground than some other organizations for definite conclusions about the structure of influence on the different types of decisions. It seems fair to say that the Executive Board has greatest influence on representational decisions, while the staff influence is paramount on operational decisions. But where the distinction between decisions is blurred, or where a single process of decision making has at one and the same time programmatic, rule-creating, and rule-supervising aspects as well as operational implications, the difficulties of precisely analyzing the structure of influence multiply too fast. On programmatic questions and on rule-creating and rule-supervising matters—and indeed on the comparatively rare symbolic decisions—there is close interaction between executive directors and staff. And on both boundary and programmatic decisions, decision making within the organization has been greatly subject to external influence from the United States in the early period and later from the Group of Ten.

Representational Decisions

The Fund conducts its choice of managing director, top officials, and executive directors with a quiet discretion that verges on the hush-hush. (No important representational questions arise in selections for the Board of Governors; each state is represented on this board, and only plenary sessions are held.) All four managing directors have been selected in solemn conclave of interdelegation discussions with as much secrecy as if they had all been cardinals: one might almost have expected white or black smoke to come from the building on H Street. The details of these conclaves are unrecorded, but the point is generally taken that the managing director must be acceptable to the United States and henceforward also to the other members of the Group of Ten.

As to elections for the Executive Board, the convention that these should also be uncontested was adopted at the Savannah Conference in 1946. When the members tried to follow the electoral procedures laid down at Bretton Woods, they found themselves in a farcical impasse; not enough free votes were available to produce the number required for seating the last two nominees, Ahmed Zaki Saad of Egypt and Camille Gutt of Belgium. Pragmatically deciding to elect them nonetheless, the board resolved to forestall any such complications in the future by always arranging beforehand that no more candidates come forward than could be seated.[18] This means that head-on clashes and confrontations are avoided and that representational decisions have to be taken behind closed doors before general meetings. There is by now a well-established system of caucuses and lobbying. This reaches its peak among the Latin Americans, the Francophone Africans, the Commonwealth, and the Asian groups in the two weeks before the annual Fund meeting.

As the Fund's membership has grown, so has the number of elected directors on the board; from an original seven, the number reached eleven by 1952 and fourteen by 1968. In that year, the number should have been fifteen, but it happened that the Italian was sitting as special appointed director under the provisions for the representation of creditors in the Fund. An elected director may represent anything from three or four other states to as many as fifteen or sixteen.

This arrangement would have been unworkable if elected directors had depended solely on their constituents for their individual influence. Individual influence does vary. It may be due to a director's length of tenure, or it may come from his having been nominated by a state that is much more important within his group than any of the others. Occasionally, a director's influence is enhanced by a balance between divergent interests among his constituents, liberating him from the need to stay too close to the views of any one of them. Compared to the United Nations, there has been little resort in the Fund to the system of rotating turns in representing the various groups. Only the Scandinavian group, one of the African, and two of the three Latin-American groups have taken turns. Throughout the years 1952 and 1968, the other groups, electing nine executive directors, have been content to be represented by a national from the same country. Representational questions have been much less important in the Fund than in other international organizations. There have even been occasions when members have cheerfully abstained from voting in elections for the executive directors in order to avoid anomalies and difficulties that would upset the orderly conduct of the organization. On at least one occasion a member not only abstained from voting but also allowed its votes to be cast by one director and its views stated by a different one.[19]

Nor has there been a strong competitive tendency among the elected directors to increase the number of their clients, even though more clients would have increased their voting power on paper. As it is, one elected director may have almost twice as many votes to cast as one of his colleagues. But it will not necessarily follow that he has greater influence on the board.

The question of Chinese representation after the communist victory in 1949 also caused only a flutter in the Fund, compared to the heated arguments over this issue in the United Nations and elsewhere. India, Czechoslovakia, and Yugoslavia, aware of the capitalist bias of the Fund and their own ideological isolation on its left wing, proposed the exclusion of the Chinese representatives at the 1950 annual meeting. By a show of hands, the members agreed that this was a "purely political" issue, that it was already before the United Nations, and therefore that it was out of order. It was ten years before China's place among the appointed directors was taken by West Germany, the "Chinese" director then continuing to be elected to the board by the combined votes of Taiwan, Korea, and South Vietnam.

Symbolic Decisions

The Fund's revulsion from the Chinese representation question was typical of its disdainful reaction to political matters generally. Moreover, its dominant ideology, especially in the early period, was frankly system preserving rather than system challenging or reforming. Its symbolic decisions therefore ignored the questions of race relations and colonialism so popular in other organizations and dwelt rather on the need for members to fight the destructive dragons of inflation and monetary anarchy.

Of course, there was always underlying disagreement about how, in terms of practical policy, inflation could be avoided—especially in a poor, developing country. Yet finance ministers and central bankers assembled at annual Fund meetings found it natural to pronounce an anti-inflationary credo in heartfelt unison. Some Fund ideologies would hold that these were not purely symbolic decisions, since their authors were firmly convinced that these pronouncements exerted real political influence. Others are more skeptical. Later on, the original simplistic Fund orthodoxy, which held that all a primary-producing country had to do was fight against inflation, became eroded through contact with the practical problems of policy making for economic development. As Fund membership grew, its officials who were sent out on missions could see that the rich countries also shared some responsibility through the shortcomings of their trade or aid policies and that too strict anti-inflationary policies could sometimes hinder development. [20]

Boundary Decisions

In the beginning, the Fund faced boundary questions toward the United Nations proper and toward the World Bank. The Bank and the Fund were the only two agencies belonging to the United Nations family to be located in Washington. They were also the only two that had asserted their right not to transmit their administrative budgets to the General Assembly. And though the managing director has always made an annual speech to the Economic and Social Council, the action has been only a routine courtesy. Furthermore, when the Fund and the Bank were invited by the UN General Assembly to take part in the Technical Assistance Board (TAB) at the inception of the Expanded Program for Technical Assistance (EPTA), both declined out of a jealous regard for their special responsibilities and their financial independence. The same touchiness has resulted, as Horsefield explains, in the Fund's practice of sending parallel rather than joint technical assistance missions to member countries.[21]

Since that time the United Nations generally has left the Fund pretty much alone. Confrontations have been comparatively minor and unpremeditated. They have have been with the UN General Assembly or sometimes with the Economic and Social Council, and they have concerned such matters as the Fund's part in the Congo restoration program, the collection of balance-of-payments statistics, or the independent status of the Fund's technical assistance missions.

Toward the Bank, the Fund has always shown a cool but sisterly helpfulness. The Executive Board agreed, for instance, in 1953 to accept World Bank bonds as collateral security if central banks that invested in them later found it necessary to borrow from the Fund.[22] The twin organizations also got together about that time—when the Fund was then running a sizable deficit—to explore the financial savings they could realize by sharing not only a library but other services as well. Nothing much came of the idea, and on the whole the two organizations go their own ways on policy matters, though they are located side by side. The Bank is much more sensitive than the Fund to the welfare side of development and to the need to please the United States Congress and others who control the purse strings in the chief aid-giving countries of the world.

If the plan for a large and powerful International Trade Organization had ever materialized, the ITO and the Fund might have faced serious boundary questions in relation to their roles. Indeed, the precaution was taken, in an early draft of the American White Plan, of cutting out certain clauses concerning the elimination of trade barriers and export subsidies, though this was done primarily with the idea of anticipating possible boundary trouble between the U.S. State Department, which was mainly responsible for trade policy, and the U.S. Treasury, which was mainly responsible for monetary policy. The Fund itself, however, was well aware of the danger of conflict with ITO; and when preparations were being made in 1947-48 for the Havana Conference to draft the ITO charter, the Fund sent along two of its executive directors and a staff team. At the suggestion of one director, Ahmed Zaki Saad of Egypt, a carefully instructed Liaison Committee was set up and provided its usefulness in subsequent relations with the GATT. Later, the same precautionary spirit led the Fund to set up a branch office in Geneva, the better to regulate its relations with UNCTAD.

Thus while collision with trade organizations was avoided by careful steering, clashes with other monetary organizations overlapping the Fund's general issue-area were avoided by means of decisions taken outside the Fund itself. In the early phase, when the European Payments Union (EPU) was set up, the Fund dutifully responded to a decision by the United States as to what was to be accomplished, with whom, and by what means. Later, in the 1960s, the United States had to negotiate directly with the most powerful or recalcitrant of the highest-ranking states in the specific environment in order to set up the machinery for such monetary cooperation and mutual support as were considered necessary.

As a result the Fund has had to work alongside other monetary agencies. There is the loose but powerful association of the Group of Ten, whose deputies met sometimes in that capacity and sometimes, under different hats, as Working Party Three of the OECD; and there is the Bank for International Settlements at Basel, whose monthly meetings of central bankers achieved new importance after 1961 as the United States and other developed countries came to rely on swift short-term credit between central banks, and as each country became more vulnerable to monetary policies pursued by other central banks. As explained earlier and in the next section, the liquidity issue has played a part in boundary decisions affecting the Fund, as well as in programmatic and rule-creating decisions.

Programmatic Decisions

One important programmatic decision has already been mentioned as a turning point for the Fund. This was the ERP decision to shut off the European countries from Fund resources from 1948 to 1952 and, in effect, until about 1955.

The next, known as the Rooth Plan, was taken in 1952 and was in a way a composite preparation to reserve the restricted program of the Fund's earlier years.

The Articles of Agreement had not made clear precisely how the Fund should operate its multicurrency kitty. And they were especially vague about what should happen in the transitional period—mistakenly expected to be brief—between the end of the war and the general convertibility of currencies.[23] Did the members have an automatic right to draw on the Fund, or could they be refused, and on what grounds? These were the key questions. The British and French argued that they could each draw up to a quarter of their country's quota in any one year at their own discretion. The United States disagreed, and its view prevailed. Then, about 1950, the United States was becoming concerned that the Fund would be dissipated if its currency sales, or drawings, failed to be repurchased with reasonable speed and became, in effect, long-term loans. It therefore wanted the Executive Board to agree that all drawings should be repaid within five years. "This the other Executive Directors were not prepared to concede without a quid pro quo in the form of a concession which would go some way to meet their view that drawings should be automatic."[24] The result was the package deal suggested by Ivar Rooth soon after he became managing director. Drawings within the *gold tranche*[25] would be allowed automatically. But they would have to be repaid in three to five years, and higher charges would be made for extended drawings. Additionally, members would be allowed to arrange short-term "standby" credits on terms individually negotiated.

This last provision was perhaps, programmatically, the most important.[26] It was a foot in the door of the Fund for developing countries, and it gave the Fund a built-in right, like that of any bank, to bargain with the customers according to their respective credit ratings. By 1961, when, for example, Australia, Guatemala, and Peru were all given standby credits at about the same time but on very different terms, Joseph Gold, the Fund's general counsel, blandly confirmed that "the terms of stand-by arrangements were varied according to the conditions and problems of the members to which they were granted." [27]

Another point left unclear by the Articles of Agreement, whose resolution gave rise to two important programmatic decisions, was whether the Fund could be used to cover members' deficits arising from anything other than seasonal, cyclical, or emergency fluctuations in the balance of payments.[28]

This was the phrasing not of the Bretton Woods Agreement but of the

United States' Bretton Woods Agreements Act, which was much more precise and—understandably so, since it had to pass the Eightieth Congress—more restrictive too. The Executive Board had either to concur with or qualify this interpretation. The board temporized and compromised by declaring that the use of its resources was to be limited "in accordance with its purposes to give temporary assistance in financing balance of payments deficits on current account for monetary stabilization operations." [29]

This rule effectively excluded deficits, however temporary, resulting from capital outflows. For most members this was not an important consequence so long as currencies were not convertible and exchange controls restricted capital transfers. But after 1957 it began to become more crucial, especially for sterling, which, as an international vehicle currency, was particularly subject to shifts of short-term capital and to leads and lags in invisible payments. The Fund therefore responded in 1961 with a clarification of its earlier decision, which said that it did not, after all, preclude the use of the Fund's resources for capital transfers.

Whether the Fund's decision to increase the members' quotas should be counted primarily as a programmatic or a regulatory or rule-creating decision—or even as an operational one—is not easy to decide. On each occasion that the decision has been taken to expand quotas, the Fund has deliberately engaged in what the political scientists call *task expansion,* inasmuch as it sought to increase its capacity to make an impact on the international monetary system. Moreover, it has also used the general change in quotas to alter the relation of members' quotas to each other, affecting in this way both their contributions and also their rights to draw on the Fund. Thus the general quota increase in 1959 was by 50 percent; but with special increases to particular members the total was increased by about 55 percent. In 1966 the general 25 percent increase was accompanied by a total net addition of about 8 percent. The 1970 overall increase was by 35 percent, including special quota increases. By this means, the role of the European countries, especially of West Germany, in the international monetary system has been acknowledged by the Fund—though perhaps with a slight time lag in every instance. The quota increases have also reflected the growing orientation of the organization toward the developing countries. Not only have the quotas allocated to the new members added to the combined total for all developing countries, but also the average increase for the twenty-five developing countries that were founder-members has been 183 percent compared to 109 percent for the founder-members classed as developed countries. Some figures calculated by Edward Bernstein show that in 1967 the developing countries constituted three-quarters of the membership; they were allocated 27 percent of total quotas (25 percent if China is excluded) but had made 31 percent of total drawings from the Fund. [30]

In 1963 a programmatic decision was made that seems to have marked a significant and later a progressive easing of Fund attitudes toward the developing countries, which by then had at least a numerical majority in the Fund. This was the decision concerning compensatory financing for exports of primary products. As pointed out by Bernstein, the developing countries, especially the Latin Americans, had been disappointed at the Fund's not fulfilling the promise implied in the preface to Keynes's *Proposals for an International Clearing Union* to furnish "protection from the loss and risk for which extravagant fluctuations in market conditions have been responsible in recent times."[31] At last the Fund responded to the agitation in its report *Compensatory Financing of Export Fluctuations,* which indicated the Executive Board's decision to adjust some quotas for primary producers and to introduce a system of special drawings for this purpose. Like normal drawings, they would be repayable after three to five years, but they could not exceed 25 percent of quotas, and they could be given only when statistical analysis showed the shortfall in a country's balance of payments to be due to circumstances beyond its control.[32] In 1966, under urging from UNCTAD, the board raised the limit for outstanding drawings under the scheme from 25 to 50 percent. By 1967, eight countries had made use of it. They included several that had been on the brink of default (Ghana, the United Arab Republic, Ceylon, and Brazil), and a few that would probably have been unable otherwise to draw on the Fund.

Operational Decisions

Most of the operational decisions of the Fund have arisen either out of the day-to-day management of the Fund's accounts or out of the management of the Fund's relations with particular countries that have drawn on its resources. Financial management has involved decisions on the general rules governing drawings from the Fund, including the rate of charges to be made and the arrangements for repurchase of currencies so as to conserve and maximize the Fund's resources. I have considered these decisions as programmatic for taxonomical purposes, although they also clearly affect the Fund's operations. I have considered as operational what Tew calls "local decisions." These local operational decisions have evolved with the elaboration of the Fund's mission procedures since these began in 1952. The chief role here is played by the area departments of the Fund and also by the Exchange and Trade Relations Department, to whom any important policy question has to be referred. An important shift of responsibility from the United States to the Fund took place in the mid-1950s when the Fund, partly through its missions, began to negotiate directly with members and no longer went first to the United States, as the sole creditor country, to get approval. Until this change, Tew says, "No drawing was approved by the Executive Board without it being made clear in advance that the U.S. authorities were in agreement."[33]

Some of the Fund's staff recognized that from then on the United States was using the Fund to promote policies and advice that—in Latin-American countries, for example—would have been rejected out of hand if proposed directly from Washington. In this role, between about 1957 and 1962, the Fund became noticeably more meddlesome and ended by being engaged in almost uninterrupted dialogue with almost all the Latin-American countries and with at least some of the African and Asian ones.

Though they often deal with matters of detail and affect only one country at a time, these operational decisions are politically important to the countries concerned. They invade the delicate common ground between the state's responsibility for the domestic economy and relations with the external monetary system of which the Fund is guardian. In this role, the Fund believes that it can subject Latin-American countries, for example, to a much closer scrutiny of their economic policies than even Western Hemisphere organizations like the Latin-American Committee on the Alliance for Progress (CIAP) can do. And this is concurrent with the continued casting of the Fund, in deference to local nationalism, as the bogey of foreign imperialism. It is significant that the Fund's turnover of middle-ranking staff members who are of Latin-American nationality has often been high. Recalled to serve at home in the finance ministry or the central bank, many Mexicans, Brazilians, Chileans, and so on have then kept up close and collaborative relations with the Fund in private, while allowing xenophobic sloganeering to persist in public.

Rule-Creating Decisions

The Fund's rule-making activities have always been directed toward two simple but basic objectives: stability and orderly growth in the international economy. Opinions have differed among participants and over time about precisely what measures were necessary to attain these objectives. And, as Lenin advised the strategists of revolution, it was sometimes necessary to go two steps backward in order to make any progress at all. Thus, there have also been rule-canceling decisions along the way.

Stability, it was decided at Bretton Woods, was to be found through fixed, not floating, exchange rates. Therefore a fundamental rule was that any member must fix a par value for its currency as a condition of access to the Fund's resources. [34] Having set a parity, a member might not change it without consulting the Fund and was also to see that, in transactions across the exchanges, rates did not vary from parity by more than 1 percent (article IV, sec. 3). In 1959, however, the European currencies became convertible, and arbitrage dealings multiplied in foreign exchange markets. It then became possible for the margins from par for exchange rates between EPU currencies and the dollar to move 1 percent down from par in one case and 1 percent up in another, so that the cross rate between them could then vary by 2 percent on either side of parity. Regarding stability, standard rules, and good monetary order as more important than the strict letter of article IV, the board accepted a staff suggestion that countries should fix a margin with a reserve currency (normally the dollar) within 1 percent and should then keep cumulative margins with other convertible currencies within 2 percent. [35]

Then, if the rates were to be fixed, there must be just one single rate for each currency and not a bundle of multiple rates. At an early stage, however, in December 1947, the board sent out a circular letter directed at the many countries—especially in Latin America—who disagreed with the Fund on the grounds that multiple exchange rates were less offensive than tariffs and had little restrictive effect on trade or on the general stability of the international system. The letter,[36] though it admonished, did not wholly condemn the offending members.

As to orderly growth, the predominantly American philosophy of Bretton Woods was that this required the eventual removal from the international monetary system, as from the international commercial system, of as many stultifying restrictions on free trade and investment as possible, particularly those that offended against the most-favored-nation principle of nondiscrimination. However, in case the monetary system should be so out of balance that one currency became scarce, the Bretton Woods rules allowed for controlled discrimination by other members—and in the Fund itself—against this surplus country by the so-called scarce currency clause (article VII), or as it was jokingly spelled by some American officials, the "$carce currency clause."

A nondecision of some significance was surely that of August 1947, when the intensity of the postwar dollar shortage was first becoming apparent, and it was agreed not to invoke article VII. As already explained, the way out of the scarcity—which was of course an aspect of what was later called the liquidity problem—was to husband the Fund's resources while using other channels to dispense American aid.

A corollary of the provisions regarding currency relationships was the relation of each currency to gold. It was originally believed in the Fund that in order to avoid a situation where the gold market and arrangements governing changes in gold prices would undermine the stability of the carefully ordered nondiscriminatory monetary system, it was necessary to prevent sales of newly mined gold at premium prices. Particularly in its first five years, the Fund tried to deal severely with countries seeking to offer subsidies to gold production (Peru, Colombia, Canada, and Australia). Thanks largely to Canadian ingenuity, its efforts were ineffective, and in September 1951 it abandoned the attempt to cope with the threat by starving the market. For about ten years the whole problem was left more or less in abeyance, and the precise meaning of the Articles of Agreement concerning the sale and purchase of gold remained unsettled.[37]

In 1960-61 a real, as opposed to an imagined, threat to the system occurred when the dollar-gold price came under such speculative pressure that it was decided to defend the price by means of the Gold Pool

(1961-68). This was an arrangement for collectively financed market intervention, a gold-price stabilization scheme operated by the Bank of England in London, the world's leading gold market. When the sterling devaluation of November 1967 set off a still greater wave of speculative gold buying, the dollar came under acute pressure, the demands on contributors increased, and the Gold Pool agreement came unstuck. As a substitute for it, the two-tier system was devised to separate the private market for gold from the price system governing gold sales and purchases by central banks and by the Fund. The ambiguities of the Fund toward gold (reflecting the divergent concerns of the members) permitted a long-drawn-out argument in 1968-69 between the United States and South Africa, the issue being whether the Fund was obliged to buy gold for currency from a member or whether in its discretion it could refuse to do so. The United States wished to force South Africa to sell on the private market, bringing prices down and closing the gap between the two tiers. The Fund uncharacteristically took no firm stand on the legal question, avoided an open commitment to either side, and left it to the United States and South Africa to face each other out and eventually to reach a practical compromise arrangement.

Rule-Supervisory Decisions

Hardly a single rule created by the Fund at Bretton Woods and after for governing international monetary behavior has not had to be changed or bent in some degree during the Fund's career as an organization for rule supervision. As things turned out, the problems of the postwar world were not those of the 1920s or the 1930s. Moreover, the Fund lacked the support of the strong International Trade Organization which had been planned as its ally and accomplice in international rule supervision. Here is a brief summary of the modifications:

1. The Fund has had to allow members with no par values to use its resources. According to Horsefield, by the end of 1965 there were twenty-three of these and seventeen more whose parities were wholly or mainly ineffective.[38] And from 1964 on, the board openly acknowledged that any member might draw on the Fund before it had fixed a par value.

2. Despite early fears of unstable exchange rates, major devaluations have been rare. But in practice many members have decided to devalue first and consult the Fund perfunctorily or ex post facto.

3. Fluctuating or "floating" exchange rates have been tried by member countries—most notably by Canada from 1950 to 1962 and briefly by Germany in 1969 and 1971—and the Fund has had to tolerate and even encourage them in certain situations.

4. Multiple exchange rates also have had to be much more freely tolerated than the original rules implied. Indeed, the whole idea of the

Fund as a blind goddess of monetary justice, dealing firmly, impartially, and indiscriminately with all, has had to be entirely dropped. Particularly in rule supervision the Fund has had to be partial toward the weak and poor and toward the reserve currencies.

A significant example of the last change occurred in 1951. According to the GATT rules, members in no difficulty over balance of payments should drop discriminatory exchange controls if and when the IMF certified such controls to be no longer necessary. At the GATT conference at Torquay the Fund reported in this connection that a number of sterling area countries had rising reserves but were maintaining dollar-discriminatory controls. The report was defiantly rejected by the Australians and others—who probably guessed that the Fund's lawyers and statisticians lacked the wholehearted political support of the Truman administration. And so no more was heard of it.[39]

Paradoxically, although it has had to leave in abeyance many of its formal powers of rule supervision, the Fund has yet been able to exercise, through the development of techniques of multilateral surveillance over individual members, much closer real supervision than was originally envisaged. One French economist already quoted concludes that the Fund

> a acquis une autorité réelle grâce à sa compétence, à son expérience et à sa sagesse. . . . Dans toutes les questions monétaires les gouvernements le consultent et l'écoutent volontiers comme un grand médecin ou une société d'études et pas simplement comme un banquier dont on dépend.[40]

Essentially, its role as a banker and its control of substantial financial resources are the sources of the Fund's supervisory powers. As one official mainly concerned with developing countries crudely but aptly put it, "We use our money to increase our leverage." The detail and sophisitication of letters of intent has been increasing, from the time when they were first discovered by the Fund as a way around the difficult question of automaticity of drawing rights to the 1968 codification of past practice in a single declaration of Fund policy in 1968.[41] This in itself indicates the increase in the Fund's supervisory authority, at least over those that have drawn heavily on it. (Indeed a specific decision of June 1960 records the Fund's successful extension of its advisory and consulting role to include not only the weaker brethren still inscribed under article XIV, but also members that had undertaken convertibility obligations under article VIII and who were not formally bound to consult with the Fund.)[42]

Actors and Their Sources of Influence

National Government Representatives

The only time when each member of the Fund has its own delegate is at the annual meetings of governors, where the performances are largely ritual, and significant decisions are only rarely taken. In the Executive Board, only five directors represent a single country. These countries are: the United States, Britain, France, India, and West Germany (replacing China in 1960). The Italian director, who became a formally appointed director in 1968, nevertheless continued by agreement to represent the interests of Spain, Portugal, Malta, and Greece. And in 1958, when Canada briefly acquired the right to an appointed director as a result of heavy use of Canadian dollars by the Fund, Louis Rasminsky, the Canadian director, continued to speak for Ireland.

Middle-rank members like Canada, Japan, Belgium, the Netherlands, and Brazil have the most votes of the countries in their electing group and effectively nominate their directors, subject to the agreement of their clients. Argentina and Mexico are also heavyweights in their respective groups; and if they content themselves with supplying the alternate, leaving the next most influential in their group to fill the directorship, they nevertheless control the nomination. Inevitably the result of the arrangement is that some members are oddly represented—Guyana by Canada, Cyprus by the Netherlands, and Turkey by Belgium, for example. Only in rare cases, however, as when Malaysia was openly at war with Indonesia, have members objected.

The most instructed representative, the United States executive director, is the most powerful. By act of Congress,[43] the United States president's choice of governors and executive directors and their alternates to both the Bank and the Fund are not only subject to the "advice and consent" of the Senate (as with other high diplomatic offices); but, once appointed, they were by statute under the instruction of a special National Advisory Council (NAC) whenever an act of the Bank or Fund required the approval, consent, or agreement of the United States; whenever any change was proposed in the United States quota or the par value of the dollar; and whenever any amendment to the Articles of Agreement or any loan to the Fund was under discussion. The National Advisory Council on International Monetary and Financial Problems was the monetary complement in the United States government to the National Security Council in the military. It consisted of the secretaries of state, the treasury, and commerce, with the chairman of the Board of Governors of the Federal Reserve and the chairman of the U.S. Export-Import Bank. In 1965 the United States amended the statutory arrangement by giving the right of final decision to the secretary of the treasury, rather than to the NAC as a collective body.

The United States executive director's power was never derived from the NAC, however, but ultimately from the president of the United States. And with each administration the influence of such statutory watchdogs and councils, as compared with private advisers to the White House, varies quite capriciously. During the Kennedy administration, for example, the NAC was soon superseded by a more flexible and informal policy-making body. Out of an ad hoc group set up in 1962 to consider long-term strategy for strengthening the international monetary system,[44] there grew a policy group under Secretary Douglas Dillon and an operating group under Robert Roosa. Significantly, this latter group felt that its prime task was guiding the United States delegation to Group of Ten meetings, rather than acting as watchdog on the American executive director, William Dale, at the Fund. Later, when Roosa was succeeded by Frederick L. Deming as under-secretary for monetary affairs, the group generally became known as the "Deming Group."

The American executive director is also one of those who has been least often replaced. In twenty years, from 1949 to 1969, the United States changed its director only once, when Frank Southard became the Fund's deputy managing director in 1962 and was succeeded by William Dale. The United States executive director has always had so important a part to play in Fund business, as controller and initiator, that seniority was obviously helpful to him.

The contrast with the relatively rapid turnover of British executive directors is striking. The British government is also understood to instruct its executive director rather closely from London when any important issue is under discussion. But the British have rarely been initiators; and when, as in the Maudling Plan of 1963, they tried to deviate from United States policy, they met with little success. It has apparently not been felt necessary, therefore, to have a director with long familiarity in Fund ways. Except for Sir George Bolton, who stayed at his post during the Fund's first six years, the typical turn of duty for a British executive director has been about two years.

Length of tenure by itself may make it easier for a director to play his part on the Executive Board, though it does not always, or necessarily, add to a representative's influence in decision making. Pieter Lieftinck of the Netherlands was a senior director; helped by this fact and the Netherlands' keen interest in Fund affairs, his voice was said to carry weight in board meetings. Two other active and articulate "old hands" in Fund history have been the late Jean de Largentaye of France and Ahmed Zaki Saad of Egypt. During most of de Largentaye's tenure, however, the French government, if not openly hostile to the Fund, showed little interest in it. The United Arab Republic under President Nasser was also critical and resentful of the Fund but prudently left Zaki Saad, a devoted elder of the Fund, undisturbed.

A much surer recipe for influence is for the member whom the director represents to establish a strong net creditor position. This, more than personalities, explains the recent importance in Fund decision making of both the Japanese and the West German executive directors. Since about 1965 it has been taken for granted that no proposal before the board will be pressed to a decision if Germany opposes it. The Japanese power to control decisions is probably more recent.

The Managing Director

The managing director of the Fund must be a dignified figure, of suitable seniority, but this side of senility,[45] generally respected in central banking circles, acceptable to the United States, but not himself an American national. This latter convention was established at the Savannah Conference, when it was believed that the World Bank president needed to be from the United States, so that the Bank could float successful bonds in United States markets, but that it would not be diplomatic for the United States to hog both the top jobs. (Oddly enough, in spite of their disagreements, Keynes badly wanted Harry White to be the Fund's first formative managing director and was disappointed by the convention.)

Conceivably, the convention could be reversed at some future time; the World Bank might perhaps choose a German president and thus leave the United States free to nominate, if it wished, an American as executive head of the Fund. So far, however, the custom has persisted, and the office has been filled by Camille Gutt (1946-51), a former Belgian finance minister; Ivar Rooth (1951-56), a former governor of the Swedish Riksbank; Per Jacobsson, (1956-63), also Swedish and an experienced and distinguished economist and top official of the Bank for International Settlements; and finally, since Jacobsson's untimely death in 1963, Pierre-Paul Schweitzer, a former deputy governor of the Banque de France and the favored nominee of his predecessor.

Indeed, the managing director's constitutional position is much stronger than that of the United Nations secretary general. Each is the chief administrative officer of his organization, but the managing director is the permanent chairman of the Fund's Executive Board and is thus in a position to control the agenda, direct the discussion, and by this means influence the board's decisions. He is therefore in a much stronger position than the secretary-general, who merely has a right to attend and to draw the attention of the Security Council to any matter that he thinks may threaten international peace and security.[46]

In the first decade or so, the main qualification required of the managing director was the possession of *gravitas,* the expression of financial rectitude and respectability. Only when the Fund began to emerge from its early doldrums did opportunities begin to occur more frequently for him to exercise his two prime functions—the diplomatic and the dogmatic. Both Jacobsson and Schweitzer have acted effectively not only as brokers and mediators defining doctrine, but as financial prophet-popes, uttering warnings, pronouncing anathemas, and pointing the way ahead.

Unlike the United Nations secretary-general, who especially in U Thant's administration has often had his diplomatic role usurped, as at Tashkent, or pushed to one side, as in Cuba, the Fund's managing director has played a central part on a number of important occasions. Per Jacobsson personally handled the delicate negotiations with the French government that preceded the franc's devaluation in 1958 and the large French drawing on the Fund. Even more important, he took a direct hand in 1961 in the preliminary exploration with the ten developed countries that eventually negotiated the General Arrangements to Borrow.

The result was twofold: as finally formulated, the initiative for activating the GAB was laid firmly on the managing director; and the whole procedure was integrated into Fund procedures and subjected to the Fund's established policies and principles.[47]

The prophetic role of the managing director, as distinct from the diplomatic role, has been exercised in turn by Rooth, Jacobsson, and Schweitzer. The adjective *prophetic* is used more in the Hebraic than in the Delphic sense; it does not refer to predictions but to public utterances on current economic and financial developments that may affect the Fund's operations or statements in which the managing director uses his supranational position of authority and his supposed expert, inside knowledge to influence opinion outside the Fund—for example, on financial aid for developing countries. Another instance was Jacobsson's speech at the 1959 annual meeting, in which he declared that the distinction previously drawn between "hard" and "soft" currencies had become invalid, and hence that there could no longer be any justification for exchange and trade policies and controls that discriminated between member states on these grounds.[48]

Segments of the Bureaucracy

Two departments of the Fund secretariat play an especially creative role in its decision-making processes: the Legal Department and the Research Department. The one reflects the organization's concern with legitimacy, the other its need to respond to changes in a highly dynamic specific environment.

The Legal Department's position of power followed from the members' original decision, expressed in article XIX of the Bretton Woods Agreement, to entrust interpretation of the agreement to the Executive Board (with a right of appeal to the Board of Governors) and not to any outside body or court—an arrangement then peculiar to the Bank and the Fund among international organizations.

Since the Articles of Agreement had left a number of matters vague or undecided—a practice common enough in the constitutions of all international organizations and probably more than usually so when complex financial or commercial matters are involved—a large part of the Executive Board's time in the early years of the Fund was taken up with elucidating the precise terms on which members could gain access to the Fund's resources. The board soon found itself seeking the help and advice of the Legal Department.

In the early years, while the United States was taking a conservative and restrictionist view of the functions of the Fund, the Legal Department, like the Fund itself, was headed by a Belgian, André van Campenhout, whose attitudes were no doubt influenced by Belgium's strong monetary position in the late forties and early fifties and were therefore broadly sympathetic to the United States view. Van Campenhout was succeeded as general counsel to the Fund by two distinguished British lawyers: in 1955 by James Fawcett and from 1960 onward by Joseph Gold. Gold, particularly, has played a unique role in the evolution of Fund practice. A series of impressive staff papers and other monographs have made him, if not quite an *éminence grise* of the organization, or a Thomas Cromwell to Schweitzer's Henry VIII, at least a very influential departmental head.

In fact, far from the Legal Department's losing influence with the growth in staff and the number of separate departments (from five in 1946 to fifteen in 1968), its influence has rather increased as it became apparent in the early 1960s that reinterpretations were needed of overly rigid decisions taken earlier,[49] and as the late 1960s showed that it was necessary to reform and amend the mechanisms of international monetary cooperation of which the Fund remained an integral part.

In a different way, the influence of the Research Department has also derived from the pressures of a highly dynamic specific environment. The Fund has had to run continually to catch up with the procession of events in the world outside. The papers, reports, and memoranda originating in the Research Department have been the chief engine of change and adaptation in Fund policy. (Even the United States director now finds it better if the staff present a proposal favored by Washington than if he personally puts it to the board.) It is illuminating to contrast the highly political role of the Fund's Research Department with the much more detached and academic role of, for example, the Research Department of the UN Economic Commission for Europe under Gunnar Myrdal at the height of the cold war. However brilliant the ECE economists and statisticians were, they were condemned to total impotence by the East-West deadlock in the economic environment.

In a dynamic environment like that of the Fund a research department must not be so inventive and innovative as to outrun the adaptability of governments. On the other hand, if it is too slow off the mark, it risks losing the initiative to rival organizations. It therefore needs to have not only technical and intellectual resources, but sound political judgment as well. Since 1958 the department's head has been Jacques Polak, a shrewd and canny Dutch economist with long experience in the Fund.

The importance of close working relations between the managing director and the head of the Research Department is obvious. Differences of temperament and opinion between two such strong but contrasting characters as Per Jacobsson and Edward Bernstein led to the Fund's loss of one of its most distinguished and creative officials. Indeed it is fair to say that in Bernstein's day the Research Department was probably a more influential segment of the bureaucracy than the Legal Department. Later, the two were bracketed by insiders as being of roughly equal influence.

Eminent Persons and Expert Advisers

The Fund's relations to a number of eminent economic experts (of whom Keynes, White, Bernstein, and Triffin are likely to be best and longest remembered) has been a close and remarkable one. But it is easy to overestimate the positive and decisive influence of these seers on the actual developing structure of the organization. In the history of economic thought their names are enshrined like those of saints and martyrs in the Church. In neither case, however, does it follow that on practical questions of organization their precepts and admonitions have been closely heeded.

What is certainly true is that in the issue-area in which the Fund operates, its potentialities have always generated a measure of intellectual excitement among some (but not all) of the best-qualified brains. The contrast between the apparently rational processes of economic theory and the apparently irrational intervention of national governments in the development of an expanding international monetary system seems to have sparked inspiration here and there to find ways of resolving the conflict.

Whether in the beginning at Bretton Woods or with the SDR scheme at the end of the period under consideration, what has actually emerged in Fund practice has always been far short of the original proposal. Keynes's dream was of an international currency called "bancor," whose Anglo-American administration would impose an equal duty on the surplus country as on the deficit country using it. White's original plan described a stabilization fund, with managers, primarily American, who could decide when national policies were legitimate and when they were not and who could use their power in the international monetary system to enforce "good" behavior on recalcitrant member governments, as the United States had been used to doing in Central if not in South America.

Triffin, too, has made no secret of his ultimate aim: a world central bank. His original plan, and most of its subsequent variations, would have replaced dollars and sterling as reserve assets and substituted Fund deposits or Fund certificates. The management of these would then have been entrusted to the Fund—in practice, to the staff under the direction of the managing director.[50] In Maxwell Stamp's plan, expounded rather later in 1962, the reformist aim was also explicit, though different: to increase the flow of development aid to poor countries. The rich countries would acquire their Fund deposits to add to their existing reserve assets, only at second hand, by providing the developing countries with exports of capital goods which they would finance with loans from the International Development Association (IDA).[51] Bernstein's plan simply proposed an addition of multiple-currency reserve units to the reserves of the rich countries. But it added the proviso—which proved unacceptable to these countries when it came to the negotiations—that gold holdings would have to be uniformly matched by a minimum holding of the new reserve units.[52]

When the Fund members at last came round to the reformers' view that the international monetary system could no longer continue to work satisfactorily on gold, dollars, and sterling as reserve units, they drew also on other plans for reform, selecting those elements that interfered least with their freedom of action in monetary policy, including their freedom to choose and manage their mixture of reserve assets.

However, that they did even this much, rather than merely trusting to the expansion of quotas plus some constitutional amendment, must be ascribed in part to the indefatigable nagging of the reformers, who alternately issued dire warnings of the consequences of doing nothing at all and soothing reassurances of the ease and simplicity of the reform measures.

Thus, the source of these eminent persons' influence on the Fund's development lay partly in the ominous creakings and groanings of the monetary system itself and partly in their own dogged persistence. Equally important, perhaps, and marking a significant difference between these people and the blueprint-mongers of an earlier generation who had concocted schemes for the resuscitation of the League of Nations, was that the latter were mostly amateurs, while these were all professionals. That is, they were either central bankers like Ossola, Posthuma, Carli, and Emminger, or they had themselves worked as international officials and thus understood the Fund's machinery, were accustomed to its procedures, and were on familiar terms with its officials and Executive Board.

Bernstein had been the Fund's first research director, appointed in 1946 and continuing in this post until he retired to private consultancy in 1958. It is difficult to overemphasize the influence his ebullient and fertile mind exercised on the Fund in those twelve years. Triffin had been the first head of the Fund's European office, in Paris, from July 1948 to January 1951.[53] Maxwell Stamp had also served as a Fund official, after a period as the British alternate on the Executive Board. It is interesting that some other eminent economists who are thought by professional colleagues to have had a better understanding of the basic issues and problems—Fritz Machlup is an outstanding example—have nevertheless been content to play the more passive role of spectators and analysts. By contrast, Tiffin, Bernstein, and Stamp all bore witness, in their continued concern with the future progress and development of the Fund as an embryo of a global central bank, to the powerful organizational ideology that the Fund spread among its staff.

Representatives of Other International Organizations

More than any other international organization, the Fund has regarded itself as a separate and distinct entity, independent of all others. It has shown itself generally to be aloof and jealous of its independence. Only in two respects in the period from 1947 to 1967 has the Fund been at all sensitive to the influence of other organizations' representatives. In field operations with developing countries—especially those countries that have been deeply or dangerously in debt or have suffered a period of chronic monetary difficulty—the missions sent out by the Fund and World Bank have perforce been obliged to pool their information and coordinate their advice. In some countries, Indonesia for example, World Bank officials found their IMF colleagues still hopelessly fundamentalist and doctrinaire; in others, their assessments more closely coincided. On the whole, the Fund has been content to take a back seat and to let the Bank run the aid consortia and even the creditors' clubs—ad hoc groups that arrive at the same function from an opposite starting point. Only in Ghana, from which the Bank had prudently extracted itself before Nkrumah's fall, did the Fund take charge.

Perhaps a more important and pervasive influence on Fund activities since about the mid-1960s has come from the various organs devised by the rich and developed countries to permit mutual consultation on economic and financial matters of common concern. The chief ones have been the meetings of deputies of the Group of Ten, [54] which was widely believed by the end of the period to be the main source of policy-making decisions. There was also the very similarly composed Working Party Three of the OECD and the parallel consultations of governors and officials at the monthly sessions in Basel of the Bank for International Settlements.

This challenge the Fund has met by following the maxim, "If you can't beat 'em, join 'em." [55] It has refused to be left out of whatever new move was planned, always determined to defend its status as the one central, universal, and truly legitimate intergovernmental agency charged with the proper functioning of the whole international monetary system (i.e. excluding China and the Soviet bloc). Its trump card, which has made this strategy successful, has been its large resources of staff and statistics and its command of extensive and intimate economic information about every country involved in the system. Only rarely did it seem to be overtrumped.

Representatives of National and International Private Associations

The influence on the Fund that most nearly corresponds to that exercised in other organizations by representatives of national and nongovernmental associations comes from the profession of economics, and more specifically from the gathering of interested individuals each September at the annual meeting of the World Bank and the Fund. [56] Some eminent bank officials and academic people are invited to the meetings by national governments; some are invited by the managing director and president of the Bank as special guests. A large number of unattached journalists, scholars, writers, and others are also present, taking part without official status in the round of receptions and gatherings that accompanies each annual meeting. Indirectly and collectively, they add some unquantifiable ingredient to the development of ideas in Fund policies. One cannot deny or ignore the importance of this ingredient, which has a much more predominantly American flavor than the comparable sources of influence affecting other organizations. This is because no other continent has a body of professional economists—industrial, managerial, academic, and pedagogic—in any respect comparable to the North American profession. Although there is often no deliberate intention to do so, this body nevertheless reflects the political attitudes, the value judgments, and the ranking of political priorities, which at any given time are the prevailing ones in the United States. It is a factor that cannot help but increase any tendency in the Fund toward a dollar-centric skew in its approach to world problems.

Organizational Elites, 1958-67

In the difficult and dynamic sixties, and particularly during Schweitzer's tenure as managing director, there seems to have developed beneath the formal arrangements for interdepartmental committees a hard core of top Fund officials who could properly be described as making up an organizational elite.

Tew reports that in 1967-68 there was an inner group of four, consisting of Schweitzer himself, Southard, Gold, and Polak.

> It is informal in the sense that it has not been constituted as a group, but it meets frequently, always to discuss matters of major importance, including matters of strategy, and often to decide what to bring up in the other (larger) policy group.[57]

This latter group, which Tew referred to as the "steering group," began to function in the long process of studying international liquidity. Tew thought that it usually included the heads, or their deputies, of the Exchange and Trade Relations Department, the Treasurer's Department, and the European Department.[58] Until Oscar Altman, who was an American, died in 1968 and was replaced by a German, Walter Habermeier, the group was entirely American or British except for Jacques Polak, who is Dutch.

Environmental Impacts

It has already been made clear that the stratification of influence in the Fund very closely fits the stratification of power in the world, when allowance is made for the fact that the Fund is an organization of the international economic system, and powerful communist countries, which participate only to a very limited extent in that system, are not members of the Fund. The somewhat diminished predominance of the United States in the decision making of most international organizations, which elsewhere began to show up from 1955 onward, did not really become apparent in the Fund until the decade of the 1960s. Presumably, the explanation lies in the fact that the United States predominance was less contested in the specific environment of international monetary relations than in the general political environment and that the dollar remained the effective top currency in the international economic system.

The whole notion of a distinction between general and specific environments, which works for other specialized international agencies, needs, however, to be qualified in the case of the Fund, whose general environment is both political *and* economic.[59] In its earlier period the Fund's relegation to the sidelines was the result of political factors—but political factors with a high economic content. The cold war heightened the concern of the United States to restore Western Europe to economic vigor. Given that this economic objective had a new political priority and urgency, the Fund was a less suitable instrument than the OEEC, providing less leverage over European governments and less enthusiastic financial backing from the congress.

Later, the comeback of the Fund must be ascribed primarily to the rapid development of an international economy—an economic factor, however, with a high political content, since it put increasing strain on an international monetary system based on national currencies (and using two of them as reserve assets). None of the Group of Ten developed countries wished to see the system crack under the strain, yet they were divided by the fundamentally political question of how, when the precarious balance was disturbed, the adjustment process was to be accomplished.

Nothing could show more clearly the impossibility for analytical purposes of any attempt to divide the political from the economic. How, for example, should the more recent environmental impact of the North-South gap on the Fund be designated? Is it political or economic? It is hardly political in the accepted sense, since although the developing countries have been an important influence on decision making in the Fund, this is not because they have organized (as in UNCTAD) a populist lobby. They are influential because their economic weakness has constituted—and, more important perhaps, has been seen to constitute—a potentially dangerous threat to the growth, stability, and general welfare of the whole international economy.

The Specific Environment

The outstanding features of the specific environment can, for simplicity, be reduced to five. They bear out my contention that for this organization the specific environment—that is, the international monetary and financial system—does not have an independent impact, since it is itself a dependent variable of the general politicoeconomic environment.

Briefly listed these features are:

1. *The United States deficit.* This had the result of unexpectedly requiring the assistance of the Fund (as of the other major central banks in accepting the GAB, supporting the Gold Pool, etc.) to defend

the dollar. The deficit was the product of the United States reaction to the general political environment (Vietnam, NATO, and military and economic aid costs) and also, since it is the top currency state, to the general economic environment (overseas investment, concern for sterling).

2. *The European surpluses.* These unexpectedly enabled the developed countries of Western Europe to assist the United States and to do so on their own terms of limited retractable commitment, thus indicating their incomplete confidence in (not to say doubt or suspicion of) the political purposes and priorities of the United States as well as its reliability in the fight against inflation. The surpluses marked the European recovery, after a twenty-year interlude, of at least some of their former economic status; the use made of the surpluses was an assertion of a corresponding political recovery.

3. *The weakness of sterling.* This weakness unexpectedly increased British dependence on the Fund and the Fund's involvement with Britain. Such a development was partly the consequence of British failure to adapt to the loss of status in political, economic, and monetary matters and partly traceable to the role of London as financial marketplace in the international economy.

4. *The debt positions of the developing countries.* These debts created a second symbiotic relationship between the Fund's staff and a numerically large, though constitutionally weak, group of members. The accumulation of more debt servicing and greater repayment commitments than these countries could handle without defaulting or checking their growth forced the Fund to choose between excluding them as worthy of credit or organizing some rescue for them.

5. *The international capital market.* This is one of several related aspects in the accelerating development of an international economy, another being the growth of international production by large multinational corporations, mostly American. The expansion in the volume of international financial transactions and in the market, for Eurobonds and Eurodollars, in the 1960s created conditions in which maladjusted exchange rates set off major movements of short-term money, adding enormously to the problems of adjustment and liquidity with which the Fund is closely concerned.

Pattern of Polities

There is a significant division of polities from the point of view of the Fund, but it is not the one expressed in the matrix of chapter 2. It is the division by which all those states (competitive, mobilizing, and authoritarian) whose primary economic relationships lie in the international market economy are separated from those whose do not. (The first and largest group includes those sterling area and franc zone countries whose most important economic relations are or were with their respective master-currency state, Britain or France.) The minority are noncompetitive and ideological; but, more important, they are closely allied by monetary as well as military ties to China or to the Soviet Union. The list has changed little since 1950: only through the delayed exclusion between 1950 and 1958 of Czechoslovakia and Poland and the addition between 1958 and 1967 of Cuba. Shifts of states from one class of polity to another have not noticeably affected their behavior in the Fund. Ghana and the United Arab Republic are good examples. The Indonesian withdrawal between 1965 and 1967 was less a matter of polity or ideology than of the greater mutual suspicion between the debtor country and her uneasy creditors.

Conclusion: A Prospective View

The Fund in its decision making has always been quick to reflect any changes in the specific environment. But I have argued that the specific environment is itself in very large part the product of much more widely felt developments in the broad political and economic environment. If this is so, the Fund's course in the future as in the past will be determined mainly by how the most important governments, especially that of the United States, will react to these developments in the international political economy.

The only perceptible difference within the Fund in the 1970s will be that resulting from the constitutional amendments that have given the EEC countries, when they are united, an effective veto over certain Fund decisions. The United States will still be the chief initiator (still being ensconced in a constitutionally predominant position) but no longer the sole controller and potential vetoer—unless of course the six EEC countries are divided among themselves.

Outside the Fund, the alternative prospects before it could be briefly outlined under more or less the same heads as those suggested by the previous section:

1. *The United States deficit.* Many economists at the time of this writing seem to believe that if the United States does not radically change its way of reacting to the general political and economic environment, the result will be a continuation of the United States payments deficit, taking one year with another. If they are right, one might expect a sharper necessity for the United States to choose between either retreating toward modified isolation or advancing toward international cooperation. Retreat to an entrenched position accompanied only by the closest allies would be expressed militarily in a "Fortress America" policy and monetarily in a strictly controlled but preferential dollar area on the pattern of other earlier master-currency areas. In this case, the Europeans might conceivably leave the Fund to be run as it wished by the United States. They would very likely stay

in; but the Fund itself, paralyzed by blocking vetoes in both directions, would be left high, dry, and inactive save as an aid agency and a glorified research institute—much as the UN Economic Commission for Europe under Myrdal was left by the onset of the cold war.

If, on the other hand, the Americans opt for further advance toward international monetary cooperation and coordination, the Fund could expect the accretion of new decision-making responsibilities. How much of these fell to it would depend on the share accorded other organizations, such as the BIS and the Group of Ten, within the issue-area.

2. *The European Economic Community.* As before, the choices for Europe will depend partly on the choices taken by the United States. One possibility likely to be favored by an American retreat is somewhat faster progress toward a common external monetary policy and the establishment of a common reserve, which would not altogether replace separate national reserves but would be a rival European mini-fund—initially smaller but capable of growth. Hitherto, when one of the six (Italy in 1963 or France in 1969) have been in trouble over payments, they have turned not to the other five EEC countries, but to the United States and the Fund. Progress by the community toward closer monetary union, if it were to prove more than a wishful blueprint, could be a threat to the Fund's authority.

3. *Sterling.* The above development would be less likely if by the mid-1970s Britain were to be part of an enlarged European Economic Community. British links with the United States and with the Fund tightened during the 1958-68 decline of sterling. But though the decline is probably almost complete, the tighter links will not so easily vanish, not least because of London's value as a financial center to United States banks and their large corporate customers.

4. *The developing countries.* The prospect for the debt position of developing countries will be mainly determined by future growth rates for world trade and investment and for the gross national product in the rich countries that are the developing countries' chief markets and which set the limits for their export prices and earnings. Against an adverse tide from these sources, anything the Fund could organize on behalf of the developing countries would be no more than a sand castle. The Fund's self-interest in steadily upward trends for aid, trade, and investment (public, private, and mixed) hardly needs spelling out.[60]

5. *The international economy and its capital markets.* What new demands may be made on the Fund in its role of international guardian of stability and order in the system, as a result of rapid change and expansion in the international economy, can only be guessed. Thanks to the pressures on the United States, the first demand for the Fund to exercise a kind of central banking function concerned additional liquidity—a demand met in limited degree by the activation of the

scheme of Special Drawing Rights. There could conceivably be others. For example, central banks are expected to exert some control over interest rates and the direction of investment. Both matters are arousing international concern. And, in their earlier days especially, central banks may be called on unexpectedly in a financial crisis to intervene in a panicky market or to prevent the collapse of a private bank or enterprise—which might otherwise bring down the whole system in chaos, panic, and confusion. In both respects, demands now quite unforeseen conceivably could be made on the Fund. How it would respond would depend primarily on the political attitudes and alignments of the United States and the other developed countries at the time, and these cannot safely be predicted.

9 GATT: Traders' Club

Gerard and Victoria Curzon

The General Agreement on Tariffs and Trade (GATT) is a commercial treaty that embodies a number of generally accepted principles of commercial policy according to which its signatories have agreed to live.[1] GATT is best known as a forum for consultation, discussion, and negotiation in Geneva; but it is also a code of behavior upon which countries base their commercial relations, and as such it is in constant use all over the world in the normal bilateral diplomatic channels.

Evolution, Functions, and Structure

Seen historically, the GATT is the expression of its founding members' desire to enjoy once more the stability and simplicity of trade relations achieved in Europe in the latter part of the nineteenth century, later shattered by two world wars and the Great Depression.

In 1946 the United States proposed a tariff negotiation to a Preparatory Committee of the Economic and Social Council of the United Nations, which was then drafting the charter for an International Trade Organization. These developments were the result of thought that had gone on for a generation and had been inspired by Cordell Hull, who was the prime mover behind the first Reciprocal Trade Agreements Act of 1934. During World War II the United States had pursued the practical implementation of Cordell Hull's ideas on freer trade (i.e. that free trade was necessary in order to maintain peace) in all allied discussions on postwar arrangements, such as the Atlantic Charter, lend-lease agreements, and so forth. Anxious to make use of congressional permission to negotiate tariff reductions, which was limited to three years, the United States suggested that a series of commercial negotiations should be entered into among interested countries under the auspices of the 1945 Reciprocal Trade Agreements Act. The United States proposed that these negotiations should take place simultaneously and that they should be embodied in one multilateral treaty with more or less similar rules for all participating countries, the rules differing only in the individual tariff schedules applied by each country. It was suggested that this General Agreement on Tariffs and Trade should provisionally incorporate the commercial policy provisions of the draft ITO charter. The following year a tariff conference was held in Geneva, and the GATT emerged from it in October 1947.

The authors wish to thank the Graduate Institute of International Studies, University of Geneva, for the research grant which permitted them to complete and revise this chapter for publication.

Its purpose was to provide a general framework of rights and obligations for countries participating in the tariff negotiations sponsored by the United States. This general framework corresponded fairly well to the American view of how international trade relations should be organized, namely, that tariffs should be applied in a nondiscriminatory manner, that tariff concessions should be passed on to all countries subscribing to the general agreement, irrespective of whether or not they had negotiated specific tariff agreements, and that a series of elaborate escape clauses should ensure the collective supervision of any unavoidable departures from either the general or specific trade obligations entered into by the members of the system.

Part I of the general agreement obliged all contracting parties to grant general most-favored-nation treatment to each other and enshrined the principle of nondiscrimination. Nevertheless, existing preferential trading arrangements, like the British system of imperial preference, were expressly permitted.

Part II of the general agreement contained the remaining rules of good behavior, but its provisions did not apply to inconsistencies existing before October 1947, or, for other than founding members, before the date of accession. It contained a number of rules dealing with transit trade, antidumping duties, customs valuation, and the like. More important, it contained a general prohibition of quantitative restrictions and laid down the conditions of balance-of-payments disequilibrium under which they might exceptionally be used. Further exceptions were permitted in emergency situations, for reasons of security, or for the purpose of economic development.

Part III of the general agreement defined the general principles that should govern GATT tariff negotiations and the conditions under which contracting parties might modify former concessions. It contained the "waiver" provision which allowed the GATT to relieve any member of any obligation

> in exceptional circumstances not elsewhere provided for. *Provided* that any such decision shall be approved by a two-thirds majority of the votes cast, that such majority shall comprise more than half of the contracting parties.[2]

Part IV, "On Trade and Development," added in 1965, set out new guidelines for good behavior with respect to the trade of less-developed countries.

The cumulative effect of all the permitted exceptions to GATT's two main rules—nondiscrimination and the prohibition of all forms of protection save the customs tariff—prompted many critics to maintain that the principal rules had been rendered meaningless. GATT, however, was never intended to be more than a flexible and pragmatic document representing the maximum that countries were prepared to agree upon when it was signed. It was not meant to last very long. In the end it proved fairly relevant to the trade problems of the fifties and sixties and became an adequate alternative to the formal international trade organization, which failed to materialize.

The United States Congress failed to ratify the ITO charter because the traditional protectionist lobbies objected to its free trade content, while the free traders objected to its protectionist elements. The administration found itself caught in a pincer movement and, realizing that it could not obtain a majority, never submitted the charter to Congress for approval. As a result, the general agreement became the only document on which to base the gradual reconstruction of trade relations that had been so frequently attempted without success since the time that World War I put an end to nineteenth-century free trade. A move to make GATT into a formal international organization by the establishment of the Organization for Trade Cooperation (OTC) in 1954-55 met with the same fate as the ITO, since the forces in the United States that had objected to the latter in 1950 were still latent five years later.

The Formal Framework for Decisions

The General Agreement on Tariffs and Trade, signed by twenty-three countries on 30 October 1947, was a temporary arrangement to be incorporated in the International Trade Organization at a later date. It thus contained none of the normal attributes of the founding document of an international organization, such as provision for an executive body or a secretariat; nor did it even have *members* in the strict sense of the term, but only "contracting parties." (We hope nevertheless, to be forgiven for using the terms *members* and *membership* throughout this study as shorthand substitutes for more correct but unwieldy phrases.) In spite of these institutional shortcomings, the general agreement contained all the commercial policy rules of the stillborn ITO (but not the chapters on commodity arrangements and restrictive business practices), and the code itself proved sufficient in the end to give international trade cooperation the framework it needed.

Lacking an institutional structure and therefore obliged to improvise, GATT used article XXV, entitled "Joint Action by the Contracting Parties," as the legal basis upon which to build what became, in effect, an international organization without a charter. Article XXV provided for joint action by the signatories of the agreement to give effect to its provisions, to facilitate its operation, and to further its objectives. When joint action was taken, the agreement specified that the contracting parties as a group should be referred to as the Contracting Parties, which thus became the only body in GATT resembling a general assembly.

To begin with, GATT did not exist as an organization except at the periodic formal meetings, held usually once or twice a year. But it soon became clear that GATT's supervisory functions had to be exercised on a continuous basis. Since no one could expect all members to sit permanently in Geneva throughout the year, a Committee for Agenda and Inter-sessional Business was formed in 1951. Its main purpose was to discuss exceptional restrictive measures imposed by various members to safeguard the balance of payments. The Inter-sessional Committee, as it came to be called, was permitted to organize intersessional voting by air mail or telegraphic ballot on questions concerning balance-of-payments restrictions. This device permitted the Contracting Parties to take joint action whether or not they were in session.

After the failure of the OTC a greater effort was made to render GATT's presence continuous between sessions, and after much discussion a Council of Representatives was established in 1960. It replaced the old Inter-sessional Committee and was given far broader powers. So extensive were these powers that it was able to take over all GATT's general housekeeping. Nevertheless the council could not act on behalf of the Contracting Parties in matters of substance unless it collected the same number of affirmative votes as would be required if the Contracting Parties were meeting in full session. Since the council was to have forty-nine members, it contained almost two-thirds of GATT's contracting parties (seventy-six in 1969) and could almost invariably achieve the consensus necessary for run-of-the-mill decision making.

In addition to the council, a certain amount of intersessional work was conducted in a number of committees and working groups. In 1958 the Contracting Parties embarked on a Program for Expansion of International Trade and created three committees to discuss the possibilities of expanding trade in industrial products, in agricultural products, and for less-developed countries. First known simply as Committees I, II, and III, their names were changed to the Committee on Trade in Industrial Products, the Committee on Agriculture (in 1967), and the Committee on Trade and Development (in 1965). These committees, with their various subsidiary working parties and groups, also formed part of GATT's improvised organizational structure.

Sessions of the Contracting Parties were to be "held from time to time as required," the date of each session being fixed during the previous one. Sessions were in fact held at intervals of about a year. Each contracting party was entitled to one vote and had a right to participate in all postal ballots initiated by the council. Voting rules varied according to the subject under discussion. An amendment of part I of the general agreement, containing the obligation to grant most-favored-nation treatment, and of articles XIX and XXX, could only take place if it was unanimously agreed upon. Amendments to other parts of the agreement became effective once they had been accepted by a two-thirds majority of the contracting parties, but were only effective among those who had subscribed to them. The accession of new contracting parties was similarly subject to a decision by two-thirds of the existing signatories, but was effective for all members unless they disclaimed the links thus created by invoking article XXXV (see below). Permission to suspend a GATT obligation could only be given by a two-thirds majority of those voting, provided that this number was equivalent to more than half of the contracting parties. All other decisions were taken by a majority of the votes cast.

Voting and formal decision making are not normal features of GATT's existence, however. Its principal purpose consists in offering members a common meeting ground to exchange views, air complaints, and take one another's commercial temperature. It is not a decision-making machine, but a forum for discussion, and since discussing is something that government delegations do quite naturally, no elaborate procedures are needed to encourage it.

The very lack of formal institutions allowed GATT to take the changes of two decades in its stride. Large sections of the agreement itself were seldom, if ever, used, and most of the adaptation to change was made painlessly via the mobilization and demobilization of committees.

The year 1958 stands out as a major turning point in GATT's history. Internally speaking, it was the year of the Haberler Report, which laid out the three broad trade policy issues with which GATT was to occupy itself during the sixties—industrial trade, agricultural trade, and less-developed countries' trade. Independently of GATT, but having a profound influence on trade relations, 1958 marked the end of currency controls on current account in Europe and the establishment of the EEC. The first caused an unprecedented upsurge in foreign trade; the second eventually provoked the United States into offering in the Kennedy Round the largest and most comprehensive tariff cuts witnessed in GATT since the first 1947-48 conference. From 1958 onward, GATT ceased to deal with postwar problems and began to occupy itself with the questions raised by peace, prosperity, and economic development.

The Secretariat and Budget

The GATT secretariat has a curious position among intergovernmental administrations. The general agreement itself made no provision for secretariat services, and the Contracting Parties used the secretariat of a largely defunct body called the Interim Commission for the International Trade Organization (ICITO). ICITO was created in 1948 at the end of the Havana Conference to deal with the current trade business of the time and prepare for the entry into force of the ITO charter, but it was subsequently asked to supply the Contracting Parties with secretariat services until such time as the ITO should come into existence. ICITO remained an organ of the United Nations, and it was this body to which Contracting Parties paid their annual contributions and which employed the GATT secretariat—its only function. ICITO was also, incidentally, GATT's only formal link with the United Nations family.

The GATT secretariat is known for its modest size. In the early years it consisted of 6 professional staff members and 12 typists and general staff employees. Only in 1951 did the Contracting Parties make their first financial contribution to the costs of running the ICITO secretariat, which until then had been paid for by the United Nations. And it was not until 1955 that the secretariat left the Palais des Nations in Geneva to take up permanent residence a little farther up the road in Villa le Bocage. But if the total size of GATT's secretariat remained small even in 1969, its growth rate had been formidable: it employed 85 professionals and 112 general service staff members permanently. Temporary staff members varied according to work in hand, and they accounted for about another 150 employees at the end of the Kennedy Round.

GATT's budget reflects a similar trend. It remained below $500 thousand for the first decade. From the late 1950s onward it grew steadily and topped the $3 million mark in 1968, reflecting the growth in GATT's range of interests, a large increase in membership, and, of course, inflation. The largest single item in GATT's budget related to salaries and other staff costs; this item alone accounted for about two-thirds of the total. Office overhead, including buildings, took up about $250 thousand, and the remainder was accounted for by the International Trade Center, whose cost was shared by UNCTAD. The trade center is GATT's only significant outside activity and, along with a scheme for training foreign service officers, the only one that might be described as a technical assistance program. The increase in GATT's budget has been particularly marked since 1958, reflecting the change from the old GATT to the new.

On the income side, GATT had a small annual income of about $15 thousand a year from the sale of publications, and a larger, more variable income from interest on investments—some $50 thousand a year. The remainder came from assessed contributions calculated on the basis of each member's share in the total trade of all the contracting parties, computed on a three-year average of the latest available trade figures. Nevertheless, when a member's trade share was less than 0.12 percent, a minimum contribution was required of it. Of GATT's seventy-six contracting parties, plus the three associated governments, thirty fell into this category in the provisional scale of contributions calculated for 1969. Only nine members contributed more than $100 thousand in 1968,[3] but among them these nine accounted for over $2 million, or approximately two-thirds of the total contributions. The United States, although it made the largest single contribution, by no means shouldered a major part of GATT's running costs. A few of the smaller developed countries, especially the Scandinavian states, made voluntary contributions to the International Trade Center, and the UNDP planned to finance selected trade center projects as from 1969. GATT's contribution to the trade center was frozen at $671,600 in 1969 in order to keep the total budget down and discourage GATT from entering the race to provide multilateral technical assistance to developing countries.

Decision Making: A Taxonomical Analysis

GATT takes decisions on two very different planes. It occasionally takes decisions that relate to the general agreement as such, although the procedure is usually long winded and often results in no decision being taken at all. Even recommendations can only be squeezed out with the greatest difficulty. On the other hand, decisions to create a working party are taken readily, and a problem can shuttle back and forth from working party to council, from council to session, and back again for two or three years before it is shelved or otherwise disposed of. In spite of the absence of much visible output, this process is by no means sterile. It gives governments a chance to find out exactly what other governments think about an issue of general trade interest; it gives them time to work out their own positions; it clarifies frequently obscure aspects of trade policy, and it is a constant reminder that the system can only work if the habit of cooperation is fostered and maintained.

Besides decisions and discussions relating to the general agreement, a major part of GATT's output consists of specific and usually bilateral decisions taken during tariff conferences as a result of negotiations held under GATT's auspices. The gradual accumulation and consolidation of these specific decisions to lower tariffs on a reciprocal and multilateral basis over two decades has led the world from the tariff and quota-bound state of the early postwar years to the comparative freedom of trade among industrialized countries enjoyed at the end of the sixties. Each specific tariff bargain is insignificant in itself, but the effect of all tariff bargains struck since 1947 is considerable. The general agreement provides a bag into which specific agreements are dropped from time to time. Since the fabric that went into the making of the bag was never very strong in the first place, GATT spends about as much time mending the holes in it as adding to its contents. The great question is whether the bag will not one day split open, allowing its painfully acquired contents to escape. So far, attempts to make a new and stronger bag have failed, and the old one is the best we have, although it is generally agreed that it is extremely vulnerable to both internal and external attack.

Of the types of decision selected for investigation in the general framework of this book, the only ones that are of significance in GATT are rule-supervisory decisions (mending holes in the bag) and rule-creating decisions (filling it up). Representational issues often provide interesting anecdotes, but not much time is spent on them. Symbolic and operational decisions are unimportant, unless one holds the extreme view that all international forum activity is symbolic anyway—a position we do not take. Questions of boundary have not been important during the first twenty years of GATT's existence, with the exception of the GATT-UNCTAD question, but they may become more important in future as other international organizations or informal groups, such as the OECD, the Group of Ten, and so on, offer alternative forums for international trade cooperation.

Representational Decisions

When the general agreement was signed in 1947, it had 23 contracting parties. However, its territorial application was far wider than mere membership figures might suggest, since countries possessing colonies undertook, for the most part, to apply GATT's trading rules in respect to the trade of these possessions. In point of fact GATT applied to 105 states and territories at its inception. Since then most of these territories have become independent, and many of them have maintained their relation to GATT. In all, there have been 57 accessions and 4 withdrawals from 1947 to 1968.

Any country may accede to the general agreement. But because every newcomer automatically benefits from the cumulative effect of all tariff concessions negotiated in GATT before its arrival (since on accession it becomes entitled to most-favored-nation treatment), the newcomer is expected to enter into tariff negotiations with existing contracting parties before becoming a member of the club. The acceding government thus pays an entrance fee in exchange for all the benefits and concessions that have already been negotiated in the past. One might think that this custom would make it harder for new members to join as time went on and as concessions piled up in the GATT schedules. In fact, since most newcomers are newly independent and not very well off, established GATT members do not normally drive too hard a bargain, and many former dependencies enter without any payment at all if they happened to be within GATT's territorial application before they gained independence.

On the other hand, there have been examples of very thorough negotiations for accession. Switzerland, for instance, took two years to negotiate provisional accession and a further eight years to achieve full membership because a number of agricultural exporters (notably New Zealand) objected to Switzerland's all too efficient form of agricultural protection and felt that it could afford to import more cheap food. Germany and Japan were only able to join in 1950 and 1955 respectively, after the United States' perception of the Soviet threat had brought a modification in its attitude toward its former enemies.

It may happen that a contracting party does not wish to give GATT treatment to a newcomer for political or economic reasons. This situation has arisen on numerous occasions. Article XXXV states that GATT shall not apply between two contracting parties if they have not entered into tariff negotiations with each other and if "either of the contracting parties, at the time either becomes a contracting party, does not consent to such application." Since then, article XXXV has been used for political reasons by eight countries that hold certain other states in great odium, and for economic reasons by forth-three countries against Japan. (Most of the latter reservations had been dropped by the end of the sixties and more sophisticated ways of controlling the inflow of Japanese goods developed.)

Article XXXV is an admirable safety valve, which permits GATT debates on accession to remain relatively unpoliticized. It is noteworthy that India and Pakistan have remained the only countries to invoke article XXXV against South Africa and that there has been no attempt to make that country withdraw—indeed, GATT has no powers of expulsion.

The United States furnished the only example of one contracting party's unilaterally suspending its contractual obligations toward another when in 1951, during the McCarthy period, it declared that "the Government of Czechoslovakia, through its actions, has nullified benefits that should have accrued to the United States under the General Agreement on Tariffs and Trade."[4] Czechoslovakia made a similar declaration and the Contracting Parties took note of the situation, declaring that the United States and Czechoslovakia were free to suspend their GATT obligations toward each other, providing they did not modify their obligations toward other members. The United States did not repeat this form of protest when Cuba became a communist state.

Any contracting party applying the agreement in its entirety may withdraw after giving six months notice to the secretary-general of the United Nations (article XXXI). Under the "Protocol of Provisional Application" only six weeks' notice is required. However, the right to withdraw at sixty days' notice may be invoked by a contracting party under article XVIII, "Governmental Assistance to Economic Development," or article XXIII, "Nullification or Impairment." The countries that have withdrawn from GATT so far are: Nationalist China, Syria, Lebanon, and Liberia. All of these withdrew in the early days.

The general political environment has had great influence on GATT's membership. Until the thaw in East-West relations, Czechoslovakia was GATT's only communist contracting party, and it was almost completely dormant as a GATT member, emerging only once, in 1950, to record its protest against the accession of West Germany and Korea.[5] By 1958 East-West relations had improved to the point where Yugoslavia applied for full membership. After three years of examination and reporting, it became a provisional member in 1962 and a full one in 1965. Poland made an official request for full accession in March 1959; but it became a full member only in 1967, as part of the Kennedy Round. The presence of Cuba, Czechoslovakia, Yugoslavia, and Poland in GATT is proof of a general interest in developing trade links between planned and market economies, but there has been little real trade expansion between these two groups of countries. The political aspect of these accessions was illustrated by a marked deterioration in the climate of consultation after the August 1968 Prague coup. Despite a definite setback in East-West trade conversations in GATT, Hungary and

Rumania nevertheless applied for membership in 1969. They were reportedly given a cool reception.

Most accessions take place on the initiative of the applicants themselves, though a former colonial power may act as a broker for a former colony. No one country can exercise a veto, for admission is decided upon by a two-thirds majority; article XXXV allows contracting parties to avoid newcomers if they wish to. As a result GATT has some strange bedfellows, but politicization of debates is almost unheard of. Furthermore, nonmember governments can obtain observer status. Thus for many years most Eastern European countries, and some other nonmembers have regularly followed the work of the Contracting Parties by sending permanent representatives to GATT meetings; they may, on occasion, even speak on behalf of their governments.

Executive or Examining Bodies. GATT has become progressively more informal in composing its executive organs—the former Inter-sessional Committee and the Council of Representatives described earlier—and as far as working parties or committees are concerned, informality has been the watchword from the outset. When the old Inter-sessional Committee was formed in 1951, its membership, initially limited to fifteen countries and later expanded to seventeen, was drawn from those countries possessing permanent delegations in or near Geneva. About ten countries were usually reelected automatically: namely, Australia, Brazil, Canada, France, India, Italy, Pakistan, the United Kingdom, the United States, and West Germany. This list gives a fair indication of the locus of influence in GATT in the early fifties.

When the Council of Representatives replaced the old Inter-sessional Committee in 1960, the decision was that it should be composed of "all contracting parties willing to accept the responsibility of membership therein."[6] The 1969 list of forty-nine members, therefore, no longer indicates the locus of influence in GATT, but only the incidence of keenness. Only very small countries (or a political pariah like Rhodesia) are not on the council, and even they can be co-opted as full members if the discussion turns on an issue of particular interest to them. The council itself, however, is at the center of GATT's decision making, for it has gradually taken the place of the full-dress sessions in handling most of the forum functions for which GATT is responsible.

Membership on the main committees and working parties is not limited to any specific number, and in principle any country that wishes to be a member of a committee or working party has only to ask. This means that some committees and working parties of general interest—on such matters as development questions, agriculture, nontariff barriers—may have as many as fifty delegations present at a sitting. On the other hand, when the Balance-of-Payments Committee discusses Korean import restrictions, one can expect the Japanese to be there in force but not, perhaps, the Dutch or the Danes: the Balance-of-Payments Committee, which is one of the important standing committees, numbers fourteen countries,[7] including the six largest trading countries of GATT. A country not normally on the Balance-of-Payments Committee but interested in a particular consultation is free to participate if it wishes to.

Symbolic Decisions

GATT has its fair share of symbolic decisions nowadays, especially in the field of trade and development. At their annual sessions the Contracting Parties adopt resolutions affirming, for instance, "the crucial importance of a maximum expansion in the export opportunities of less-developed countries to the development of their economies."[8] But, as these latter countries do not cease to point out, much remains to be done in this respect. There are also some rather symbolic activities, such as consultations on balance-of-payments restrictions applied by less-developed countries. The original purpose of such consultation and scrutiny was to make sure that measures inconsistent with the general agreement would be applied temporarily and removed as soon as the original reasons justifying their imposition no longer existed. Nowadays, except in the case of rich, developed members, GATT turns a blind eye to many inconsistencies. Indeed, one can even say that GATT has a double standard by which it judges breaches of the code—a severe one for the developed and a lenient one for the underdeveloped.

Because GATT has had the good fortune to remain aloof from the mainstream of political affairs (it exists only to serve the commercial interests of its members), it has avoided being mesmerized by a number of difficult issues, such as the South African question, the Israel-Arab conflict, the Anglo-Spanish disagreement over Gilbraltar, the Indo-Pakistani situation, and so forth. Symbolic decisions condemning or condoning one side or the other and the mustering of votes for such decisions are quite unknown in GATT.

Programmatic Decisions

Since GATT is primarily a forum organization, programmatic decisions are not taken in the framework of the budget committee as is the case in service-oriented organizations. The main use to which GATT's resources are put is in organizing tariff conferences and in supervising its rules, but these activities will be more appropriately discussed in the sections dealing with rule-creating and rule-supervisory decisions. However, the GATT forum is also used to discover new directions for international trade cooperation, notable examples of which are the Haberler Report and the inauguration of GATT's Program for the Expansion of International Trade in 1958.

Third World Challenge and GATT's Trade Expansion Program. One of the trade policy issues that began to arise after the end of the postwar reconstruction period was what to do about less-developed countries' trade.

In point of fact, the GATT secretariat can claim to have discovered, in its annual review of international trade in 1954, "the relative decline in trade between non-industrial and industrial areas, accounted for by the failure of the value of exports from the non-industrial areas to expand."[9] This theme was subsequently taken up by delegations and soon became a regular subject of discussion at GATT sessions. It led in 1957 to the appointment of a panel of experts who were asked to examine past and current international trade trends and their implications, taking note especially of

> the failure of the trade of less developed countries to develop as rapidly as that of industrialised countries, excessive short-term fluctuations in prices of primary products and widespread resort to agricultural protection.[10]

In retrospect the report of the panel of experts, produced by four scholars outside the organization—Professors Haberler, Meade, Tinbergen, and Campos—turned out to be a basic piece of rethinking about the role that GATT should play in international commercial arrangements. On the basis of this report, the Contracting Parties inaugurated the Program for the Expansion of International Trade in 1958, according to which economic development was included in GATT's range of interests; and agriculture, excluded as a result of an earlier decision, was grudgingly readmitted.

When it first attempted from 1958 to 1961 to find a solution to the problems of developing countries within its traditional framework, GATT took the lead from its senior members, the secretariat, and two of the more dynamic less-developed countries, Brazil and India. When nothing happened, external pressure from UNCTAD and internal pressure from other less-developed members caused a shift in policy and methods. Further work in the course of 1962 and a suggestion from the director-general led to the creation in 1963 of a Committee on the Legal and Institutional Framework of GATT in Relation to Less-Developed Countries. This in turn resulted in the adoption of part IV of the general agreement, which added three new articles by which the Contracting Parties pledged themselves to joint action to increase the exports of poorer countries. In accordance with a Brazilian proposal, they also agreed that "developed contracting parties do not expect reciprocity for commitments in trade negotiations to remove tariffs and other barriers."[11] The new chapter on trade and development was worked out in order to put less-developed countries' demands on a legal footing within the general agreement. The principle of reciprocity was abandoned on paper, in the interests of development; but one cannot get much for nothing in commercial diplomacy; part IV has therefore turned out to be largely symbolic.

Besides drawing up part IV, the Contracting Parties also departed from traditional GATT work methods by embarking on a large-scale operational activity—the International Trade Center—to help its less-developed members.

GATT's programmatic decisions related to economic development have been initiated principally by the Committee on Trade and Development as a result of collaboration between the secretariat, developed countries, and less-developed states. Developed countries have usually made conservative proposals, appealing to developing states to use the opportunities offered by the GATT forum and its secretariat services to negotiate trade concessions. These proposals have met with little success, and the substantive discussions have migrated to the OECD (for developed states) and UNCTAD (for developing states).

Boundary Decisions

GATT's external relations with other international structures are limited almost entirely to those which, in one way or another, have a bearing on international trade. The most important of these are the IMF, UNCTAD, the regional integration groups and the OECD, and they are discussed in this order.

GATT and the IMF. One of the principal derogations from GATT's rule that quantitative restrictions were not to apply to members' trade was the balance-of-payments escape clause, which permitted quotas as an emergency measure. Balance-of-payments disequilibria, however, were daily bread for the International Monetary Fund, one of whose tasks was to investigate the balance-of-payments position of those who applied for loans to tide them over a payments crisis. A country experiencing a temporary disequilibrium in its international payments could address itself to the Fund for money and notify GATT (if possible ahead of time) of emergency quota restrictions. All that remained for GATT to do was to discuss the propriety of such emergency action and take into account "all findings of statistical and other facts presented by the Fund relating to foreign exchange, monetary reserves and balances of payments" (GATT, article XV). The same article enjoined GATT to "seek co-operation with the International Monetary Fund" so that their policies with regard to balance-of-payments crises should coincide.

GATT's relationship with the IMF was important as long as large European trading countries maintained quantitative restrictions on dollar trade for balance-of-payments reasons. Since the end of 1958, however, widespread currency convertibility and the end of quotas on dollar trade have confined this relationship to investigating the balance-of-payments position of some less-developed countries (with the exception of the United Kingdom import surcharge in 1964), for whom the criteria of control tend to be lenient.[12]

GATT and UNCTAD. UNCTAD was the first to rival GATT's position as the world's universal trade organization. Ever since some of the smaller

Eastern European countries began showing an interest in GATT, in the mid- and late-1950s, the Soviet Union has pressed in various universal organizations, such as ECOSOC and the General Assembly of the United Nations, for a world trade organization that could deal with East-West trade problems and that would put a stop to the Eastern European drift into GATT.

After the 1961 Ministerial Meeting in GATT, which failed to take positive action on the problems of the underdeveloped countries, the Soviet Union saw that it could muster a majority for its new world trade organization by combining the East-West trade problem with the North-South one. Successful canvassing in ECOSOC in the summer of 1962 led to a resolution that a world trade conference should be held. [13]

Though some authors see antecedents to UNCTAD in such events as the Bandung Conference in 1955, the Belgrade Conference in 1961, and the Cairo Conference in 1962, [14] the political impetus was given by the USSR, determined to discuss the communist countries' commercial problems in a trade organization less committed to market principles than GATT. The less-developed countries were willing cosponsors but did not possess the strength to create UNCTAD alone, and the United Nations secretariat gave the scheme its wholehearted support because it seemed a wonderful opportunity to get its hands on the fertile field of trade and commerce, which until then had been GATT's preserve.

It is worth noting that the underdeveloped countries who are members of UNCTAD but not of GATT belong to three broad groups. The largest of these is the Latin-American group (along with some Asian countries) whose trade is closely linked with the United States and who have bilateral commercial treaties embodying the most-favored-nation clause. These countries, numbering about twenty, therefore obtain the benefits of concessions negotiated by the United States in GATT without "paying" for them; they therefore need neither GATT nor an alternative organization for these particular benefits. The second group consists of countries with a unique market situation for a single export product, like the oil-producing countries of the Near East; and the third is a miscellaneous group of countries whose interest in trade is still minimal—Afghanistan, Nepal, Yemen, and others. GATT therefore covers substantially the same territory as UNCTAD in North-South trade, but not in East-West trade.

The overlap led inevitably to rivalry in the early years. During the period of the Kennedy Round negotiations, it has been said that UNCTAD had more people working on the Kennedy Round than GATT. Indeed, UNCTAD followed the negotiations very closely and, with a speed untypical of organizations, produced a report at the end showing how few benefits there were for less-developed countries.

Competition from UNCTAD may have made GATT more sensitive to the problems of North-South trade than it was before. The GATT secretariat now devotes considerable resources to the development of North-South

trade, mainly by helping countries to negotiate and by spotting opportunities for them. The developed members in GATT, furthermore, now make
little attempt to enforce GATT's rules when developing countries break
them, but it is difficult to say whether this is the result of indulgence or
indifference.

On the whole, however, GATT's senior members were glad (in the end) to
have UNCTAD take the pressure of developing countries' demands out of
GATT, leaving their habitual trade policy forum clear for more substantive
negotiations. If anything, UNCTAD did not prove successful enough, and
enough disturbance was still felt in GATT to make one or two developed
countries take some of their trade problems to the OECD instead.

Relation to the EEC, EFTA, and LAFTA. GATT is the legal base upon
which regional integration projects of the EEC-EFTA type are built, and
their founding documents all refer to article XXIV of the general agreement
in explanation and justification. GATT, in turn, retains the right to examine
these treaties and pronounce itself on their compatibility with the general
agreement. In point of fact, the Contracting Parties have come to no decision
regarding compatibility of any one of the regional economic integration
projects claiming legal status under article XXIV. In each case the
Contracting Parties felt that there were "legal and practical issues" that
could not be "fruitfully discussed further,"[15] and they postponed their final
judgment for an indeterminate time. In the meantime, they reserved the
right to conduct annual consultations under article XXII.[16]

An interesting example of overlapping supervisory authority occurred in
November 1964, when the United Kingdom, claiming serious balance-of-payments difficulties imposed a 15 percent surcharge on all imports. This action
was contrary to both GATT and EFTA, which allowed only the use of
quantitative restrictions in such circumstances. GATT and EFTA reacted in
two completely different ways, EFTA making an impassioned issue of the
case and GATT treating it with the composure taught by experience. The
usual working party was convened, and the problem was discussed at the
leisurely pace of three meetings in two years. EFTA's stronger reaction
succeeded in bringing the surcharge down from 15 to 10 percent, but failed
to make the United Kingdom conform to its treaty obligations. The United
Kingdom abolished the surcharge before the GATT working party could
draw up a report.

GATT and the OECD. During the 1950s GATT overlapped with the
OEEC on the question of liberalization of quantitative restrictions but did
not begin overlapping with OECD until the end of the 1960s. During and
after the Kennedy Round GATT members took up the question of nontariff
barriers, which they had largely ignored in former tariff conferences. The
debate started harmlessly enough in a typically piecemeal fashion—discriminatory European road taxes that put powerful American cars at a

competitive disadvantage vis-à-vis European ones; the American Selling Price valuation technique for a small range of chemical products, and so on. However, after the Kennedy Round GATT members agreed to let the secretariat make a thorough investigation of all nontariff barriers, prior to staging a formal negotiation at a later date. After a little delving it became clear that much general research on the subject had already been done in the OECD, and that if a nontariff barrier negotiation were ever to be held, the OECD's claim to be the forum would be as good as that of GATT, especially since the nontariff barrier question is definitely an issue for developed, and not developing, countries.

Besides the nontariff barrier issue, the OECD's principal function of providing developed countries with a forum to discuss their policies toward less-developed ones began to tread heavily on GATT's toes as the discussion turned to working out a tariff preference scheme in response to demands made in UNCTAD. Toward the end of the 1960s, the OECD emerged as a serious rival to GATT's forum function.

Boundary questions in GATT are of several sorts. With UNCTAD and the IMF, GATT is on the receiving end of initiatives and information; where regional groups are concerned, the Contracting Parties try to keep a collective and parental eye on their evolution and ask them to account for themselves once a year. As no decisions are ever taken, however, the problem of identifying initiators and obstructionists arises in a very shadowy way. No one really bothers too much about what the African and Latin-American regional groups are up to, but the EEC and EFTA are carefully watched. The enthusiasm of the United States for being economically discriminated against has waned since 1957, and the EEC's agricultural policy is under constant fire. EFTA, especially since the end of the Kennedy Round, arouses fewer passions. The United States and the large Commonwealth countries, along with a few advanced developing countries like Argentina, Brazil, and India, are the principal collective watchdogs of European integration. The EEC and EFTA are careful not to criticize each other, for obvious reasons.

Rule-Creating Decisions

GATT Tariff Conference. One of GATT's outstanding achievements has undoubtedly been the organization of six tariff conferences since 1947. These have probably reduced protectionism to a level well below the most optimistic hopes of the early postwar years. The tariff conferences involve any contracting parties willing to negotiate and may last a few months or a few years. The decision to hold a tariff conference is taken by the Contracting Parties at one of their periodic sessions. Until now the United States has been the usual initiator. GATT has, in fact, lived according to the rhythm of United States trade legislation.

The first six rounds of tariff negotiations organized under GATT's auspices corresponded to repeated renewals of the Reciprocal Trade

Agreements Act; and the last and most important one—the Kennedy Round, lasting from 1964 to 1967—was the international counterpart of the U.S. Trade Expansion Act of 1962. On the other hand, since the economic recovery of Europe and the emergence of the Third World, American commercial policy has been formulated in response to external challenges, and it has been this process of challenge and response that has characterized GATT's activity since 1958.

It is one thing to decide to hold a tariff conference and another to make a success of it. The actual agreements that are reached during the conference are the result of essentially bilateral concessions, which accumulate and are automatically made multilateral by the most-favored-nation clause. The process whereby bilateral concessions are accumulated and generalized is the key to GATT's relative success as a forum for tariff reductions, for it limits the effective negotiators to those who have a genuine interest in the subject under discussion, namely, the principal supplier (or suppliers) of the product being negotiated. Subsidiary suppliers are either taken for a free ride or asked to provide a small concession in exchange for their windfall gain. Countries that refuse to do this (as is their right) are not well regarded, and most countries genuinely interested in trade cooperation are usually glad to reduce tariffs on a reciprocal basis as long as no strong domestic pressures oblige them to do otherwise. The final result is a large, frequently untidy package, involving most of the main trading countries of GATT and many thousands of products. The elements that go into the decisions by individual delegates in the course of these negotiations are determined largely in the home country, where governments are confronted with the difficult task of trying to please everyone—protectionists and free traders alike.

The system of item-by-item negotiations just described was used very successfully during GATT's first tariff conference of 1947. After that it proved more and more disappointing at each successive round. As early as 1951 the Europeans, particularly the French, pressed for so-called linear, across-the-board, tariff cuts; but the United States considered itself unable to accept the automaticity implied by linear tariff reductions at a time when Congress was in one of the periodic troughs of its trade policy cycle. Once the EEC's common external tariff was in place, however, that organization had no other way to negotiate as a single entity save on the basis of linear cuts; item-by-item negotiations would have torn holes in the common tariff.

The real initiator in the decision to change from item-by-item negotiations to across-the-board tariff cuts was the EEC; before the Dillon Round it was France. But until 1962 the United States vetoed the idea, and only when led by a Democratic administration and faced with the threat of discrimination by the EEC (not to speak of EFTA) did Congress agree to it.

While it is clear that the United States and its domestic legislation imposed the timetable of the GATT tariff rounds, it was nevertheless the interaction of United States and European trading interests that determined the issues involved. The growth of European power in GATT, from the creation of the EEC onward, meant that by the 1960s the United States was no longer alone in its role of initiator and vetoer in trade cooperation matters. Its position was now shared by the EEC, and they became jointly responsible for the success or failure of international trade cooperation from then on.

Rule-Supervisory Decisions

There are two sides to GATT. One side, which we have just described, is the creative job of reducing the barriers to trade that exist among its members. The other is the rather thankless task of mending the holes that appear in the GATT bag.

The examination of breaches of its trading rules takes up a goodly portion of GATT's time. Some exemptions are foreseen in the treaty itself. Thus, the most-favored-nation clause may be set aside by countries forming a free trade area or a customs union, operating already existing preference systems, recovering from World War II, or applying import restrictions for the purpose of economic development. In the last-named case, however, deviation is permitted only if it is temporary, if it covers only a small part of the country's external trade, and if it confers benefits that substantially outweigh any injury that other contracting parties might suffer. The rule that the customs tariff be the only permitted form of import restriction for GATT members may be shelved to safeguard the balance of payments and to promote economic development. Any other deviation from these two broad rules must be formally waived by a two-thirds majority. The waiver procedure is GATT's principal escape clause, and it permits a member under certain conditions to discard any obligation arising from the agreement. Waivers were asked for less often in the sixties than in the fifties, either because the need for them declined or because countries became reluctant to submit to the rigors of the waiver cross-examination technique. Waivers have usually been granted on request, after examination of the amount of trade affected, but have usually been subject to annual review and have been, in principle, temporary. The only permanent waiver GATT ever granted was to the United States for certain agricultural products in 1954-55.

A more usual procedure is to call a working party to study a breach of the GATT, usually after the guilty party has notified its partners of an action already taken and the reasons that have impelled it to act in this manner. If heavy trade interests are involved, the debate will be lively, and the defendant may consider it diplomatic to make concessions (e.g the case of Germany in 1959-61). If, on the other hand, the defendant chooses to be obstinate and undiplomatic, there is little the others can do save register disapproval and, in an extreme case, seek authority to retaliate (e.g. the EEC's Common Agricultural Policy or the problem of its Associated Overseas Territories). Finally, if the senior GATT members consider that the defendant's action is justified, the working party is likely to do nothing but discuss it (e.g. the United Kingdom's import surcharge in 1964).

Another common pattern in the control process is a complaint by country X that country Y is in breach of its GATT obligations and is nullifying or impairing country X's rights as a result. Faithful to its pragmatic tradition, GATT has no full-fledged procedure for handling such complaints. This is a result of the historic accident that made it the founding document of a de facto organization, while the real charter with detailed provisions for dispute settlement remained a dead letter.

The main characteristic of GATT's system of dealing with disputes is the policy of encouraging their settlement through bilateral consultations between the parties concerned. This is called the conciliation procedure, and it usually ends in a negotiated settlement. Only if the matter cannot be settled bilaterally, will it be referred to the Contracting Parties. A small panel is then appointed, composed of a few representatives chosen for their neutrality and extensive knowledge of GATT. If its recommendations are not accepted by the disputants, the plaintiff may ask for authority to retaliate. At this stage, the Contracting Parties may act jointly to grant this authority. The decision is taken by a simple majority of the votes cast. Some two dozen cases have been settled by panels of conciliation; and so far only in one case have the Contracting Parties recommended retaliation as a solution (the Netherlands versus the United States in 1950).

Few panels of conciliation have been called in recent years. In the 1960s the last one met in October 1964 to put the final touches to its report on a Uruguayan complaint that seven European countries were restricting their imports of beef and wool products and thereby nullifying or impairing benefits accruing to it under the general agreement. Countries seem to be increasingly reluctant to let a dispute get to this stage and prefer to settle bilaterally if possible.

Many blatant cases where countries flout the general agreement are never challenged because it is obvious to all from the outset that nothing would be gained. Two examples among many are the United States' petroleum import regulations and the United Kingdom's Coal Board's embargo on imports.

Operational Decisions

Since GATT is almost 100 percent a forum-type organization, operational decisions are not important. The International Trade Center is GATT's only significant operational activity, but it does not loom large in its overall work.

Actors and Their Sources of Influence

National Government Representatives

We have tried, for the purpose of this book, to shed light on the role of individual government representatives in GATT affairs. From our own knowledge of the way GATT conducts its work, we were inclined to believe that the individual did not play a decisive part, and interviews confirmed this belief. Personalities abound in GATT's twenty-years' existence, but they have rarely succeeded in shaping the course taken by world trade cooperation, except perhaps at the very beginning, before the GATT system jelled. At the very most, they may have achieved some above average tariff bargains for their governments or pleaded a weak cause well, but this cannot be said to be part of GATT's collective' decision-making process. Governments remain the true actors in the forum for international trade cooperation that GATT provides, and their delegates are closely briefed. The impact a country may have in GATT, however, is partly determined by the quality of its delegates which, in turn, is a function of the interest it takes in the GATT forum as a means of furthering its commercial interests. The quality of United States representation in GATT, for instance, varies according to the priority given to international trade policy by the administration of the day, while that of most European and white Commonwealth nations is usually consistent within a competency band ranging from sufficient to good. No delegation, however competent, can take initiatives and make a mark in GATT unless it is supported at home by a trade ministry that has a well-defined international trade policy and knows where it is going. Some countries fail to make an impact in GATT because their trade ministries have no clear policy and, when presented with a problem, will dither for months before deciding on one. In the meantime their GATT delegations are condemned to inaction. On the other hand, some countries pursue a consistent policy and have well-briefed delegates in Geneva. It stands to reason that the latter will have greater influence on the course of collective decision making than the former.

Representatives of Private Associations

Protectionist lobbies influence commercial policy decisions in every capital in the world, but they rarely come to Geneva to exercise their pressure.[17] The fact that GATT's tariff conferences are geographically isolated from domestic lobbying arenas may contribute to the generally quiet atmosphere of GATT's deliberations. Apart from a few informal contacts between the secretariat and some national chambers of commerce or producers' associations, NGOs are not actors in the GATT system.

Caucuses

Caucuses were unknown to GATT until recently, and even now they are only rudimentary. Although GATT has not taken over the caucus structure of UNCTAD, one caucus has definitely been formed within it—the so-called Group of Less-Developed Countries—and it represents a complete departure from GATT tradition. Its antecedents go back to the late 1950s and early 1960s, when some twenty less-developed countries would occasionally meet and try to formulate a common position in Committee III. As a result of these efforts the Ministerial Meeting of 1961 had before it a Program of Action submitted by a well-defined group of less-developed countries.[18]

But the more direct origins of the present group are to be found in the secretariat's desire, encouraged by the developed members, to give delegations from less-developed countries technical help in the Kennedy Round negotiations. Early in these negotiations it became clear that poor countries did not have the necessary expertise either to follow what was going on or to see when trade items of importance to them were being discussed and where possible advantages for them lay. The secretariat, largely on its own initiative, began to provide less-developed countries with this information. Ever since then, these states have held regular meetings with the help of the GATT secretariat. These meetings may take place as often as once a month. The group has not been officially or legally integrated into GATT; but its existence is acknowledged in GATT's pragmatic manner, and the secretariat keeps the records, provides a meeting room, and sends out the circulars. Similarly, the group makes its wishes known without issuing them as formal resolutions of the less-developed countries.

The only other fairly persistent grouping in GATT is composed of producers of the temperate zone agricultural goods (Australia, New Zealand, Argentina, Uruguay, Canada, and sometimes the United States), who have a common interest in improving access to Western Europe's large consumer markets for food. They work together in the Agricultural Committee, but nowhere else; and they remain a nebulous group without formal structure.[19]

The Director-General and His Immediate Entourage

If it were not for Eric Wyndham White at the head of the GATT secretariat for twenty years, one could dismiss the question of the individual's role in GATT as being interesting but inessential. No one can doubt, however, that Sir Eric influenced the course of events in GATT not once, but many times.

Part of his influence derived from his position, but much of it was built up over the years through his own efforts and the way he conceived of his job. Throughout his period of office he took an active part in all the more difficult negotiations; delegations that were unable to work out an arrangement between themselves turned to him, knowing him to be technically competent and impartial. Sometimes with the help of the secretariat, and sometimes without, a formula would be devised to resolve the difficulty. Indeed, this role of honest broker is an integral part of the work of the director-general of GATT and of the secretariat.

There is no doubt that Sir Eric made himself extremely useful to GATT's members, and when he in turn suggested a new course of action, they considered it seriously. He was therefore one of the actors in GATT who took initiatives, though whenever possible he would persuade a government to put them forward for him. Thus the director-general is said to have initiated the 1955 Review Session, the Haberler Panel, and part IV of the general agreement. Sometimes, however, an idea of Sir Eric's did not obtain the approval of the important contracting parties in spite of all the informal pressure put upon them. For instance, the GATT Plan for Tariff Reductions and the OTC were both initially his ideas, but they did not come about.

Sir Eric's influence reached its climax during the Kennedy Round, when his diplomatic sense for compromise was in great and constant demand. The control center of this hive of diplomatic activity was known as the "Bridge Club" because no more than four people were usually present at the discussion. There is no doubt that these private meetings between the director-general, on the one hand, and the representatives of the United States, the EEC, and the United Kingdom, on the other, contributed to the success of the Kennedy Round negotiations.

Segments of the Bureaucracy

The three departments of GATT's secretariat and the office of the director-general are unevenly staffed. There is no doubt that the Department of Trade and Development nowadays takes pride of place, at least as far as sheer numbers are concerned. A few years ago this department did not even exist, and in 1965 it was still only a division. In 1968 it had a professional staff of twenty-four, compared to fourteen for the Department of Trade Policy, which supplies the services for GATT's forum role. Since the less-developed countries in GATT are not very well organized, the road is clear for initiatives from the Department of Trade and Development.

Besides this segment of the secretariat, the only other department that is directly involved in decision making is the Department of Trade Policy. This unit is important for rule creation, (i.e. to officiate during negotiations), but examples of its initiatives are less easy to find than in the case of the Department of Trade and Development. The reason may be that the countries it serves know fairly well what they are about, and there is less room for maneuvering by the secretariat. This in no way detracts from the essential nature of the work of the Department of Trade Policy, for without the centralization of trade information that it undertakes, multilateral commercial diplomacy would be difficult.

At certain periods, such as during tariff and trade conferences, the secretariat is perhaps 70 to 80 percent occupied with the negotiations or with organizing negotiations between governments. When no large-scale trade conferences are going on, the secretariat is mainly occupied in conducting research for the prenegotiation stages of current issues.

Eminent Individuals

The role of outside consultants has been significant only once in the life of GATT: when the Contracting Parties appointed Professors Haberler,

Meade, Tinbergen, and Campos to the panel of experts that produced the Haberler Report. At the end of 1968, the Contracting Parties once more affirmed their desire to follow the guidelines that the report had laid down ten years earlier. That the Haberler Report should have marked GATT so deeply is particularly interesting when one considers that it is attributed to four academics unconnected with the organization. In point of fact Professor Meade, whose role is said to have been preponderant, worked in close collaboration with Wyndham White and the director of the Trade Intelligence Division, the late Dr. H. Staehle. There seems to be little doubt that the academicians and the international civil servants agreed on the basic issues and that Sir Eric got the report he wanted.

Sources of Personal Influence

Probing to discover the most influential individuals in GATT's history, with the help of half a dozen independent interviews, yielded surprisingly little. Memories did not seem to be at fault, since more names were cited for the 1940s than for the 1960s. The reason seems to be this: in the 1940s GATT had a huge and challenging task that inspired people to independent action, rather as UNCTAD did in 1964. With the gradual accomplishment of the task, GATT became identified with what it had achieved. Since maintaining the status quo is less inspiring than changing it, individuals in GATT have tended to be less colorful in later years than in earlier ones. Furthermore, governments tend to send their best and most senior people to conferences that are building something new. Once the edifice is in place, the level of representation declines and routine takes over.

Of the seven influential individuals named for 1950, two were secretariat officials, Eric Wyndham White and Jean Royer. The remainder were representatives of influential states. In 1958, when five influential individuals were named to us, two were once more members of the secretariat (the same ones as in 1950); one was an outside academic, Professor J. E. Meade; and of the two remaining persons, both government representatives, one was from a small state, the other from a large one. In 1967 the influential persons seemed to be limited to those who took part in the Kennedy Round; and they were all representatives of important trading countries, apart from the executive head (from England) and his deputy, Finn Gundelach (from Denmark). See table 9.1 for a complete breakdown by nationality.

In short, this attempt to define the qualities in people that help to make them influential in GATT shows one thing clearly—that all influential figures have a strong constituency behind them, either in the post they hold in the secretariat, in the intrinsic strength of the countries they represent, or in the interest in trade policy shown by their governments and trade ministries.

Organizational Ideology

To what extent does GATT have an organizational ideology, and does it have a bearing on decision making in the organization? At first sight, GATT appears to have a well-defined organizational ideology with its origins in Cordell Hull's ideas concerning free trade and world peace. Very briefly stated, the credo is this: freer trade and nondiscrimination are conducive not only to material prosperity but to peace among nations. However, it would be difficult to prove that such lofty thoughts had guided GATT for twenty years. The unwritten credo by which it in fact lived was more prosaic: international trade cooperation can only be founded on freer trade and nondiscrimination provided that it is based on reciprocity because under fixed exchange rates each individual member must preserve a certain balance between exports and imports.

Table 9.1

Nationality of Influential Individuals in GATT

	1950	1958	1967
United States	2	–	2
United Kingdom	2	2	1
France	2	1	–
Canada	1	–	1
India	–	1	–
Belgium	–	1	–
EEC Commission	–	–	1
Denmark	–	–	1
Total	7	5	6

GATT is therefore a forum where all obligations, both under the general agreement and under the specific agreements, are as nicely balanced as possible. When unforeseen disturbances occur to upset this balance (usually a payments crisis or difficulties in a particular sector due to import competition), the organization's energies are devoted to restoring the original balance as quickly as possible.

The official ideology is therefore largely irrelevant in explaining the course of GATT's history, while very few events and decisions cannot be traced back to the unwritten one. In fact the fifties and the sixties have shown that members of GATT generally subscribe to the unwritten law of international trade cooperation under fixed exchange rates: reciprocity first, nondiscrimination second, and free trade third—all subject to the balance-of-payments constraint.

Environmental Impacts

While the previous section minimized the role of the individual in GATT's decision making (with the notable exception of the executive head), the present section will show that the specific environment has been very important in explaining the locus of power in GATT.

The Network of World Trade

The outcome of all major collective decisions in GATT is strongly influenced by a few important countries. Their power to shape the course of decision making in GATT is directly related to the extent of their participation in world trade. As long as the United States was the only contracting party to account for more than 16 percent of world trade, it was able not only to veto initiatives (like the GATT Plan for Tariff Reductions),[20] but to impose its will upon the others for better or for worse (as in later decisions to hold tariff negotiations or to grant the United States its unconditional agricultural waiver).

The United Kingdom, which in GATT's early years accounted for over 10 percent of world trade (see table 9.2), was also able to wield some influence. It succeeded in maintaining imperial preference, for instance, in the face of American opposition, but it usually chose to use its weight in support of American policies.

Table 9.2

Shares in World Trade of Major Countries and Trading Groups
(In Percentages)

	1950	1958	1967	1970
North America, of which:	20.5	19.8	19.7	18.9
United States	(16.8)	(17.0)	(12.5)	(16.3)
Western Europe, of which:	32.4	37.7	42.4	44.3
United Kingdom	(10.3)	(8.9)	(8.2)	(6.1)
EEC (external trade)	—	(15.1)	(14.8)	(14.4)
EFTA (external trade)	—	(11.9)	(10.1)	(10.1)
Japan	1.3	2.7	4.8	6.2
Nonindustrialized areas	37.7	28.3	21.6	20.1
Eastern Europe, USSR, and				
Communist China, of which:	8.1	11.5	11.5	10.5
External trade	(1.0)	(4.4)	(4.3)	(4.2)

Sources: Various issues of GATT, *International Trade;* and OECD, *Overall Trade by Countries.*

However, the most important single change in the network of world trade during GATT's twenty years of existence was undoubtedly the emergence in 1958 of a large trading group in Europe accounting for 15 percent of world trade. The EEC carried great weight in GATT from the outset because of the relative volume of its world trade; and when it is well represented, it is equal in stature to the United States. Both the EEC and the United States have the power to initiate or to veto important proposals; and, perhaps unhappily for the smaller planets in this dual constellation, both of them are to some extent restricted—the United States by Congress, and the EEC by the Council of Ministers.

Nevertheless, the individual members of the EEC continue to be active in GATT in their own capacity, not in tariff matters but in discussions on balance-of-payments restrictions, trade and development, waivers, conciliation panels, and so forth. In other words, the EEC brings its full weight to bear only in rule-creating and programmatic decisions, while rule supervision still brings forth individual attitudes. EFTA, despite the fact that its external trade accounts for 10 percent of the world total, does not wield commensurate power in GATT because it does not have a common commercial policy and its members act individually in all GATT forums.

Decisions relating to trade between less-developed countries and developed ones depend heavily upon the attitudes of the United States and the EEC, despite the fact that this trade accounts for over 20 percent of the world total. The reason is that the developing countries' apparently large share in world trade is composed of about a hundred heterogeneous fragments that no amount of political pressure has yet succeeded in fusing. Nevertheless, developing countries in GATT enjoy a certain amount of strength through weakness, and their demands for waivers and other derogations from the general agreement are always treated with indulgence.

The rapid growth in Japan's share of world trade has increased that country's potential power in GATT, but it will not be realized fully for a few more years because of Japan's attitude toward trade liberalization.

Eastern Europe, the Soviet Union, and the People's Republic of China account for a very small proportion of world trade if one treats them as a single trading block and discounts their trade with one another. In 1950 the external trade of the East accounted for only 1 percent of the world total, and although this share increased to 4.3 percent in 1967, it still remains very small for the size and importance of the countries concerned. Since GATT has always been a traders' club, its members never felt that the absence of such marginal traders was a serious departure from universalism, even if it had been possible politically and economically to include them.

Changes in the network of world trade take place very slowly, and usually their effects are not noticed in GATT for a long time—unless, as in 1958, a sudden change occurs with the fusion of several trading countries as a result of a politicoeconomic event.[21] A more dramatic and almost as important environmental change for GATT has been the uninterrupted growth in world trade since the agreement was established in 1947.

Growth in World Trade

The dollar value of world exports (f.o.b.) rose from $58 billion in 1948 to $239 billion in 1968, a threefold increase in twenty years. From table 9.3, giving ten-year growth rates in world exports since the 1880s, it can be seen that the (nominal) rate of growth has probably been considerably larger in the 1960s than during any comparable peacetime decade in the last century.

The percentage growth rates given in table 9.3 are necessarily simplified, but they are telling even if one does not attempt to take price changes into account. Even in an inflationary period like the sixties many prices remain stable or decline in world markets; and while inflation might explain much of the difference in growth between the 1900s and the 1950s, it certainly cannot explain the difference between the fifties and the sixties.

Table 9.3

World Trade Growth, 1880s to 1960s

Decade	Annual Average	World Exports (in Billions of Dollars)	10-Year Growth Rates (in Percentages)
1880s	1876-80	6	50[a]
1890s	1896-1900	9	
1900s	1896-1900	9	50
	1911-13	18	
1930s	1926-29	32	-28
	1936-38	23	
1950s	1948-50	60	93
	1958-60	116	
1960s	1958-60	116	137
	1968-70	275	

Sources: Up to and including 1936-38, P. Lamartine Yates, *Forty Years of Foreign Trade*, Ruskin House (London: Allen and Unwin, 1959), p. 28. From 1948 on, figures published in various issues of *International Trade*, based on the UN *Monthly Bulletin of Statistics*.

[a]Twenty years' growth.

The latter difference can be attributed to the effect of trade and payments liberalization after World War II, which reached a first point of culmination in 1958 with the abolition of quotas and exchange control on dollar trade in Europe. GATT played a part in this process, as did the IMF and OEEC. It therefore contributed to, and was able to bask in, the favorable atmosphere for trade cooperation that prevailed during the sixties. The Kennedy Round marked another high-water mark in postwar economic cooperation, but by that time the effects of different national aspirations concerning desirable growth rates, inflation, and employment levels were beginning to take their toll on countries' balances of payments in a fixed exchange-rate system, causing deep and growing disequilibria in all major trading countries. Unless more flexible exchange rates are adopted in future, the seventies will see a return to trade and currency controls between the principal GATT members. On the other hand, if the senior members adopt a more flexible international monetary system, the prospect for the complete abolition of tariffs and the adoption of a new code to deal with nontariff barriers would be considerably brighter. What happens in GATT is very clearly determined by what happens in the general economic environment: only the bravest "Gattophile" would maintain the inverse.

Stratification of States' Influence

GATT had seventy-six contracting parties and three associated states in 1968. The great majority of these countries conducted their trade and commercial diplomacy more or less according to GATT's rules and within its framework but did not exercise influence in collective decision making.

GATT can be said to have a senior and a junior school. The seniors at the end of the sixties were the developed countries of North America, Western Europe, and Japan. The juniors were the less-developed countries. There were also some intermediates—Australia, New Zealand, South Africa, and Israel—in the process of moving from the junior to the senior school.

Influence in GATT is clearly situated in the senior school, where there are two heads and a number of prefects. What has kept them interested in GATT for twenty years is the fact that their steadily growing economies clamored more loudly for free trade than for protection. There is no guarantee that they would remain interested in GATT if, in a stagnant or declining world economy, the claims of protectionism rang more loudly than calls for freer trade. Influence in GATT, therefore, is a function not only of a country's share in world trade and its stake in the system (roughly measured by the share of imports in domestic consumption or the share of exports in domestic production), but also of the balance, at any given point in time, between protectionist and free trade forces in the domestic political arena.[22] Negative influence must nevertheless be accounted for and was included in the rank ordering of influential GATT members in table 9.4.

Patterns of Conflict and Alignment

A glance down the list of the nineteen most influential countries in GATT will show that with one or two possible exceptions the organization is run by like-minded democracies of the Western type. The result is that GATT has escaped at least one of the main patterns of conflict in the general environment—the cold war. Indeed, broad patterns of conflict and alignment in GATT did not emerge until the end of the 1950s, with economic integration in Europe and decolonization in Africa and Asia. Before then, conflict in the general environment was reflected only spasmodically and bilaterally in GATT. When the United States suspended its obligations to Czechoslovakia in 1951, it did so alone; as an organization GATT was shocked but not deeply wounded or divided. Similarly, the fact that India and Pakistan refused to apply GATT rules to South Africa in 1947 reflected their own conflict with the South African government; but the issue in

Table 9.4

Comparison of Influence in GATT with Status in the Specific Environment

Country	Negative Influence (A)	Positive Influence (B)	(Index) Total Influence (C)	Rank Order in Influence (D)	Percent Share in GATT Trade (E)	Rank Order in GATT Trade (F)
United States	7	11	18	1.5	18.6	1.5
EEC	8	10	18	1.5	18.6	1.5
United Kingdom	5	5	10	3	8.1	4
France	5	4	9	4	6.6	6
Federal Republic of Germany	3	5	8	5	12.7	3
Canada	2	5	7	8	6.2	6
Japan	3	4	7	8	6.1	6
Switzerland	2	5	7	8	2.1	12
Italy	3	4	7	8	5.1	9
Australia	2	5	7	8	2.0	12
Netherlands	2	4	6	13.5	4.4	9
Belgium	2	4	6	13.5	4.1	9
New Zealand	2	4	6	13.5	0.6	26
Argentina	3	3	6	13.5	0.8	21
Brazil	3	3	6	13.5	0.9	21
India	3	3	6	13.5	0.9	21
Sweden	1	4	5	17.5	2.6	12
Denmark	1	4	5	17.5	1.5	16
Nigeria	2	2	4	19	0.4	33.5

Note: The scoring used for columns A, B, and C was as follows for all significant types of decision in GATT—representational, programmatic, and rule-creating:

	Score
Negative Influence. Prevents on important issues.	
Frequently	3
Occasionally	2
Rarely	1
Never	0
Positive Influence. Initiates successfully on important issues:	
Often	3
Occasionally	2
Rarely	1
Never	0

Insofar as rule-supervisory decisions were concerned, the scoring used was as follows:

Negative Influence. Acts contrary to GATT and gets away with it:	
Often	3
Sometimes	2
Rarely	1
Never	0
Positive Influence. Protests about others breaking GATT rules:	
Often	3
Sometimes	2
Rarely	1
Never	0

GATT remained strictly local, and all alignments were studiously avoided. In the same way, the black African governments' passionate disapproval of South Africa, which found its economic expression in a trade boycott, did not become a cause of cleavage in GATT because South Africa was persuaded not to complain.

Since the beginning of the 1960s, when many saw Europe becoming an economic and political rival to the United States through economic integration, the resulting alignment in GATT was modified by several degrees into a constructive pattern of challenge and response. During the same period the process of decolonization and the deepening conflict between North and South appeared in GATT in milder form than elsewhere. Indeed, GATT seemed to have succeeded in putting a veil between itself and the outside world, which warded off the sting of conflicts that oppose its members. Israel and the United Arab Republic signed the same agreement[23] but had nothing to do with one another in the GATT forum, which functioned perfectly well with or without them. Cuba and the United States ignored each other; Malaysia and Indonesia did not mention confrontation once in GATT as long as their war lasted; Greece and Turkey did not raise the issue of Cyprus. Since all these disagreements were treated with discretion, there was no need for other contracting parties to take sides in GATT. Even when a conflict arose within GATT's own terms of reference, like the chicken war between the United States and the EEC, the contracting parties did not neatly line up on one side or the other. They remained grouped in the background until asked to supply a compromise solution. (If a commercial conflict comes to GATT at all, it is because efforts to reach a bilateral settlement have failed.)

There seem to have been two reasons for this happy state of affairs. The first resided in the value that the contracting parties themselves placed on GATT's work. They found it useful to have a forum for multilateral commercial diplomacy, however informally constructed; and they did their best to isolate it from the political side of international relations.

The second reason for GATT's rather uneventful existence seems to have been that its more important members saw eye to eye on most issues. There was always a majority of Western states on the old intersessional committees, and even in the loosely constructed Council of Representatives they still made up 51 percent of its membership in 1967, although they accounted for only 35 percent of the total membership. It was also from Western states that the GATT secretariat recruited its senior members, with very few exceptions (see table 9.5).

Classification of Membership according to Political Regime

Classification of the contracting parties according to type of political regime suggests that free trade and democracy were closely related. In 1950, twenty-three out of thirty-one (74 percent) sovereign contracting parties possessed competitive political systems; in 1958 the proportion was twenty-eight out of thirty-eight (73 percent); and in 1967, in spite of the increase of authoritarianism in the world at large, the proportion of politically competitive regimes in GATT was still 44 percent of the total. In the Executive Body, the proportion was higher—57 percent. If one looks at the list of influential and active countries in table 9.4, the proportion was seventeen out of nineteen, or 90 percent. This surely goes some way toward explaining the absence of deep conflicts in GATT. Although there were nineteen cases where a change of polity occurred in the general environment from 1950 to 1968, none had a noticeable effect on GATT's internal affairs.

Table 9.5

Distribution of Representation in GATT

Contracting Parties

	1950		1958		1967	
	Number	*Percentage*	*Number*	*Percentage*	*Number*	*Percentage*
Western	16	51.61	21	55.26	28	35.44
Socialist	1	3.23	1	2.63	4	5.06
Other	14	45.16	16	42.11	47	59.49
Total	31	100.00	38	100.00	79	99.99

Executive Body

	1952[a]		1958		1967	
	Number	*Percentage*	*Number*	*Percentage*	*Number*	*Percentage*
Western	10	66.67	11	64.72	25	51.00
Socialist	0	–	1	5.88	4	8.20
Other	5	33.33	5	29.40	20	40.80
Total	15	100.00	17	100.00	49	100.00

Higher Staff (D.1 and above)

	1950		1958		1967	
	Number	*Percentage*	*Number*	*Percentage*	*Number*	*Percentage*
Western	2		2		10	83.40
Socialist	0	–	0	–	0	–
Other	0	–	0	–	2	16.60
Total	2		2		12	100.00

[a]No intersessional procedures were agreed upon until 1951.

Conclusions and Prospective View

The general environment seems to be of little importance in explaining the structure of influence in GATT unless the decisions concern the accession of new contracting parties, especially Eastern European ones; it is important in relatively few programmatic or symbolic decisions. Individuals do not wield autonomous influence in GATT with the exception of the executive head, who derives his power from being the guardian of the collective conscience. He appears as broker in all types of decisions and as initiator in one or two. The secretariat also derives influence from its central position in GATT's informal structure. Such informality of structure, however, does not mean that the secretariat enjoys much autonomy, and it acts more often as a broker than as an initiator.

There remains the specific environment to explain the interplay of influence in GATT—and more precisely, the pattern of trade. Although trade patterns turn out to be the most important single explanation, the actual constellation of influence varies considerably from decision to decision, both among the different types of decisions and among decisions of one type because trade structures vary from country to country. As a general rule, large traders or trading blocks dominate the structure of influence; but small countries with an overriding strength in just one product can do so, too, when their product comes under discussion. The great majority of GATT's contracting parties have neither the overall size nor the degree of specialization necessary for the acquisition of influence in GATT. Very few compensate for this lack of economic base with energies stemming from political ambition because GATT is not a satisfactory forum for political action.

As a result our list of influential countries in GATT contains only nineteen entries, counting the EEC and its members separately because they do not always act as a unit. The structure of influence appears to be diffuse for most types of decisions because of the infinite variety of trade patterns and possible subjects of discussion. However, because GATT has only nineteen states, at the most, that wield influence, it is not difficult to estimate the power constellation in the background of most decisions. In rule-creating decisions, for instance, one has but to observe the subject under discussion and look at the trade figures to see which contracting parties are most interested in it, both on the exporting and on the importing side. Generally speaking, the exporters will be the initiators, and the importers, the interlocutors. The negotiation process will usually be painstaking and slow. But GATT is effective as a forum because, by and large, both sides stand to gain from the contact. A tariff negotiation typically produces a multitude of crosscutting groups whose behavior leans more toward consensus than conflict.

Rule supervision, the other major branch of GATT's activity, also works by consensus; and the moral pressure of consensus is often effective in redressing even situations that have started with conflict. Programmatic decisions concerning the trade of less-developed countries seem to be the only ones that could become truly a source of conflict because of the hostility engendered by the subject; but until now difficult situations in the organization have been dealt with cooperatively.

How stable is this picture of GATT? And are there any discernible independent factors that might affect it? We have already remarked that, because trade patterns shift slowly, changes in the pattern of influence for any given problem may seem imperceptible for a long time. On the other hand, nothing is immobile in applied economics; and changes, however minute, do occur continually. In the end, an accumulation of changes in the same direction will shift the pattern of trade and hence the structure of influence for a given product. It is just as possible, however, that changes may cancel each other out, leaving the structure of trade unaltered.

Since the Kennedy Round free trade in industrial products among developed countries is almost an accomplished fact. A few hard-core tariffs remain, but most of them are low; and it is possible to foresee a time when they will no longer be considered essential to the well-being of the countries imposing them. The relative freedom of industrial trade enjoyed at present by the countries of the North Atlantic area will tend to favor increased specialization and division of international production. To the extent that a high degree of specialization can compensate for economic size in conferring influence in GATT, as was suggested above, one might predict that the coming decade or two may see more smaller countries emerging and wielding influence in GATT through their respective specialities. At the same time, medium and large countries will also become more specialized, thus gaining influence on some issues and losing it on others. In short, increasing international specialization will tend to make patterns of influence in GATT more precise, at least as far as trade negotiations are concerned.

The most noticeable change that took place in GATT's typical pattern of influence in its first twenty years was the switch from domination by a single country, the United States, to what is to all intents and purposes a condominium. From 1958 to 1968 the United States and the EEC both wished to reduce tariff barriers on their trade with each other and succeeded in doing so. During the same period, however, they failed to agree on a common policy in relation to less-developed countries. Should GATT's two rulers disagree on any fundamental policy questions in the future, nothing will be achieved; each side will cancel the other out. It is even possible that one or the other may cause an involuntary halt in GATT through constitutional paralysis. For instance, it seems likely that the reduction of nontariff barriers to trade will occupy the Contracting Parties for at least the next ten years, if not longer. It seems equally likely, however, that the EEC will be in no position to negotiate until it has settled its own numerous internal problems with respect to nontariff barriers and that the United States will not move until the EEC can do so too. The whole nontariff barrier negotiation may therefore be put off for several years because of constitutional paralysis in the EEC. The United States Congress, though renowned in GATT for going back on the administration's word, is probably less subject to paralysis than the EEC's commission, which will always find it difficult to agree on a common policy, either to propose or respond to. Consequently, one can foresee certain difficulties—for instance, in future programmatic decisions—that will require the unanimous approval of six plus one, instead of the leadership of one alone.

GATT's most fruitful working years may conceivably be over, since free trade in industrial goods is almost a fact among the influential GATT members and since most of the other, less-developed members wish to exchange the most-favored-nation rule for preferences. Nontariff barriers and agriculture, the two major commercial policy problems that remain, may be so difficult that GATT will be reduced to the output level of a disarmament conference, while the problem of development may be taken out of its hands completely by UNCTAD and the OECD.

The great and unknown independent variable to which GATT is subject is the general economic situation. If the developed world prospers, GATT will prosper with it. But if Europe or the United States suffer an economic setback, GATT will suffer with it, and the work will have to be done once more. Because history does not repeat itself, however, and because the climate of international cooperation changes from period to period, no one can guess what form the new arrangements might take.

Exploring the more promising fork in the road, one might suggest that great and fundamental changes are currently taking place in the traditional trading relations between countries. In our brave new world, where some corporations have annual turnovers larger than the GNP of sovereign countries, where capital is increasingly mobile and becoming a substitute for trade, where multinational corporations play havoc with trade theory, tariffs, and tax authorities, perhaps we need something more up to date than the rather dog-eared general agreement. Protection and regionalism—two anti-GATT trends—seem to be on the upswing; and for the next few years GATT will probably be more occupied with rule supervision than rule creation. A period of great change—the sudden growth of membership due to decolonization, the appearance of the EEC, the unprecedented growth in world trade—made GATT a dynamic organization from 1958 to 1968. The commercial map for the 1970s has already been drawn over the unpromising and rocky landscape of emergency import surcharges, nontariff barriers, agricultural protection, and economic development. On the other hand, if the international monetary crisis, which the world waited for in vain during the sixties, is constructively resolved in the seventies, bringing the majority of countries out of the constraints of maintaining fixed exchange rates in a reserve currency system into a more flexible world monetary order, the implications for world trade cooperation would be positive. The balance-of-payments constraint on tariff and nontariff negotiations would disappear, making it easier for countries to relax the rigid ideology of perfect reciprocity in international trade cooperation, which has characterized most of GATT's work during the fifties and the sixties.

10   UNCTAD: Poor Nations' Pressure Group

Joseph S. Nye

Every international organization seems unique from some point of view. UNCTAD is unique by definition if one accepts the waggish interpretation of the acronymn as meaning "Under No Condition Take Any Decisions." This bit of humor underlines an important point. In its first five years, under the leadership of the dynamic Argentine economist, Raul Prebisch, the United Nations Conference on Trade and Development housed an effort to use international organization not to serve the activities of governments but to create a forum in which the more prosperous member countries would come under pressure to agree to measures benefiting the less-developed member countries. More specifically, under Prebisch, UNCTAD was the scene of a deliberate effort to use international bureaucracy and conference diplomacy to alter current norms affecting trade and development. Given this objective, there was often a sense of wordy unreality about decision making in UNCTAD. And the anatomy of influence within UNCTAD was affected by the fact that the organization was designed primarily for the exercise of influence by some members against others.[1]

Structure, Functions, and Evolution

Founded in 1964, UNCTAD was a product of the explosion of membership in the United Nations system that followed the process of decolonization. Deliberately and to a considerable extent overlapping in subject matter with the earlier established General Agreement on Tariffs and Trade (GATT), UNCTAD under Prebisch reached a total of 135 members compared to the 87 contracting parties of GATT.

The major impetus for UNCTAD came from less-developed countries dissatisfied with the unfavorable economic trends of the late 1950s. At first it appeared as if UNCTAD represented an economic alliance between these countries and the Soviet bloc, because the USSR had been pressing since the mid-1950s for a world economic conference to promote East-West trade. The Western countries, satisfied with the GATT arrangements (which had followed the failure of the 1947 International Trade Conference) and fearful of Soviet efforts to disrupt them, had consistently resisted the Soviet initiatives. However, when the East European and less-developed countries

The author is grateful to Marina Finkelstein, Branislav Gosovic, Jean Siotis, Anne Winslow, and several officials who wish to remain anonymous for their comments on an earlier version of this chapter. It was researched and written in 1968-69 while the author was Visiting Research Scholar at the Carnegie Endowment for International Peace in Geneva. Unless otherwise noted, quotations are from interviews in Geneva in 1969. The present tense is used to make the style consistent with the other chapters in this study.

joined forces in proposing a conference on trade and development, the Western countries found their own refusal to enter into multilateral talks over trade problems increasingly untenable.[2] Their subsequent agreement to call a conference in 1964 represented reluctant concessions to political expediency rather than any positive acceptance of the idea of UNCTAD.[3]

UNCTAD was born at the 1964 Geneva Conference. The most striking feature of the conference was the emergence of the seventy-seven less-developed participating countries as a unified group. This had several important effects. First, it came as a shock to the Western countries and gave the conference as a whole a sense of enhanced political importance. Second, Third World unity meant that the Western and socialist countries were nearly always in minority positions; this led to the special conciliation provisions we will describe below. Third, the emergence of a cohesive voting coalition of poor countries stimulated the Western countries to strengthen their own solidarity by prior coordination in the Organization for Economic Cooperation and Development (OCED). This had both a rigidifying and a conservative effect, since Western group solidarity was essentially based on an agreement not to embarrass each other on vulnerable points. Finally, the Western countries had to accept an organization that was more independent of the United Nations than they would have preferred. The Geneva Conference also set the pattern of closeness between the secretariat and the less-developed countries that has distinguished the organization and caused considerable mistrust among the Western countries.

The Formal Framework for Decisions

UNCTAD is an organ of the UN General Assembly, and its constitution is General Assembly Resolution 1995 (XIX), passed unanimously in December 1964. Formally, UNCTAD reports annually to the General Assembly through ECOSOC, though in practice it is virtually independent of ECOSOC. The UNCTAD secretariat is part of the United Nations secretariat in the sense of being subject to United Nations regulations on salaries, promotions, and so on, but its location in Geneva (over United States objections) gives it a considerable degree of independence. On the other hand, UNCTAD is not as independent of New York as most of the specialized agencies of the United Nations. One reason is that its secretary-general is appointed by the United Nations secretary-general and confirmed by the General Assembly, and another is that its budget is part of the regular budget of the United Nations and is handled by the standard procedures in New York.

The main deliberative organs of UNCTAD are (1) a triennial conference open to all state members of the United Nations, the specialized agencies, or the IAEA; (2) a Trade and Development Board of fifty-five members elected by the conference and meeting twice a year (once a year after 1969); (3) four permanent committees of forty-five members (fifty-five in the case of commodities), elected by the board and reporting to it, which meet at least annually to consider commodities, manufactures, invisibles and financing, and shipping, respectively.

The first two conferences were huge affairs—the second in New Delhi in 1968 lasting eight weeks and being attended by 1,436 delegates from 121 countries. Board and committee meetings are also large and last for several weeks. Governments not represented on the board are allowed to attend as observers and to speak on cases of special interest to them, with the result that several hundred people may be in the room at its meetings.

The formal provisions of the resolution that created UNCTAD are worth noting. An annex to the resolution classifies member states into four groups or lists for purposes of election to the board. States in group A (the Afro-Asian states plus Yugoslavia), together with the Latin-American group (group C), in practice form the Group of 77 less-developed countries.[4] Group D (the communists) and group B (developed market economies or the West) form the other two points in the triangle of UNCTAD groups.

The second exceptional feature of Resolution 1995 (XIX) is the provision that a small group of states can postpone a vote until the next meeting of whatever UNCTAD organ is involved by requesting the formation of a conciliation committee. In Gardner's words, "the conciliation procedure provides a 'cooling-off' period, usually about six months, during which agreed solutions can be sought through quiet diplomacy."[5] Formal conciliation is to be used in regard to subjects substantially affecting economic or financial interests of countries, but not on matters of procedure, principles, or the establishment of subsidiary bodies. In practice, the formal conciliation procedure has never been used, but the concept of prolonged consultations rather than summary votes has been widely employed in UNCTAD, even in some procedural cases where it was technically not necessary.

Assigned Functions of the Organization

The developed countries remained skeptical about UNCTAD and wished to restrict it to the general role of providing a forum in which broad problems of trade and development would be discussed. Group B countries were concerned with preserving GATT with its more congenial charter, membership, and secretariat as the sole forum for binding trade negotiations. In contrast, many less-developed countries pressed for a concrete negotiating role for UNCTAD.

It is worth noting, however, that delegates from a number of less-developed countries were privately content with the division of labor between GATT and UNCTAD—UNCTAD serving as a public forum for pressure to improve their bargaining position in the negotiating forum of GATT.[6] And those less-developed countries that advocated a greater "negotiating" role for UNCTAD rarely wanted to see it give up its role as a public forum for pressure.

Western countries also resisted those activities of UNCTAD that they felt to be encroaching upon the jurisdiction of ECOSOC (an organization they considered better balanced). Many developed countries also tried to prevent UNCTAD from having a service role as a participating agency in the United Nations Development Program. In 1967, however, the GATT and UNCTAD secretariats worked out an arrangement for joint management of the International Trade Center that GATT had started in 1964. At the seventh session of the Trade Board in September 1968, the richer countries finally dropped their opposition to an UNCTAD service role.[7]

Budget and Staff

UNCTAD's budget[8] and staff have grown rapidly. In 1966, the first year that the secretariat reached its full planned strength, the budget was $5.45 million, and the total staff consisted of 361 persons, including 164 at the professional level. By 1969 the budget had grown to $8.37 million, and the total establishment comprised 478 posts, including 209 at the professional level.[9] The structure of the secretariat is given in table 10.1.

Since the UNCTAD budget is part of the regular United Nations budget, the scale of assessment is the regular United Nations scale. In 1967 the largest contributor to the United Nations budget was the United States, with 31.91 percent of the budget; the USSR was second, with 14.92 percent. At the other extreme, fifty-nine states paid the minimum assessment of 0.04 percent. In 1967 Western member countries paid 63 percent of the regular United Nations budget, Socialist countries paid 21 percent, and Others paid 16 percent.[10]

During the Prebisch era, UNCTAD's expenditures were almost entirely related to its forum role. The two main activities of the organization were research and conference services. The latter accounted for 26 percent of the total budget. Most of the research was oriented toward service related to the forum role.[11]

Major Turning Points in the History of the Organization

UNCTAD's history is rather brief for major turning points. But, as we shall see below, the central role played by Raul Prebisch as the organization's first secretary-general meant that his retirement and replacement in March 1969 by Manuel Perez-Guerrero, a Venezuelan diplomat with long United Nations experience, was doubtless one such turning point.

Another was the unwieldy second conference held in New Delhi in 1968. Though the conference may not have been so complete a failure as the press declared it to be, the general feeling was one of disappointment. However, many delegates also felt that the meager results of the conference had a sobering effect and that the conference did lead to such changes as (1) the acceptance of proposals for minor improvement of the UNCTAD machinery at the September 1968 board meetings, (2) a more moderate and conciliatory approach among the Group of 77, (3) the beginning of a lower level of group B representation, and (4) enhanced importance of the board vis-à-vis the conference as the key institution of the organization.

Decision Making: A Taxonomical Analysis

Decisions in UNCTAD under Prebisch tended to result from bargaining rather than analysis. Initiatives came almost entirely from the less-developed countries, though some members of the secretariat also made some contributions. Group D countries, having very little to give, and disappointed by the failure of the organization to reflect their interests in East-West trade, made few suggestions. The same was true of most group B countries, which saw themselves in a defensive position. Some of the smaller Western

Table 10.1

UNCTAD Staff: 1968

Division	Professional	General Service	Total
Office of the Secretary-General Office of Administration	14	19	33
Research Division	17	20	37
Trade Policies Division	9	9	18
Commodities Division	25	21	46
Manufactures Division	12	9	21
Invisibles Division	22	18	40
Trade with Socialist Countries	7	5	12
New York office	19	28	47
Trade Expansion	4	1	5
Conference Affairs and External Relations	10	16	26
Subtotal	139	146	285
Conference, Administration and Other Common Services (Interpretation, Translation, etc.)	59	110	169
Total	198	256	454

Source: UN Doc. TC/B/181, 2 August 1968, Annex, p. 3.

countries argued that group B should have taken more initiatives. If they had done so, according to these members, more time at UNCTAD meetings would have been spent discussing more tolerable draft resolutions. However, their position was weakened by the lack of reciprocity in the organization. As one delegate from the 77 put it, "We make demands that involve no commitments, but their responses involve commitments." No matter what positive motion group B proposed, there was an incentive for some members of the 77 to press for more because of the one-sided nature of the pressure group process. The net result was to strengthen the position of the conservative delegates from the larger group B countries and to increase group B's difficulty in agreeing on positive—as contrasted with defensive—positions.

Among the less-developed countries there tend to be two types of initiators—depending on the general or specific nature of the subject. On specific substantive questions, initiation has usually come from the countries with the most direct interests—for instance, from African states on questions of a cocoa agreement, Malaysia on questions of rubber and synthetics, Afghanistan on questions of access to the sea for landlocked states. General questions might involve substantive issues, such as whether developed countries should meet an aid target of 1 percent of the GNP, or matters of procedure, such as setting up a new committee or finding a compromise resolution. As a rule, initiatives on both types of general questions have come from states like Brazil, Chile, India, Yugoslavia, Nigeria, or the Philippines, which, because of their administrative capacity and depth of expertise or the personality of their representatives, see themselves (and are seen by their fellows) as leaders of the 77 and wish to preserve that position. On major questions initiatives have come less often from the secretariat than from the delegates, at least after the 1964 conference. However, specific members of the secretariat have played important roles in persuading delegates to sponsor resolutions in such fields as shipping, commodities, and trade among developing countries.

The same leading countries in the 77 and the largest countries in groups B and D sometimes also have played the role of potential vetoers, capable of blocking undesired initiatives, though no country has possessed a consistently effective veto power. (Nor has the secretariat been very effective in blocking undesired initiatives, as was shown by the lengthy agenda for the New Delhi Conference and the plethora of unwanted studies arising from board or committee decisions.) The prestigious leaders among the 77—as mentioned above, Brazil, Chile, India, Yugoslavia, Nigeria, and the Philippines—and the large countries of group B, particularly the United States, the United Kingdom, and France, are to some extent controllers whose known or surmised views are generally taken into account by other actors without any specific act of accountability taking place. The less-developed countries have played this role more often in relation to symbolic, representational, or programmatic issues; the richer countries more often in relation to major programmatic issues that affect the total resources of the organization and in relation to decisions on rule creation that affect their substantive trade interests.

Finally, the brokers who act as go-betweens among participants in decisions tend to come either from the smaller countries in group B with more liberal policies (for example, Norway, Sweden, the Netherlands) or from the leaders among the 77. The brokers are often named by their major groups to sit in the small contact groups that try to work out compromises. These groups frequently have been chaired by secretariat officials, some of the most important by Prebisch himself. Aside from such meetings, however, the secretary-general has not played as constant a brokerage role as did, for example, Eric Wyndham White in GATT.

Representational Decisions

Qualifications for membership in UNCTAD were set by the General Assembly in Resolution 1995 (XIX). New members meeting these qualifications are admitted as a matter of routine. Sometimes credentials have been challenged (the larger the forum, the more likely the challenge), but such challenges have also become a matter of form. Election to the board follows the formula in Resolution 1995 (XIX).[12] Each group decides on its candidates. Despite occasional complaints by countries like Cuba and Israel, which were excluded from the four groups, it has become more or less routine for the board to accept the amalgamated list unanimously.

Within groups, a general understanding has been worked out about representation. The largest states are always represented on the board and on whatever committees they wish. As one delegate of a large Latin-American state expressed it, "We cannot be expected to let one of those small states represent our interests, and they realize it." As for committees, it is generally agreed that where specific interests are concerned, states can be nominated to committees as they wish, so long as they are not, in the words of one delegate, "too greedy."

The interesting differences over representation have occurred in reference to general interests and primarily among the middle ranges of the African and Latin-American groups, where an understanding about the ranking of states has not been as easy to reach as it was among the less-numerous and more-developed states of group B.

The chairmanships of the groups, positions that the discipline of the group system renders very important, generally rotate in alphabetical order every few months. Chairmen usually act as spokesmen for their groups, though they sometimes appoint others to speak on particular issues because of their personal competence or interest. Board and committee offices rotate among groups on the basis of an agreed formula, the nominations ordinarily reflecting the structure of influence mentioned above, modified by judgments on personal capacity in some cases and a need for representation of different factions in a group. The United States and the Soviet Union rarely accept nomination to offices.

When the question of geographical representation on the secretariat was raised by the delegate of Tanzania in 1966, the secretariat responded by recruiting more Africans, but this did not become a major issue. While some group B governments have been concerned about the staffing of a few top posts, Western countries are in general already heavily represented, and their governments do not make major efforts to second important officials to the UNCTAD secretariat. Personnel from group D countries tend to staff the Division of Trade with socialist countries.

Of the fifty top officials of UNCTAD in May 1968, twenty came from United Nations service, including ten from the regional commissions. Six high officials including the secretary-general, had at one time or another served in ECLA.[13] The regional distribution of fifty top officials in UNCTAD and forty-seven top officials in GATT is shown in table 10.2. The fact that nearly half the top officials came from Western countries was not, however, a good index of the influence of group B governments in the secretariat, as we shall see.

Table 10.2

Regional Distribution of Fifty Highest UNCTAD Staff Posts Compared
to Forty-seven Highest Staff Posts of GATT (1968)

Region	UNCTAD		GATT	
	Number	Percentage	Number	Percentage
Western (group B)	22	44.00	35	74.47
Socialist (except Yugoslavia)	8	16.00	0	—
Other (Group of 77)	18	36.00	9	19.15
Africa	(7)	(14.00)	(1)	(2.13)
Asian (including 1 Yugoslav)	(6)	(12.00)	(5)	(10.64)
Latin American	(5)	(10.00)	(3)	(6.38)
Unknown	2	4.00	3	6.38
Total	50	100.00	47	100.00

Source: Internal secretariat lists and interviews.

The top personnel of UNCTAD did not change much between its organization in 1965 and the New Delhi Conference in early 1968. The most significant change came in November 1968 when it was announced that Prebisch would retire early, in March 1969, because of failing health. As far as is known, United Nations Secretary-General U Thant seems to have acted after only a few consultations in appointing Prebisch's successor, Perez-Guerrero, who had previously had no important direct connection with UNCTAD. Thant acted quickly and without extensive consultations, as if to avoid being caught up in the Byzantine complexity of the UNCTAD group system. In any case, the announcement came as a surprise both in Geneva and in many important national capitals.

Symbolic Decisions

UNCTAD under Prebisch was characterized by a number of symbolic issues that did not have immediate practical consequences but tested the acceptability of goals or ideologies held intensely by the different groups of actors. Since symbolic issues are not subject to the formal conciliation procedure, the possibility that the less-developed countries might use their latent voting strength gives them greater influence over symbolic issues than over substantive ones. Symbolic issues can be divided into two types: those inherent in the nature of the organization and those arising from extraneous political issues. Leadership on the latter type of issue sometimes deviates from the usual UNCTAD patterns. For instance, Algeria and Uganda played important roles in walkouts and—despite the objection of group B—in the eventual vote during the final hours of the New Delhi Conference to recommend that the General Assembly amend Resolution 1995 (XIX) so as to expel South Africa from UNCTAD.

UNCTAD's relationship to the United Nations—as a subsidiary of the General Assembly rather than as a specialized agency—accounts for South Africa's remaining a member. Although the absolute number of votes for expulsion is slightly higher, a two-thirds majority for expulsion was not available at the Twenty-third General Assembly in New York, where the legal staff declared the measure at odds with the United Nations Charter. It is interesting to note that in smaller UNCTAD forums, the South African issue has not been raised. South Africa has not been elected to the board, but neither has its presence as an observer been challenged. During negotiations for a sugar agreement, African representatives participated fully with South Africa (as they did in GATT). In the view of an African diplomat, only the large forums, such as the New Delhi Conference, are useful for pointing up issues like that of South Africa to the world. There was a walkout each day during the first four days of the New Delhi Conference: two concerned South Africa; one was by Arabs on the Israel question; and one was by group D over South Korea.

More significant symbolic issues in UNCTAD concern the politics of trade and the role of UNCTAD itself. In some cases these issues have started as substantive issues of rule creation or boundary problems with other organizations. But after a certain amount of fruitless debate made it clear that a meaningful compromise could not be reached because national positions were too inflexible and too far apart, the discussion of the issues began to take on a symbolic character—asserting or testing intentions rather than aiming at concrete consequences. For example, at first the new principles for trade raised at the 1964 Geneva Conference represented potentially important cases of rule creation. By the end of the conference, when the principles were voted by vast majorities over Western (especially United States) objections and despite the certainty that they would have no immediate substantive consequences, the principles themselves had begun to take on primarily symbolic importance.

Boundary Decisions

As we have indicated, boundary issues are important in UNCTAD, since UNCTAD overlaps with so many other organizations, particularly GATT. In general, group B countries are concerned about boundary issues and problems of duplication, while the less-developed countries are inclined to welcome the pressure that duplication puts on other organizations.[14] The strategy of the UNCTAD secretariat varies on this problem. Prebisch was careful to keep good relations with the UN Department of Economic and Social Affairs in New York, even when this policy cost him support among the 77 who wanted more duplication. In return, when issues such as UNIDO's establishment of a Department of Foreign Trade arose, Prebisch was able to get support in New York by changing its name to "Department of Export Oriented Industries" and to obtain an admittedly vague understanding that the new department would concentrate on production rather than trade issues.

Prebisch was also careful to stay on good terms with the Advisory Committee on Administrative and Budgetary Questions (ACABQ), which played a central part in approving the UNCTAD budget. Prebisch did not press the ACABQ for overly dramatic increases, and it in turn did not recommend drastic cuts in his budget proposals. In his relations with the ACABQ, Prebisch had less difficulty in finding a middle ground between the demands of the Group of 77 and United Nations bureaucratic pressures because most of the less-developed countries were aware of the strong position of the Western countries in the ACABQ.

For the secretariat the main boundary question, however, has been its relations with GATT. Prebisch frequently talked about the need to avoid duplication, but usually in general rather than specific terms. On the other side, the GATT strategy was to minimize boundary problems by avoiding discussion of duplication and denying that it really existed. In 1967 Prebisch and Wyndham White worked out arrangements for converting the GATT Trade Center into a jointly managed International Trade Center. By and large, however, cooperation between GATT and UNCTAD has been quite limited and daily contacts are few—a situation that seems to suit most of the parties concerned.

Programmatic Decisions

Until 1969, when it began to move into the field of providing services for states through participation in the International Trade Center and the UN Development Program, UNCTAD was an organization for meetings and studies. In general, Prebisch preferred this approach. Pressing for a greater service role were some members of the secretariat, some governments of less-developed countries that hoped to benefit from additional services, and some developed countries which felt that a service role would divert the secretariat from sensitive issues in the philosophy of trade relations. But Prebisch believed that in the early years the best way to use the organization to promote changes in the norms governing international economic relations was by having an intellectually independent secretariat producing studies closely geared to UNCTAD international meetings. Consequently, UNCTAD's budget has been devoted primarily to meetings and studies.

The choice of such issues as tariff preferences, commodity policies, and supplementary financial measures reflected the initiatives the less-developed countries had taken in the Preparatory Committee for UNCTAD, which Prebisch subsequently synthesized. Among the problems the secretariat faced, however, was maintaining a single set of priorities. The divergent interests and levels of development among the 77 made it difficult for them to agree upon the ranking of issues; one way of maintaining their political unity and avoiding divisions was by adding new demands to an already long list. While the surfeit of projects allowed the secretariat some leeway in choosing its own research priorities, simply because it would have been impossible to do everything at once, the problem of priorities remained. For instance, in a list of some eighty-seven major research projects being undertaken by the secretariat, each related to a specific conference, board, or committee resolution, some sixty were assigned to the first of three classes of priority.[15]

Interesting examples of the problem of establishing priorities were the decisions, or lack of decisions, on the agenda for the second conference. As we argued above, this was perhaps the crucial event during the Prebisch era. Both within the secretariat and within the groups there was division over the nature of the agenda for UNCTAD-II. Some people wanted to concentrate on a few issues; others argued that an attack along a broad front would be the only way to preserve UNCTAD's key feature, the coalition of 77. Concentration on a few issues eventually became the official policy of the secretariat. But Prebisch was unable to persuade the 77 gathered at Algiers in October 1967 to place any limits on the demands catalogued in what they called the Charter of Algiers.

Each developing country insisted that its particular interest should be represented; and acceptance was certain because of the group system and the generally agreed need to keep the coalition of 77 together. As one delegate explained it:

If Afghanistan wants the problem of land-locked countries to be discussed, India and Pakistan each have to support Afghanistan for local reasons. The Asian group supports the position taken by two of its leading countries; the other less-developed countries accept the decision of the Asian group, and the item goes on the agenda.

And finally, of course, the Western countries had no strong incentive to prevent the conference from becoming overburdened.

Power over the program through control of the budget rests in part with the secretariat. Such power is held particularly by the secretary-general who formulates the budget on the basis of estimates from his division, by officials at United Nations headquarters and the ACABQ, and by the Western countries, who provide more than two-thirds of the funds for the United Nations budget. Early in the process the informal Geneva Group of large donors indicates what they consider to be a tolerable budget level; but the large contributors have more influence on total sums than on allocations between fields, and despite their complaints the budget has grown quite rapidly.

Rule-Creating Decisions

Much UNCTAD activity concerns rule creation, though positive decisions are rare. On such issues as trade principles, amounts of aid to be given by donor countries, buffer stocks for commodities, and tariff preferences the less-developed countries have initiated measures and the Western countries have resisted them. But even though agreement on formal instruments like conventions has been rare, secretariat officials and representatives generally feel that the principles they reiterate in their speeches, reports, and resolutions are helping to establish a new set of economic norms. They point to the fact that the idea of tariff preferences for less-developed countries had been unthinkable under the most-favored-nation philosophy of trade that prevailed at the time of UNCTAD-I, but that some three years later, it was accepted in principle by the United States. While the Western countries refused to negotiate the details of such a scheme in UNCTAD bodies, it was UNCTAD pressure that led to their formulation of a weak scheme in the OECD. Though UNCTAD had a very limited direct role in the formal process of rule creating in most fields, its pressure has been felt nonetheless.

One exception is with commodities, where UNCTAD inherited the authority of the United Nations to arrange formal negotiations for commodity agreements. Two major efforts were made to negotiate commodity agreements during the Prebisch years. Efforts to reach a cocoa agreement broke down, but in 1968 the secretariat was able to negotiate a modest sugar agreement for that limited and extremely depressed part of the market not subject to preferential schemes. Behavior at the sugar agreement meeting reflected the specific interests of countries rather then the normal UNCTAD political patterns. It is interesting that in this decision area, in which UNCTAD dealt with specific economic interests, the behavioral roles

and structure of influence in decisions closely resembled the pattern in
GATT.

Rule-Supervisory Decisions

During the early sessions of the Trade and Development Board, the
less-developed countries pressed for detailed investigation of how the
developed states carried out the resolutions voted against their will by the
first conference. It soon became clear that the Western states would regard
such an "inquisition" as intolerable and that they might even quit the
organization. A compromise—in which Yugoslavia played a major mediating
role—was reached at the second session of the Trade Board in September
1965, when the secretariat was given the task of preparing a general annual
report on the implementation of UNCTAD measures. Realizing the
sensitivity of the issue, the secretariat responded cautiously, and its reports
did not have a very significant effect. In short, UNCTAD's role in rule
supervision has been minimal.

Operational Decisions

As mentioned earlier, until the very end of the Prebisch era, UNCTAD was
limited to meetings and research. But in 1968 it began to participate in the
International Trade Center and, in 1969, in the UNDP.

Actors and Their Sources of Influence

In this section we will classify the actors in UNCTAD, assess their relative
influence, describe their attitudes, indicate persistent groupings, and point
out cohesive or moderating factors.

Classification of Actors

National Government Representatives. One of the surprising things about
UNCTAD under Prebisch was the relatively high level of representation it
attracted. While political ministers came only at the beginning and end of the
triennial conferences (despite Prebisch's desire for ministerial representation
on the board) representatives at board meetings generally held high
bureaucratic posts, which handled political aspects of apparently technical
subjects. Since UNCTAD was primarily a forum for putting pressure on
developed countries, its effectiveness depended upon their listening. How
attentively they listened was reflected by the level and nature of the
representatives they sent.

In the words of a Western diplomat, "no group B country has made
UNCTAD its chosen instrument for policy." Group D diplomats privately
expressed disappointment with the way UNCTAD had become so thorough-
ly the instrument of the less-developed countries. One would therefore have
expected the more-developed countries gradually to lower their level of
representation and to shift UNCTAD affairs from substantive departments to

branches of foreign departments concerned with routine affairs of international organizations. As one United States official said, "When delegations to UNCTAD are staffed primarily by the Bureau of International Organization Affairs instead of the Office of Economic Affairs in State, then you will know that UNCTAD has become like ECOSOC and the pressure is off." Toward the end of the Prebisch era signs of a lowering of representation began to appear, and the level of representation at the eighth Trade Board in 1969 was lower than at the seventh board in 1968.

Why do relatively high-level officials sit through interminable and repetitious meetings whose outcomes, as they complain, they could predict in advance and where they are frequently subjected to harsh criticism?[16] When this question was put to Eastern and Western diplomats, they usually gave the following three reasons (in descending order of importance): (1) They have economic motives for attending. As one group D diplomat put it, even though UNCTAD discussions are usually abstract, "if you are not there when the principles are made, you may be hurt in the action." (2) Short-run political gains are possible through attendance. Many governments wish to present a favorable political image to the less-developed countries for the sake of other foreign policy objectives. (3) A number of representatives cited the long-run political importance of the development problem and saw the UNCTAD forum as a safety valve, providing both education and catharsis for the less-developed countries.

The UNCTAD policies of most governments in groups B and D are commonly formulated in the national capitals, and delegations are closely instructed. Insofar as delegates from developed countries are influential, it is far more because of their nation's role than because of their personal qualities. The situation is almost the opposite with regard to governmental representatives of the less-developed countries. While delegates from some of the larger countries, like Brazil and India, receive detailed instruction from home and are always influential because of their national role, for many of the less-developed countries personal character and long experience in Geneva are most important. As the delegate from an important African country proclaimed, "We are the only real plenipotentiary diplomats left. Those others are always on the Telex to their capitals." To be more precise, among the heads of delegations to the Seventh Trade Board in 1968, all of those from Eastern Europe came from the national capitals; 61 percent of group B's delegates came from the national capitals; but only 17 percent of the delegates from the less-developed countries came from the national capitals. In contrast, 67 percent of the delegates from less-developed countries were permanently stationed in Geneva, and the rest came from other posts in Europe.[17]

Interest Groups. The rules of procedure of the UNCTAD board provide for representation of nongovernmental organizations (NGOs) and their right to address the board or its committees on relevant subjects. By early 1969 the organization had accepted twenty-one NGOs in a general category allowing them to participate in the plenary meetings of the board, and nine in a special category with rights before specific committees of the board. Of the total of thirty organizations, eighteen could be said to represent business and commerce, four represented labor confederations, two were agricultural or cooperative NGOs, and six came from other groups. In general, NGOs do not play a major role at the larger UNCTAD sessions. The more specific and technical the subject, however, the larger their role.

The Executive Head and His Immediate Entourage. The record of UNCTAD in the 1960s was intimately connected with Raul Prebisch. Both delegates and secretariat officials agree that under Prebisch UNCTAD was an "executive head-oriented organization," reflecting both his merits and faults.[18] This is not to say, however, that Prebisch controlled the delegates or even the Latin-American delegates. On the contrary, he often found himself criticized for his moderation by delegates from less-developed countries; and one of the sharpest attacks on him at New Delhi was launched by the ambassador of Brazil. Unlike, for example, Eric Wyndham White of GATT, Prebisch was criticized for spending too much time in New York or in national capitals instead of in Geneva and for not being more available to delegates. As evidence, consider Prebisch's activities from the middle of May to the end of August 1968. In the second half of May he had consultations with ECLA officials in Chile, consultations with government officials in Colombia, and consultations with United Nations officials in New York. During June he consulted with United States officials in Washington, again with ECLA officials in Chile, introduced the 1969 UNCTAD budget at the ACABQ, and attended meetings of the Appointments and Promotions Board at New York. The next month he attended meetings of ECOSOC in Geneva and of the Administrative Committee on Coordination in Bucharest and addressed the Group of 77 at its request in Geneva. August was taken up with an official visit to Czechoslovakia, consultation with ECLA officials in Chile and with United Nations officials in New York. Obviously Prebisch considered the national capitals and the United Nations headquarters of higher priority than the delegates in Geneva.

Raul Prebisch has been one of the most successful men in the twentieth century in the use of an international organization—first ECLA, later UNCTAD—to affect governmental policies. He was not, however, a particularly good administrator. Both within UNCTAD and among outsiders, the UNCTAD secretariat had a reputation for very uneven administration. One reason was governmental rejection of Prebisch's request for a deputy; another was the United Nations nationality quotas, which led to some disastrous appointments; and a third was that Prebisch was not really interested in administration. High-level staff found it difficult to see him; junior staff almost never saw him. He rarely held internal meetings or took steps to improve staff morale. In short, he sacrificed internal efficiency for the sake of external effectiveness. [19] He usually worked "bilaterally," through a small group well known to him from previous United Nations service. However, although Prebisch was not a good bureaucrat in the administrative sense, he was a good bureaucrat in the sense of knowing how to work within the larger United Nations bureaucracy. As has already been pointed out, after UNCTAD's establishment he adopted a conciliatory attitude toward the Department of Economic and Social Affairs, and he always kept on good terms with the ACABQ. For a man who was sometimes thought of as a troublemaker, he was a surprisingly firm believer and practitioner in the United Nations system.

What then was the secret of Prebisch's success in using international organization to force ideas upon governments' attention? Prebisch achieved his effect by catalyzing an inchoate set of ideas prevalent among less-developed countries into a clear doctrine and then tirelessly repeating it in fluent, moving speeches that reflected his honesty and conviction. Among the "overdocumentation" for the 1964 conference, Prebisch's personal analytical report "proved to be almost the only one constantly referred to and used as a basis for discussion by the delegates." [20] Prebisch's style was that of a prophet, and his chosen instruments were words. This is not to say that Prebisch simply imposed his ECLA ideology on UNCTAD. As we saw earlier, a good deal of the UNCTAD agenda had been settled before his appointment. In fact, Prebisch had changed much of his early ECLA ideology when he came to UNCTAD, particularly his ideas on import substitution and the downgrading of trade. Moreover, Prebisch's ideas were continually evolving. During his five years as secretary-general he revised many of his ideas in response to criticism.

Prebisch did his own thinking. He would closet himself in his office for weeks, painstakingly writing out his own reports. His speeches were always delivered without notes, and he generally disregarded drafts submitted by secretariat members. Ideas in UNCTAD came more from the top down than from the bottom up. The role of the secretariat was not so much to generate ideas as to work out supporting documentation. This had the effect of making the secretariat—with the exception of two divisions under the direction of old colleagues of the secretary-general—a rather passive instrument.

Prebisch's style had the faults and virtues of personal control. On the one hand, it made for an uncoordinated secretariat and encouraged the prevalence of a particular theoretical point of view, with which many group B countries disagreed more or less strongly. On the other hand, it meant that UNCTAD had a coherent doctrine, which was not bureaucratically created, but reflected the earnest conviction of its secretary-general and provided a reference point for its major political feature—the coalition of the 77 less-developed countries.

Segments of the Bureaucracy. National origin is not a major source of cleavage in the UNCTAD secretariat; and, with the possible exception of the minor Division of Trade with Socialist Countries, which has been described by one participant as "a group D fiefdom which does no one any harm," bureaucratic segments do not tend to align themselves with particular states. In particular, Prebisch was very careful not to appear to favor Latin Americans in the secretariat. As we said earlier, Prebisch was to a surprising degree a man of the United Nations system. Probably the most important informal division in the secretariat was that between the "old United Nations hands" and the "outsiders" who came to UNCTAD from governments or universities.

In October 1968, just before his retirement, Prebisch established two small committees of high secretariat officials to assist in the discharge of his administrative and substantive duties. Both were staffed entirely by old United Nations hands. The membership of the group charged with substantive affairs was a good index of the most generally influential members of the secretariat.[21] Of the six top officials, three were of Western European origin, one was Eastern European, one Asian, and one Latin American. But none could be said to reflect their governments' positions. On the contrary, all had nearly two decades of United Nations service and were inclined to share a similar set of ideas that could be called an UNCTAD doctrine. Other secretariat officials, some sharing the ideology, some not, often had influence over specific subjects within their competence. For instance, both P. Judd on commodities and C. Eckenstein on trade expansion among less-developed countries, were mentioned by more than two-thirds of the panel. But all those with generalized influence were old United Nations hands.

Eminent Individuals. In the commodities field, UNCTAD has an institutional provision for eminent advisers in the form of the Advisory Committee on Commodities, which replaced the United Nations Interim Coordinating Committee for International Commodity Arrangements. The advisory committee consists of seven experts, including one nominated by FAO and one nominated by GATT. Its influence is minor, however, partly because of its infrequent meetings, partly because of an objective but daunting first report. More informally, the secretariat sometimes commissions research from prominent outside economists, but their role is not important in the organization.

Representatives of Other International Organizations. Representatives of a number of other international organizations have played roles in specific UNCTAD activities, for example, in studies by the FAO on commodities, and by the IBRD and IMF on financial questions. In addition, the OECD, CMEA, CECLA, and the United Nations regional commissions have taken part in preparing group positions before UNCTAD meetings. GATT is a perpetual presence, though one cannot really say that its representatives play an active role in the UNCTAD system. The major actors from other international organizations are from the United Nations in New York. As we saw earlier, the United Nations secretary-general seems to have acted almost autonomously in appointing Perez-Guerrero as Prebisch's successor. Moreover, the head of the Department of Economic and Social Affairs and the members of the ACABQ were all potentially important enough to cause Prebisch to conciliate them. In short, UNCTAD's institutional relationship to the United Nations has made a difference.

Representatives of the Mass Media. One would expect that in an organization whose main function is to serve as a forum, and which aims at pressing for changes in group B countries, the mass media would play a major role. In practice, however, they have not played an important part in UNCTAD, except perhaps during the 1964 conference. It is interesting to note that the *New York Times* ran forty-five articles and editorials on UNCTAD-I, but only eighteen on UNCTAD-II. [22] Dissatisfaction with inadequate press coverage led to the less-developed countries to propose a resolution at the eighth Trade Board that the secretariat study means to improve UNCTAD's public relations. The ability of the secretariat to increase its public relations work independently was limited, however, by its having to rely on the United Nations information services and by the concern of group B countries with the financial consequences of any expansion.

Resources

Ability to Mobilize Votes. Despite the fact that voting in UNCTAD rarely has significant effects outside the organization, the potential of the 77 to mobilize an automatic majority, along with memories of the "voting machine" at the 1964 Geneva Conference, have been important latent sources of influence for the less-developed countries. Consequently, they are a source of influence for those Third World delegates whose leadership is generally accepted and for the few members of the secretariat who are adept at lobbying among delegates.

Budgetary Contributions. As we saw earlier, group B countries provide two-thirds of the UNCTAD budget. Delegates of the larger countries informally discuss the budget with the secretariat in Geneva at an early stage of its preparation. In addition, at UNCTAD meetings they frequently stress the financial implications of various actions, and this emphasis has some effect as a signal to the representatives from less-developed countries. But since group B countries have no item veto, representatives of the less-developed countries who feel intensely about a point can pass it over Western opposition. Thus the fact that an individual represents a state that makes a large contribution to the budget may sometimes be a source of general influence for him, but the influence is often not sufficient to make his will prevail on specific issues.

Material Resources. On substantive matters the knowledge that the Western countries account for some 70 percent of the world's trade and that they cannot be voted, but only persuaded, into making important concessions to the less-developed countries gradually has come to be widely accepted in UNCTAD circles. The possibility that group B countries and, to a much lesser extent, group D countries might refuse to go on playing the game is their major source of influence in UNCTAD. This influence is greater, however, in substantive than in procedural decisions.

Permanent Representation. The fact that they are on the scene in Geneva is an important source of influence for delegates from the less-developed countries. The permanent representatives in Geneva tend to be better informed on the workings of the organization and thus in a position to brief and lead their regional colleagues who arrive for meetings loosely instructed and generally out of touch. While the Asians and particularly the Latin Americans are generally represented in Geneva, less than one-third of the African members of UNCTAD have permanent delegations in Geneva. This situation weakens African influence in general, but it increases the personal influence of the more able Africans in Geneva who thus come to be regarded as representatives of all Africans.

Among developed countries, on the other hand, the most influential delegates are those who come from the national capitals. While permanent representatives in Geneva sometimes acquire detailed knowledge and contacts, which enhance their influence, their presence in Geneva is not nearly as important as their country of origin in accounting for their influence. [23]

Functional Position and Access to Decision Makers. Since Prebisch played a central catalytic role but was frequently absent, those officials and the one or two delegates who were personally close to him derived a certain influence for that reason. Individuals holding positions as conference officials or as chairmen of their groups also derived considerable influence from these posts.

Flexibility in Position. The rigidities of the group system in UNCTAD tend to reward inflexibility, at least in the early stages of meetings. Given the imperatives of group unity, one or two countries willing to press a point ad nauseam are often able to bring a group to accept it. Also, the forum role of UNCTAD, particularly among the 77, makes it difficult for a moderate to prevail over a more legitimate extremist in the early stages of discussions. The need to refer matters back to groups also dampens independent initiatives by those individuals who have good intergroup contacts. On the other hand, flexibility and diplomatic skill are useful resources in the final stages of discussion when it becomes clear that something must be done to salvage a meeting. At such a time an individual who is known as a good broker becomes more influential. But a flexible position alone is not a major source of influence in UNCTAD.

Administrative Competence. Administrative depth, resulting in well-prepared positions and evoking a general feeling among other delegates that a delegate has an effective administrative machine behind him, is an important source of influence for individual delegates. This advantage was frequently cited by other delegates to explain the continued influence of such countries as Brazil, Chile, India, and Pakistan. In the secretariat certain individuals benefit from a reputation for administrative competence; but, as we saw earlier, this was not Prebisch's major interest; nor is it the strong suit of some of the most influential secretariat members.

Expert Knowledge. The lower the level of the UNCTAD organ and the more specific the subject of concern, the greater the role of expert knowledge. Even at the level of the board, however, a particular delegate's expert knowledge sometimes leads a group to designate him their spokesman on an issue, although when a chairman of the group has been chosen by alphabetical rotation, he generally serves as spokesman.

Doctrinal Legitimacy. The economic doctrine elaborated by Prebisch, discussed below, has become a point of common reference for delegates from the 77, but not for the other states. In short, in determining the influence of delegates, factors other than belief—the UNCTAD doctrine—are more important. Inside the secretariat, however, ideological legitimacy in the sense of generally sharing most of the major points of the UNCTAD doctrine is a necessary condition for influence in general programmatic decisions, though it is not necessary for influence on specific technical issues.

Continued Association with the Organization. When a delegate comes from a large developed state, his country of origin is a sufficient source of influence. In contrast, delegates from the smaller Western states and from most of the less-developed countries, derive influence from continued association with the organization. Long association provides the knowledge of detail and the sense of "being in touch" that is essential to actors whose power comes from their reputation for leadership as initiators or brokers. In the secretariat, long association with the United Nations system and with UNCTAD was characteristic of the most influential members under Prebisch.

Attitudes

Organizational Ideologies. UNCTAD has a broad doctrine, primarily articulated by Prebisch in speeches and reports. It is quite widely shared in the upper levels of the secretariat (particularly among the old United Nations hands) and widely referred to by representatives from less-developed countries. Although group B or D countries rarely mention it, at a more general level everyone at UNCTAD proclaims his devotion to the task of "development"—the central point of the doctrine.

The roots of the UNCTAD doctrine can be found in the 1962 Cairo Conference, at which thirty-six less-developed countries discussed problems of economic development, as well as in the proposals of the less-developed countries for the agenda of UNCTAD-I at the Preparatory Committee meetings and in the work of the United Nations regional economic commissions. However, the most coherent presentations were in Prebisch's two conference reports *Towards a New Trade Policy for Development* (1964) and *Towards a Global Strategy of Development* (1968). Prebisch portrayed the world as divided into a developed center and an under-developed periphery. Technological changes and social structures in the rich center prevented the nineteenth-century free trade mechanism from working fast enough—if at all—to transmit the development process to the poor periphery. Thus new principles in international economic organization and specific compensatory programs were needed, which were not based on a mythical equality of states but took special account of what less-developed states were lacking. In light of these general principles, Prebisch suggested a series of specific programs which were more or less the agenda of UNCTAD-I. In his second report Prebisch stressed the need for acts of political will in which developed and less-developed countries would converge to reach agreement on a global strategy for development.

Although most people agreed about the need for development and at least with part of Prebisch's interpretation of the environment, many Western economists and officials were unhappy with the economic reasoning in his arguments. [24] The communist countries felt they already had an adequate broad-based ideology; they also felt that UNCTAD's programs did not take into account the uniqueness of their historical experience or their economic systems. According to their argument, since they were not colonial powers, they were not responsible for the development gap, and most of UNCTAD's corrective measures were not relevant to their planned economies. Among the less-developed countries, there have been frequent general references to the UNCTAD doctrine, but likely disagreement over translating it into a strategy of action. It is one thing, for example, to agree with Prebisch on the evils of "vertical spheres of influence," but another thing for Francophone African states to give up their preferential association with the EEC. Nonetheless, in general terms the UNCTAD doctrine is vital to the maintenance of the coalition of the 77.

Other Attitudinal Issues. Men do not live by doctrine alone. Personal goals have also played a significant role in UNCTAD decisions. Within the secretariat some divisions are led by men who have the reputation of being time-servers, others by men with reputations as bureaucratic entrepreneurs.

The effects of these personal characteristics are reflected in the growth and changes that have occurred in the bureaucracy, for instance, in the size of the Invisibles Division and the creation of the Trade Expansion Program.

Looking at the conference diplomacy activities of UNCTAD, one sees that personal goals have also had a marked effect in this sphere. Conferences are a social arena where delegates project their personalities, engage in personal competition, applaud certain speeches, and maneuver for the prestige of election to conference offices. Even when they have nothing of substance to concede, some group B delegates have admitted that they were willing to spend long hours attempting to agree on compromise wording for resolutions, not just to serve their national interests, but because of their personal reputations as diplomats. For the same reason, other delegates have cultivated a reputation for cynicism. Among the Group of 77, vying for the personal prestige of leadership has accounted for difficulties at several UNCTAD meetings.

From the perspective of government policies, however, personal goals and varying attitudes do not play a significant role in UNCTAD decisions. The delegate who becomes so converted by the speeches he hears that he exceeds his instructions quickly loses his effectiveness at home. As one Western delegate remarked, "You don't advance in our bureaucracy by preaching UNCTAD doctrines." Occasionally an individual in a political post has played an important role. For instance, Edward Heath as president of the British Board of Trade helped to create a positive atmosphere at the end of the 1964 Geneva Conference; and United States Assistant Secretary of State Anthony Solomon did much toward changing the United States position on tariff preferences for less-developed countries. In general, however, except for the Nordic countries and the Netherlands, politicians in the developed countries have not found a domestic constituency that makes it profitable at the ballot boxes to preach UNCTAD doctrines.

The extent of dual loyalties among the delegates is difficult to judge. Certain diplomats who have earned a reputation among their peers as particularly hard and effective workers in UNCTAD were questioned by the author at length and in detail about this factor. Some group B diplomats confessed sympathy with UNCTAD aims, and a few even said they had used demands made at UNCTAD as an excuse to press for liberal policy changes at home. But most found UNCTAD too frustrating an organization, both as a forum and in their relations with the secretariat, to feel loyalty toward it. (This attitude contrasted in many cases with their more positive feelings about GATT.) Diplomats from both developed and less-developed countries tended to cite professional pride and career advancement as the main motives for their diligence at UNCTAD.

Persistent Groupings

UNCTAD under Prebisch was an organization built on groups. The institutionalization of the group system was probably the single most important factor in UNCTAD's decision-making process. Countries like South Africa, Israel, and Cuba, which were excluded from regional groups, were effectively excluded from general influence (and election to the board). UNCTAD meetings invariably started at least half an hour or more late, while the major groups met to hammer out common positions. But as a harried board president confessed, it would have saved no time to start a meeting before group positions were clear.

A number of delegates criticized the rigidity of group discipline because of the premium it gave to extreme positions. Some diplomats from the larger group B countries admitted privately, however, that the group system protected them from the stronger pressure they might have experienced had they been more isolated, as they had been in 1964. On the other hand, some delegates argued that the formal group system made UNCTAD manageable and gave it whatever political force it had. Suggestions for minor relaxation of group discipline ran into the problem of low degree of trust within each of the group coalitions.

In general, by the end of the Prebisch period there was a sense of frustration with the ponderous nature of the group procedure. Some of the more influential delegates had begun to arrange informal meetings with members of other groups; and the new secretary-general had begun to hold informal consultations with members of various groups in his office. Even these modest initiatives, however, were criticized by some of the persons not included.

Within the groups important cleavages exist. Group B is often divided into the important subgroups of the British and Americans, the EEC, and the more liberal Nordics, who are sometimes joined by the Netherlands. The Africans tend to divide by language, the Latin Americans by size. But these cleavages are more significant inside group caucuses than outside them. Cross-group alliances are rare, except for the coalition of the 77. To a minor extent such alliances have developed on specific issues like shipping or commodities, where some of the developed countries have interests similar to those of the 77. Within the 77 the beginnings of a de facto alliance between the least-developed Latin-American and African states appeared at the 1967 Algiers Conference, called to prepare the position of the 77 on the agenda for UNCTAD-II. However, diplomatic pressure and an appeal for regional solidarity by the larger Latin-American states eventually prevailed.

Conflict and Cohesion. As we have noted, the net effect of the group system has been to polarize positions and dramatize conflict in the forums. At the same time, the group discipline that exists and the appointment of group representatives imposes a sort of order on UNCTAD meetings and generally, in its cumbersome way, leads to what might be called compromise in words, if not always in policy.

Organizational Elites. Helped by a fellow scholar of UNCTAD and a secretariat official, the author selected the names of ten persons representing the secretariat and the major groups in the organization whose experience encompassed the entire UNCTAD history. These persons were asked to identify "individuals who had been the most generally influential in the UNCTAD system as a whole up to 1968" and to give the reasons for their influence. [25] With the exception of Prebisch, the panel described delegates as far more influential on general programmatic and substantive issues than the secretariat. It is interesting to note that all members of the panel proceeded by identifying the key leaders of each of the groups. Of the sixteen influential individuals identified by the panel, half came from the less-developed countries; that is, three were Asians, three Latin Americans, and two Africans. Half were from the Western countries of group B; four came from the large countries and four from the smaller. None came from the communist countries of group D.

Impact of the Environment

Despite its brief history, the general and specific environment of UNCTAD has had considerable impact on the organization. The specific environment has been marked by a growing dissatisfaction among less-developed countries over declining terms of trade, their diminishing share of world trade, and the existing institutional structures in the field. The general environment has been marked by the salad days of nonalignment, when the sharpness of thy East-West cleavage—and some illusions—gave the new states a short-run appearance of political importance that became rather diminished by the end of the decade.

These environmental conditions at the time of its birth left their mark on UNCTAD as an organization. The composition of the executive organs reflect the political division of the world into Eastern (group D), Western (group B), Afro-Asian (group A), and Latin-American (group C) groupings. The composition of the bureaucracy, compared to GATT's for example, also reflects the pressures of the new states for representation. Indeed these pressures for rapid improvement of geographical distribution of posts have led to some unsuitable appointments that have seriously crippled certain branches of the secretariat. The orientation of the organization toward Third World goals (rejecting Eastern preferences calling for attention to East-West trade) and the nature of its program and policies as described above are all evidence of how the environment of the early 1960s has affected the organization.

Several changes in both the general and specific environment between 1964 and 1968 contributed to the paucity of results at the second conference in New Delhi (February-March 1968). While one must be careful not to overstate the difference in results between the Geneva and New Delhi conferences, the Western countries did make an important concession about

Table 10.3

Influential Persons in UNCTAD
(In Alphabetical Order in Each Category)

Identified by All 7	Country	Sources of Influence
Adebanjo	Nigeria	Personal expertise, experience, status as "spokesman for Africa"
Brillantes	Philippines	Personality, interest, experience
Lall[a]	India	Personal expertise, importance of his country, administrative competence
Santa Cruz	Chile	Long United Nations experience, senior standing, closeness to Prebisch
Silveira	Brazil	Being spokesman for 77, importance of his country, personality

Identified by 3 or More		
"Anyone from United States"	United States	Material resources of his country
Everloff	Sweden	Sympathetic reputation of his country
Forthomme	Belgium	Sympathetic individual character
Goldslag	Canada	Standing of his country, parliamentary skills
Golt	United Kingdom	Importance of his country, experience
"Ivory Coast"	Ivory Coast	Strength in French Africa, expertise on commodities
Jolles	Switzerland	Sympathetic nature, expertise, detailed knowledge on specific issues
Prebisch	Argentina	Position as secretary-general
Reed	Norway	Sympathetic reputation of his country, diplomatic skills
Viaud	France	Importance of his country, experience, skills

[a] Identified by 6.

institutions at Geneva. And some countries presented initiatives that were well received by the less-developed countries, for example, Britain and Sweden on supplementary financing. According to well-informed observers, many less-developed countries persisted in believing until the late hours of the New Delhi Conference that the Western countries could "not afford to let the conference fail" and that they had some "concessions up their sleeves."

What had changed between 1964 and 1968? In the general environment the stratification of power and the distribution of states according to their economic and political characteristics remained more or less the same. Ordinarily, and at least partly because of the group system whose discipline somewhat diminished the effect of national differences, political changes of regime rarely had a pronounced impact on UNCTAD except in so far as they affected the general political climate. The main changes from 1964 to 1968 were that the ideological sharpness of the East-West cleavage diminished, marking the apparent beginnings of a United States-USSR détente—and that both camps showed a growing disillusion with the short-term political importance and development prospects of the Third World. As an Eastern European official put it, "The Russians have turned to a much more selective approach to the Third World." Another observer said of the change in the Western position, "1964 was still close to the great illusions of the independence year, 1960." [26]

Another major change in the specific environment of UNCTAD over the same period was the dramatic increase in world trade accompanied by a continued decline in the less-developed countries' share of that trade. The rapid growth of the developed market economies helped cause a 6 percent annual growth of exports from the less-developed countries in the 1960s, a rate 50 percent higher than that projected by the UNCTAD secretariat and twice as high as the rate in the late 1950s. However, the increased burden of debt service, higher cost of invisibles, and declining aid meant that the ability of these countries to import grew at the same 4 percent rate that prevailed in the latter 1950s. Thus a gap, dramatized by UNCTAD-I, remained; but it did not show up as an export gap in the way that UNCTAD papers had predicted. [27]

Western countries concentrated on the Kennedy Round reductions of tariff barriers in GATT and urged the less-developed countries to do likewise. They argued for the most part that those less-developed countries that had taken the Kennedy Round seriously had profited more than those that had restricted themselves to discussing questions of trade philosophy in UNCTAD. At the same time, however, the very success of the Kennedy Round tariff reductions led to a certain protectionist swing of the trade politics pendulum, particularly in the United States. At the same time growing problems in the international monetary system reduced still further what little flexibility there had been in the aid policies of some of the most important countries in UNCTAD. With no articulate body of opinion among politicians, the press, universities, or youth, which would serve as a countervailing constituency, except in a few small group B countries, the pressures on Western officials came primarily from the conservative direction.

Finally, the communist countries were unhappy not only because of the criticism they received in UNCTAD, but also because the less-developed countries were unwilling to devote attention to East-West trade issues that were of greatest material concern to the group D countries. Fear that the Soviet Union would reap political gains was one of the factors that had caused the Western countries to take UNCTAD seriously at the Geneva Conference. The decline of Soviet interest in the organization substantially reduced this threat.

One of the interesting questions about international organizations is the extent to which the structure of influence in the arena they provide differs from what one would expect the structure of power in the general political environment to reveal. To get some impression of how much the influence in UNCTAD differs from influence in both the general environment of international politics and the specific environment of trade and aid, the author ranked the most influential states in UNCTAD according to a behavioral index. Although influence is a notoriously slippery concept, it was clear that we wanted a measure of actual behavior in the organization rather than a measure of potential capacity. Accordingly, we distinguished between negative and positive influence in different types of decisions in UNCTAD, treating the unweighted sum as an indicator of general influence.[28] States were scored by the author on the basis of interviews, analysis of documents, and observation of meetings, according to the scheme shown in table 10.4.

From table 10.5 we see that the United States, France, and Britain were the three most influential states in UNCTAD under Prebisch, despite its reputation as an organization for less-developed countries. On the other hand, the USSR ranked much lower than one would expect on the basis of its power; and a number of developing countries ranked much higher than we would have expected on the same basis. When we look at table 10.6, however, we find interesting differences in the type of influence. The United States is first in negative influence but tied for eleventh with the USSR in positive influence. India, Chile, and Brazil have the greatest positive influence, but all ranked quite low in negative influence.

It is also interesting to note that of the twenty-two most influential states in general, thirteen were Western (group B); two were Socialist (the USSR from group D, and Yugoslavia from group A); and seven were Others (from the 77).

Table 10.5 compares the ranking of the most influential states in UNCTAD with their order on the Cox-Jacobson scale of power in the general

Table 10.4

Behavioral Index of Influence of States in UNCTAD
1968-69

Type of Influence	Negative	Positive	Total
Representational			
Symbolic			
Programmatic			
Rule-Creating			
Rule-Supervisory			
Operational			
Boundary			
Total			

Scoring Rules

Direction of Influence	Action	Score
Negative	Prevents frequently on important issues (would include use of formal veto or blocking at an earlier stage)	3
	Prevents occasionally	2
	Rarely prevents	1
	Never prevents	0
Positive	Frequently initiates successfully on important issues	3
	Occasionally initiates successfully on important issues	2
	Rarely initiates successfully on important issues	1
	Never initiates successfully on important issues	0

environment of international politics. (One of the ten most powerful states, the People's Republic of China, was not a member.) Six of the nine other most powerful states were also among the nine most influential in UNCTAD, but not always in the same order as in the general environment. Kendall's tau beta correlation coefficient, which measures the degree to which pairs in the proper order on the two scales exceed those in the reverse order (and gives scores between -1.0 and +1.0) is .43 in this case. Influence in UNCTAD is positively related to power in the general environment, but the relation is far from perfect. International organization is a special type of power arena.

Comparing the order of the ten most important states in the world as measured by share of world exports or by amount of aid given (see table 10.7) shows that only five of the top ten exporters and five of the top nine

Table 10.5

Influence by Behavioral Results in UNCTAD

Group 1 (score over 20)	Rank Score in Environment	General (P + N)	Positive	Negative
1.5 France	3	23	9	14
1.5 United States	1	23	7	16
3 United Kingdom	5	21	7	14
Group II (score 15-19)				
4 Brazil	15	17	10	7
5.5 Australia	15	16	9	7
5.5 India	9.5	16	12	4
7.5 Chile	below 39	15	11	4
7.5 Japan	5	15	4	11
Group III (score 11-14)				
10 United Arab Republic	31.5	14	9	5
10 USSR	2	14	7	7
10 Yugoslavia	15	14	9	5
14 Canada	9.5	13	6	7
14 Italy	8	13	4	9
14 Federal Republic of Germany	7	13	4	9
14 Netherlands	15	13	5	8
14 Belgium	21	13	5	8
17.5 Nigeria	36	12	8	4
17.5 Norway	31.5	12	7	5
20.5 Pakistan	21	11	7	4
20.5 Sweden	11	11	6	5
20.5 Ivory Coast	below 39	11	7	4
20.5 Switzerland	15	11	4	7

Note: Maximum score = 42; 10 and under not counted.

aid donors (excluding China) were among the equivalent most influential states in UNCTAD. The values of Kendall's tau beta for these two indices of the specific environment (.41 and .52 respectively) indicate an almost equally imperfect correspondence between influence in UNCTAD and rank in the specific environment as between influence in UNCTAD and rank in the general environment. This fits our description of UNCTAD as a political forum rather than a technical agency concerned with trade and aid.

The USSR, though one of the two superpowers, was in the second category of influential members in UNCTAD. One reason is shown in its lower ranking (seventh and fourth) in trade and aid, which meant that it had less control than the large Western states over the material resources that the

Table 10.6

Positive and Negative Influence in UNCTAD
of Most Influential States

		Positive					*Negative*	
I.	1	India	12	I.	1	United States	16
	2	Chile	11		2.5	France	14
	3	Brazil	10		2.5	United Kingdom	14
II.	5.5	Australia	9	II.	4	Japan	11
	5.5	France	9		5.5	Federal Republic of Germany	9
	5.5	United Arab Republic	9		5.5	Italy	9
	5.5	Yugoslavia	9		7.5	Belgium	8
	8	Nigeria	8		7.5	Netherlands	8
III.	11.5	Ivory Coast	7	III.	11	Australia	7
	11.5	Norway	7		11	Brazil	7
	11.5	Pakistan	7		11	Canada	7
	11.5	United Kingdom	7		11	Switzerland	7
	11.5	United States	7		11	USSR	7
	11.5	USSR	7		15.5	Norway	5
	15.5	Canada	6		15.5	Sweden	5
	15.5	Sweden	6		15.5	United Arab Republic	5
	17.5	Belgium	5		15.5	Yugoslavia	5
	17.5	Netherlands	5		20	Chile	4
	20.5	Federal Republic of Germany	4		20	India	4
	20.5	Italy	4		20	Ivory Coast	4
	20.5	Japan	4		20	Nigeria	4
	20.5	Switzerland	4		20	Pakistan	4

Note: Maximum score = 21.

UNCTAD forum was concerned about. As one delegate to UNCTAD put it, "When it comes to concrete issues, everyone knows that they have nothing to offer." It has been reported that Soviet initiatives toward making some concrete concessions at the end of the New Delhi Conference were thwarted by its group D partners, who argued that as semideveloped states themselves they could not afford them.[29] Moreover, as we mentioned above, many of the group D states were somewhat disillusioned with the unwillingness of the 77 to get into the subject of East-West trade and with their own treatment as part of the developed "North."[30] Nonetheless, its importance in world politics made the USSR a weighty political presence at UNCTAD conferences, but more on symbolic, representational, and programmatic issues than on regulatory or substantive ones.

Two other states among the ten most powerful in the general environment of international politics—Germany and Italy—ranked much lower among the influential than was expected. Germany was also among the ten most

Table 10.7

Comparison of Rank inside UNCTAD with Rank in Specific Environment

General Environment

Rank Order of Power (1967)		Rank in UNCTAD
1	United States	1.5
2	USSR	10
3	France	1.5
5	People's Republic of China	NM
5	United Kingdom	3
5	Japan	7.5
7	Federal Republic of Germany	14
8	Italy	14
9.5	India	5.5
9.5	Canada	14
11	Sweden	20.5
14	Switzerland	20.5
14	Australia	5.5
14	Brazil	4
14	Netherlands	14
14	Spain	below 22
18.5	Argentina	below 22
18.5	South Africa	below 22
18.5	Belgium	below 22
18.5	Poland	below 22
21.5	Denmark	below 22
21.5	Indonesia	below 22

Specific Environment

1. Share of World Export Rank

Rank		Rank in UNCTAD
1	United States	1.5
2	Federal Republic of Germany	14
3	United Kingdom	3
4	France	1.5
5	Canada	14
6	Japan	7.5
7	USSR	10
8	Italy	14
9	Belgium	14
10	Netherlands	14
11	Sweden	20.5
12	Switzerland	20.5
13	German Democratic Republic	NM
14	Australia	5.5
15	Czechoslovakia	below 22
16	Venezuela	below 22
17	Denmark	below 22
18	Poland	below 22
19	Brazil	4
20	South Africa	below 22
21	Austria	below 22
22	India	5.5

2. Amount of Aid Given Rank

Rank		Rank in UNCTAD
1	United States	1.5
2	France	1.5
3	United Kingdom	3
4	USSR	10
5	Federal Republic of Germany	14
6	People's Republic of China	NM
7	Japan	7.5
8	Canada	14
9	Belgium	14
10	Australia	.5
11	Czechoslovakia	below 22
12	Italy	14
13	Netherlands	14
14	German Democratic Republic	NM
15	Rumania	below 22
16	Sweden	20.5
17	Poland	below 22
18	Portugal	below 22
19	Switzerland	20.5
20	Austria	below 22
21	Hungary	below 22
22	Norway	17.5

Note: NM = Nonmember.

important states in the specific environment of trade and aid, and this was true of Italy on trade. Since both were among the defeated states of World War II, that fact may have somewhat inhibited their ability to capitalize politically on their economic strength. But their ranking also reflected the rather low priority they assigned to UNCTAD, the quality of their delegations, and the fact that France, with its influence upon its former colonies and its more assertive foreign policy tended to fill the leadership role among the EEC states insofar as they acted in common.

It is interesting to note that in GATT, during the 1967 Kennedy Round negotiations, which dealt with concrete trade problems, officials and delegates sometimes referred to the "Bridge Club" or the "Big Four." In UNCTAD during the same time the analogous expression was the "Big Three." Japan was frequently one of the Big Four in the GATT negotiations but not one of the Big Three in UNCTAD discussions. Similarly, in GATT one of the Big Four was the EEC, with the representatives of the commission and the council playing important roles. In the political forum of UNCTAD, however, the members of the EEC frequently took different positions; the commission played a minor role, and the member of the Big Three was France, not the EEC. However, the smaller the forum and more specific the subject in UNCTAD—for instance, shipping questions or the negotiation of a sugar agreement in 1968—the more influence in relation to the issue involved was found to vary with the specific economic power of a country.

The countries that ranked higher in influence in UNCTAD than would have been expected from their power in the general environment were less-developed countries such as Brazil, India, Chile, the United Arab Republic, Yugoslavia, and Nigeria. While the first two of these were among the most important less-developed countries in their share of exports and receipt of aid, the major source of influence for all was their ability (because of size, administrative capacity, ideological legitimacy, and the personalities of their delegates) to establish positions as leaders of groups and of the 77 in a forum as unique as UNCTAD.

The Structure of Influence: Past, Present, Future

If we conceive of an international organization as a regularized diplomacy and a secretariat, the structures of influence in UNCTAD have been described. There is no single elite for UNCTAD decisions, nor is the structure of influence completely the same for all decisions. Yet there is less variation by type of decision than one might expect. One reason might be that ubiquitous feature of UNCTAD, the group system. The rigidity of the group system, its effect in obscuring national differences within groups, the emergence of group leaders for the reasons we have already discussed, and the use of the UNCTAD forum for general discussion rather than specific negotiations means that the leaders tend to be generalists rather than specialists. One delegate said, "In GATT a different man handles each issue.

When I first came to UNCTAD I was astounded to see the same faces discussing everything from shipping to commodities." As we have already seen, the more specific the subject matter of the meeting, the greater the influence of states with particular interests. For instance, Cuba was one of the most influential states at the sugar conference; Norway was one of the most influential states in the Shipping Committee, and Sweden (a large contributor to UNDP programs) in the Finance Committee. But even in smaller groups—and this is true of the less-developed countries—the same countries are likely to have the administrative capacity and group leadership that make them influential on most questions in a general forum like UNCTAD.

The secretariat is most important in relation to programmatic, boundary, and, to a lesser extent, rule-creating decisions. Within the Prebisch secretariat, influence was concentrated at the top and flowed downward. Certain divisions run by long-time colleagues of the secretary-general tended to be autonomous fiefdoms. The same divisions did well in the allocation of the budget; in some cases they were the ones whose directors made contact with delegates. These directors, along with some members of his office staff, were closest to Prebisch in helping to determine general policy of the secretariat, unless the subject was a technical one; in that case their influence was temporarily supplemented by the officials concerned. Relations between this inner circle of the secretariat and the delegates from the developed countries were not close. Consultants were hired, the budget slightly altered, or programs slightly changed in response to group B governmental concerns—but none of these were major changes.

Vis-à-vis the representatives of the less-developed countries, the situation was somewhat different. Relations between the less-developed countries and the secretariat were not as close as one might have expected from the public image. Nonetheless, the strategic program of the secretariat had to include the broad list of demands formulated by the 77; and although there was some leeway for secretariat discretion, the secretariat was careful not to offend members of the less-developed countries' coalition.

While Prebisch frequently acted as a mediator among the less-developed countries, as for example in such cases as the efforts to reach agreement on the Algiers Charter, he was not sufficiently available to or trusted by group B countries to shepherd negotiations in UNCTAD in the way that Eric Wyndham White did in GATT. Wyndham White has been described as spending much of his time talking to delegations in his office, keeping his finger on the pulse of a meeting, and knowing what to suggest and the right moment to suggest it in order to dissolve deadlocks. Except at the 1968 sugar conference, Prebisch almost never played such a part.

In short, if we take an international organization to mean both a secretariat and its corresponding permanent conference diplomacy, then the UNCTAD we have described is a strange, complicated machine that produces very little in real output, but whose internal wheels and gears move according to more or less regular patterns.

We can also think of an international organization in a still broader sense, however, as including all the relevant roles—even that of national politicians—that affect an organization's achievement of its declared and derivative goals or its failure to achieve them. We are then faced with the questions of how the strange machine affects national policies and how national decision makers restrict, enlarge, divert, or ignore its output. From this "national policy perspective," the crucial actors in UNCTAD are the bureaucrats and politicians in the national capitals of a handful of countries. The extent to which the strange machinery of UNCTAD affects those national policies is difficult to determine. The constant meetings of the organization politicize trade matters and prevent national bureaucracies from sweeping awkward matters under the rug. For example, the Geneva mission of a crucial group B country was forced to devote about half as much time to UNCTAD as to GATT, though it considered GATT many times more important and infinitely more sympathetic than UNCTAD.

In some cases, as with invisibles, UNCTAD has broken new ground for international consultation. Topics like freight shipping rate policies became subject to study by intergovernmental organization for the first time. In other cases, its criticisms have caused changes in organizations like the IMF and GATT, which were the preferred policy instruments of the relevant governments. On one question—tariff preferences for less-developed countries—pressure from UNCTAD's forum was partly responsible for a change in group B policies, the depth of which remains to be seen. But, at best, the most influential actors from this perspective see UNCTAD as a necessary evil; and until domestic incentives impel them to pay more heed to it, there will be a discrepancy between decisions and influence in UNCTAD in the narrow sense—an international organization defined as a secretariat and associated conference diplomacy—and UNCTAD in the broad sense—an international organization defined as the total set of actors affecting its goals. [31]

Judging the impact of an international organization (narrowly defined) upon its environment raises the question of what is the relevant period over which to judge the impact. Prebisch's aim was to change UNCTAD's environment over a longer period. In Prebisch's view this was already occurring by the end of his five-year service as secretary-general. It did not matter that the developed countries at New Delhi had agreed to a resolution creating a formula for granting more aid at the same time that actual aid allocations were declining or that a preference scheme might lead to quotas and licenses, which could have both a discriminating and a hegemonial effect. [32]

From this view of the world, the gap between international organization in word and reality is only a temporary problem. The role of resolutions, including one-sided ones, is an ideological one: to establish principles and set the direction of pressure. Eventually governments will respond. As evidence, Prebisch cited the incorporation of what had been heretical ECLA ideas of the 1950s in the Kennedy administration's Alliance for Progress in the 1960s. He might also have pointed to the inclusion of a number of UNCTAD ideas in the celebrated Pearson Report submitted to the IBRD in 1969.

In Prebisch's view, one must approach the question of the role of international organization from a dynamic rather than from a static perspective. Essentially, an effective international economic organization goes through three major stages. The first is the stage of setting forth and dramatizing the problem. During this stage an intellectually independent secretariat must separate itself from powerful governments and put forward a common problem in a new light. Although such action may (and, in fact, did) lead to charges of bias, that is the price that must be paid if one makes life uncomfortable for established bureaucracies. In Prebisch's view the charge of bias was a temporary mistake in perception by the developed countries. Governments have a common interest in the development problem, and the UNCTAD secretariat was no more biased in suggesting measures that would use developed countries' resources as a remedy than WHO is biased in suggesting that developed countries' resources be used to attack the problem of malaria in the tropics. In any case, the secretariat must play an independent and intellectual role in stating what is desirable in the first stage.

During the second stage, the secretariat must withdraw and allow government discussions with their attendant controversy and confrontation (the conference diplomacy) to take the center of the stage. By and large, this was the stage of UNCTAD at the end of the Prebisch era.

Only in the third stage, when there are signs of willingness to compromise, does the secretariat reenter in an active role—as a broker now rather than a prophet, stressing the possible rather than the ideal and patiently exploring with each side the possibilities of a negotiated solution. By the end of Prebisch's tenure the one piece of evidence hinting that UNCTAD might be entering this stage was the successful negotiation of a sugar agreement in 1968, in the course of which the secretariat dropped its ideal scheme and helped establish an imperfect compromise. According to Prebisch the two roles of a secretariat are not incompatible if it is understood that they occur at different stages and if a secretariat maintains enough flexibility to perform well in both stages.

Ideological resolutions can also help to establish norms for the young people in rich countries who are becoming disenchanted with affluence and can ultimately become a domestic constituency for UNCTAD. In his farewell address at the eighth Trade Board, Prebisch predicted to the government delegates that such bodies of opinion would eventually appear in their countries. If the environment should change in that way, many of the

UNCTAD secretariat studies and Group of 77 resolutions that had been regarded as unacceptable and that offended even those group B officials who were most sympathetic to the development program would eventually become "negotiable reality."[33]

At the end of the Prebisch era, however, a change in environment of this kind, one that might make governments ready for the meaningful compromises necessary for stage three, had not yet occurred, and the UNCTAD pressure strategy was beginning to yield diminishing returns. If, as a secretariat official said, the task of UNCTAD was "to shell the beaches," the result for many group B officials was, in the words of one, to leave them "shell-shocked." In consequence, a distrust of UNCTAD as an organization developed that may keep it from having a more concrete negotiating role. One group B official put it this way: "We will agree to some things in GATT that we would not agree to in UNCTAD, because we know where we stand there."

Those in the secretariat who were less sanguine about the future direction and stages of change argued that the UNCTAD secretariat should not let itself become identified so closely with the less-developed countries. Rather, it should—like the EEC commission—represent the current structure of power as accurately as possible and concentrate on finding solutions within the range currently available, that is, go directly to stage three. Others argued that it was too late for this role, but that UNCTAD's secretariat should encompass a broader range of ideas about development in order to generate a livelier intellectual climate. In other words it should stay in stage one but incorporate a broader set of ideas.

In any case the situation at the end of the Prebisch era was marked by a decline in the level of representation at UNCTAD meetings and a continued hardness in the positions taken by the major group B countries. In the general political environment, the continued détente between the super-powers and the disillusionment with the difficult problems of development kept on dimming the political importance of the Third World, an idea that had given UNCTAD much of its earlier political impact. In the specific environment of trade and aid, there seemed no reason to believe that the downward trends either in the share of trade or in the absolute magnitudes of aid would soon be reversed.

Faced with this situation, some observers felt that Prebisch's successor had no choice but to preside in an orderly fashion over UNCTAD while it declined into general irrelevance. Others, however, felt that UNCTAD was indeed entering Prebisch's stage three. In their view many issues that had only been discussed in general terms during the first five years would come to fruition during the second five years, even if they were not always negotiated in detail in UNCTAD.

Perez-Guerrero is not a prophetic type like Prebisch. He has brought a new style of leadership to the post of secretary-general that is more closely attuned to bargaining over concrete issues than dramatically asserting new norms. He travels less to national capitals and United Nations headquarters than Prebisch did, and he spends more time with his staff and with delegates. One of his changes was to institute regular meetings of directors and to try to break down the separation of divisions into isolated fiefdoms. He has also tried to enliven the intellectual atmosphere of the secretariat at lower levels. In contrast to Prebisch, he is more interested in matters of detail than in global strategies. At the same time, among the member states, one begins to see signs of a loosening in the rigidity of group discipline.

In short, the new style fits in with Prebisch's view that after he left UNCTAD its future lay in implementing the ideas generated earlier during the pressure group stage. Whether UNCTAD can (or in the view of some, should) become less of a populist pressure group and adapt to a new role remains to be seen. And whether Prebisch's strategy will pay off in the long run, proving UNCTAD to be one of those rare international organizations that has contributed to re-creating its own environment, will be one of the intriguing questions of the next decade. UNCTAD under Prebisch was a pressure group, with all the merits and faults those words imply. UNCTAD under Prebisch was also the symbol of some men's concern about the enormous challenge of development, their refusal to accept the existing patterns of bureaucratic and international norms, and their attempt to use international organization in an innovative way.

11 The Anatomy of Influence

Robert W. Cox and Harold K. Jacobson

How are decisions taken in international organizations and who most influences these decisions? These are the central questions of this book. Its purpose is, however, not limited to providing more exact and precise answers on these two points but includes an attempt to understand their wider implications. Rather than to produce a politician's manual on how to get results through international organizations, the aim has been to know more about how the structure of influence in present international organizations may determine their future roles and how their decisions are likely to affect the distribution of wealth and power in the international system. We want to know whether and how international organizations may strengthen the weak and temper the strong; whether they will support the status quo or work for redistribution of the world's wealth; whether they will reinforce or undermine the institution of the nation-state. The question "Who governs?" directly implies the question "Who is likely to benefit most and who least from a particular form of government?" This study stops short of analyzing the actual consequences of action through international organizations, but it is intended to throw light upon the implications for the international system of the structure of influence in international organizations.

Initially, we should recall the limits of our data. Each of the eight agencies treated here exhibits a distinct pattern of influence. These eight are a reasonably representative sample of economic and social agencies having world scope within the United Nations family of organizations. They are not, however, necessarily representative either of the United Nations itself or of the many organizations of more limited membership, regional or other. It will be for other studies to ascertain how far our findings are relevant to these other organizations.

Methodological weaknesses must also be acknowledged. Although it is possible to define influence in reasonably precise terms and even to illustrate its components with mathematical symbols and equations, no method has yet been discovered for satisfactorily giving quantitative expression to influence in the context of international organization. Who is more influential, an initiator, a vetoer, a broker, or a controller? How can one compare the influence of a government representative who is particularly active with respect to symbolic decisions with that of an international official whose activities are confined to the programmatic and operational decisions? Such comparisons, of course, have been made implicitly and even explicitly in the preceding chapters and will be made here; but they are at best inexact approximations that depend greatly upon the judgment of the analyst, and they must be made with caution and subtlety. Our conclusions cannot therefore be quantitative, though we seek to use quantitative measurements whenever they are possible and relevant in order to inform and control qualitative judgments.

The purpose of a comparative study is to enable one to go beyond the particular situation of each case and to see whether there are recurrent patterns having similar structures and processes of influence. If such recurrent patterns could be analyzed so as to describe types of influence structures, each displaying characteristic features of certain key variables and typical interrelationships among these variables, such a typology could be useful both for classifying international organizations and for making short-range predictions of what their implications—whether stabilizing or de-stabilizing—are likely to be for the international system.

Such ambitious hopes can only be realized to a very limited extent in our present state of knowledge. The methods used in the case studies reported here are various, and none yield conclusive results. Modesty with regard to results is a becoming correlative of ambition with regard to goals in an initial inquiry. Our conclusions as developed below are tentative hypotheses. They seem to be valid within the limitations of data and methods just mentioned, but they are not proven theorems of general application.

The first step in constructing models of influence in international organization is to sift carefully the findings from the discrete analyses of each of the eight agencies. This involves returning to the framework outlined in the first chapter and attempting to answer the questions raised there.

Functions, Structure, and Evolution

As in the individual chapters, a consideration of the organizations' functions, structure, and evolution is a necessary prelude to the analysis of processes and influence.

It has already been pointed out that all of the eight organizations have relatively specific mandates. All of them also perform both forum and service functions, but the mixture of these functions differs among the agencies. One way of viewing these mixtures is to examine the proportion of funds each agency expends on the two types of functions. Interpreting 1967 budgetary figures, the eight agencies seem to fall into four groups. More than 90 percent of the expenditures of IMF and WHO appear to be allocated to service functions. UNESCO and ILO appear to allocate from 65 percent to 85 percent of their expenditures to service functions. ITU and IAEA seem to divide their expenditures about equally between the two types of functions, with IAEA putting slightly more emphasis on forum functions. GATT and UNCTAD, in contrast to the other organizations, perform principally forum functions. Neither allocates more than 10 percent of its funds to service activities.

The rank orders of the eight agencies according to the proportion of their expenditures devoted to service activities and according to the size of their staffs and budgets correspond closely (see table 11.1). In general, the higher the proportion of an agency's expenditures devoted to service activities, the larger its staff and budget. The notable exception to this rule is IMF. IMF's case can be explained by the fact that its service activities are different from those of WHO, ILO, and UNESCO, which relate principally to technical assistance. IMF provides technical assistance, but its principal service activities are more like banking functions and apparently demand less staff and a smaller administrative budget. Furthermore, the administrative budget of the IMF cannot, strictly speaking, be compared with the regular budgets of the other agencies.

Table 11.1

Comparative Rank Order of Agencies by Service Activities
and Size of Staff and Budget, 1967

Proportion of Expenditures Devoted to Service Activities		*Size of Staff*		*Size of Budget*	
Rank Order		*Rank Order*	*Total*	*Rank Order*	*Total[a] (in millions of dollars)*
1	IMF	1 WHO	4,367	1 WHO	83
2	WHO	2 UNESCO	3,600	2 UNESCO	54
3	UNESCO	3 ILO	2,500	3 ILO	38
4	ILO	4 IAEA	1,127	4 IMF	22
5	ITU	5 IMF	921	5 ITU	12
6	IAEA	6 ITU	502	6 IAEA	11
7	UNCTAD	7 UNCTAD	454	7 UNCTAD	7
8	GATT	8 GATT	201	8 GATT	3

Sources; Preceding chapters or *Yearbook of the United Nations 1967* (New York: United Nations, 1968).

[a]Includes UNDP and Voluntary Funds, but not UNICEF. Rounded to the nearest million.

Although UNCTAD is very much like GATT in the proportion of its expenditures devoted to service activities, it has a much larger staff and a correspondingly larger budget. This difference should merely be noted now; an explanation will be sought later.

In a certain sense the differences among the agencies portrayed in table 11.1 represent structural differences. Size as measured by staff and budget is an important aspect of structure. There are also other structural differences among the agencies. One important difference relates to membership. Figure 11.1 shows the total membership of the eight agencies for 1950, 1958, and 1967 and also divides the member states of each agency into the three categories of Western, Socialist, and Other. Table 11.2 presents these data in percentages. Communist China, East Germany, North Korea, and North Vietnam did not belong to any of the organizations treated here. Putting these exclusions aside, over the entire period ITU and WHO have most consistently approached universality. In 1950 they were the only two of the six existing agencies to include the USSR; and the year previously the USSR ceased participation in WHO. In 1967 five of the agencies—UNCTAD, ITU, WHO, UNESCO, and ILO—were much more universal in membership than the other three. With respect to these other three, some poorer states were

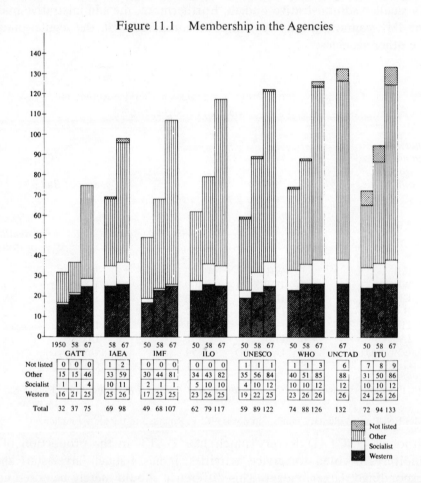

Figure 11.1   Membership in the Agencies

	1950	58	67	58	67	50	58	67	50	58	67	50	58	67	50	58	67	67	50	58	67
	GATT			IAEA		IMF			ILO			UNESCO			WHO			UNCTAD	ITU		
Not listed	0	0	0	1	2	0	0	0	0	0	0	1	1	1	1	1	3	6	7	8	9
Other	15	15	46	33	59	30	44	81	34	43	82	35	56	84	40	51	85	88	31	50	86
Socialist	1	1	4	10	11	2	1	1	5	10	10	4	10	12	10	10	12	12	10	10	12
Western	16	21	25	25	26	17	23	25	23	26	25	19	22	25	23	26	26	26	24	26	26
Total	32	37	75	69	98	49	68	107	62	79	117	59	89	122	74	88	126	132	72	94	133

Not listed
Other
Socialist
Western

not members of IMF, as is reflected in the smaller proportion of member states in the Other category, which is largely made up of less-developed states; and several Socialist states also were not members. IAEA included several Socialist states, but many poorer countries chose not to join. GATT, with the smallest membership of all the agencies, has only a few Socialist members and includes the fewest poorer states. Interestingly, GATT is the only one of the agencies to have a membership fee; that is, a state that joins GATT must extend tariff concessions to the contracting parties. Of course, it will also receive tariff concessions from the members of GATT at this time. The jump in membership for all of the agencies between 1958 and 1967 is principally the consequence of the onrush of independence in Africa, which started in 1960. As can be seen from figure 11.1, all of the agencies have shown a substantial increase in the proportion of their membership falling in the Other category.

Other structural differences among the agencies can be listed quickly. The IMF is the only one of the organizations to have weighted voting; all of the others operate on a one-state, one-vote basis. All of the agencies have at least three principal components: an assembly or conference, which meets periodically and includes all members; a smaller council or board, which meets more frequently; and a secretariat. Four of the agencies—ILO, IAEA, IMF, and UNCTAD—have constitutional provisions that specify certain aspects of the composition of their smaller councils. In the first three, the purpose is to ensure that those states with resources that are important to the agency will be represented; in the last, UNCTAD, the purpose is to ensure a composition in which the significant interests are carefully balanced. ILO particularly, and ITU also, provide for considerable direct participation by representatives of private associations. WHO has the most extensively developed system of regionalism of the agencies. UNESCO is the only agency to have national commissions, which in the terminology employed in this study, represent an attempt to organize country subsystems in a particular manner by giving them a formal structure that its creators thought would skew influence in ways favorable to the organization. From its earliest period ILO attempted similarly to organize its country subsystems through the appointment of national correspondents who were to be the director-general's ambassadors to the relevant trade union, employer, and governmental actors within the country subsystem.

The budgets of the organizations have grown concomitantly with the growth in their membership; and, as with the membership, the most substantial increases have occurred since about 1960. Budget growth has been related to growth in service functions. The WHO, among the eight agencies, has had the most substantial increase in its budget, and it has always stressed service functions. As the budgets of several of the other organizations have grown, they have also come to place increasing emphasis on such activities. This is particularly true of ITU and ILO. Before World War II, these two organizations, the only ones among the eight to have been created prior to that war, were both primarily engaged in forum activities; but this began to change after 1950, and by 1967 both were deeply involved in service activities. The other agencies have also shifted their emphases in varying degrees in the direction of service. The shift has been accompanied by an increasing reliance on funds other than regular budget funds, principally those allocated from the United Nations Development Program. By 1967, as figure 11.2 shows, UNESCO, ITU, and ILO were heavily

Table 11.2

Data from Figure 11.1 in Percentages

	GATT		IAEA		IMF		ILO	
	Number	%	Number	%	Number	%	Number	%
Not Listed								
1950	0	0	–	–	0	0	0	0
1958	0	0	1	1.5	0	0	0	0
1967	0	0	2	2.0	0	0	0	0
Other								
1950	15	46.9	–	–	30	61.2	34	54.8
1958	15	40.5	33	47.8	44	64.7	43	54.4
1967	46	61.3	59	60.2	81	75.7	82	70.1
Socialist								
1950	1	3.1	–	–	2	4.1	5	8.1
1958	1	2.7	10	14.5	1	1.5	10	12.7
1967	4	5.3	11	11.2	1	0.9	10	8.5
Western								
1950	16	50.0	–	–	17	34.7	23	37.1
1958	21	56.8	25	36.2	23	33.8	26	32.9
1967	25	33.3	26	26.5	25	23.4	25	21.4
Total								
1950	32	100.0	–	–	49	100.0	62	100.0
1958	37	100.0	69	100.0	68	100.0	79	100.0
1967	75	100.0	98	99.9	107	100.0	117	100.0

dependent on UNDP funds. WHO and IAEA also relied on UNDP funds, although to a lesser extent. In contrast, IMF, GATT, and UNCTAD received no money from the UNDP in that year.

The staff of each agency has also grown, and the size of an international organization's budget and staff may be factors conditioning its growth potential. A very limited organization seems to lack the reserves of personnel and funds to take initiatives for expansion. Beyond a certain threshold, however, planning of growth becomes possible. A large bureaucracy enjoying long-term contracts and having support from a variety of national interests not only has a built-in momentum for survival, but its very size allows a margin of resources to be devoted to planning and stimulating outside support for expansion. The number of cases studied here, however, is too small to determine either whether there is such a threshold marking the point where international organizations have a built-in expansive capability or—if it exists—what that threshold may be.

Table 11.2 (Continued)

UNESCO		WHO		UNCTAD		ITU	
Number	*%*	*Number*	*%*	*Number*	*%*	*Number*	*%*
1	1.7	1	1.4	–	–	7	9.7
1	1.1	1	1.1	–	–	8	8.5
1	0.8	3	2.4	6	4.5	9	6.8
35	59.3	40	54.1	–	–	31	43.0
56	62.9	51	58.0	–	–	50	53.1
84	68.9	85	67.5	88	66.7	86	64.7
4	6.8	10	13.5	–	–	10	13.8
10	11.2	10	11.4	–	–	10	10.6
12	9.8	12	9.5	12	9.1	12	9.0
19	32.2	23	31.1	–	–	24	33.3
22	24.7	26	29.5	–	–	26	27.6
25	20.5	26	20.6	26	19.7	26	19.5
59	100.0	74	100.1	–	–	72	99.9
89	99.9	88	100.0	–	–	94	100.0
122	100.0	126	100.0	132	100.0	133	100.0

Decision Making: A Taxonomical Analysis

The taxonomy of decisions outlined in the first chapter was developed to facilitate exploration of whether patterns of decision making and influence differed with different types of decisions. That question has been probed in the analyses of the individual agencies. But at this stage a second question can also be asked; that is, whether the same or different processes prevail for the same types of decision. As the patterns in the eight organizations are compared, another issue also must be considered: the importance of each type of decision within each of the various agencies. As used here, importance is an aggregate concept including frequency of occurrence, salience to the participants, and consequences. It is possible that differences among various agencies in their patterns of decision making and influence for particular types of decisions may be related to the comparative importance that these classes of decision have for the agencies.

Representational Decisions

Representational decisions are relatively important in all of the organizations, but they have generally been least important in IMF and
GATT—significantly, the two agencies that include neither the Soviet Union

Figure 11.2   Expenditures of Agencies and Share of Funds Provided by UNDP

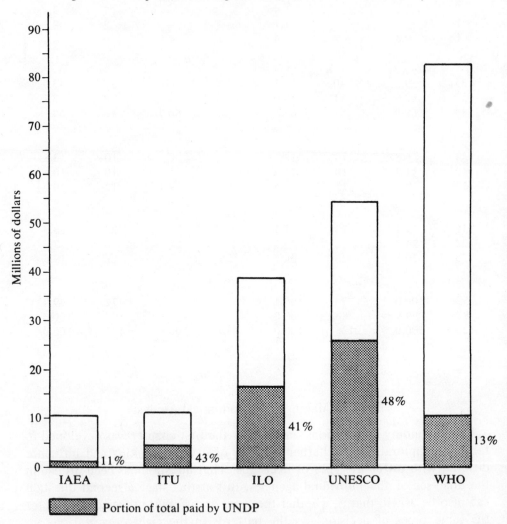

SOURCE: United Nations, *A Study of the Capacity of the United Nations Development System*
(Geneva: United Nations, 1969), vol. 2, table 11.

nor several other socialist states. In addition, in IMF the weighted voting
system predetermines what in other agencies would be the outcome of
certain representational decisions. It is noteworthy in this connection that
for a long period representational decisions were of little or no importance in
IMF. Then a major question was raised concerning the voting power of

various states in certain decisions involving procedures for issuing Special Drawing Rights, the intention being to secure a blocking veto for the combined EEC countries. The controversy was related to major changes in the Fund's environment.

In all of the agencies, representational decisions are primarily the province of government representatives, who influence these decisions in all four ways: as initiators, vetoers, brokers, and controllers. Only in ILO are representatives of private associations actively involved, and there, like governmental representatives, they too exercise influence in all four ways. Generally, executive heads influence significantly only those representational decisions that concern appointments of high secretariat officials; in these decisions they are often initiators and can always be vetoers. In other representational issues, the executive head in ILO has occasionally intervened, principally to serve as a broker in the highly contentious issues that grew out of the Soviet Union's resumption of membership in 1954. In this instance the director-general saw in the issues a threat to the nature and perhaps even the life of the organization, and for that reason he intervened. GATT is the only agency whose executive head plays an important role in representational decisions as a matter of course, and this peculiarity seems to be related to the unimportance of such decisions in that agency.

Bargaining techniques generally prevail in determining the outcome of representational decisions. In ILO, however, procedures that seemingly called for analytical techniques were followed in an attempt to solve some of the representation issues involving employer delegates from socialist states. The final decisions were actually the result of negotiating a consensus, in other words arrived at by bargaining, but the analytical procedures helped to make the result acceptable to important actors.

The selection of the executive head is a critical representational decision in all eight of the organizations. Four different formal procedures are followed: (1) In ITU until 1959 and in IMF, ILO, IAEA, and GATT[1] the executive head is appointed by the council or smaller body; (2) in WHO and UNESCO the executive head is nominated by the council but elected by the assembly; (3) in ITU since 1959 the executive head is elected by the assembly; and (4) in UNCTAD the executive head is appointed by the secretary-general of the United Nations.

These formal differences have an effect both in determining who has influence in making the decisions and on the outcomes. The first method and, to a lesser extent, the second skew influence in favor of those states most likely to be represented on the councils. As was indicated earlier, it is significant that three of the agencies using the first procedure, IMF, ILO, and IAEA, also have constitutional provisions by which the major states in the international system that are members of the agency are ensured a place on the council. Except in ITU, executive heads chosen by the first procedure have always been nationals of Western states. The other three procedures have resulted in the choice of nationals from Western and Other, but not Socialist, states. The analysis of the individual agencies revealed that in IAEA, IMF, and GATT the executive head must be acceptable to the United States; in other words the United States government has an effective veto. In IMF and GATT the European Economic Community may also approximate such influence in the 1970s. The secretary-general of the United Nations is a vetoer as well as an initiator in the case of UNCTAD. In no other agency are there vetoers, although some actors would be powerful controllers.

Symbolic Decisions

Symbolic decisions are very important for ILO and UNCTAD but have little importance for all of the other organizations. Like representational decisions, they are of least importance for IMF and GATT, the two agencies to which the USSR does not belong. The importance of symbolic issues for UNCTAD is the least complicated to explain. This agency's origins can be traced to demands by poorer countries for changes in the international system, which were calculated to hasten their development. Such demands can be articulated most forcefully in the General Assembly of the United Nations, where representatives of poor states predominate. Given the nature of the international system, the United Nations cannot authoritatively legislate change, but it can urge and demand change. UNCTAD has been labeled a populist pressure group, and as such its principal functions have been symbolic. Through it poor countries use symbolic issues and symbolic decisions as means of mobilizing opinion in favor of redistributionist policies, for lack of alternative means which could give real effect to such policies.

The ILO's preoccupation with symbolic issues is to be explained by the fact that the status and role of organized labor and of employers lie at the heart of the ideological differences between Western, Socialist, and Third World concepts of how economic and social welfare activities should be organized. The ILO was thought by many workers' representatives in the past to have its raison d'être in its role as international spokesman for the interests of labor. They looked upon the ILO as their organization and identified it with the independence of trade unions. If Western employers could not identify their interests so closely with the ILO, they saw it as an organization that at least conferred a kind of moral sanction upon employers' independence and free labor-management relations. But the behavior of Soviet representatives and of some developing countries' representatives following the mid-1950s called this view into question. Symbolic issues became important as a means by which these new members could acquire recognition for new goals and old members could reiterate old and continuing goals. The struggle for the ideological identity of the ILO was fought through symbolic issues.

Symbolic decisions in the international organizations reviewed here were more frequent during two periods following World War II. The first period was in the mid-1950s, when the Soviet Union joined or resumed membership in ILO, UNESCO, and WHO. The second was in the early 1960s, when several newly independent states, mainly in Africa, joined the agencies then in existence. It was in this period that UNCTAD was created. During each of these two periods the relationship of the organizations to their environments underwent a change. New demands were raised in the organization, and eventually some new programs were adopted. The symbolic decisions had a great deal to do with identifying the demands that would be met and the ways of meeting them.

Like representational decisions, symbolic decisions tend to be principally the province of government representatives; in ILO representatives of private associations also play an active part. Executive heads and even segments of bureaucracies occasionally become involved in symbolic decisions. Usually both serve as brokers and attempt to moderate tensions.

In both ILO and UNCTAD, though, where symbolic decisions are important components of the organizations' activities, the executive heads have been more than just occasionally involved. Raul Prebisch, through his writings and reports, supplied the intellectual content of many of UNCTAD's symbolic resolutions. He also played a crucial part as a broker in securing the adoption of these resolutions. In general the UNCTAD bureaucracy has also seemed to be aligned with the majority, or the 77, on symbolic issues. The substantial size of the UNCTAD bureaucracy can largely be explained by the fact that the bureaucracy plays an important role in the forum activities and particularly in the symbolic decisions of the organization. David Morse in the ILO followed a policy that was the reverse of Prebisch's. He made use of symbols with a view to moderating symbolic politics, appealing simultaneously to universality and to tripartism with its implications of trade union autonomy. Morse tried consistently to play down the East-West symbolic issues that were usually raised, many times in the form of draft conference resolutions, by those challenging the traditional conception of the ILO's role in the world. Acutely aware of the ideological character of the issues, he urged that politics should not intrude into a technical body.

Symbolic decisions are almost invariably the result of bargaining rather than analytical procedures. To render issues less explosive symbolic demands sometimes are turned into requests for analytical studies, as in WHO; subsequent decisions must then have a certain analytical component. But in the initial decision analytical techniques are hardly ever introduced.

Boundary Decisions

Boundary decisions can stem from several different circumstances. Three in particular have occasioned boundary decisions in the organizations considered here. First, two organizations can have overlapping mandates.

This frequently occurs when one organization has quasi-universal membership and the other limited membership, but it can also occur between organizations that have memberships constituted on a similar basis. Working Party Three of the Organization for Economic Cooperation and Development and the Group of Ten work in the same field as the IMF, and both GATT and UNCTAD have broad mandates with respect to international trade. WHO and IAEA each have valid bases for undertaking programs in radiation, and a long list of similarly overlapping areas of jurisdiction could easily be compiled. Second, organizations working in different fields can compete with one another for limited funds. For example, seven of the eight organizations in this study are recipients of allocations from UNDP. Since in any given fiscal period UNDP's funds are a fixed quantity, if the allocation for one agency is to be increased, that for another must be reduced. Third, boundary problems arise when organizations collaborate in the execution of work. GATT and UNCTAD, for example, share responsibilities for the operation of the International Trade Center.

Boundary issues have arisen with respect to all eight of the agencies included in this study. Because of the different circumstances that might give rise to boundary decisions, the frequency of such decisions does not necessarily correspond with the extent to which they involve conflict. Another point to be noted is that procedures in settling boundary decisions frequently involve actors from political systems outside the organizations, and sometimes these decisions are even settled exclusively by such actors. The extent of conflict inherent in an issue and the extent of involvement of external actors in boundary decisions appear to be related.

In general, executive heads tend to be the most active with respect to boundary issues. Probably more than any other actors, they are professionally concerned and identified with the survival and growth of their organizations. Furthermore, the executive head of an international organization will generally be best informed about boundary problems. In this sense his position is like that of a president or prime minister of a state with respect to foreign policy. The same reasons that impel executive heads to play a leading part in boundary issues also push the bureaucracies of international organizations and segments of the bureaucracy toward active roles. Frequently government representatives also play a role.

Boundary decisions relating to the definition of jurisdictions were particularly frequent in those of the organizations that existed during the late 1940s and early 1950s and were again frequent in the early 1960s. The first period coincided with the establishment of the United Nations system; and indeed UNESCO, WHO, IMF, and GATT were themselves created during this period. At that time all of the agencies fought to defend their spheres of competence as they defined them. Actors in ITU wanted to ensure that the United Nations would not usurp some of the union's traditional functions. Several actors in ILO wanted to achieve this and more; they sought special standing for the organization within the United Nations system. WHO had the problem of making already established organizations part of its structure. The other agencies then in existence sought to stake out their jurisdictional claims. In all instances a coalition of international and governmental officials was readily formed and dominated the decision making. Initiatives were taken by both groups. Vetoers were generally external actors, as when the Soviet Union blocked the special status within the United Nations system that ILO was seeking. After a few years, the issues tended to become less intense, government representatives became less active, and the predominant roles in boundary decisions reverted to executive heads and members of the international bureaucracies.

Boundary issues stemming from competition for limited resources occasioned a number of controversies and decisions in the 1950s, the period that produced the UN system's extra-budgetary funds, on which several of the agencies soon became heavily dependent. When the Expanded Program of Technical Assistance was first created, the participating specialized agencies were each allocated a certain share of the funds. Only three of the eight agencies considered here—ILO, UNESCO, and WHO—were included in that original allocation. Their shares were respectively 11 percent, 14 percent, and 22 percent. Although by 1967 the basis for the allocation of funds in the United Nations Development Program had changed, giving more emphasis to the demands of country development programs and more central authority to the UNDP, in that year the three agencies received 10 percent, 18.7 percent, and 6.1 percent of the available funds.[2] Thus, except for WHO, the allocations have been relatively stable. This is also true for the agencies that joined the program later—ITU, IAEA, GATT, and UNCTAD. Even for WHO, the decline in its allocation has been gradual.

The WHO case is interesting, for it reflects a strong bias within the organization, articulated particularly by the executive head and the bureaucracy, favoring reliance for program activities on internally rather than externally controlled funds. The policy of the United States and other major Western contributors has been that technical assistance funds should be voluntary contributions channeled to the agencies through a central point—the UNDP. These countries have thus also opposed any tendency toward increasing credits for technical assistance in the regular budgets of functional agencies. That WHO was able to develop its operational activities despite these general policies was a triumph of functionalist politics, which seems to have been attributable both to the determined leadership of the WHO bureaucracy and to support from the medical profession and national public health authorities.

The stability of the allocations made through the UNDP to most of the participating agencies suggests that the international officials from these various agencies were able to agree broadly about the sharing of resources. "Dividing the pie" became a less difficult issue in the 1960s than it had been in the preceding decade. One reason why this could be so is that in the 1960s the resources available to the United Nations Development Program increased enormously. In 1967 the expenditures under the UNDP were $161.3 million; in 1960 expenditures under comparable programs had been only $35.5 million.[3] Dividing an expanding pie is a much less contentious task than dividing one of fixed size.

In the final period, boundary issues relating to jurisdictions became acute again. This change was related to the entrance of a large number of new states into the United Nations system. Two different developments occurred. Representatives of new and poor states coalesced to press for the establishment of new organizations with mandates that would overlap those of ILO and GATT but have different formal structures, the hope of these representatives being that the new structures would be more responsive to the demands of their countries. ILO and GATT each responded initially by reordering their programs slightly, then by being intensely concerned about the mandate of their rival organizations, and finally by working out a division of functions with their erstwhile competitors, the United Nations Industrial Development Organization and the United Nations Conference on Trade and Development. In each case the executive head took the initiative and set the tone for the organization's response. The issues were not, however, such as could be settled between executive heads. Government representatives both in the agencies and in the General Assembly of the United Nations became involved, often as a result of executive heads' seeking support. To some extent the issue between rival international agencies was pushed back to the national level. Accommodation followed a demonstration of support for both rivals through their respective country subsystems.

The second development concerned particularly the IMF. In the early 1960s—for a variety of reasons, some related to the expanded membership in the organization—the richer states began to show a propensity to meet in smaller bodies to settle their monetary affairs, namely in the Group of Ten and Working Party Three of OECD. In this instance the executive head's strategy was to take steps to ensure that representatives of the Fund would be included in these smaller bodies and thus to maintain a link with them that was both formal and meaningful.

Boundary decisions stemming from day-to-day service activities are almost exclusively the province of members of the international bureaucracies. Occasionally, in cases where tensions are high or important consequences are at stake, executive heads and perhaps even governmental representatives will intervene. When they do, it is often more as vetoers, controllers, and brokers than as initiators. A great number of routine boundary decisions are taken in UNESCO, ILO, and WHO and a somewhat smaller number in IAEA. There seems to have been an interagency process of learning collaboration. As already suggested, the resources available through UNDP provided an incentive to interagency agreement; and the prospect of governmental intervention in case of open conflict between agencies was an incentive to limit interagency rivalry.

In the relationship between the level of conflict and the involvement of actors external to the participant subsystem mentioned earlier, three patterns of boundary decision making emerge. The first takes the form of a cartel of executive heads or representatives of international bureaucracies acting for them. This is a low-conflict pattern in which competition is kept within the family. Competition exists among the representatives of international bureaucracies but is not allowed to become visible to other actors. Although the relations among these international bureaucratic actors essentially involve bargaining, analytical arguments are an important element in decision making, that is, arguments based upon agreed jurisdiction, acquired capabilities, and budgetary history. This pattern of decision making probably depends upon a continuing if not increasing flow of resources. It is adequate for allocations of resources in a situation in which no major changes in relations between organizations occur, but would probably not do if any significant change did take place.[4]

A second pattern is one of intergovernmental decision making. Sometimes this takes place entirely outside of the formal structure of an international organization but has important consequences for its mandate, consequences that become apparent within the organization as programmatic decisions. Examples are the implications of the nuclear Non-Proliferation Treaty for IAEA and the negotiation of agreement about Special Drawing Rights among the Group of Ten, an agreement subsequently given effect through the IMF. Whenever the boundaries of international organizations are thus determined externally, it is because the stakes are important to the policies of the major states. Interorganizational conflict does not arise in such cases because the decision is taken out of the hands of international bureaucracies. At best, they can keep themselves informed and show readiness to respond.

The third pattern is a mixture of the first two, in which both executive heads and government representatives are involved. When it occurs, there is a higher evident level of interorganizational conflict than appears in the first two patterns. Executive heads may take the initiative to bring government representatives into the issue in order to be able to demonstrate support for their organization's position or claims. This is a crisis pattern of decision making that is likely to become transformed into one of the first two patterns. Executive heads will gamble that after a show of their organizational strength they may revert to the cartel type of decision making, their power position clarified. It is conceivable, although we find no illustrative case among the limited number studied, that an issue involving such conflict might be taken out of the hands of the executive heads and a decision might be imposed by governments. Awareness of this possibility has undoubtedly moderated the use by executive heads of an appeal for constituent support in interagency disputes.

Programmatic Decisions

Programmatic decisions tend to be of two types, although both involve the strategic allocation of the organization's resources among different types and fields of activity. Some have consequences that would make them appear retrospectively as turning points in the evolution of an organization. Examples of such decisions would be: those in which several of the agencies decided to participate in the United Nations Expanded Program of Technical Assistance; WHO's decision to embark on a worldwide program of malaria eradication; the decision that caused IAEA to become the chief inspecting instrument under the Non-Proliferation Treaty; and the initiation of new rounds of tariff cutting through GATT. The second type of programmatic decision also manifests itself in incremental change rather than as a turning point. These decisions concern shifts in emphasis among programs. Examples here would be UNESCO's decisions about the proportion of its resources it should devote to promoting of education, as opposed to communications or the social and human sciences, and similar decisions in ILO involving the development of human resources, as opposed to industrial relations. Cumulatively, over a certain time, such decisions may be as important in their consequences for program change as the more dramatic results of the first type. Programmatic decisions of the first type have occasionally affected all eight of the organizations; those of the second type have been particularly frequent in ILO, UNESCO, and UNCTAD, somewhat less frequent in WHO and IAEA, rare in IMF and ITU, and almost absent in GATT. The frequency of this latter type seems to be inversely related to the specificity of the mandates of the organizations; those with the least specific mandates take them most frequently.

An impressive number of major programmatic initiatives were taken outside of the organizations studied here. The initiative for the Expanded Program of Technical Assistance, which had consequences that substantially altered several of the agencies, was taken in the United Nations; and the origins of the proposal can be traced to the United States, in President Truman's inaugural address of 1949. The Non-Proliferation Treaty was negotiated completely outside of IAEA. Decisions to hold tariff-cutting rounds in GATT have really been dependent upon action by the United States Congress, giving the United States president authority to engage in such negotiations. In most of these circumstances, the executive head of the organization involved is most often limited to reacting; when the opportunity is presented he can seize it eagerly or unenthusiastically; or he may even be able to ignore it. He is then a controller. He may become an initiator when it comes to defining precisely how the organization will implement the new program.

Because their consequences are so serious, programmatic decisions of the first type, whether taken within or outside of agencies, necessarily involve government representatives. Among other things, these representatives are usually the only actors who have the legal authority to take initiatives. And if the programs have substantial costs, only the representatives of major governments are in a position to pledge the necessary funds. More broadly, only government representatives can make the commitments necessary to carry out programs in such matters as tariff reduction or monetary policies. The actual source of initiatives, of course, can be more inclusive. Executive heads, bureaucracies, and eminent individuals can all articulate ideas that could become the basis for new programs. Where the key decisions concerning future tasks of an international organization are taken by a very few governments, the ability of an executive head informally to draw attention to his organization's qualifications for the required task may be critical. This means he must have the political talent, contacts, and acceptability to intervene effectively through the representative subsystems of key countries in their domestic decision making. The managing directors of IMF, some more effectively than others, have all maintained close contact with the financial decision-making authorities of the rich Western powers. David Morse, fresh from Washington in 1948, reoriented the ILO for a role in technical assistance while keeping in close touch with the preparation of President Truman's Point Four proposals.

The executive head plays a much more important part in programmatic decisions of the second type—those that involve the allocation of the agencies' resources among different fields of activity within broad spheres for which assent has already been given. In these decisions, the executive head is frequently the initiator, and representatives of the major states are controllers. In the agencies in which decisions of this type are taken frequently—ILO, UNESCO, and UNCTAD—the executive heads have been very active. In WHO eminent individuals who are members of expert committees may also take part in the initiation of new programs.

The nature of a new program might be the result of analytical processes, but its dimensions, measured by the resources allocated to it, will always be the result of bargaining. Executive heads and segments of bureaucracies are inevitably actors in this bargaining. Government representatives may or may not be. It strengthens the executive head's hand in relation to segments of his bureaucracy if government representatives are not involved. WHO provides an example where the part played by government representatives in decisions of this nature, particularly those relating to the Geneva headquarters, is minimal; and this circumstance constitutes an element of the director-general's strength. In UNESCO, in contrast, government representatives are as a rule much more deeply involved. One consequence has been noted: it is much easier to secure approval for a program in UNESCO than to have a program effectively implemented. Government representatives are reluctant to oppose each other's favorite projects for fear of retaliation against their own, but the executive head and segments of the bureaucracy may effectively determine what gets done about them.

Rule-Creating Decisions

All of the agencies attach some importance to rule creation. The agencies differ significantly, however, in the extent to which rule-creating decisions constitute a significant element of their activities. ITU, ILO, IMF, and GATT take rule-creating decisions frequently; WHO and IAEA somewhat less frequently; and UNESCO and UNCTAD only occasionally. UNESCO's failure to develop rule-creating activities more fully represents a frustration of the early hopes some held for the organization. UNCTAD's failure represents a lack of authority by the organization.

Organizations also differ in the significance of the consequences stemming from their rule-creating decisions. Basically, the eight organizations fall into two categories in this respect. The rule-creating decisions of ITU, IAEA, IMF, and GATT can have substantial economic and political significance; those of ILO, UNESCO, WHO, and UNCTAD are less likely to have such significance.

Patterns of decision making with respect to rule creation vary greatly among the agencies. In one pattern government representatives have the predominant role. In GATT government representatives invariably are the initiators; the executive head is the crucial broker, with representatives of several smaller states also frequently playing this role. The representatives of the United States and, since the mid-1960s, of the European Economic Community generally have the power to be vetoers. Representatives of governments are also the sole initiators with respect to some of ITU's rule-creating decisions, particularly those relating to frequency allocation; but the initiative in recommendations for equipment specifications generally comes from representatives of manufacturing concerns—or, in the terms employed in this study, private associations. Which actors, if any, shall have the power to veto depends on the particular issue. If it concerns telephones, since half of those in use are in the United States, the United States would have this power; but it would not have the same power in all issues.

A second pattern gives members of the international bureaucracy the preeminent role. In the ILO the initiative has generally come from the international officials, with conference delegates from all three groups—workers, employers, and government—serving as controllers. In UNESCO initiatives come from international officials, government representatives, and representatives of nongovernmental organizations; and there is no clear vetoer.

In other organizations, presenting a third pattern, the initiative and major influence over rule creating appears to be a combination of the two above-mentioned patterns: coming in part from government representatives and in part from the international bureaucracy. In the IMF government representatives of the United States and perhaps of the leading EEC countries are vetoers. There is no vetoer in WHO, and initiatives can come from government representatives, international officials, and private individuals. The pattern with respect to initiatives is similar in IAEA, but representatives of both the United States and the Soviet Union can be vetoers. IAEA is somewhat special in that some of the rule-creating decisions that have the greatest import for the agency are made outside of its framework.

The contrast between the first two basic patterns in rule creating is shown pointedly by comparing UNCTAD and GATT, which operate in the same field of trade policy. Whereas in GATT the government representatives have a monopoly of initiative, in UNCTAD the executive head has been perhaps the most important single source of initiatives, with representatives of poorer countries also providing some, often with the advice and assistance of the UNCTAD secretariat. The difference is to be explained by the nature and the consequences of the rule-creating decisions of the two organizations. GATT's rule-creating decisions usually result in legal instruments with substantial consequences; those of UNCTAD more often result in hortatory statements that have less tangible consequences, at least in the short run.

This factor of practical consequences provides, indeed, the only basis for generalizing about the differences observed in decision-making patterns for rule creation. The greater the immediate practical consequences are in material terms, the more the predominant influence is likely to be exercised by the governments—and also by those private associations with a large stake in the outcome. Conversely, the slighter the immediate consequences, the greater the scope for influence by international officials.

The mixture of analytical and bargaining modes of decision making also varies among the different agencies. All rule creation involves bargaining because rules benefit some interests more than others. The issue of whether or not a rule is to be created is always a matter for bargaining. In most cases, too, the nature of the rule offers wide scope for bargaining. The prevalence of analytical methods in determining the content of rules is a function of two variables: the nature of the subject matter and the influence of the international bureaucracy.

Rules about some subjects are constrained by scientific procedures and possibilities. In WHO, preparing a standard course of treatment for the cure of yaws by penicillin is a relatively fixed matter that allows little variation. There may be certain trade-offs between, for instance, the cost of treatment and the probability of definite cure, but these are relatively limited. Similarly, many of the subjects dealt with in ITU involve physical properties that allow little variation in the form of rules concerning them, although in general the possibilities for trade-offs in telecommunications are probably greater than they are in matters of health. The subject matter of IAEA is probably roughly in the same category as that of ITU. The economics applicable to the subject matter dealt with by IMF and GATT, by contrast, has tended to be normative and is less bounded by physical properties, thus leaving substantial scope for bargaining over the content of rules. In general, then, the more the work of an international organization corresponds to a developed field of exact science, the greater the scope for analytical methods in decision making about rule creation.

However, even in fields where scientific expertise is least exact, for example, in issues of labor policy, international bureaucracies will endeavor to use analytical methods, since their influence over decisions largely depends upon the use of these methods. The ILO has, for example, developed procedures for analyzing national laws and practices with reference to proposed new international standards which give international officials considerable initiative as to the way in which proposals are framed. Some of the organizations in which scientific expertise is least relevant, notably ILO and UNESCO, are among those in which international bureaucracies have the greatest influence because the consequences of decisions are less directly important.

Rule-Supervisory Decisions

The eight organizations differ widely in the attention that they give to rule supervision. IMF is more attentive to this issue than any of the others, with GATT, ILO, and IAEA coming close behind, in that order. However, if IAEA's supervisory activities increase, as they may be expected to do with the coming into force of the Non-Proliferation Treaty, IAEA's position will rise, and eventually it may head the list. All four of these agencies were established to perform what were conceived of as important regulatory functions. ITU, WHO, UNCTAD, and UNESCO all devote less attention than the other four to rule supervision, and again the order probably shows roughly the relative amount of attention each organization gives to this issue. It may well be that ITU and WHO are relatively unconcerned with rule supervision because in matters of telecommunications and health it is greatly to the interest of actors to comply with regulations.

In IMF, ILO, and IAEA the secretariats are deeply involved in rule-supervisory functions, especially in detection. They audit government reports; and in IMF and IAEA they can in certain instances conduct direct investigations. GATT is rather different, for the refusals to meet obligations in this area are relatively open. Governments do their own monitoring and bring charges before GATT. If the secretariat is involved, it is simply to assert that particular obligations do in fact apply in the circumstances. Government representatives closely supervise the detection functions performed by IMF's bureaucracy; and they are deeply involved in all four agencies at the verification stage. Formal legal sanctions tend to be the exclusive preserve of government representatives, but in IMF and ILO the international bureaucracies also play a part.

One might think that rule-supervisory decisions relating especially to detection and verification would be arrived at almost exclusively in the analytical mode, but in actual practice in IMF and GATT a good deal of bargaining takes place, not so much because the rules are not clear as because the strict application of them might so gravely affect a member country as to overstrain its loyalty to the system of regulation. Furthermore, attenuating circumstances can usually be advanced to ensure that a de facto infringement of rules will be overlooked. Thus when the British government imposed a 15 percent surcharge on imports in 1964, the GATT machinery took a tolerant view. Instead of risking a breakdown in the system of rule supervision by enforcement in hard cases, actors in international organizations often prefer to tolerate infringement while they use the utmost persuasion to bring the defector gradually back into line. Sometimes, however, strict rule enforcement has symbolic value for actors. Examples are the charges of alleged infringement of trade unions' freedom of association brought against Czechoslovakia and Hungary before the ILO during the 1950s and the allegations of forced labor in Portuguese African territories brought forward in the 1960s. In some cases, like those in the socialist countries mentioned, there is small likelihood that an international organization can exert influence on a domestic situation, and condemnations may be merely symbolic acts. In some other cases the international bureaucracies may be successful in using the analytical techniques of factual inquiry, including on-the-spot missions, as a means of putting pressure upon the country concerned to modify its practices but at the same time keeping it within the system of regulation. In such cases analytical techniques are really instruments of bargaining pressure.

Operational Decisions

The importance of operational decisions for the agencies varies directly with their proportion of service functions. Thus such decisions are most important for IMF and WHO, quite important for ILO and UNESCO, somewhat less important for ITU and IAEA, and least important for GATT and UNCTAD. Since the late 1950s, however, operational decisions have acquired more importance for UNESCO, ILO, and ITU than they had before that time.

Operational decisions are usually bargains struck between international officials and representatives of clients who may or may not have other connections with the organization in question. Both can be initiators and vetoers. With the growth of international technical cooperation, an underlying theme of the relationship between national and international officials has been a jockeying for predominant influence in determining operational decisions. *Country programming* has been seen as a way for the recipient government to gain more effective influence over the aid it receives from international agencies and as a means of shifting the initiative in proposing aid: instead of being in the hands of the international agency interested in enlarging its own program, determining influence would go to the government concerned with the coordination of all developmental activities in its territory. But the competition for influence between national and international officials is complex, and each party may often have some allies in the camp of its rival. Officials in sectoral ministries of recipient countries may support the initiatives of the international agency that corresponds to their ministry (i.e. public health officials will follow that course with WHO; labor ministry officials with ILO, and so on), fearing that centralized decision making in their own government would give other ministries greater power over them. On the other hand, some centrally placed international officials believe that country programming is not only a more rational method for allocating resources for development but also a way to limit the expansive entrepreneurial proclivities of sectoral international agencies.[5] In one sense, the struggle is also about patronage, especially patronage in the form of travel opportunities, which have been multiplied through international fellowships. Fellowships that are the gift of international officials can be a means for them to acquire the support of national officials for expansion of international programs. At least partly from a wish to dispense this patronage for themselves, national governments in less-developed countries have tended to centralize control over the granting of fellowships to their own nationals.

For those agencies that are dependent on UNDP for financing some or all of their operational activities (all of the eight but IMF), UNDP officials are controllers; and UNICEF officials are controllers for WHO and, to a much lesser extent, UNESCO.

Government representatives, particularly those representing donor countries, may intervene in particular instances, and they do so rather frequently in IMF. In fact, in IMF's early years the approval of the United States representative seemed necessary for any operational decision. In other agencies the intervention of government representatives is less frequent, and it usually has the purpose of changing the "rules of the game" rather than merely affecting particular operational decisions. Even without direct intervention by government representatives, international officials will often be guided by their own perceptions of how key governments would react to certain operational decisions; and thus the representatives of these governments have the status of controller conferred upon them. Of course, among the eight agencies considered here the stakes involved in individual operational decisions are greatest in IMF. Furthermore, in IMF, operational decisions frequently have a substantial bearing on rule creation and rule supervision.

Executive heads also sometimes intervene in operational decisions to ensure that these decisions really implement their programmatic goals and to use such decisions to build and maintain the support of clients—to name two important motives.

Obviously, operational decisions cannot be made without bargaining, but analytical techniques are also employed in all of the agencies. They generally set certain broad parameters within which bargaining can occur.

Actors and Their Sources of Influence

What has just been said here about classes of decisions and those who make them needs to be analyzed further in reference to the participant subsystem, that is, those who directly participate in the decisions of the international organizations. We are concerned with identifying sources of influence so as to explain the structure and processes of influence in organizations. Those sources that generally account for the influence of the organizational elite may be different from those that might enable an individual to become influential. We are interested in both and will try to deal with both, but they must be kept distinct.

Representatives of Governments

The representatives of key member states were among the most influential in all of the agencies and, potentially at least, with respect to all types of decisions. The list of such key member states is small. In most instances it probably consists of the United States, the Soviet Union, the United Kingdom, and France, although in some agencies the list would be limited to the first two, and in others it might be expanded to include West Germany and Japan. In any list the representatives of the key states, whoever they might be, were influential. Depending on the policies of their governments and, to a lesser extent, upon their individual inclinations, they might be initiators or vetoers or both, and in all cases they were among the controllers.

For these actors, position is the principal explanatory variable. The assets available to a representative of a key member state are many, and they are cumulative. Not only will his state have high status in the general environment, it will probably also have high status in the specific environment of the organization. This means that his state will be relatively wealthy and will have control of resources vital to the functioning of the organization; these assets carry prestige. His state will also be among the principal contributors to the budgets of all those organizations—most of which depend on annual assessments paid by their members. Furthermore, the resources of his state are such that it can support him with one of the largest delegations in the meetings of the organization, a substantial bureaucracy in his own national capital, and a large foreign service. This support will help him to be better informed than most of his colleagues and will give him a greater capacity for lobbying, both at the site of the meeting and in national capitals throughout the world. With such a combination of assets even an ineffective person could be influential; but in fact the key member states appoint effective individuals more often than not. Even if their interest in the organizations is marginal, the opportunity costs of appointing effective individuals to represent them are not great because these states have a wealth of trained and talented manpower.

One other factor helps explain why the personal attributes of these actors are relatively unimportant. Because of their place in the general and specific environment, the United States and the Soviet Union cannot afford a casual involvement in international organizations; and they have large and efficient bureaucracies that can issue detailed instructions and monitor the way they are carried out. Particularly in the United States, the bureaucracy will begin with conflicting views on an international question that must be resolved before the state can act, and the reason why instructions of American delegates are at times so rigid and detailed is that they are almost treaties among warring entities within the state.

To return to the symbolic formulations developed in the first chapter for the representatives of the key member states, P (or position) is much more important than A (individual attributes) in the formula $P \pm A = C$, when C represents their capacities as individual actors. And P is consequently a more important element explaining influence, in the symbolic representation $X_a \cdot C \cdot D = I$, where X_a represents the actor's decision to convert his power into influence, D the distribution of all other forces in the organization, and I the influence he possesses.

Representatives of smaller states have fewer assets, but these states also have a tendency to allow their delegates greater freedom; and thus individual inclinations and attributes become for them much more important determinants of their influence. Or in symbolic terms, for them A is generally a more important explanation of their capacity than P. While the representatives of the key member states could exercise influence as initiators, vetoers, and controllers (and perhaps even as brokers, though the constraints of their position generally militate against this), representatives of other states are much more likely to exercise influence in one or at most two ways. It is also more likely that they will be forced to specialize in particular subject areas.[6]

A big power's representative can make his power felt unilaterally, but a small power cannot exert influence unless its representative has attained influence as an individual or unless there is concerted action by a large number of representatives. The caucus has become an important instrument for aggregating the influence of small powers' representatives. This is one reason why delegates of such powers are relatively free from detailed instructions, since the effectiveness of caucusing depends upon the members' aligning their votes behind a common position arrived at through political processes within the participant subsystem. At the same time, their lack of detailed instructions sometimes creates a need for them to caucus; they may need and want guidance.

In the discussion about government representatives the treatment of the position variable P has thus far been limited to distinguishing between representatives of powerful member states and those of other member states.

Other useful distinctions can be made. One relates to the manner in which the representative is linked with his government, whether through the foreign office or a functional ministry; the other relates to his location, whether he is permanently stationed at the headquarters of the organization or based within his own country and sent abroad only in connection with particular meetings.

Because foreign offices are generally concerned for the most part with representational and symbolic issues, wherever these issues have received greatest attention, foreign office representatives have been most numerous. Foreign office representatives also tend to deal with budgetary questions, since national legislative procedures often provide that government contributions to international organizations be approved as part of the foreign office budget. The concern of foreign office representatives is mainly with the aggregate levels of international organization budgets, whereas representatives from the functional department of government concerned with a particular agency are more interested in allocations to different programs within the budget.

Permanent representatives are important principally in two different circumstances: where decisions regarded as important are continually arising, as in IMF; and where the organization's program is so loosely defined that it must be constantly monitored, as in UNESCO.

In addition, a distinction must be made between large rich states and small poor states. The latter tend to constitute their delegations to the conference machinery of organizations—for example, UNCTAD—principally by drawing on the staffs they maintain at the headquarters of the organization, while the rich states are much more inclined to send officials from their national capitals to fill leading positions in their delegations, utilizing their permanent representatives as advisers and assistants.

The foregoing suggests general sources of influence for government representatives. Studies of individual organizations in the preceding chapters of this book have also attempted to indicate sources of influence of those individuals, including government representatives, who have been most influential. Most of the authors did this by consulting a panel of persons with knowledge about the organization. Some authors attempted to trace changes over time by focusing where possible on the years 1950, 1958, and 1967. Variations in the methods used preclude treating the data rigorously as a basis for precise calculations; but there is a sufficient correspondence in the results to warrant certain inferences, the validity of which might be explored further in more systematic studies.

Aside from the representatives of key member states, the attribute most widely shared among the more influential individual actors in the participant subsystems of the international organizations studied here was long association with the organization. Such association is not by itself a sufficient condition for an actor to exercise influence in the organization, but except for the representatives of the key member states it does seem to be a necessary condition. In the quarter-century since the end of World War II, long association has become an asset of increasing importance.[7]

Corresponding to the growing importance of long association is the declining importance of prominent personalities who owe their influence to their achievements or status outside the organization, for example, figures prominent in national political life or in the scientific or industrial worlds. During the early 1950s such persons were more frequently found among those most influential in the organizations studied than in more recent years.[8] The job of government representation has become a more specialized career.

Expert knowledge, in the sense of having a modicum of professional or scientific proficiency in the field in which the organization in question operates, also seems to be a frequent source of influence in most of the organizations. A person who owes his influence to his expert knowledge need not be a great contributor to thought in his field, though some have been, particularly in the 1950s.

The importance of other individual attributes as sources of influence for government representatives varies with organizations, with ways of exercising influence, and with subject matter. Personal charisma and intransigence can both be important attributes in UNCTAD, an organization where symbolic decisions are important and where the group structure allows a determined individual to block agreement. Personal charisma can also be important in the other agencies, especially in symbolic and representational decisions and to a lesser extent in programmatic decisions, but charisma was generally less important in the 1960s in all of the organizations than it was in the 1950s.

Ideological legitimacy is probably more important in UNCTAD and ILO than in the other organizations; again the link with symbolic decisions and their importance is obvious. In both organizations, however, ideological legitimacy is more important for some actors than for others. In UNCTAD it is essential for representatives of the poorer states, but of little importance to those of many richer states. In ILO, at least a measure of ideological legitimacy is a condition of entrance into the establishment. Negotiating ability is a useful asset in any of the organizations, but it is particularly so in GATT and for those who aspire to be brokers there and in other agencies. Administrative competency does not seem of itself to be a very important source of influence.

The evolution over time of some of these various sources of influence seems to describe a general trend. There has been a decline in the significance of personal eminence acquired outside the organization and of charisma, and at the same time an increase in the importance of knowing the ropes and knowing the relevant people through long association with the organization. This suggests a growing bureaucratization of decision making common to all the agencies studied, a trend that seems to apply to the United Nations as well. The decision makers belong increasingly to specialist groups who devote so much of their time to the politics of their particular international organization that other activities are excluded or subordinated. Personal characteristics are still important in determining influence, but they are those qualities that generally make people effective in bureaucratic structures, such as drive, tenacity, expert knowledge, and negotiating skill.

Representatives of Private Associations, National and International

As was pointed out in the preceding section, representatives of national and international private associations are important in decision making, but they exercise substantial direct influence only in ILO, ITU, and UNESCO, in that order. Almost the same things could be said of such actors in these three agencies as were said of representatives of states in the discussion of sources of influence. Again, the distinction between the representatives of key entities and of others would hold, and the list of key entities would be small. Being the representative of the American Telephone and Telegraph Company would bestow upon the incumbent a capacity for influence in ITU in certain circumstances equal to that of the representative of the United States, but there are few similar examples.

Executive Heads of Organizations

Executive heads inevitably are influential in many decisions in international organizations. They occupy the key administrative post in the agencies. At the very least they are controllers with respect to programmatic decisions, but they can also be initiators, vetoers, and brokers in these and other decisions. As with other actors, the amount of influence a particular executive head will have and the ways in which he will exercise it will be determined both by the characteristics of his position and by his individual attributes. In general the latter are probably the more important.

The resources available to executive heads are limited. All of them have some control of appointments in the secretariat and to ad hoc committees, and they can also affect the allocation of some resources—for instance, for technical cooperation projects and fellowships. All of them have an ability to use the international bureaucracy or elements of it in ways that they choose: for research to document arguments or to explore alternatives or for maintaining contacts and negotiating with states. Two other assets, however, are perhaps less tangible but even more important. All executive heads occupy strategic locations in the communications networks of their organizations, and their positions afford each of them platforms from which they can make their views known. The term *platform* does not necessarily imply great publicity and large audiences; executive heads can use their official standing in that manner, but they can also use it to speak to more limited groups, and this mode is probably more effective. Given the structure of the international system, the chances that an executive head of an international organization will obtain his goals by appealing to the populace of states over the heads of their governments are nil. Instead, he must appeal to the government itself or to a segment of it or to some relevant organized interests. But the important fact is that his position as the executive head of an international organization gives him a legitimate and sure means of stating his views. He has a right to speak and can be virtually certain that the audience he chooses will listen.

The key task for any executive head is to use his strategic location in his organization's communications network and the platform his position affords him to mobilize a consensus in support of organizational goals. How influential an executive head will be depends in large measure on his success in performing this task. The dimensions of the task vary with circumstances and time, and prescriptions for success have been highly individual.[9]

The executive heads who have led the organizations studied in this volume have displayed a variety of qualities. Raul Prebisch articulated an ideology that gave purpose and direction to his organization. David Morse adapted the tasks of his organization to a changing environment. Eric Wyndham White excelled as a broker in delicate negotiations. Marcolino Candau will be remembered as an efficient administrator of the complex organization that WHO became under his direction. There is no generally valid list of qualities required of an executive head, no robot portrait of an ideal director-general. The requirement for success is an effective relationship between the personality and particular talents of the incumbent individual, the characteristics of the organization, and the opportunities presented by its world environment. Thus different qualities are required in different organizations at different times.

But if there are no certain formulas guaranteeing success for an executive head, there are several minimum requirements. He must maintain effective working relations with at least some of the key member states that control the resources essential for the organization's functioning (or in the case of IMF, those states that have the greatest stake in it). This usually means gaining contacts in these member states through the country subsystem, which can give him support and leverage on important issues likely to arouse opposition from other quarters within that country. He must also maintain effective working relations with the voting majority in the organization's conference machinery. At times, in organizations that use majority voting and give each state a single vote, these two requirements impose contradictory demands; but the executive head cannot afford to become the prisoner either of large powers or of a voting majority of small powers. Finally, even if he does not fully control it, the executive head must ensure that segments of the international bureaucracy do not work against his policies. Executive heads are in every case called upon to be a bridge between the participant subsystem and the representative subsystems. Thus they cannot afford to become identified exclusively with the one or the other. An executive head requires the ability to assess the comparative need for attention to "inside" and "outside" aspects of the job and to perform effectively to take care of whichever aspect is the more important at a particular moment. In view of these requirements and the limited resources available, we should perhaps be surprised that several executive heads have been quite influential instead of wondering that some have not. Those who have been most successful have been alive to the fragility of their position.

Members and Segments of the International Bureaucracy

Either individually or collectively, members of international bureaucracies are usually most influential in operational decisions, but they may also be influential in other types of decisions. They often exercise this broader influence in the name of the executive head of their organization—in matters that receive little personal attention from him and that he cannot effectively control—but sometimes segments of bureaucracies act quite independently. Whether or not they will be influential in decisions other than operational ones and how they will exercise their influence depend upon a variety of circumstances, including the nature of the organization and its activities, the characteristics of the executive head, and the personal qualities of the bureaucratic leaders.

In the IMF two segments of the international bureaucracy, the Legal Department and the Research Department, were particularly influential because of the importance of their work to the Fund. Legal interpretations of the Articles of Agreement have been crucial in determining what the Fund could do—or at least in lending legitimacy to what the Fund sought to do—in certain instances; and the reports of the Research Department were important in stimulating, or sometimes in discouraging, change and adaptation within the international monetary system.

In several of the organizations, but particularly in WHO and UNCTAD, individual members of the bureaucracy have gained influence by becoming important aides to the executive head. In WHO the organization was so well run as to preclude any other route to influence for members of the bureaucracy. In UNCTAD on the other hand, it was not good administration but the high standing of Prebisch with the voting majority within the organization that made access to the executive head one of the best of the available routes to influence.

ITU provided a third pattern. Segments of the bureaucracy had their own supporters among the conference machinery of the organization and exercised influence independently of the executive head. This situation was built into the constitutional structure of the ITU. The large number of elected officials in ITU was, among other things, a device for ensuring that no single individual would have complete control over the bureaucracy and for limiting its autonomy. In ILO, the growth of the organization's activities and their changing orientation toward services, created new divisions of functions within the bureaucracy. Similar situations have prevailed in UNESCO and to a lesser extent in IAEA. When the strength of segments of the bureaucracy is not built into the constitutional structure of the organization, the crucial ingredients for it to develop are a bureaucracy of a certain minimum size—so that the executive head cannot maintain personal control—and a multiplicity of organizational tasks.

Individuals Serving in Their Own Capacities

Individuals serving in their own capacities have been involved in decision making at one time or another in most of the eight organizations. They have played the most substantial role in WHO, IAEA, and IMF, a somewhat more modest role in ILO, a lesser one in UNESCO and UNCTAD, a still lesser one in GATT, and virtually no role in ITU. Deeply involved individuals have been a significant force in programmatic and rule-creating decisions. In other cases, however, their primary function has been to legitimate or lend authority to opinions or policies of other actors.

Individuals owe their appointment to advisory panels, consultative committees, and the like—and to the reputation they have acquired with influential decision makers in an international organization, in particular with senior international officials or the executive head. The assets they trade on in decision making within the organization are their expert knowledge and the status that they have gained outside of the organization as well as possibly their informal access to influential decision makers within the organization. Expert status has a self-reinforcing and self-perpetuating quality. Appointment to a committee generally contributes to an individual's stature and thus makes his subsequent reappointment more likely. Organizations tend to consult the same individuals again and again; indeed in IMF most of the individuals who have been influential in their own right were at one time or another closely associated with the Fund, most often as members of its staff.

Experts and expert panels are, in political terms, often primarily a legitimating device, a means of obtaining authoritative support for policies or programs. The initiative for nominating panels and for referring issues to them usually lies with the executive head or segments of the international bureaucracy. Thus predictability and reliability will be important criteria in making appointments. Another consideration is representativeness; legitimation can only be effective if different currents of opinion recognize among the experts some persons whom they trust.

Representatives of Other International Organizations

Representatives of other international organizations have played a relatively limited role in the eight organizations. Such people have naturally been involved in boundary decisions and to some extent in operational decisions in all of the organizations. In boundary decisions they have been initiators, vetoers, and controllers, and in operational decisions, mainly vetoers and controllers. They have become involved in programmatic decisions sporadically, most often as a consequence of the cumulative effects of operational decisions, and again generally as vetoers and controllers.

The distinction between the limited active influence of representatives of other international organizations and their more passive influence as controllers is important, particularly in the relations of UNDP to those agencies that depend upon this source for a substantial share of funds to finance their programs. The fact that UNDP itself has had few effective powers of central planning either at the international level or the level of country development programs has been forcefully criticized as an abandonment of development goals in favor of the satisfaction of the sectoral interests of agencies.[10] Nevertheless, the influence of UNDP as controller should not be underestimated. The availability of voluntary funds has been important in reorienting the activities of the major agencies toward development and technical cooperation. Agencies have been induced to design their programs so as to meet the basic criteria of UNDP financing. If ILO is giving emphasis to human resources development and UNESCO to education for development, one basic reason is UNDP's influence as controller and the influence of other sources of additional funds. This influence as controller may also extend more subtly to preference among countries, although little information is available to illustrate this point. It is noticeable, however, that Cuba has received less assistance from UNDP than other states of comparable economic level and size.

In contrast to the UNDP, the United Nations Economic and Social Council appears hardly to have figured in decision-making patterns in the agencies, despite the fact that about 30 percent of ECOSOC's own decisions have concerned the specialized agencies and related organs.[11]

Employees of the Mass Media

Employees of the mass media are hardly involved in decision making in the organizations considered in this book. The reason is that the organizations seldom deal with matters that arouse wide public interest. Instead, their subject matter is largely and primarily the concern of various bureaucracies.

The politics of these organizations tend to be politics among bureaucracies, and communications in systems of this type are served by official documents, personal contact, and informal networks, rather than by the mass media. This conclusion does not mean that employees of the mass media could not be important actors in decision making in international organizations, but merely that they are not likely to play an impressive role in organizations similar to those considered here.

Attitudes and Ideologies

Having examined the actors in international organizations individually, we can now consider how they interact and what motivates them. In the eight organizations considered—as in all organizations—the actors have been driven by a mixture of personal and public goals. Tourism, prestige, and prospective salaries and careers are the stuff from which private satisfactions can be derived. For most people such incentives are an essential condition of their participation in organizational activities. Many, of course, want other less private goals as well—peace, security, and social equality, to list just a few of the broad objectives often sought through organizations similar to those studied here.

That personal and public goals should be found to mingle in international organizations is not surprising, since they are characteristically found together in all types of organizations.[12] If the fact has hitherto escaped attention, the reason is perhaps the legal bias that has prevailed in international organization studies and that tends toward a normative view (and thus one oriented toward public goals) rather than a behavioral view of decision making. More recently an awareness has developed in the milieus concerned with international organizations of the extent of self-serving activity that goes on within these organizations and that—although its real importance may well be exaggerated—has contributed to a certain disenchantment with international organization.

Authors of all of the studies of organizations included in this book shared this awareness that self-serving motives were important as an explanation of actions. Even with this recognition, however, a number of unanswered questions remain. It is difficult, in the first place, to assess comparatively for the eight organizations the prevalence of public and private goals. One hypothesis inviting further exploration is that in those organizations most closely tied to state policies—such as GATT and IMF—the scope for pursuit of private goals is limited or in any event subordinated to public policy. This constraint would be less effective in organizations, such as ILO or UNESCO, in which individuals rather than states have the most initiative. In such cases, one would have to look more to ethical norms of behavior as a restraint upon conduct prompted by private motivatons. A further question is whether such codes of conduct have not been somewhat eroded with the greater heterogeneity of values present in international organizations in recent years.

Another difficult question to answer is whether private and public goals are necessarily opposed: Does an increasing prevalence of self-serving action necessarily mean a decline in service to public interests? The private incentives and ambitions of organizational leaders may serve public goals. Private incentives to lesser actors—such as travel opportunities to attend conferences or pursue educational programs—may be used as a way of gaining support for public goals. In political terms, the more relevant questions are: Who is manipulating whom through private incentives? And what difference does it make to the decisions taken and the consequences that flow from them? To these questions, no firm general answers can yet be given.

A second attitudinal issue of greater importance than the distribution of private and public goals relates to organizational ideologies. Emerging from World War I and maturing in the 1930s was a functionalist theory of international organization. According to this theory, the building of contacts among technical specialists in different areas of public policy, the "multilevel interpenetration of governments" (a phrase of Sir Arthur Salter's), and the creation of transnational alliances among interest groups presented potentialities for organizing many of the functions of government internationally in such a way as gradually to erode the scope and authority of the nation-state in favor of world institutions. World government would be gradually built upon a series of sectoral bases. Because of its similarities with some of the economic and political theories of the early nineteenth century (particularly that of Saint-Simon) and because of its concentration on solutions rather than on the analysis of conditions, this strain of internationalist theory had strong utopian overtones. It was always the doctrine of a minority, but of a minority very influential in drawing up the institutional blueprints for the system of international social and economic cooperation set up in the United Nations and specialized agencies at the close of World War II. In its pluralism, functionalism was an international extension of Western democratic theory, stressing the rights of individuals and of private associations as well as the autonomy of professional and specialist interests as values having primacy over the state. The number of adherents to functionalism in the agencies has declined, however—at least relatively, and perhaps also absolutely—since the end of World War II.

There are several reasons for the decline in the relative popularity of functionalism. While functionalism may have been attractive to many individual Americans, it was never very congenial to the official policy of the United States government. Functionalism implies a gradual erosion of sovereignty, something that the United States as a collective entity has been most reluctant to allow. The reasons for this reluctance are obvious. Since the struggle for independence, American doctrines have emphasized the uniqueness of the United States and of its historical experience and role. The United States has been large enough to achieve most of its purposes wthout the need for extensive collaboration with other states. And as the richest major state in the system, the United States has been vulnerable to limitless claims and demands.

Nor was functionalism congenial to the Soviet Union. The leaders of this state have been imbued with an even stronger sense of their historical mission than have American leaders. Acquiescence in functional penetration would be seen by them as an abdication of the Soviet role in the dialectic of history. Moreover, if functionalism were applied to the Soviet sphere of the world, it would result in a loss of control by the USSR. Then too, functionalism is a gradualist doctrine that purports to solve by reform the sort of problems that according to Marxist tenets can only be solved by conflict and revolution.

Finally, the new states that have come to constitute the majorities in the agencies were not attracted by functionalism either. They were interested in building rather than in breaking down national sovereignty, and they looked to international organizations to effect redistribution so as to facilitate their development, something about which functionalism had little to say.

A basic reason for the decline of functionalism is, therefore, that it had the support of neither the two superpowers nor the majority of the member states. Furthermore, individuals became disillusioned with functionalism when its promised benefits with respect to peace and security failed to materialize. Nor were younger recruits to international organization, reading the historical record of functionalist activities and noting its ineffectiveness in broader issues, attracted to the ideology.

The ideology that has supplanted functionalism for general purposes is developmentalism. In all of the agencies, one can find some persons—and more frequently large numbers of them—who are dedicated to the notion of development. Development, though, is a value commitment rather than a carefully articulated, coherent ideology. It is not relevant, as was functionalism, to the transformation of the international system by strengthening authorities other than those of nation-states. It is a pledge to do something for the poorer parts of mankind, a pledge to which both the United States and the Soviet Union could subscribe, albeit for their own reasons, and one warmly welcomed by the majority of member states, the recipients of the proffered assistance. Moreover, it is a pledge to attain a tangible goal: progress toward it can be measured and actually achieved. Consequently, the doctrine is infinitely more satisfying to individual participants than is functionalism.

Developmentalism in many respects contradicts implicitly if not explicitly the political values underlying functionalism. Developmentalism stresses the coordination and coherence of economic policy at the national level, whereas functionalism seeks to stimulate sectoral interests and their transnational linkages. Developmentalism leads to stress upon centralization of policy control and action at the international level, whereas functionalism favors the autonomous growth of sectoral international agencies. Developmentalism stresses the primacy of the general interest of the collectivity in development, whereas functionalism places a higher value upon the freedom of individuals and of associations distinct from the collectivity.

Beyond these general ideologies, all eight of the organizations were found to have their own particular ideologies, which have been especially strong in ILO, IMF, GATT, and UNCTAD. These four agencies have more in common than might appear at first glance. Symbolic or rule-creating decisions—in ILO, decisions of both types—have constituted important activities and were more important in these agencies than in the other four. To a certain extent both symbolic and rule-creating decisions can be regarded as concrete formulations and expressions of ideological tenets. Both involve the enunciation of norms; the difference is in the consequences. Beyond being ways of looking at the world, ideologies are normative statements; thus organizational ideologies are strongest in agencies where normative functions constitute an important branch of their activities.

Another distinction relating to organizational ideologies can also be made among the agencies. In four of the agencies—ITU, WHO, GATT, and IMF—all of the actors subscribed to the ideology, although clearly in varying degrees. In the other four—ILO, UNESCO, IAEA, and UNCTAD—however, either there was dissent from the dominant organizational ideology or there were competing ideologies. This phenomenon was most pronounced in ILO and UNCTAD—of the four agencies, the two in which organizational ideologies were most pronounced.

The four organizations in which all of the actors tended to subscribe to the organizational ideology can be subdivided into two categories. In IMF and GATT the organizational ideologies were written into their constitutional documents, and membership carries with it something of a commitment to this ideology. At least those who want material benefits are expected, as in some charitable institutions, to acclaim the revealed truth, wherever their hearts may be. Significantly, neither agency includes the Soviet Union or several other communist states. ITU and WHO, on the other hand, have been among the most inclusive organizations; but their tasks are relatively specific, technical, and essential. The organizational ideologies have stressed these points, and beyond serving as cohesive forces within the organizations, they also serve to insulate the organizations from the broader political environment.

In the four organizations where divisions about the organizational ideologies were found, these divisions permeated decision making. In UNCTAD the divisions were in effect written into the group structure and have legal status. Broadly there are three groups: the 77 (groups A and C) for which Prebisch formulated the UNCTAD doctrine; the Western states (group B), which were the principal targets of the demands posed in the doctrine and hence opposed to it; and the socialist states (group D), which had their own problems concerning international trade and their own prescriptions. In ILO there was a division between those who thought the organization's functions were primarily normative and those who saw them as primarily developmental, and another between those committed to a liberal pluralistic view of social order and those who espoused more unitarian forms of socialism. There is a similar conflict in IAEA between those interested in control and those interested in development. In UNESCO developmental enthusiasts also compete with those who advocate other goals; but the general configuration is much more complex in UNESCO, and it defies any easy dichotomy. Rather than two, there are many competing ideologies.

Persistent Groupings

All of the agencies contain a group of actors committed to budgetary expansion and another committed to controlled growth or perhaps even stability. The advocates of expansion include international officials and many representatives of the poor states; those who want controlled growth include primarily some representatives of the Western states and of the socialist member states, as well as those of a few poorer states. During the 1960s, the noncommunist major contributors to the budgets of international organizations have created in the so-called Geneva Group, a caucus whose primary purpose is to make critical reviews of agency programs and budget proposals. In those agencies in which the Soviet Union participates, the Warsaw Pact countries act, with rare exceptions, as a unit in decision making. In all eight organizations representatives of states tend to coalesce on regional bases with respect to representational issues. The Africans further divide into Francophone and Anglophone groups. To some extent the 77, which became institutionalized in UNCTAD, can also be found in the other agencies. This group is most cohesive in symbolic decisions; with other types of decision, even in UNCTAD, it has great difficulty acting as a unit.

These are the only persistent groupings common to all of the organizations; all other groupings tend to be specific to the agencies. The constitutional documents of two agencies formally establish groupings. UNCTAD, as noted, formalizes regional groupings. In ILO, delegates to conferences are divided into three groups: employer, worker, and government.

In none of the agencies, therefore, is there a single persistent grouping that prevails for all categories of decisions. Instead, there are several crosscutting coalitions.

The Establishment

The foregoing are groupings that serve to organize and to aggregate the views of actors who have like interests in the participant subsystems of international organizations. They thus perform functions analogous to those of political parties in national political systems. The studies of individual organizations have also revealed another persistent grouping, whose function is to reconcile views among the various divergent elements within the organization, to place limits on conflict, and to aggregate policy at the higher levels of the organization itself. This consensus-minded grouping has been called the establishment. To a varying extent such a grouping is present in all of the organizations. Its existence is clearest in ILO, but to a varying extent such a grouping is also present in other organizations. It consists of a relatively small number of actors—international officials, representatives of states, and, where they are important, representatives of private associations—who have had a long association with the agency. The international officials in this group occupy key posts in the secretariat, and the representatives usually hold seats on the council and key committee assignments. These people, because of their long association with the agency, will have developed a certain identification with it. They will be intimately familiar with the agency and able to get things done within it. They will be controllers and many times probably brokers, and they will seek to manage business within the organization. They will know one another well; and although they may have strong differences among themselves on policy questions, they will have learned to temper these differences with concern for the organization. Their disputes will be conducted according to the rules of the game. Indeed, they will have played an important part in constructing those rules. The rules will have been designed to protect the organization, but they will also facilitate and preserve the influence of members of the establishment and their status as controllers. Establishments, by their nature, are conservative.

Establishments moderate conflict, construct consensus positions, provide orderly ways of doing business, and manage this business. They manage communication among relatively discrete parts of organizations. At the same time, establishments can have a stultifying effect on organizations. Establishments can lose touch with important organizational constituents; and, because their members are controllers, they can complicate and even block adaptation to changed conditions. To avoid this, establishments need to ensure their own self-renewal. The establishments of the organizations considered in this book all took action to recruit new members, but whether or not this recruitment was rapid and widespread enough to foreclose the possibility of petrification was not clear.

The Organizational Elite

Like all organizations, the eight studied here had some actors with greater influence than others. Those with the greatest influence constitute the organizational elite. This group overlaps with that identified as the establishment, but it is not identical. Some members of the establishment would not qualify for membership in the elite, and the reverse would also be true. The term elite as used in this study does not signify a cohesive group. Membership in the elite is a measure of influence. Membership in the establishment is determined by behavior.

At the outset, in chapter 1, we questioned whether there were elites with general influence in each international organization or whether a number of different elites would be found, depending upon the type or subject matter of decisions in the organization. Insofar as there are elites with general influence, it would be important to know their chief characteristics. Since the eight studies employed somewhat different methods of identifying organizational elites, it is difficult to compare the results; but certain generalizations can be made on the basis of the data available.

First, it was more difficult to identify organizational elites in UNESCO, IAEA, IMF, and GATT than in the other agencies. The reason for this difficulty in UNESCO seems to have been that different actors were influential in different issues; there was a plurality of elites, none having general influence. In the other agencies, except for a small number of individuals, influence seemed to be more a property of states than of individuals.

Second, in some organizations in which an organizational elite with general influence could be identified, the members of this elite did not necessarily have the determining voice in all major decisions. In the ILO, for example, a plurality of elites exists according to types of decision: the people who determine rule-creating decisions are, on the whole, different from those who determine operational decisions. The meaning of general influence here is influence over those types of decisions that are preeminently important in the organization. In ILO this means representational and symbolic decisions, but it differs with organizations. In WHO, programmatic decisions have been of overriding importance, and in UNCTAD symbolic decisions.

Third, to the extent that an organizational elite could be identified, it consisted predominantly of individuals who were nationals of Western states or principally of states with high per capita GNP and competitive polities. These individuals set the cultural tone of the organizations. Nationals from communist states and from poor states with authoritarian or mobilizing regimes were much less numerous among organizational elites.

Nevertheless, differences came to light among the organizations with respect to Western predominance. Perhaps the easiest way to show the facts with some precision is to rank the agencies according to the proportion of the members of their councils who were nationals of Western states. The percentage of the council membership from the three groups in 1967 was:

	Western	Socialist	Other
IMF	55	0	45
IAEA	44	12	44
ILO	41.6	8.3	50
ITU	34.5	10.3	55.1
UNESCO	33.3	10	56.6
UNCTAD	32.7	12.7	54.5
WHO	20.8	12.5	66.6

No figure was computed for GATT, since any state that desires to do so may serve on its Council of Representatives. A comparable statistic, though, might be derived from the composition of the Executive Committee of ICITO, the group that formally chose the director-general of GATT.

Exactly half of this group were nationals of Western states, and thus GATT would rank immediately after IMF in the accompanying list.

While these figures show certain differences among the organizations, they should be interpreted with caution. In the case of IMF they do not even signify voting power because the weighted voting system gives the Western states even more power than the number of seats held by their nationals would indicate. More important, the figures imply greater influence for nationals of Other states than they are reputed to have in any of the agencies. Nevertheless, in terms of Western predominance among the influential, the rank ordering of the agencies is probably roughly accurate.

A final generalization is that nationals of Western states accounted for a higher proportion of the organizational elite in the agencies in 1950 than in 1967. A rough notion of their distribution can again be obtained by comparing the 1950 percentage of nationals from the three groups who held seats on the councils of those agencies that were in existence then.

	Western	Socialist	Other
ILO	62.5	3.1	34.4
IMF	57.1	7.1	35.7
UNESCO	55.5	0	44.4
ITU	44.4	16.7	38.9
WHO	44.4	11.1	44.4

The decline of Western nationals within organizational elites has been accompanied by an increase in the number of nationals from Other states, although the latter still constitute a much smaller proportion of the organizational elite in the agencies than the proportion of the total memberships that their states account for. The identification of influential individuals for some organizations by expert panels suggests that the predominance of persons from Western countries has been even greater than that indicated by figures for memberships of councils and that the decline since the 1950s has been less marked. In other words, according to evidence based upon the opinions of knowledgeable persons, continuing Western predominance in most of the organizations that were covered is rated to be somewhat greater than formal representation reveals.

Environmental Impacts

Participant subsystems provided more complete explanations of the processes of decision making and the structure of influence in some organizations than they did in others; but in no case did they furnish a complete explanation. The environment, to varying extents, had an impact on all agencies.

The Stratification of Power

As we shift to this second level of analysis, our attention will move from individuals to collectivities and principally to states. It should already be obvious that a strong relation was found between a state's power in the environment and its influence in international organizations. Lists of the most influential states in international organizations invariably included most if not all of the most powerful states, provided of course that they were members. However, the rank ordering of influence in the organization was seldom if ever identical with that of power in the general environment. The influence of some states in some international organizations is greater than their power in the environment; with others it is less. There are three explanations for this finding. The first is that organizations also have specific environments, and states may be more or less influential in these environments than they are in the general environment. The second is that influence is at least partly a consequence of a deliberate attempt to convert power, and states may not choose to do this. Finally, since influence is a reciprocal phenomenon, a state's lack of influence may be the consequence of decisions and actions of other states.

To illustrate these points, IMF, GATT, and UNCTAD are all concerned with international trade. The USSR's share in world trade appeared to be low compared to its general world power; or, in the terms used in this study, its rank in the specific environments of IMF, GATT, and UNCTAD was lower than its rank in the general environment. The explanation is that the USSR participates only to a very limited extent in the trading and monetary system dominated by Western countries. Its own trading and payments are organized in a separate system. Rank order here was but an indicator pointing to broader explanations. But it did suggest, in part, why the USSR was not a member of IMF and GATT and why its influence was relatively low in UNCTAD, in which it did participate. To take other cases, the Netherlands and Norway ranked much higher in the specific environment of health than in the general environment, and their influence in WHO was closer to their status in relation to health than in the general environment. The United States was the leading state in the specific environment of UNESCO, yet its influence has not been impressive in that organization because it has not tried to be influential except on an extremely limited number of issues. Canada, on the other hand, has been shown to have greater influence in several international organizations than in their specific environments or the general environment. The reason is that for a number of years Canada chose to make international organizations a principal vehicle for the expression of its foreign policies.

Finally, the Federal Republic of Germany, to a lesser extent Italy and Japan, and in the 1960s the Republic of South Africa have each had less influence in all of the organizations than their status in the general and specific environments would make them appear capable of exercising. Clearly the potential influence of the first three states suffered because they were defeated in World War II, and that of South Africa has suffered because of international opprobrium aroused by its racial policies.

Since the end of World War II, the United States, the United Kingdom, and France have consistently ranked among the top states in the general environment. They have also been among the top states in influence in each of the organizations. The Soviet Union has held second place in the general environment and in all the organizations of which it has been a member (with the exception of UNCTAD, for reasons already suggested); it has also been among the most influential states. Though these states comprised only a small share of the world's population, 15.8 percent in 1967,[13] their combined GNP accounted for more than half of the world's total, or 57 percent in 1967.[14] Their relative national wealth was a major factor contributing to their influence in the organizations. It allowed them to do other things outside the organizations that gave them power, such as expending substantial sums for military purposes and economic assistance. It was a factor in their having high status in specific environments. It enabled them to have substantial administrative resources to deal with international organizations, and it placed them among the principal contributors to the organizations' budgets. Since these four states were so important to the agencies, their policies deserve individual scrutiny.

The United States has been the most powerful state in the environment since the end of World War II, and it undoubtedly gained this status some years before that war began. It has also been a moving force in the creation and life of international organizations. During World War II the United States devoted more resources than any other state to planning for the postwar world, and international organizations came to play a prominent part in these plans. They were to bring peace and prosperity to a world of sovereign states. In 1945 the United States was clearly the most enthusiastic supporter of international organizations among the four major victorious powers. The extent of this enthusiasm may have been related to its failure to join the League of Nations, but the fact that the United States would be extremely influential in the postwar international organizations was undoubtedly another reason. United States enthusiasm, though, did not carry with it a willingness to cede any significant degree of sovereignty. On the contrary, international organizations were never viewed as something that would seriously hamper American freedom of action; and whenever this came to be in question, the United States drew back.

As an extension of its postwar planning, the United States played a prominent role immediately after the war in all of the international organizations then in existence. Given its stature in the world, it could not have helped being influential, but generally the United States actively sought influence and was usually successful. The United States saw international organizations as places where it could achieve important policy objectives, and it frequently gained its goals. It exercised influence in all ways, as an initiator, a vetoer, a broker, and a controller.

Extensive and indeed almost overwhelming American influence extended well into the postwar era. As one indication of the influence of the United States, in 1958, when seven of the organizations considered in this study were in existence, the executive heads of four were American citizens: Gerald Gross, secretary-general of ITU; David Morse, director-general of ILO; Luther Evans, director-general of UNESCO; and Sterling Cole, director-general of IAEA. An American, Eugene Black, was also executive head of the World Bank.

By 1967 United States influence in the agencies had waned somewhat, but it was still substantial. The United States remained the largest contributor to the budgets of all of the agencies and the largest supplier of extrabudgetary funds. The sharp increases in the budgets of the agencies in the early 1960s were dependent on American decisions, and American decisions were major factors in the slowdown in the budgetary increases that occurred in the late 1960s. One sidelight illustrating the agencies' financial dependence on the United States is that in the late 1960s Americans held assistant executive head positions overseeing administrative matters in UNESCO, WHO, and IAEA. At that same time the director-general of ILO, the deputy managing director and secretary of IMF, and the administrator of the UNDP were all Americans. Thus in all of the agencies that had substantial budgets, Americans were either in one of the top two positions in the secretariat or in charge of financial matters.

Perhaps the decline of American influence was most notable in GATT, where the European Economic Community began in the 1960s to act as a unit, which in terms of international trade was even more important than the United States. In no other agency was there a group with as much power as the EEC had in GATT, and consequently no agency presented a comparable challenge to American influence. In the 1970s the EEC countries may come close to the same influence in IMF. The negotiations leading to the creation of Special Drawing Rights were an indication in this direction, although the EEC did not negotiate as a unit in IMF as it had done in GATT.

Of course, American interest in the agencies has varied. Generally, the United States has seen ITU, IAEA, IMF, and GATT as places where its own interests were at stake; in contrast, the others—and particularly UNESCO and WHO—though relatively expensive, could do little that might harm the United States. In the 1950s, when the Soviet Union rejoined ILO, the United States took a more serious view of ILO for a while, regarding the agency as a forum for a propaganda battle that it did not want to lose. Because UNCTAD could strongly affect United States interests if it gained substantial authority, at first the United States sought to block that agency's creation. But once it became clear that the organization could not be prevented, American policy has been careful to circumscribe its authority. In sum, the United States has pursued a basically negative policy toward UNCTAD.

The influence of the Soviet Union in the agencies has grown more than that of any other state since the end of World War II. In 1950 the USSR was a member of ITU, but not participating fully, and it had withdrawn from WHO. It was not a member of the other four organizations studied here that were then in existence: ILO, UNESCO, IMF, and GATT. In 1967 it was an active member of six of the eight organizations (ITU, ILO, UNESCO, WHO, IAEA, and UNCTAD), and it was among the most influential states in all of the six but UNCTAD. As one rough indication of Soviet influence, in the late 1960s, nationals of the USSR held posts as assistant executive heads in UNESCO, WHO, and IAEA. A Soviet citizen was also a member of ITU's International Frequency Registration Board. The high status of the USSR in the agencies represented considerable acculturation on its part to the international system. But even so, the organizations did not present themselves to the Soviet Union as important places for the accomplishment of Soviet objectives. It constantly sought to minimize its financial commitment to them and seldom took initiatives, except on representational and symbolic issues. In other types of decisions its usual way of exercising influence was as a controller. In contrast to the United States, the Soviet Union could seldom act as a vetoer. The relatively low influence of the Soviet Union in UNCTAD, which has already been mentioned, was evident in rule-creating and programmatic matters; but in representational and symbolic matters the Soviet Union was highly influential.

The relatively high influence of France and the United Kingdom in the organizations in part derived from their status in the general environment, but it was also a carry-over from an earlier period. In the years between World War I and World War II these two states were the dominant powers in international organizations; and even when organizational discontinuities occurred, the influence of France and the United Kingdom generally extended into the postwar era. Their status as colonial powers was also a source of influence. Despite decolonization, both powers continued to exert influence on some former colonies, particularly in Africa, through national bureaucracies. Decolonization also left these states with a surfeit of administrators some of whom joined the staffs of international organizations.

As with the United States and the Soviet Union, the high secretariat positions occupied by the nationals of these two states give some indication of their standing in the agencies. In 1967 French citizens were the executive heads of UNESCO and IMF and assistant or deputy executive heads in ILO and WHO. In ITU a French citizen was on the International Frequency Registration Board, and another was head of one of the international consultative committees. (The other international consultative committee was headed by an American.) British citizens held the posts of executive head of GATT and assistant or deputy executive heads in ILO, WHO, and IAEA and in addition headed two of IMF's five departments. (The other three were headed by two Americans and one Dutch citizen.) France and the United Kingdom have exercised influence frequently as initiators, brokers, and controllers, but hardly ever as vetoers. In recent years French policy toward international organizations has seemed more generally active than British policy, which has been more selectively focused on those organizations, such as the IMF and GATT, whose activities impinged significantly upon British policy.

In the late 1960s the People's Republic of China, the Federal Republic of Germany, and Japan also had substantial power in the general environment. China was not a member of any of the eight organizations. To a certain extent this may have been a matter of its own choice, but it was more clearly attributable to policies engineered by the United States. Germany had influence equivalent to its general standing only in IMF and GATT. These two organizations were important to Germany, and it ranked high in their specific environments. There had been a time lag between German attainment of high status in the economic environment and its acquisition of influence in those economic organizations. When Germany did acquire influence in them it was made easier because these agencies had relatively restricted memberships. Germany's disability as a defeated power after World War II was particularly important in IAEA; but its relatively low influence in ITU, ILO, UNESCO, WHO, and UNCTAD may, in addition, have reflected a lower priority which Germany accorded to the affairs of those agencies. German political leaders may also have felt that it was both unnecessarily costly and politically inadvisable to suggest any wish to play an active "great power" role. Japan's influence, though it had increased greatly, nonetheless still lagged behind Germany's, despite the fact that Japan's GNP surpassed that of Germany by the close of the decade. Clearly, though, if patterns of influence among states in international organizations were to change, China, Germany, and Japan would be the most obvious potential recruits for leading roles.

The Distribution of States according to Their Economic and Political Characteristics

The distribution of states according to their economic and political characteristics constitutes a second variable in the environment. In this respect the most dramatic change since the end of World War II has been the large number of states that have gained independence. In 1950, of the 154 political units that we have classified, 72 or nearly 47 percent were not independent. In 1967 only 23, or less than 15 percent, remained in that category. This change has sharp consequences for all eight of the organizations. Among the six that were in existence in 1950, memberships had grown to be at least 70 percent larger by 1967. In all instances this increase necessitated some structural changes. As the size of conferences or assemblies grew, that of councils also tended to expand; otherwise they would have become less representative, and the competition for seats would have become more intense.

Beyond this dramatic change, there have also been other changes in the distribution of units in the environment. The most significant change is that decolonization has been accompanied by an increase in the proportion of independent states with authoritarian polities, from 39 percent in 1950 to 45 percent in 1967; at the same time the proportion of states with competitive polities has declined from 42 percent to 33 percent. Contrary to some popular views, the changes in the distribution of states according to their per capita GNP were much less significant. Although the absolute number of poor states (i.e. those with per capita GNPs lower than $600 annually) had increased substantially with decolonization, poor states actually constituted a smaller proportion of the total number of independent states in 1967, when they accounted for 75 percent, than in 1950, when 79 percent were classed as poor.

In an analysis of collective demands on the agencies, relative figures alone provided no basis for expecting that pressures for redistribution would be greater in 1967 than in 1950; but such pressures were actually much greater, and the agencies were doing much more for poor countries in 1967 than they had done in 1950. Perhaps in this instance absolute numbers were more important than proportionate shares. As another possibility, states that gained their independence in the late 1950s and the 1960s may have been more vocal in pressing their demands than the other poor states that had been independent longer.

Other explanations for this change in international organizations are to be found in changes affecting the international system itself. In 1950 the international system was polarized by the cold war, and other issues tended to be subordinated to this cleavage. Subsequently, the developed-underdeveloped cleavage gained greater preeminence, initially because of the competition between the superpowers for support among emerging nations and ultimately in its own right. The recognition that economic development has an important bearing on the equilibrium of the international system originates as much from rich countries' foreign policies as from poor countries' pressures. Indeed, the United States government's policy was probably of equal or greater importance as an influence moving international organizations in this direction than was the articulation of poor countries' opinion in these organizations.

Whether or not the increasing proportion of the agencies' membership in the authoritarian category has affected the organizations is moot. The most likely impact seems to have been to discourage competitive states from seeing these organizations as clubs composed of states like themselves. This change may have led them away from emphasizing rule creation in areas relating to polities. It is significant that the two agencies where such rule-creating decisions might have been taken, ILO and UNESCO, have increasingly turned toward service activities, but so has ITU, where the nature of polities makes little difference to the subject matter of rules.

Shifting the focal point for analysis to individual states and groups of states, the scheme of categorizing units has proved only partially useful as a predictor of their behavior in these agencies. As has already been mentioned, states with low per capita GNP do seek redistribution through international organizations, but to discover that the poor seek to better their lot through available institutions is hardly a surprising finding. These states also stress representational decisions, but personal goals often outweigh broader considerations in their policies concerning these matters. Many of the leaders in the group of poorer states are drawn from those with a per capita GNP from $200 to $599 per year; but some influential states such as India and Nigeria also come from the lowest economic category. Generally, whether a state is in the lowest or the second lowest economic category seems to be only marginally important in determining the demands that it will place on an international organization. Such factors as the power of the state, the orientation of its broad foreign policy, and the characteristics of its elite are much more important.

Richer states—those in the top two categories of per capita GNP— generally do stress regulatory decisions and to some extent demand technically sophisticated services in ITU, IAEA, IMF, and GATT, but not in the other four agencies. They demand these services, though, only as an adjunct to facilities for conference services. The richer states are not particularly interested in having the agencies become independent sources of technical expertise; they prefer that technical expertise should have national bases. The richer states are not totally uninterested in rule-creating decisions and technically sophisticated services in ILO and UNCTAD and even UNESCO and WHO, but they generally prefer to organize these matters nationally and to engage in whatever collaboration might be necessary in international organizations with restricted memberships, such as OECD, or where decision-making procedures placed less emphasis on majority votes, such as GATT.

The divisions by type of polity were also found to be of only limited explanatory value. Representatives of mobilizing regimes do frequently initiate symbolic decisions, but representatives of other types of regimes often do this too. Competitive regimes are likely to be especially careful before they agree to rule-creating decisions relating to such domestic matters as the ILO's labor standards, but all types of regimes are equally watchful of rule-creating decisions in such agencies as ITU, IAEA, IMF, and GATT. Rarely have internal struggles for power within competitive regimes been directly or even indirectly relevant to the policies these countries have pursued in international organizations. Some representatives of authoritarian regimes have been brokers, but so have several representatives of competitive regimes. Only mobilizing regimes hardly ever supply brokers.

Since the end of World War II several states have undergone changes in regimes. The only changes that substantially affected the policies that states pursued in these international organizations were shifts into and out of the mobilizing category. Regimes could change from competitive to authoritarian or vice versa with hardly any perceptible effect on states' policies; but shifts to or from the mobilizing category usually had noticeable effects.

In a broader sense than that with which we have been dealing, however, the classification of states by polities and economic status was important, for—as has been pointed out more than once in this study—by far the largest number of influential actors in international organizations have been citizens of rich, competitive states. The culture of international organization reflects the values of these polities, modified by a growing acceptance of a diversity of regimes and a consequent restraint in pressing to extreme conclusions the implications of a liberal ethic.

The Pattern of Conflicts and Alignments

The final variable in the environment is the pattern of conflicts and alignments. The four broad currents—the conflict between communist and anticommunist states, the struggle for decolonization, the controversy between rich and poor states, and the movement toward regional integration—have all left some mark on the organizations.

The last of the four currents has had the least impact. The European integration movement had great consequences for GATT. Economic integration involved matters that were clearly within the agency's mandate and had to be discussed there; and by the late 1960s the European Economic Community became a collective actor within the agency. Movements toward economic integration in other regions were occasionally discussed in GATT, but beyond that they had few consequences for the organization. The EEC may well have a similar effect on IMF in the 1970s.

None of the regional integration movements has been very significant to the processes of decision making and the structures of influence in the other agencies, not even in UNCTAD, whose activities cover the same field as those of GATT. Members of regional groupings revealed little homogeneity of outlook except on issues that brought together much more inclusive alignments. This fact illustrates the limited extent to which regional integration movements have succeeded in evolving common policies and the mechanisms necessary for their creation.

The East-West and North-South controversies affected the agencies much more deeply. The communist-anticommunist conflict has been profoundly felt in all of the eight organizations. It kept all of them from becoming completely universal; none included in their membership the People's Republic of China, the German Democratic Republic, the Democratic Republic of Korea, and the Democratic Republic of Vietnam. Furthermore, during the height of the cold war in the early 1950s the Soviet Union and several other communist states in Eastern Europe participated in ITU, but not in ILO, UNESCO, WHO, IMF, or GATT. Subsequently, these states became active in ILO, UNESCO, and WHO; and they joined IAEA and UNCTAD when those agencies were created. WHO welcomed the USSR back to membership. Resolutions had been adopted in Health Assemblies during the Soviet Union's absence asking this state to reconsider its position; special efforts were undertaken to make its resumption of membership as easy as possible; and when it did come back, it was immediately accorded high status in the organization. Soviet entry into UNESCO occasioned no controversy. When the USSR rejoined ILO, in contrast, the event provoked an organizational crisis. The Soviet Union has never shown an interest in IMF or GATT, although other Eastern European states have done so.

IAEA, though created on American initiative, could only take on significant tasks in an era of Soviet-American détente. The détente that prevailed following the Test Ban Treaty of 1963 was limited to security matters (the purview of IAEA) and had little effect on economic cooperation. Consequently there was no movement toward Soviet membership in IMF and GATT.

Simply in terms of membership, in the early 1950s all of the eight agencies that then existed, except ITU, were aligned with the West. In the same period the United Nations could also be considered Western aligned because the United States and its allies were consistently able to muster a majority in the General Assembly on security issues. During the 1960s only IMF and GATT appeared to be aligned with the West. The voting predominance of the Western countries has become much less certain in the other agencies, and the Soviet Union has assumed active membership in them. The Western orientation of IMF and GATT is explained by the fact that the international economic system to which both are linked does not include the Soviet bloc, which has its own separate system for trade and payments.

The issue concerning the alignment of the agencies' policies with Western policies—on which the dispute about membership hinges—is complex. The main function of IMF and GATT is to facilitate the development of that system of international economic relations in which the United States and other Western countries have the biggest stake and to protect this system against instability. In that sense the two organizations are clearly aligned with the West. The measure of ILO's alignment is to be found more in the outcome of representational and symbolic decisions than in program matters or rule creating, about which there has been relatively little overt East-West controversy. In ILO the Soviet group gained ground since the 1950s without, however, displacing Western preeminence. The other agencies have appeared less completely aligned with the West. During the Korean War the United States actively sought the support of UNESCO for its policies but failed. Issues that provoked East-West divisions seldom arose in WHO and ITU. To a substantial extent, IAEA could not carry out its functions without Soviet-American agreement. By the time that UNCTAD was created the cold war had waned. Furthermore, many secretariat officials and government representatives felt that if the organization were to become aligned in the conflicts dividing the relatively rich countries of the world, it would weaken its ability to advance the interests of the poorer countries.

The two North-South controversies, centering on decolonization and development, can be considered simultaneously. To assess sensitivity to these questions, particularly to the conflict over decolonization, membership can again be used as an index. The Republic of South Africa is an anathema to the new states, and to them a change in its racial policies is an essential aspect of the struggle to end colonialism. South Africa voluntarily left UNESCO in the 1950s; it was driven out of WHO and ILO in the middle 1960s and barred from certain ITU meetings, but not from others. An attempt to exclude it from UNCTAD failed, but only because of the organization's connection with the United Nations; and no attempt was made to exclude it from IAEA, IMF, or GATT. Reflecting a roughly similar pattern, symbolic issues relating to decolonization and development have been raised most frequently in UNCTAD and ILO, less frequently in UNESCO, and least frequently in ITU, WHO, IAEA, IMF, and GATT.

In all of the agencies created before 1960 (all but UNCTAD) the issue of whether more attention ought to be devoted to development problems has received considerable attention; and all seven organizations have shifted their program priorities somewhat over the years. Perhaps WHO and GATT have shifted the least. WHO's activities were heavily oriented toward problems of poor states from the outset. In contrast GATT's activities have centered on the problems of the richer countries; and it could not change its orientation without changing its nature as an institution. GATT might have changed, had it not been that a new agency, UNCTAD, was established with an overlapping mandate, but one directing the new agency toward activities that would favor the poorer countries. In ILO, UNESCO, IAEA, and IMF there has been continual discussion since the mid-1950s about the amount of attention these development-oriented programs were receiving and the amount they should receive.

Has the growing complexity in the pattern of conflicts and alignments enhanced the ability of the executive heads and the international bureaucracies to become more independent of the powerful controller countries in the management of their organization's affairs? The United States, the most powerful state in the environment, has been the principal contributor to the budgets of all of the agencies; and the executive heads of the agencies maintained effective working relationships with the United States. The Soviet Union's entry into several organizations did not offer an alternative source of budgetary support, but rather a second superpower whose views had to be considered. As new states swelled the ranks of the organizations, the opportunities for executive heads to mobilize a voting majority among the poor states increased; but this tactic had limited utility, for in the end the great powers would not be coerced. The increased voting strength of the poorer states was a potential danger, since the majority might take action, even against the executive head's urging, which would diminish the willingness of the most powerful states to support the organization. The loosening of the bipolarity of the early postwar years, therefore, has not had the effect of increasing the independence of action enjoyed by international officials; rather it has complicated their problem of coalition building by adding new dimensions to it.

Functionalism has been discussed previously as an organizational ideology. Scholars have also used and elaborated some of the concepts of functionalism as a framework for analysis of international organizations. Although functionalism as an organizational ideology and functionalism as a framework for scholarly analysis have many elements in common, our discussion is confined to the first of these meanings. Used in this sense, conventional functionalist theory has stressed that agencies should meet the criteria of being *technical, functionally specific,* and *essential.*[15] An agency is called technical when there is a body of sophisticated professional or scientific knowledge that is necessary to the conduct of its work. It is functionally specific when its work relates to one specialized area of public policy. It is essential when the function performed is necessary to minimum intercourse among nations. According to this theory, organizations having such characteristics should not be much affected by *world political cleavages* or what we have called the pattern of conflicts and alignments. The experience of the eight agencies studied should make it possible to review the validity of these concepts and these assumptions.

We do not propose a critique of the theory of functionalism as developed by scholars, but rather an analysis of functionalism as an organizational ideology from the point of view of its adequacy and effectiveness as a guide for action. The foregoing analysis has suggested, however, the relevancy of another factor beyond those normally considered in conventional functionalism, namely, the *salience* of the agency's tasks to the most powerful governments. Do they consider the agency's tasks to be highly important in terms of their own interest? Of course, none of the organizations listed in table 11.3 possesses any of these characteristics to an absolute degree, just as none is utterly devoid of them. It is however possible to show the relative extent to which each of the eight agencies possesses each characteristic.

Certain relationships seem to stand out from table 11.3. In the first place, the functionalist hypothesis is partially confirmed in that some organizations that are both technical and functionally specific (ITU and WHO) have been affected less than the others by world political cleavages. However, IAEA, which is both technical and functionally specific, has been much affected by world political developments. The difference may be that WHO and ITU appear to be more essential than IAEA.

Of all the concepts, that of essentiality presented the greatest difficulty when it came to assigning values for the eight agencies. Essentiality refers to the nature of the task, rather than to the organization. The concept depends entirely upon functionalist theory, since it assumes that if a task is both essential and on an international scale, some international structure or organization must exist or be created to carry it out. Thus, arrangements to deliver mail between countries seem both to be essential and to require

Table 11.3

The Agencies Viewed according to Functionalist Criteria

	High	Low
Technicality	GATT IAEA IMF ITU WHO	ILO UNCTAD UNESCO
Functional specificity	GATT IAEA IMF ITU WHO	ILO UNCTAD UNESCO
Essentiality	ITU WHO	GATT IAEA ILO IMF UNCTAD UNESCO
Salience	GATT IAEA IMF ITU	ILO UNCTAD UNESCO WHO
Sensitivity to world political cleavages	GATT IAEA ILO IMF UNCTAD UNESCO	ITU WHO

international agreement. On the same line of reasoning, ITU's task of securing international agreement on the use of radio frequencies and standards for equipment and WHO's task of providing information vitally important to the control of epidemic diseases may be considered as both essential and international in scope. Some other tasks, however practically useful or morally desirable, such as promoting education or improving labor conditions, or even furthering broader humanitarian goals like the defense of human rights, cannot be considered essential in precisely the same sense. It is perhaps more debatable whether the tasks of IMF and GATT are essential in this sense. The regulation of exchange rates and of trade relations can be considered an essential function, if not for the world as a whole, then at least for the trade system dominated by the United States and major Western countries. But it could also be argued that such a system could conceivably be self-regulating, for example, through some mechanism like the gold standard. Thus for purposes of classification here, the tasks of these organizations are regarded as less universal and less essential than those of ITU and WHO.

The very process of arguing over classification of agencies according to the essentiality of their tasks, however, throws doubt upon the validity of the concept itself and thus upon a pillar of functionalist theory. It is doubtful whether any specific tasks are in themselves essential to the international system. What is implied in the use of this term is a propensity of states to organize the performance of certain tasks internationally. If this propensity is very high, the task may come in time to be regarded as essential because the actors will have become used to having it performed internationally. Whether one considers the work of existing international institutions or the possible creation of new ones, however, the politically relevant questions concern the propensity of states to organize the performance of tasks internationally, rather than the inherent nature of the tasks themselves. Writings in economic theory have discussed some of the factors that relate to a propensity to organize the production of public goods collectively,[16] and some of these economic concepts have been applied to international organization.[17] This approach to the study of collective action draws attention especially to the existence of marked differences in capabilities and what they imply for the propensities of the actors. Countries with sufficiently high capabilities—for example, the two superpowers—could probably organize for themselves many of the kinds of services usually regarded as essential. If they prefer a collective production of such public goods through international organizations, it is either because other countries might otherwise have a free ride at their expense, or because of other noneconomic reasons. In other words, international organization of these services is a convenience to, rather than a necessity for, states with high capabilities; and these states are prepared to provide the incentives or coercion required to secure the participation of other states. The convenience usually depends upon having all relevant countries participate; and universal participation is likely to depend in turn on the avoidance of issues that are not directly relevant to the tasks entrusted to the organization. In other words, the pursuit of symbolic issues dividing the members would be likely to undermine the continuing effectiveness of such an organization. Pressure to take on new tasks may also raise tensions within the organization, unless this pressure develops from the same consensus and the same incentives and coercion as the initial task. Quasi-universal international organizations carrying out technical tasks about which there is broad consensus thus tend to remain limited in scope and nonpolitical, but these characteristics should not be attributed to the essentiality of the task itself.

A Summary of Conclusions

The preceding sections of this chapter have analyzed separately the different variables used in this study of influence, treating them comparatively for the eight organizations covered. From the foregoing analysis, certain conclusions of general significance are clear.

A first finding is that there is a common stratification of influence, with minor variations, in all of the organizations. Whether we consider the national origins of individuals or participating states, the rich Western countries with competitive polities are the predominant influence in all the organizations. Their influence has remained remarkably stable, declining only marginally with the accession to membership of many new nations. This is not a surprising finding in view of the structure of power in the world as a whole. But it is a little surprising, given the different reputations of the organizations studied, to find, for instance, that the effective influence of individuals from the rich Western countries is only marginally less in UNCTAD than in the IMF.

The consequences that flow from this predominant Western influence differ depending upon whether the influence is primarily that of states or of individuals. Where, as in the case of IMF, state policies are determining, the policies of the organization may be expected to serve Western states' objectives to the extent that the countries concerned can agree upon these objectives. In the case of IAEA these objectives include collaboration with the Soviet Union and its allies. Where influence is primarily a property of individuals, the policies of the organization may be less likely to be an extension or aggregation of Western states' policies. Western influence may be more subtle and indirect, being the expression of common cultural attitudes: those characteristic of the rich, competitive polities. Variations in the degree of alignment of international organizations with the policies of the major Western states also derive from differences in the degree of participation of the socialist countries, highest in IAEA and lowest in IMF, but nowhere do these seriously affect the general pattern.

Second, there has been a general shift in the preoccupations the eight organizations have shown since the 1950s with problems of the less-developed countries. Here the pattern is general, but its incidence has had more variation. WHO from its origins leaned primarily toward services to less-developed countries. GATT, by contrast, has exhibited this orientation to the least degree among the organizations, and there it is mainly symbolic. In IAEA, services to poorer countries have had somewhat more practical significance for programs than in GATT, but possibly the reason lies only in the organization's search for a useful transitional role while awaiting an opportunity to undertake more substantial functions. In all the other agencies, program reorientation toward the concerns of less-developed countries has been the main theme in the story of their work during the past twenty years and especially during the past ten. That even those international organizations which seem least apt for such action took part in the general movement is an indication of its force.

The control by rich countries of action directed to poor countries, most of them newly independent, is a good definition of what might be called *collective colonialism.* (The term *neocolonialism,* now applied widely and loosely, might also be used here but for the fact that it often appears to refer more especially to the mechanisms of direct influence retained by former metropolitan powers in their former colonies.) International organizations have taken over some of the burdens formerly carried by the colonial administrations of a few metropolitan powers. They have spread the financial burden more widely, altered the symbolism of colonial rule by making the administration of these services consistent with accession to formal sovereignty by the recipient country, and even eased the transition for some individuals from the old to the new colonialism by providing many jobs for former colonial administrators.

Third, the growing preoccupation of the more nearly universal international organizations with the problems of the Third World has been accompanied by the creation of a number of shadow organizations to deal with business of direct concern to the rich countries. When these countries have felt a need for direct international consultations or services, they have tended to organize these outside the more universal agencies. Thus the Group of Ten and other similarly limited meetings of finance ministers and central bankers have prepared the important decisions affecting the monetary relations of the rich Western countries. When it comes to policies regarding incomes or wages, industrial relations, and manpower, these same countries talk to each other in OECD rather than in ILO.

Fourth, there has been a general trend toward the bureaucratization of decision making in all organizations, though the process has gone further in some than in others. Charisma and the status of individuals outside the organization have become less important sources of influence over the years, while long association with the organization and the holding of strategic functional positions within it have become more important.

Bureaucratization implies giving institutions an interest in their permanence and growth. Specific initial goals may be somewhat obscured if they cease to appear relevant to the current concerns of nations; but the organizations that have been set up to achieve these goals, once they have crossed a certain threshold of size, do not diminish comparably when this happens. They find new jobs to do. The existence of a large organization is itself a potentiality and a pressure for the expansion of tasks. ILO and

UNESCO expanded into new fields of activity during the 1950s and 1960s; and UNCTAD, with its relatively large staff and diffuse mandate, may show a similar expansiveness.

Fifth, there has been a shift in the dominant ideology of international organizations from functionalism to developmentalism. Insofar as ideologies legitimize structures as well as policies, this trend may have important implications. The structures of the eight agencies are based upon functionalist precepts, linking sectoral national agencies and interests together transnationally. Developmentalism has weakened the justification of these sectoral structures, particularly as regards their freedom from central control in planning development and the legitimacy of their appeals for support from special interests. This ideological weakness is probably neither very marked nor very serious for IMF. It seems potentially most important, however, for the future of those agencies—notably ILO and UNESCO—that defend their independence with functionalist ideology but have come to depend most heavily upon UNDP funds.

Sixth, there is a difference between those agencies in which there is a strong and distinctive organizational ideology and those in which it is less pronounced. ILO, UNCTAD, IMF, and GATT are in the first category; and ITU, UNESCO, WHO, and IAEA are in the second. The organizational ideology provides an orientation and legitimation for the activities of the agencies in the first category. In two of these agencies, IMF and GATT, all of the participants tend to adhere to the organizational ideology, though to a varying extent. These are also agencies to which socialist countries generally do not belong and in which representational and symbolic issues are played down. ILO and UNCTAD come much closer to having universal membership, and within these two agencies one finds strong dissent from the dominant organizational ideologies. Representational and symbolic issues are much more prominent. The other four agencies also have organizational ideologies, but they are much less pronounced features of the life of these bodies.

Seventh, international organizations are distinguished from each other according to whether the participant subsystem or external factors are dominant in decision making. The framework employed in this study has distinguished the participant subsystem from other factors in two different ways. One referred to the participant subsystem and representative subsystems as different though overlapping components of international organization, the other to the participant subsystem and the environment as different levels of explanation of decision-making processes and influence in international organization. Both ways of distinguishing the participant subsystem are linked to each other because the representative subsystems are closer to environmental pressures. They are channels for the expression of demands and vehicles for the mobilization of support. The organizations studied in this book fall into two groups of four each: those in the first group are dominated by their participant subsystems, those in the second by their representative subsystems.

What went on in ILO, WHO, UNESCO, and UNCTAD could be explained mainly in terms of the actors in the participant subsystems of these organizations—that is to say, delegates, international officials, and associated independent specialists—but the internal patterns of influence differed among these organizations. In ILO and WHO the secretariats played a major role, while in UNCTAD the regional caucuses of delegates were more important. Their common feature was, however, that the participant subsystems of these organizations had achieved a degree of autonomy in relation to their environments. Another key feature was that in these organizations the representatives of the most powerful states tended to exercise influence mainly as controllers. Unless key decision makers were to misjudge the political limits within which the participant subsystem could work and overstepped these limits in some serious way, states or other environmental forces were unlikely to interfere in a way that would disturb the decision-making processes of the subsystem. The autonomy of a subsystem of this type is relative, not absolute; it depends upon the tolerance of key forces in the relevant environment and upon an awareness by key decision makers in the subsystem of the probable limits of this tolerance.

What happened in ITU, IAEA, IMF, and GATT by contrast had to be explained largely in terms of their representative subsystems. Governments— and in the case of ITU, private associations—consider these organizations to be direct instruments of policy or places where policies can be harmonized. More than the decisions taken by the first-mentioned group of agencies, their decisions have been responsive to the conditions of their specific environ- ments, for example, changes in international economic relationships affect decisions in IMF and GATT. This is not surprising, since state policies also are to be understood mainly in terms of environmental factors: economic, technological, or political.

The essential distinction is between organizations that must be thought of as a set of individuals, and those that must be thought of as a set of states or, in the terms of this study, between organizations dominated by participant subsystems and those that are dominated by representative subsystems. Organizations of the latter sort have, by definition, little or no autonomy. What they can do is always limited by the decisions of states. The full implications of this distinction must be examined in the last section.

An eighth conclusion can, however, be drawn from the distinction made in the seventh: organizations subject to participant subsystem dominance are those whose work has little salience for states, especially powerful states; and organizations characterized by representative subsystem dominance are those whose work has great salience. The issue of salience relates to the consequences of the rule-creating and the rule-supervisory decisions taken by the organization. Of all the actions taken through international organizations, those that make and apply rules have the greatest implications for the behavior of the major states. Participant subsystem dominated organizations are those that do not take rule-creating and rule-supervisory decisions or take only such decisions that have minor immediate consequences. The organizations that do take rule-creating and rule-supervisory decisions that have important immediate consequences—or, to put it in other terms, organizations with substantial authority—are dominated by their representative subsystems. By adding this conclusion to that discussed above, about the relative importance of organizational ideologies in the agencies, we can arrange the agencies in a two-by-two matrix.

	Strong Organizational Ideology	Weaker Organizational Ideology	
Rule-creating and rule-supervisory decisions have important immediate consequences.	IMF GATT	ITU IAEA	(Representative Subsystem Dominated)
Rule-creating and rule-supervisory decisions do not have important immediate consequences.	ILO UNCTAD	WHO UNESCO	(Participant Subsystem Dominated)

This matrix suggests that the importance of certain decision types for an international agency and the prominence of its organizational ideology, as well as its membership and the type of political system that it will have, are crucially related. The membership of those organizations in the upper left cell does not include the bulk of the states belonging to one significant group in world politics, namely, the socialist states. This may be a condition of their having significant authority. Conversely, the more universal membership if ILO and UNCTAD may be related to their lesser degree of authority. In a sense these two organizations might be regarded as abortive attempts to gain substantial authority. Although many poor countries would have liked to give UNCTAD substantial authority, this was blocked by the rich countries. ILO's case is more complicated. During its early period in the 1920s and 1930s, ILO's rule making probably had greater relevance to the preoccupations of its major member states than has been the case more recently. Particularly since the 1950s, the expansion of membership has brought greater ideological diversity into the organization and has shifted emphasis from rule creating to services. In these two organizations symbolic decisions have come to assume greater importance and to be more controversial than in any of the other organizations. In other words, an accent on symbolism appears to be a surrogate for substantial rule-creating and rule-supervisory authority. The fact that decision making in these two organizations is dominated by their participant subsystems reflects their failure to gain substantial authority. Organizations in the upper right cell have substantial authority, but the exercise of this authority is not associated with a strong organizational ideology, since these agencies have precise and limited tasks that have been defined for them through agreement by the major states. Organizations in the lower right cell concentrate on providing service of a kind that can be carried out essentially by international bureaucracies, rather than by collaboration among national experts. This explains the importance of programmatic and operational decisions in such organizations and the tendency to leave such decisions, within wide limits, to their participant subsystems.

The broad conclusion that organizations dominated by their participant subsystems are those whose work has little salience for the major states is another sobering reflection on conventional functionalist theory, which in the past conveyed the message that autonomy for international organizations was universally a "good thing" because world government would gradually be built on the basis of a series of autonomous, functionally defined centers of power. On this assumption, the record of the past two decades is not very promising. But perhaps the functionalist stress on organizational autonomy as a general goal has been misplaced.

A ninth and final conclusion from the foregoing analysis suggests an alternative approach: viewing international organizations according to how far they involve the effective policy-making processes of governments rather than how independent of states they have become. This view leads toward a fuller understanding of the role of international organizations in international relations, though their role does not appear to conform to the ultimate goals of functionalism.

In this perspective, international organizations are sensitive communications networks within which the power holders in world affairs have been responsive to signals from the less powerful without abandoning the control of action to them. International organizations facilitate the orderly management of intergovernmental relations witout significantly changing the structure of power that governs these relations, at least in the short term and somewhat beyond. Over their longer history, the greatest potential for change from international organizations may lie in the opportunity they give the less powerful to influence the climate of opinion and the accepted values according to which action is determined.[18] Thus, international organizations have been a medium for gaining widespread acceptance of the obligation on the part of the wealthier and more powerful to give economic assistance to the poorer and weaker; and they may become a means of giving the less powerful majority of countries a greater collective voice in the management of world affairs, to the extent this majority is able to take advantage of the available communications network by aggregating persuasive views.

Present Trends and Future Prospects

What does all this mean for the future, in regard not only to decision making within international organizations themselves but to their role in world politics? It would be helpful, in trying to answer this question, to have some general models of influence in international organizations, to know which of these models might be best able to respond effectively to emerging issues and what consequences each type is likely to have upon the distribution of world power and wealth. This would, of course, be looking toward the future from the standpoint of the present structure of influence. It would be reasoning forward from the results of our analysis in this book.

The distinction between organizations in which the participant subsystems dominate decision making (those covered in this book being ILO, UNESCO, WHO, and UNCTAD) and those in which representative subsystems dominate (ITU, IMF, GATT, and IAEA) provides one major criterion of structural types. Representative subsystem dominance, almost by definition, means that an organization is governed in the main by the most powerful states. In the classical tradition of politics we can call this the *oligarchic model*. There are two distinct patterns in the way influence is structured in organizations where decision making is determined by the participant subsystem. One is what can be called a *monarchic model,* the other a *pluralistic-bargaining model*. These models are ideal types in the Weberian sense. Each of the organizations studied has some elements of each type, but each also tends characteristically toward one of the three types. The principal properties of these models are outlined in the following paragraphs.

The monarchic model is characterized by the importance of the executive head and of other actors who belong to the organization's establishment, regardless of whether they are members of the international bureaucracy, representatives of states and other entities, or independent personalities. The model has certain analogies with monarchies of fifteenth-century Europe. In these monarchies the king is the central, most powerful figure, but his power has limits. He must retain support among the barons, for he has not the power to crush them. He can strengthen his own position by enlarging his own court. Courtiers are dependent on him for favor; but he must always be watchful of courtly intrigue, of the ambition of courtiers to become barons. The establishments of the monarchic type of international organizations are composed of a mixture of barons and courtiers—both to be found among influential representatives and international officials—often quarreling among themselves and nourishing rival ambitions, but united in their loyalty if not to the king at least to the crown, that is, the institution. Establishments may sometimes be divided about goals and often about policies, but they unite in defense of the organization and of the existing structure of influence.

The important decisions in monarchic organizations are thus made by the executive head and the influential individuals forming the establishment, who together manipulate the participant subsystem. These individuals are in theory accountable to states; but in practice they enjoy much latitude and autonomy in what they do within the organization. Members of the establishment are more accountable to each other than to states. The most powerful states tolerate this situation so long as the activities of such organizations do not seriously affect them. ILO and WHO tend to resemble this model.

The oligarchic organization is a second type. The activities of such agencies are considered highly salient by the most powerful states, and a frequent activity of the agencies is to create rules that apply to these states, as well as to others, and have important consequences. The authority of the executive head and of the international bureaucracy is defined with precision, and wherever possible it is constricted. Such tasks as they must perform are carefully monitored by representatives of states. The most influential actors are the representatives of the most powerful states, and they are accountable to the highest levels of national government for what they do. State policies, rather than the participant subsystem, explain decision making and the structure of influence. ITU, IAEA, IMF, and GATT most closely fit this model.

The third type is the pluralistic-bargaining model. In organizations of this type the pattern of influence is extremely diffuse and fluid. What goes on in the organization can be explained largely in terms of the participant subsystem, but there is no single network through which this subsystem is manipulated, no cohesive establishment. Different coalitions pursue different goals and negotiate understandings on the allocation of resources. These crosscutting alliances of individuals in the participant subsystem are the salient characteristics of the model.

This model has to be explained largely in negative terms. Either because of personal inabilities or because of constraints on his authority, the executive head has not been able to establish his dominance. Because there is not sufficient consensus on objectives, and there is considerable divergence of interest, no establishment has formed upon which leadership could rely. The most powerful states are not interested in playing a leading role because the organization's activities do not affect them. This situation, in turn, is a consequence of the very nature of the activities or of a conspiracy on the part of the most powerful states to limit the authority of the organization. UNESCO and UNCTAD are organizations roughly of this type.

How the organizations' resemblances to these decision-making models bear on their output would seem to be clear. Those agencies whose activities will have the most substantial immediate effects are also those in which influence is most closely held by the rich, established states, in other words by the states least interested in redistribution. The output of other agencies may be more oriented toward redistribution, but the immediate consequences of their work will be less. Since all international organizations comprise individuals drawn from national establishments, even those agencies that have advocated redistribution among countries are unlikely to urge redistribution within countries.

It is not sufficient to outline the properties of these models as though international organizations were stable political systems enduring indefinitely in the same form. In looking toward the future, it is important to understand how each model might respond to the changing conditions of the larger international system within which it operates.

Conventional functionalist theory is a point of reference. Functionalism posits that organizations should be grounded upon a perception of common functional problems requiring action at a level beyond that of the nation-state. Functionalism sees the growth of autonomy of international organizations as a way of transforming the nation-state system and tends to link autonomy with a leading role for the executive head and international bureaucracy. How likely is it that future developments will follow the path started by functionalism? The matter may be approached by considering how the nature of the issues may affect the selection of structures of influence. Issues may be a forcing-ground for organization.

The substantive business of the eight organizations studied—and by extension the business of other organizations as well—forms three big clusters of issues. First are the issues concerned with East-West relations. These begin with arms limitation and arms control, extend to nuclear questions, and also include other scientific and technological matters. The second group are issues concerned with the functioning of the world market economy, including regulation of international trade and payments. Third, there are the issues of development assistance.

East-West issues have been dealt with only to a limited extent through international organizations, IAEA being the outstanding exception to this general rule. Insofar as international organizations have been involved, these issues have been handled through structures of influence approximating the oligarchic model. Some organizations in which the participant subsystem dominates, such as ILO and UNESCO, have attempted on occasion to play a role in this area; but even in these organizations East-West issues tend to be determined by the relevant representative subsystems.

The world market economy is the economic system in which the large, free-market national economies are the principal components. It is a transnational system in which private organizations—and notably among them the large multinational corporations—interact with states. Though it is the largest economic system, measured by wealth and geographical extent, it is not the only one, since the Soviet-dominated world socialist economy coexists with it. The world market economy requires certain regulatory mechanisms; these were institutionalized at the beginning of the period studied in this book, that is, following the Bretton Woods conference of 1944. The structure of influence in these institutions conformed to the oligarchic model.

Changes have taken place in the system during the intervening period; and these have been followed by some adaptation of the institutions. At their origins, IMF and GATT were the servants of the Western countries, functioning for a trading area that also included the colonial territories of these countries. When most of these colonial territories became independent, the new countries continued to be part of the same transnational economic system as before, but now in many cases they participated as independent members of the two organizations.

Although the expansion of membership did not significantly alter the structure of influence in IMF and GATT, it did tend to diminish the real importance of these organizations to the richer countries, which began to transact the economic business of most concern to themselves in more restricted forums. Monetary negotiations are initiated and agreements prepared through OECD and the Group of Ten; and, with the completion of the Kennedy Round, GATT's significance for the world's biggest traders may have been reduced at least temporarily.

Thus with regard to the issues of the world market economy, oligarchic structures of influence prevail in international organization. In addition, a hierarchy of organizations has arisen according to the relative importance of decisions for the richest countries.

Less-developed countries have reacted by converting UNCTAD into their pressure group. The minimal contacts that both IMF and GATT have acquired with socialist countries of Eastern Europe (*not* including the USSR) can be seen as testing the extent to which the world market economy may establish links with the socialist area.

Development assistance, by contrast, seems to have become the sphere of activity of organizations in which the participant subsystems dominate. It has been the principal factor in the growth of ILO and UNESCO and was from the outset the main task of WHO. Development assistance activities require large international bureaucracies for their execution, and strong international bureaucracies have been regarded as the necessary underpinning for the autonomy of international organizations. Is development assistance then perhaps the road toward greater autonomy and authority for international organizations at the present time?

We think the answer is no and that the autonomy apparent in some of these organizations in the 1960s was based on an illusion. This semblance of autonomy has to be explained largely in terms of the ways in which influence is exercised among international organizations.

In the early 1950s, the United States was the dominant influence in all of the organizations studied here, as well as in other specialized agencies and in the United Nations itself. In many cases the executive heads were Americans;

and even if they were not, their acceptability to the United States government was a major consideration in their appointment. These separate institutions were each subject to a common predominant state influence.

Since the 1950s, a more complex situation has developed. Other Western countries have gained in power relative to the United States. The dialogue between these other Western countries and the United States on issues of direct concern to them has shifted to the more restricted international organizations. At the same time, the United States and the other Western countries have sought to direct the international agencies with a large membership from less-developed countries into a more exclusive preoccupation with development assistance, since they no longer wished to use them for issues of concern directly to themselves.

The success of this policy in certain organizations, such as ILO and UNESCO, has however been accompanied by a withdrawal of the United States and other Western powers; from positions of active influence they turned to positions as controllers within these organizations. Seen from the perspective of the political system of that particular organization, that is, ILO or UNESCO, the United States appeared to be more retiring. Seen from the perspective of the whole system of interagency relations, however, the continuing expansion of these agencies was dependent upon voluntary funds provided outside their assessed budgets mainly by the United States and other Western countries. Most of these voluntary funds came through the UNDP, and the United States seems to have retained a de facto right to appoint the administrator of that program and an undoubtedly great—albeit indirect—influence over its management.

In very rough terms the arrangements that have been worked out might be described as follows. The most powerful states, particularly the United States, have determined the level at which the UNDP would be supported financially; a cartel of agency executive heads and bureaucrats has determined the proportion of the funds that each agency would receive; and the management of the program has been carefully overseen by the United States. In this way it has been possible for the rich Western countries to give these universal organizations a general orientation toward development, but no one has really been in a position to determine development policies. In practice, these have been shaped through the cumulative impact of countless operational decisions and individual bargains struck between international and national bureaucrats. Frustration of the major contributors because of their lack of influence in this latter respect has led to the reappraisal of UNDP through the commission headed by Sir Robert Jackson. This body has advocated more centralized management of all development assistance activities.

The illusory aspect of the autonomy of the service-oriented international organizations during the 1960s lay in the fact that the ultimate control of the powerful states was always there, even though it was seldom asserted directly. International organizations could provide only the services that governments would accept, and the levels were determined by the decisions of a few of the most powerful states. Now that some governments want to go further and have a more active voice in shaping development policies, the job of development assistance may be reorganized so as to diminish the role of those specialized agencies of the monarchic and pluralistic-bargaining types, which had the biggest programs in the 1960s.

Are new issues looming that might alter the tendency toward oligarchic organizations? The emerging functional opportunities have not been examined systematically in this book, although some new problems and opportunities have been touched upon incidentally in the chapters dealing with different organizations. Arms control and related issues have been mentioned already, but there do not seem to be any real prospects that these will be resolved by giving wide authority to an international organization. The two issue areas most charged with new, unresolved, and growing problems are the world market economy and world ecology.

Past experience would suggest that economic as well as ecological issues, both of which have high priority for powerful countries, will be dealt with under the direct control of these states, either through ad hoc intergovernmental consultations designed to harmonize national policies or through international organizations of the oligarchic type in which the representative subsystems of these states effectively determine decisions. The trends apparent in the present evolution of international organization would thus be reinforced. Having structures of influence in which rich and powerful countries are preponderant, international organizations would continue to be supports for the existing ordering of power and wealth. They would be unlikely to act toward redistribution of world power and wealth.

This prospect in itself, by demonstrating the power relations inherent in an extension of international organizations on their present basis, raises the possibility of a dialectical reaction. If international organizations appear to be controlled by the interests of the rich, the poor may seek their own defense through a resurgence of nationalism. This could apply to the new issues as well as the old. Population control has already become politicized, being represented as the instrument that the rich and the white have chosen to contain the poor and the colored. Other proposals for ecological controls may be similarly interpreted as attempts to stabilize the planet in favor of the already developed areas. The nation-state is the only available instrument capable of controlling multinational corporations and other external influences on national economies. Small nations fearful of foreign economic domination may use it, despite contrary advice from the World Bank, to control these external influences. Nationalism in these circumstances is not an irrational reaction to the need for orderly management of the world's resources. It may be but the subordination of this need to what the poor of the world regard as a greater need—redistribution of wealth and power. As future changes in the stratification of world power give China greater influence, this tendency is likely to be strengthened. Like all dialectical reactions, this one will probably have its limits in time. After that limit is reached, the need for international organization of economic and ecological affairs will still remain, but it may perhaps be posed in terms of altered power relations.

Two prospects and one problem for the future of international organizations appear from the foregoing. The first prospect is negative: the monarchic model of international organization is not the wave of the future. Not that the monarchic institutions of today are in danger of disappearance. Some may continue to perform their low-salient tasks without challenge and with an efficiency born of routine. Others may face the subtle danger of fossilization, a gradual voiding of substance in favor of empty ritual, as the vital forces in the environment steadily lose interest. The autonomy that these organizations have gained may have been bought at the price of irrelevancy and of a diminishing involvement of persons and interests in the national capitals, where the real source of power over men and material continues to rest. Some functionalists saw in the monarchic model a step toward world government; but their hope has failed.

The second prospect is positive: the oligarchic model, in contrast to the monarchic, will continue to be the most effective way of handling important business. Any significant future growth or task expansion of international organization is likely to be through this type. The people who make these organizations work have never entertained any thoughts of building world government; but they have had the more immediate and practical goals of maximizing international cooperation without seeking to supplant the state system. They have penetrated more deeply into national policy making by involving influential national policy makers more fully in their work. This they can do because the decisions made in such organizations are often of great consequence for powerful states.

The problem ahead is how the prospect of future vitality for the oligarchic model—which will reinforce the existing distribution and stratification of power and wealth—can be squared with the rising demands of the poor.

One answer may be an increasing prominence of nationalism in world affairs. Poor countries' nationalism is more and more a transnational phenomenon. Radical and revolutionary elites from different countries have contact with one another. Nationalistic movements no longer focus on the glories of the particular country's past, but assert the personalities of particular peoples allied in protest against established power. The primary issue for nationalism is not economic growth—any classical liberal economist could demonstrate that poor countries would have higher growth by relying on the functioning of the world market economy. The issue is who should decide questions affecting economic growth and other vital matters that concern the nation. The nationalist reaction gives precedence to the goal of acquiring effective local control over local affairs, economic as well as political. Nationalism may be expressed through international organizations. Or it may bypass them.

Another partial answer is that international organizations are supports for the established order only in the short run. Their more lasting effect may be different. Such organizations may lead to new insights, perspectives, and understanding on the part of individuals who participate in their work, as well as by others less directly involved.[19] This is the raw material from which new policies and ultimately new orders are forged. The long-range effect of international organization as a medium through which governments of powerful countries learn adaptive behavior is likely to be most significant when the organizations are those that deeply involve influential policy makers—that is, the oligarchic type.

The resolution of the problem posed by resurgent nationalism can be sought in this direction. There is nothing final in the threefold typology suggested here. In particular, there is no reason to believe that the oligarchic model cannot be transformed in new ways toward a broader diffusion of influence. Its great assets as a new point of departure for the evolution of international organization are the ability to deal with important questions and to involve important people.

Appendix A

The Stratification of Power

Robert W. Cox and Harold K. Jacobson

"Power" is used here in reference to states. It is the potential of a state for wielding external influence. Power is conceived as a function of a number of component factors: the amount of resources, the extent to which these resources can be effectively mobilized to exert influence, skill in using resources, and willingness to use them.

Resources are both material and psychic. Economic and military capabilities are material resources. Reputation, prestige, and morale are psychic resources. Skill is a property of individuals rather than of states, but the general level of skills in the population may be considered an element in a state's power. Willingness to use resources is also a property of individuals; but certain aspects of a state's psychic resources, such as a reputation for determination and a spirit of independence, express potential in this respect.

We have used five indicators for the concepts of the components of power mentioned above. Each indicator has been reduced to a scale. Each country's position on the five scales was recorded and the resulting points added to yield the country's score or "power rating." States were scored for the three base years, 1950, 1958, and 1967. They were then put in rank order for each of these years according to their scores.

The five indicators used are:

1. *Gross National Product (GNP).* A state's GNP is probably the best single indicator of its overall resources.[1] Even with all the qualifications one must make about the unreliability of data from most parts of the world, the difficulties in aligning national accounting systems, and the problems in converting many different currencies to a single one, GNP is a measure that can be used for ordering states according to their economic capacities. It is a comprehensive figure that subsumes several factors, including natural resources, population, level of technology, and capital stock. Although one may question some figures in any table of GNPs, and the figures undoubtedly demonstrate certain disparities, the scoring scheme that we utilized reflects only those substantial differences that are certainly significant. Because GNP data were not available for all thirty-nine countries for 1950, in certain instances we used data for the period 1950-53. Since GNP changes only slowly, and the scoring categories are relatively broad, this should not seriously affect the comparability of the data. In order to be able to use the same scale for the three base years, the figures for 1950-53, 1958, and 1967 have been converted into 1965 prices.

The authors are indebted to Hans Günter, of the International Institute for Labour Studies in Geneva, for advice, criticism, and help in constructing the composite index presented here.

2. *Per capita GNP.* The per capita gross national product is often used as a general indicator of a country's economic development. Here it is especially relevant as indicating a state's ability to mobilize its economic capacity (per capita GNP being an approximate measure of productivity) and thus potentially to use it for external influence—for example, through military action or economic aid. Per capita GNP also correlates fairly well with indicators of the general level of skill in the population.[2]

3. *Population.* A large population may be a handicap to the mobilization of resources in a state with a low level of economic development; but it represents a potential for development and may also be a significant military factor. It should thus be taken as an additional indicator of resources.

4. *Nuclear capability.* Because of the enormous destruction that can be caused by nuclear weapons, nuclear capability has become a unique factor of military power in international relations. Even if a state does not possess nuclear weapons, its known or reputed ability to have them within a few years if it so decides is also to be regarded as a resource for influence.

5. *Prestige.* The international prestige of a state can add to (or conceivably detract from) its objectively assessed economic and military capabilities. Prestige must be assessed by judgment rather than by computation. Ideally, some measurement of the attitudes of other populations toward each state might be desired. The criterion used here is the degree of autonomy or independence of a state's foreign policy, considered as an indicator both of a psychic resource in dealing with other states and of willingness to exert influence in external relations.

The scales used for the five indicators are as follows:

GNP at 1965 prices (in billions of dollars)

1	under .9	7	30-39
2	1-3.9	8	40-59
3	4-6.9	9	60-99
4	7-9.9	10	100-199
5	10-19.9	11	200-499
6	20-29	12	500 and over

GNP per capita at 1965 prices (in dollars)
1 under 200
2 200-599
3 600-999
4 1,000 and over

Population (in millions)
0 under 2
1 2-19
2 20-59
3 60-99
4 100-249
5 over 250

Nuclear capability
0 no foreseeable nuclear capability
1 ability to acquire nuclear weapons by 1980-85
2 possession of nuclear weapons
3 developed "second strike" capability

Prestige
0 nonindependent foreign policy
1 alliance-aligned
2 neutral or nonaligned, independent foreign
   policy
3 leader of alliance system or recognized
   leadership of a group of states or
   active independence in a hostile
   environment

The scores yielded by this method do not show a sufficiently wide spread to give a proper reflection of *relative* power. For example, the United States in 1967 scores 26 and Switzerland 13; it cannot be concluded that the United States is only twice as powerful as Switzerland. The aim of the exercise is to give a realistic rank order of power, and the method seems ·adequate to this purpose. Changes in rank order can thus be traced over the period 1950-67. Further refinements could be introduced in weighting and scaling, but these do not seem to be necessary for the purpose of rank ordering.

The basic figures yielding the score for each country are given in the following table. Only thirty-nine countries are included, the others being all small powers. The five figures that are added to form the total are given in the order: GNP (1-12), GNP per capita (1-4), population (0-5), nuclear capability (0-3), prestige (0-3).

	1950-53	1958	1967
Argentina	5 + 2 + 1 + 0 + 1 (9)	5 + 3 + 2 + 0 + 1 (11)	5 + 3 + 2 + 1 + 1 (12)
Australia	5 + 4 + 1 + 0 + 1 (11)	5 + 4 + 1 + 0 + 1 (11)	6 + 4 + 1 + 1 + 1 (13)
Austria	3 + 2 + 1 + 0 + 0 (6)	3 + 3 + 1 + 0 + 2 (9)	5 + 4 + 1 + 1 + 2 (13)
Belgium	5 + 4 + 1 + 0 + 1 (11)	5 + 4 + 1 + 0 + 1 (11)	5 + 4 + 1 + 1 + 1 (12)
Brazil	5 + 2 + 3 + 0 + 1 (11)	6 + 2 + 3 + 0 ı 1 (12)	6 + 2 + 3 + 1 + 1 (13)
Canada	7 + 4 + 1 + 1 + 1 (14)	7 + 4 + 1 + 1 + 1 (14)	8 + 4 + 2 + 1 + 1 (16)
Cuba	2 + 2 + 1 + 0 + 1 (6)	2 + 2 + 1 + 0 + 3 (8)	4 + 2 + 1 + 0 + 3 (10)
Czechoslovakia	4 + 3 + 1 + 0 + 0 (8)	5 + 3 + 1 + 0 + 0 (9)	6 + 3 + 1 + 1 + 0 (11)
Denmark	2 + 4 + 1 + 0 + 1 (8)	3 + 4 + 1 + 0 + 1 (9)	5 + 4 + 1 + 0 + 1 (11)

	1950-53	*1958*	*1967*
Federal Republic of Germany	8 + 3 + 2 + 0 + 1 (14)	9 + 3 + 2 + 1 + 1 (16)	10 + 4 + 2 + 1 + 1 (18)
Finland	3 + 3 + 1 + 0 + 0 (7)	3 + 3 + 1 + 0 + 0 (7)	4 + 4 + 1 + 0 + 0 (9)
France	8 + 4 + 2 + 1 + 1 (16)	9 + 4 + 2 + 1 + 1 (17)	10 + 4 + 2 + 2 + 2 (20)
German Democratic Republic	4 + 2 + 1 + 0 + 0 (7)	5 + 3 + 1 + 0 + 0 (9)	6 + 4 + 1 + 0 + 0 (11)
India	6 + 1 + 5 + 0 + 2 (14)	7 + 1 + 5 + 1 + 2 (16)	7 + 1 + 5 + 1 + 2 (16)
Indonesia	4 + 1 + 3 + 0 + 2 (10)	5 + 1 + 3 + 0 + 2 (11)	4 + 1 + 4 + 1 + 1 (11)
Israel	1 + 2 + 1 + 0 + 3 (7)	2 + 3 + 1 + 0 + 3 (9)	2 + 4 + 1 + 1 + 3 (11)
Italy	6 + 2 + 2 + 0 + 1 (11)	7 + 3 + 2 + 1 + 1 (14)	9 + 4 + 2 + 1 + 1 (17)
Japan	6 + 2 + 3 + 0 + 1 (12)	7 + 2 + 3 + 0 + 1 (13)	10 + 4 + 3 + 1 + 1 (19)
Luxembourg	1 + 4 + 0 + 0 + 1 (6)	1 + 4 + 0 + 0 + 1 (6)	1 + 4 + 0 + 0 + 1 (6)
Mexico	4 + 2 + 2 + 0 + 1 (9)	5 + 2 + 2 + 0 + 1 (10)	6 + 2 + 2 + 0 + 1 (11)
Netherlands	4 + 3 + 1 + 0 + 1 (9)	5 + 3 + 1 + 0 + 1 (10)	6 + 4 + 1 + 1 + 1 (13)
New Zealand	2 + 4 + 1 + 0 + 1 (8)	2 + 4 + 1 + 0 + 1 (8)	3 + 4 + 1 + 0 + 1 (9)
Nigeria	2 + 1 + 2 + 0 + 0 (5)	2 + 1 + 2 + 0 + 0 (5)	3 + 1 + 3 + 0 + 2 (9)
Norway	2 + 4 + 1 + 0 + 1 (8)	3 + 4 + 1 + 0 + 1 (9)	4 + 4 + 1 + 0 + 1 (10)
Pakistan	3 + 1 + 3 + 0 + 1 (8)	3 + 1 + 3 + 0 + 1 (8)	5 + 1 + 4 + 1 + 1 (12)
People's Republic of China	7 + 1 + 5 + 1 + 1 (15)	8 + 1 + 5 + 1 + 2 (17)	9 + 1 + 5 + 2 + 2 (19)
Philippines	3 + 2 + 2 + 0 + 1 (8)	3 + 2 + 2 + 0 + 1 (8)	4 + 2 + 2 + 0 + 1 (9)
Poland	4 + 2 + 2 + 0 + 0 (8)	5 + 2 + 2 + 0 + 0 (9)	6 + 3 + 2 + 1 + 0 (12)
South Africa	3 + 2 + 1 + 0 + 3 (9)	4 + 2 + 1 + 0 + 3 (10)	5 + 2 + 1 + 1 + 3 (12)
Spain	5 + 2 + 2 + 0 + 1 (10)	5 + 2 + 2 + 0 + 1 (10)	6 + 3 + 2 + 1 + 1 (13)
Sweden	4 + 4 + 1 + 0 + 2 (11)	5 + 4 + 1 + 0 + 2 (12)	6 + 4 + 1 + 1 + 2 (14)
Switzerland	4 + 4 + 1 + 0 + 2 (11)	4 + 4 + 1 + 0 + 2 (11)	5 + 4 + 1 + 1 + 2 (13)

	1950-53	*1958*	*1967*
Turkey	3 + 2 + 2 + 0 + 1 (8)	3 + 2 + 2 + 0 + 1 (8)	5 + 2 + 2 + 0 + 1 (10)
United Arab Republic	2 + 1 + 2 + 0 + 3 (8)	2 + 1 + 2 + 0 + 3 (8)	3 + 1 + 2 + 1 + 3 (10)
United Kingdom	9 + 4 + 2 + 1 + 1 (17)	9 + 4 + 2 + 2 + 1 (18)	10 + 4 + 2 + 2 + 1 (19)
United States	11 + 4 + 4 + 2 + 3 (24)	11 + 4 + 4 + 3 + 3 (25)	12 + 4 + 4 + 3 + 3 (26)
USSR	10 + 2 + 4 + 2 + 3 (21)	10 + 3 + 4 + 3 + 3 (23)	11 + 3 + 4 + 3 + 3 (24)
Venezuela	3 + 3 + 1 + 0 + 1 (8)	4 + 3 + 1 + 0 + 1 (9)	4 + 3 + 1 + 0 + 1 (9)
Yugoslavia	3 + 2 + 1 + 0 + 3 (9)	3 + 2 + 1 + 0 + 3 (9)	6 + 2 + 1 + 1 + 3 (13)

The rank order of states based on the above scores is shown in table A.1. This stratification of power may be compared with those used by other authors. While recognizing the limitations of gross national product, A. F. K. Organski has used GNP as a single indicator subsuming many of the factors of power.[3] His scheme has the merit of greater simplicity than ours. Its disadvantage is that it does not include the psychic element in power. A more complex computation is involved in the method used by F. Clifford German.[4] This does include morale and gives a special weighting for nuclear power. (It does not, however, include the notion of prestige as a resource for influence.) The disadvantages of German's method are its unnecessarily complicated (for our purposes) ways of estimating the strategic advantages of land space and economic resources. Furthermore, the complexity of the method makes it troublesome to apply to large numbers of countries. Both the Organski and German methods have the apparent advantage over ours of suggesting measurement of relative power by showing the intervals between states on a scale, as well as their ranking. That this advantage is more apparent than real is suggested both by Organski, who does not make much more of a claim for GNP than that it shows a ranking of power,[5] and by German, who acknowledges that the dissatisfied reader can change the coefficients to his indicators according to his own aesthetic judgment.[6]

The broad similarity of the results given by all three methods is striking. Where they differ, we feel our method gives more satisfactory results. Among the leading states the use of GNP alone seems to underrate the power of France, China, and India and to overrate that of the United Kingdom, the Federal Republic of Germany, and Canada. (These limitations are recognized by Organski.) The effect is to shift their ranking within the top ten, but it does not change their status as members of the top ten. German's method seems to underrate France, which has eighth place in his ranking compared

Table A.1
Rank Order of States according to Power

Rank Order	1950	Score	Rank Order	1958	Score	Rank Order	1967	Score
1	United States	24	1	United States	25	1	United States	26
2	USSR	21	2	USSR	23	2	USSR	24
3	United Kingdom	17	3	United Kingdom	18	3	France	20
4	France	16	4.5	China	17	5	China	19
5	China	15	4.5	France	17	5	Japan	19
7	Canada	14	6.5	Federal Republic of Germany	16	5	United Kingdom	19
7	Federal Republic of Germany	14	6.5	India	16	7	Federal Republic of Germany	18
7	India	14	8.5	Canada	14	8	Italy	17
9	Japan	12	8.5	Italy	14	9.5	Canada	16
12.5	Australia	11	10	Japan	13	9.5	India	16
12.5	Belgium	11	11.5	Brazil	12	11	Sweden	14
12.5	Brazil	11	11.5	Sweden	12	15	Australia	13
12.5	Italy	11	15	Argentina	11	15	Austria	13
12.5	Sweden	11	15	Australia	11	15	Brazil	13
12.5	Switzerland	11	15	Belgium	11	15	Netherlands	13
16.5	Indonesia	10	15	Indonesia	11	15	Spain	13
16.5	Spain	10	15	Switzerland	11	15	Switzerland	13
20	Argentina	9	19.5	Mexico	10	15	Yugoslavia	13
20	Mexico	9	19.5	Netherlands	10	21	Argentina	12
20	Netherlands	9	19.5	Spain	10	21	Belgium	12
20	South Africa	9	19.5	South Africa	10	21	Pakistan	12
20	Yugoslavia	9	26	Austria	9	21	Poland	12
27.5	Czechoslovakia	8	26	Czechoslovakia	9	21	South Africa	12
27.5	Denmark	8	26	Denmark	9	26.5	Czechoslovakia	11
27.5	New Zealand	8	26	German Democratic Republic	9	26.5	Denmark	11
27.5	Norway	8	26	Israel	9	26.5	German Democratic Republic	11
27.5	Pakistan	8	26	Norway	9	26.5	Indonesia	11
27.5	Philippines	8	26	Poland	9	26.5	Israel	11
27.5	Poland	8	26	Yugoslavia	9	26.5	Mexico	11
27.5	Turkey	8	26	Venezuela	9	31.5	Cuba	10
27.5	United Arab Republic	8	33.5	Cuba	8	31.5	Norway	10
27.5	Venezuela	8	33.5	New Zealand	8	31.5	Turkey	10
34	Finland	7	33.5	Pakistan	8	31.5	United Arab Republic	10
34	German Democratic Republic	7	33.5	Philippines	8	36	Finland	9
34	Israel	7	33.5	Turkey	8	36	New Zealand	9
37	Austria	6	33.5	United Arab Republic	8	36	Nigeria	9
37	Cuba	6	36	Finland	7	36	Philippines	9
37	Luxembourg	6	38	Luxembourg	6	36	Venezuela	9
39	Nigeria	5	39	Nigeria	5	39	Luxembourg	6

with a rank order of 4.5 in ours for 1958, as well as India and Italy; it apparently overrates Japan, giving it seventh place in his ranking compared with tenth in ours for 1958. German also ranks Poland, Czechoslovakia, and the German Democratic Republic in tenth, thirteenth, and fifteenth places, respectively, whereas in our computation they come out much lower, sharing a rank of 26. Rated by GNP alone, Czechoslovakia and the German Democratic Republic, by contrast, seem to fall too low, perhaps as a consequence of the use of different statistical concepts. Our method includes countries like Cuba, Israel, the United Arab Republic, and Yugoslavia within the 20-30 rank range, thus recognizing their importance in world affairs and the influence they may wield because of their ideological position, their assertions of independence, or similar reasons related to prestige.

One objection to our index might be that the scoring system produces a number of equal scores, resulting in a ranking by groups of countries that tend to increase in size at the lower ranks. GNP or the German index, by contrast, gives a precise rank to each state. The concepts and measurement of power are, however, so rudimentary that small differences in the ratings of states would be illusory. It thus seems more in keeping with the real state of knowledge to work with measures that do not pretend to too much precision.

Differences in the indices discussed here reflect different concepts of power. GNP is a very comprehensive indicator of economic potential. German's composite index seems to reflect a Clausewitzian view of power as consisting ultimately in military capabilities; and its stress on land space and self-sufficiency implies strategic concepts of variable validity depending upon the technology of warfare. If, however, power in international relations is thought of as potentiality for influence in the normal business of world affairs, then other factors should be included. Among these other factors, our composite index gives some—but probably not enough—weight to prestige. In a search for better and fuller indicators of power, it should be possible to devise more sophisticated measures of prestige than we have used.

Another factor that would merit inclusion (and was referred to by Organski) is the effectiveness of political systems: to some extent this may be represented by GNP per capita, but measurement specifically both of the level of administrative efficiency of a government and of the degree of commitment or involvement of the population in support of government policies would be a valuable addition. Self-sufficiency has advantages in a state of siege; but interdependency—for example, a large share of world trade—would be a potentiality for influence in more normal circumstances. Finally, consideration should be given to the power that stems from weakness; for example, a state like India can exert influence because its low level of development is a matter of concern to richer countries.[7] The volume of external aid received by a country might be an indicator of this particular potentiality for influence. These are directions that new efforts toward the measurement of power might explore.

Appendix B
Capacity in the Organizationally Specific Environments

Shown in this appendix are rank orders of states in the specific environments of the International Labor Organization (see table B.1), the International Telecommunication Union (see tables B.2, B.3, B.4), the World Health Organization (see table B.5), and the International Monetary Fund (see table B.6).

Rank orders of capabilities in the specific environments of the organizations not given in this appendix are included in the chapters relating to them: for UNESCO, see tables 5.3 and 5.4 (pp. 169-72); for IAEA, see table 7.5 (p. 251); for GATT, see table 9.4 (p. 326); and for UNCTAD, see table 10.7 (p. 364).

International Labor Organization

The composite index of labor policy capabilities of states, constructed for the three base years 1950, 1958, and 1967, is designed to give a rank order of states according to their capabilities in the field of activities of the ILO.[1] Capabilities is used to mean both the possession of resources and effectiveness in using them. Defining this field and selecting indicators necessitates some bias. For example, to stress industry and industrial employment implies the judgment that the ILO exists primarily to deal with questions of industrial labor, although some countries' delegates are maintaining that now the ILO should give more attention to rural workers. Nevertheless, the structure of representation in the ILO reflects organized industry, so this bias may be justified in an attempt to categorize the environment.

Variables included in the composite index are—
- A. the aggregate importance of industry in the country
- B. the total number of workers potentially unionizable
- C. the strength (in numbers of members and in effectiveness of organization) of trade unions and employer organizations
- D. the objective success of the country in managing the critical problems affecting labor (such as unemployment, level of earnings, and rights of the worker)
- E. the international prestige of the country in the fields of labor and social policy

The indicators chosen to measure these variables are (in parentheses is the letter of the component to which the indicator relates)—
1. *Total industrial production.*[2]   (A)
2. *Share of industrial production in total production.*   (A)

This appendix was prepared jointly by Robert W. Cox, who wrote the section on ILO; Harold K. Jacobson, the sections on ITU and WHO; and Susan Strange, the section on IMF.

3. *Total industrial labor force.* (B) The labor force figures are based on census data and are available only for 1950 and 1960. The 1960 figures have been used in both the 1958 and 1967 indices. The result is probably to understate in most cases the 1967 indices, but this is unlikely to bias the resulting rank order significantly.

4. *Industrial labor force as a percentage of total labor force.* (B) Same observation as for 3.

5. *Prestige of industrial relations system.* (E) The index is based on replies by a number of specialists in industrial relations to a questionnaire seeking their opinion on the extent to which some countries' industrial relations systems are or were "models" for those of other countries. It takes account of historical impact, efforts actively to promote one's national system or some significant part of it as a model, and the extent of actual emulation in other countries.

6. *Importance of trade union members as a percentage of the total labor force.* (C) Trade union membership figures vary in reliability. Figures used for some countries are only approximations. Data are not available in all cases for 1950 and 1958. If such data were missing, the same rating as in 1967 was used whenever assumed trends in membership and available figures on labor force changes indicated that a change in rating was unlikely.

7. *Effectiveness of trade union and employer organizations.* (C) The index is based on a number of specialists' replies to a questionnaire. Trade union effectiveness is rated according to unity of action, unity of organization, and authority over members. For employer organizations, there is a simple judgment of relative effectiveness, taking into account the degree of organization of individual employers, the number of powerful outsiders, acceptance of decisions by members, established relations with representative trade unions, and successful protection of the interests of members. It is likely that this index is most accurate for 1967, as the fullest data are available for that year.

8. *Level of unemployment and underemployment.* (D) These are the indicators used for the objective success of labor policy. Where appropriate, these indicators have been supplemented by migration data. For the majority of countries, unemployment figures are available from the ILO *Yearbook of Labour Statistics*. For most developing countries, however, estimates had to be made, basing judgment upon the prevailing economic conditions (in a few cases conclusions were sustained by indications found in reports by ILO employment experts).

The scales used for rating of components are as follows:

1. *Total industrial production.* A ten-point scale, with ten equal to the proportion of United States gross national product derived from industrial production (the largest of any state). Others were rated proportionately, with figures rounded off upward. On this basis, only nine countries score one or more for 1967. All others score zero.

2. *Industrial production as a percentage of total production.*

Percentage	Points
under 20	0
20-29	1
30 and over	2

3. *Total industrial labor force.* A ten-point scale, with ten equal to the industrial labor force of the USSR (the largest) and others rated proportionately. This gives scores of one or more to nineteen countries for 1960.

4. *Industrial labor force as a percentage of total labor force.*

Percentage	Points
under 20	0
20-29	1
30 and over	2

5. *Prestige of industrial relations systems.* Countries are rated on scales of zero to two for each of the three factors considered.

Factors:	historical impact on other countries
	efforts currently to promote one's national model
	extent of emulation in other countries
Scores:	0 little or no influence on other countries
	1 influence in a few (i.e. from three to six) other countries
	2 influence in many (i.e. more than six) other countries.

6. *Trade union members as a percentage of total labor force.*

Percentage	Points
under 10	0
11-24	1
25 and over	2

7. *Effectiveness of trade union and employers' organizations.*

	Yes	No
Trade unions		
unity of action	1	0
organizational unity	1	0
authority over members	1	0
Employers' organizations		
effectiveness	1	0

8. *Objective success of labor policy.*

Percentage of unemployment or underemployment	Points
under 4	4
5-14	2
15 and over	0

Table B.1 shows the rank order of states resulting from the composite index of labor policy capabilities.

Table B.1
Rank Order of States according to Labor Policy Capabilities

Rank	1950	Rank	1958	Rank	1967
1	United States	1.5	United States	1	United States
2	USSR	1.5	USSR	2	USSR
3	United Kingdom	3	United Kingdom	3	Federal Republic
4	France	4	France		of Germany
6	Federal Republic	5.5	China	4	United Kingdom
	of Germany	5.5	Federal Republic	5.5	France
6	Sweden		of Germany	5.5	China
6	Spain	8	Japan	7	Japan
8	Israel	8	Sweden	8.5	Sweden
11.5	Switzerland	8	Australia	8.5	Australia
11.5	Australia	10.5	Spain	10	Israel
11.5	German Democratic	10.5	Israel	12.5	Italy
	Republic	14.5	Switzerland	12.5	Spain
11.5	Norway	14.5	Netherlands	12.5	German Democratic
11.5	Czechoslovakia	14.5	German Democratic		Republic
11.5	New Zealand		Republic	12.5	Czechoslovakia
17	China	14.5	Norway	18	Switzerland
17	Canada	14.5	Czechoslovakia	18	Denmark
17	Netherlands	14.5	New Zealand	18	Netherlands
17	Poland	20	Italy	18	Austria
17	Luxembourg	20	Canada	18	Cuba
22.5	Japan	20	Poland	18	Norway
22.5	Italy	20	Finland	18	New Zealand
22.5	Argentina	20	Luxembourg	24.5	Canada
22.5	Denmark	23.5	Denmark	24.5	Belgium
22.5	Austria	23.5	Austria	24.5	Poland
22.5	Finland	26	Argentina	24.5	Yugoslavia
26	Belgium	26	Belgium	24.5	Finland
27	Yugoslavia	26	Yugoslavia	24.5	Luxembourg
28	Venezuela	28	Venezuela	28	Venezuela
29.5	Cuba	29.5	South Africa	29	Argentina
29.5	Mexico	29.5	Cuba	30	India
31	South Africa	31.5	India	31.5	South Africa
32	Brazil	31.5	Mexico	31.5	Mexico
33	India	33	Brazil	33	Brazil
34	Turkey	35	United Arab	35	Philippines
35	Philippines		Republic	35	Turkey
37.5	Indonesia	35	Philippines	35	United Arab
37.5	United Arab	35	Turkey		Republic
	Republic	37.5	Indonesia	37	Indonesia
37.5	Nigeria	37.5	Pakistan	38	Nigeria
37.5	Pakistan	39	Nigeria	39	Pakistan

International Telecommunication Union

Table B.2

Rank Order in Telecommunications: 1950

	Telephones in Use (units)	Rank Order	Radio Receivers Produced (thousands)	Rank Order	T. V. Sets Produced (thousands)	Rank Order	Total Score	Composite Rank Order
United States	43,004,000	1	14,590	1	7,464	1	3	1
United Kingdom	5,376,053	2	1,809	3	541	2	7	2
Canada	2,911,900	3	821	6	30	3	12	3
France	2,405,802	4	963	5	5	5	14	4
Federal Republic of Germany	2,393,013	5	2,008	2	—	22.5	29.5	5
Japan	1,664,490	6	287	10	—	22.5	38.5	6.5
Australia	1,109,984	9	343	7	—	22.5	38.5	6.5
USSR	–	36.5	1,071	4	12	4	44.5	8
Denmark	721,821	13	109	12	—	22.5	47.5	9
Czechoslovakia	385,000	19	293	9	—	22.5	50.5	10
Austria	412,989	18	199	11	—	22.5	51.5	11
Norway	451,727	17	102	13	—	22.5	52.5	12
Poland	230,000	24	294	8	—	22.5	54.5	13
Finland	328,394	21	57	15	—	22.5	58.5	15
New Zealand	369,986	20	54	16	—	22.5	58.5	15
Sweden	1,615,200	7	—	29	—	22.5	58.5	15
China	244,028	23	100	14	—	22.5	59.5	17.5
Italy	1,244,152	8	—	29	—	22.5	59.5	17.5
Switzerland	896,398	10	—	29	—	22.5	61.5	19
Argentina	798,391	11	—	29	—	22.5	62.5	20
Netherlands	781,678	12	—	29	—	22.5	63.5	21
India	168,397	25	44	17	—	22.5	64.5	22
Belgium	687,012	14	—	29	—	22.5	65.5	23

	Telephones							
Spain	651,516	15	—	29	22.5	—	66.5	24
South Africa	458,851	16	—	29	22.5	—	67.5	25.5
Yugoslavia	110,170	27	26	18	22.5	—	67.5	25.5
Mexico	285,600	22	—	29	22.5	—	73.5	27
United Arab Republic	115,500	26	—	29	22.5	—	77.5	28
Turkey	65,150	28	—	29	22.5	—	79.5	29
Indonesia	43,000	29	—	29	22.5	—	80.5	30
Israel	29,761	30	—	29	22.5	—	81.5	31
Luxembourg	23,412	31	—	29	22.5	—	82.5	32
Philippines	19,675	32	—	29	22.5	—	83.5	33
Pakistan	19,364	33	—	29	22.5	—	84.5	34
Brazil	—	36.5	—	29	22.5	—	88	37
Cuba	—	36.5	—	29	22.5	—	88	37
German Democratic Republic	—	36.5	—	29	22.5	—	88	37
Nigeria	—	36.5	—	29	22.5	—	88	37
Venezuela	—	36.5	—	29	22.5	—	88	37

Sources: Except for China: Telephones—United Nations, *Statistical Yearbook: 1952* (New York: United Nations, 1953). Radio Receivers and T.V. Sets—*Statistical Yearbook: 1957, 1959,* (New York: United Nations, 1958, 1960). For China: Telephones—*The World's Telephones: 1967* (New York: American Telephone and Telegraph Company, 1967). The figure noted is for 1948. Radio Receivers and T.V. Sets—UNESCO, *Statistical Yearbook: 1967* (Paris: UNESCO, 1968). The figures available indicate radio receivers and T.V. sets *in use.* To get figures roughly comparable to those used for the other states, they have been divided by ten which, in the case of India for example, is the rough ratio between the number of sets in use and those produced annually in this period.

Table B.3

Rank Order in Telecommunications: 1958

	Telephones in Use (units)	Rank Order	Radio Receivers Produced (thousands)	Rank Order	T.V. Sets Produced (thousands)	Rank Order	Total Score	Composite Rank Order
United States	66,630,000	1	12,734	1	5,281	1	3	1
United Kingdom	7,469,000	2	1,774	5	1,985	2	9	2
USSRa	5,324,523	3	3,900	3	1,000	5	11	3
Federal Republic of Germany	5,090,102	5	3,075	4	1,487	3	12	4.5
Japan	4,334,602	6	5,028	2	1,191	4	12	4.5
Canada	5,113,308	4	695	10	420	6	20	6.5
France	3,703,578	7	1,543	6	372	7	20	6.5
Australia	1,936,960	10	381	11	283	8	29	8
Czechoslovakia	789,679	19	303	13	134	10	42	9
Denmark	978,398	16	85	19	119	11	46	10
Poland	446,236	26	790	7	57	14	47	11
China	531,981	24	700	9	1	17	50	12.5
Mexico	447,984	25	328	12	84	13	50	12.5
Austria	615,328	22	279	14	54	15	51	14
Argentina	1,223,593	14	–	30	90	12	56	15.5
German Democratic Republic	–	39	718	8	180	9	56	15.5
Finland	545,338	23	87	18	9	16	57	17
Italy	2,988,465	8	–	30	–	28.5	66.5	18.5
New Zealand	641,342	21	126	17	–	28.5	66.5	18.5
Sweden	2,409,842	9	–	30	–	28.5	67.5	20
Spain	1,477,904	11	–	30	–	28.5	69.5	21
Switzerland	1,475,003	12	–	30	–	28.5	70.5	22
India	367,000	27	198	16	–	28.5	71.5	24
Netherlands	1,402,155	13	–	30	–	28.5	71.5	24
Yugoslavia	217,542	28	259	15	–	28.5	71.5	24
Belgium	1,031,703	15	–	30	–	28.5	73.5	26

Brazil	928,117	17	—	30	—	28.5	75.5	27
South Africa	828,434	18	—	30	—	28.5	76.5	28
Norway	672,406	20	—	30	—	28.5	78.5	29
Israel	93,280	33	33	20	—	28.5	81.5	30
United Arab Republic	185,452	29	—	30	—	28.5	87.5	31
Cuba	170,092	30	—	30	—	28.5	88.5	32
Turkey	167,230	31	—	30	—	28.5	89.5	33
Venezuela	158,575	32	—	30	—	28.5	90.5	34
Indonesia	90,968	34	—	30	—	28.5	92.5	35
Philippines	74,047	35	—	30	—	28.5	93.5	36
Pakistan	63,905	36	—	30	—	28.5	94.5	37
Luxembourg	42,411	37	—	30	—	28.5	95.5	38
Nigeria	29,349	38	—	30	—	28.5	96.5	39

Sources: Except for China: United Nations, Statistical Yearbook: 1959, (New York: United Nations, 1960).
For China: Telephones—The last figure available is for 1948. An estimated figure for 1958 has been computed using the same growth rate as for India between 1950 and 1958. Radio receivers and T.V. sets—UNESCO, Statistical Yearbook: 1967 (Paris: UNESCO, 1968). The figures available indicate radio receivers and T.V. sets in use. To get figures roughly comparable to those used for the other states, they have been divided by ten, which, in the case of India for example, is the rough ratio between the number of sets in use and those produced annually in this period.

aEstimated.

Table B.4

Rank Order in Telecommunications: 1967

	Telephones in Use (units)	Rank Order	Radio Receivers Produced (thousands)	Rank Order	T.V. Sets Produced (thousands)	Rank Order	Total Score	Composite Rank Order
United States	104,073,849	1	19,272	2	9,586	1	4	1
Japan	18,216,767	2	31,624	1	7,038	2	5	2
USSR	9,680,000	5	6,416	3	4,955	3	11	3
Federal Republic of Germany	10,321,281	4	3,751	4	1,917	4	12	4
United Kingdom	12,008,000	3	1,532	8	1,272	5	16	5
France	6,999,621	8	2,208	6	1,242	6	20	6.5
Canada	8,345,000	6	1,604	7	577	7	20	6.5
Spain	3,359,029	10	277	15	551	8	33	8
German Democratic Republic	1,780,319	14	932	10	475	10	34	9
Australia	3,178,278	11	444	13	255	14	38	10
Poland	1,530,479	18	612	12	495	9	39	11
Czechoslovakia	1,678,717	16	305	14	256	13	43	12
Mexico	1,045,506	25	1,035	9	274	12	46	13
China	1,462,947	21	3,000	5	10	23	49	14
Austria	1,163,194	23	238	17	192	16	56	15
Yugoslavia	506,039	29	240	16	252	15	60	16
Brazil	1,472,677	19	—	31.5	417	11	61.5	17
Argentina	1,553,789	17	—	31.5	155	17	65.5	18
New Zealand	1,119,422	24	80	22	54	20	66	19
Finland	949,976	28	103	21	85	19	68	20
India	1,017,990	26	850	11	—	31.5	68.5	21
Italy	7,057,187	7	—	31.5	—	31.5	70	22
United Arab Republic	352,316	31	161	19	48	21	71	23
South Africa	1,322,101	22	184	18	—	31.5	71.5	24

Sweden	3,757,495	9	—	31.5	—	31.5	72	25
Netherlands	2,718,792	12	—	31.5	—	31.5	75	26
Switzerland	2,533,684	13	—	31.5	—	31.5	76	27
Norway	987,264	27	—	31.5	102	18	76.5	28
Philippines	207,593	35	122	20	18	22	77	29
Belgium	1,746,170	15	—	31.5	—	31.5	78	30
Denmark	1,469,195	20	—	31.5	—	31.5	83	31
Israel	344,487	32	18	23	—	31.5	86.5	32
Turkey	427,770	30	—	31.5	—	31.5	93	33
Venezuela	327,038	33	—	31.5	—	31.5	96	34
Cuba	238,224	34	—	31.5	—	31.5	97	35
Indonesia	169,142	36	—	31.5	—	31.5	99	36
Pakistan	162,642	37	—	31.5	—	31.5	100	37
Luxembourg	93,767	38	—	31.5	—	31.5	101	38
Nigeria	77,883	39	—	31.5	—	31.5	102	39

Sources: Except for China: United Nations, *Statistical Yearbook: 1968* (New York: United Nations, 1969).

For China: Telephones — The last figure available is for 1948. An estimated figure for 1967 has been computed using the same growth rate as for India between 1958 and 1967. Radio Receivers and T.V. Sets — UNESCO, *Statistical Yearbook: 1967* (Paris: UNESCO, 1968). The figures available indicate radio receivers and T.V. sets *in use.* To get figures roughly comparable to those used for the other states, they have been divided by ten, which, in the case of India for example, is the rough ratio between the number of sets in use and those produced annually in this period.

World Health Organization

Table B.5

Rank Order in the Specific Environment of WHO: 1966

	Number of Physicians[a]	Rank Order	Inhabitants per Physician[a]	Rank Order	Infant Mortality Rates[b]	Rank Order	Female Life Expectancy at Age 0[c]	Rank Order	Total Rank Order Scores	Composite Rank Order
United States	305,453 (67)	2	650 (67)	10	23.7	15	73.80	10	37	1
Australia	19,351	18	600	7	18.2	8	74.18	7	40	2
France	58,000	7	850	19	21.7	11	75.40	4	41	3
Federal Republic of Germany	94,593	5	630	9	23.5	14	73.57	14.5	42.5	4
United Kingdom	55,000	8	870	21	19.6	10	74.73	5	44	5
Netherlands	14,550	21	860	20	14.7	3	76.10	1	45	6.5
USSR	503,220	1	460	2	26.1	19	70[d]	23	45	6.5
Czechoslovakia	27,096	13	530	3	23.8	16	73.57	14.5	46.5	8
Denmark	6,550	31	570	5.5	16.9	5	74.70	6	47.5	9
Japan	108,290	3	910	23	19.3	9	73.61	13	48	10
Norway	5,020 (67)	33	750 (67)	13.5	14.6	2	75.97	2	50.5	11
Canada	23,990	16	820	17	23.1	13	74.17	8	54	13
Sweden	8,840	28	880	22	12.6	1	75.70	3	54	13
Switzerland	8,857	27	680	12	17.1	6	74.13	9	54	13
Italy	91,519 (67)	6	570 (67)	5.5	34.3	22	72.27	21	54.5	15
German Democratic Republic	21,365	17	750	13.5	22.8	12	73.53	17	59.5	16
Israel	6,339	32	410	1	25.3	17	73.73[e]	12	62	17
Austria	13,108	24	550	4	28.1	21	73.54	16	65	18
Poland	41,331	10	770	15.5	38.9	24	72.90	19	68.5	19
Belgium	14,176	22	670	11	25.4	18	73.51	18	69	20
Spain	41,932 (67)	9	770 (67)	15.5	36.0	23	71.90	22	69.5	21

New Zealand	3,270 (67)	36	18	17.7	7	73.75	11	72	22
Argentina	37,732 (67)	11	8	—	33	68.87	24	76	23
Finland	3,797	34	28	15.0	4	72.60	20	86	24
Yugoslavia	16,976	20	26	62.1	25	65.58	27	98	25
Mexico	24,342	15	31	62.9	26	60.32	28	100	26
India	103,184	4	35	—	33	40.55	34	106	27
Philippines	24,385	14	29	—	33	53.36	31	107	28
Luxembourg	332 (67)	38	24	26.8	20	65.75	26	108	29
Venezuela	7,497	29	27	—	33	66.41e	25	114	30
Brazil	35,200	12	33	—	33	—	37	115	31
United Arab Republic	13,640	23	32	—	33	53.80	29	117	32
Pakistan	17,570	19	36	—	33	48.80	32	120	33
Turkey	11,335	26	34	—	33	53.70e	30	123	34
Cuba	6,862	30	25	—	33	—	37	125	35.5
South Africa	12,473 (67)	25	30	—	33	—	37	125	35.5
Indonesia	3,644	35	37	—	33	47.50	33	138	37
Nigeria	1,982 (67)	37	38	—	33	—	37	145	38
China	—	39	39	—	33	—	37	148	39

a United Nations, *Statistical Yearbook: 1967, 1968, 1969* (New York: United Nations, 1968, 1969, 1970). Where noted, the only figures available are for 1967.

b United Nations, *Statistical Yearbook: 1968* (New York: United Nations, 1969).

c United Nations, *Demographic Yearbook: 1967, 1968* (New York: United Nations, 1968, 1969). The figures should be considered as the latest available, up to 1966.

d Jewish population only.

e Both sexes.

International Monetary Fund

Table B.6

Rank Order in the Specific Environment

1950 Rank Order		Score	1958 Rank Order		Score	1967 Rank Order		Score
1	United States	157	1	United States	(302)	1	United States	(457)
2	United Kingdom	22.5	2	Federal Republic of Germany	(50)	2	Federal Republic of Germany	(82.5)
3	Canada	14	3	United Kingdom	(38)	3	France	(78.5)
4	India	9.7	4	France	(27.5)	4	United Kingdom	(76)
5.5	France	8	5	Canada	23	5	Japan	(53)
5.5	Australia	8	6	Italy	(18)	6	Italy	(51)
(7	Switzerland	9)ª	7	Japan	15	7	Canada	36.5
8	Brazil	6	(9	Switzerland	11.5)	8.5	Netherlands	22.0
10	Italy	4	9	India	11	(8.5)	Switzerland	22)
10	Mexico	4	9	Netherlands	11	9	Belgium	20.0
10	Netherlands	4	11	Belgium	10	10	India	18.8
12.5	Belgium	3	11	Australia	10	11	Australia	17.6
12.5	South Africa	3	12	Venezuela	8	12.5	Sweden	12
15.5	Germany	1	13	Brazil	7	12.5	Mexico	11.5
15.5	Sweden	1	14	Sweden	6	13	South Africa	8
15.5	Venezuela	1	15	Mexico	5	14	Venezuela	7
15.5	Japan	(0)	16	South Africa	3	15	Brazil	—

ªSwitzerland is placed in parentheses as a nonmember of the Fund.

Note: This order is based upon the position of the member country's economy in respect of trade and monetary considerations. The indices are reserve holdings, reserve or master currency position, overseas investment income, and estimated GDP.

Appendix C

The Distribution of Units by Political and Economic Characteristics: Criteria and Classification

Robert W. Cox and Harold K. Jacobson

This appendix presents a matrix classification of countries according to type of political regime and level of economic development. The classifications refer to three key years used in the study for comparative puposes: 1950, 1958, and 1967. The present note also explains the definition of the universe of countries, the principles for the classification of polities, and the method followed for classifying by levels of economic development.

The Universe

All states or geographically distinct territories with a 1967 population of more than 200,000 in round figures are included. Political units are included irrespective of their constitutional status; for example, French and Portuguese overseas departments are listed separately, not subsumed under the metropolitan country. The list includes 154 units, of which 131 were independent states in 1967. Independence is considered to mean having de facto independent international relations regardless of how widely this status is formally recognized. For example, the People's Republic of China, the German Democratic Republic, and Rhodesia (following its unilateral declaration of independence) are all included. Colonial territories, overseas departments, and protectorates like Bahrein are regarded as nonindependent, as are countries whose foreign relations are handled by another state, as Bhutan's are by India. Austria prior to the 1955 peace treaty is similarly regarded as nonindependent, as is Syria during the brief period of union with Egypt, when it had no separate foreign relations or separate membership in international organizations. Diminutive states like Andorra, Lichtenstein, Monaco, and San Marino, even though formally independent, are excluded from the list because their populations are less than 200,000.

For purposes of comparison over time, the same list of political entities (composed, as noted, on the basis of 1967) is used for the three years. Thus, countries that became independent in the 1960s are classified as nonindependent in earlier years and listed under the 1967 name for 1950 and 1958 even though they may have been part of a differently defined geographical entity during the colonial period. For example, Mali was part of French West Africa in 1950 and 1958. The figures for nonindependent countries in 1950 and 1958 are thus to some extent artificial. They reflect what subsequently happened rather than the then state of affairs. This may be regarded as both a convenience for analysis and a shadow statistic expressing potentiality for independence.

This matrix is used first to express the total general environment. Subsequently it is used to express the membership of the different international organizations studied. Adjustment of membership has been necessary in the case of some organizations whose membership includes some units not figuring in the list of 154. This has the effect of reducing the membership of the following organizations:

ITU: nine fewer members (Holy See, Lichtenstein, Maldive Islands, Monaco, French overseas territories, Portuguese overseas territories, Spanish territories in Africa, United Kingdom protectorates and overseas territories, and United States territories) [1]

UNESCO: one fewer member (Monaco)

WHO: three fewer members (Maldive Islands, Monaco, and Western Samoa)

IAEA: two fewer members (Holy See and Monaco)

UNCTAD: six fewer members (Maldive Islands, Monaco, Holy See, Lichtenstein, San Marino, and Western Samoa).

Polities

A threefold classification of polities is used. A first basic dichotomy is between competitive and noncompetitive political systems. The noncompetitive category is then divided into mobilizing and authoritarian regimes.

Although it is difficult to determine the extent of competition in some marginal cases, we have preferred not to have recourse to a middle term like "semicompetitive" or "unstable democracy."[2] We prefer to dichotomize according to the dominant tendency of the regime during the year in question, using criteria that are as objective as possible.

In a mobilizing regime the political leadership intends to use the political system to transform the society in accordance with a more or less systematically formulated ideology (Marxist, populist, eclectic, and so on). This category reflects the beliefs of leaders and followers about the ultimate goals of the regime, rather than the achievements of the regime.

The authoritarian category includes what are diversely referred to as traditional monarchies or oligarchies, military regimes without a specific ideology, and modernizing monarchies or oligarchies. Also classified here are regimes, notably Rhodesia and South Africa, ruled by a substantial racial minority within which competitive politics exist; thus, to some extent this is a residual category.

Operational criteria to distinguish competitive regimes include:

1. Competitive regimes have two or more political parties or other important autonomous organizations, such as trade unions, which legitimately or legally compete for office or influence.

2. The government results from a recent election freely contested by more than one party with credible chances of winning. (Criterion 2 may justify reclassifying a hitherto noncompetitive regime as competitive, though perhaps only temporarily.)

Operational criteria to distinguish noncompetitive regimes include:

1. A single party has a monopoly of government.
2. Opposition by mass-based political parties has no major political influence upon, or constitutes no threat to, the powers of government.
3. Competition is limited to a power struggle within a small oligarchy.
4. Government results from a military coup d'etat.
5. Opposition activities are suppressed by force, or there is an increasing use of force by the government. (Criteria 4 and 5 suggest reasons for reclassifying a hitherto competitive regime as noncompetitive, even though there may have been no change in the formal structure of government.)

In general, no single criterion will determine the classification of a regime. Marginal cases require judgment based upon these criteria.

Mobilizing regimes are broadly of three subtypes: first, Communist party regimes in countries undergoing industrialization, for example, the Soviet Union and Eastern European countries; second, Communist party regimes in less-developed countries, for example, the People's Republic of China, Cuba, North Korea, and North Vietnam; third, a variety of populist single-party regimes in less-developed countries, with eclectic doctrines sometimes not much more systematic than a set of slogans, for example, Nkrumah's Ghana and Sukarno's Indonesia during the "guided democracy" phase. The first two subtypes have tended to be stable systems, while the third has been highly unstable and vulnerable, especially to a military coup transforming the system into an authoritarian subtype.

The authors have checked their classifications of regimes with a number of specialists—Henry L. Bretton, Ernst B. Haas, Martin C. Needler, Roy Pierce, A. F. K. Organski, Dankwart A. Rustow, and Bryce Wood—but are alone responsible for the results to be found in the matrix.

Economic Levels

Countries are divided into four groups by GNP per capita: (1) up to $199; (2) $200-$599; (3) $600-$999; and (4) $1,000 and over. The figures have been chosen arbitrarily, but they result in groupings that accord with conventional ideas about economic levels and also with other divisions that have been achieved more systematically.[3] In very general terms, the first group includes states where deep poverty is widespread and it is not yet possible to speak meaningfully of economic development; the second includes countries in an initial stage of economic modernization, where a modernizing economic sector may coexist with an archaic sector in which poverty is widespread, and also countries in the initial stages of industrialization; the third comprises states in an advanced stage of the process of industrialization, where participation in modern production and welfare is fairly widespread; and in the fourth group are states in high mass-consumption societies.

Most of the basic data for the classification of countries according to per capita GNP (expressed in United States dollars at 1965 prices) have been drawn from publications of the United Nations.[4] These contain consistent worldwide tables of per capita gross national product (GNP) or gross domestic product (GDP) in United States dollars at current prices. Where only per capita GDP data were available they have been converted into per capita GNP data, adjusting for the numerical difference of both concepts in each country and year in question. For a number of countries, in particular certain developing countries and the Eastern European countries, rough estimates of per capita national accounts data in United States dollars had to be obtained among other methods by converting into United States dollars the global data in national currencies divided by population. Owing to divergencies in national accounts compilations and the fact that the official exchange rate used for conversions may often not fully reflect the purchasing power ratio of currencies, the result of these calculations can be regarded as rough approximations only, requiring judgment to be exercised in borderline cases. Special mention should be made of the fact that the national accounts data available for the Eastern European countries relate to the net material product concept, which excludes activities not contributing directly to material production, such as public administration and defense, personal and professional services, and similar activities.[5]

In order to obtain more comparable information, the figures for the three years have been expressed in 1965 dollars, using for this rough evaluation an index derived from the comparison of GNP at current and at fixed prices.

The Matrices

The matrices resulting from classifications according to the above criteria, for 1950, 1958, and 1967 are given in tables C.1, C.2, and C.3. The capital letters are keyed to the list of countries accompanying each matrix.

Table C.1

The Distribution of Units by Political and Economic Characteristics: 1950

Political Regime	Per Capita GNP				
	0-199	200-599	600-999	1000-	Total
Competitive	A	B	C	D	
	4	14	4	12	34
	2.60%	9.09%	2.60%	7.79%	22.08%
Mobilizing	E	F	G	H	
	6	9	1	–	16
	3.90%	5.84%	0.65%	–	10.39%
Authoritarian	I	J	K	L	
	22	7	1	–	30
	14.28%	4.55%	0.65%	–	19.48%
Nonindependent	M	N	O	P	
	57	16	–	1	74
	37.01%	10.39%	–	0.65%	48.05%
Total	89	46	6	13	154
	57.79%	29.87%	3.90%	8.44%	100.00%

List of Countries, 1950

A. Burma, Ceylon, India, Indonesia
B. Brazil, Chile, Costa Rica, Cuba, Greece, Ireland, Israel, Italy, Japan, Lebanon, Mexico, Philippines, Turkey, Uruguay
C. Federal Republic of Germany, Finland, Iceland, Netherlands
D. Australia, Belgium, Canada, Denmark, France, Luxembourg, New Zealand, Norway, Sweden, Switzerland, United Kingdom, United States
E. Albania, Bulgaria, People's Republic of China, Guatemala, Mongolia, North Korea
F. Argentina, Byelorussian S.S.R., German Democratic Republic, Hungary, Poland, Rumania, Ukrainian S.S.R., USSR, Yugoslavia
G. Czechoslovakia
H. –
I. Afghanistan, Bolivia, Ecuador, Ethiopia, Haiti, Honduras, Iraq, Iran, Jordan, Liberia, Nepal, Nicaragua, Pakistan, Paraguay, Peru, Saudi Arabia, South Korea, Syria, Taiwan, Thailand, United Arab Republic, Yemen
J. Colombia, Dominican Republic, El Salvador, Panama, Portugal, South Africa, Spain
K. Venezuela
L. –
M. Angola, Bhutan, Botswana, Burundi, Cambodia, Cameroon, Cape Verde Islands, Central African Republic, Chad, Comoro Islands, Congo (Brazzaville), Congo (Kinshasa), Dahomey, Fiji, Gabon, Gambia, Ghana, Guinea, Guyana, Ivory Coast, Jamaica, Kenya, Laos, Lesotho, Libya, Madagascar, Malawi, Malaysia, Mali, Mauritania, Morocco, Mozambique, Niger, Nigeria, North Vietnam, Papua-New Guinea, Portuguese Guinea, Portuguese Timor, Rhodesia, Ryukyu Islands, Spanish Guinea, Spanish North Africa, Swaziland, Rwanda, Senegal, Sierra Leone, Somalia, South Vietnam, Southern Yemen, South West Africa, Sudan, Tanzania, Togo, Tunisia, Uganda, Upper Volta, Zambia
N. Algeria, Austria, Bahrein, Barbados, Cyprus, Guadeloupe, Hong Kong, Malta, Martinique, Mauritius, Netherlands Antilles, Puerto Rico, Réunion, Singapore, Surinam, Trinidad and Tobago
O. –
P. Kuwait

Table C.2

The Distribution of Units by Political and Economic Characteristics: 1958

Political Regime	Per Capita GNP				
	0-199	200-599	600-999	1000-	Total
Competitive	A	B	C	D	
	3	12	9	13	37
	1.95%	7.79%	5.84%	8.44%	24.02%
Mobilizing	E	F	G	H	
	10	6	5	—	21
	6.49%	3.90%	3.25%	—	13.64%
Authoritarian	I	J	K	L	
	20	13	—	—	33
	12.99%	8.44%	—	—	21.43%
Nonindependent	M	N	O	P	
	42	19	1	1	63
	27.27%	12.34%	0.65%	0.65%	40.91%
Total	75	50	15	14	154
	48.70%	32.47%	9.74%	9.09%	100.00%

List of Countries, 1958

A. Burma, Ceylon, India

B. Brazil, Chile, Colombia, Costa Rica, Greece, Japan, Malaysia, Mexico, Peru, Philippines, Turkey, Uruguay

C. Argentina, Austria, Federal Republic of Germany, Finland, Ireland, Israel, Italy, Netherlands, Venezuela.

D. Australia, Belgium, Canada, Denmark, France, Iceland, Luxembourg, New Zealand, Norway, Sweden, Switzerland, United Kingdom, United States

E. Albania, Bolivia, People's Republic of China, Ghana, Guinea, Indonesia, Mongolia, North Korea, North Vietnam, United Arab Republic

F. Bulgaria, Hungary, Iraq, Poland, Rumania, Yugoslavia

G. Byelorussian S.S.R., Czechoslovakia, German Democratic Republic, Ukrainian S.S.R., USSR

H. —

I. Afghanistan, Cambodia, Ethiopia, Haiti, Iran, Jordan, Laos, Liberia, Libya, Morocco, Nepal, Pakistan, Paraguay, South Korea, South Vietnam, Sudan, Taiwan, Thailand, Tunisia, Yemen

J. Cuba, Dominican Republic, Ecuador, El Salvador, Guatemala, Honduras, Lebanon, Nicaragua, Panama, Portugal, Saudi Arabia, Spain, South Africa

K. —

L. —

M. Angola, Bhutan, Botswana, Burundi, Cameroon, Cape Verde Islands, Central African Republic, Chad, Comoro Islands, Congo (Brazzaville), Congo (Kinshasa), Dahomey, Gambia, Ivory Coast, Kenya, Lesotho, Madagascar, Malawi, Mali, Mauritania, Mozambique, Niger, Nigeria, Papua-New Guinea, Portuguese Guinea, Portuguese Timor, Rhodesia, Rwanda, Senegal, Sierra Leone, Somalia, Spanish Guinea, Spanish North Africa, Southern Yemen, South West Africa, Swaziland, Syria, Tanzania, Togo, Uganda, Upper Volta, Zambia

N. Algeria, Bahrein, Barbados, Cyprus, Fiji, Gabon, Guadeloupe, Guyana, Hong Kong, Jamaica, Malta, Martinique, Mauritius, Netherlands Antilles, Réunion, Ryukyu Islands, Singapore, Surinam, Trinidad and Tobago

O. Puerto Rico

P. Kuwait

Table C.3

The Distribution of Units by Political and Economic Characteristics: 1967

Political Regime	Per Capita GNP				
	0-199	200-599	600-999	1000-	Total
Competitive	A	B	C	D	
	3	15	5	20	43
	1.95%	9.74%	3.25%	12.99%	27.92%
Mobilizing	E	F	G	H	
	13	8	6	1	28
	8.44%	5.19%	3.90%	0.65%	18.18%
Authoritarian	I	J	K	L	
	36	18	5	1	60
	23.38%	11.69%	3.24%	0.65%	38.96%
Nonindependent	M	N	O	P	
	13	9	–	1	23
	8.44%	5.84%	–	0.65%	14.93%
Total	65	50	16	23	154
	42.21%	32.46%	10.39%	14.94%	99.99%

List of Countries, 1967

A. Ceylon, Gambia, India
B. Barbados, Colombia, Costa Rica, Dominican Republic, Equador, Guyana, Jamaica, Lebanon, Malaysia, Malta, Mexico, Peru, Philippines, Singapore, Turkey
C. Chile, Ireland, Trinidad and Tobago, Uruguay, Venezuela
D. Australia, Austria, Belgium, Canada, Denmark, Federal Republic of Germany, Finland, France, Iceland, Israel, Italy, Japan, Luxembourg, Netherlands, New Zealand, Norway, Sweden, Switzerland, United Kingdom, United States
E. Albania, People's Republic of China, Congo (Brazzaville), Guinea, Mali, Mongolia, North Korea, North Vietnam, Southern Yemen, Syria, Tanzania, United Arab Republic, Uganda
F. Algeria, Bulgaria, Cuba, Iraq, Rumania, Tunisia, Yugoslavia, Zambia
G. Byelorussian S.S.R., Czechoslovakia, Hungary, Poland, Ukrainian S.S.R., USSR
H. German Democratic Republic
I. Afghanistan, Bolivia, Botswana, Burma, Burundi, Cambodia, Cameroon, Central African Republic, Chad, Congo (Kinshasa), Dahomey, Ethiopia, Haiti, Indonesia, Kenya, Laos, Lesotho, Madagascar, Malawi, Mauritania, Nepal, Niger, Nigeria, Pakistan, Rhodesia, Rwanda, Senegal, Sierra Leone, Somalia, South Korea, South Vietnam, Sudan, Thailand, Togo, Upper Volta, Yemen
J. Brazil, El Salvador, Gabon, Ghana, Guatemala, Honduras, Iran, Ivory Coast, Jordan, Liberia, Morocco, Nicaragua, Panama, Paraguay, Portugal, Saudi Arabia, South Africa, Taiwan
K. Argentina, Cyprus, Greece, Libya, Spain
L. Kuwait
M. Angola, Bhutan, Cape Verde Islands, Comoro Islands, Mozambique, Papua-New Guinea, Portuguese Guinea, Portuguese Timor, Spanish Guinea, Spanish North Africa, South West Africa, Swaziland, Bahrain
N. Fiji, Guadeloupe, Hong Kong, Martinique, Mauritius, Netherlands Antilles, Réunion, Ryukyu Islands, Surinam
O. –
P. Puerto Rico

Ernst B. Haas has compared our classifications with those that he has used.[6] His classifications involve somewhat different and longer periods of time than our three base years. Nevertheless, where it is possible to compare his classifications with ours he found 88.3 percent agreement with respect to regime types and 50.5 percent agreement with respect to levels of economic development. The principal reason for the substantial disagreement concerning economic development is that although, like Haas, we use four categories, we have relied on per capita GNP as our index, while he relied on per capita energy consumption. Our system consistently places states in higher categories. Haas prefers per capita energy consumption because he feels that it is a better index of the welfare of those in the working population who are likely to join trade unions, a subject of particular concern for his purpose. We preferred a more general measure.

Notes

Chapter 1

1 These figures are from Michael D. Wallace and J. David Singer, "Intergovernmental Organizations in the Global System, 1815-1964: A Quantitative Description," *International Organization* 24 (Spring 1970): 239-87.

2 There seems to be increasing consensus among social scientists on such a definition. See Robert A. Dahl, *Modern Political Analysis* (Englewood Cliffs, N.J.: Prentice-Hall, 1963), pp. 39-54; and also Dorwin Cartwright, "Influence, Leadership, Control," in *Handbook of Organizations,* ed. James G. March (Chicago: Rand McNally, 1965), p. 3.

3 The phrase is from Geoffrey Barraclough, *History in a Changing World* (Oxford: Basil Blackwell, 1955), pp. 183-84. Barraclough was referring to "three great turning points when European society swung upwards on to a new plane" (p. 79). The same concept can be applied in the microcosmic history of international organizations.

4 See Robert A. Dahl, *Who Governs?: Democracy and Power in an American City* (New Haven: Yale University Press, 1963); Theodore J. Lowi, "American Business, Public Policy, Case-Studies, and Political Theory," *World Politics* 16 (July 1964): 677-715.

5 See, for example, James N. Rosenau, "Pre-theories and Theories of Foreign Policy," *Approaches to Comparative and International Politics,* ed. R. Barry Farrell (Evanston, Ill.: Northwestern University Press, 1966), pp. 27-92.

6 The stages outlined here were suggested by the work of Fred C. Iklé. See especially his *Alternative Approaches to the International Organization of Disarmament* (Santa Monica, Calif.: RAND Corporation, 1962).

7 Ernst B. Haas, *Beyond the Nation-State: Functionalism and International Organization* (Stanford, Calif.: Stanford University Press, 1964), pp. 103-13; James G. March and Herbert A. Simon, *Organizations* (New York: Wiley, 1958) distinguish four "processes" whereby organizations react to conflict: "(1) problem solving, (2) persuasion, (3) bargaining, and (4) politics." The first pair they call "analytic," and the second pair "bargaining" (pp. 129-30). Our usage corresponds to theirs.

8 The studies of permanent missions are steps in this direction. The most detailed study published to date is Arnold Beichman, *The "Other" State Department* (New York: Basic Books, 1967). An ambitious comparative study of permanent missions is currently being conducted by the Carnegie Endowment for International Peace.

9 Various attempts have already been made to identify groupings. See especially Chadwick F. Alger, "Interaction in a Committee of the United Nations General Assembly," in *Quantitative International Politics,* ed. J. David Singer (New York: Free Press, 1968), pp. 51-84; Arend Lijphart, "The Analysis of Bloc Voting in the General Assembly," *American Political Science Review* 57 (December 1963): 902-17; and Bruce M. Russett, "Discovering Voting Groups in the United Nations," *American Political Science Review* 60 (June 1966): 327-39. However, neither participants' observations of interactions in a committee room nor the analysis of roll call votes, the two techniques involved in these attempts, fully measures what is involved in the concept of persistent groupings of actors used here. Among other things neither gives adequate attention to actors who are not representatives of states.

10 See in particular Hayward R. Alker, Jr., and Bruce M. Russett, *World Politics in the General Assembly* (New Haven: Yale University Press, 1965), chap. 9, "Who Initiates, with What Success?", pp. 167-90.

11 The manner in which the ranking in this study has been constructed and its relationship to other attempts to measure power are discussed in appendix A.

12 The way in which the typology has been worked out is described in appendix C.

13 See Morton A. Kaplan, *System and Process in International Politics* (New York: Wiley, 1957).

14 Ibid., p. 21.

Chapter 2

1 The nineteen countries whose type of polity changed according to a comparison of the three base years are:

	1950	1958	1967
Argentina	M	C	A
Bolivia	A	M	A
Brazil	C	C	A
Burma	C	C	A
Colombia	A	C	C
Cuba	C	A	M
Dominican Republic	A	A	C
Ecuador	A	A	C
Ghana	NI	M	A
Greece	C	C	A
Guatemala	M	A	A
Indonesia	C	M	A
Iraq	A	M	M
Lebanon	C	A	C
Peru	A	C	C
Syria	A	NI	M
Tunisia	NI	A	M
United Arab Republic	A	M	M
Venezuela	A	C	C

C = Competitive
M = Mobilizing
A = Authoritarian
NI = Nonindependent

2 Raymond Dennett and Robert K. Turner, *Documents on American Foreign Relations, 1947* (Princeton, N.J.: Princeton University Press, 1949), p. 7.

3 George McTurnan Kahin, *The Asian-African Conference* (Ithaca, N.Y.: Cornell University Press, 1956), p. 81.

Chapter 3

1 There is only one comprehensive scholarly study of ITU: George A. Codding, Jr., *The International Telecommunication Union: An Experiment in International Cooperation* (Leiden, Netherlands: Brill, 1952). ITU itself published a popular history of the organization on the occasion of its centenary entitled *From Semaphore to Satellite* (Geneva: ITU, 1955). Delbert D. Smith has several sections on ITU in his *International Telecommunication Control* (Leiden, Netherlands: Sijthoff, 1969); and David M. Leive has published an elaborate study of one aspect of ITU's activities, *International Telecommunications and International Law: The Regulation of the Radio Spectrum* (Leiden, Netherlands: Sijthoff, 1970).

2 ITU, *International Telecommunication Convention* (Montreux, 1965), article 4, para. 1a.

3 Ibid., para. 2.

4 Ibid., Annex 4, *General Regulations,* chap. 9, rule 2, para. 3(1).

5 ITU, Resolution 42.

6 ITU, Resolution 35.

7 ITU, Resolution 30.

8 ITU, *Radio Regulations* (Atlantic City: ITU, 1947), chap. IV, article 12, para. 3(3).

9 ITU, Resolution 25.

10 Consisting of two former ITU officials, one present official of the union, and one scholar who has had long familiarity with the agency.

11 The Ordinary Telegraph and Telephone Conference that was held in 1958 and the World Administrative Radio Conference that was held in 1967.

12 ITU, *International Telecommunication Convention* (Montreux, 1965), article 12, para. 2(1).

13 The following ITU members were not included in the basic classification for 1950: Belgian Congo and territory of Ruanda-Urundi; French protectorates of Morocco and Tunisia; Monaco; Portuguese colonies; colonies, protectorates, overseas territories, and territories under mandate or trusteeship of the United Kingdom; territories of the United States; and Vatican City. For 1958, the

following were omitted: Belgian Congo and territory of Ruanda-Urundi; territories represented by the French Overseas Postal and Telecommunication Agency; Monaco; Portuguese overseas territories; Spanish provinces in Africa; colonies, protectorates, overseas territories, and territories under mandate or trusteeship of the United Kingdom; territories of the United States; and Vatican City. For 1967, the following were not included: French overseas territories, Liechtenstein, Maldive Islands, Monaco, Portuguese overseas territories, Spanish provinces in Africa, United Kingdom overseas territories, United States overseas territories, and Vatican City.

14 ITU, *International Telecommunication Convention* (Atlantic City, N.J.: ITU, 1947), article 7, para. 1(b).

Chapter 4

1 Memoirs and accounts by participants describing the origins and early years of the ILO include James T. Shotwell, ed., *The Origins of the International Labor Organization* (New York: Columbia University Press, 1934); George N. Barnes, *From Workshop to War Cabinet* (London: Jenks, 1923); Sir Harold Butler, *Confident Morning* (London: Faber and Faber, 1950); and Edward J. Phelan, *Yes and Albert Thomas* (London: Crescent Press, 1949). Phelan also wrote some reminiscences of the World War II period during which he was acting director, in *Studies* (Dublin) 44, 45 (1954-57). A detailed historical reconstruction of the 1919-20 period is Daniel P. Moynihan, "The United States and the International Labor Organization" (Ph.D. diss., Fletcher School of Diplomacy, 1960), which is available on microfilm. An older study is Leon-Eli Troclet, *Legislation sociale internationale* (Brussels: Librairie Encyclopédique, 1952). *The International Labour Organisation: The First Decade* (London: Allen and Unwin, 1931) is an anonymous account by ILO officials; B. W. Schaper, *Albert Thomas: Trente ans de réformisme social* (Assen, Netherlands: Van Gorcum, 1959) is a study devoted to the first director; and Francis G. Wilson, *Labor in the League System* (Stanford, Calif.: Stanford University Press, 1934) is a political study of the interwar period.

Ernst B. Hass, *Beyond the Nation-State: Functionalism and International Organization* (Stanford, Calif.: Stanford University Press, 1964) is a case study of the ILO used by Haas to test and refine functionalist theory. See also his statistical study, Ernst B. Haas, "System and Process in the International Labor Organization," *World Politics* 14 (1962): 324. Another study that makes considerable use of statistics, especially voting analyses, is Torsten Landelius, *Workers, Employers and Governments: A Comparative Study of Delegations and Groups at the International Labour Conference 1919-1964* (Stockholm: Norstedt & Soner, 1965).

There are a number of legal studies on the constitutional and standard-setting aspects of the ILO, of which the one most relevant to this chapter is Wilfred Jenks, *Trade Union Freedom* (London: Stevens, 1957).

On the controversy over Soviet participation, see Bernard Beguin, "ILO and the Tripartite System," *International Conciliation*, no. 523 (May 1959); and Harold K. Jacobson, "The USSR and the ILO," *International Organization* 14 (1960), pp. 402-28. A Soviet viewpoint is to be found in V. G. Shkunaev, *Mezhdunarodnaya Organizatsiya Truda: Vchera i Segodnya* (Moscow: Institute of World Economics and International Relations, 1968). As a fiftieth-anniversary project, the ILO commissioned the preparation of an official history by Antony Alcock, *History of the International Labor Organization* (New York: Octagon Books, 1971). A general description of ILO structure and activities is George A. Johnston, *The International Labour Organisation; Its Work for Social and Economic Progress* (London: Europa, 1970).

2 See John W. Follows, *Antecedents of the International Labour Organization* (Oxford: Clarendon Press, 1952), and the criticism of his approach in Robert W. Cox, "The Idea of International Labour Regulation," *International Labour Review* 67 (February 1953): 191-96.

3 Butler, *Confident Morning*, pp. 175, 240; Moynihan, "The United States and the International Labor Organization," pp. 204-05, 250.

4 Phelan, *Yes and Albert Thomas*, pp. 15-18.

5 ILO, *Programme and Structure of the ILO: Report of the Director-General*, Report 1, Part 1, 1963.

6 ILO, "Report of the Committee on Freedom of Employers' and Workers' Organisation," *Official Bulletin*, 39 (1956): 475-599.

7 *John Herling's Labor Letter*, 13 June 1966. See also John P. Windmuller, "The Foreign Policy Conflict in American Labor," *Industrial and Labor Relations Review*, 82 (June 1967): 205-34.

8 See Norman F. Dufty, "Technical Assistance and the International Labour Office," *Journal of Industrial Relations* (Australia) 9 (November 1967): 245-57.

9 Butler MSS., dated 27 December 1930, cited in Moynihan, "The United States and the International Labor Organization," p. 485.

10 See Ernest A. Landy, *The Effectiveness of International Supervision: Thirty Years of ILO Experience* (London: Stevens, 1966).

11 International Labor Conference, 53d Session, *Provisional Record*, no. 41 (June 1969), p. 479.

12 During the summer of 1970, the U.S. Congress decided not to provide funds for payment of the United States' assessed contribution to the ILO. This action was taken as a reaction to the appointment by Morse's successor, Wilfred Jenks, of a Soviet assistant director-general. The response of the Congress represented a new use of the financial weapon by the major contributor to the ILO's budget.

13 ILO, *Industry and Labour* 12 (15 December 1954): 541-42.

14 Also significant was the 1965 decision of the French government to include the WFTU-affiliated CGT in the rotation system for French worker delegates (alongside the CGT-FO and the CFDT); the CGT represented the French workers as delegate in 1967.

15 WFTU, Executive Committee, 34th Session, *Report on the Second Point on the Agenda: Development of the WFTU's Work in the United Nations and Its Specialized Agencies* (Prague, 25-27 October 1967), p. 8. The speaker was Stana Dragoi, secretary of the WFTU.

16 Wilfred Jenks in a lecture to the Graduate Institute of International Studies, Geneva, 27 October 1969, published in *Annals of International Studies* (Geneva: Alumni Association of the Graduate Institute of International Studies, 1970), p. 60.

17 Landelius, *Workers, Employers, and Governments*, pp. 53 ff.

Chapter 5

1 Figures from Unesco, *What Is Unesco?* (Paris: Unesco, 1968), p. 13. Extended works on UNESCO and UNESCO activities include Julian Huxley, *UNESCO: Its Purpose and Its Philosophy* (Washington, D.C.: Public Affairs Press, 1947); Theodore Besterman, *Unesco: Peace in the Minds of Men* (London: Methuen, 1951); Charles S. Ascher, *Program-making in Unesco, 1946-1951* (Chicago: Public Administration Service, 1951); Brenda M. H. Tripp, "Unesco in Perspective," *International Conciliation*, no. 497 (March 1954); Walter H. C. Laves and Charles A. Thomson, *Unesco: Purpose, Progress, Prospects* (Bloomington: University of Indiana Press, 1957); Jean Thomas, *U.N.E.S.C.O.* (Paris: Gallimard, 1962); George N. Shuster, *UNESCO: Assessment and Promise* (New York: Harper & Row, 1963); T. V. Sathyamurthy, *The Politics of International Cooperation: Contrasting Conceptions of U.N.E.S.C.O.* (Geneva: Droz, 1964); René Maheu, *La civilisation de l'universel: inventaire de l'avenir* (Paris: Laffont; Gonthier, 1966). The author of this chapter is preparing a study, entitled *Engaging Internationally*, which includes consideration of UNESCO participants.

2 ECO/Conf/13, 14 November 1945.

3 Cf. Laves and Thomson, *Unesco*, p. 34.

4 Ascher, *Program-Making in Unesco*, p. 1. Ascher adds that the Fifth General Conference was told of 279 separate actions required in 1951.

5 The address by Kingman Brewster, Jr., president of Yale University, at the Sixth Conference of the Institute of International Education on 20 February 1969 in Washington, D.C., may serve as one example. Brewster likened the problem of international educational development to "the challenge to systems analysis caused by the effort to fill the gallon jug with the contents of the quart bottle."

6 Those interviewed were asked, "In the judgment of your government, what is the greatest single limiting factor which restricts UNESCO from being even more effective than it is now?" They represented Australia, Austria, Belgium, Brazil, Canada, Congo (Kinshasa), Ethiopia, Finland, France, India, Italy, Netherlands, Nigeria, Rumania, the Soviet Union, Sweden, United Arab Republic, United Kingdom, United States, West Germany and Yugoslavia. The author is obliged to the Social Science Research Council, which gave the necessary support, and to Mietta Manca, whose interviewing virtuosity made possible these data and others to be utilized later.

7 U.S. Assistant Secretary of State Archibald MacLeish commended a UNESCO radio network "capable of laying down strong signals in every inhabited spot on the earth" during the First General Conference in 1946. "MacLeish Asserts U.S. Favors Unesco Radio," *New York Herald Tribune* (Paris), 20 November 1946.

8 As used here, rule creation and rule supervision parallel the setting and applying of general standards, and programmatic and operational decisions parallel the promoting of programmatic and structural extension. The latter types in each case are delineated in my "Policy Processes and International Organisation Tasks," in *International Organisation: World Politics,* ed. Robert W. Cox (London: Macmillan, 1969), pp. 98-112. A programmatic decision that aroused widespread recognition of an impending redistribution of resources would be comparable to legitimizing reallocation, another policy process. As indicated early in this chapter, founders of UNESCO also contemplated its animating mutual concessions to realize mutual gains.

9 On collective legitimation, see Inis L. Claude, Jr., *The Changing United Nations* (New York: Random House, 1967), chap. 4; and idem., "The Vogue of Collectivism in International Relations," *Interstate* 1 (November 1968).

10 The tendency for those in UNESCO to be tempted by exotic program morsels might be represented in a bureaucratic directive following the UNESCO acronym: *U*ndigestibility *n*ever *e*xcuses *s*ecretariat *c*opping *o*ut. On UNESCO and the natural environment, see the author's *Engaging Internationally.*

11 For 1967, the Participation Program offered thirty-two substantive categories of promotional assistance totaling $2,046,754. Unesco, *Report of the Director-General on the Activities of the Organization in 1967* (Paris: Unesco, 1968), Appendix 3.

12 For an apparently divergent view, see T. V. Sathyamurthy, "Twenty Yeats of UNESCO: An Interpretation," *International Organization* 21 (Summer 1967): 632.

13 UNESCO Doc. 13C/PRG/31, 24 July 1964; UNESCO Doc. 14C/32, 21 October 1966. NGOs and their relations with UNESCO and with other intergovernmental organizations are listed, and often tabulated, in the Union of International Associations' *Yearbook of International Organizations* (Brussels).

14 As of 21 October 1966, UNESCO classed its NGO affiliates as follows:

		Number
Category A	(consultative and associate relations)	25
Category B	(information and consultative relations)	127
Category C	(mutual information relations)	102
Total		254

15 For more about UNESCO directors-general, see Sathyamurthy, *Politics of International Cooperation;* idem., "Twenty Years of UNESCO"; and Sewell, *Engaging Internationally.*

16 Unesco, *Report of the Director-General on the Activities of the Organization from October 1949 to March 1950* (Paris: Unesco, 1950), p. 13.

17 On early attempts at a UNESCO credo, see Basil Karp, "The Development of the Philosophy of Unesco" (Ph.D. diss., University of Chicago, 1951).

18 I am grateful to the Royal Institute of International Affairs (United Kingdom) and the Council on Foreign Relations (United States) for access to their files of press and other clippings in the course of my research for this and a subsequent study.

19 Cf. Ernst B. Haas's "minimum common denominator," e.g. in "International Integration: The European and the Universal Process," in *International Political Communities* (Garden City, N.Y.: Doubleday, 1966), p. 95.

20 I have sought to develop this point for UNESCO and other United Nations agencies in the final part of "Functional Agencies," in *The Future of the International Legal Order,* ed. Cyril E. Black and Richard A. Falk, vol. 4 (Princeton, N.J.: Princeton University Press, 1972).

Chapter 6

1 For a popular account of the origins of international collaboration in health see Timothy J. Larkin, "The Great Ghat at Harwar," *Bulletin of the Atomic Scientists* 18 (January 1962): 6-11. The same material is covered in the only scholarly book in English that deals with WHO, Robert Berkov, *The World Health Organization: A Study in Decentralized International Administration* (Geneva: Droz, 1957); and in the first volume of WHO's official history, *WHO: The First Ten Years of the World Health Organization* (Geneva: WHO, 1958). A second volume of the official history has been published, *WHO: The Second Ten Years of the World Health Organization, 1958-1967* (Geneva: WHO, 1968). One book dealing with some of the organization's early activities has been written by a former

assistant director-general, Dr. Neville Goodman, *International Health Organizations and Their Work* (London: Churchill, 1952); and another by a journalist, Murray Morgan, *Doctors to the World* (New York: Viking, 1958). The literature on WHO is relatively sparse; aside from these five works, there are only brief articles.

2 U.S., Congress, Senate, *Providing for Membership and Participation by the United States in the World Health Organization and Authorizing an Appropriation Therefor,* 80th Cong., 1st sess., 1947 S. Rept. 421, p. 7.

3 See U.S., Congress, House, Committee on Foreign Affairs, Subcommittee on National and International Movements, *Hearings, United States Membership in the World Health Organization,* 80th Cong., lst sess., 1947, pp. 113-18.

4 This phrase was contained in a resolution approved by the House of Delegates of the AMA in July 1946. It was repeated by the secretary and general manager of the AMA in testimony before the U.S., House of Representatives, ibid., pp. 49, 58.

5 WHO, *Constitution,* Article 29.

6 WHO, *Official Records,* no. 31, p. 29; no. 88, p. 3; and no. 163, p. 2.

7 Ibid., no. 31, p. 19; no. 88, p. 3; no. 163, p. 3.

8 U.S., Congress, House, *United States Contributions to International Organizations,* 90th Cong., 2nd sess., Doc. 375, 1968.

9 WHO, *Official Records,* no. 151, p. 21.

10 WHO, *Official Records, Eighteenth World Health Assembly,* part I, p. 33.

11 See WHO, *Official Records, First World Health Assembly,* pp. 39-43.

12 WHO, WHA 19.31, May 1966.

13 WHO, *Constitution,* Article 52.

14 WHO, WHA 2.73, June 1949.

15 See Walter Judd's remarks in U.S., Congress, *Congressional Record,* vol. 95, part 11 (Washington, D.C.: GPO, 1949), p. 14165.

16 WHO, WHA 20.50, May 1967; 21.47, May 1968.

17 This process has been analyzed in Charles S. Ascher, "Current Problems in the World Health Organization's Program," *International Organization* 6 (February 1952): 27-50; and in Walter R. Sharp, *Field Administration in the United Nations System* (New York: Praeger, 1961).

18 WHO, *Constitution,* Article 29.

19 EB5.R33, February 1950.

20 However, Rule 10.7.2 of the *Regulations for Expert Advisory Panels and Committees* provides that "the Director-General may direct to the attention of the chairman of an expert committee any statement of opinion in its report that might be considered prejudicial to the best interests of the Organization or of any Member State. The chairman of the committee may, at his discretion, delete such statement from the report, with or without communicating with members of the expert committee or, after obtaining their written approval, may modify the statement. Any difficulty arising out of a divergence of views between the Director-General and the chairman of the committee shall be referred to the Board."

21 Thus the following WHO members were not included in calculating the percentages. For 1950, Monaco, Albania, Bulgaria, Byelorussia, China (Taiwan), Czechoslovakia, Hungary, Poland, Rumania, the Ukraine, and the USSR; for 1958, Monaco, Byelorussia, and the Ukraine; and for 1967, Monaco, Maldive Islands, Western Samoa, Byelorussia, the Ukraine, and South Africa.

Chapter 7

1 There is a limited body of literature on the IAEA, most of it referring to particular programs or functions rather than to general structure and development. Useful background information can be found in Bertrand Goldschmidt, *Les rivalités atomiques, 1939-1966* (Paris: Fayard, 1967); Arnold Kramish, *The Peaceful Atom and Foreign Policy* (New York: Harper & Row, 1963); John G. Stoessinger, "The International Atomic Energy Agency: The First Phase," *International Organization* 13 (Summer 1959): 394-411; Bernhard G. Bechhoefer and Eric Stein, "Atoms for Peace: The New International Atomic Energy Agency," *Michigan Law Review* 55 (April 1957): 747-98; and Lawrence Scheinman, "Nuclear Safeguards: The Peaceful Atom and the IAEA," *International Conciliation,* 572 (March 1969). A recent comprehensive study of the IAEA is Paul C. Szaz, *The Law and Practices of the International Atomic Energy Agency,* Legal Series no. 7 (Vienna: IAEA, 1970).

2 IAEA, *Statute,* Article V, sec. F2.

3 Glenn T. Seaborg, "The Promise of the International Atomic Energy Agency" (Address presented at the International Theoretical Physics Conference on Particles and Fields, University of Rochester, 31 August 1967).

4 Approximately $20 million was expended by the agency for these types of technical assistance between its inception and 31 December 1967. See, generally, IAEA, General Conference, *The Provision of Technical Assistance by the Agency with Special Reference to 1967: Report by the Director-General,* GC(XII)/INF/100, 13 August 1968.

5 More precisely, the IAEA is charged with the responsibility of verifying that states are meeting their treaty obligations; and provision is made for individual states or groups of states to negotiate appropriate agreements to this effect with the agency. It is therefore possible, and indeed probable, that the relationship between the IAEA and different states will vary. In the case of the European Atomic Energy Community, for example, it is to be expected that that community's safeguarding system will remain intact and that IAEA's relation to nuclear activities will be more indirect in EURATOM countries than in other countries like Japan, Sweden, or Mexico.

6 What really is involved here is mobilization of support from developing countries by some dissatisfied advanced states to help the latter gain a privileged status in the agency. It is not at all clear that everyone understands what is going on.

7 IAEA, *Statute,* Article VII, secs. D and C, respectively.

8 The equipment in question, a low-temperature irradiation loop, was not suited to military purposes in the first place.

9 For an analysis of the CNNWS see Scheinman, "Nuclear Safeguards," esp. chaps. 1 and 3.

10 IAEA, General Conference Resolution, GC(XII)/RES/245, September 1968.

11 IAEA, General Conference Resolution, GC(I)/RES/5, 22 October 1957.

12 IAEA, Board of Governors, *Provisional Rules of Procedure,* Rule 8a, as amended, GOV/INF/60.

13 A "developing country," for research allocations and other developmental purposes, is one that is receiving assistance under the UNDP.

14 Politicking in the contract field also occurs within the secretariat. Thus, it has happened that high officials have sought to curry a country's favor for their governments by intervening to ensure that a research contract should be awarded to that country.

15 IAEA, General Conference Resolution, GC(XI)/RES/230, 2 October 1967.

16 Noncompliance reports are also made to the General Assembly.

17 Thus, the board held forty-nine sessions in 1961, but only sixteen in 1967. The volume of agency work had remained constant during this time (although 1961 was one of the years in which safeguards were heavily debated), while the board's relation to the director-general in terms of his autonomy and capacity for discretionary action did not undergo significant change.

18 Capability in the specific environment, for the purposes of this discussion, is determined by the following indicators: possession of nuclear weapons; infrastructure for nuclear research and development; installed and forthcoming capacity for nuclear power; and control of source materials. The first ten states are ranked in terms of capability; the remaining ten are divided into two groups; countries in each of those groups are listed alphabetically because of the absence of significant differences between the states.

19 It is important to remember, however, that most of the permanent appointments were made in the earlier years where recruitment was largely from other secretariats, which themselves had large Western components. This circumstance somewhat limits the significance of these figures.

20 The magnitude of the problem is considerable. As of March 1966 nearly 40 percent (76 out of 193) of the research and power reactors operating outside of the United States and the Soviet bloc were located in EURATOM countries. At the time of this writing the EURATOM countries are negotiating collectively with the IAEA. For an analysis of the problems involved see Lawrence Scheinman, "EURATOM and the IAEA," in *Nuclear Proliferation: Prospects for Control,* ed. Bennett Boskey and Mason Willrich (New York: Dunellen, 1970).

Chapter 8

1 The dollar is the top currency of today's international economy, as sterling was in the nineteenth century. The term *top currency* is used to denote the generally preferred monetary medium for international financial transactions. It will be used as a reserve currency, as a vehicle or trading currency, as an intervention currency for market stabilization, and as a unit of account. But though a top currency role is usually the product of economic leadership in the international economy, it also

has important political implications for the issuing state. See the present writer's *Sterling and British Policy* (London: Oxford University Press, 1971) especially chapter 1.

2 There is an extensive literature on the IMF and relevant matters. Much of it, though, is either parti pris or concerned primarily with arguments over economic mechanisms and theories.

A recent major source is the Fund's own three-volume study of its first twenty years, *The International Monetary Fund, 1945-1965: Twenty Years of International Monetary Cooperation* (Washington, D.C.: IMF, 1969). Volume I, *Chronicle,* by J. Keith Horsefield is a careful chronological account of the Fund's development. Volume II, *Analysis,* edited by J. Keith Horsefield, contains some analytical contributions on special questions or aspects of the Fund's work by Margaret de Vries, Joseph Gold, and other Fund officials. Volume III, *Documents,* also edited by J. Keith Horsefield, includes the texts of all the pre-Bretton Woods proposals, basic Fund documents, decisions, and pronouncements, the second *Compensatory Finance Report* of 1966, and the Special Drawing Rights proposal in the form agreed to at Stockholm in 1968. It also has a full list of the Fund's own extensive publications. Valuable current bibliographies are compiled for the IMF journal, *Staff Papers,* by Martin L. Loftus (e.g. 12 [November 1965]: 470-524 and 15 [March 1968]: 143-95). An earlier study by a Japanese former executive director is Shigeo Horie's *The International Monetary Fund, Retrospect and Prospect* (London: Macmillan, 1964). In French there is Pierre Turot's *Le fond monétaire international, son évolution, son actualité* (Paris: Epargne, 1966), and M. Robert Mossé, *Les problèmes monétaires internationaux* (Paris: Payot, 1967). Mossé also wrote on the Bretton Woods conference, *Le système monétaire de Bretton Woods et les grands problèmes de l'après-guerre* (Paris: Recueil Sirey, 1948); much better is Richard Gardner's classic study of Anglo-American economic diplomacy, *Sterling-Dollar Diplomacy: The Origins and the Prospects of our International Economic Order,* recently reissued with a retrospective introduction (New York: McGraw-Hill, 1969). For a general introduction to the issue-area, Fred Hirsch's *Money International* (London: Penguin, 1967) is excellent; it has a separate chapter on the Fund. For more critical material, see Robert Mundell's article "The International Monetary Fund," in *The Journal of World Trade Law* 3 (September-October 1969): 455-97. A succinct survey of the prospective alternatives is Harry G. Johnson's "The Decline of the International Monetary System," *World Today* 25 (March 1969): 103-09, and Terence Higgins's "Into the 1970's with the IMF," *World Today* 26 (February 1970): 47-53. The Princeton series of Essays and Studies in International Finance has closely followed the course of international monetary debates; the late Henry Aubrey's *Behind the Veil of International Money,* Princeton Studies in International Finance, no. 71 (Princeton, N. J.: Princeton University, International Finance Section, Department of Economics, 1969) would be helpful to nonspecialists, as would Richard Gardner's contribution, "The Politics of Liquidity," in *International Organisation: World Politics, Studies in Economic and Social Agencies,* ed. Robert Cox (London: Macmillan, 1969), pp. 275-85. For an official survey see "The IMF: Use and Supply of Resources," in the *Quarterly Bulletin* (Bank of England) 9 (March 1969): 37-51; and Martin Barrett, "Activation of the Special Drawing Rights Facility in the IMF," *Monthly Review* (Federal Reserve Bank of New York) 52 (February 1970): 40-46. For the Fund's relations with developing countries, the defendant's case is put in Edward M. Bernstein's "The International Monetary Fund," in *The Global Partnership: International Agencies and Economic Development,* ed. Richard N. Gardner and Max F. Millikan (New York: Praeger, 1968), pp. 131-51, also published in *International Organization* 22 (Winter 1968): 131-51.

In the following pages I have also made use of Brian Tew's mimeographed study, "The International Monetary Fund" (Nottingham, 1970). Students will find the latest edition of his *International Monetary Cooperation, 1945-67,* 9th ed. (London: Hutchinson, 1967), a concise and intelligible introduction to the issues.

3 See IMF, *Articles of Agreement,* Article XII, sec. 2(b), which lists eight questions on which the governing board may not delegate its powers.

4 These provisions have not been substantially changed by the revisions negotiated in 1968-69 as part of the package deal on Special Drawing Rights. The minimum total votes on issues requiring qualified majorities was altered from four-fifths to 85 percent, thus giving a veto to the European Economic Community. A new Committee of Interpretation was also set up to safeguard the EEC's interest.

5 M. Robert Mossé, quoted by Oscar Altman in "Quotas in the International Monetary Fund," *Staff Papers* (IMF) J (August 1956): 141, and in Hirsch, *Money International,* p. 264.

6 For the quotas of leading members and the relation of these amounts to the share of total voting rights, see appendix A. The 1970 revision of quotas will put Canada, Japan, and Italy ahead of India, which now drops from fifth to eighth place in the ranking by quotas.

7 An exchange first considered and approved by the Executive Board in 1951 and effected three years later when the United States wanted the gold.

8 Hirsch, *Money International,* p. 266.

9 Despite the name, the country club is not jointly owned by the World Bank, though the Fund generously opens membership to the latter's staff at a "concessionary rate" of $400 a year.

10 Horsefield, *Chronicle,* p. 86.

11 In 1952 only six countries had accepted the obligations of convertibility under article VIII (secs. 2, 3, and 4) and therefore did not need to consult the Fund in the manner prescribed for "article XIV members."

12 In recent years this training function has been extended through the expansion of the IMF Institute, which runs courses for junior officials.

13 Tew, "The International Monetary Fund," p. 68.

14 See, for example, *International Reserves and Liquidity: A Study by the Staff of the International Monetary Fund* (Washington, D.C.: IMF, 16 September 1958), reproduced in Horsefield, *Documents,* pp. 349-410. See also Mundell, "The International Monetary Fund," p. 495. Mundell himself was for a short time a Fund official.

15 It is true that the way ahead had been prepared some five years earlier by the basic decisions contained in the Rooth Plan, but the harvest of activity was some years delayed.

16 Embodied in Executive Board Decision No. 1289, 5 January 1962, and an exchange of letters between the ministers of finance of the countries concerned.

17 This is what Hans Aufricht, an eminent authority on comparative central bank law and a former chancellor in the Fund's Legal Department has well described as "living law." See Hans Aufricht, *The Fund Agreement: Living Law and Emerging Practice,* Princeton Studies in International Finance, no. 23 (Princeton, N. J.: Princeton University, International Finance Section, Department of Economics, 1969). See also Joseph Gold, "Constitutional Development and Change," in *Analysis,* ed. Horsefield, pp. 513-605.

18 Horsefield, *Chronicle,* pp. 27-29.

19 The member was Denmark. In 1947, by arrangement, Denmark's votes were cast by Guido Carli of Italy, while the Belgian director, Hubert Ansiaux, continued to speak for her. Horsefield, *Chronicle,* p. 166.

20 The conflict is briefly dealt with in connection with the Fund staff's report in 1960 to the UN Commission on International Commodity Trade. See Horsefield, *Chronicle,* pp. 532-33. Some Fund officials also felt that the 1969 decision on commodity stabilization could be counted as a symbolic decision.

21 Horsefield, *Chronicle,* pp. 286-87.

22 The Bank later withdrew its proposal, perhaps because it thought the charges suggested by the Fund for its services were too steep. Horsefield, *Chronicle,* p. 349.

23 In Fund language, the transfer of countries from article XIV status to article VIII status, a change made by most European countries in 1961.

24 Tew, "The International Monetary Fund," p. 23.

25 I.e. so long as the Fund's holding of a member's currency did not exceed 100 percent of its quota.

26 Tew rightly included this as a fourth point in the Rooth Plan, although strictly speaking it was accepted a little later than the other three points. See Emil G. Spitzer, "Stand-by Arrangements: Purposes and Form," in *Analysis,* ed. Horsefield, chap. 20, pp. 468-91.

27 Gold, quoted in Horsefield, *Chronicle,* pp. 490-91.

28 Article VI, sec. 1 denied the use of the Fund for a "large or sustained outflow of capital" and threatened sanctions against any member failing to prevent the Fund's use for such a purpose. However, it expressly excepted use in respect of "capital transactions of reasonable amount" or "capital movements met out of a member's own resources of gold or foreign exchange."

29 IMF, Executive Board Decision no. 71/2, 26 September 1946, quoted in Horsefield, *Documents,* p. 245.

30 IMF, Executive Board Decision no. 1238 (61/43). For details, see Horsefield, *Chronicle,* pp. 503-06.

31 Bernstein, "The International Monetary Fund," pp. 133 and 137.

32 In practice, this condition was liberally interpreted: for example, the Football War between Honduras and San Salvador was counted by the Fund as a circumstance beyond the control of the belligerents.

33 Tew, "The International Monetary Fund," p. 86.

34 Article XX, sec. 4c. Enemy-occupied states were exempt, an exemption used by Italy, for example, to avoid setting a par value until as late as March 1960. For the underlying philosophy, see Ragnar Nurkse, *International Currency Experience: Lessons on the Interwar Period* (Princeton, N. J.: League of Nations, 1944) (A.4. 1944.II).

35 See Margaret G. de Vries, "Setting Par Values," *Analysis,* ed. Horsefield, chap. 4, pp. 51-89. This decision, plus the provisions of the two-tier gold price arranged in 1968, finally established the international monetary system de facto on a dollar standard.

36 Reproduced in Horsefield, *Documents,* p. 261.

37 For details, see Joseph Gold, "The Ambiguities of Gold," and J. Keith Horsefield, "Subsidies to Gold Producers," in *Analysis,* ed. Horsefield, pp. 559-64 and 203-16, respectively.

38 Horsefield, *Chronicle,* p. 597.

39 Margaret de Vries relates this incident in "The Consultations Process," in *Analysis,* ed. Horsefield, chap. 11. It is barely mentioned in Horsefield, *Chronicle.* There is a good acount of it in Gardner Patterson, *Discrimination in International Trade: The Policy Issues, 1945-1965* (Princeton, N. J.: Princeton University Press, 1966) pp. 71-74.

40 Mossé, Les problèmes monétaires internationaux. See also Turot, *Le Fond monétaire international.*

41 Horsefield, *Chronicle,* p. 613.

42 See Executive Board Decision No. 1034 (60/27), Horsefield, *Documents* pp. 260-61. Fund practice regarding letters of intent was greatly developed during successive negotiations with Britain.

43 U.S., Bretton Woods Agreements Act, Public Law 171, 79th Cong., 1st sess.; text reproduced in *Selected Decisions of the Executive Directors and Selected Documents,* 3rd issue (Washington, D.C.: IMF, 1965), pp. 146-56. A comparable constitutional arrangement, but of less immediate significance in Fund decision making, is the German law under which the executive director is subject to a Committee of Instruction consisting of the chairman of the Bundesbank and the foreign, economics, and finance ministers. See Germany, "Gesetz betreffend das Abkommen über die Internationale Finanz-Corporation und betreffend Gouverneure und Directoren in der Internationalen Bank für Wiederaufban und Entwicklung, in der Internationale Finanz-Corporation und im Internationalen Währungsfonds, vom 12. Juli 1956," *Bundesgestzblatt,* Part II, no. 21 (1956) pp. 747-56.

44 The Long Range International Payments Committee (LRIPC).

45 At the end of Camille Gutt's first five-year term in 1951, the board decided that future managing directors should retire at age seventy. By implication, therefore, they are ineligible for election to a five-year term once they have passed sixty-five.

46 United Nations, *Charter,* Chapter XV, Article 99.

47 See Horsefield, *Chronicle,* pp. 50 and 511-13; and Horsefield, *Documents,* pp. 246-54 for the terms of the GAB and the accompanying letter from Wilfrid Baumgartner of the Banque de France to the other nine countries.

48 A more recent example can be seen in Schweitzer's address of 2 June 1969, at Queens University, Kingston (Ontario). See Pierre-Paul Schweitzer, "Bretton Woods, Twenty-Five Years After," supp. 10 to *International Financial News Survey* 21 (6 June 1969): 177-80.

49 For example, the "classification" that reinterpreted the 1966 decision that Fund drawings were available only for deficits on current account transactions. See Horsefield, *Chronicle,* pp. 504-06.

50 E.g. Robert Triffin, *Gold and the Dollar Crisis: The Future of Convertibility* (New Haven: Yale University Press, 1960).

51 Hon. Maxwell Stamp, "The Stamp Plan: The 1962 Version," *Moorgate and Wall Street* (issued by Hill, Higginson, Erlangers) (Autumn 1962), pp. 5-17.

52 Edward M. Bernstein, *Quarterly Review and Investment Survey* (Model, Roland & Co.) (Fourth Quarter 1963).

53 One of his first proposals for extended use of Fund resources as a means of improving European payments arrangements was put forward while he held this office. The Executive Board declined to back his ideas but allowed him to present them to OEEC governments as a private individual. See Horsefield, *Chronicle,* p. 223.

54 Deputies of ministers of finance or their equivalent and of governors of central banks.

55 See the previous section entitled "Boundary Decisions."

56 See Horsefield, *Chronicle,* pp. 590-91.

57 Tew, "The International Monetary Fund," p. 49a.

58 Ibid., p. 77.

59 On this point, both Richard Gardner and William Diebold, Jr., have much that is pertinent to say in "The Politics of Liquidity" and "Commentary," in *International Organisation,* ed. Cox, pp. 275-85 and 286-93. See also Aubrey, *Behind the Veil of International Money.*

60 Cf. *Partners in Development: Report of the Commission on International Development (Pearson Commission) to the International Bank for Reconstruction and Development* (London: Pall Mall Press, 1969).

Chapter 9

1 A short GATT bibliography would comprise the following works: Gerard Curzon, *Multilateral Commercial Diplomacy* (London: Michael Joseph, 1965); Kenneth W. Dam, *The GATT: Law and International Organization* (Chicago: University of Chicago Press, 1970); Thiébaut Flory, *Le GATT: droit international et commerce mondial* (Paris: Librairie Generale de Droit et de Jurisprudence, 1968); John H. Jackson, *World Trade and the Law of GATT* (New York: Bobbs-Merrill, 1969); Karin Kock, *International Trade Policy and the GATT: 1947-1967* (Stockholm: Almquist & Wilsell, 1969).

2 General Agreement on Tariffs and Trade, Part III, Article XXXV.

3 In order of importance: United States, $502,750; West Germany, $335,060; United Kingdom, $333,170; France, $205,900; Japan, $176,900; Canada, $169,270; Netherlands, $148,070; Italy, $142,430; and Belgium, $113,370.

4 GATT, *Basic Instruments and Selected Documents* 1 (May 1952): 36.

5 In the end Korea did not accede until 1967, at which time no formal protest was made.

6 GATT, *BISD,* 9th Supp. (1961), p. 8.

7 Australia, Belgium, Brazil, Canada, Finland, France, Germany, Ghana, India, Japan, Sweden, United Kingdom, United States, Uruguay.

8 GATT, *BISD,* 13th Supp. (1965), p. 68.

9 GATT, *International Trade, 1954* (Geneva: GATT, 1955), p. 4.

10 *Trends in International Trade* (Geneva: GATT, 1958), p. 1.

11 GATT, Article XXXVI, sec. 8.

12 The IMF, however, significantly affected the work of GATT after the announcement of the Nixon measures in 1971 by supporting the United States request for exceptional measures to protect their balance of payments, declaring that the United States was in "fundamental disequilibrium." The relationship between the two organizations does not permit the IMF to go beyond this statement and pass judgment on the particular trade measures to be taken to correct the situation. This is left to GATT's Contracting Parties.

13 UN, ECOSOC, Resolution 917 (XXXIV), 3 August 1962.

14 A. S. Friedeberg, *The United Nations Conference on Trade and Development of 1964* (Rotterdam: Rotterdam University Press, 1969).

15 E.g. GATT, *BISD,* 9th Supp., *Report of Working Party on the European Free Trade Association* (February 1961), p. 20.

16 GATT has studied ten regional treaties: the Arab Common Market, the Australia/New Zealand Free-Trade Area, the Central American Free-Trade Area, the Equatorial Customs Union, the European Economic Community, the European Atomic Energy Community, the European Free-Trade Association, the Latin-American Free-Trade Association, the South Africa/Rhodesia Customs Union, and the United Kingdom/Ireland Free-Trade Area.

17 As an exception to this general rule, United States congressmen visit Geneva regularly during tariff negotiations; and textile lobbies also did so during the critical phases of negotiation leading to the cotton textile arrangement.

18 They were: Argentina, Brazil, Burma, Cambodia, Ceylon, Chile, Cuba, Ghana, Haiti, India, Indonesia, Israel, Federation of Malaya, Federation of Nigeria, Pakistan, Peru, Tanganyika, Tunisia, United Arab Republic, Uruguay, and Yugoslavia. GATT, *BISD,* 12th Supp., p. 89, n. 1.

19 In 1971, when the GATT system was seriously in jeopardy, a group of stalwarts drew together and began to make joint statements concerning the value of the multilateral trade system; they were Sweden, Switzerland, Canada, and Japan–the principal nonapplicants to the EEC. They became known as the "Ginger Group."

20 The GATT Plan for Tariff Reductions was an imaginative proposal to reduce tariffs on a linear basis by 30 percent over a period of years. The idea was enthusiastically pursued by the smaller European states, who worked on it for several years before it was rejected by the United States and the United Kingdom and finally shelved in 1955-56.

21 The rapid rise in Japan's share in world trade during the sixties seems to be the exception that proves this rule. It remains true, however, that a time lag appears to exist between achieving the critical mass (say 8 percent of world trade) and making a sizeable impact in GATT—and, similarly, in the inverse situation, e.g. the United Kingdom, where loss of the critical mass is not felt in GATT for some time after the event.

22 These three factors of influence in GATT account for the fact that most less-developed countries do not figure in table 9.4, although they formed almost a two-thirds majority in 1968 and, in the mass, had an effect on development trade policy of developed countries outside GATT.

23 The United Arab Republic has been a provisional member since 1962 and became a full member in 1969.

Chapter 10

1 Among the major sources on UNCTAD are: Richard N. Gardner, "The United Nations Conference on Trade and Development," *International Organization* ·22 (Winter 1968): 99-130; Branislav Gosovic, "UNCTAD: North-South Encounter," *International Conciliation,* no. 568 (May 1968), pp. 5-80; Diego Cordovez, "The Making of UNCTAD," *Journal of World Trade Law* 1 (May-June 1967): 243-328; Kamal Hagras, *United Nations Conference on Trade and Development* (New York: Praeger, 1965); A. S. Friedeberg, *The United Nations Conference on Trade and Development of 1964* (Rotterdam: Rotterdam University Press, 1969).

2 David Kay, *The New Nations in the United Nations: 1960-1967* (New York: Columbia University Press, 1970), pp. 95-100. See also Charles L. Robertson, "The Creation of UNCTAD," in *International Organisation: World Politics, Studies in Economics and Social Agencies,* ed. Robert Cox (London: Macmillan, 1969), pp. 258-74.

3 On the problems and politics of preparation for the conference, see Cordovez, "The Making of UNCTAD," pp. 265ff.

4 The name comes from the seventy-five countries that issued the Joint Declaration of Developing Countries at the 1963 General Assembly and a Joint Declaration of the Seventy-seven Developing Countries at the end of UNCTAD-I. Cuba, China (Taiwan), Israel, Mongolia, and South Africa are not included, although they are on the A and C lists. The name was kept for political reasons, though the membership of the "77" had grown to eighty-seven by the time of the New Delhi Conference. For a good account of the UNCTAD group system, see Gosovic, "UNCTAD: North-South Encounter," pp. 9-30.

5 See Gardner, "The United Nations Conference on Trade and Development," p. 118.

6 See, for example, the replies of governments in UN Doc. TD/B/175, 22 July 1968.

7 In terms of bureaucratic politics on the American side, this reflected a victory for the U.S. State Department bureau concerned primarily with substantive trade issues over the bureau that was concerned with the "neatness" of the United Nations development system.

8 Contained in section 20 of the United Nations budget estimates.

9 See UN Doc. TD/B/181, 2 August 1968, Annex, pp. 2-4.

10 See chap. 1. In addition, eight states that were not members of the United Nations but were members of UNCTAD (West Germany, Switzerland, Liechtenstein, Monaco, San Marino, Holy See, South Korea, South Vietnam) made contributions equal to 8.6 percent of the budget.

11 This is in contrast to UNCTAD's counterpart, UNIDO, which was heavily oriented toward technical assistance.

12 Gardner, "The United Nations Conference on Trade and Development," p. 116.

13 The background of the others: eleven, government service; seven, academics; two, other IGOs; and ten, unknown.

14 See UN Doc. TD/B/L.156, 6 February 1969.

15 See UN Doc. TD/B/207, 30 December 1968.

16 As it was jokingly said, the difference between an UNCTAD meeting and a football game was that in football you knew in advance how long it would last but not the outcome, while in UNCTAD you knew the outcome but never how long it would last.

17 Calculated by the author from UN Doc. TD/B/INF.15, 19 September 1968.

18 See Robert Cox, "The Executive Head: An Essay on Leadership in International Organization," *International Organization* 23 (Spring 1969): 205-30.

19 See Chester Barnard, *The Functions of the Executive* (Cambridge: Harvard University Press, 1938), p. 60. See also Ernst Haas, *Beyond the Nation-State: Functionalism and International Organization* (Stanford, Calif.: Stanford University Press, 1964), chap. 4.

20 Johan Kaufmann, *Conference Diplomacy: An Introductory Analysis* (Leiden: Sijthoff, 1968), p. 48.

21 All its members were mentioned by two-thirds or more of the panel, described below. The panel also added an official from the New York office, Sidney Dell. Members of the substantive committee were: W. Malinowski (Chairman), P. Coidan, P. Berthoud, R. Krishnamurti, and J. Viteri.

22 Calculated by the author from the files of the Council on Foreign Relations. These figures seem representative for the European press as well.

23 For a more detailed discussion and evidence see Jean Siotis, "Les missions permanentes à Genève et la CNUCED: Rapport préliminaire," mimeographed (Geneva: Carnegie Endowment, 1968).

24 For a sympathetic, yet quite critical, appraisal of the economic reasoning in the UNCTAD ideology, see Harry Johnson, *Economic Policies toward Less Developed Countries* (Washington, D. C.: Brookings Institution, 1967). See also Friedeberg, *The United Nations Conference on Trade and Development,* chaps. 3 and 4.

25 Seven persons complied. Two refused: one of these was an Eastern European who felt that to mention names would be misleading; the other was an Arab diplomat who gave no reason. One request was impossible to follow up because the person had left Geneva.

26 Aid figures showed a like trend. According to the Pearson Report, grant and grantlike aid from the richer, noncommunist nations fell from \$4.5 billion in 1961 to \$4.1 billion in 1968. *Economist,* 1 November 1969, p. 29.

27 See Isaiah Frank, "New Perspectives on Trade and Development," *Foreign Affairs* 45 (April 1967): 522-24.

28 Weighting by type of decisions would probably add only slightly to the validity of the results. In any case, small differences in rank might be accounted for by scoring errors, and they should therefore not be taken too seriously. Only the general pattern is significant.

29 *Washington Post,* 26 March 1968.

30 See S. Mihailovic, "Confrontation without Real Solutions: Second United Nations Conference for Trade and Development," *Review of International Affairs* 19 (March 1968): 5-7.

31 Incidentally, whatever the merits of the latter perspective for the analyst, it is interesting to note that most participants conceived of the organization in the former, more restricted, sense.

32 As one cynical observer put it, the price of preferences is quotas and licenses; and when licenses are given out in Europe, they tend to go to former French colonies.

33 This account of Prebisch's strategy is based on his "farewell addresses" (UN Docs. TD/B/222, 22 January 1969; TD/B/AC.6/2, 23 January 1969) and on personal interviews with Prebisch and his colleagues.

Chapter 11

1 In GATT the Executive Committee of the Interim Commission for the International Trade Organization had the nominal authority to appoint the executive secretary.

2 United Nations, *A Study of the Capacity of the United Nations Development System* (Geneva: United Nations, 1969), 2:12a and table 4, app. 6 (hereafter referred to as United Nations, *Capacity Study*).

3 Ibid., table 7, app. 6.

4 Writing of the Administrative Committee on Co-ordination, which is composed of the executive heads of the specialized agencies, and on the basis of his close experience of more than two decades in interagency coordination machinery, Martin Hill said bluntly that the ACC "cannot easily take a position detrimental to the interests of any agency, or in opposition to the wishes of its executive head." "The Administrative Committee on Co-ordination," in *The Evolution of International Organizations* ed. Evan Luard (London: Thames and Hudson, 1966), p. 129. Walter R. Sharp quoted a member of ECOSOC who put it even more bluntly, stating that "ACC has tended to be used by the agencies as an instrument to safeguard entrenched interests and limit interference by the Council." *The United Nations Economic and Social Council* (New York: Columbia University Press, 1969), p. 148.

5 See United Nations, *Capacity Study,* especially 1:iv-v, 9; 2:2

6 Although his purposes were not the same as those here, Johan Kaufmann has noted in some detail the qualities that he thinks are needed for what he calls "conference diplomats." See chapter 7, "Conference Diplomats—Requirements and Characteristics," in his *Conference Diplomacy: An Introductory Analysis* (Leiden: Sijthoff, 1968), pp. 139-40. All of these are individual attributes, and many can be important sources of capacity and ultimately of influence for individual actors.

7 Although accurate comparisons are impossible because of inadequacies in the data, this situation seems to contrast with that in the United Nations, where long association appears to be a less important attribute of influential actors than it once was. See Robert O. Keohane, "Institutionalization in the United Nations General Assembly," *International Organization* 23 (Autumn 1969): 859-96.

8 Sharp has noted a similar phenomenon with respect to ECOSOC. See his *The United Nations Economic and Social Council,* pp. 32-33.

9 This seems to be a general characteristic of organizations. See Chester Barnard, *The Functions of the Executive* (Cambridge: Harvard University Press, 1946); and also Richard E. Neustadt, *Presidential Power: The Politics of Leadership* (New York: Wiley, 1960).

10 United Nations, *Capacity Study,* passim.

11 Sharp, *The United Nations Economic and Social Council,* pp. 65-71.

12 See, for example, Abraham Zaleznik, "Interpersonal Relations in Organizations," pp. 574-613, in *Handbook of Organizations,* ed. James G. March (Chicago: Rand McNally, 1965).

13 United Nations, *Demographic Yearbook* (1967).

14 Arms Control and Disarmament Agency, *World Military Expenditures, 1969* (Washington, D. C.: Government Printing Office, 1969), p. 17.

15 For a detailed discussion of both meanings of functionalism see Ernst B. Haas, *Beyond the Nation State: Functionalism and International Organization* (Stanford, Calif.: Stanford University Press, 1964). See also Inis L. Claude, *Plowshares: The Problems and Progress of International Organizations,* 3rd ed. (New York: Random House, 1964), chap. 17.

16 For example, Mancur Olson, Jr., *The Logic of Collective Action* (Cambridge: Harvard University Press, 1965).

17 John Ruggie, "The Strategies and Structures of International Organization: The Theory of Public Goods, Science and Development Plan and Consequences" (Paper submitted to the American Political Science Association, Los Angeles, Calif., September 1970).

18 Inis L. Claude, Jr. has made this point cogently and persuasively. See his article "Collective Legitimization as a Political Function of the United Nations," *International Organization,* Vol. XX, No. 3 (Summer 1966), pp. 367-79. See also his *The Changing United Nations* (New York: Random House, 1967).

19 Chadwick F. Alger has done some stimulating and pioneering work in this area. See his articles: "Non-resolution Consequences of the United Nations and Their Effect on International Conflict," *Journal of Conflict Resolution 5* (June 1961): 128-45; and "United Nations Participation as a Learning Experience," *Public Opinion Quarterly* 27 (Fall 1963): 411-26.

Appendix A

1 See Klaus Knorr, *The War Potential of Nations* (Princeton, N. J.: Princeton University Press, 1956); and A. F. K. Organski, *World Politics,* 2d ed. (New York: Knopf, 1968), pp. 208-15.

2 Bruce M. Russett, Hayward R. Alker, Jr., Karl W. Deutsch, and Harold D. Lasswell, *World Handbook of Political and Social Indicators* (New Haven: Yale University Press, 1964), p. 283, shows a product-moment correlation coefficient of .80 with the percentage of literate population aged fifteen and over; .80 with primary and secondary school pupils as a percentage of population aged fifteen to sixty-four; and .58 with students enrolled in higher education per 100 thousand population.

3 Organski, *World Politics,* pp. 209 ff.

4 F. Clifford German, "A Tentative Evaluation of World Power," *Journal of Conflict Resolution 4* (March 1960): 138-44.

5 Organski, *World Politics,* p. 215.

6 German, "Evaluation of World Power," p. 141.

7 Inis L. Claude, Jr. has dealt with this phenomenon in terms of the concept of *passive provocation* in an essay entitled "Economic Development Aid and International Political Stability," in *International Organisation: World Politics,* ed. Robert W. Cox (London: Macmillan, 1969), pp. 49-58.

Appendix B

1 Preliminary result of work undertaken jointly by R. W. Cox and Hans Günter.

2 Including mining, manufacturing, construction, electricity, gas, water, and sanitary services (International Standard Industrial Classification divisions 1-5).

Appendix C

1 The last five members in this list are groups of nonindependent territories, which include 18 units in our list of 154: (1) Comoro Islands, Guadeloupe, Martinique, and Réunion; (2) Angola, Cape Verde Islands, Mozambique, Portuguese Guinea, and Portuguese Timor; (3) Spanish Guinea and Spanish North Africa; (4) Bahrein, Fiji, Hong Kong, Mauritius, and Swaziland; (5) Puerto Rico and the Ryukyu Islands.

2 James S. Coleman "Conclusion: The Political Systems of the Developing Areas," in *The Politics of the Developing Areas,* ed. Gabriel Almond and James S. Coleman (Princeton, N. J.: Princeton University Press, 1960), pp. 532-76, uses the concept of "semicompetitive"; and Seymour Martin Lipset in *Political Man* (Garden City, N. Y.: Doubleday, 1959), pp. 45-46, uses "stable" and "unstable" democracies and dictatorships. Our usage is closer to that of Ernst B. Haas, whose classifications are adapted from those of David Apter. See Ernst B. Haas, *Collective Security and the Future International System* (Denver: University of Denver, 1968); "Future Worlds and Present International Organizations: Some Dilemmas," in *Bulletin* (International Institute for Labour Studies), no. 6 (June 1969), pp. 4-20; and *Human Rights and International Action: The Case of Freedom of Association* (Stanford, Calif.: Stanford University Press, 1970), Methodological Appendix, pp. 135-59.

3 For example, all of the states in the highest GNP per capita group fall in the "High Mass-Consumption" category according to the classification scheme derived by Bruce M. Russet, Hayward R. Alker, Jr., Karl W. Deutsch, and Harold D. Lasswell, *World Handbook of Political and Social Indicators* (New Haven: Yale University Press, 1964), p. 298.

4 United Nations, Secretariat, Department of Economic and Social Affairs, *Yearbook of National Accounts Statistics: 1967* (New York: United Nations, 1968), and earlier editions, especially 1965 and 1966; and, United Nations, Secretariat, Department of Economic and Social Affairs, *Statistical Yearbook: 1968* (New York: United Nations, 1968).

5 Sources used in connection with these rough estimates include the following: Organization for Economic Cooperation and Development, *National Accounts of Less Developed Countries, 1950-1966* (Paris: OECD, July 1968); Organization for Economic Cooperation and Development, *National Accounts of OECD Countries, 1957-1966* (Paris: OECD, 1967); United Nations, Economic Commission for Latin America, *Economic Survey of Latin America* (New York: United Nations, 1955, 1960, 1966, and 1967); International Monetary Fund, *International Financial Statistics* (Washington, D. C.: IMF, 1965). We are indebted to Hans Günter for his help in preparing these statistics.

6 See Ernst B. Haas, *Human Rights and International Action,* pp. 135-59.

Contributors

Robert W. Cox is professor of political science at Columbia University, an appointment he took up after resigning as director of the International Institute for Labour Studies during the summer of 1972. He held the directorship of the IILS from 1965 to 1972 and previously held various posts in the International Labour Office. Since 1963, he has also been professor at the Graduate Institute of International Studies, University of Geneva, Switzerland. During the academic year 1971-72 he was visiting professor in the international studies program at the University of Toronto.

Gerard and Victoria Curzon are economists who have written several studies together, including *After the Kennedy Round, Hidden Barriers to Trade,* and *Trade Policy in the 1970's.* Gerard Curzon is professor at the Graduate Institute of International Studies, University of Geneva, Switzerland, and editor of the *Journal of World Trade Law.* He has been visiting professor at the University of Chicago (1968) and at the University of Carleton, Ottawa (1971). His study of GATT, entitled *Multilateral Commercial Diplomacy,* was published in 1965.

Harold K. Jacobson is professor of political science and chairman of the department at the University of Michigan. He is also a member of the Center for Political Studies and director of the International Organization Program there. His previous publications include *The USSR and the UN's Economic and Social Activities* and *Diplomats, Scientists and Politicians,* which he coauthored with Eric Stein.

Joseph S. Nye is professor of government and program director of the Center for International Affairs, Harvard University. He is the author of *Peace in Parts, Pan-Africanism and East African Integration,* and other works.

Lawrence Scheinman is professor of political science at Cornell University. His previous publications include *Atomic Energy in France under the Fourth Republic* and two issues of *International Concilation,* "Euratom: Nuclear Integration in Europe" (no. 563, May 1967) and "Nuclear Safeguards, the Peaceful Atom and the IAEA" (no. 572, March 1969).

James P. Sewell is research associate at the Center for International Studies, the Woodrow Wilson School, Princeton University. His interest in UNESCO does not end with this contribution; a larger study is forthcoming. He has authored *Functionalism and World Politics,* emphasizing IBRD, and other studies focusing upon the specialized agencies and upon the superpowers' security policies.

Susan Strange has been a research specialist at Chatham House, the Royal Institute for International Affairs, since 1965. She has taught at University College, London, and at the London School of Economics. Her book *Sterling and British Policy* was published in 1971.

Index

Access, 400

Accountability, 429, 430

Actors, 35, 393-409; defined, 12; in GATT, 316-21; in IAEA, 238-49; in ILO, 114-28; in IMF, 283-92; in ITU, 76-87; persistent groupings of, 23; in UNCTAD, 346-57, in UNESCO, 153-61; in WHO, 194-205

Administrative Committee on Co-ordination (ACC), 348

Administrative competence: as source of influence, 243, 352, 396

Afghanistan, 46, 461-63; in GATT, 311; in UNCTAD, 339, 344

Africa, 32, 44-45, 52, 54, 57, 375, 413; in IAEA, 217, 226; in ILO, 105, 107, 108, 109, 118, 119, 120, 126; in ITU, 73, 82, 98, 99; levels of economic development, 46-48; in UNESCO, 144, 147, 150, 152, 160, 162, 165, 167; in WHO, 182, 186, 187, 189, 200, 204

African states: in GATT, 328; in IAEA, 253, 257-58, 259; in IMF, 274; in UNCTAD, 336, 339, 340, 341, 347, 352, 356, 357; in WHO 212

Ago, Roberto, 116

Agriculture: in GATT, 309, 315, 322

Aid: as source of power, 411

Albania, 31, 46, 461-63; in IAEA, 259; in ITU, 95, 98; in UNESCO, 144, 167; in WHO, 183

Alcock, Antony, 467

Alger, Chadwick F., 465, 478

Algeria: 46, 461-63; in IAEA, 259; in UNCTAD, 342

Algerian War, 270

Algiers Conference (1967), 356

Alker, Hayward R., 465, 478, 479

All-African Trade Union Federation, 108

Alliance for Progress, 368

All Union Central Committee of Trade Unions, 117

Almond, Gabriel, 479

Altman, Oscar, 292

Amazon, 152

American Federation of Labor-Congress of Industrial Organizations (AFL-CIO), 117, 118, 119-20

American Medical Association (AMA), 178

American Selling Price: valuation technique, 313

Analytical decision making: defined, 13; employment of mode, 112, 379, 381, 385, 389-90, 391, 392-93

Andorra, 457

Andrada, Marco Aurelio, 76, 87

Andrews, Paul, 139n

Anglophone African states, 406

Angola, 461-63

Apartheid, 109

Apter, David, 479

Arab Common Market, 475

Arab-Israeli conflict, 342

Arab League, 125, 149

Arab states: in IAEA, 227, 229, 232; in UNCTAD, 249, 342; in WHO, 184

Argentina, 44, 46, 54, 439, 442, 447, 448-49, 450-51, 452-53, 454-55, 461-63, 466; in GATT, 313, 318, 326; in IAEA, 226, 245, 255, 258; in IMF, 284; in ITU, 70, 79, 87, 89, 91; in UNCTAD, 358, 364; in UNESCO, 168, 169, 170; in WHO, 186, 208

Arms control, 216, 229, 250, 431, 434

Aron, Raymond, 269

Ascher, Charles, 152, 468, 470

Asia, 32, 45, 46-48, 52, 53; in IAEA, 249; in ILO, 106, 118, 119, 125, 126; in ITU, 73, 98, 99; in UNCTAD, 147, 152, 156, 166; in WHO, 200

Asian-African Conference (1955), 52

Asian states: in GATT, 311; in IAEA, 253, 257-58, 259; in IMF, 269; in UNCTAD, 336, 341, 344-45, 352, 357; in WHO, 212-13

Association with an international organization: as source of influence, 198, 245, 395-96

Aswan, 152

Atlantic Charter (1941), 298

Atoms-for-Peace, 218, 222

Attitudes and ideologies, 22, 402-06

Aubrey, Henry, 472

Australia, 31, 32, 39, 46, 439, 442, 447, 448-49, 450-51, 452-53, 454-55, 456, 461-63; in GATT, 307, 318, 325, 326; in IAEA, 225, 235, 237-38; in ILO, 126; in IMF, 269, 277, 281, 283; in ITU, 70, 87, 89; in UNCTAD, 362, 363, 364; in UNESCO, 166, 168, 169, 170; in WHO, 186, 207, 208

Austria, 31, 32, 39, 46, 439, 442, 447, 448-49, 450-51, 452-53, 454-55, 457, 461-63; in IAEA, 235, 250; in ITU, 89; in UNESCO, 166, 168, 169, 170; in WHO, 208

Authoritarian polities, 41, 44, 93, 130-33, 211-12, 252-55, 329, 408, 415-17, 458-59, 466; defined, 29-30

Bahrein, 457, 461-63

Balance of payments, 278, 279, 283, 307-08, 310, 315, 321, 333; U.S., 271

Balance of terror, 51

Balfour, Lord, 142

Bancor, 289

Bandung Conference (1955), 52, 311

Nations Conference on International Organization

San Marino, 457, 458

Sarawate, Manohar Balaji, 76-77

Sathyamurthy, T. V., 468, 469

Saudi Arabia, 46, 461-63; in UNESCO, 161

Scandinavian states: in GATT, 303; in IAEA, 225; in IMF, 274; in UNESCO, 154

Schaper, B. W., 467

Schweitzer, Pierre-Paul, 269, 286-87, 288, 292

Seaborg, Glen T., 471

Seluman, Robert, 50

Senegal, 46, 461-63

Service: activities, 100, 105-06, 122; functions, 136, 218-19, 372-73, 415, 423-24, 427-28; organization, 5-6, 308

Shapiro, Robert, 139*n*

Sharp, Walter R., 470, 477, 478

Shkunaev, V. G., 467

Shotwell, James T., 467

Shuster, George, 468

Siegel, Milton P., 201

Sierra Leone, 46, 461-63

Simon, Herbert A., 465

Singapore, 46, 461-63

Singer, J. David, 465

Sino-Soviet split, 53

Siotis, Jean, 334*n*, 477

Smallpox eradication, 191, 209

Smith, Delbert D., 466

Socialist states, 373-74, 380, 406, 408-09, 423, 425, 427; defined, 31; in GATT, 329; in IAEA, 220, 221, 224, 225, 227, 228, 229, 247-48; in ILO, 128, 133-35; in IMF, 291; in ITU, 65, 80, 85-87, 97, 98; in UNCTAD, 335, 337, 341, 350, 360; in UNESCO, 144-45, 147; in WHO, 181, 185, 205

Social Science Research Council, 139

Solomon, Anthony, 355

Somalia, 46, 461-63

South Africa, Republic of, 31, 32, 39, 46, 410, 419, 440, 442, 447, 448-49, 450-51, 452-53, 454-55, 458, 461-63; in GATT, 308, 325-28; in IAEA, 224, 226, 237-38, 245, 248, 249, 251, 255, 257-58, 261; in ILO, 105, 107, 120, 125; in IMF, 282; in ITU, 68, 89, 98; in UNCTAD, 342, 356, 364; in UNESCO, 146, 168, 169, 170; in WHO, 182-83, 187, 208

South African/Rhodesian Customs Union, 475

South East Asia Treaty Organization (SEATO), 49

Southern Yemen, 46, 461-63

South Korea. *See* Korea, Democratic Republic of

Southland, Frank, 285, 292

South Vietnam. *See* Vietnam, Republic of

South West Africa, 461-63

Sovereignty, 149-50, 403-04, 424

Soviet Union. *See* Union of Soviet Socialist Republics

Space communications, 60, 64, 73, 87-90, 152, 159

Spain, 31, 39, 46, 440, 442, 447, 448-49, 450-51, 452-53, 454-55, 461-63; in IAEA, 250; in ITU, 66, 80, 89, 90; in UNCTAD, 364; in UNESCO, 146, 166, 168, 169, 170; in WHO, 182, 208

Spanish Guinea, 461-63

Spanish North Africa, 461-63

Spanish territories in Africa, 458

Special Drawing Rights (SDRs), 3, 10, 266, 271, 289, 297, 379, 385, 412

Specificity, 420-21

Spitzer, Emil, 473

Staehle, H., 320

Stamp, Maxwell, 289-90, 474

Stein, Eric, 470

Sterling, 278, 294, 296; area, 294-95; convertibility of, 270; crisis, 271; devaluation of, 282

Stoessinger, John G., 470

Stratification of state power, 27-28, 34, 37, 38, 40, 55-56, 409-14, 423, 428, 435, 437-43; and GATT, 325; and IAEA, 250-52; and ILO, 129-30; and IMF, 292; and ITU, 88-90; and UNCTAD, 360-64; and UNESCO, 168-73; and WHO, 209-11

Structure of influence, 25, 27, 34, 35-36, 346; in GATT, 330-32; in IAEA, 260-62; in ILO, 124-27, 135-38; in IMF, 295-97; in ITU, 99-101; in UNCTAD, 360-70; in UNESCO, 173; in WHO, 213-15

Study of the Capacity of the United Nations Development System, 173-74, 270, 477

Sudan, 46, 461-63

Sudjarwo, 227

Suez crisis, 266, 270

Sukarno, Achmed, 132, 459

Surinam, 461-63

Swaziland, 461-63

Sweden, 28, 31, 32, 39, 46, 53, 440, 442, 447, 448-49, 450-51, 452-53, 454-55, 456, 461-63; in GATT, 326; in IAEA, 239; in IMF, 270; in ITU, 70, 90; in UNCTAD, 340, 358, 362, 363, 364, 366; in UNESCO, 166, 168, 169, 170; in WHO, 208, 214

Switzerland, 31, 32, 39, 46, 53, 439, 440, 442, 447, 448-49, 450-51, 452-53, 454-55, 456, 461-63; in GATT, 305, 326; in IAEA, 250; in IMF, 265, 270; in ITU, 70, 80, 87, 90, 91; in UNCTAD, 358, 362, 363, 364; in UNESCO, 154, 166, 168, 169, 170; in WHO, 208

Symbolic decisions, 15, 29, 380-81, 395, 405, 408, 413, 418, 422, 425; defined, 9; in GATT, 304, 306, 308; in IAEA, 229-30, 239; in ILO, 109, 136; in IMF, 273, 274-75; in ITU, 67-68,